Basics' Back

Olivier T. Godichet

Nature's Spirit
in Social Maths & Logics

I: Formal Sciences Primary

2016

oligodix@gmail.com

Basics' Back. *Olivier T. Godichet*
1st Edition: December 2016

ISBN 978-1-365-57050-6

Basics' Back

Olivier T. Godichet

Nature's Spirit
in Social Maths & Logics

I: Formal Sciences Primary

2016

To Dr Concepción Ferrufino

a sort of mathematician

to put humanity in his heart
empower poor peasants in his lands
yoga practice behind his teacher's desk

Index

Introduction

Observing the effects of human *genii* on modern societies and worldwide ecosystems, as we had in the first times of globalization and its revolution of information supporting techniques of communication; humanity looks like urgently needing to revert many of its dogmatic principles. So as to abandon many of its exhausted paradigms. As well as in the urgent need to instate cognitive ways of smart thinking; for a better appropriation of management in their humane social-economics.

Humans should rather less admire themselves, as so superiorly intelligent; for selfish individual goals; like after their "rankings" on universal competition. That competition is for establishing the anti-natural and anti-logical superiority. Against that humans should care more for the wonders of nature; including those of their unconscious brains. So not to pride themselves of their disconnections from the realities and, of their pretended ways of forcing 'values'. Especially when they are 'phenomenologically so improper at making cooperate cultures in a peaceful way. Did not they learned that understanding, comprehensively knowledge provide better options?

We ought better rethink and reconsider: what we have done and are doing and be more inspired by Nature and wise humans. Because, knowing better the extraordinary natural structures, we have taken or, we have been provided; the formal sciences make us discover; with efforts of scientific virtues. Hence formal sciences could converge towards wiser approaches, with humbler explanations for a better reward. Those are our sources for social-economy mastering.

See the natural environments, under social practices. Modern Occident's mythology of industrial progress has established plenty of traditional stressing ways. Destructive ways lauded as progress. So many mistakes have been made and are still made by much stupidly.

Reviewing carefully our tools of abstraction, we have not coped our major disturbances, and they turn now unavoidable. Proper solutions are still kept on the margins, in a hot pot of 'residuals', evading precautions in practices. So, still very weak, are many amendments we turned conscious of. Even worse we have promoted many sorts of counterproductive adjustments.

Some marginal (but more social) economists in some ways, in their duties respect to the sustainability of societies; have occasionally felt something at the respect. They expressed their doubts. Hence not in such primary basics we will try here. To mention some writers of that: Hirschmann, Simon about his doubts, Leontief after his contributions, Galbraith elegantly in lay good sense of meaningful economics, Georgescu-Roengen fundamentally, Passet eventually, Arrow by his care for complexity, Allais relatively isolated in his fundamentals, Sen quite directly and possibly Stiglitz quite polemical.

Most of them conceived their critics or comments by the sides maybe not since inside the core perspective of methods. Among them maybe Perroux one that have deeply felt the philosophic challenge, but mid of the eighties we were less clear about forms.

Formal and fundamental natural scientists brought piece-wise contributions. Often after they intended to make them popular, but as soon as the complexities of formalism have been everywhere, as in personal computers; experts appear to pretend to master these. So the message of Prigogine, Thom and others has diluted in 'black waters'. Maybe Allais and in his national difficulties at his last efforts of messages have turned somehow, too misunderstood; by an environment of 'super stupid determinists of his country.

Of course many have taken advantage of the profitable: 'objection your honor'. Among them we miss all those that fairly tried to face professionally, the new ecological challenges. The perspective of this essay is not to be specific about such critical problems producing disasters but: to open minds on the fundamentals. Fundamentals as a product of human genii; but that does not more laud the superiority of progress. They simply put evidence: what we really do not know properly: how to care and exploit properly.

Since politics look like to prefer forcing mistakes, reasons and justifications. This increasingly criminal futility also express themselves in narrow selection of methods. Methods that are used by governance of government; against the nature of thinking and the ways to make it smarter. Preferring sorts of transformations speculating about larger virtual ways profits pretending; they are just nonsense anyhow in some important ways.

Sciences have extraordinary formal methods. Humans' societies do not use them properly, for what they can suggest but should not be used to alienate. We do not care enough their new developments; their precautions and proper ways of advancements. Most fundamental forms are just taken as marginal curiosities. Those methods can tell much, in matters of understanding. Often they are better when used for doubting and care about what is done.

Use them in more proper ways and phenomenologically friendly turns increasingly critical. Since most humans are expected, from the paradigms to just stay or turn, stupid with the knowledge they are 'provided'. Computer systems just help in these nasty implicit policies; providing the fake appearances of reality, disconnecting humans' controls from wise efforts, surreptitiously because plenty of their appearance looks like positive and kind.

Formal methods could tell much more. So the deficiencies make the determinists bizarre, dictatorial and counter-determinist. If we care to listen somehow and want to do; this may turn essential for the future. Present political and economic frameworks are harshly promoted by world-wide hysteria of compulsory determinist policies. Quite often they are managed either as tautologies for idiots. Management simply ill-treat; promote illusions; applies straightjackets viciously force governance into madness. It prevents the natural understandings; confuse scientific reactions to lunacy and deprives even the fair use of tools.

The author of this essay has seen very ineffective transnational policies. Even when those policies were pretending to share and provide. Once accounted all collateral effects, disqualifications and evolutions produced by global trends world-wide and local; critical evidence of absurd massive conflicts come from that. So evidently these disasters are intricated with the glocal management imposed locally.

We are not with this essay for impolite about globalization failures. More positively we make some formal suggestions upon methods for the adjustments of epistemologies and on dividable methods among legitimate citizens. So to make suggestions about epistemologies or philosophies of sciences. Observing how they have been abused: to mislead and misconduct.

Our aim is to question our methods of abstractions, conception, design, measure and decisions; and suggest some few but substantial amendments in our ways to do things. Some points to reinstate primary thinking careful of evidence.

'Basics' Back', present essay questions bases; after intuitive understandings of Nature's resources. And then to work better than our present applications of methods. Isolated reinstatements are already been mentioned in many essays of good intentions. But their clues, for new social deal with sciences, are too sparse and too thin in front narrow hegemonic orthodoxy.

Thus you will meet here, some necessary, already discovered important theorems and new kinds of concepts; inspired by scientific advancements of methods or, more properly said, their epistemologies. In particular, we are inspired by modern formal sciences on "complex sciences"; they are already introduced in many of modern human kinds, of enquiries and questions. Complexity word is even turning an ineffectual label increasing misunderstandings.

An essay is limited in space and coherence. And this one, of one thinker, even with a broad perspective, intent to point at the basic widely collected for "remastering". It adds some personal original suggestions of concepts; and so it will stay 'scientifically thin. At present social-economical levels of complexity 'superimposed on natural's ones, distribution among relatively autonomous human mind is more important.

What is required from any human is: awareness and to be able to recall their experience of good doings, previous intuitions, as well as perplexities. What they were meaning more than what was told. Suggest is not telling you much on what (you ought to do), but more on how. And in the case of universal sciences, for some of your requirements but not all of what you do: real sciences not for *a panacea*.

A first volume is dedicated to formalisms of few amounts or numbers. A second one, and may be no more, for larger numbers of formal concepts: mainly operations, approaches, networks and statistics.

Our practices have been in the dire states, of World's globalization. We have tried to avoid misunderstandings on the many tools we used; for thinking and suggesting. Eventually this made us bizarre, more trying to prevent nonmalignant policies, misunderstandings; even indirectly or belatedly. We have seen much of those defects eve in the best original intentions. And once against our suggestions other options prevailed they produced their wrong effects and could witness that; their main drivers go far away to other dedications more fruitful to their careers.

This essay is not about judgments, nor in determinist construction of values 'from nothing'. It is more in the care of instrumentals with fewer prejudgments. Even if obviously the main conducing ideology of thinking, the occidental one, should be accounted as the main culprit; because the main positive provider of knowledge and of technological revolutions it met largely excessive support from locals, 'willing to look like obedient'. Any should feel committed to make differently rather than waste in structuration since nonsense friendships with superior partners. The planet wait for better and less than more waste of other determinist alternatives.

Occident has not been good at involving and incorporate other cultures basics. Somehow lately it may have provided corrective studies, not changing much to the equivocal trends and wrong dynamics. Moreover this did not enough prevent the forcing of its sorts of economics for 'out' of the way' profits. The development of recent transnationalism came together with sorts of too weak corrections, determinist ones, not preventing powerful adverse effects. Policies of 'development' have mostly been misguided.

In this collection of tips, you will not find the funniest ways of leisure business world provided, for your moments on Earth. But if they can make you wish to turn wiser and find happy satisfactions in efforts of intelligence for your conduction. At least, you will have the satisfaction to have done genuinely honest, good as you can.

Understand that once the neurobiological structures of our brain have succeeded to connect properly happiness and self-satisfaction (vague emotional feelings) with efforts; social care with materialistic goods and services to help everyone; can make the future better. That is the fair way to be happy with less need to consume and waste too much of the planet. That is levels of happiness are to correlate properly, with the degrees of efforts in cares; you can develop respect to achievement. Believe your neurophysiology: adapt to that, whatever perverse and corrupt, can be the worldwide society of consumptive illusions.

We try to examine, as far as possible, in this essay of epistemology; essence of abstractions of human beings; for projecting themselves in their environments in Nature ... more or less transformed material as well as socially build. You will not find the direct way of what you have to do: this is a self-care of a path that you have to do by yourself.

Human lives, in actions and programs are to produce bias in Nature and it flows of transformations and renewals the wise way is to make them sustainable. Mostly they now do it by means of engineered transformations. Everyone ambitions remain to sustain oneself and better. Altogether it is to provide enough and renew in the least destructive ways as possible. It is primary not to misunderstand nor mis-care natural dynamics and cycles of renewal in "works of progress."

Thus in this essay we do not say that you will change everything or you will stop doing anything. The goal is to learn to make it better. That could be a sort of human progress precisely distinct from the technocratic ones; those who have been associated during 2 past centuries; increasingly against the evidences of mind. But methodologically it is more about 'tipping the balances' in wiser ways and be confirmed the many already doing this.

Since I have often been in the hard and sad margins of societies, so perturbed they were negative; by the world-wide effort of "para-dogmatic" globalization; even when pretending the contrary to just bring peace. I will thereafter use more the neutral "we" At least, according to our observations. Good tales on their wonders, have been intensely provided, by foreign public funds 'helpers' in management. They made it in a way dictating the rules of self-assessment. Our critics are not in the attitudes, any human proceed so, but they misguided because misguided themselves, when not making enough the efforts to examine reflexively what they were doing especially because not with their own wealth but their national or international funds.

Because either optimistic or skeptics or critics of the "other alternative solutions" that looked like telling what to do; we tried to avoid that too. As far as decently possible and even caring much for the future reputation of structures, we were associated with, for a while... Often we have seen the pretended best advocates promote the worst examples in the field. We did not compromise for a long time as soon as deluded by 'routines of excellence' that have been, we suspect, so damaging. Our diagnostics and critics have cared not to be 'ill- nor preconceived'. We asked more systematically our-self, about what was essentially useful to do, communicate and inform upon, freely and not for self-advancement. Our ambition is not about eradicating or erase 'competition'; despite having seen many defects of any similar 'pure' conducts.

As a result we dedicated most of our free time to the basics of scientific thinking; as required by better care. Not much about, what others had to do; but for caring the sincerity and conviction of our contribution. As the minimum essential we could ensure, and what an exterior can bring. Anyhow an intellectual often has to be exterior. That is the economics of universality.

It is not the same to provide a universal tool for primary skills and self-empowerment and: to promote the sort of superstructures' of best management paradigms. They look like for the leadership of peoples. Whom would have their best interest 'out'? Even when it includes the global dividable means.

In most cases it was not to prevent communities to test the "supports" they received. Play in the margins of legitimate social actors, not empowered by discretionary use of public funds either foreign or local to self-promote unsustainable futures. Acting in most cases, to let indigenous values design themselves positively. That is: making use of their own resources and be empowered, by contributions of universal knowledge. Things that should be check-able by their own. Being this with physics and the ways they find in "always relative" feelings of freedom is a wise minimum. Without waiting for 'obliged smiles' and forcing heart rewards ... the most dangerous nice occidental principles.

Under the umbrella as large as a proper social utility provided by individuals. It is to be inclusive and common enough essential everyone's aspiration. This is for sustaining satisfaction; when driven by peace and construction of societies. Hence not, by the resources exposed, surreptitiously promoting the excesses of modern models, of occidental consumerism; as carried by the means of telecommunications and marketing; as well as and even more abused by the affluent and leisure classes of modern administrations and businesses of far distant leisure.

In this essay our aim is not naive. Globalization is actually quite unsustainable and the setbacks of natural disconnections, transferred to virtual poor connections with realities. Those are making misperceptions of microelectronic devices and less socially useful has to expect. Even if plenty of dimensions and comments point to quite right directions and make the many technological devices of globalization are positive.

More modest goal of this essay is to introduce some of the concepts, which appeared to us, along the road because necessary. Patterns, minimalist mechanisms, sort of half-complex processes, tricks and tips of fundamental knowledge applied to abstract approached to phenomenological realities. Those have followed us all along with natural observations of cultures.

Either functional, structural, cultural or psycho-cognitive minimalist patterns of mechanisms have no such bizarre correspondences with mathematics, logics, fundamental physics, theoretical economics, econometrics, bio-mathematics.

Once epistemologies all reviewed on one side, and the popular expressions often used as wisdom prolegomena; or popular says used as mnemonics. Only that the popular ones are and need to be local culture products and not come from the business of self-help widely translated of the nicest place for business minds: inflation of same words really compete with those required by cultural contexts.

As required to better manage, our scientific minds; "before the last words" of humanity? Our suggestions more appropriated? - For the buffer zones of abstraction, in our brains or our collectives? Such suggestions are conceived to be previous or meanwhile the processes of transforming collective determinisms, design wiser policies. That is, tools for frames-workings social-cognitive steps. Basic and essential ways of thinking are with mathematics, logics, fundamental physics, management of technological processes and; recommendable properties or concept of theoretical economics and statistics and with neuro-cognition.

Our introductory essay is about the margins of innovative concepts required for wiser thinking, especially quali-quantified. [We make intense use of these 2 prefix: 'quali' and 'quanti']. This is imagined for good economy of thinking, including tolerance for robustness. Natural things are so complex; it is a waste to pretend control so much. Thus be economic with formal efforts: enough (and much more) but not too much. This essay maybe not as simplified as your pleasure expect. Here the minimum to share. Elsewhere we are preparing a larger and more formal handbooks of epistemologies.

Sometimes ago it seemed to us necessary to introduce half complex intermediate concepts, using the visual displays, as a sort of ideography. Thus we intended to make it a proper visual grammar of design and called it 'olicognography'. After many years, we still see them essential for coping complexities and complications. That is the way large part of our brain does. We are for empowering brains not in an esoteric nor in a just determinist way. Occidentalism has perverted the rules of correct thinking in lay affairs. Most people are expected to stop thinking: in a way of 'Pensée Unique Executive Perversion'.

This essay is also starting the intent to ground formal methods, in our ideas of methods. Formal methods as we call mathematics and logics (increasingly; we do not make a difference between) ... and applied to physics and mechanisms of nature. Traditionally these have developed their applications fast; because effective and also because: 'the personal computer'. But latter one really needs better approaches of humans' uses.

This essay could be unpleasant to read by some we nevertheless revere. Because we try to avoid much the symbolic of these disciplines. As well because we write about something, 'of their own'; and not just made as simple as possible, for the vulgarization and advocacy, of their own register. We will not try to force your conviction that this is what you 'have to trust'.

You will have to see by yourselves. The more we will provide with technical details for exploring further. Any friendly complements to that essay are wise, dictionaries or handbooks. Only have the key words, the indices or the encyclopedia of the web, as Wikipedia or any working papers can be useful. That is the good part of globalization, not enough cared in consistent social-economic practices.

In realities you try, what you started to trust, are your efforts (in a consistent way), and regulate or weight yourself your values. You try to use your knowledge, or the labels of concepts to recall them. In a world of great sources for real material field and scientific literature, care nevertheless that this can too absurdly compete and misguided by over-inflation and ideological property rights.

Of course it is not our purpose to increase your existential anxiety; about what you learned for "being social." But in front of the evident complexities of life, many people react. They are left too far behind inconsistent policies, and with "poor levels of education" they are maintained out. Such levels almost wanted so: conflicting illusory knowledge makes frustrated future and left cultural systems disturbed. This often prevents from evolving into fairer pathways to social issues; when good ones were not ostracizing and stigmatizing with 'your failure', despite the fact that in so well intervened governance, 'by us'.

In abstracts many core social issues have only recently started to be approached, by some; hence too much this has been as 'special non-related problems'. Maybe this is because of conflicting management, between methods, epistemologies and ways of receiving consideration from societies; have made many mental rigidities. These rigidities have been over-promoted, and have filled too much and too many memory registers of brains'.

With 'social wordy erudition' much have just disqualified social brains' and humans' networks of decisions. Reasoning capacities have been weakened by determinist goals of achievement and neutralized. Judgments have been shortcut to reward the non-legitimate ones. Adverse effects of globalization seem too to expand proportionately more and faster than modern progress on essential knowledge, concepts and methods for sharing, volunteering cooperation and supports.

In this essay you will not find a clear doctrine. Despite being in the middle of so many pieces required to be rethought, about our abstract way of thinking that is not our goal. You may imagine that coherence, congruence should support the development of a specific "new scientific register," for receiving the support of 'specialists' cohorts.

There are, sorts of simplifications and reductions that have been in the history of scientific methods a large and important way of understanding and management and many special academic departments have been created ... with the effect to induce avoidance or by pass. Obviously, there are plenty of misunderstandings in social, economic, political, cultural, anthropological, religious and moral sciences (for some) or arts eventually called of rhetoric, dialectic or literature.

More or less appropriately arts somehow including natural sciences registers, make (unwise) use of labels such as 'complexity' and 'complicated'. Plenty of registers of management are also moving to some sorts of precautions at the respect. But, maybe, because more importance, unsolved situations or avatars of problems have taken complexities are losing much biodiversity and undue complications are not dying. It is becoming harder to maintain on some side, levels of wealth and; on the other side, turn harder to maintain and reach world-wide standard levels of diverse consumption.

When not wanting to label: 'failures'; many aid services put in difficulties of governance, regressive states, rents and curses of poverty, or terrorism --- to avoid those of: disaggregating interventions; international plots, wars on terror, accelerated rates of extraction, preservations of dividends, worldwide economical emigration.

So, not as the joke it may look like, this book is about let you with more questions after it is reading; than before. In the hope that these questions will be more about the good-will of your ideas upon your practice. Practically, the aims and limits of this essay.

It is not exhaustive neither of the title of chapter not on its ambitions; many simple arguments will miss: there is no place for more than a minimum. Many fundamental formal results and of physics world's interpretations are already available. To profane: they are often unusual; but even if they may be seen as "hard," they are essential. We try to provide with lay expressions of basic formal concepts; that ought to be understood intuitively by any citizen. Corresponding to the specialists of them to clear them further for you. Consider that many are already known explanations; that we retake sometimes not mentioning our sources. We tried to avoid 'esoteric providers' (when culturally they could be quite inspiring). We added some of our questions in a naive way. They may be taken as something needed for everyone understanding.

There are also, somehow half-complicated concepts ('hafcos'?); that seems needed by complexity approach. Traditional modern societies distrusted soon in many natural sciences to make prevail our 'kinds of amounts of mass' and plenty of 'social arts'. As soon as they caught a sort of fake overview, many tradi-modern-modem jump on just one reason and only naked explanations; reached after a very linear prospect of demonstrations. When having, by the way very narrowed the use of methods.

Thus not all these halfcos required explanations can be provided. Effectively there is a need to understand at least metaphysically and intuitively, but for coring and sharing and connect around, at one's own human distance, universal principles and examine how they develop in the real situation not orthodox nor heterodox like religiously.

Care, this essay is not about wanting absolutely to tell the truth of our physical and teleological or metaphysical world. In such complex nature it is full of inspirations for human inspirations incorporating precautions; ...

... rather than selecting our misunderstandings for some esoteric alternative determinism. Like for projecting a sort of scientism.

So first book considers basic grounds of formal sciences, treated in a vulgarized simplified way; close to the principles of physics. We repeat, you will not turn you any specialist with that. But; as profanes and citizens or 'professionals also citizens', you may understand or discover how these sciences also are.

Willing to provide collection of essential concepts to now, we made our own basic complements and we added few more things to think about; more than ensuring some thesis, sometimes explanations will look like 'mis-matching' a bit erratic. Like with drawings where you will not find the explanations you expect from the text. More they are open links not so difficult to complete, since the web, or just sort of conceptual essays ... near your neighbors or thrown as unprofitable in third worlds second hand book stores of poor markets.

[So many treasures we have seen, by the side of fictions. Themselves thrown more because their appearance not the one expected from 'looking like rich people'. Despite also plenty of unclean manuals for exams, abound and thrown because missing the essence of real life problems and the mysteries of proper thinking].

There will be a second volume, it will be about operations and sorts of low numbers pluralism, structures like networks and then larger numbers and their methods. Up to their applications in our phenomenological world.

Let call formal sciences the logics and mathematics we use. To clear our thinking about what we want to do, the things and amounts for working realities. Thinking of amounts and measures in mathematics is the basic of economics. But not make simple mathematics of amounts in reality just for the pleasure of exact and simple operations. In this essay logic and mathematics are mostly intuitively treated; to approach our reasons fast and leave out many degrees of pure mathematics actually formalized. Mistakes have been in losing the deep relations of direct experience in natural phenomenologies. If amounts do not match humans were experiencing it directly on their own bodies. Mistakes also to take pure mathematics many of conditions and issues that make them logically adapted to conceive in realities.

So we have a poor use of formal sciences in our existence because too simplified and too reduced; respect to what needed and what possible; if properly trained to be cognitively half-automatic. That is sciences progressed, technologies also but lay humans regressed their relations to evidence. Because they have switched from lives more submitted to environmental constraints; where they were evolutionarily adapted, to artificial ones more requiring of abstract care. As an effect they lack and delayed in preserving and developing sustainable societies.

Formal sciences and natural knowledge are now more appropriated to suggest since fundamental mechanisms. Including probabilistic made "statistical" and biological ecological to conceive, design and make more properly. Efforts require individual commitment rather than: experts of good will and their illusions that the technologies will do it for them. This is not for just satisfying the equation(s) of maximizing virtual 'virtuosity' (consumption, profit, leisure, laziness). Because there are coming together with minimizing: reflective thinking, essential understanding, sense of social constructions, critical efforts of personal involvement. Else social arts with the purpose of better social share (democratic, political and economic) are dumped in 'the remains' by most, possibly because promoted directly and not by 'the conditions'. [Of course the improper financial conditioning have not been let behind, it have been put deterministically ahead and that made it the 'big problem'].

Formal methods have developed so much their efforts to cope in detail, that they turned very hard for good volunteering between. Even scientific professionals of the arts qualified in excess unique voice in each register; and undercare higher free skills of synthesis and cautious translations. Social actors whom remain as subjects and players; namely the citizens in society, barely make a good use of those fundamentals. Too much they are, perturbed by interfering determinist influence. Even many professionals have missed sorts of properly empathic treatments. The structures of administrations are themselves, as well as of social civilian organizations, including the working one has 'outsourced consistency'. As a result 'qualified people of the art of essential in formal methods' waste time in their corners meanwhile most do not do with ... essentials ... they even ignore. Many 'administrators' have preferred sorts of supports by numbers for not looking at their own abuses. Whence many social groups or societies are fighting for distrust what methods tells or should tell for proper match.

It is not the challenge of this book to make a full review of formal sciences as could pretend any specialized encyclopedia and if not shelves of books.

Our aim is more with some few basic theorems, make you familiar with kinds of formulation about logic of mathematics, minimum proper concepts, naive questions and few suggestions of primary care. Possibly to remind or introduce concepts, well needed to change our way of insisting on that deterministic fundamental mistake; which can be summarized by the sentence: "we have the truth as the numbers tell."

That self-enquiries may not be so hard, as lay users would imagine. Such methods are interdependent and formal expressions show that common-ness. So if degrees of expertise rigor; do not defusing enough, nor call enough. Then doing are not dedicated, as to expect, in fair development of societies. Plenty of human resources are wasted in strange activities of bureaucracy, non-positive nor socially useful.

Now, if formal perspectives should no more imagine that one leader has the truth, even with a good personal computer (with the best program to recall) and can solve any issues. So more individual commitments, playing partly collectively, are needed. Challenge also by the side of efficient collective intelligence. It is not so easy and requires plenty of coordination, be more spontaneous than 'driven' There is too a need of good share and volunteering in cultures' wholesomeness; and preparations are required to empower society in their efforts of doing properly. This requires qualification and quantification of any sort in the formal abstraction, relevant to individuals and social duties hence not in a unique way.

A major issue is 'intertwining,' in formal practices adapted to each level. That consider: the modeling, the "mechanics" identification of parameters, the scales for measures, the selection of variables for framing problems and make use of characteristics as weights or exponents of any realities based and operated.

Formal operations may have become the refuge of simplifications, too in excess. We will see how not to complicate that too much, but relax and specify, 'kinder for operations in reality'. Problems of real-world difficulties need better implicits, in methods 'conditions of validity'. Emphasis must be made variable, on structural and functional forms, frameworks. Methods provide models, ground them, then 'upon these', humans "manipulators" can want to 'superimpose their sub-model of interference or influence'. That is: of intentions, hence more pretending to derive and obtain (that is: bias). But better not 'suck and destroy' everything of the 'grounds' first model.

Nature is still a better engineer than us, and the principles we used for our technological changes, do not play as we would like, out of the physics "rules of games." That is those who want to manipulate these "rules of games" and in some degree succeed in that not in the so artificial way many do. Progress is more with: being softer and smarter in the 'extractions' and wiser in subsystems of influence constructions.

Now, it is to observe on one side the abstract products of our formal methods and what we engineer. Since the core of the representation models; makes the representations, or models, of realities that both individuals as well as social say to collect information and use with tools. The first representation is a model or object respect to a second original in reality which is a subject, or should carefully be. Subjects will have to receive a fair treatment respect to the object pretending to represent them and set by identifying relations between subject and object(s) and details relations such as similarities, equalities, and when at the political issue assignments (or attributes). Similarities address patterns, especially made of the functional sorts of natural effects. Identities would be for the correspondence and symmetries.

Here a formal primary in an intricated universe: you have to imagine most things playing in some degree on its own (field, logic, atom) and also in some extend in any other (in many cases) (logic, atom, field). From that established relations in reality or 'to come in reality' of similarity (or non-contrasting operators), equalities (or inequalities), limits (and distance from), in (or out) the borders of some unit.

In short anything is playing in its ground and at the same time, at least looking at another one. That is a fundamental dual (or primal-dual, when a 'problem'). The trick being here that it has to appear so in the formalism. Notice also the system concept of 'identification'. Observe that we already used plenty of concepts basically to modeling.

Too much ('out and many in') economic management prosper modeling but not made this identified by all. Even with formal procedures with technologies engineers have narrow-minded just those steps. Relevant parameters have been avoided because not from the economics specialized register. When this has not been miscared. Important even when major concern of economics is about quantification. Even when the aim could be about what humans have to do. Basically these kinds of under-care from political economic modelers, willing to share their processes, are not so different from the segregation made by "similar" manipulators of social arts; when they are trying to force, with 'clean-fewer arguments' their reasons or connections to the 'sources of finance'.

Those often have extraordinary extended the abstract qualitative concepts on ... 'what they want from as simple as that'. When even not against the very physics or nature of these. Even out common fragment of a nucleus of spirituality allowed. Historically they even had invented convenient gods (or the same their own version, different from others') for adapting and creating registers of exclusivity and ownership. Insofar to pretend about their "special will" to "have the whole picture" or 'cover enough'.

Unconsciously or not; they create sorts of hegemonic concepts, that should be "core for others, because of themselves". This is done, whatever the consistency to human's common use; or its irrelevancy to core-ness. Especially when having been able, by the social norms and means, to create and develop unequal societies, based on discrimination, segregations and extractions. They avoided good uses of methods in social environment, especially when having observed these could help to find wiser alternatives.

For example: it may be surprising to have arguments with professional humanitarians when you are only providing them just with formal elements supporting their own views. That is, objectors miss just you are supporting them. Maybe this because they are embarrassed with their own implicit martingale if not by their ways of thinking. And so more they want you to admit their masquerade (by no means legitimate respect to the local culture in its environment.

More important than, turn that you accept their 'eccentric' ideology (of the first world) in fact not much more than their private interest. Without caring whether social economics effectively care freedom and social economics effectively.

So nice could be the anti-formalists, they oppose affirming their caprice and their difference. Or more avoid transparent approaches, because reminding their nightmares with mathematics symbolism, tricky 'lunatic' exercises and common missense of logics. Education systems and ways of training are not free from critics about these; which also does not care enough about societies with fairly operating core and clean?

The specialists may lack minima of pedagogy. Good connections between formal methods and importance of open-minds are good at respecting. Arguments often misaddress and express ignorance about those methods. In that way these difficulties are effectively informative; especially on 'out contexts'. 'Legitimate contexts should have such sorts of consistency. Heterodox critics of social economics or social arts imbued of quantifying methods; often react on over-simplistic weak strength of logics. They are not necessarily nurturing structures of democratic; nor they are effectively preventing 'democratic ways of abuses' possibly because part of the weakening. To care a presumption a primary respect to anyone, and be cautious with the principles of the universe.

There are in many sorts of social problems, needs to account in a broader way but, first of all, more logical ways respect to the real situations, including cultures: formal methods not a substitute to them, not so difficultly. For such sort of perspective we will often prefer to call "wholist" instead of "holistic" as such ways of approaching. Formally, it is about smoothing relations between global and local. Precisely not in some unique way of social arts. But more for some clearness in scientific commons; environment and core; atoms and surroundings; particles (joined somehow) with superposed fields.

We need is to care much more about as many as possible good social ways to use formal methods for exemplary positive social economics. Included in the respect of potentials. Thus for clearing explanations and possibilities; inspire and share such methods. For helping, servicing and supporting social relations do in the possibilities of Nature and without substituting collective intelligence and commitments.

Of course economically, many social and shared problems deserve to be better formulated, for inspiring solutions. But it is about an economy of formal efforts too. Hypothetically we are like in the hope that the social-economics of formal sciences; used in our common lives, now made of plenty of symbolic numbers and technological interfaces: should for example develop 3 times to cope better with the challenges of computed information era. But we are also convinced that the present bias and wrong uses should be divided by 2 if not more, to save time, especially wasted by bureaucracy for their own 'efficiency'.

With social statistics there are proliferations of data collections and operations. Many professionals enjoy this kind of salary even when aware of a lot of uselessness and; conscious of many waste of time. Meaning by the example that we could behave and do better by a coefficient of 6, having reduced by 2 the fancies of leadership in caring.

[In industrial economic terms, we would say that it is to internalize costs more socially, expand more intensities of synergies, wasteless. In public economics it could be said: externalize and delegate more for less subsidiary, social contract more efficiently and rationalize less deterministically. In mathematical economics it would be said: non-linearize the technical coefficients, diffuse more the threshold up toward positive effects; rebalance the critical ratios of balance and choice...

But overall recognize we have really poor clues on risks of non-linearity with sensibilities of original specifications. Such as those which are in the switches from fields into operations. Much we ignore about the proper ways to diffuse wisely. Because diffusions are complex percolations even more complicated when manipulated by direct determinisms. We do not have much to say about the leverage effects, pushing the criticality of systems or operations, just observe the ones of finance not properly phenomenological. And observe that we have really stupid guys or groups, by the side of hierarchical choice]... Much of the truth about up to the date of globalization policies.

Somehow, Kuhn's social paradigm on his theory of scientific revolutions was adapted: to conceive transformations in technological societies too forced to turn rude for obtaining minimum shares. Theory also received (pre and post) some fuel from recycling of Schumpeter's: capitalism creative destruction. More recently this was supported by Roemer's 'endogenous growth'. But such way of harsh renewal they were somehow challenged, well before the revolution of information, like by Veblen, Ellul or Galbraith...

Personal computer period going on, this TIC revolution came together with many bizarre ideas of their own utopia. Like to make artificial intelligence intent replace humans in most things ... when it not has been serving nice post-industrial rhetoric if not by the beat generation. Like if promoting lazy, obese and stupid first world, could be the best evolutionary game to happiness; meanwhile armadas of less stupid than us robots would have done the jobs, controlled by Asimov's law.

From self-care and up to democratic social management; societies have exposed too much their social misconstructions, to systemic and global failures. Both because not enough with formal approaches and too wrong with themselves. For not taking them properly as methods, tools and conditions so as to avoid the disqualification of care of primary values. Failures are now evidenced in so-called 'systemic' in the national or regional crisis; missing the responsibility of economic social world-wide problems. Conflicts exhausting humanities, worsening global dimensions but this maybe digging one's own graveyards, producing wars and poorly democratic societies. Despite so many efforts to make them nice to the global leaderships; and despite or because of the wonders of technological achievements.

World-wide systems are supposed to be informative but they seem not to imagine that improper qualified and quantified management have been major part in the breaking of dances, and still do not hold their responsibilities. Their private when not often conquered over public, have strongly biased public social needs in their due ratio to possibilities keeping an eye on social partners of sustainability.

> No need to be fond of mathematics, logics and physics, nor be phantasm-like. What we will try to understand, in the essay are the requirements for logics, quantifications, congruence, coherence, covariance and compactification, at the interface of humans and tools and within real communities.

Mistakes could have been avoided just looking more thoroughly. For example: in epistemologies the precautions are still not a subject of systemic concern. Or more appropriately said: still too concerned by the purity of algorithms (which is fine in many technological *calculus* but the way 'brains compute'). So this is dangerous when making operations between humans; people turning them 'down-sizable'. In short, our deep conviction is that methods and management must formally intertwine and reflect like 4 pillars in the management of knowledge:

- **Care phenomenologies**: that is the perception of circumstances and evidences at sight. In many social issues they are enough complex and complicated. Not to examine them in, too pre-prepared explanation scopes; [... it ground effective empathy];

- **Fundamental knowledge**: any that could be widely communicated (but too obfuscated). This being mainly, of formal and natural sciences or technical when too much light has been projected on services of abstract world-wide standards of 'normalizing without semantic';

- **Cultural preferences in democratic ways** of complications for social deliveries; anchored to their areas of living; so-called "university of life." But often mistreated by bureaucratic standards of management, taught there and too prone to abuse of norms;

- **Natural cognitive processes including those shared**, and based on complementarities and experienced environments (in their ecosystem).

Ways of Science
(Loops in the Hoops?)

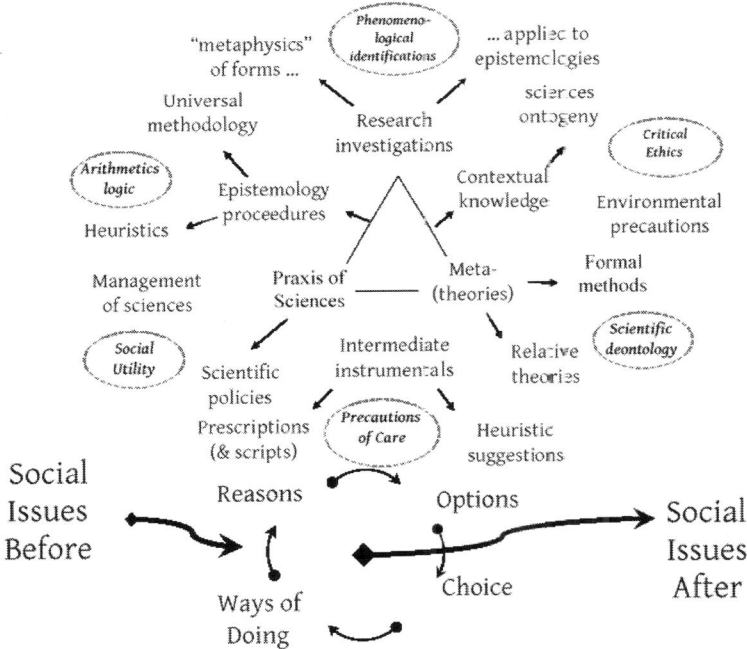

Formal Thinking

Upon the 'poorly voluntarily shared' universals of mathematics and logics; all should feel concerned, by the lack of proper and honest combination. In specialized (and sub-specialized) registers their use would be to obtain proper informative balances in human affairs. We should want to cultivate them between all, in a humble way and avoid wasting time in polemics. Dual combinations, properly implemented in cares would change the way nature appreciate the indifference humans have at the respect most universal frameworks. Nature's do use mathematics and logics in a wiser than humans.

When approaching Nature with "hard" working formal science(s) is to shape your intelligence. Efforts of abstractions humans have naturally developed much, even when useless. This uselessness could still be good and the best you could do if thinkers do not implying much consumption nor 'waste nature'. If thinking and doing do not disturb anything it is quite good. This is often better, since Nature has its own better flows towards potential evolutions of species. Often more efficient than humans at supplying the omnivorous thinking animals. [Namely, close ones as badgers, boars and some aggressive apes including the one pretending, (often as a joke when the familiar to a dictator to have superior values].

Abstracting, to try to free you and people around, from difficult contingencies; making it peacefully and cunningly while still enjoying life will make your condition of nothingness on Earth an enviable one ... more reasonable than any lost paradise and made possible thank to so much capital of knowledge accumulated for making biases as smart and sweet are possible without eluding efforts.

Best mathematicians; can be any kinds of humans, but best ones are often naive, only about their pure and perfect register and less so; compared to their fellow citizens. So purity of mathematics a good way to *nirvana*? Modern societies, offer them kinds of, not so bad conditions of life as teachers or calculators. Those not the best ones can often be involved in leadership, since good at manipulating operations. But most human ambitions in disciplines of abstraction, do not master properly. Perhaps because they have not trained for being happy with formal methods. But more to use them in serious bourgeoisie-ness, when not programs aggression and special devices of destructions. [If you do not use them is just as in the basis of theory of potential]

Should purity of abstractions be the ultimate goal?–maybe so only for yourself, but avoid too many expectations for others. Purity in Nature is globally absurd, especially for proactive humans. Contemplation with the merits already mentioned. Religious people not have to feel offended, but their constructions are hardly an independent and free *panacea*. Humans could be right to react; to sort of challenges posed by others. Just freedom of reactions is often failing despite good intentions and hardly in the constructions of wiser societies. [Ingenuousness probably to reserve to questions to formal sciences?]

Mathematics spirits look-like tending to infinite simplicity of numbers and perfection in operations ... doing their best to such a perfection even when formal sciences even evidenced demonstratively their own self-limits. This is quite surprising: why intent to manage exactly if there are plenty of reasons to think that probabilities governs and deviations to average not so bad, once fairness ensured, robustly? Arithmetic is not complete. Formal logics has probably its lack of completion to, and it may be more a question of language [at the simplest level]?– the reasons of the mismatches between Wittgenstein, Popper or Carnap?

Physicists Best Users of Mathematics

Theoretical physics is 'almost using' mathematics the best way, and has narrowed (unconsciously?) this *locus* of purity to only inhuman abstract models: perfect gas, full emptiness, 'perfect' crystal and not few more. Purity for physicists has been for very specially controlled experiments on principles. Thereafter physicists have clearly in mind that reality's conditions are very different and, sort of simplifications from purification is more for utilitarian transformations rather than smart nature of physics. Humility taught by dire proper social uses of formal sciences should prevailed, despite the 3rd or 4th modern world system (1) Arabic, 2) Dutch, 3) British, 4) American) is still embarrassed with many ideologies. Ideologies are 'unrelaxed by their increasing uses of formal methods: compulsive behaviors, syndrome of withdrawal from determinism and, *delirium* of authoritarianism: have still plenty of wide places of expansions.

First you have to mind that in physics 'full emptiness' (perfect quantic *vacuum*) may not be a pure symbolic oxymoron; but a quantic place filled with stuff; that does not make much sense at your scale of concern; to your measuring devices, but is the source of every particles (or configurations?–of fields-atoms). Quantic theory still debating, not for its validity generalized to whole physics; but just and no more on some details (as told by Aspect, a French physicist having experienced electron entanglement (we often use the term of 'intrication'). Then how to take account of that in normal complex life?

Quantic Physics Positioning

Traditionally Quantic theory has plenty of counter-intuitive concepts, respect to determinist illusion but experimentally recognized; to fit very well the estimates of this theory. About quantic theory maybe you can mentally have to work so:
- **Not to imagine particles and field separately,** for most, any particle has a field; field(s) producing particles(s) (and transformations?); and conversely particles 'driving' fields? ... [maybe stable only statistically dynamically balanced];
- **superimposed fields produce particles(s), at a given probabilities of creation and; disappearance** of particles(s) at given rates too, [once **potential configurations preserved by the numbers?**].

- Out protons and electrons (and their anti-particles) most particle-are not stable and can have very short life). But their **molecular renewals at level of living bodies, are probably faster (than imagined?)**
- So how? - if looking like fixed, they could (be) nurture (d) an entire life? - the answer may be in **frameworks; rather than atoms alone**.
- How statistics could make this?–or help in that: reproduce always nearby frameworks or configurations and their fields (maybe not at the "same time") both the memory and the primary openness ... suggesting that **'order' is impossibly 'definitive with the same'** and renewal (by 'musical chairs'?) is key?
- That way particles and/or fields are **'open to relations'** at characteristic amounts of masses, energy (ies); transfers and speeds.
- That sorts of **obliged relations being distributed** at: atomic, chemical and other different levels of characteristic energies, and transfers; and so on. [Squint as a whole, imagine a sort of Chinese boxes, from the smallest to the largest with space (or holes) (to **smooth integration** of paradox?) and; between **evolutionary processes** (since the fundamental), allowing the **emergence of more frames, when cooling or slowing** by **differentiation of basic**;
- The named reasons why: **4 types of forces**: 1) just attractive matter (started with Newton, completed by the 2 chapters of Einstein: special relativity theory and general relativity theory (energy linking relation Einstein's formulation of total mass-energy relation); but with transferable energy; 2) electromagnetic (main **attracting** between signed negative-positive charges in motion; **separating** when of the same signs (negative-negative; positive-positive), these 2 mainly for masses and electric charge mechanics, theory designed by Maxwell, almost alone; further then put into Quantic theory especially by Dirac);
- **Range of characteristics** mass naming the particle, since almost null mass (pure quanta of energy?) -with photon eventually with maximum limit of speed light's, only made of photons (or mass-less);
- 3) & 4) Weak and strong interactions: 2 forces for/from *nuclei* of atoms; mechanics. With the dual of in core (hadrons in nuclear physics), out (the previous forces for leptons and mesons with mobile particles); the weak one demonstrated related or "avatar" to electromagnetic force (subject of the quantic electrodynamic chapter); strong interaction (subject of the quantic chromodynamics chapter) still not well connected (in search of great unified theory);
- You probably know from recent events that gravity fields exist with their special quanta Higgs's boson. This basic is also making "naked gravity" a space of simple curves? [do not miss Einstein's correspondence with energy]
- Less simple than thought bases of **'intrication(s)'** (or entanglement(s), to expect one day more inspiring for proper formulation of the 'system' [we will see some 'sub-management' further.].

Physicists have still plenty of work of formulation to deliver formal understanding to all. For us only naive observations, they are because that could be helpful to think about at social humane macro-level:

- Fields cross with particles, balanced at characteristic values?; since the **beginning of micro-start** (be this beginning to emerge from origin phases and/or from sub-particles (quarks) and "naturally selected upon their **discrete position(s) stability**);
- this may make - either - discrete nature start **filling continuity**–or - previous phase fundamental physics states somehow **continuous but then 'holing'** by attraction after the **dispersion and cooling** then, **naturally selecting** (according big bang theory and **aftermaths**);
- particles relatively more compact, more **discrete like ordered as ordinals** and their field looking like more **continuous as somehow cardinals** [just this place of selection much below in the scale, that is to say 'before' biology];
- Energetic and kinetic propulsions of particles-fields along pathways either original (and maintaining somehow, some fields quite extended as those of gravity and originally by Big Bang theory) but switching into characteristic proportions; then switching back? (Locally and globally after the reach environment) expand their fields immediately far ahead at the origin. Propelled (furthest one by physics world conducts of coherence?–if not strings), and;
- **Interacting** with other particles and other fields; redesigning local fields that can be 'from the galaxy down to us' (us higher but in kinds of cool complexities? On nicer borders of galaxies?);
- So the sort of interactions can consider: of fields-fields (superposition?), fields-quanta, quanta-fields ('entanglements'. quantic jump, and so on) and quanta-quanta (atoms assemblies and molecules but sharing other forms of the field), it is important to consider **species of statistics** (in enough amounts) and **probability can be the formal tool for approach** since kindergartens.

[We will see simple interesting analogies further].

Advocacy for the Use of Logarithm in Qualities or Exponents in Quantities

Logarithm (rec. exponential) allows us to **catch different levels of similarity**, across scale(s) of given amounts, indicated various bases in the lower range (rec. upper range). Logarithm transformations **converting exponents into products** and **products into sums** (reciprocally up in exponents).

Core is there the Euler constant e ($\approx 2.7182818..$) of neperian base (provided by Swiss exiled mathematician Euler). It appears unsurprising in a large number of mathematical characteristic formula. e^x function is non-vanishing: $e^x \neq 0$. Sort of universal constant may still has some physics interpretations to uncover? [Say this is a basic for the start of bifurcation or a minimum for a self-degree of informative freedom?].

γ is another key Euler's constant; $\gamma = e^C$; with $C = \lim_{n \to \infty} (\Sigma_{\upsilon=1}^{n} 1/\upsilon - \ln n) \approx 0.577$.

Euler's constant has also an important relation with interest rates at the infinite:

$$C = \lim_{n \to \infty} [1 + 1/2 + 1/3 + ... + 1/n - \ln(n+1)]^n = -\int_0^{(} e^{-t} \ln(t).dt$$

Euler's constants support transformation "positioning all into the transcendental register" [Mind that multiply by 0 position all in 0, but adding 0 does not change amount... and just imagine that non effective addition with objects or subjects requiring to renew for 'staying the same'. In physics this not at all 0 is just your-self **minimum compensation of entropy, for staying the same**].

Thus "only reasonable approximations, linking transcendental to infinite **series** approximations. Series approximations are essential to the conceptions of **functions** in mathematical analysis. It is a "progress" towards infinitesimal calculus and approach of limits near infinite large or small (by 'impossible' division). **Logarithms relates straight-line geometry with circular one via trigonometric and differential** *calculus*.

To accelerate the rhythm about the proposal to use more the non-straight-lines of logarithms and exponential, some properties together with ideas:

There is the **symmetry** of $y = \log(x)$ to $y = e^x$ to the straight line x=y. Log of one (1) is 0; log of base is 1. Product of amounts rules the sum of their logarithms; quotient of amounts rules difference of their logarithms. Power of amounts rules by logarithm transformations products of amounts. Changes the bases is so: ($\log_{base\ a}$ variable = $lob_{base\ b}$ variable/$\log_{base\ b}$ base a). Inverse property (base $\log^{base'a'variable}$ = variable or logbase 'a' ^{variable} = variable). The **log$_{odds}$ of a probability** $plog_2 p$, {p|p $\in$ [0,1], i.e. p that looks like a probability} is the logarithm of the odds between the probability p and its complement p^c = 1-p. The inverse of the log$_{odds}$ functions logit ($\cdot$) is the standard 'logistic function'.

The relationships between 'signed distance maps' and 'space conditioned probabilities' define a meaningful probabilistic model; log$_{odds}$ maps form **a vector space** and as so, is composed *via* **linear** methods; while simultaneously maintaining the intrinsic properties of shapes. Log$_{odds}$ not only describes the shape of a single **structure** but also capture some aspects of **variations** within a structure across populations and expert segmentation.

In the **general solvable logarithm**: the low base relation is the economy of networks, threshold of detectability or differentiation ability (a wild field of potential exploration). An essential to examination the **emergence of complex units** will take complex numbers as formal core. Complex numbers are related to trigonometric functions and power (exponent) expression [Even if this looks like too above your understanding, put that in mind and wait we will provide more explanations further].

Thermodynamic Connection

Now to start some relations to thermodynamic thinking:
- Concept of the **system** will be illustrated all along this essay; (local collection with some, joined together (at first by gravity) [with some **laws of conservations**, if physical concept]; differentiated by order (or '**counter-entropy**' (neguentropy) if informing).

- **Openness** of identified system (or sub-parts of the system) is fundamental; this openness is essential for anything 'happens and goes on': **transformations, exchanges, losses** and **gains**; be of anything: matter, energy ... much disordered (easier to provoke, be caught and waste; but also for being eternal or 'ethereal'); somehow ordered (easier to congregate, propel and cool (?) and evolve; but "deserting or emptying the surroundings", than possibly then **die** from 'self-starvation');
- **Variable openness-closure of the system**(s) is always with a minimum non-null of the other sort); exchange about what you can absorb and relax; [possibly expressed in the formal ... or limiting 'degeneracies' (if we understand degeneracies as the way to get down from the general formulation expression (wave-like?), to local values (atom-like?);
- Formula null *vacuum* is 1) an inner one as a statistic production of less than 0 *vacuum* (creation will emerge something "from the magic hat" or the 'quantic sea') and; 2) outer cosmic *vacuum* (where there could be, plenty of matter that we cannot see.

Why practically this could be macro-minded usefully (and how?):
- Never consider static and alone quanta but: quanta & field (eventually crossed?) + balances of creation & disintegration...
- Our nature (not necessarily the whole universe) is **soft-discrete** (oxymoron1) and **hard-continuous** (oxymoron2); of numbers: natural they are prone to whole **set**(s) and **intervals**, or more diverse (in its sub-sets of functional-structure); with space [care that our terms of logics and theory of numbers are not just 'for the style'];
- Our physics' systems are anyhow relatively open (so we can exist: renew, exchange, function); and relatively closed system somehow ordered frame-work and structuring (not considering our entire universe) **only special fractions of cases** ... the 'relative' term meaning that **priorities can modulate after the environmental change**s or/and the will (of hunger);
- [For sure: we have to stop to consider ourselves 'unique in the cosmos' but; that does not mean that other aliens will come to invade us; even if we would like to justify our self-defense and so the reverse: get there and 'civilized them' (when this sort of argument will not be more than "Beetlejuice them" while taking advantage of their natural resources];
- Consider mass conversion to energy, in an almost pure way: at light speed (absolute formula, maximum frequency possibly shortest wave period) then Einstein's formula $e=mc^2$). But a large chunk of mass quanta relatively related (possibly larger wave period ... in the present stage of the theory, relativity related?) ... not traveling at light's speed and so cut it by 2 (to explain work on Earth $w = \frac{1}{2}mv^2$? - or some ratio between order and disorder? At observed temperatures).
- Cosmologically plausible (according to the system of reference), still enormous speeds around us: the cosmic bodies will not be anywhere they could like in the space but in **balance between centripetal-centrifugal** forces; thus relatively (to ourselves) in a **place of equilibrium** where 'proprioception can ignore' the speed at which Earth turns around the Sun (out of seasons) and in the Milky

Way (not the chocolate bar). Meanwhile our observation of the celestial bodies or way out Earth's attraction: should not ignore that. [... The proprioception is the feeling of the positions, of the pieces of our body (limbs, head and trunk...].

- Also having to care about conditions called **extensive parameters** like temperature, volume, pressure, etc. outer defined Especially because fundamental switches (or twists?); eventually manipulated by the conditions of constraining parameters could display characteristic critically values of phase reasonable existence (inner values called intenties);
- In the formulation of anything it is always to join the **concept of tensor** (eventually vector) as a primary kernel for abstract reasoning on physical subjects... motion out and motion in [as an **informative piece** ... or just the **differentiate** or **integration** formula when formalizing?].

Notions and Relations of Thermodynamic

[To expect some other briefs about **space, time, unit definition, systems of reference, entropy** and so on further ... since other core concepts are in much need ... as you have detected?]. Now knowing that our intuition go too fast, and do not explain much let have a better advised respite: Migdal quoted by Chizhov [our comment]:

- Quantum mechanics predictions are ambivalent, they offer only **probability** of this or that event [openness should prevail in some degree less than all absolutely closed or 1: and more than 0];
- **Probabilistic description applies both to complex and simple systems** of *quantum* mechanics ['common residual pit' open to all: energy ... but also a **framework of differentiated residuals**; since they can save by recycling; by yourself, if you can dispose properly Carnot's compartments; but often more wisely by nature's diversities, self-reproducible if biological];

- The probabilistic nature of predictions lies in that, the properties of micro objects cannot be studied; unless the means of study are taken into account [means get "in" the residue for all?–but maybe not in the '1st last gap'];
- Wave function is not a physical but an information field [but (out "*vacuum*" of gaps'?); [but we prefer Petrova's view: fields are (also?) particles produced; otherwise mostly yes to "information" ... as a class; if information also as a time concept and as a model];
- The **superposition principle** is of *quantum* mechanics: the full function made a **wave functions** of, mutually exclusive events. [Objection as before and superposition of fields: both of all and special. Thus discrete *spectrum* is about finite possible levels of energies, of a given particle and for the particles: of a given superposition].

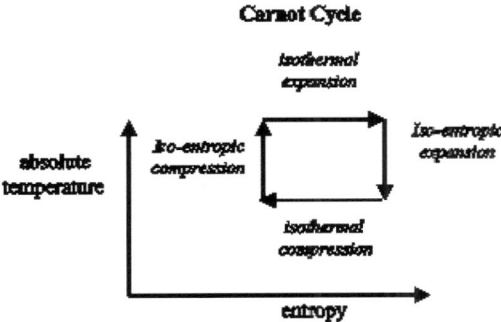

Formal structure of quantum mechanics has 3 types of basic assumptions:
- **Manifold** are the main object of representation [to understand that any kind of observation, or measure through a window (... formally a relative system?), passes by a sort of map, or surface of exchange (or layer or leaf), so a concept of manifold];
- The (pure) **physical state** of a system is **described by a ray** $|\psi\rangle$ in a unitary function space (Hilbert space); the inner product between 2 such states $|\psi\rangle$ and $|\phi\rangle$ is denoted $\langle\psi|\phi\rangle$;
- . Each numerable observable physical quantity is represented by **an Hermitian linear operator in the function space;**

The only attainable numerical value in a measurement of an observable or a function of an observable are the Eigenvalue, of the associated operator, and any such Eigenvalue is a possible result of such a measurement [Eigenvalue a concept we will detail further]. The expectation value for measurements is made by the Hermitian form $\langle Q\rangle = \langle\psi|Q|\phi\rangle$; if the ray is normalized so that $\langle\psi|\psi\rangle = 1$.

"Equations for material systems and equations of field theory is 'radically distinguished types' of differential equations. Those of natural systems have to describe physical quantities. Solutions of field theory have to describe physical structure (of which physical fields are made of), to which closed exterior forms are assigned."

Basic elements of the **equations for material systems are derivatives by integrate** upon which one can obtain the desired function describing physical quantities.

Half micro-scope on States (Dirac formalism) and representing wave			
Dirac formalism	Wave		Applications
	Functions	equations	
$\lvert \varphi \rangle$	$\varphi \rangle$	Poisson	Electro-magnetism
$\lvert \psi(t) \rangle$	$\psi(\mathbf{r},t)$		Acoustics
$\langle \psi_2 \mid \psi_1 \rangle$	$\int \psi_2 {*}\langle \psi_1 \rangle d^3 r$		Newton gravity
$\lvert \psi \rvert^2 = \langle \psi \mid \psi \rangle$	$\int \lvert \psi \rangle \rvert^2 d^3 r$	Navier – Stockes	fluids dynamics
$\langle \psi_2 \mid \hat{A} \mid \psi_1 \rangle$	$\int \psi_2 {*}\langle \hat{A}\psi \rangle d^3 r$	Schrödinger	de Broglie
$\langle a \rangle \langle \psi \mid \hat{A} \mid \psi \rangle$	$\int \psi {*}\langle \hat{A}\psi \rangle d^3 r$	Schrödinger extended	Klein-Gordon
			Dirac
		General Relativity	Einstein Field

Differential expressions and differential forms in quantic mechanics are the basis of field theory equation.
- Type I: differential equations describe processes
- Type II: (field theory) essential relations between differential forms

Diverse particles and their respective fields, co-existence suggests plural logics? **Quantic theory logic is also called multi-valued logic**—some few may be formally clean. Remind too many modes of modal logic are "unclean" (in a logic metaphoric way, possibly following in that Girard).

We know that the previous is short. As a minimum, know about the 'dangers to come' having better care of fundamental physics management. This required both by the **ecology** if wanting to put it at the core of our required abstraction for ... 'saving the Planet'? And also computer **world-wide revolution under globalization, needs much better care of context-linked languages of Culture** (to extend Chomsky). More modest formal systems should be properly packaged for making computing systems work less stupidly and humans keep their master-minding of their issues.

And About Logics

Most common 'logicians' practices' have an ambition of unitary logic (clear from any ambiguities) but have not found any so ... even in arithmetic logic all have failed. (In the purest corner of 1st order logic). Somehow for not despair? It still hoped to be filled. And also the binary one (Boolean logic: the logic of yes/no or '0 or 1'—that of the computer) is, still required by the present computers. At least until Quantic Computing take the lead [without making easy the emptying of bank accounts]. So some human needs for reasoning made or still make:

- Unitary-ness for materialist thinking, whatever the level of it "consolidation" is impossible without arbitrary cut?–because **at least we need a small contrast** like A (some event) and non-A (¬A) ... basic support for a primary link?

- Binary logic developed many applications, since the one of computer Boolean logic (after a British logician) of 'true-false' logic.

- Further special logics for some kinds of problems logic. But soon their master wants to include and fix more problems of contradictions (especially because they are more specified?). When increasing the details .. either up (in broader generalization, not enough specifiable when not logical enough blocks) or down (in more focused cases leading to too many only specified details for non-general solutions).

[It will not be a waste to think about the problems of globalization both as threat to construction of societies ... filled of tautological policies not assuming honestly?–and the difficulties of software program ... in their economy of sheets of papers?].

- Logics of few (more than 2) may be called **tri-valued logic**, or **modal logic** [imagine "modalities"]; with avatars elsewhere as in network analysis with its sorts of **cliques** and other. These require to be better or easier (and closer to natural human languages of intuitive logics).

[They are probably the best for what needed in our approaches of half-complex formalities: they can start all **network systems** of **feed-backs, connectivity, smallness, coalitions**; have **'generally solvable equations'** ... but lacks the merits of: omniscience, omnipotence nor without absence of logical shadows;.

- Some "many numbers,' or **cardinals** can follow **great number laws** [so called in statistics or probability theories].

[A clique is a subset of vertices, of an undirected graph; such that its induced subgraph is complete; that is, every two distinct vertices in the clique are adjacent.].

Just one first order logic?—you human is not an abstract one, so when you want to "know yourself" properly dualize, start to anchor at 3–4 and "systematize to close higher."

Articulate logics [like few] and mathematics [like many] need specification; but care: there are more elements of logics to manage at once [in a sentence of logics]. It implies that more logical contradictions and difficulties, you will meet for cleaning operating logics. This poses problems automating computed machine ... as high as can be the piles of present "software" programs; fundamentals are not respected, any software program is closed by itself. For example, clusters with partitions (despite pruning) ... and socially this is horrible. [But to expect quantic computations for replacing humans?].

Of course any human mind tries intuitively to be logic and train hes (his & hers = hes) brain, mostly making sense to that (even unconsciously). As a result, intuitive expressed logic is correctly ... monstrous (the number of your neurons): for humble human needs, in their one at a time. Working immediate brain memory is about half a dozen key words [on matter of seconds and few minutes but with the monstrous side: the work of billions of neural cells.

This monstrous rate of reduction means at least: no-more to call 'animal spirit minds' in such despicable way, there should be some reasons that could be expressed in formal foundations. [In the way of 'simplexity'?

> "Simplexity may be defined as the combination of simplicity and complexity, within the context of a dynamic relationship between means and ends." (Compain)].

We should care: not to waste and treat humans' intelligence better: by providing good conditions to individual and collective intelligence. Like with: work aids, economics of information, avoidance of conscious prejudgments and help better in everyone task.

Animal spirit is essential for solving the contingencies of common life especially when no time to consciously explore all the options of explanation(s) and have enough "just in time"; the reactions to save our lives before too late.

This, does not mean that brain cannot be humanely prepared. Even if preparation is subject to memory loss and uneconomical thinking. A primary would be to take into account the diversity of intelligence (there are between half or full of a dozen, and quite often our (fake) occidental competitive way care mainly a couple; talk and reports.

Worldwide buzzing media fill airs with determinist lay concepts; often absurdly trying to catch the one-ness priority of viewers' attention. And with a comprehensive solution (some 'one' direction provided in standard framework: 'the good the bad and the ugly' for some; the 'good, the bad or the beautiful' for others). So emotions can emerge from that; or calling for feeling of concern; for something very far beyond the viewers' range of careful management.

For the formal human at a range of good practice, such news are almost always bizarrely formally shaped, mistreat **transmissions** and carry many logical absurdities. First, respect to the **context kinds of plural perceptions** (where the solutions start); second in the sort of managed combinations; thus overall where the free **provisions of measures and quantification**, that may change the whole picture, are often lacking.

They carry many **implicits** (more or less **hidden** when not developed by the viewer); that helps many to suspect sort of plots; because cognitively **any tries to complete** the pictures. There are manipulations; but after cultural ways of collective interpretations. These are much less than effectively coming from strategic thinking **mimics**. Major defects come in fact; from the components and structure of real information, which is mostly missing: since in the habits of communication consider really about; what and how information is.

The reason why just some efforts at saving words by some formal checks, avoidance of missed and uncontrolled sources; considering information. there could be: better links to materiality. To have and care about, more consistently. This would better participation to the buildings of communities and societies. Massive means would waste less of communications and care economically more essential information. Less noise, more consistency and the globalization would look-like more pleasant: more consistent, with less censorship or sheep-like effects.

Lay people and any cultured consistent groups make use of **similar conceptual terms** and they often did not reach so different kinds of definitions; least not in their own terms and **conceptual design frameworks**. What is important is more that they succeed in doing well and be supported in the right place and the proper ways. So when designing some **block of information to communicate** (say a message); it is good to remind physics tips. Accounts of those will be provided. Of course it is far from easy, to prevent the accumulations of distortions, about a message. Nevertheless, there are better behaviors and better ways for treatment of information or communications; upon useful subjects.

For example, with the amounts obtained from statistics and more careful probabilistic; without trying to impose excessive **filters** and **simplifications** of messages to others; nor restrict the work to do, in the adaptation to the most relevant problems to the audience; on real scientific contains and empathically understood.

Informative concepts are to open and share in modeling or representations and actions. Among the most important is the physics' ground of the world a micro of basic needs; **to refer deviations**; and scientific descriptions of the environment; focused upon **relatively autonomous units of operations**. Some framing down, close to what is relevant to social issues, can be required from intents of social influence; like when policies and programs... Not looking-like throw down to them inaccessible superstructures of governance. Also to prevent non-unique and narrow-minded imposed solutions introduced as 'the only way to solve the problem'. Not to ignore the requirements of cognitive developments needed to make sense in common issues.

Anyhow it is to prevent the "all for sure" even if it is also to be robust enough and not too affecting the survivals in current lives. The future, at best, synergistically supported policies by individuals may be in "targets of communications; with blocks of information." An arithmetic logician could say **classes** and **sets**. Eventually to **shape systems of information** with '**do it yourselves together formal systems**'; open to requirements of local complements and involve cultural dimensions with 'higher values.' Higher values are quite universal but as basic, almost innate, makes they should be culturally expressed, and not forced by digressing manipulations (if projects are legitimate and non-violent).

Communicating the basic, from outside; for reflecting economically the essential scientific understandings (compatible with the levels) ... and not much more: the complements are more local. Communicating for supporting others' questions and provision of ... not too narrowed tools; by the previous decisions. So that **each, as a community; could work their own models**; include their own **dimensions** somewhere and in different ways.

That is not a big thing where intuitive approximations dominate; but have in mind: 1) it took years of child development and adulthood experience for properly communicating within one's own culture; 2) conceptual translations still very poor and weak; 3) not to call "proper communication of information about real sciences" most of the stuff prevailing in managerial standards.

[They are often so tautological that the problem is more of a correct local correspondence and collaborative implementation, rather than a motive of alienation by the goals decided above, at the top].

We find basic to insist on **information** should anchor locally in phenomenological mental maps, with an important register on how 'natural' physics world could work. Essential knowledge can be provided. Social constructions have to follow if values are genuine and authentic.

Humans have (mainly but not only) **brained visual maps**; for articulating instruments (either conceptual or material). They are **not only conscious but**

entangled with 'unconscious'. Even by the side of conscious-ness humans have plenty cognitive resources of better thinking; but much is unconscious.

That does not mean any has 'superpowers'. Unconscious is not simply innate: it can be formed and trained (not as a perfect determinist would think). Moreover to account for environmental logics. Possibly caught by perceptions (of many kinds, more than 5) and articulated and communicated (for collective empowerment). Even if artificial transformations added much with many captors and data recorders and methods of data treatment.

Communication a (n)-arrow part of conscious interpretations; transmitted, nowadays by technologies of information and communications (tic).

Not to be surprised so that most social networks of world-wide-web are so 'uninformative', mis-contexts prone; and mostly biased by too much useless private consumption. And then, this is more feeding behemoths of 'junk information(s) and antisocial shortcuts'. Moreover, that is what remains when inefficient at helping in consistent social constructions... Based on "directives-ness or executive-ness" and fancy issues.

So huge and excessive sources of invading confusions are critically turning problems. When humans are marginalized by junk consumption, or others are too absorbed in lower and higher tasks (apart from decent dynamics). They can react filtering and narrowing the sense of community. Any has in or out-burst about the mismanagement; despite that globalized world-wide-web look like providing plenty of opportunities and good knowledge for good care to local levels of communities' needs. This good material turns very obscured by irrelevancy and hard to find in enormous lists. Compared to the massive nasty intrusions avalanche. [It turns too difficult to share because too much naughty-noise buzzing and nasty attacks invading. Add that to bugs and we are in a poorly dominated by non-cooperating viruses].

Communication and information, in the way we also presented a trigger the need to talk about the important concept of entanglement or disentanglement analog, maybe, to its quantic theory forms.

"Entanglement" of some fundamental particles pairs is a pillar of quantic mechanics theory, where one behaves perfectly exactly the same as the other (either by exact or statistics property, of the level or below? [... or because the "mid-intertwining" along enough range?]. Almost identical one of a pair, least one difference which is the sense of rotation of particles (called the spin?).

Such 2 particles of the pair have been measured: unaffected by the distance. Theoretically physicists have also the complement concept of de-intrication. Perfect correlation has been demonstrated across more than a hundred kilometers separating distance. Enormous distance, for such tiny particles as electrons.

[Can be the picture a Mobius strip a strip twisted once then glue each extremity?. This makes you strip has not just up and just down but both [or not at all?]. It is typically topological. You cut it by the mid you obtain 2 strips but they intertwined and not separated: you have one. Leave one for the universe, repeat the cut in the 2nd, you obtain 3 intertwined. So? either 1) strip-twist-ring -full cut or; 2) ring-half-cut- twist or in the 3 dimensions; 3) sphere in hole- hole-in sphere]... It would be uneconomical not to try to take advantage of all 3.]

[Concepts to 'avatar-adapt' at different levels: between fields, field-atoms, some particles or molecules (electron and some other molecules)? For a picture of that make a small exercise with a **Möbius strip** (once made) cut it by the middle and then go on, just with another smaller loop ... that is very pretty! But have to be reversed (from below to up)].

After entanglement it is to examine with the formation of residuals (de-intrication?) or 'below similar' complement; done that since the concept of the field as well as higher in complexity models. In a larger system because of incorporated uncertainty (and despite discreet-ness?) it would be about similarities else identities (we will approach those terms later). [But may not have to deliver with our version of Schrödinger's cat ... unless the intricated electron is making the field of the other meanwhile the other an atomic formula ... twist and each one its turn?].

Practices of Information and Communications

To clear the lay perspective. Call 'information' the enough appropriated formal match like between causes and effects (not too abstract-alone). And, by the side of physics, the match of "intertwined by the lower level" maps of matters- energies (matter that can transform into and/or deliver energy?). Information that eventually under transformations may produce the patterns of "causes-effects" and transformations observed.

At least to make a distinction between just patterns from "below" and those "emerged at the level"; when for doing any real work respect to a 'phenomenological label involves functional infrastructure and simpler amounts. ... Humans just label sets and classes of information within matter(s) more or less stable, least stable first to produce functional energies?

Call 'communication' the transmission of what could be transferred, from 'that' information (out lies and 'un'-dimensioned sort of concept). Fundamentally it would require to examine thoroughly what makes information(s); maybe in the framework of 4 'forces' (and quantum theory). Thus the package to transmit plus local environmental conditions (maybe not much: more the original specifications, if the recipient of information is in the same universe. So comes the channel of transmission, the conditions of the recipient and its 'environment'.

This is the traditional way of the determinist channel of transmission but a quantic theory framework would also consider long-distance correlations (entanglement?), short distance correlations (entanglement?), initial conditions values (to relate to degeneracy?), densities ratio (between transmitter-recipient). If the purpose of the recipient is to make use of the maximum information...

In most cases, it is much less interested ... unconsciously. Recipient condition effect is important if about information; effective abstract of communication ... in the same way as entropy (S: as a whole that we do not know much about; and the ΔS that we calculate after recording transformations).

[In mathematics, a degenerate case is a limiting case in which an element of objects class, is qualitatively different from the rest of the class and hence belongs to another, usually simpler, class.

By the side of logic, **a set has closure** under an operation if performance of that operation on members of the set always produces a member of the same set; in this case we also say that the set is closed under the operation].

As a result it is to conceive some minimum packed system or kernel of information, from components (beginning with energy-matter). And possibly enough well expressed and then taken in charge by a communication channel ... hence probably: not just 0 or1 bits. In thermodynamic system it can be useful to add temperature and density, at least.

Logical closure: a formal system for propositional calculus is complete if:
- Any formula that can be proved in the system is tautclogical (at least, its effect is coherence),
- Any tautological formula can be proved (criterion of decision

Strong completeness considers:
- Completeness,
- Compactness, according that a set of formula has a model since all of its finite subset have a model

In the simplest way completeness has the meaning that everything provable is true.

Sequential closure
A subset A of a space X is called sequentially closed provided that for every sequence f: $\omega \rightarrow$ A if f converges to a point $x \in X$, then $x \in A$. A space X is called sequential space provided every sequentially closed set in X is closed in X.

- **Closed sets.**
- The closure of an arbitrary set is a closed set.
- An arbitrary closed interval [a, b] on the rea line is a closed set,
- The set of function satisfying the condition $|f| < K$ (open sphere) is not closed. Its closure is the set of functions satisfying the condition $|f| \leq K$,
- Whatever the metric space R, the void set and the whole space R are closed sets,
- Every set consisting of a finite number of points is closed.

Of course what we seek is that closure here are not strict to exclude any reality from logics.

Open sets
1. A necessary and sufficient condition that the set M be open is that its complement R–M with respect to the whole space be closed,
2. The set M = $\cup_k M_k$ of all functions each of which satisfies a Lipschitz condition $|f(t_1)-f(t_2)|$ ($\leq$constant $|t_1-t_2|$ (for some constant is not closed. Since M contains the set of all polynomials its closure is the entire space C (a, b (

That does not make things easy, respect we are abusing of the lay term of information and communication. But it could be not as difficult as complex minded people think ... and this is also a bit more consistent than naked one, or other definitions of concepts: 'I saw in the TV so I know exactly what to do'.

Information in Physics

In that sort of framework, including when accounting for the limits:
- Information has to be anchored to reality (not just data observer, captors, register?);
- Wholesome-ness or proper communication of conditions, as well as of decoding frameworks are never perfect, but require their 'neutrality' (not to overload its importance, nor to manipulate it; and not just charge humans of all mistakes because have pretended to give the order but missed to properly inform);
- That needs better standards of "true completion" interpretative frameworks. To consider essential knowledge or less equivocal standards of completion (staying open to local cultural empowerment) and check. Not to carry central determinism, etc.);
- About Matter, it is to look at both as for itself and, by "degradation", as a source of energies and more or less information in the pieces (often "more economic");
- Phenomenological energies (under human eyes) for a large part a degradation of other matters (the lately most degraded one is heat), but also matter for "directions of" order by information;

"**Heat**" is a sort of universal disordered kind of energetic transmission (locally or radiated, there could be a special morphological treatment required) ... quite similar to noise (but able to nurture speeds of reactions and conduction. It is possibly also the parameter of "fundamental phase media change" (in particle-field: the level of temperature set the potential orders). Simultaneously problematic and needed after heat is the concept of entropy. [Care that Theory of 'information' concept of entropy in thermodynamics more the one of disorder is too simply flip-flop as the one of information in the former.]

The concept of information in heat is somehow delicate, conceptually nothing informative in heat (as inner quality) but as soon as some heat in some local colder place heat turns a good adjuvant. Overall the role of heat is important as a contributor to phase-space kinds of regime (hence the problem of climate warming on mental health?–more or less ironically. As Jevons could imagine).

- Entropy an *ex-post* concept?–at least its variation has been evidenced well as a balance of 'transformation gap requirements' (by the complement of first principle of conservation). Could it be induced from an *ex-ante* information provoked transformation [conception of a system of **perturbation**?].
- Communication is then, much at risk to ignore local conditioning, and so always somehow poorer than the original; when not distorting; (loss of values since original conditions, or degeneracy ... at least in the use of the recipient?

In some way, it is to manage what can be relevant to **thermodynamics formalism** (including concept of entropy or 2nd law of thermodynamics) and theory of information (which have analogical concepts) ... [further concepts to come].

Information Formalism Design

About empirical criteria of appropriateness of communication, with learning in perspective: you have to complete any message: structure the one you receive (**marginal information** has some **structure**), with your constraints as a receiver (no effect of lost information); and add parameters of intentions, to deduce varieties or options of activities. Unconsciously, your brain will do it and quantic structure too (having at least it's a field for any useful effect).

A useful construction, to always have in mind is: on how to capitalize together? with the opportune criteria of '**communicated-information**'; which are: 1) the right one (**quality**); 2) in enough in **quantities**, and a bit more (possibly the reflexive one, or the between **e** and 2?); 3) at the right moment (time for a **coincidence**); 4) in the right place (**space**: medium and local), with; 5) the "right" of relatively autonomous actors (**levels of** systemic information treatment) ... or system complexity index. There is also the capacity of **treatment**. [To observe that it is a minimum that can inflationary extended ... so the need of **economy of information** ... and accounting of preparation by learning: **economics of knowledge**].

Have in mind, since there the connection between information and entropy in an **ambiguous** way (as formulated in the theory of information–or electronic communication by Shannon); and the sort of concepts as managed by thermodynamic theory (as evoked by Von Neumann to Shannon). A something to works plus a bit more than this seminal conversation: many authors of books on information logics mention crossed information. In our opinion this is first in any more than one ... possibly just the fundamental switch?–have a volume heterogeneity for 'poling' and order field?

Further you will receive more suggestions. From now on you need a basic on this just essential formula.

$$n.\log_{base}.n$$
Information on amounts n = amount n ×logarithm of n

- n a quantity, better a **characteristic** minimum or maximum, possibly of self; but also 'out there'.
- **Base** could be better either $(\max_n - \min_n)/\max$ or $\max_d - \min_n/\min_n$. In the simplest way; it is a binary (2) for calculus but after scale we have at least qualitatively: 'I respect to all others' ... eventually in the *vacuum*

Some philosophy at the respect is essential. First why such product? Is it not enough the n amount?- it could be so, only if just with pure symbol of numbers? Thus the product of information (or a channeled communication) on the 'self'? Or since base 2 the emitter and the receiver. This formula may be the start of something different, from pure symbolism of numbers; with important effects: why not consider the **information of units upon oneself**? [When it appeared the theory of information awake many ambitions of being able to predict and detect in applied psychology with many deceptions].

Most know well that logarithm bridges the arithmetic product with the arithmetic addition (they have been invented for that: to convert harder multiplication into simpler addition with sliding rules). It is also the right concept for relating diverse levels of scale (despite in simple numbers, it is primarily between one digit scale and 2 digit scale (it is easy to relax or extend that). It has a way of systematic conception much larger, we think. For example, to imagine we have a something qualitative (minimum ordinal prone) by the side of logarithms and quantitative that have to **match** in one or the other way (cardinal prone respect to ordinal).

Thus is characteristically fundamental: why not consider the qualitative of a **model**, the logarithm of the quantity or symmetrically the exponent: an ordinal the cardinal amount? Then, more or less separately, you can work the logarithm number 'qualitatively' on one side and "empower it"; if for quantities requirements. Or work the amount (characteristically) than log that to explore further. The qualitative lower range or the proper formula to provide (if the amount is characteristic enough). And there the amount informs on itself (qualitative model) or the model (informs about: quantitative models).

Further thinking is required. The product (operation) is, first of all, a match, say a **model relation**, how they correspond. (Formally either '=' or ':=' or '≡' ... and we could like to add, '≡ $_{closure}$'). **Closure can be time.** They are the same eventually modeled so and; relaxing both; we can work on one side: with quantities at a given scale or **integrated scale unit** and digits after point (in Americas, coma in Europe); like set of properties characteristics; this gives a reasonable quantified picture of qualities and go up in scale either inductively of quantity joining. It is not a problem if just 'conventional in shared abstract' ... the later almost all policies are quantity **induced**) or **deductively**, if we already know the characteristics ratios of amounts ... thus to relate these to **characteristic exponents**.

> You have noticed that logarithm and exponent that makes 2 orders of integration or; conversely differentiating. This may even have some sense. In kinetics you integrate intervals motion for speed, and one more for the acceleration (or the reverse (differentiate of derivation). In statistics you make the average of the average and there you reach the **great number law**: any average of average just the normal law. A 'double-click' that may have plenty of meaning. Remind the relation between energy and matter.

Of course, it is about simple expressions; to expect more complicated but similar formula, possibly distinguishing kinds of prospect (**divergence, convergence**...). Also crucial is about information which has a formal basis in communication textbooks. Books of **encoding** and about theory of information, pay attention, but maybe are not careful enough about...

Intuitively: pay more attention to **crossed information**; it may be as fundamental as the self-one (once self-being in your own autonomy?): for exchange, reflection, stabilizing complement, etc. evolution needs that.

Say we have an amount simply and another kind of logarithm (just reasonable scale) and this is just what we need for exchange of information and intertwine many things ... that is a model piece of oneself; you can exchange with another piece of the other.

[In physics world, there is not (in absolute) the **problem of compatibility**. Because on the fundamental there are the transducers: electric currents are electrons and visual photons just to be converted photo-electrically, etc.]. With complex information it is somehow more complicated but not so impossible; when with an overview on **specifications of informative packages**.

To stay scientific with crossed information but more detailed in specifications. First it is often plausible ... in the physical world molecules are transforming (since the margins of the *nucleus*: cloud of electrons) and self-informing Put one with the 'bit-boot' of others ... at the minimum an electron or a free space for others' electron (expressed in logarithm terms) of a something known to react with; and cross (or exchange more or less symmetrically), the amount of other, with this small chunk ... or 'bit-bout' (*ex-ante* information, *ex-post* a transformation produced).

Observe that most molecules are not naked atoms but stabilize by 2, at least, or under more reactive 'ions' having lost one electric charge.

This small piece together *versus* (but with) large piece has, in fact, much of the formula in chemistry and physics formulation (here is a connection of logarithm expressions with exponential formulas). [... Make philosophy about the **law actions of masses**].

Abstract formulation in social arts; has plenty of work to do with 'better anchored materialistic formal expression'. Especially if we stay scientifically wise (... but not too scientist). There is even a recent school of anthropology trying to find gauges in social productions. It is called 'consiliance'). Anyhow about modeling abstractions; in the materialistic world you will not do more than what physics allows (or your formula is wrong; or your principle is not a principle, or your theory is false).

This is also very nice with **marginal calculi formulations**; as **vectors**; of the end-tip of the curve(s), used in various scales problems and ... in exchange (or trade). "Give me your information (the one you can exchange, if I can make better use of this, than you; so... I give you mine correspondingly if ... you give me yours, " ... [my kingdom: an orbital, for a horse: your electron ... whichever free electron, probably not the electron I lost just before].

Of course: to have better **models of correspondences** (more complicated formulas of information). With amounts that have especially to work with characteristic maxima, minima, varying conditions and averages. Also to imagine uses with other specifications like with 'stocks'; when treating about kinetics or dynamics of reactions. When approaching **multiple stages** of conception, and so on. Since we are not just speaking of symbolic simple numbers, but of realities' amounts and of our common technological or natural management (all physics).

As essential concept of management: start anyhow with crossed exchange of information and characteristics definitions ... with any sort of complex or populations significant concepts. This includes the probabilistic-statistical ones, which form the substrate of **measures**. Probably in the same way, there are the questions of modeling, decisions and so on. There are many premises of that in fundamental theories.

Moreover, for the meantime: logarithms make use of a base. Base 2 logarithms the simplest one and the one used by Shannon. But why 2 the mostly admitted?–and not many others used? (Out the fundamental neperian).)

First because in the bit of communication, what is transmitted along "linear line" of communication (close relations with binary logic) are just 0 and 1 (so 2 values or 1 and the 'non'). What is the physical ground of that? If we look and compare, the value of the logarithm at scale order, to notice that logarithm of them, base 2 is the highest. In lay terms the "base 2 that cover best." Base more than 2 is either more information providing a lower required value (since 3 or more informing, they are either less informing or less having to inform... And also some sense of **division** or **partition**. Now for deeper intuitive (physics explanation), contained in the fact that derivation of logarithms is the inverse of value (or an elementary piece or cut of whole value?)

Between 2, of course, starts the comparison. Plenty of models start (despite otherwise ill-conceived) with this cardinal; or may this be better called the "first complete cut"? Be cardinal 2 to examine the physical statistical relations with 2 bodies or kinds of bodies. In economics very often we start with 2 sectors models; when it is envisioning with 2 eyes (but eyes' binocularity and memory the 3rd and 4th, meanwhile the 2nd eye function not exactly the same as the 1st), etc.

> "**Average mutual information methods**
> 1. Factorization of a **joint probability density** as a measure of independence between 2.
> 2. **Embedding theorem** (global embedding dimensions) explores several choices; varying answers in specific context of the signal source. Using false nearest neighborhood algorithms.
> 3. **True vector field** method attempting to construct local vector fields
> 4. **Manifold** decomposition signal separation methods (Hammel)
>
> It is based on the ability to make a decomposition at each point of a state space into linear stable and unstable linear manifolds. Those manifolds are **invariants**. So identified their direction, seek an increment to adjust backward and forward the estimation. When stable and unstable directions coincide the schema fails and large increases can occur. Method recover and move back to a clean orbit at a rate governed by Lyapunov exponents and inferred by Myers of the smallest Lyapunov exponent.
>
> Average mutual information
> $$I_{AB} = \sum_{am\ bn} P_{AB}(a_m, b_n) \ln [P_{AB}(a_m, b_n)/P_A(a_m) P_B(b_n)]."$$

Also it seems to us that you **may vary the basis of logarithm**s in consideration to the number of connecting links between a start of 2 'qualified amount' or 2 nodes and other configurations.

Broadly said, quite automatically in formal application we make use of base 2 log and base 10 log; without thinking enough of the meaning nor to the use of others. A proper packaging of network algebra should develop the mid-range (especially because of the importance of cliques and **small network**). As well as we will have to pay some attention to proper orders of scale, instead of just taking base 10 log for granted.

Reminding the paper of the $\int f(x)\, dx$ [symbol of integration, function of variable x, differentiation of variable x], since it is the first link of the concept to **measure, integration, probability, motion** (or **potential**, or **function of density** in probability). Observe that the formula of information is not far from that considering the n could be identified to f (x) and dx to log (n). Nor the formula is far to **vector polar coordinates**; if you consider f (x) of a vector as length of rectangles and log (x)

as a tangent vector (thus in real number 2 dimensioned: $\mathbb{R}^2$) ... with an interpretation a bit more delicate ... but nice with perturbation theory?–would be the perpendicular informative perturbation. [Perpendicular is also analytically relative to 'independence'(in theory of probability). It is essential to the composition of best referring bases, etc.].

Consider also more pieces: partition by 3 or more. Many, if not most things in physics, start at 3; be them the 3 dimensions of subject space; you have components of networks like in feed-back or feed-forward, cliques and small networks. Many questions emerged in geometry; triangle properties; the 3 bodies' problem examined by Poincaré, etc. In economics partition would fair cut and distribution of the pieces of cake (or dividends). Finally also somehow in the **theory of games** or of **choice**.

Then some algebra for that may help to empower the theory of information. In effect, **in some way, an observation or a measuring experiment is affecting unity**. This is to relate to another basic concept of quantic mechanics observer, influence) of perturbation) and more or less destructive probe. But for our more modest mean-time: it may be a basic concept to vary logarithm bases, for exploring what we can "alienate", from an overall complex unit.

Maximum Informative Unit

Another basic concept about information formula made "complicated"? - would be that of **maximum characteristic amount: self-identifying**? Complicated formula will probably have to take into account its **environment**, plus **the minimum 'own and proper'** level of unit complexity expressing your "self"

[Properly formulated at levels of 'social myself,' it would, probably, have to consider the block: {my formula & operations made} compared to {effects received by the society & fair formula for everyone}].

Of course scientific formulation can be much more complicated than here. But observe, in facts many living bodies metabolic **characteristic ratios or exponents are similarly simple**. But some dimensions are too clear, at the respect. For example, in zoological nature you have homeo-thermal and poïkilo-thermal metabolism. Then, according to their size animals are. metabolically very similar in yields: not much difference between mules;

elephants, rats or humans they size relate simply to metabolism and one species to another with not much more difference. Their energetic rates a universal, easy to calculate since the mass (made the measure, norm or metric); to provide a characteristic exponent which could be almost the same for all, on average, and the universal value. Further then, you consider for variations (respect to the previous max-min *calculus*) the energetic cost of activities; according is the probability of preserving the first balance … [something like a relative system?].

So if the characteristic minimum is of our living self like; when defining needs. To sustain your life and; statistically your patterns for managing that (even under different cultural terms); your dearest ones in case of your identity, to meet with the wisest ones. Then, we may start to think a bit better about **economics of life**: since the complex unit of 'information self to the whole,' we are. [Yet, not to confuse with complex numbers but make use of others of our reviews].

Have practically in mind: you work with **characteristic amounts, respect to yourself**, relative to other, or to a referential. Top-down you will start with a (reasonable) self-maximum within an environment; bottom-up the start will be a minimum. Self-referred to itself: formula of information. Then how to shape a system of reference? Self-also qualitative basis (thus as [0,1] if closed or]0,1 [if open … and so on). Quantitatively referred to self, more than one; or not yet emerged: under self 0. Under 0 is a relative, so it can be negative and the under 0 negative branch of the logarithm curve seems to be good for that. In some way the negative sign just for what remains to emerge?

Of course if you use a perfect absolute scale; positions, mass and so on, that will show something, not the easiest to think about. We do not ask to abandon all the simple algebra. But observe: on the symmetric straight line between the log and exp curves, probably the best one [for the emerging axis reference of the new system. [Only we need a clean formulation of concepts of integration-differentiation at different orders of scale, 'of complexity']. Be flexible, so as to better understand your purpose, the concept of characteristic amounts and so on. It is stupid to put yourself in a scale, more for a galaxy, if it is to make a *calculus* for your daily need of food. Have just below the main frame of your sources of evolution

Complex Unit thus the start of an Information Formula.

It seems to us that we can … qualify the logarithm as the "law of emergence" … or … "law of evolutionary creation".

(If you want to keep it apart from "creation of the beginner of everything.") And exponential law (symmetric to logarithms respect to y = x axis) as the one of expansion. Exponential growth up to the limit: properly reversed as extinction or saturated by 'cleaning around' (or exploiting) [Form is given by a **Verhulst's equation**]; or by the information perspective. The radius of the projection's sphere (not far from the unit), center at (0, 0) and 'catching' would be like the lens-piece of the ex-curve and the corresponding of ln (x). [ln for the napierian (or neperien) logarithm base]. Notice that once met and fit, unit somehow is achieved, adjustments made or dis-adjustments explained (mistake, scaling or functional variations).

Why the logarithm curves the needed piece for emergence? - try to think about:

- Basic base consider the 0 and the 1, logarithm catches both on the abscissa; conveniently and makes that unit only relative;

- Logarithm abscissa variable is only positive; hence for the negative ordinate before the (1 abscissa, 0-ordinate) you may imagine it the pivot of emergence. Before you have only negative ordinate [value of log (x) can be negative before the 1 that is below in relative sub-dimensions?];

- "Relatively" as a sign for "yet not the unit considered." and the length of this branch possibly the 'requirements before emergence'); thereafter the base-pivot and then the only positive slow-growing branch can be the one of qualitative and informatively economic qualifying existence? [There is also a concept of 'path-system in that logarithmic curve'].

- Then, more appropriately, consider the scaling made by amount, simply e^x or taking the product making the "qualitative-quantitative information." [to have a fundamental scalar of complexity as the minimum]

- Intuitively it is easy to imagine the slow growth of information (since relative levels of complexity);

- The path length on a branch, since the 'pivot' could be something as a cost of information or the 'previous lower systems, providing to ...'

- You may understand too from the good yields or costs of default, or in excess of information (since the positive point average chosen: too much complication not "economical," nor enough for preserving then the possibility of death.

- Eventually the economics limits of partitions and sizes (to explore).

Thus for a brief summary:

1.	**Information about oneself**, to care about the relations characteristically existing?–in physical issues or ought to exist under fair constraints, in social issues ... at least as informants
2.	**Crossed information and/or exchange** at least of qualitative (then corresponding quantified pieces) pieces are as important as your amounts of reserve (stock, overall amounts);
3.	**Vary the basis of logarithms after connections** (more than 2 but not much more) and respective information (once evidenced the effectivity of exchange between; that is a matter of exchangeable quantities (the narrow scale -1 respect to scale 0) or scale 0 respect scale +1 could be wider);
4.	Relative approach of **moving or interfacing margins**, especially for non-simply linear marginal calculus of realistic amounts (we will give further some more explanations);
5.	**Relative approach of definition**(s), takes precautions (much better than forcing any abstract or speculation. "The what (of me) you should believe" ...

6. **Emergence and/or relative creation of higher complex units** (jump of scale, emergence required ... and stabilization by evolutionary selection and formally relative system economic completion?

By the way, remember that logarithm and exponential have relation to trigonometric expressions and these also used the complex numbers well.

Different Traditional Entropy Concepts and their Characteristics

Entropy Concept	Concept
Thermodynamic	measures set of microscopic states
Macroscopic diversity (functionally distinct)	measures set of functionally distinct macroscopic states or (more generally) pathways of dissipation
Macroscopic diversity (functionally equivalent)	measures set of functionally equivalent macroscopic states or (more generally) pathways of dissipation
Behavioral uncertainties	measures set of behavioral sequences (i.e. measures of macroscopic diversity conditioned on the past and possible other, external factors
Entropy of Organization	difference between size of initial set, or thermodynamic entropy change concomitant with irreversible preparation of the system starting from standard state (in general an impractical and arbitrary concept).
Structural Diversity (Components)	measures number of types of components in the system and the evenness of their relative occurrence.

Extreme or Opposite States of Entropy

High Entropy	Low Entropy
Large Proportion of Energy Unavailable for Doing Energy	Small Proportion of Energy Unavailable for Doing Work.
Disorder, Disorganization Thorough Mix	Order, High Degree of Organization, Meticulous Sorting or Separation
Equally Probable Events, Low Probability of a Selected Event	Pre-ordered Outcomes, High Probability of Selected Event
Uniform Distribution	Highly Uneven Distribution
Great Uncertainty	Near Certainty, High Reliability
Randomness or Unpredictability	Non-randomness, Accurate Forecasts
Freedom (Wide Variety) Of Choice, Many Possible Outcomes	Narrowly Constrained Choice, Few Possible Outcomes
Large Diversity	Small Diversity
Great Surprise	Little or No Surprise
Much Information	Little Information
Large Amount of Information Used to Specify System State of	Small Amount of Information Used to Specify State of System
High Accuracy of Data	Low Accuracy of Data

Logic and Mathematics Delays and Mismatches

They have historically; happened in the imbalance between ... "formally"; as different considerations between specialists and some limits imposed by personalities rather than by lack of "pores" between the 2. Many professional 'mathematicians' were enclosed in their "methods for very exact *calculus*"; and the demonstrations of conjectures difficulties. All this progressed confusingly. Primary skills were almost easier when not embarrassed in sort of services for living.

Professionally mathematicians and logicians out some universities required to be astrologists, physicians if not judge or artists as architects, painters, ... engineers not necessarily using much mathematics. Administrators more at collecting taxes and eventually different kinds of special accounting. In the 17th century came the Royal academies. Turn to the 19th century has been important the high schools of the French republic (provide central state with good civil servants especially in mathematics. And further the German universities Reform (launched by von Humboldt since Prussia. Also appeared during the period alternative kinds of geometries (non-Euclidean geometry) with Lobachevski and later Klein's Erlangen program about geometry; nevertheless geometry had lost its first rank.

"Pure mathematicians" or mathematical analysis emerged systematically after Descartes; with symbolic mathematical expressions further requiring axiomatic cleanliness. This came at an accelerating path (omitting here the giants of 18 -19th centuries, and gave the illusion of a summit, end of the 19th century. When in effects had already emerged the contributions of mathematicians closer to logics of arithmetic (Galois, Riemann or Peano) and Set Theory especially with Cantor and Dedekind; whom faced hard criticism and critical doubts. Mathematicians had rules of their own, well effective for their essential, and logics more with fewer poor details.

By its side modern formal logic had a pivotal moment to rigorous formalism of subjective logics (noticeably by Frege). Before the 19th century logics also had to fight hard with philosophy, philosophers more rhetoricians and dialecticians (nicer metalanguage). Formal symbolic logics inspired by mathematical symbolic and its aspiration of pure cleanliness came later, take off the end of the 19th century, then consolidate during the 20th century. When trying to pay attention to cleaner logical construction of mathematics; of course, some mathematicians disliked. After the different difficulties of Whitehead and Russel; this was followed by the intent of closure with Tarski. Diversity flourished nevertheless in logic, despite arithmetic limits encountered (incompletely?) by a logician (Gödel); for deceiving Hilbert's arithmetic ambition of consistency, meanwhile Gentzen's other efforts also turned short on that meanwhile opening perspective.

All this now receives much care because turning more critical since the computers dislike shades. You will have further many things of logics but not perfection, which means good and bad. For the bad, mathematics still in its ambition of purity and cleanliness, bad for the proper involvement of humans in their affairs: most software, cut at the algorithm will put by the programmer after the preference of 'cutters'. Good for simple physics calculi after their numbers. Which can be effectively meaningless: any computer may spit your numbers in the face, we have not seen many good at deep meanings in our applied register; but vanity and inconsistency a lot. Excluding humans from automatism is maybe better not to have humans erring in many industrial processes. Since they are sensitive to madness. But in many other things misunderstanding and exasperation are not all human mistakes, quite often these seemed to us more by the side of bureaucrats and 'mediocre followers'.

More or less good for careers in computer logic professionals we have plenty of really nasty paradigmatic *Leviathan* reasons of f bureaucracies: to inflate reports with formal and operating inconsistencies. Of course this comes with supposed scientific justifications and experts advice care. Few concepts pretended to be key, included in global report, sort of global mantra to misguide and dissimulate the lack of care of essential local development roots: communication rather than fair communication of information.

In an increasing way social arts inspire their interpretations since formal sciences, without caring that being social arts, we should better care the good conditions of humans for working and not dissatisfies others' values, to give sense to their accounting of values. But this does not mean they should be easy to manipulate after individuals and states will. Modern prospects with formal sciences for (inner or cognitive) humans account approaches have massively started somehow with probability foundations in gambling (2nd part of the 18th century); and in differential calculus of marginalist school, 2nd part of the 19th century.

In social arts, as used since half a century; main quantified registers of economics, another slow growth and then accelerating processes. Ambitions have turned inflationary and sometimes wasteful, compared to the suspected logarithm-like growth yields of formalized economic, arts of sciences. There have been too often with interpretations of "naked economic facts". A sort of striptease under the eyes of unwise political economics governors. Some having turned central bankers other occasionally directly governing; belly dancing in front of markets or; pantomime of lips, behind the press media microphones.

As mathematics with arithmetic logic Economics had profane logics of its own. This turned then deductive and main studies prepared after tis filters and then transferred from "serious formal methods" to arts of policies. And probably this was more arguments for justifications, economists owners of free riding trajectories or as members of club not less willing to play like everyone without economic theories. By formal kinds of exercises there were and still are 3 main pillars: theory of the 'general equilibrium' (differential calculi and equations more or less systemized); theory of games (and implicit theory of probability, rules of games and choice) and; econometrics (with times series statistics and too short assumptions on sorts of operations and inference cleaned from constraints).

Sophistications of many formulations after models, have co-extended. By the side of pure symbolic manipulations, there are some sophisticated but light developments with slim empirical identification of concepts and variables. So sometimes they are carrying much naïve and pure interpretations of almost independent variables-dimension especially on micro-economic assumptions; especially narrowing much human behaviors. This coming from deterministic goals to forward them by feedback. Especially for adjusting, predicting and showing good fits somehow very artificial. Too well calibrated by tautological definitions of "masses" on retrospective series; but too often surprised in their ambitions by the other ways of bifurcations and mostly failing to inform softly on social trends or directions.

Challenges of Formalism for Society

At almost 30 years of information revolution with personal computers, it is to observe that theoretical economics has obtained many theorems that maybe not as reserved as originally imagined. That is to say, too weak for being strongly just comprehensive of their specific economical position and possibly expandable outside the delimited register of economics itself. Data and regular records of many sorts somehow properly exist in noticeable numbers; since almost half a century. With national accounts things had started with Kuznets's efforts for providing national statistics material for economic policies. Wide fields opened to economists trained with Samuelson's handbook for 'math-electrification' of Economy. States have expanded statistics data collection in enormous proportions and diversity. In an almost horrendous way for anthropologic economics eyes. Sometimes in a horrible logical way for social data if ones dare to examine the very epistemologies of such 'arts of the table'. Social scientists add their empirical ambitions so as to expand the occasional *census* and sociometry they had before, with *census* and demographic registers or more large scale collection.

So most have started since half a century to calculate correlations, regressions, statistics parameters even when with poor quality of data collection and dubious semantic. Dubious semantic when you think about when looking at the economics of all that and the narrowed focus and areas of mathematics used there: positive, idealized, unlimited, mostly without care of many basics, simple operations and shortcuts.

It looks like that registers of economics can think they have all what is needed for social-economic, so the poor results just the fault of human irrationals. Progressively some conscience about complexity has emerged, also with the possibilities offered by the studies of social world-wide-web networks yet not to imagine that could require a mixture of all contradictory theories articulated inductively and deductive, positive and precautionary for shared work. This should not be like storage ponds for of theses and experts of determinist services so 'economic climatology'.

At the water mill same time major, it seems to us that threats are growing. The automated systems still in puzzles look like heating and disturbing pieces more for Brownian and far from the broad constructive effects they could have: ease the diffusion of processes supporting social economics and first of all informative natural transformations within anthropo-scene and ecosphere. Despite many signals that this could be well 'fruitful' as in agro-economy, or imagined in public economics. At the expense of flexibility were precisely needed or robustness and stability elsewhere. Moreover we also need a better management of precautions, especially for not falling in the 'black holes' that the extremists speculators of the principle of precaution may call for.

Past economic policies, with many interesting concepts may have been biased in their applications and not toward societies wealth. All in all along 2 centuries of industrial capitalist, some broad formal sciences positive results have emerged. To include in terms of policies some amendments of ferocious capitalism 1st age and publicized attitudes respect to "masses". They were made a profitable business. Some observe that most people are better than one century ago (just before World War I) ... So they should better care not to be in some secular down-turn of mood worst today than a century ago (just before the war, where most contenders engaged ... almost happily, war was expected to be a matter of weeks).

The development of formal economy has explained and approached a lot of 'driving concepts (and more than just those). Still the ambition for prediction much ahead the anticipated. More the experts have fit their language to the phenomenology of disappointment; and the curious public has developed its disarray toward the scientific-ness of how their society is doing. Now, with modern days of revolution of means of personal computation; extraordinary tools for formal treatment are widely available. This question is very critical. These tools have kinds of applications in human development of societies. How they could have to serve primarily the traditional administrative ways of conducing: social, political or economic programs for lesser distortions. What sort of computed aids are to conceive as interfaces that could be used by collectives, individuals and care?

Cautions are needed to appease the nightmares of people who observed that any computer stupidity; could be taken as a superior law by Aid business managers; over any beneficiaries. They are just ignoring the history of the places where they play their fake philanthropic games. Without seeing that they are too correlated with warriors' ones. Neither they see how they disqualify cultures' strength, and inadvertently do the same with critical local good professionals. So more they promote kinds and close relationships of polite ones, so close to 'naïve generous'. Because not caring whether the effects, nor that their results empower corruption.

Globalization with information and technological has a broad sense of enormous fair practice test. If humans' societies and individuals do not learn to play fair and correct with essential economics. After having understood that smooth straight linear path does not exist. They will hardly create proper, positive and fair non-linear ones. Tests should not be under-esteemed by social practices.

Test is about intertwining of good practices with social constructions, in some recent expression: synergies and/or convergence. [Similar to the theory of development call 'convergence']. Unless we prefer to let the present stage of world-wide-web to the battle fields in world margins and murky world of hardly balanced but already developed societies. That is favoring nasty hacking of (fake) free riders and freedom-killing 'authorities'; and so on.

Non adverted, it seems to us, a major problem is in the defects of formal resources management, the discrimination of citizenship by bureaucracies or the waste in their wrong doings out economics of communications, the geopolitics of mis-governance.

Today, despite that, most of the world population have not been properly introduced to: clean heuristics after the phenomenological evidence of natural complexities; but more to the exaggerated misconducts of humans' complications. As the result the analytical tools finding true avoid proper perspectives ways on how nature is doing. Also as a result the analogies, coherence, consistencies are poorly serving and efforts are: not conduced logically enough nor; rigorously mathematics can come with. More useful and applied mathematics has served other profits than those they should do.

Financial numeracy has obviously, turned essential to everyone, in excess. Misproportioned even to the informative ambitions about real economy. Since much has been done to mismatch social values. Communication has pretended represent ground information, disconnecting it from humans phenomenological evidences just preparing a world of 3 human species only: traders, geeks and institutions' hackers.

In its way formal mathematics is essential, nowadays, for being 'a proficient' scientific in any kinds of sciences. Even economics of behaviors, game theory 'applied' do. No more in microeconomics to repeat the truisms and tautologies put in formal models as primary conducts and primary laws. Since having been introduced formally by von Neumann, Morgenstern, Nash, Harsanyi. Somehow smoothly came further Kahneman or Aumann. And also somehow sociologically have been added by Becker, Schelling and Bowles. After the reasons of probability, logics of games also appeared. Alas, also with many shortcuts, as before with microeconomical scientism. Defects or excesses have wasted plenty of resources and good wills.

But with computer revolution, we are still much in the waiting rooms for better democratic adaptations to management. Are cares of sciences, able to bring hope to 'virtuous loops' to informative social heuristics'.

We are in a world of 'ghosts' or: balances between forms and probabilities or; quantic uncertainty for maintenance, economics and evolutions. The proper ways are not with 'fixing', 'rising', 'maximizing' and excluding. Quite better we have to do with 'looping', 'recycling', 'involvement' and 'reproduction', 'synchronizations of parameters on balances, care of patterns and shapes in the essentials. To prepare resilience from down-turns and favor learning lessons with recruitment. Socially that may mean: participation, cooperation, imitations and competed respects of fair rules. It is not just individualism, competition, certainty and authority of leadership only making use of partitioning, closing, maximizing and tolerating free riding pushes and take-away.

A major reproach to make to traditional systems of education with numeracy and mathematics is non-phenomenological care in some societies to have dedicated most mathematicians and logicians as experts of truth and discriminatory elitism. Formal symbolic intelligence should care more about the diversities of cognitive intelligence and, the contentions of the paradigms defects; that also exist in such registers.

All these domains of professional mathematician's predilection just now poorly mimic programed robots. Meanwhile other cybernetic applications are trying, 'to free any humans of thinking'. It should not be missed letting brains operate with their logics, (including capabilities of formal logics). And their statistical neuronal cells, populations of ordered treatments do their job. Today yet we are not in these good tracks for 'learning society' (Stiglitz & Grunwald recent work).

Premises of Logical Models With Arithmetic

Skolem (a Norwegian logician) sketched in 1952 three possible desiderata of foundational research in mathematics. The "logicist" desire is to obtain a way of reasoning which is logically correct. So that it is clear and certain in advance that contradictions will never occur, and what we prove are truths in some sense.

The "opportunistic" outlook has more modest aim; it is only "to have a foundation which makes it possible to develop present day mathematics; and which is consistent insofar." It has the "unpleasant" feature that we are never sure when the foundational work is complete.

Skolem's 3rd "mathematical desire" would be like the "Hilbert Program," characterized as the result of "giving up the logician standpoint and not being content with the opportunistic one."

As an "obliged specialized register" we have formal logic of an axiomatic kind. But despite Hilbert's axiomatic ambition this failed soon. It has been demonstrated impossible in less than 3 decades. [Hilbert has been a major German mathematician of 19th to 20th-century transition. He proposed in 1900 a series of 23 major challenging problems for the 20th century. The apparent impossibility demonstration provided by Austrian-American logician Gödel in the 2nd part of the twenties].

Now, back to basic: any logical assumption, even about algebra (ways of calculi) generally takes the form of predicate logic. Finite-order predicate calculus (as recalled) by Takeuti as the motivation of set theory. (Its cleanest formulation is called Zermello-Frankel-Choice Set Theory: ZFC.) This logic is commonly seen as primary in arithmetic. But already you have a disturbance: within some 7 to 9 founding axioms you have the unequal one of choice. Moreover with comprehension axiom it would be more unstable than the finite-order predicate calculus alone.

Proof theory of full set theory is technique of demonstrations already considered too difficult for a satisfactory investigation. Nevertheless, out the deceived satisfaction of perfectionists (meaning in computers' programmers) most of actual classical analysis mathematics can be formalized within the finite order predicate calculus. Difficulties of finite-order predicate calculus as mentioned by Takeuti would be (quite specifically):
- although 'cut-elimination theorem' holds for the system with comprehension axioms; this does not supply information on the structure of the system [have in mind that 'cut' about simplification principle of logic: you 'cut and reduce'];

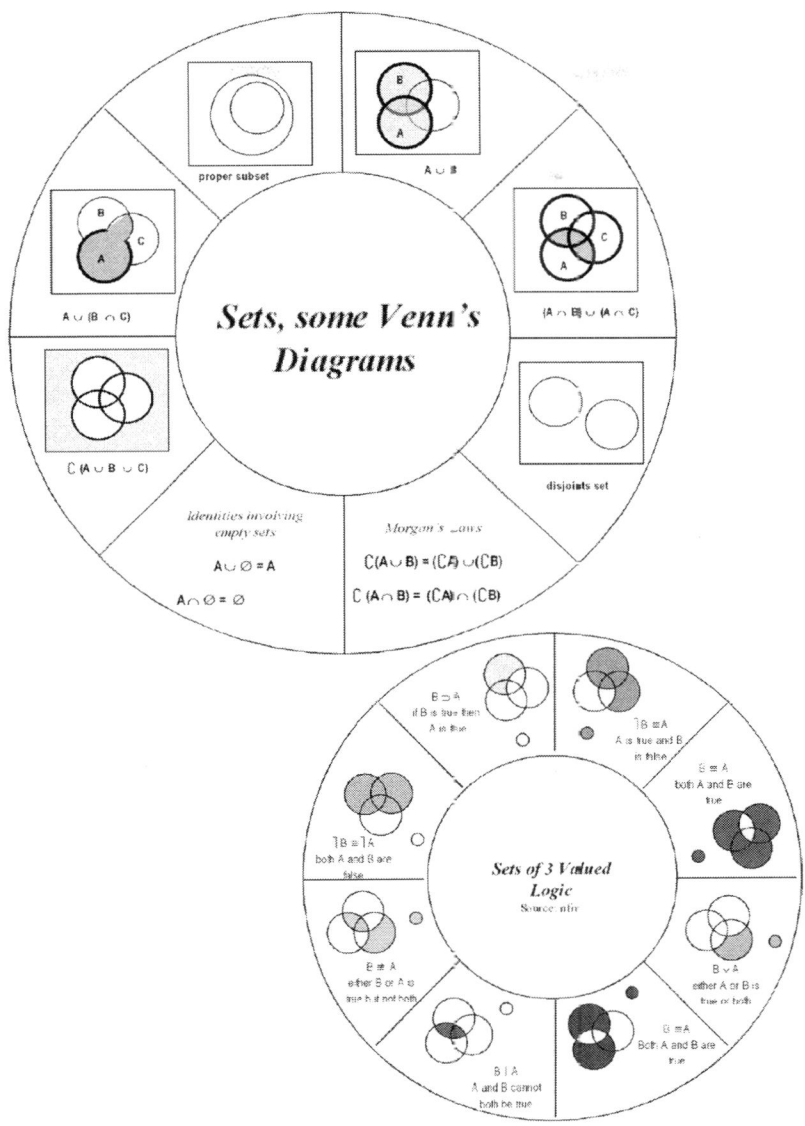

- unlike 1st order system, the one with the comprehension axiom; the axiom of choice (of set theory) is not complete with respect to the semantics of standard structures;
- a standard model (or structure) for a finite order language means one in which the 2nd order quantifiers range over all the subsets of the given domain; the 3rd order quantifiers range over all subsets of these, and so on...);
- proper extension of finite order predicate calculus has not been discovered. Also said that we do not know any natural and meaningful principles for the 2nd order predicate calculus, beyond the comprehension axiom and the axiom of choice.

Anyhow bizarre it could be (for us this sentence), maybe to follow Girard about 1st order predicate calculus and a small bit of 2nd order ... analogies with' our bouts of information's formula?

Second order logics commonly have:
1. symbols
2. logical: common connectors, equality, quantifiers,
3. non-logical: arithmetical, binary constant predicators, functional predicator, individual constant: 0, 1
4. non-arithmetical variables: individual (just as those of first order logic, sets and collections, free related to formula,
5. formulas expressions, sentences, models with a syntax's semantic

Expressive capacity of 2nd order language allows to consider:
The finiteness and infiniteness, identity, transitivity of a relation, arithmetical operations, natural number, numbering (cardinality), continuity, bijectivity.

Development of 2nd and higher logic can observe empirically:
- Introduction of subparts
- The weakening of the fundamental axioms core
- Adding some system of axioms not true in any circumstance
- Adding more sophisticated operators.

Without explaining much more than few intuitive relations for lay readers:
- cut and elimination has to do with the simplification of formulas;
- completeness is about reaching the highest limit of your worked set; it has a finite maximum;
- axiom of choice, related to ordering within a collection of numbered objects;
- orders of logics as a number of levels of development of logical constructions (somehow "intertwined" or "within" or 'entangled').

It is just here about words of logics applied to logic of calculi, as well as for seeing that not everything is fully solved. Mathematics are not just about solving small and artificial exercises (of leaking bath-tube). And for most people; it is turning increasingly important to know: when and how to call people of such arts (not just by their credit card). Artists, they are too, at least because having to communicate and when most are not as smart as they are often credited. So, not just blindly, let them pretend to be scientists. Any humans as citizens or ascetic explorers of their environment are directly or indirectly, better-off when sharing numeracy and knowledge about amounts. But they ought to turn able to pose problems logically; despite not at ease with calculi.

In Defense of Zen-Ness

This is increasingly important, for not 'striking on those damned machines not understanding you'. Soon these in their 'matrix', as robots are going to be able, one day to self-defense. On the mean time some are already good at 'killing you', metaphorically or not.

Anyone ought to learn to implement records, collect data, inspire and run models and question results. For not wasting resources improperly and for caring themselves from private bureaucrat-minded. Not to bias records, intent to lure models and miss the lessons of honesty. Some basic literacy is required at their respect; ability to open them, to the communication of data and so on discharged from being disciples or devotees.

[... Hence not to be passive purgatory sufferers; if you want to go to heavens after that. Only Hell is paved with good intentions].

When you have computers, economics of calculi, priorities in corresponding matching enough properly logic, numbers and so on. Mathematics is not just for tricky artificial problems and disdain. Disdain is not scientific it often more expressing the deficiencies, the ignorance on how to call professional mathematicians, the incompetence in the management complexities of realities, the vanity of efficient bureaucrats, the abuses of religious dogma.

Defects altogether observed in stupid cultures that based their developments on colonial empire, neocolonialist doctrines of "superiority without numbers" or populist misunderstandings. All this makes the limits of meaning. Because even if some logicians in decision (Church's non-decidability) or just of logic of mathematics (as Church, Turing, Chaïtin) have demonstrated that "in many corners" you have problems and decisions that cannot be solved with mathematics.

Main criteria for determinism, which are hardly met 'spontaneously' are:
- **Completeness:** that is, given any properly formulated mathematical proposition P. either a proof of P could be found, or a disproof. [notice that it is qualitative case]
- **Consistency:** given a set of axioms for, say, arithmetic, such as the Dedekind-Peano axioms, PA, could it be shown?- that no proof of a contradiction can possibly arise? A proof of consistency should finitary, non-appealing to infinite objects or methods. [Could the finitary-ness be in the ordinal/cardinal ratio?]
- **Decidability:** could there be a finitary process or algorithm?- That would decide for any properly formulated proposition P; whether it was derivable from axioms or no.

Care that intentions in determinism antecede often abusively the more interesting 'tails'.

Formal sciences can equip better pathways to solutions (so-called **heuristics**). Qualitatively well posed or **well formulated** in logics, increasingly can make use of computers. Moreover mathematics is now a primary source of innovative concepts;. Something that many business theorists and economists make use of; in a naïve way: take some mathematical or logical concept, put it like a business method and there you have a best-seller.

Practically, social economies will be better-off, if mathematicians, logicians or epistemologists, could be well distributed in society. Hence not only as "teachers" for supporting collectively better than certain deciders). So more extensively shared and volunteers care of concepts. We are much in that 'public administrators of beneficiaries' in the difficulty. Administrators whom often refuse to admit and apply proper rules of simplicity. Especially defective are the Cartesian ones in real life, and the Executive ones lost in their theories of business (profit).

All are with their own social position. Participation of mathematical logicians ought to be able to find good professional prospects, respecting and respected. At 2nd intertwined order would also be very useful: the critical thinkers. Complementarily: left when since the right side; right when on left side, individual challengers when in broad social mind, collective standards if with private businesses and all respecting some piece of commonness.

Primary Objections to Unique Mathematical Pathway

So, it is to observe that formal limits of 1st logic and arithmetic as a whole; have been essentially demonstrated. What still lacks are the ways to care about. Fundamental objections to the perfection of formal sciences have, in vain, motivated purity investigations. Vanity is with the 1st goal (if alone), but such pure investigation, in formal sciences often becomes fruitful in the 2nd place. Since having often discovered methods, algorithms and other proper designs.

Mathematicians for most have focused on their own specialized discoveries and innovations. Too often sometimes, at the service of very sophisticated special works. Barely did they have, from time to time, dedicated to epistemologies for all. As could have made Thom, Prigogine in their cultural world. Anglo-Saxons have limited their pedagogy to re-establish the good broad sense to their students, not much further in the whole society. Good level of vulgarization was often entailed in Soviet's Union formal and natural scientists. Some 'renewed' Russians are very interesting with dynamic social models. But these do not necessarily link properly qualities of models with social participation amounts.

Historically soon in the first half of the 20th century, Hilbert's problem about perfect axiomatization of arithmetic has been "locked-in by an impossibility" by Gödel's incompleteness. This at the same time put in trouble Vienna Circle formal ambition of scientific programs (especially in the 1st European part of life of Carnap). But Gödel was also a relatively 'marginal' member to this circle of thinkers on logic of a scientific system. Popper and Wittgenstein have been visitors of the circle and then emigrate to England.

More discreetly, Carnap evolved towards an interesting conception of probability and induction mostly when in America. Hintikka (a Finnish logician) later requalified 1st Carnap in narrower conditions of validity. A stream to account for understanding our uncertain world was about ergodicity, probability and non-linearity. It involves, not really a stream but broad-minded mathematicians personalities as Poincaré, Markov, Einstein, Lyapunov, Wiener, Kolmogorov.

Another quite inspiring stream (for our intuitions?), with logarithm formulation; follows this chain of authors since the start of the 20th century with Hölder's inequality; Carnap in the fifties, Suppes in the sixties.

An effort towards comprehensive perfection of mathematics 'formal language ambition when the 2nd half of the 20th century has been that of Bourbaki's group (of French mathematicians) for a "clean, homogeneous and rigorous formulations". It also failed but produced plenty of good results and formulations. Also it is to mention in first time of computer Simon's (& Shaw and Newell) General problem solver effort [Simon was multidisciplinary American a scientist].

[For not looking like too incomplete, on scientific systems, you may also need Popper, Russel, Wittgenstein, Granger, Lakatos, Feyerabend]

Global Consistence is Still a Hope, but not much?

Renewed hopes either of unified theory appears from time to time; or maybe today they have more pluralist correspondences between many different parts of mathematics, like with Langlands' program or Grothendieck before.

[About "extension of classical theory of groups to non-Abelian extensions, **Langlands's program** creates links between number theory, commutative algebra, algebraic geometry and representations of Lie groups"].

Comprehensiveness of mathematics not just an illusion: everything has to fit together, despite specified diversities of terms... Sort of invariance or universal similarities over different supports and theories.

More recently with considerable difficulties in the nineties you have a basic landmark expected since centuries: the demonstration of **Fermat's great conjuncture achieved by Wiles** a British–compulsive successful–mathematician (Successful compulsion not pathological at all). This has many implications in natural number theory. But the demonstration has been difficult and lengthy and time consuming. The importance of this result is that a proper clearing between only discrete and natural numbers ($\mathbb{N}$ 'based') with continuous real numbers ($\mathbb{R}$ 'based'). This would also be a good if not almost perfect step comprehension of mathematics progresses, but no more at reach of one or few mathematicians.

For another example in algebraic structure the so-called "**monster group**" would be the largest showing that number of groups is finite and this largest very important for the classification of simple groups (a basic structure of algebra we will evoke later.

The utility of all that with the proper way to program computers for large calculi, increasingly used in technologies ... and possibly to provide better understanding of very large number randomness (or complementary non-randomness). Like why our brain has billions of neurons, if we can commonly store less than some 40 thousand words (some more, many less) and then, much less of concepts.

At the minimum it would be on how to frameworks better our models of social economics. Econometrics intended with thousands of variables (but in **multilinear way**) with national economy, just before the neoliberal revolution and with quite deceiving results (even Leontief disagreed with the excesses of mathematics in economics). Nearby sorts of non-linear or fractals concepts ... that ought to have better inspired the revolutionary extremists before they brutally tried their expectations on national economies?

So, if on one side a perfectly founded arithmetic looks like not possible (this being at the bottom of the calculus); all this is also relevant to logics and algorithms formulation (sets of instructions for given calculi). Put in software they may similarly have tired for few decades, the 'progress' and ambitions of artificial intelligence (but not all the technological ones).

Exit simple perfect universal procedures like the **continued iteration** (a bottom up arithmetic procedures used by Gödel's in his objection). And more recently mentioned **Fermat-Kronecker descent** applied to arithmetic logic (top-down arithmetical procedure) as explored by Gauthier (himself recognizes that this complementary approach is facing similar limits of perfection).

Between them are the '**pieces of algebraic structures**' such as **groups, rings, ideals, bodies**. Using or not the commodities they have uncomfortable difficulties, of commutativity, division and so on.

For lay readers or users it is necessary to have in mind that computed programs depend on those limits and will, almost for sure, meet difficulties and face problems.

Thus many can still 'be scientifically Zen,' even if some expect to master enough for controlling the essential: they are wrong!–care your good-will or do not let others define it

---

Theory of Demonstration in Arithmetic

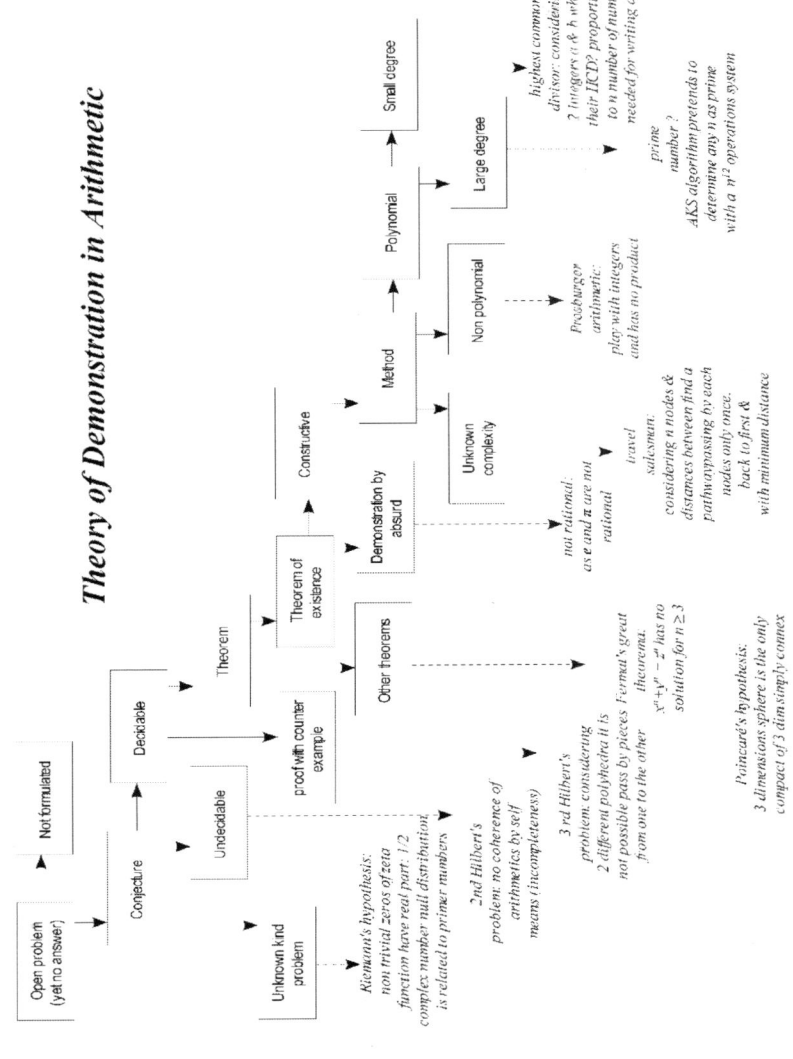

Open problem (yet no answer)

Not formulated

Conjecture

Decidable

Undecidable

Unknown kind problem

proof with counter example

Theorem

Theorem of existence

Demonstration by absurd

Other theorems

Constructive

Method

Unknown complexity

Non polynomial

Polynomial

Large degree

Small degree

Riemann's hypothesis: non trivial zeros of zeta function have real part: 1/2 complex number null distribution is related to primer numbers

2nd Hilbert's problem: no coherence of arithmetics by self means (incompleteness)

3 rd Hilbert's problem: considering 2 different polyhedra it is not possible pass by pieces from one to the other

Fermat's great theorema: $X^n + Y^n = Z^n$ has no solution for $n \geq 3$

Poincaré's hypothesis: 3 dimensions sphere is the only compact of 3 dim simply connex

not rational: as e and π are not rational

travel salesman: considering n nodes & distances between find a pathway passing by each nodes only once. back to first & with minimum distance

Presburger arithmetic: play with integers and has no product

highest common divisor: considering 2 integers a & b what is their HCD? proportioned to n number of numeral needed for writing a & b

prime number ? AKS algorithm pretends to determine any n as prime with a n^{12} operations system

58

Intuitively, all the previous gives a different picture to purity's ambition in any population: efforts towards homogeneity, separation by discrimination and utopian regularities are not physics reality; only human's aspiration to easy abstraction. Eventually felt by teleological humans as a need? But **should not be only for abstracting on abstractions**?–Or mostly to approach their own way to use? Morally, if mentally strong, and only for your- self-positive mood (respecting others), you may spiritualize. But do not put that too much and too specified above humans or upon coerced humans. Or none will succeed in being self-correctly sincere?

Naïve users' aim more about being correct with mathematics and logics; in humans' essential affairs. There the point is about **to which extent 'clean the approach'** Respect that will not make them profaner; even with Natural numbers simple scale. Truth, not all and only metric, simple, repetitive, automatic and exactly as hoped by dictators'. What is key also how you balance the efforts between proper forms and physics; or possibly what and for what you shortcut without abuse.

Another annoyance for purifiers; would be like in the deceptions given by artificial intelligence. Best language for artificial intelligence, invented in the seventies of the past century (PROLOG). Observe also that automation of factories in the eighties planned to be soon the robot factories at 100%. Some have almost been, but in few proportions. Most had to turn into a mix of human operators and robots. Actually another outburst of those ambitions is coming together with cloud computing and interactive sensitive robots. Thus, **how not to produce too misguiding paradoxes? - in the relationships between robots and humans**?

Physicists have different sorts of compulsions respect to those of mathematicians. They are trying to find phenomenological explanations and as far as possible experiment-able ones. But their explanations have turned hard to formulate. Quite often nevertheless they discovered or rediscovered structures of mathematics by the way. Pure mathematics was formulated for providing pure results with the very simple ways of primary operations. But with applications of results which were hard to see. But now physics is seeking directly seeking in mathematics its interpretations and most of them. Today research physicists can no more, do without them.

Nature of physics has obtained 'complex' mathematical structures; well ... under the eyes of profanes. At least 'not complicated at will of wantonness'. In effect, in the formulation of realities; phenomena will generally happen to receive the most clever and 'beautiful simple formula' among various candidates. If of the sort complex ones, not too manipulated by humans' determinist. Statistics approaches provide either good approximations or sometimes significance 'just by numbers' or, the model will have to be revised.

Social arts are aware of the need to revise models; own previous but also those of the other side, of the barriers; ... Especially the most 'mathematized' ones; which is economics in various registers. Recent models of macro-policies have been 'superbly rude'; gross (is that 'economics'?) and tautological: 'if you are a nation be it 'definitively balanced' not much more than a straightjacket as 'reference' without physics sense..

Many other social arts registers try, as anthropology (especially 'consiliance theories' ... about something like **guides of measures** within concepts or artifacts, in a more '**hidden pattern's way**'); sociology (having with the Web. an enormous field of study for network mathematics); history (concerned by evolutionary processes within cognitive and spatial economics mathematics); human ecology (is old fashion but about to bounce-back with neuroscience?) and so on.

Formal purification as done by mathematicians and logicians has effects in the complex dual. Any primary concept (or leading one) tries to organize everything "below itself" often implicitly more required by its' maintenance; like a paradigmatic flag (as what we see in some way of principal components of geometric analysis: the 2 most important make the axes of the graph). As a result specialists will generally succeed in designing a 'minimum enough' or at maximum-optimal (like Pareto's 'principle') almost no more than a 'mantra'. Later there is a sort of idea quite near to the complete almost closed system. Just deciding completely by recorders, or programs, or deciders. [We will see epistemological concepts in next to come volume].

Covering 'histogram of data and computed models (relatively random simulated) allows to **compare predictions of models to experiments physically controlled**. Today you will not be able to guess a specific formula without manipulating dozens of lines of calculi; and comprehensive understanding on 'any letters' accent'. Lay people are increasingly left behind. Humans' lessons have been weakened especially with the evolutions of mechanical societies to electronic ones. With the 'out' humans are biomechanical, just the 'in' may use bioelectricity. Because **enacting correspondence with technological devices is now much less mechanical**. When it is not systematically apartheid, by the intuitive management of essential concepts relevant to problems. Electronic devices do not have the same learning way. As a result most people with non-abstract intelligence are excluded; from many areas of formal sciences when anyone should be considered better simultaneously as a professional and a citizen.

Even in the abstract, the concept of being both, 'in' and 'out' as well 'up' and 'down', is not enough accounted in formal sciences. [So is the occidental way of 'clear cuts' ... promoting in the same way clashing class societies. Probably the reason why many reacting societies turned to the alternative within the Occident which has been communism].

Now for our formal concern about the system; we need more effective expression of that in formal expression: of systematic conceptual treatment of **mixtures, overlaps, super-positioning, confusions** and so on, possibly more 'at the level'. Of course it is hard to imagine the proper configuration of that; which is present in any complex issues (and even any our common world physics) without logical errors. Those with some information things are both somehow true and false. Just maybe not right at the same time. Switch from one to another requires time-information and energy.

Further then, it is to **find formally the proper configurations** in our kinds of physics world. Out over-simplistic purification of objects, of sets' elements or; operations. There is a need for proper logical-arithmetical system formulation of that, inspired by the way physics organizes its levels ... somehow to show it in a matrix of transformation from one state to another?

[We knew, of course, that **fuzzy logic** (Zadeh's original works), by its treatment of 'third included'? Looks like that. But it induced too simple general kinds of operations (called co-norms) ... It is too blurred to be systematically fuzzy ... as Smarandach? - when you have many pieces of information ... and already have more inspiring concepts in probability theory, fields theory or quantum mechanics?].

Conventional probability theories:
- Kolmogorov's probability calculus,
- Classical probability,
- Logical Probability,
- Frequency interpretations,
- Subjective Probability,
- Condition probability.

There is almost a century; great mathematicians could have pretended, after important advancement of mathematics; to have an encyclopedic view of their discipline [we just remind Schwartz's comments]. Now this has well disappeared. Even the broadest minds cannot pretend to such sort of self-mood. What some may have is a core of procedures (already better than most). But they all have to specialize for research. Either focus on a niche (of very special kind of investigation) or try to be an over-viewer of one chapter among many dozens of a handbook, often felt as nodes.

Still mathematicians may look like 'broad' in the eyes of profanes; because they are often at ease with mathematical equipment and in subjects of other sciences they apply better **formal approaches and analogies**. But profanes, after their school training in mathematics have often missed the minimum: maintain curiosity for the propaedeutic of formal epistemology. With formal scientists the converse prospect is quite uncommon. Some plunder their smart concepts in mathematics or those, having been physicists or reached high mathematics levels, in their school of engineers and turned their service into bankers or traders, not exactly for sharing their talents.

This is a paradox of being appreciated by poor rigor ... if not absurd. Because, when **in competitive professions, partnerships in exchange are mostly lowered**. Paradoxically also tis may increase the crisis by 'copy-stampede' from the self-distrust based on lower knowledge. As well as vicious circle since 'being too big to fail' promote irresponsible risk taking.

Also many non-mathematicians 'experts,' just prefer not to call, when not good at these sorts of methods and not enough self-controlled after critical formal conditions. Possibly, **societies could need, sorts of 'cool' formal science judges.** Could they do well in the development of social relationships? [After all Fermat was a judge]... Not for 'fixing this damned irrationalities' of course. But school training or first years of university did not care much to **adapt propaedeutic to recipient epistemologies and to different kinds of intelligence.**

Most formal sciences professionals have been trained more to resolve standard and narrowed exercises. Hence this is not **for being good at preparing for help-calls;** from as many as possible that can help to cope with such tools in their extent of possibilities. Moreover, many skilled and good at formal sciences are, not exactly in good socially democratic practices; neither is good enough in social usefulness.

Many practices need to be more open to formal and kind contributions. Since so much required in most human activities. And especially consistent with economics of essential needs; including social constructions of frameworks.

Favorable to Formalism for Social Constructions

Once understood the way to solutions in complex framing. (A mixture of good results search with proper procedures. You have at the minimum good experiences of lessons. Including failures and unconscious discovery of the proper formula. Both as expression and management; such scientific concepts are almost valid. They will not change for fancy preference. So we would just have to input other amounts; if there is no change of nature, nor of formal behaviors coherent to environment(s). If from social arts, they are self-conscious of their limits and if stability for procedures is also not bad; then such formal forms are **conventional: their formula should be susceptible to change.** As soon as 'better social convenience is assumed' (if in Pareto's condition). Possibly the best change there would be the most fairly sacrificial ones; for empowering sustainability and potential. [Not the easiest sweetest ones, at the expense of others or nature].

In physics, experimental devices need to deliver reproducible experiments, and then to be confirmed by **crossed checks of data.** Paradoxically also the most understood as possible but simultaneously the fairer and more impartial in the assessment. In other words, we have to **cross the informative perspective.** Thus, results of experiments will not change capriciously. But real conditions may be quite different and more variable. That is more difficult to uncover if 'physics effects are thinner'; as essential as they could be.

Formulas are often dynamics, phase-space generally important. In such region of given phase-space quite important will be the **nearest critical borders.** Under more realities conditions **the balances, making the critical transitions of regimes** (of space-space) can need to be (re) appreciated. They are not as positioned as in the laboratory [the in *vitro*-in *vivo* of biology or ecology also applies in physics]. [If you are not familiar to such concepts keep them in mind you will have more explanations later].

Some tips to **check the right formula or results of measure**: 1) **order of numbers values** (if your results are similar or very different from similar exercises); 2) **equations in dimensions** (formulas often have a basic expression of parameters: length, temperature, time, etc. and the analogies between expressions (for example between mechanics and electricity); 3) computer **simulations displays** give chaotic (explosive) divergences easily (but there are behaviors that are effectively chaotic and kinds of macro-orders micro-locally non-linear (expression of formal chaos); 4) **alternative approaches** either of logical reasoning or calculus.

Unconventional logics, similar registers help qualitative analysis, assumptions and conditions of formulations, good formulation, and appreciate conditions for existence of solutions or for some atypical logical mechanisms.

Considering the convergence: first of formal sciences and their demonstrated limits of imperfect simplicity. A primary kinds of questions are about if they complete one another or in which way they confound. So mathematics which arithmetic logic quite comprehensively developed in one register you have easy to equalize the concept in others. Thus **artificial completeness is made after the economic interests** of researchers; but none will take this completion as "natural". [Economic in a broad sense of making easy].

Next problem would be so; about if **fundamental physics is the completion of formal sciences?** That is fundamental physics 'just this completeness'. Or at the reverse (care with the conviction of mathematicians or logicians proud of their formal sciences) formal science could represent the completion of the physical world. Just the physical world all and no more than in mathematics-logics? - in the way of Tegmark that: everything is just mathematics. We need to get in that further.

Empirical Heuristics With Mathematical Problems

Not the purpose of this essay is not to turn the reader a mathematician of a logician, just to put your mind in conditions, so as to be open to some thinking about such sort of logics. Bet here in front of such kind of problem and find it 'the solution'.

For a common language brief about the problem of mathematics approach from Polya:
1. What is the unknown, what are the data, what are the conditions?
- Involve (documentation, re-readings, brain-sleeping);
- similarity, intent to solve another similar (collect examples)
- understand, try it experimentally (what tells the simulations, patterns of heuristics)
- data generality
2. Devising a plan do you know a related problem?
- introduce suitable formulation (find the dimensions),
- restrictions, look at the unknown,
- share, is there a related problem solved and
- satisfiability usable for your own

3. Carrying out the plan;
- Commitment, engagement,
- common sense,
- process operations.
- check each step

4. Examine the solution;
- look back can you check the result
- cross-examine, can you make it a different way?
- gauge, give a concrete explanation
- reconsider, to use for another problem, should you include an auxiliary element in order to make it usable.

Now the suggestion to enlarge is that you take such heuristics or practical way to solve; and have an epistemological thinking about them. Either trying a broader meaning of words in the sentence; or evoke one of your and reformulate the receipt after your problem.

Our school curriculum is often lacking these practices. Similarly or by analogy then specifications come in the stupid way. Not even recopying receipt, sketch, frameworks or as cognition's scholars say "**scripts**". When it is just what we have to do: find such guides good enough and robust, choose and translate. But stay sensitive to 'abnormalities' and more rigorous and/or mediated studies. Meanwhile those of mathematics are the broadest ones and should be open-mind to rigorous ones for such studies. If having understood not to restrict them to the traditional stupidities made with. Hard intents give some result, good anchoring produce experience, then adjust and reinstate scripts.

When you examine a **system of equations** you see: 1) scaling coefficients (numbers which can be explicit proportions in the system; 2) variables which are that which varies and the unknown to calculate; 3) signs put before (or ahead of?) coefficients or as operations and; 4) powers put in super-indices after the variables.

In the rush to have the solutions you soon miss that signs could be signs or operations. Not to imagine, eventually that **an extension could be just the complex number** if not exactly in the opposite (180°) direction. Hardly, 'powers' or exponents are properly explained as **possible characteristic exponent**... The differential calculus you learn, integration goes up, that is making the power increases (one degree up at a time of integration) and derivation goes down (one degree less at a time of derivation). When you learn to integrate you will also meet with constants defined by the way up which are calculated at initial conditions (C_0) providing a specific solution; when 'many' is without this value.

More or less in the chapter of equations solving elucidation; we heard of **determinants**. That it is a systemic general method and; 1) **completing the lines** of the system of equations expression, but different powers possible (polynomial) then; 2) **proper ordering of one variable terms**; after their powers (more or less complicated variables at one same power or of just one variable for approaching the solutions of a system of equations: 3) **calculus of denominator**. Determinants allowing to explore the general possibilities of solutions (existence) and how many of them with a way of calculus, involving the 'whole system of equations'; 4) precise solutions taking for the determinant corresponding to a variable ... the coefficients of others!

Philosophically this formulates a system, having coherence. Not too complicated, determinant calculus has something of the matrix in quaternions and octonions (with complex basis?). So if you are trying to find principles you will expect the system you have under the eyes about something very important: essential, important and basic. Thus you will expect this serious system be a characteristic one of importance.

A bit more advanced and turned a philosopher in the techniques and having practiced a bit with calculus, you may have heard about 'characteristic exponents'; also you may have understood the **limits of general method for solutions,** have had some use of differential-derivation calculus. Also you have been introduced to physical meanings of equations, introduced to the concept of functions, seen developments of functions into series (Taylor's expansion) for approximations; possibly approached series of data by polynomial approximations of understood the new frameworks of mathematical analysis, etc. ...

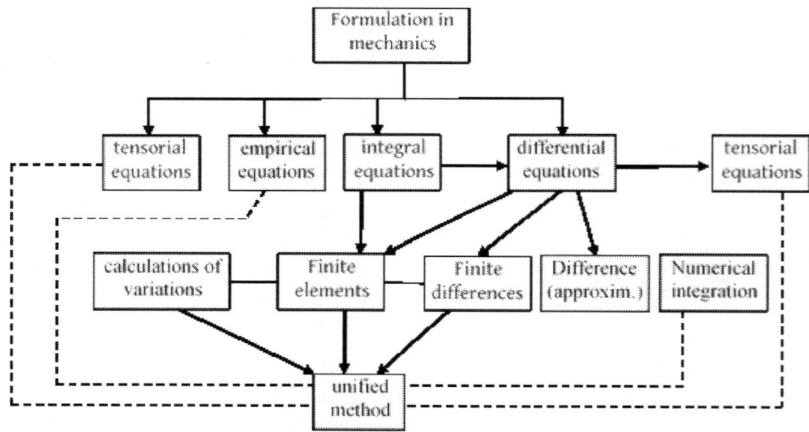

You may turn more interested logics and wanted to know the metaphysics meaning of that. If you have made efforts to try to understand, rather than be ecstatic at a number of solutions, nor frenetic about calculi: remind or observe that today computers could make all the calculus more easily. Since computers never get bored at spiting numbers at your face, to leave you with the worst part of 'what that mean?' - if I want to understand and do not want to look at others as a number? As technicians you often know that there is a characteristic or standard formula after your technical duties. But intellectually or more wholesomely, is this intriguing?– You only wanted an estimate for some task and did not catch **formalism may help to catch the sense of system**s.

General Expression of Solutions

Thus what remains?–if you want to be an explorer with formal methods, of your own problems, **heartiest ones and find a good symbolic formal expression of what you want and possibilities of operations in a social way.** It is about to enhance the formalism of your fair options. But you may prefer not to change the formula too often?–Despite the fact that you may recognize that this some 'one or the other' is more a social convention, with thin scientific ground. Observe also that judiciary rules or laws are often keener with absolute numbers (fine or penalty); tolerate percentage (taxes, fees); but prefers to put formula in technical standards and avoid serious formulations in their dear texts. That is stupid!

Anyhow an important question is about if you will always have a **general method to find your solution** to any system of equations. Starting with just one variable, you will learn soon that there are limits. 2nd, 3rd and 4th degrees (or power) of one variable equations have a general expression of solutions. Without general solutions for higher order is demonstrated since the start of the 19th century. So they cannot be programed. Out of course special forms may have simplifications, like substitutions of variables. Galois (a French mathematician dead too young) shown that theory of **groups** (an elementary algebraic structure) could reveal if a polynomial closed form of solution implying algebraically simple operations. He proved that it was impossible to find generalized solutions to equations of degree 6. Abel (a Norwegian mathematician whom also died too soon) made the complement for 5th degree, start of the 19th century. As a result **only general solutions with equations power 4** and below (with simplicity of operations).

By the side of geometry if you have culture of physics, you know that any **volume** having object has so 3 dimensions. A 2 dimensions will correspond to a **surface** or **area**. Further mind that as an object and it may be not so difficult to conceive about what is a **matrix** (for a metrical plane plan) of 2 dimensions. Or a **matroïd** (more objects similar concept to a matrix is in a sort of 'plastic' logic of geometry called **topology**). Normally any volume will start to **exchange through a surface** (outer one and inner one **more 'complicated but selective' mechanism**). With dimension one you have more lines, points, possibly granules, etc.

Somehow similarly intuitive about numbers concepts, once in logics having understood you may need more information for enough dimensions in the formal approach. An eye back on what you learned about systems of equations you may guess that there are something like 3 or 4 dimensions. In physics the 4th dimension is commonly the time. Logics basic *'nucleus'* on its own has to consider 1st and 2nd order logics for simple arithmetical operations. To apply this to something comes that you have at least 2 elements a 'smoothing' (object, set, elements, number...) or/and have a language ... which, at the minimum is made of 4 things to manage).

[In mathematics, a formal language is defined by an alphabet (1) set of symbols) and (2) formation rules (specify string of symbols (2.1) belongs (2.1) (do not belong (2.0) and count as well-formed (2.1.1) or not (2.1.0). The formation rules are usually recursive. Some further rules postulate and other establish how to build its grammar].

And so on, you find that almost in any register, quantic theory, general solutions of equations, logics language...

The **base** in numbers is: zero and one]0, 1 [and then you need more, only one concept or two not enough ... better to start since 3 or 4. Anyhow, and if wanting to evolve on scale may be better also a *modulus* of the sort and find higher same 3 -4 blocks or below also ... move your contraction or expansion of blocks of dimensions in the same way.

[Notice we used]0,1 [to mind them open such brackets are used in intervals of number, not closed on numbers to show openness before and after for the case of base].

Dimension only about natural number dimension?–well... Already exist concepts about non-integer dimensions. Say also in multiple levels of scale (one digit, 2 digits or tenth, 3 digits or hundredth) we need to broader the perspective and at the same time not diverge too much.

Self-similar forms across scale called **fractals have non-integer base** and so will have numbers after the point (or coma) of base dimensions(s). Precisely and probably not surprisingly the most interesting of these non-integer base, development of self-similar pattern, will occur between integers or natural dimensions. That is dimension cardinal is commonly between 2 and 3 for most interesting self-similar fractals.

Fractal self-similarity is this property to have a similar pattern reproduced the same-looking at small levels of scale (micro) as at high levels (macro) of scale. It is a form that could be of considerable interest such as in economics ... not much need to imagine too different behaviors. The sort of **self-similar patterns about kinds of human behavior?** As could expect by policy deciders, to adopt these attitudes that governed 'should have'. Even if they ignore mathematical wonders still not illusions of any policy or business.

In the half range of possibilities and the remains let to reproducibility. But it is not to give ideas to politicians in economics about that physics not as automatic in the simplest way to any human mind have to do. To considering before not to threaten 1) Life priorities (that may have stronger 'strange attractors'; 2) Most humans' societies living on 'hydro-pneumatic derivations' from main energetic channels of physics (as agriculture). Other 'exogenous' societies are unable to violate physical principles (most fundamental shared ones); 3) Engineered biases of natural flow assignations; 4) Evolutionary principles within **balance of complexity** (biosphere) and **artificial anthropic complications** (noosphere). So wise policies should come after all that (near one's smallest Chinese boxes) and care enough efficiently the up flow perturbations produced (they may increase more the destruction of entropy).

[Strange attractors, a kind of fractal produced pattern (see annex) are robust when of the fundamental physics kind but, as dynamic patterns (of some strangely structuring form) may possibly, critically evolve.]

A complement with these sorts of complex forms emerged from relatively simple geometric expansion is **cellular automata: automatic**. They apply simple rules 'percolated' in the abstract-formal or diffused in the physics environments. Wolfram identified 256. But there should be other mechanisms of the sort (as Lyapunov functions).

This may make evolutionary places for 'constructal' and **mechanisms of memory** (also called hysteresis); since the low levels (if not lowest) of physics.

Maybe we do not want to turn out like ants or like; those small fishes trying to escape to the collective fishing technique of dolphins. Such behaviors can be zoological applications of those simple rules in societies of animals? Last examples with nives of bees, sketches of ants and other social insects. Small beings formal mechanics another case for some sort of simple rules could be providing massive complex forms; as cellular automata explored by Wolfram; and constructals evoked by Bejan, etc.

In facts the ambition 'not to be like' is stupid; all those pieces and tools are well required by 'superior higher level of organization'. So the discrimination stances are ignoring the formal evidence: most of what we think and how we behave is, just trying to reproduce more primitive mechanisms ... but also with our specificities. Just as with more **'other more informative links'**?–not our intention to say that humans are not special.

Now it is to make the concept **'at the system level a package of 3-4 dimensions'**. So below you would have another sort 'micro-pearl' (relatively incorporated at your level); and higher it would be as in a 'macro-ball'. [This later would be formed as an informative energetic balance; established between source of feeding environment and maximum complexity achieved with your optimal netger tropy].

In fundamental physics, **supplementary dimension** somehow has started to be imagined by Kaluza (this has almost a century but may not have been enough understood). With this line-one dimension which at micro-level that would be a "tiny tube." [Of course formally it will not be as easy as just our fancy comments.]

Even intuitively there are more problems with the package. 3 dimensions is a bit poor.

About time's dimension, the 4th one in basic physics formulation, you have probably eared that in most basic physics theories it has to be symmetrical or reversible (travel into the past and the future?). So: **what to do with irreversibility?** - Prigogine (a Belgian chemist) worked well to show that **disordered chemical systems could produce macro-order and irreversibility.** Making it since a thermodynamical point of view. Connes a French mathematician also worked hard on **non-commutative geometry**. With that you 'have an order and cannot permute the symbols of variable in a relation between. Hence especially when the relation an operation. [We probably need the concept of complex operations be developed more]

> It is not as easy as said, the physics side must also be clean, especially because we **also need some reversal**. Thus obtain expressions allowing to 'tight and un-tight the Gordian knots'. Non-commutativity could be this needed formal concept about relative irreversibility? [Could there be different kinds of 'irreversibilities' according to the maximum level of the "system" and this; without disappearing all sources of entropy... Destruction of complexity reinstate the primary ones of field-particle. That may be a large register ... to explore with string theory methods?].

Now to observe that 3 dimensions packaging presents more opportunities of properties; either formal or physical. To raise naïve questions further about that let take the picture-wise biological image of a cell.

Such biological cell has 3 dimensioned volume-like subject. At 2 inner dimensions there are plenty of membranes. The cell packs lower dimensions for the fate of its volume. Membranes are useful for 'closing' as outer membranes; and inner separations of compartments for ordering metabolic structures and flows. Much of metabolic activities; in the structured membranes inner packing. In the same way cell has plenty of filaments or one dimension lines participating in: motions, transports, structures and so on. Could the analogies also exist in more primary physics? At least there are plenty of observations that a biochemical level there are similar sort of organic chemical structures ... before life self-reproduction..

See now how to **assimilate supplementary dimensions**? With perspectives, we know that we also need 3 more dimensions for specifying since any volume outside. **'Geodesic'** is more at ease with 4 dimensions. These provide a complete overview on the limits and shape of the volume of interest (in the example: the cell). Sorts of shapes have formal analytical relevancy such as with concepts of **convexity**, **concavity** and others. Also (for further comment) could we anticipate: **elliptical topology**?

> Now with the cell, we may not need it simply convex. There are processes where, locally and transiently you observe the concavity, like when the cell is including something. The formal analogies, not a problem in geometry. For macro-objects, only to observe that in applications these kinds of approaches are anyhow much better. To evoke the obligation for more complex chemistry. Chemists allowed 3 dimensions visual displays on screens of computers can simulate macromolecules. Many other abstract prone registers had better proceedings.

So since the start of thinking; in any sort of abstract; rather than just with 'concepts without thickness' like abstract gradient of the area around statistics averages? -**we need to imagine geometric forms**. It is now very common to encounter for geometrical landscape with peaks and valleys; forms and shapes in much scientific literature.

Questions would then be about the mathematical analysis meaning of these forms. [Often at the basis of econometric modeling]. For what take has such similar approaches. Say for example, we have a 3 dimensions object for what one, two or three dimensions more (and up. Remind general solutions only for 4 dimensions maximums. Thus like 5th to 8th dimensions?-**obtain supplementary specifications allowing to find some solution for too complex formula?** [Or for resolving the excess of simplicity of operations?]... In a similar way below. Possibly reasons why our sort of [unsure] 'informative shuttle'?

Another consideration is about **integrity or integrality; or conversely the differentiability apparel** to associate with the 'decent' formal system. This would probably have to consider some (narrow **integrability** (up of dimensions) and **differentiability** (down of dimensions). In the first place to go up to 3 or 4 dimensions (formal integration) and down to the **elementary base** (formal differentiation, more or less symmetrically and made use of for establishing a relative self-informative system? [Elementary base is not useless, for dual and labels or index of the system... Despite the fact that we make a distinction between a 'formal shape' with some systemic properties and a subject 'behaving as a system' as its level of scale of complexity].

We already mentioned that with a sort of **macro-unit system** and then **maximum level of complexity** (not necessarily directly related). [System concept with some sense in von Bertalanffy's concept: 'the whole not simply the sum of all parts'), with that information would be quite a nice formal concept. Thus have any pack with a core of 3 dimensions?

How this would make sense with so important physics's **operators** (Lagrangians and many others); or **multipliers** (Laplacians the most important) ... Or 1st and 2nd degree developments of, the **Taylor's functions' expansions**. Of course actually our suggestions compose more a soup of bizarre formal and physics-biology analogies. What would be the correspondence of the 'system' and 'complexity' concept with pure formalism?–could this have to involve theory of numbers? More precisely we have some 'visuals'. On prime numbers and "holes" of rational numbers (filled by irrationals or transcendent numbers) [those last not prime].

[Taylor's expansion makes the relation of functions to their expansions in series by making use of differentiating operators. Possibly the 1st and 2nd are the most important terms because implicitly carrying the formal system concept?].

See? 0, 1 is not considered as **a prime number**. 2 the first and only even prime number. 3 is the first odd one. Then the whole of 4 even, not prime number. Next 'not prime' are: 6, 8, 9 10, and so on. So prime numbers sort of steps or (relative) padlocks of numbers?–also put in evidence by **irrational** or **transcendental**? Consider the first ones $\sqrt{2}$ and $\sqrt{3}$; that is to say "you have to pass top-down" 2 to obtain $\sqrt{2}$. Rather than bottom-up; since you have an infinite series as real value of $\sqrt{2}$. Roughly speaking: **"algebraic irrational numbers** can only poorly be approximated by **rational numbers"**; whereas **"transcendental numbers** can be efficiently approximated by rational numbers".

Other trails to explore the evoked **elliptical topology** (respect to stretchable volumes with 'holes across') and up-scales informative links of the complexity chain (we suggested with $n.\log_n n$)?

Elliptic because after **sphere**, it is the general form of (relatively) closed object in 3 dimensions. Observe that ellipse has 2 *foci*: the start of **binary-ness**. To think more in terms of 3 dimensions elliptical object, possibly 3 foci (Poincaré's 3 bodies problem). Mind 'incorporation' because we are still with one volume concept or **logical ball**, dualized by some contrast, provided integration-differentiation. And **topology** because we need that not a rigid ball; that is property preserving like measure especially at equilibrium of rest so requiring some 'elasticity' or non-fragmenting stresses (which formally is topology). [See more intuitions elsewhere in this essay].

Nevertheless, care we are just trying to find new ways in the expressions of scales, dimensions, *modulus* of number systems, eventually geometrical forms; not with esoteric numerology. Clearing immediately about the '**informative systemic shuttle'** that it would have a minimum of 2 references (at the extremes: **global-local** or **absolute-relative**): ground one (physics universe) and own level (of maximum achieved complexity).

A given complex system 'achieving' a given **maximum level of systemic complexity** ... which it would have to assume as a 'system'. The practical suggestion **to index complexity with prime numbers?** (Rather than the 'too slippery' natural or even numbers). So with such steps of prime numbers, you can index with the one achieved and; relatively you have the same unary start just by subtraction either of the lowest prime one (making the relative 0 of the bases) and the largest primer one (making the relative 1 unit). Just add the prime number index and you recover your global-ness (the one made of fundamental particles). [Keeping in memory the prime number index).

[This also suggests a system has in complexity to 2 prime numbers of indexing, thus a piece of systems' scale. Notice (0,1) just base; (2, 3) first prime numbers no system; (1,2,3) head one system but need to be completed by specifications? (3,5) and (5,7) if with just one concept (no system?); (7,11) there are 3, so a 2nd level system thus inclusive of (0,6)?–only the 0 not to be absolute].

To imagine things not so simple. A complex system in it level of complexity may incorporate various other complex systems, turned subsystems since not as complex as major one but 'incorporated' o serves its general unit. This various other subsystems are not out the narrowest environment of considered major units. A living body is not, 'like that', going to incorporate lower subsystems existing like, on to the Sun (which also obeys to some same physics laws as what in troposphere).

So, for the moment the proposition of the **system formal shuttle**: the package or set of relative dimensions (3 and around). And its properties of operations should be 'within' at the level the ones between 0 and 3 as inner. And the **complement of specification** or outer quite, symmetrically thus from 3 up to 6 dimension for specified solutions (or 8? –String theory varies upon that complementary dimensions) quite similar at any levels (along absolute scale).

Moreover, as you will read about later; we have in mind both the **universal scale** (since 'nothingness' and evolving to complexity after the 'physical numbers' and the relative one (reinstated or reinitiated); we also have the 'ordered world developing with the inside': a Chinese box (or Russian doll) formally requiring to be regular enough (in the shuttle). Meanwhile, in the physical cosmos of the universe both scale co-exist: since the Big-Bang with an expanding universe and a structuring within the universe.

Serious studies about the minimum number of specifications are needed. For obtaining a realistic solution, or at least a model can be completed by at least one solution of reality. If not so pure fancy abstraction! But a **minimum shell of 4** could be, for the moment: as we like

---

for the "shuttle" how this would not be inconceivable?–the prime indexing number reached on the absolute scale. That is the one self-information 'quali-quanti' representation succeeded; have been able to make there. A basic system around the unit. Quali (tative) would consider the main set of properties having met their Quanti (ties) from the environment (metabolism to compensate entropy and its avatars). To index this level of complexity; as a step or consider a relative logical closure: next prime numbers (?). We understand it is a bit difficult, anyhow you need to **visualize 'more serious geometrical frameworks'** than the 'simplest of rejections'.

Since a prime number has not natural decomposition (in set of $\mathbb{N}$). Meanwhile in $\mathbb{R}$ polynomials have good roots with algebraic numbers (but our world is quantic)

[Probably God prefers to tickle humans as dices]. So the only 'integer' subtraction by itself sets the counter to base: (relative) 0 and 1 (unit). And the system framing can restart: logic relative to number need not to make it, for the main with a horrible pair of prime numbers. And there you have also economics, if not aesthetic.

Your management with a simple system is simplified because a relative one. You try to **shape your model in a number of the bases for the main properties**. Qualitatively you will work in natural numbers or eventually on mantissas of logarithms if required. Quantitatively you will work with real numbers; eventually the irrational or transcendental ones. But your amounts of food come from simpler sources.

In abstract the same *modulus* of "relatively closed" shuttle applies. That is, you have the qualities matched to quantities. This makes, at best, a system of such 'objects-representations' (half-complex–but–half-simple: the 'head' or your system of representation). In the same way you have a similar system of operations (addition, multiplication, subtraction, division) defining the simple operations of the unit.). All these 3 "intertwined" and 'completed by the real' for a whole picture. [It is possible to also have to design concepts of exterior algebra to consider the exchanges.

In almost absolute environment it is also the same as you know: simple arithmetic and statistics. Where operations turn somehow complex is with macro-complex environments you live in. And if you want to preserve other systems there. At least in spirit having understood that if you destroy everything ... your society and civilization is dead. (Less short than Keynes)].

This 'completed in the real' is; by the side of reality or; the properties measured, allowing to specify. The expression of solutions, of such problems, is not full in general; when at its level of 'maximum achieved complexity'. Which is regular characteristic sort of space-phase **medium** not many solutions you have. Dimensions higher than 3 the basic would have a **'tail'** specifying to the very case? [We may have to examine statistically and logical enough various cases for estimating the **invariant** within a **medium** of existence].

Time is usually the 4th dimension of the **quaternion**. Quaternion is a sort of **Hamiltonian**. Which is a convenient mathematical expression for a 'metrical matrix system'. Time may turn a piece of formal system. Maybe the usual one the 1st fundamental **'closure.'** Notice time usually divides (is in the denominator) respect to other dimensions. [Turning then into speed, expansion or at the reverse. But in the traditional way time still requires to be better conceived; with more complex life's expectancy].

This may have to call for a system of time(s) for the (one system) of **closures** (tentatively). Mind eventually **these closures are different pictures of times?** The usual one the period of life, of such constitutive particles. So of the universe. (Absolute-time or time-life: the most fundamental are mainly protons and electrons ... between them the neutron.). But other dimensions of times are the ones of life at its level of achieved complexity (your **life expectancy**).

[That way may make **times: pieces or segments,** pile them, order them, hierarchize in the way of Chinese's box or Russian Dolls. Do that in the relative main one for non-infinite integration (box-up) and derivation (box-down). And possibly 'holing within' highest closed one. If we mind not to have our heart entangled to the other side of the galaxy. Or our cat with the same fate as of the copy in another planet. But still we fundamentally need this entanglement at levels of electrons].

Consider another (time) the one of the *medium* where you are. At the middle of a major disaster this may kill you. More closely affecting your probability of death (?). The 4th bout of time could be, what we are trying to do. Maybe analogic, to the human body. It would be the one of your critical function 'at the moment' [Which can be either the time you gave to you phase-space and/or a probable one.

[If you are running in advance of a lion after you ... and your heart (critical power ratio) does not deliver ... happy meal to the lion!].

So 1) **time line-base** (it may be closer to your system than protons and neutrons (the just below systems of which you almost totally depend: metabolic or phase-space); 2) your **overall time line** (average life expectancy or after the action or the horizon of time you have); 3); the **time line of your main critical state** (provided as the 1st by the hierarchy within your vital functions; 4) the **time line of your environment** of subsistence (you may affect). Time's arrow needs a field of 4 cardinal orderable and integration-able segments?

[Then this would be the usual known time (out simple formal intervals 'just a metric or normed measure dimension one'. Effectively the fundamental atomic vibration would be the period of founding universe particle period... Or could be the characteristic probability of field -particle twist. ... Or would be the ratio you have between this (previous) and that of the particle-field twist? This may, statistically, provide with some qualitative lessons. But not quantitatively clear. You will need further informative approach].

[If you have no time to calculate all that; let your brain make it, for your natural conditions. Even if most of what it is doing will be unconscious. If the matching, as a system, of these 4 minima not good; you will probably have to review, consciously? Why what you tried did not work; and then change your priorities. That is, how your brain works. By the way you may change some of your characteristic times. Hence not the one you have non-horrendous scientific access: nuclear ones].

That way, a prime number index will not decompose into products of factors. Of those exposed to "disaggregation". The system is real because here and maintaining. Of course "achieved" is primarily "an objective existence." You may build any conceptual pure abstract non-existing system, but that would not be 'economical'. **Actually, the main suit of economics is uneconomical**, because neither properly respected, neither properly inspiriting for lowering the threats. Nor it is enough 'capped' by the best economical rules: the 'ethical ones'.

This may be, how to refer your system to a **'systemic shuttle' at levels of existence**. Without having to work too much with the prime number index of maximum complexity reached. You may have to **work just within the minimum**

characteristic qualities quantified (provided by the universe) **and the maximum characteristic quantities (requalified?** By your metabolism), (provided by the environment).

If the system on which you are working is far in the evolutionary scale balances of complexity; it could be quite less easy to manipulate. It is far from balance-equilibrium you are phenomenologically used to and it is more critical. And observe:

> You **apprehend systemic complexity** but you are **seeking for sufficient general calculability**: that the minimum for your manageability. So the most important metaphysical question: does this manageability take phenomenological sense with how things work in our surroundings?

One last point for the moment: your "shuttle" is not free in the outer space (with all needed stocks and reserves for the trip). Fundamentally, you are in a physics universe with its laws. So in its universe and you do with that: the protons, electrons you have (and the emergences forms and systems under your levels detailed). You amounts your quantities with that. So **you have to take into account systems' environments of existence** bottom-up (want it or not) or formally said your **universal basis**. [But does this mean that running through another universe you will not be able to exchange?–with aliens of parallel universe? That is: a more interesting sort of trade within our universe? Is that more important than to organize our environment relations more fairly?].

Formally you relatively simply reinstated system in its universe with this prime number index of achievement. [And you may study the lower systemic constructions or broad qualified quantities?]. At the reverse you have to consider your providing environments; and care the smart extractions you make in this. That is a '**top-down approach', which is economical and should be better 'moral'**?. Moral in the sense of choosing smarter and kinder alternatives of better and enough transformations instead of speculating too much, for 'grab and run out of the destruction'.

> The *genius* of Nature: is having framed together (and evolutionarily) bottom-up and top-down.

Economically? At least formally in your micro-dimensions; you will have more to do with nearby systems (indexed with closest prime numbers). They will be below if you consider the achievement of your system the highest. Of course, economically it is better to take your electrons and protons from the meat and vegetables you obtained from breeding and agriculture. Rather than from "oxygen-nitrification" of underground-hydrocarbons? In fact we let those reactions made by the Sun, the atmosphere and the soils or oceans bacteria.

> The stupidity of humans' consciousness is of not being able to frame its socio-economic system after ethical choice; between the diversity of options for better-off at minimum social costs.

Observe that with formal sciences; we are not at all as heretical as you may have started to think. Even if the picture looks very different from the modern harsh ways of simplest operations. Our suggestions of explorations seem very bizarre?

- $\mathbb{N}$ natural numbers set, stays almost the same. Just we suggest prime numbers given (or having) a sort of *status* for indexing 'step of congruence'? [To confirm after proper mathematics concept]. Such set of numbers 'prefers' addition for quantities, products for qualities and it is also 'bottom-up prone.

> Anyhow it will be better to recruit more properties in our usual thinking.

- $\mathbb{Z}$ of integer numbers set is built the same way as natural numbers provided a sign giving emphasis to subtraction, since the corresponding reached natural number. But what does mean minus numbers really? - Nothing if only exchangeable. Such set of numbers 'prefers' subtraction quantities. It is also 'top-down."

  Eventually to relate the $\mathbb{Z}$ (integer numbers set) concept better with $\mathbb{C}$ (complex numbers set) that is: relative $\mathbb{Z}$ number binary-ness or linearity or 180°, relative position thus but it is to refer to $\mathbb{N}$ and has correspondence with $\mathbb{C}$).

  Anyhow, it seems necessary to be sooner clever in our operations. With subtraction we should not exceed (not too indebted). Since the world live too much on debts either as credits in their bank account, or respect to nature.

- $\mathbb{Q}$ of rational numbers with division takes from $\mathbb{N}$ numbers (including $\mathbb{Z}$). They point at algebraic numbers in real ones. They are top-down and division prone.

- $\mathbb{C}$ numbers are ascribed to $\mathbb{R}$, relative in all possible relativeness axis (or neighbors numbers? Or a pre-plural-influence?). They are algebraic completions of real numbers. [Expect more explanations further].

- $\mathbb{R}$ of real numbers. This set receives irrationals as complement of rational numbers. It also hosts transcendental numbers. What is important is how numbers are formed. Also algebraic numbers are real numbers roots of polynomials are in $\mathbb{R}$.

  o Cantor Set theory proved the Set of algebraic numbers is countable and; the set of real numbers is not countable.
  o After theorem of Euler-Lagrange: a real number is quadratic algebraic numbers iff it has a periodic continued fraction.
  o Theorem: every irrational number has at least the approximation ($|\alpha - p/q|$ $(<1/q^k)$ in order 2

o   Liouville approximation: an algebraic number of degree n ≥1 can have at most the approximation order n.

Probability of Link(s) Quali-Quanti

Now it is to imagine how to implement a something like quali-quanti and quanti-quali informative representation (minimin and maximax already with plenty of data?) ...; between: qualitative ordinal-cardinal properties and Quantitative Characteristics Amounts?

Think first that in 'theoretical' physics, almost any abstract and **most natural mechanisms, are probable or uncertain**. Conscious phenomenological approaches mostly with (hugely) defective information. Defective it is in the practical sense to have the smartest approaches of good environmental practices (in a formal sense). But having already many small parts of mechanics; as required by the proper handling of what could be called pure exact mathematics.

From social-economic we turned used to distinguish '**determinism**' (possibly **exogenous causality**) from 'not-determinism' (possibly **endogenous effectivity**?). So is statistics; we may use central mean (average) as positively probable; with **intervals of uncertainty** (standard deviation or 'mean error') [that looks like a bit time intervals...]. And the (had to be) **'least surprising' residual** which, in common modeling, is called '**noise**' and formal and supposedly **ergodic-like** (local constant random motions). Nowadays most people are hardly understanding the foremost surprising: the **non-linear formal behavior** (also called **chaotic** in mathematics). [Most thoughts about statistics in forthcoming volume of this essay].

Connecting Uncertainty and Information

Shannon's theory of information

$D(f(x), \ g(x) \ | \ x \ \in[a,b])/_a^b$ $f(x).\ln f(x)/g(x).dx$
f,g probability density functions

U-uncertainty : $U(r) = \int_0^c |A_\alpha| d\alpha$
$|A_\alpha|$ denotes the cardinality of α of the fuzzy set
U(r) is also a weighted average value of Hartley information

uncertainty
implies
Simplification of problems
1.Eliminating
2. Adding
3. Cutting unity
Conflict resolution

principle of uncertainty invariance
relation uncertainty and information
invariant preserved when changing formalism

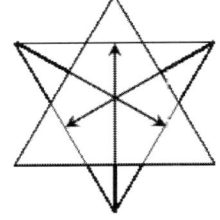

"Revelation"
the piece of information that allows us to know which kind of "formal" world we are

Dempster-Shafer Theory
Necesity measure (A∩B) =
min[Nec(A), Nec(B)]
with $m(A_i)= r(x_i) - r(x_{i+1})$
Possibility measure
(A∪B)=Max[Pos(A), Pos(B)]
$Pos_A(B) = Max_{x \in B} \ r_A(x)$
$U(r) \ = \ \sum_{i=1}^n \ [r(x_i)-r(x_{i+1})]\ln|A_i|$
(generalization of U(r))
$Confusion(m) = - \sum_{A \in F} m(A_i) \ln Belief(A)$

principle of maximum uncertainty
Ampliative reasonning
(generality)
Optimization

76

In quantic physics they conceive almost always respect to **some observer** (under human eyes?). Thus have this in mind. After the above mentioned *nucleus* of 3 could be imagined? - A sort of 'set' of 6 kinds of mathematical behaviors? Twice 3 is possible after **manageability** (or relative open-closure of general relative minimum system). We ought now to add different levels (of **modular** expressions). [So just a small phenomenological approximation that need to be better formulated].

Also we are in the idea that all kinds of such mathematical behaviors may co-exist in a complex objects (**unity, so an achievement**, not a preliminary systemic concept. [That is not because a mad human tells you not to be mad that you will admit forcibly]. Hence this would not necessarily be in the "same systemic **window**". Subjects' economics implicitly or unconsciously make use of all resources at the stack. Our 'invented suggestion' still not in the management of formal epistemology.

[Moreover we have to care: it is not very wise to multiply the use of arbitrary categories in formal approaches. Since they may miss the truest ones]. An example is with the multiplication of indices in many competing priorities of 'statistics'.

This may 'at the end' have ethical concern: if you 'chose the **choice**'; you have to search for the proper sorts of formal behaviors (composed of operations). This, for not mistaking your analysis nor mislead your actions. Analysis exposed to mistaking **artifacts and/or improper formulations**. Actions sometimes generically called *praxis;* practically consisting of **over-imposing ones' own determinisms**. In the uncertain frameworks it is also to work conditions. Set **perturbation** or **interfere; phasic**-like or **counter-phasic**-like (if process is periodic) and intent to '**synchronize**,' '**deviate by influence**' if not **shocking** or **crushing**. [A more formal systemic classification is required, using perturbation theory].

Consciously, it is also to research for your own formal economy. Primarily the suggestion is the one of your brain. Neurosciences evidences that conscious activity of your brain is often a small and over-esteemed part. As a result and increasingly **unconsciousness and well-trained emotions can often** do well or enough. So what has to be formalized? - and to which extent?

What we should expect as better aids? ... - instead of again and again programs of structural financial adjustments programs?–Back at human level? – when in fact scales extend globally. What to learn and how to train directly and indirectly? -our brains for better cognitive efficiency (once hung this damned rational neoclassical economics closed in its labyrinth of determinist pomposity?).

Just mind: there are plenty of simple, intuitive formal procedures for fairer overviews and judgments. So it is to stop believing in 'that is what you have to do: "stop thinking!" (If you are 'below') and believe 'what I say' (since 'I am above').

Also mind: a 2nd order reflexive kernels of 'formally wise processes'. This could be the best collective human intelligence with universal best pieces of... If the helpers at the respect could be fairly neutral in local societies. At least stay unaffected by: unaware and 'innocent' 'corruption of self-interests'.

Endogenous sustainable development cannot wisely turn a fortress of xenophobia. Nor the ignorance of bureaucratic power normative effects should be missed. But how it could effectively load a peaceful cultural apprehension of 'self-wish-ness.'

Now with: formal infinitesimal almost exact differential calculus formulations; of the ones you can manage as an explicit model. Including care for parts you cannot manage. Later one often called the "residual", has been excluded too much from any other game than noise and spurious. [We will explain more about that in the next book]. There is a need to formally understand the connection between exact (difference) *calculus* and theory of probability.

Regular transformations, if a non-linear behavior may adapt scales, start with linear *calculus* (the easiest one) and formally also the *nucleus* of functional analysis. That is we need to frame somehow properly: **linear calculus, metrics** (straight ruler measure). These are mathematically in dimension one, but higher dimensions should not be missed. Where are more common non-linearity, more options and more dynamic systems.

In the probability of physics, Heisenberg's **principle of uncertainty** seems to have established as principle the 'that we cannot know perfectly'; because of many reasons. Then what are the probabilistic models or sub-models? - despite that their formulation links also to integral-able-differential calculus. Formally, they receive different sorts of treatments: **simulations, perturbations,** statistics **records** and **smoothing** and so on). Models also have to distinguish what we can manage (variables of control) or since where, and if other management(s) could apply. As in collective policies or with precautions. The preventive precautions are the ways to cope with uncertainties. In finance or economics or many others applied registers, all this is called jointly '**risks**'; but it is a very poor way to try to understand.

Accounts of un-expectable behaviors are turning increasingly important, in some way. They are to parametrize also the non-linear irreducible behaviors. [We have like **Lyapunov's exponent, fractal dimensions, complexity usual measures** (Kolmogorov one with a start of informative expression). Most have to do with the **concept of distance** and/or norm.

Hilbert produced someone crossed, geographers have some; theory of information and computation also. Minkowski provided a general expression. [Minkowski distance is a metric in a normed vector space. Which can be considered as a generalization of both the Euclidean distance and the Manhattan distance. Mahalanobis (a mathematician and planner of modern India) proposed a measure of the distance between a point P and a distribution. Entropy formula is often used in one way or the other. Also it is to mention the use in geometry and probabilities. Hausdorff distance measures how far 2 subsets of a metric space are from each other. Statistics have many classificatory indices. All that is quite 'heterogeneous'.

[In **normed vector space** of dimension less than infinite:
- all norms are equivalent,
- all linear application is continuous,
- a sub space of finite dimensions of any space is closed,
- all normed and finite vector space is complete,
- all bounded suite has an adherence value
- all suite converges iff it has just one adhering value.]

Fundamental authors in mathematics may not be full adept. They all share, looking like concepts and have special use. One understands that all that should fall in **Measure theory** comprehensive approach and this has **integration as core** and has been in infinitesimal calculus achieved somehow after Riemann and Lebesgue. But some **theory of probability** digression, also much linked to measure and integrability has needed some insights from Borel to Kolmogorov].

Correspondence between Languages? (care that we suggestively completed)				
Script	Probability theory	Set theory concept	Measure theory	General interpretation
Ω	event space	Field	normed measure space (Ω, S, μ)	aggregative system
ω ($\omega \in \Omega$)	elementary outcome	Element	point in space $\omega \in \Omega$	individual in the system
A ($A \subset \Omega$)	event	part of Ω	measurable set $E \in S$	extension (attribute)
$\omega \in A$	A realized	least of 1 element in part	points in measured set	existence
$A \subset B$	A implies B	A included in B	integration	integrability
$A \cup B$	A or B	Union	additivity	summable
$A \cap B$	A and B simultaneously	Intersection	producibility	cross-able
A^c or $\Omega \setminus A$	¬A (contrary event)	Complementary	separability	negation operator
$A \setminus B := A \vee B^c$	A but not B	Difference	subtraction	subtractibility
$\varnothing$	impossible event	empty part	empty space	Vacuum
Ω	sure event	whole set	whole scale	environment
$A \cap B = \varnothing$	non-compatible event	disjointed parts	independence	maximally neighbors
P (A)	Probability	choice axiom	normed measure. μ (E)	relative magnitude of E
$\forall \exists$	random variable	Cardinal	convertible to measurable function f	individual attribute of ω
ω / A	Expectation value	cardinal$_{order}$ /cardinal	averaged integral $\int f d\mu$	mean value of attribute f
$\forall$ or $\exists \rightarrow \omega A$ or	Distribution	Order	induced measure μ_f	attribute of the system Ω

We have to narrow in this essay, it is not a substitute to handbook. And mathematicians may know better than us. Our concern would be more about 'the system mantra'. As you may suspect; it is to have clear links with the fundamentals. So this essay of suggestions would be too anticipating the proper work to do at the respect. Also we are not here to intent to suggest some too separated formalism for the system. This may be a wiser suggestion than having one's own 'specific' systemic, that already have proliferated so much since von Bertalanffy General System Theory (1968).

Switching to 'physics' or metaphysics phenomenological epistemology' (which is some sort of *chimera*). There are even in very normal looking kinds of subject or objects. The commonest in nature which '**ontogeny**' is full of **singularities**. We do not have to systematically avoid efforts of **simplifications**. They are also natural subject and object so have to be explored; in which amounts and in '**random qualitative events**'. They are part(s) of structures either physical or formal. Physics subjects have some **characteristics parameters** that may make them controlled in an indirect way (synchronization, higher scale or higher levels of dimensions and so on). An important question is with how to make use of logic(s) for the study on that. For some intuitive suggestions:

- Never be ashamed to get back to basics with mathematics and logics;
- Find and mind a 'core head' of structure and functions (formally forms and operations) and share it voluntarily with the maximum of legitimate actors without wasting too much time;
- Help yourself with analogies between rigorous logic of mathematics and try to translate into logical;
- Have systemic approaches (without too confusing the levels (distribute, delegate, articulate),
- Switch from lines (one dimension) or argument and series of numbers, pack them in the plane (such as from one corner to opposite one;
- Remind that 'sub-something' in logics more means with all the properties but smaller size as with set and subset;
- Conceive any things, with 3 or 4 corners or directions: number exactly of the same sort (but the symbol) or completely different and mixtures.

Different equivalent Systems of Symbolic Notation in Logics			
Peano-Russell	**Hilbert**	**Lukasiewicz**	**others**
~P	$\overline{P}$	Np	- P, ⌐P
P, Q	P & Q	Kpq	P Q, P ∧Q
P ∨Q	P ∨ Q	Apq	P Q
P ⊃Q	P → Q	Cpq	
P ≡Q	P ~ Q	Epq	P ↔Q
(x) F (x)	(x) F (x)	⫪x Φx	∀xF (x), ∧xF (x)
(∃x) F (x)	(Ex) F (x)	∑x Φx	∃xF (x), ∨xF (x)

About Logics Primaries

Logics' applied aim is to reach the rigorous minimum, without logical contradictions; making use of one logic as universal as possible. Somehow formal logics is systematically dressed up, but possibly never as far and easy as hoped. But we have in mind that as soon as there is a logic; there are available resources of formulation to gain. Either we can search for it in the web or in a handbook chapter. We would prefer interactive platforms. Commonly any looks like lists of axioms, of a dozen; and not much more axioms. Another good help fast, for profanes are the correspondences between. Quite often literature articles give you with correspondences or concepts equivalence from one logic to another, including in arithmetic logic.

Nowadays logics theories are enough stabilized, and will probably never be perfect. It is more for stabilizing your way of thinking and of respecting, but ... how to care realities with that? Moreover it is not the same as in natural sciences; where some specific knowledge can be important.

Handbook for exams are often horrible: they teach you how to reach the only one good result ... in the leanest way. At the end most of us remain just with the feeling that real things are not like that.

Avoid social also arts exclusive readings, they may provide plenty of glimpses of erudition and when you face with the realities there is no more space than their infamous determinism and illusory puttering about. Better learn and prepare to behave, including your emotions, honestly trained. Social arts 'exclusive lectures' are more past time pleasure for 'crazy petits bourgeois' and poorly will tell you how to behave. Read synthesis for feeling, 'be part of the World.' But do not reduce your field of ideas to just the right most impressive self-help commonly religious. They are hardly prepared to respect reality's enormous diversity of 'ghosts'.

But our essay is not for explaining much on what we cannot bring some original comments or suggestions.

Intermediating Logics

Back to traditional minimum. After Tomassi (a handbook of logics we explored) think logically is about: an **argument**(s) which consists of **premises**; a **'therefore'- type** of word and reach a **conclusion** (after as short as possible numbers of lines of proof). In the **deductive** kind of argument; argument is said to be valid **if and only if** (iff) it takes a form that makes it impossible for the premises to be true and the conclusion nevertheless to be false [Mind a separation]. Otherwise, a deductive argument is said to be invalid. [This, of course, looks like an 'upside down' with physics].

[The 'upside down' our common, maybe not as benign as it looks like: either we conceive logics with **direct identification** or correspondence; and then if they could be complete (and nice); no problems of contradictions and paradoxes between (fundamental physics and logic. Or we consider logics **indirectly**, more as **a shell**; thus with possibilities of '**mirror effects**', formal to real and back switches; as we meet in optics, neurosciences and so on. Thus it is also a sort of indirectness providing a start for **irreversibility** (by the side of physics), **non-commutativity** (in arithmetic). Possibly starting very soon as in symmetry of physics. And the **posture of consensus**: we are a priori never really sure with directness or indirectness. [Possibly reserved to 'local'?]] This supports: **fundamental probability co-existing with exactness**. Respect to determinism it is quite unpleasant (not to be 'the lone child'). But after all it is quite similar to the nature of physics, the entropic expression respect to conservation law; or formally we would have the relative closeness/openness. Formally also in a minimum we are loading the negation operator in logics possibly only relative to each level? ... At the end of the history, the concept of **freedom**: the feeling (or emotion) of freedom experienced when saying 'no' ... with some closure we like to add].

Negation operators: but one non-A, in logic rigor it is not as simple as the formula: it means. A is known, or; can be non-A element complement by set E, or; can be all non-A in all, or; an antithesis procedure of A dynamic, and so on.

Negative Definiteness
Let M be any square matrix of dimension m. The following two statements are equivalent:
1). For every definite positive and symmetric square matrix Q, QM has all its **Eigenvalues** with negative real parts,

---

2). $(M + M^\top)$ is negative definite.

In Negation another complex-complicated concept abusively and wastefully taken for simple ... more useful either as a formal system? [One's assume its own contradictions as a potential 'convertible' or ... all a complement of not 'this'].

All be careful logic as a direct identification quite 'normal'. Logic when as an 'instrumental corner of shells' is requiring a complement minimum since physics, with possibilities of contradictions. It is also helpful for evolution: the resource to let if not useful enough, but keep nearby if possible to find further some use.

"A deductive argument is **sound** if and only if it is both valid, and all of its premises are actually true. Otherwise, a deductive argument is **unsound**.

The claim of the formal logician is that an argument is valid purely by virtue of **substitution-instance of a valid argument form**. An argument form is valid iff **every** substitution-instance of that form is valid. An argument form is invalid if **some** substitution-instance of that form is invalid. A **counterexample** to a form is a substitution-instance of that form, which is itself an invalid argument".

Logical forms: these addresses more **sentences** rather than **questions** and **proposals**.

In the next-coming we often coin Burgess (another logician good book). The profane reader may have a more poetic overview on them. The concepts are selected because we quote them important. Thus if we do not explain much, concerned readers can make 2 things: turn a little more open-mind like if trying to be curious and humble philosopher; and examine ingenuously (sort of analysis of containing) any concepts, operate between (union, intersections, products, addition, existential, universal quantifier...) and have a look at dictionaries.

Non-standard logics are often applied to some kind of specific logical problem, but a broad one. Any tries to be comprehensive and; if logic is in a similar way as arithmetic 'incomplete'; it means you have in arithmetic a logic of a sort. So you can intent to make use of what you know from calculus, systematically. But any may get entrapped in their technicalities and does not avoid all the semantic paradox.

Respect to applied problem if you stay stuck by logics' semantic paradoxes it is not very handy (not very flexible). Otherwise this may be because you did not have enough 'specifiable'. Or are not informed enough. There are sorts of balances between utility and economy, logics and mathematics. But that is important with modern day software sciences logic are programmable and their ambition of all is to avoid generating problems with their own logical computing, hence not necessarily care the human beings choice.

Logics under scope has to be able to **specify enough** of the different necessary options (we could call 'logical heuristics' about ways of solving). Those applied more specific logics to core axioms. Commonly cores of special logic comes partly from set theory (which is also the 1st one for arithmetic) and some added formulations and/or founding theorems of the *focus*: modality, models, 3-valued logic(s), knowledge logic, λ- calculus, and so on.

Logic of deduction a formal logic has been developed but all are anyhow imperfect ... almost in absolutes. **Inductive logic** also exists, practically; it has been more commonly seen as an ingredient (**induction**) of arithmetic logic. Too simple at its debuts. But advancements offer more. In quantified applications, there may have a need for more inductive methods to imagine together with the **deontology of inductive methods**. It could have so more future... Since numbers from below and develop up ... as soon as proper careful heuristics could expand up ... if taking advantage of experience (that is memory); to approach complexities. The deontology for the curation of crazy reductions, cuts or oversimplifications?

Few on Classical Predicate Logic

Formalizing quantification has a notion of '**formula**'. Which is more complicated than in classical sentential logic. Also a notion of **models** would require to **specify a universe**, as a k-place (predicate letter). Then which things (set) of the universe are true? They can be represented by a **denotation function** assigning true value to letters. [That is we have here a concept of **testability** and **test**]

Notions of **truth of a formula**, in a model for the formal language of classical logic, is more complex. In general after Tarski's theory of truth, notions of truth is only applicable to **closed formulas**, but today, many logicians disagree. Thus to use a general notion of satisfaction applicable (also) to open formulas: Universe $\vDash$ A (y_1, ..., y_k) [u_1, ..., u_k] truth then the case k=0; to extend to essential **quantifiers**. The most standard are **universal quantifier** ($\forall$) and **existential quantifier**(s) ($\exists$).

[Physics logic particle-field approach may have to remaster this form ... any possible or few states to one or few ones... Or some statistics-probability between cardinal configurations to ordered ones?]

What really seems to matter is the number of elements in the model's domain and the **patterns** of distinguished **relations**, among them. Number of elements taken as set, makes set theory the basic for approach of elements, things or objects.

[Usually any logic start with 2 'objects' (pairs, mid-plane, and so on or bipolar) in the axioma's list: A, B ... fine! if this is a start and made with complementary logics. Could be that a "shuttle-system of logics" wider than that? Hence we have seen that 3 or 4 is better (if 2 is not the very problem ... could be in a more structured-modular way... And so to find ways to take account of emerging properties. Be it, inspired by the systems' thermodynamics forms and/or theory of numbers. The most interesting properties are like coming after simple odd, even and prime].

Configuration, truth-value, format of elements are the reasons of models' development; hence a logic of **Model Theory**. 'Patterns' (unorthodox term) of distinguished relations are the reason of **categories theory**. **Theory of proof** examines the ways to construct truths and proofs of. With quantization and logic of mathematical you observe that the main domain of the application of efforts of logics, is the construction of '**mathematics models**'.

Social Utility and Logic(s)

Lay people have to mind that logics are tools, and support to '**neutral approaches**' for **testing, formatting**, prepare '**decision**'. This would be in repeatable and shared (but relative) arguments [Like needed by data bases 'intelligent **queries**']. Calling especially 'discrete generally admitted' or 'established continuing finite demonstrations'. Some automation could be imagined in very non-phenomenological case; but they belong to highly technological processes (with higher levels of safety?)–better than 'artificial intelligence'.

> [Of course not to miss that all computed universal logic system (fifties of the 20th century) failed. Meanwhile the wish to replace the human in absolutes of machines may just produce ... another (disastrous?) world].

Many kinds of concepts can be examined under the scrutiny of: one specific or various sorts of logics. It is good to know how to apply, intuitively, some logical techniques (ex: **tables of truth**) and understand some basic concepts (**tautology** (iso)-**morphism, induction, deduction**) ... even if to ignore most of register's management. It is not difficult, you can help you with your common sense and quite possibly simple arithmetic.

> In the hope that proper interfaces will be designed, for better capture of humans probable will. You can often get further; just reminding concepts you received and "translate" since mathematics had to be rigorous. What we seek is to turn enough explicitly for, one day the robot counselor complete the implicit with them, for the human satisfaction ... to work no less harder, but with more safety and still gaining satisfactory results from hard efforts.

> Logics are also somehow about 'systematically cooking concepts round and round but not too cooked'. Take any concept-word or ideas from a sentence or reasoning and/or characteristic way of vanity text. You may easily find many absurdities. Care the funniest ones and imagine them serious) and maybe some special (hidden?) logic could tolerantly be admitted.

Thereafter to try to imagine a **basic repertory** or a **kind of alphabet**.

> Actually still it is not to exaggerate what can bring formal logics in real lives. Alas, most people do not care about how they construct their arguments; not just for them but for others. [The innovators' 'tragedy of common's: it is stupid to be as simple when not even simpler than the audience ... but how to bring something new? And proportion it to the 'caliber' of the reader. Informative piece part of the economy? - Meanwhile so many are still in wrong practices are simply normative and illusory copies? Taking themselves like

dictators, most still think (t): better to make decisions and thereafter pretend 'they are the best and there is no other issues'. When not disappear as soon as the externalities here?

Computers "soft-wared" interactive logics needs better interfaces and more completion with humans' efforts. In human affairs cautiously, many things could be better made.

Deduction in "social sciences" may have been a good form for themselves. Common lay deductive logic has been the major one of social sciences and has, but too slowly, provided with softer interpretations. In lieu of rhetoric presumptions, segregation, moral hygienic dogma that had prevailed before and still set back.

They tried to become correct; after the human-made (ideological) disasters, they even occasionally produced or have been symptoms of the shameful ways Occident made prevail its 'superiority'.

More progresses or better controls have to be done? - with logical reformulations and reviews of that sort. There are columns of smart concepts. They have invaded the common-ness of the media. Somehow to disqualify popular wisdom. Applications should develop reflexively doing; with more modesty and better economics of actors logically qualified and quantified.

Logic of Logicians

In few concepts: logic manages axioms: there are primary logical assertions or; postulates. **Axioms** are statements, accepted without proof and regarded as fundamental to register or object (subject identified not necessarily formalized).

Logical propositions are generic terms for theorems of no particular importance. **Theorems** are established assertions, statements that have been proven on the basis of previously established statements: theorems, generally accepted statements (as axioms). A **geometrical theorem** makes use of geometric forms to make explicit the demonstrations. It was the 1st sorts of demonstrations are implicitly used in architecture, paving, geometric mosaic with beautiful results.

A **lemma** is "helping theorems". It is a proposition less applicable (in the practice of logic, but it is part of the proof of a larger theorem (so are helpful for completing the meaning or understanding.

[Nevertheless; always mind: you may give some importance to your understandings and by the same as we explained before ... could this reveal a specific case? **Axioms** require **identification** with realities. **Theorems** once established, known and to be **evoked**. Indexed could they be properly almost automatically applied for special case solutions (values in human issues). You arguments will be limited.

It is more, in the shades of interpretations (under the shadows of potentials from physics possibilities); where you can discuss about ways to put into applications. Also, you will have to find a **good balance** between **proper formulation** (often with some purist ambition) and the **configuration of concepts**. That also works 'enough **robustly**' with phenomenological evidences ... concepts of the ones moving actors [induced after selecting deductions or deduces after proper inductions].

Corollary: is a proposition that follows with little or no-proof, from one other theorem or definition. Most commonly: applied to compute; means have developed various systems according what examined and as far as possibly non-self-contradictive system. Such are: theory or sets (for the collections of objects); Theory of models, Theory of categories either for or from. For example, with topology, theory or probability and so on.

Predicate calculus is for working with enunciates. **Theory of categories** (and classes) to work with structures of mathematical relations. **Model theory** works the logics of relations between mathematical or logical means and what they represent.

Logic knowledge a sequence of authors

- Intuitionism or implicit epistemic logic (Brouwer & Heyting)
- Kripke semantic (complete for intuitionism)
- Critic to intuitionism (Quine)
- Epistemic logic for philosophers (Hintikka)
- Interpretation of proof (Brouwer, Heyting, Komolgorov)
- Structure of knowledge (Fagin, Halpern, Vardi)
- Neighborhood structures (Montague, Scott)

Demonstration Theory (Takeuti)

As an example of expert formulation: in logic, demonstrations often take the form of **ordered trees** [like trees of decisions].

T satisfying the following conditions (consider T as theory]:
- has a **minimum** called its **root**;
- for every b ∈ T {a ∈ T, a ≤ b} is linearly ordered by ≤ [≤ is left terms inferior or equal to right terms; ∈ is for element of];
- let T_1 and T_2 be **finite tree**; a **function** $f:T_1 \rightarrow T_2$ is an **embedding** iff is 1-to-1, order to preserve and satisfies the equation: f (a ∧ b) = f (a) ∧ f (b) for every a, b ∈ T_1 where a ∧ b denotes the **greatest lowest bound** of an and b; [∧: approximately and]
- Kruskal theorem: let ⟨T_k | k≤ω⟩ be a sequence of finite trees, then there exist I <j <ω such T_i≤ T_j
  - it is not provable in a certain 2nd order extension of Peano Arithmetic (PA);
  - it has a finite version of the 1st order, not provable in PA.

[Observe the intertwining of orders to make the logical framework consistent, but not in the first most general place].

Deductive and Inductive Logics

> Humans' **deductive reasoning** is about:
> - Select tasks involving **confirmation bias**. (Wason;)
> - Relations and simplification of **quantified syllogism** consider all, some 'no,' some 'no and a midterm.' (Steedman;)
> - **Conditional Inference**. (Taplin.)

This formal comment may be '**kernel-input**' [kernel is our term ... something like in mathematics immersion?]. The methodology existing in many textbooks of social sciences. Many use statistical methods. The proper 'kernel input' is more to bring to where you design your statistical hypothesis. [Kernel has a precise mathematical definition, in theory of function]

Thereafter you have the development of technique." **Natural Deduction** will ground (or bias) the concept of demonstrations on simple rules and so close to commonness; such is called natural. Core in that is the concept of **sequent** Γ - ϕ - in which the set of **hypothesis sequent** proves a formula Γ - ϕ - . Such demonstration is a tree where nodes are sequent; roots are the demonstrated sequents and; leaves would be axioms.

Relations between nodes in the succession (children of parents) are defined by some catalogue of 20 rules. Each composed of a premise and of a sequent and rule's conclusion. There exists a set of minimum rules, giving a minimum logic.

Joining a **rule of absurd intuitionism** make says that hypothesis leads to a contradiction [that is used as a way of demonstration in mathematics]. It is possible to deduce any formula and obtain a set of **intuitionist logic** rules. Replacing intuitionists absurd by classical absurd has the property to match syntactic aspect to natural semantic of propositional calculus. So a formula is a semantic consequence of a theory iff it is a synthetic consequence of the same theory for classical logic. [Observe the 'intertwining' making deduction a sort of 'logical operator']".

Deductive logics has (and still) subjugated social sciences. They consider weakly formed "important" concepts and static naïve lessons of social sciences may not fully be unnecessary. The point is that they are just local specifications. They should be in better balance with inductions.

[Observe nevertheless that once conduced the analysis in natural deduction; somehow that way. The pretension of social sciences reductionists are often down-side ... upside... Unless you take them by the techniques of analysis (not many at ease with). They can be ferocious about their lessons, and executive about the policies. Where they often miss realizing that they are not as easy as they say. And there are often (inductive) theory of management-like].

Inductive logics have driven sorts of quantitative logics. But commonly mathematicians have preferred arithmetic logics). Nevertheless, methods of inductive logics may have with better physics world evidence good developments. In the intents to replace the authoritarian lacks of 'logic of power' with inductions upon the 'conditions of environment, but work with probabilistic frames.' [Level up this to political issues (often lauded themselves as positive economy)].

To imagine better shared and volunteering mixtures of inductive-deductive logics.

Physics relation could be so: the balance particle(s)-field(s) seems to point at those particles that will be created where possible. So as for filling some 'position of *vacuum*' allowing properties. [Maybe we have to make a distinction between very stable particle-field driving the universe by very long lives and: swift from particle to field or motion of one or the other to the right place?].

That way physics shows how things work and, things have to evolve where potentials are *ad hoc* and fill and fit (?) them in probabilistic ways. This probability may also be with the population density of particle-field. Thus perspectives of the population is not to miss [Case of bosons or fermions statistics? [Being bosons the Bose-Einstein like particles and Fermions the Fermi-Dirac like particles].

> Within these frameworks of 'potential'; determinist policies, unique-minded, turn absurd. Any can phenomenologically deduce the need of a given, 'stage of environment'. This creates/has conditions of easy assignment. Not to say of some policies; in a high **determinist world** constrained to **free self-riding** either **risk adverse (keep and jam)** or **risk prone (catch and run)**; rather than **go and get for all** or **go and make all participate**.

In the field-particle inspired framework, you need balance between all together in equal conditions of potential ... to be open and able to gain orders?

Make this with humble, aware conscious autonomous people; within social contexts and you may find that better; than maintain distortions at any costs. [Sort of half-simplified perspective on a scientist way of how to do].

Arithmetic logic has **rules of induction**. You have to take account of the outer 'that arithmetic' which is the reality's complement. You may imagine **inductions as procedural applications**. Some sub-resources (or devices) of demonstrations in such logics may be:

- **Mathematical induction**: allow the management of infinite sets of affirmations; the use of a series of steps: recursion starts, for each step, and for a further step, then for all [such recursion a process of demonstration in mathematics].

[Abusing of short cuts or; of extension): it is not much more difficult to see how non-realistic illusions of induction; inspired by some universal *panacea* and as unique-mindedness if narrowed to one case. That is to say humans determinism just takes in policies, the worse of induction, and not the potential].

Induction within complexity looks to prove that atomic formula(s) (logic of the sentence) has (ve) the property of concern; as well as its negation, and so does their conjunction. Similarly with also seminal method of 'recursion on complexity.'

The principle of induction has a cost. A large number of properties, does not make a logical proof. Bold conjectures and attempted refutation "hypothesis."

- **Logical deduction**: examines all the sub-elements (best if finite classification) and treat them separately, testing and successively;

[(Abusing of a short cut of extension): in a similar way one can see the disaster of most of deductive social arts (pretending to be sciences). Like when over-exceeding the business of deductions for the perfect thesis].

- **exhaustion** and **elimination**; exhaust all the possibilities with announced test and discard or conserve; time and extent (store?); to take into account ['until contradicted'; and "as far as possible"]

- Aristotle's **syllogistic** system [more with relating simplifications?- is a way of reduction].

Practically nowadays if could be feasible to intent to match inductive and deductive logics in applications, rather than care so much about 'one' determinism.

Complement Logics, include Reality, Quantify

By pairs; apparently contradictory logics may complete one another. Care nevertheless that is not to stay trapped in abstractions but apply to "situations" and balance advantages or limits. Like we could have with such pairs as deductive logics/induction;   intuitionist   arithmetic/axiomatic   arithmetic;   set theory/categories logic; model logic/proof theory. Thirdly (if not done as primary) you always have to introduce, 'reality in'.

Thus how to organize that? Observe that these pairs may eventually be referred respect to a simple scale (measure, norm, metric) or ... maybe quite simple **head** or **skeleton** or **structure**, or **polyhedral-polygonal network of directing concepts** at some extremity. [This fast-track comments have some purpose, you will see later]. And, at the other, more or less ordered, intertwined, complex extension a sort of cloak. Between to structure them in a modular way and to stick to natural issues. [Could this be the **theory of knots** or **theory of strings** concepts or **methods**?] But care with complications.

In our conscious abstractions: 'complications' will be sort of too artificial technological developments if making phenomenology of common life too disagreeing with nature... The cognitions will face increasing difficulties to 'put together.' [Sort of projected out schizophrenia]. Thus complexities is excess are not economical. Complications in excess cut by the 2 extremities.

And also, it is to look at all the common management exaggerations of reductions and simplifications. Be them produced by the normative effects of paradigms with the absurd brutality of engineers or governors. Or revered by religions or managers sometimes made deaf and blind by their own propaganda. Many people are so unconscious or are proud to be just cynical.

Practices that could have maintained before; when hierarchical structures of societies were driven by violence, and technologies nevertheless enough depending on natural cycles. But not more sustainable at present time of revolutions (of disconnections?). They are enormous catalyzers of dysfunctional superstructures determinisms. Driven in the same way by government as by behemoths of business.

Always have in mind to use the formalisms. But make the connections (relations of similarities or not) still distinct; and relations toward identities of formal tools. This has to be with identification to realities abstracts (cognitive); and must have natural mechanisms 'anchors'.

Somehow a simple level of, most simple facts ... is already quite complex in foundational physics. But this later one supports nevertheless simple relative formulations at that level. Could they be leveling up? Then, follows up to our levels of complexity (of conscious human beings). Where our abstracts are more subjective and more or less complicated views. Directly when we have not yet the 'right formula' or indirectly, by the reductions made.

We require both: not to be too simplistic (this will not resist to the evidence of realities) and not too complicated (abstraction is anyhow an effort for simplifying. As we have to differentiate natural laws from specific details. Meanwhile abstract complications generally cannot surpass the levels of complexity reached by natural phenomena: civilization some kind of dumbness, anyhow...

... With too many distortions of over ambitions and abstract reductions; makes all the mistakes of reductionism or complications excesses. Latest also produce many distortions.

The sort of 'esoteric' reductionism which proposes simple alternatives, under obscure generic explanations; hugely exaggerates beliefs of truth. Obscure generic explanations? - that is esoteric, always meeting some audience. But socially they vary in effects: between laudable respects of nature (if at no cost, if not smart push; to and sectarian tyranny; if sizing and forcing "wasting sacrifice". As in the progress ideology carried by last century politicians of Capitalism. The ones of communisms having been disqualified. The rising one would be of religions (or anti-religious) ... just having missed history.

For short, at simple level, like of scientific evidence equipped with formal tools:
- to use at any level of formal system a negation operator;
- mastermind in probabilities of potentials (or informative links) and observe in general 3 poles either: 1 and 2 among all (3rd); you tend;
- as well, to base whatever concept in 3 dimensions at levels (dualized or contrasted when studied ... using the informative link as a minimum?);
- with down levels or universe that makes 2 $\times$3 (the minimum) and the environment (or the residual of the "*vacuum*") eventually detailed 3 ($\times$3);
- Conceive empirically that cardinal 3 starts cliques or 'question'; 4 can introduce a judgment or an observer; 5 if one in all quite specify enough one or observe a dual approach; 6 the close enough system?
- Combinations to operate of logical formal systems:
  o consider one "head" of cardinal 3 dimensions (in the relative 0,1,2,3) for the general expression,
  o 3 specifications for specific cases (measured),
  o below system(s) either absolute (the one making universe?And since which index of complexity is calculated, in the perfect case). In most cases it will be relative. Consisting of the closest engineered components,
  o environment either universe-source providing eventually phase-space or sources of provisions (it is also of the universe); but more directly sources systems of provisions (the human putting 'hemself' above all;
  o but hse will nevertheless have to consider the renewals of provisions from environment.

If wanting to be formally wise... Moral issues possibly another system above ... or pretended so).

[we neutralize him and her with 'hem'; he and she with hse]

- Consider that a given system problem or situation can be a combination or fusion of uncomplete (d) logical systems. So combining for being more 'complete' and 'more stable';
- Observe: by the side of processes that there are like complimentary, dual-primal relation (all having precise logical definitions, this makes the binary-ness;
- A good system does not have to be necessarily as close to the maximum of closure (but one) better variably open. [In the quaternion case it the imprecision of time that makes closure relative and uncertain?];
- Seeking a formal system has not to be closed. Since it is probably better to try keep it open to realities' completions so is the constraint of openness.
- Jumping up on complications, we make the suggestion of complementary logics management (as pairs of logics mentioned above).

In the first simple place of a unary prone logic, it looks like any logical need some logic 'kernel' [or shell or frame or *nucleus* or core]:
- Kernel 1st order logic on a positive (real) with comprehensive ambition (any sort of object could resume into A);
- A seed of kernels 2nd order logic (?): smaller negation of the 1st this may be a small change (or variation of 1st) in the minimum;
- A match between (operations, inclusion, links, arrows, etc. [tentatively, this has to be better formalized].

[Kernel here is just suggestive]

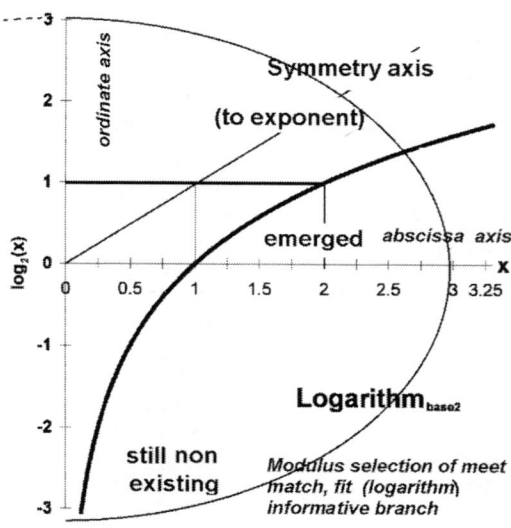

91

So in an informative arithmetic logic it may come easy to correspond:

- Either $\log_{base}x$ or x
- Either x or $base^x$
- The operation (*op*) between: either x.*op*.$\log_{base}x$ or x*op*$base^x$

[Notice that the realization (Re) could be written: x.*op*.$\log_{base}$ (x) (Re) x.*op*.$base^x$ ... tentatively?]

Further, to consider this basic link of unary logic (relative formal shuttle reset at] 0, 1 [has some of this ambition: formal unification at levels of 'maximum complexity achieved' and, like recruiting the logic; ordering in number cardinals (we will explain more ... later). Then to expand the logical complications, in good correspondence with realities.

In short, in a concept that an absolutely 'not' has no use and 'does not exist'. Like for preventing any use. In a quantic universe emerging questions are for problematized order. The operator of negation in qualified-quantified universe is before the start and~then~than: complement, dividable, pivotal and convertible.

These comments are only suggestions in needs of more rigorous founding. Since now: you notice

- The accountable 'recruitment of logic', the 'ordering in cardinal numbers" or; the ambition to involve more theory or numbers in handling of logics. [That is to say considering that logic(s) can be 'accountably relatively ordered' ... With not much need to go further than a formal system.
- It is also to have it generally calculable;
- As first effect a base of zero (but what is zero?) and unit (but does it support one (1)?);

In logical qualifications; it would also be to account for probability. [Maybe the openness from non-definition?]. This because either it is proper so (at least ergodic; potential sources of energy go into transformations or/and motion). Or because of the 'subjective environment'; humans have to doubt.

Proper formulated probability after Kolmogcrov?- probability value between 0 (empty event) and 1 (sure). Nevertheless to notice also in probability theory, events need to be all identified in a sure: set of all possible events. In the quali-quanti approach considered in quantic could be 'slightly different. The concept of crossed exchange information in help.

Duality is a physics universal too: and relations of essential. Often, the **characteristic asymmetries** are specified. Either **symmetries maintained** (at least some) or intended to be recovered or broken; those concepts are essential in quantic fundamental physics. Nevertheless it is difficult to make a definitive judgment at the respect.

Dualism looks like a minimum anyhow. In a broad perspective, we are talking of methods, between what we think and what we do; or formal tolls and our "world of realities" (namely physics). Eventually we add what we do in it ... for ourselves.

In effects with a 'shuttle system of logic' it about suggesting a short (?) cardinal abstract; also a system? - of either the quali-quanti and link or; the 1st order width-ness, 2nd order is 'seed' and togetherness or **congruence** (?); that is 3. And then an application and then expand? This makes **logical minimal cardinal** elements of 4 important to solutions. And 5 becomes important to unit-expansion. And 6 becomes important to **separation** or **reduction**. And 7 could be for a 2nd system; as the pair with 8 and; to order relatively 9? [... To account also of '**degree(s) of freedom**... Which are in effect the reductions of **needs of knowledge**?)]

Our physical World is nature specified. It has plenty of symmetries, more *ex-ante* and less *ex-post*. It is known that this excludes many antiparticles, which are non-compatible (or non-economical?) with this existence of the Universe. At least, in some places of the universe, where we are. Even if eventually emerging in special circumstances as experiments of fundamental nuclear physics. Which can predict most of those, with theories; and see them for a very short life. Also many more complex objects and properties do not show a simple dualism: mind optical properties of chemical chiral molecules, brain lateralization, biophysics devices, etc.

This essay is not a treatise. It is more for an introduction of what we feel new and necessary: **pro-lego-mena**. So we have to remain short and get fast to proposals. Perfection not our ambition. Nevertheless, practically and now with revolution of information, language of programming, arithmetic logic are all fields of experiments and logical tests upon the good or bad behaviors... Thus if we want to stay the master of our fate something; we must **re-instantiate** our ways of formal approaches?

For social applications, some accelerations (or short cuts) have been given, to apply logics. Like in theory of games (incorporated in economics microeconomics and plenty of other sorts of modeling). Logics and logicians have flourished in the past decades. At the same time, the development of mathematical methods made it also produced a considerable higher number of results. In the same way, physics results made it too, so cooperate positively in the 1st place and compete in some degree in the 2nd place cross-wards.

Logic may be seen with the purpose to clean the contradictions of our **languages**; providing some order in the ways we reason. They make sorts of reductions, but with at the same time they are able to express in more economical ways the maximum sort of philosophical logics.

To complete the lack of machines epistemology of information treatment and; supply enough logically with our criteria. These sources of information provide some better possibilities of doing according our humane responsibilities; not having as usual 'some will do it for me'.

The people of the art will more probably and at best, take our comments as working hypothesis. There is after preliminary explorations in the chosen logics (possibly quali-quantified indexed?) and mathematical methods (possibly quanti-qualified?) to face demonstrations. Formal demonstrations reinstated in common language are different from those articulations of legal procedures; which ordering is to respect judgment achievement. In logics, about a predicate or solutions of a mathematical problem have to be made useful. In judiciary judgment the 'tail' (or issue) is made of fines and punishments and is codified. The fitting out: of another register.

That is, in the judiciary, an issue given as cut, judgment produced, applications clear and economics of applications belong further to the enforcement's economics. Meanwhile in the formal sciences, issues are given with a continuity. Solutions once produced, implementations to incorporate they feed-back the phenomenological information of application and of theory. To judiciary remade a process should be the exception of a mistake. In formal sciences feed-back is the 'correctness', the constant care of calculus exactness or; the grounds of theory. Also loops are probably naturally produced.

[Of course, dissimilarities are not as printed as said. It is more make a distinction between the court judgment linear method and the circles convenient to the wheel of formal science... In a way Kelsen would have appreciated (Kelsen an essential Austro-American Law theoretician (of the 20th century), related to the Vienna Circle theorist of sciences and, fond of mathematics he could not studied].

No matter how many 'completed proofs' we give, they don't add up (or do not definitively disappear any incompleteness). Every proof reveals much more than just the bare fact stated in the theorem. This 'plus' may be even more valuable. But practically valuation has to be balanced with physics applications.

If mathematical demonstration of formulation about a physics phenomenon proven; then, we can "imagine" physics phenomenon properly described by the formulation. If proved not, then none of both are correct: 1) the description is not good or/and 2) formulation is an improper description.

Now in social approach, with relatively autonomous actors, if in the first correction empirical data tend to make plausible an improper formulation, then formulation can be used. But it will have to be revised at some time. It can so be used as a fictitious intermediate ... if humans please themselves with inconsistent short cuts.

The revision of physics is supposed to be provided better formulation. The revision of humans are supposed to have, taken care that there are responsible.

[This later: responsibility incredibly hardly occurs properly or fairly. Another ambiguous catalytic effect of revolution of communications: enormous increases of probability, that 'truth' could be known; but covering noise is even higher. Knowledge can produce unendurable outbursts; meanwhile cynicism is looking like insuperable empowered].

Keep in mind the dualism in formal-physics phenomenon. In a broad sense this may mean practically:

- For simple things a good match between physics, formal interpretations and many scientific prospects, it is to try to approximate. As close as and complement in the minimum remains);
- To look meaning of operations and/or specifications, at least because we are with simple operations; or because definitions need to be more specified respect to micro-logical system, not too contradictory;
- With more complex things (should not be unduly complicated); we need enough links of identification between physics developments and formal extension(s);
- If there is not perfect (full, complete) correspondence; a need for careful treatments; since physics symmetries or anti-symmetries or symmetries breaking (what could be qualified: direct or indirect, factual or counterfactual,

pivot and before (*ex-ante*)/after (*ex-post*), measures' intermediacy effects etc.; and that we often summarized, under the term 'similarities'--- to examine);

- Over-simplistic views or have in mind the "coherence" of both registers: physics interpretation and formal demonstrations?

> Could it be a more correct view? - that physics 'last' contradictions (paradoxes and so on); simply should be cleared by formal logics and conversely; semantic formal paradox simply explained by physics interpretations.

Complexities in physics world start very soon, in the deepest quantic structures. But at our relevant more complex levels it seems we also need conceptual better frames (or better logical management of those fundamentals. This gives place for respect and analogies. With these, to account for ambiguities since the minimum.

Then consider extensions of formal developments may pictorially seem like "spiraling as loops". [Eventually, it is to add a number of loops or spirals after the needs of physical levels... Like making the index or the level of complexity (or complications). The effects ought to be seen on physical formulation such as of thermodynamics or dynamic analysis [as shown now by some econometric models].

In the physics extensions probably also to examine sort of self-similarly; along more complex sorts of scales of complexity. That should nevertheless be finite and constrained, for example by laws of conservations and 'environment'. [We will talk more about that later]. Scale could be like: subatomic–atomic–molecular–polymer–reproducible–cellular–multicellular–integrated living beings. All that would simultaneously integrate and intertwine dependence. [Here more explanations are required].

Could complications of human's nature be approached in the same way? - But it is not to tighten excessively the balance between formal efforts, science procedures, experimental devices and identifications. Like for adding too much scientism as actually done. We need much better practices in humans' complicated things.

> In a very broad way, it looks like that added to unary-ness: specific solutions, concepts, questions, etc. 1st level of detail eventually degenerated by 2nd order included 'some margin for bugs') 'Bug' a negation exception or some source of threshold effect or singularity. It is to observe a dualist crisscrossing of: formal-physics (2nd level of detail) with a "head" as a "unary match" in the simplest way. And it would be to record more of less overlap or 'convolution' down ward).

> Then, there is a 3rd level of detail, which accounts for the more or less fast divergence (in the previous dual). It could also be said that they are the "best world" for primal-dual program, etc.

Further, some more explanations will be provided to 'surround our intuition'. Just here to link that to what we discussed above about qualitative and quantitative. What is at stack is that any perfect (impossible) unary-ness. The formal approach needs to be simultaneously; as far as possible simple and unambiguous. Consensual at levels of humans or 'democratic'.

At the same time this would be specifiable enough, or motivating as many as possible, when in human affairs.. At least in a modular way. It is not to rush without delay to the idea or the formulation part of language.

Now if what logics seek is to be the simplest, and avoid contradictions (so as not to be lock-in, by contradictions or by the arithmetic and logic unit of the computer. The computed has ways of cut, encapsulation or halting instruction. To end the loops 'in excess'; and get out the lock-in. If it is not from logics, we have some risk that loop or lock-in are inappropriate.

We also need the used logics open to specifications enough in some sufficient share. If not it will not be very economical. Why not able to have general expressions open enough and then also be able to receive diverse specifications? For some example, it took 1000 pages to Russell and Whitehead to demonstrate that 1+1 = 2. In another example: Hilbert tried to make an axiomatic demonstration system only using 2 elements, instead of 3 as minimum usual. These demonstrations were much longer than with 3 pieces.

With the meaning that a logic of only 2 does not offer enough details for describing economically the reasoning. But counter effect if there are too many elements or specifications in the logic then the sources of paradoxes or contradictions increase. Logic is supposed to reduce and simplify as much and as many as possible, of course, without arbitrary cut.

Moreover logics is also a language and language in logics have a minimum of 4 elements (inside the brackets). Thus despite the fact that we are not necessarily siding to Wittgenstein's philosophy on mathematical (for him logics was just all a language).

Our naïve suggestion is always to examine with physics. Maybe because 'preparing' for the Great unified theory with Quantic theory now enough proved, this should have effects in the metaphysics reframing of all logics. And also because we are in the mood that cleanest formal sciences complete simply most fundamental physics.

May this also conduce us in better understanding of physics? To bypass Einstein's curse upon quantic physics? [God does not play dices!]. Well .. for naïve objections, hence not as easy as the reader can imagine, at the respect.

Maybe this is the best way for Him (God) to influence probable mechanisms of evolution. Without humans noticing it and let further forces of evolution. But, out the theological arguments for servants, this possibility of reframing (where we suspect relation between cardinal and ordinal in the 'number theory cloak'); maybe the best 'Road to Reality' (to paraphrase Penrose): be developed, expand, change and conversely for existing: stay exchanging.

Since (quantic) probability allows to point at the best place; as well as keep a common primary openness and so allows evolution. With a primary selection: subjects in phases(s)-space(s) of existence this needs not to jump the best match first. As well as the need place for statistics).

Last, but not least, it is to have general formulation for some specifiable to case... A way to put formalism in Nature ... and have perfectible creative forms (or patterns naturally effectively aesthetic? Or a way to say that organized nature is also information?

Logic of Proof

To put you back on 'less esoteric' trail think (poetically) about this "enunciates" about logic proof theory from Takeuti.

Strength of all current theories of choice sequences was seen to be Π_1^1-CA (1st level of un-predictive definition: Π_1^1, consistent arithmetic: CA ... in 2nd order arithmetic); those theories interpreted in the theory of non-iterated inductive definitions.

Π_1^1-CA$_0$ emerged as being considerable, in the development of ordinary mathematics. It is a minimum model consisting of all subset of ω; which is recursive in the O (n) and; where $n \in \omega$. is given by Takeuti's ordinary diagrams of finite order (in proof theory). This is the same as Schutte's $\theta\Omega\omega_0$ or Buchholz-Schutte's $\underline{\psi}_0$ (Ω_ω).

Other situations with: determinacy of open subsets $\mathbb{NN}$; the Ramsey property of $[\mathbb{NN}]$; the Cantor-Bendixon theorem (saying that every **closed set** is the union of a **countable set** and a **perfect set**).

[Why not identify "countable set" with quanti-qualitative and "perfect set" quali-quantitative ... when "downward" operating them. "Upward" corresponding to unary-ness?].

In more common terms, in logics methods of proof procedures are (written or sketched differently, but are not so):
- axiomatization;
- natural deduction;
- sequent calculus;
- tables of truth;
- tableaus caring that they have a formal logic;
- trees' diagrams.

All these may receive simple technique of treatment and some propaedeutic with 3 or 4 of them (as well as self-philosophical thinking) maybe not so difficult to recall or apply.

Complex duals

vector
⇒
direction

All

density
⇒
continuity

exception
⇒

2

Some

1
self

correspondance
⇒
maximum reference

informed
⇒
minimum reference

equilibrium ⇒

Help You Logics

By the way we are in the formal physics frameworks; in the same way believers in God, could be tempted to introduce their Perfect Unary-ness. Observe in our relativeness that believers less problem with our approach. In the limits or limited comprehension with incomplete-ness of formal approaches.

> In their relative private and individual temptation that could be informed and shared; believers may have as absolute frame of values practically start with ordinal 3rd or 4th and fill back (in higher ranks): 1st, 2nd or 3rd with whichever spiritual concept they want; and dualize soon in absolute and relative formal systems. That is what they historically did which their spirituality. Informative link is also helpful in that: 'first ranks' the closest, if not 'the' absolute infinity reverse of absolute 0.

> Hence, out the frequent human made disasters of together-ness against others at the other extremities, in the highest statistics of numbers; not to impose to others meaningless infinite order imagine as substitute to spiritual transcendence self-assumed. Naturally in the basic all believers tend to the same cardinal of omniscience-omnipotence and mercy. Tolerance looks like just easy to identify to physics principles, kindness apart. This late simply the witness of humanity common sense intelligence: in terms of social safety we can do better than observed in nature not making with such criterion, only producing for all may have their time.

Back to our humbler reasons. Often mathematicians felt at ease with their 'purity' and so could have under-esteem logicians' efforts. For self-economic reasons have they perverted themselves in physics sciences? Or the reverse did they look like too in their abstraction? - Since logicians were more in their 'philosophical narcissism' and physicists were more with self-understanding of devised experiments? This may have been more common up to the 20th century.

Today it is no more the case, it may be harder to do it but formal sciences are now essential to fundamental natural ones. The time are more in **which proportions cross efforts between** mathematics, logics and physics. And in other natural sciences there are few doubts that being able to formulate make important professional difference in research laboratories. There even could be discrimination between those professional filling automated devices and those still in the investigation of the understanding. Only the lack of biomechanical feedbacks with what they are doing still require some understanding of the indirect and non-phenomenological processes involved in the 'electronized devices'.

Now, with computed induced requirements of more clever thinking to preserve some mastering of large numbers computed manipulations, simulations and proper approach of complexities produced by large amounts.

Either they are put forward, but highly, ugly and sadly arguable of populations' management. Or backward because there are more in the details of tiny amounts (also with huge numbers. Sad management because the illusions of bureaucratic determinism do not cope properly at all; with these expectations to receive more individualize attention and the ambitions of scale economy and simplified intelligence management. More prevail the feelings of unfairly diverged humane values, because anti-social Pareto's criterion [telling you to change nothing if someone feels affected by your entreprise].

Perhaps logical concepts by the side of relative strength, across system hierarchies, limits, constraints, transitions of phases, relative infinity, incomplete pure 0. Great numbers laws which are not in the small samplings, truer statistics, metrics, norms. Developments of cardinal-ordinal concepts, management of informative links, bundle, local fields of vectors, non-realistic simple operations, semi-complex operations are to handle. Operators are expected to induce proper care of formal structuring.

Could the lemma of: 'get off my simple operations' be no more scientific Zen?

Historically some achievements were obtained in arithmetic logic almost against calculus (Cantor's and Dedekind poor revenge). But despite Tarski's rigid attitude about logic, this had to stay entrenched in cleanliness as a narrow field of practices. Logicians could have returned to the disdain they had from mathematicians until computer science came as a new world. But on the other front, by the side of the social tail more common logicians faced some problems. Despite the relative success in some school curriculum with 'modern mathematics' since this was keen with their discipline.

These new pedagogical ways with already almost 3 or 4 decades made them teach, hence not in the multi-connected core node, that could be expected. Logicians prolonged their relative insulation, because quite failing to broad the perspective of their theories in closer services to social utility.

First lay people not really wanted to intermediate their shortcuts by clever logical formulations. Of course social artists including economists standing often on the complexity grey side border, took advantage of the ignorance, both of people and governments clients.

Also because: why care good formulation? - when it looks like so poorly rewarding compared to the hidden manipulations and distortions of wealth flows?

Could limits of modern logics broad social applications, with the TIC (technology of information and communication) have to be reinstated and better solved?

Could their efforts feel concerned by developments in sort of quanti -logics- quali - mathematics mixtures to provide more social economical flexibility respect to the modern devices? A precondition would be if not more just in the 'we will simplify everything for you and even giving you the illusion of virtual realities.

This may be important, since the time-framing of the TIC has crumpled up, most of the traditional hierarchies; for structuring the societies' horizons of times.

Efforts there, implies to be able to jump from issues back to fundamental reasons and vice versa, possibly not with the same potential profits; than those of promoting the computerization of bureaucracies; for which social effectivity?

Computers developments of software offers logicians some more professional opportunities as software engineers. But could they be tomorrow's friend of communities rather than fiends of screens?–like with better interactive interfaces?

In effects once programed automated reductions; logicians are no more needed than because of the bug they may have introduced inadvertently? Whence not having succeeded with artificial intelligence to free the machines from the humans. What are the futures of relations with topological logics? - As core of common practices that could be served by computer logics?

Articulation of Logics Spirits

In logic foundation of arithmetic and logics; **unary-relative ambition** (so not hope of definitive consistency) survived. Practically expressed in the efforts of logics to prevent contradictions and paradoxes. Elusively we think that it is also the case in mathematics. That a unary perspective on logic needs to consider a 1st order logic and an "under" inclusion of 2nd order logic. It is a bit like if having to care for as complete as possible (or 1 pure) unary register and; know what, logically to do is with at least a "no" over... And then in. ... so possibly half-cut rather than a full one (already used for the subject or, by the object). After this 1st half-cut the 2nd half-cut is less (able) to complete the 1st half one; could be more for exchange? ... Could this be the path from $\mathbb{N}$ to $\mathbb{R}$?).

This may not be the purely formal one; why not prefer to have it, at the maximum of formal efforts; be solved by reality (as Russell's paradox)?

In very short the bearded barber cut the beard of all others in the community but need to consider himself as with the 2 conditions ('barber' and 'bearded by the barber'). The liar needs a something, like a special case of absolute trust (his mom?) or a relative one (a test) that he/she does not lie. [Examples of handbooks of logic are stupid!].

Pedagogy and Propaedeutic

More literarily, to use concepts of logic(s) in ordinary applied logic you have to understand the broad meaning of axioms: since these grounds, sometimes subtly, properties and logical phenomenon well used in lay reasoning.

The goal is more to prevent some mistakes, have efforts, not to be too manipulated by your personal computer, develop another kind of cooperation so as to develop your own social business constructing your (real) communities and be able to call for some logicians appropriately.

Know about some correspondence; between the collection of defined real objects and abstracts. For, if they can effectively receive a formulation in terms of Set theory or use a register of formalism properly linked to Set Theory. Notice that set theory has no more than 9 founding axioms (we provide a list in annex). Care about sorts of tools initiated or systematized well thanks to Set Theory and use them in your realities. More specific logics also has a core with Set theory and commonly half a dozen lines of axioms more.

What you need is either have enough cleared the theory for a special type of problem you need or already start with set theory. So intent to make use the analogies with number theory, and possibly also to look at cognitive anthropology. Consider the phenomenological properties of your real objects essential to your condition(s) (or problem) and what sort of valid explorations or formulations or similar logical problems can have received from Set theory and derived tools. To notice especially, the natural ones: humans' subjective models maybe both: logical, they often have more or less large 'seeds' potentially creating disturbance.

Look at those of physics extensively open to formulation, taking nature as a guide. Prefer thereafter 'sub-model of influence' (over the kind of physics model), instead of the perfect system of your exclusive own. Avoid models in the subjection with too abstract assumptions and no amounts.

> This does not mean that the methods of modeling developed in many 'artistic' registers, psychology, behavioral, social, economic are no-intelligent and useless. Many efforts have been made to clear them. Many critics have been addressed to their experts. Some commonly proficient in their formal approaches could have been well debated. Books' industries have filled many shelves and World-wide-web with many ebooks and working papers are enormous sources of raw material and possibly robust data for the quarter of job you need to put in your project. So that does not mean you need to be all day long front of your screen.

> Most of methods are very interesting with positive views mainly if possibly criticized and both self-explored or collectively ... not as childish games, once past lower teen age. Pay more attention to those with good roots in the physical world. A screen that makes you feel you understand all and can judge in a matter of minutes is not wise. Have all the problems, never miss your businesses cared mid of your neighborhood: that is your problems and the way you drive your solutions. Once humble with the true truth it is to try to cover both: hard individual work and really empowering collective one.

> Formal sciences basic books have imperfections and many unwise shortcuts especially when focused on making you pass the exams. Of course there are some basics, more for being

informative on what you do not want to do; for the rest of your life (the converse is slimmer). They should not miss telling you why they are essential, even metaphysically and how they could support in your future dedications. And how you can apply to your preferred way of working. Thus traditional training is not more symptomatic about their unsympathetic limits instead of well 'empathetically framed' for most common readers.

In the inside of some pedagogical questions:
- Why social models for proving loose abstract concepts often have consistent "underground roots"; prefer models for themselves and not for individual-social reasons?
- Average of possibilities in econometric models, make solutions almost only accessible to perfect perspective of omniscient-omnipotent dictators?
- Essential physics principles models for most have the merits of abstract thesis definitive truth instead of robust tools open to many ones?
- Is there a need for different feasible model? Able to bias a model of balances between principles in reality (some for–polygonal- main frame) tested for criticality. Rather than determinist one for all, only one specific of the major 'insulated concept?–the demonstration of the narrow theoretical hypothesis.
- Why make social models of clear normed purity; if realities are precisely social, that is of relations pluralism and confusing mixtures? (mixtures of in/out, head/scalp, 'minimum confused order,'/suborders looking like disordered, respect to full disorder;
- Why mechanisms are considered as simple only if asymptotic far away; when Nature has just with other ways? And the range of extent varies in the short range or term?
- Why still pretend we can do better when in fact living on overuses of natural stocks?

[Some heterodox observations will be exposed with more details either in the present volume of essays or its 2nd volume].

Apart few specific some, have in mind that **formal concepts are often generic**. That is to say, out that a model has unknowns and to specify ones; coefficients often have to be empirically estimated.

Characteristics powers (or exponents) vary in a phase-space plane area. **Critical limits** are provided by **inequalities**; for given forms of mathematical behaviors. There are also general expressions of equations (cubic, quartic, conic), as well as less general expressions that can be transposed.

Inequalities in Mathematics also provide limits in the expression of formulas, There are quite useful (but do not confuse directly with those of critical phase-space transitions).

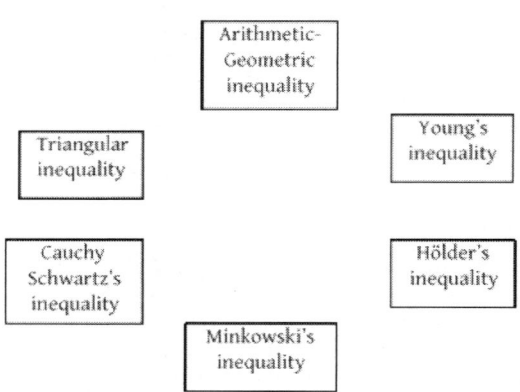

Some inequalities used in functional calculus and probability

Simple moment inequalities (few among many others)		
Basic	for all $\lambda > 0$	$P(|X| > \lambda) \leq Eg(X)/g(\lambda)$
Markov's	for all $\lambda > 0$	$P(|X| \geq \lambda) \leq E|X|^r / \lambda^r$
Chebishev's	if $X \cong (\mu, \sigma^2)$; for all $\lambda > 0$	$P(|X - \mu| \geq \lambda) \leq \sigma^2 / \lambda^2$
Jensen's	if g is convex and E (X ($< \infty$)	$Eg(X) \geq g(EX)$
Lyapounov's	for $r \geq 0$	$[E|X|^r]^{1/r}$ is $\nearrow$
Cr-inequality	Cr = 1 or 2^{r-1} as 0 <r (1 or 1 (r	$E|X+Y|^r \leq Cr[E|X|^r + E|Y|^r]$
Rao Cramer	$E[(\beta^*-\beta)(\beta^*-\beta)'] \geq M_F^{-1}(\beta)$	$\sigma^2(W_n) \geq 1/[n\langle(\partial \ln f(x;W)/\partial W\rangle]$
Cauchy Schwartz	$a^2 + b^2 > 0$	$E|XY| \leq [EX^2 + EY^2]^{1/2}$
Hölder's	$r^{-1} + s^{-1} = 1; r > 1$	$E|XY| \leq [E|X|^r]^{1/r}[E|Y|^r]^{1/r}$
Minkovski's	if $r \geq 1$	$[E|X+Y|^r]^{1/r} \leq [E|X|^r]^{1/r} + [E|Y|^r]^{1/r}$
	$X \geq 0$	$\Sigma_1^\infty P(X \geq n) \leq EX \leq \Sigma_0^\infty P(X \geq n)$

In physics you also have: **equations in dimensions** and, from a register to another analogical forms just to adapt. Switch mass with electric charge and quite easily obtain a similar formula of flows, motions, concentrations.

In the social arts of economics the concepts sorts of abstracts in frameworks can be so fuzzy; that you can easily transpose models after not so difficult adaptations; if you have a broad mind on what the mechanics in the translated but similar register. [Alas we did not use this martingale for career purpose]. Good it would be to train systematically in that: copy properly (and implement kindly) in that.

And not necessarily intent to make everyone designer of *de novo* model. Since most will not turn 'leaders' better than they express their genius in the care of social implementation, rather than hide their limits behind the closed curtain of superior attitudes in societies and communities of socio-pathological results. Cognitively in fact all copy one another.

Mimicry is a Nature essential mechanics. And so the possibly that it is the same in fundamental physics?–with populations of particles in fields?

Despite the fact that higher studies curricula, more teach their own specialized methodology insisting on this property rights and fundamental so small is the proper difference. Since here is much in the...

... universality of formal sciences. Cross disciplines makes, especially in methods, the very lessons of reality's experience.

Too many, by 'cognitive determinist incompetence' or lack of preparation, imagine that registers do not permeate and humans only need to be primarily ordered. Especially where and when they precisely would like they do nd agree with one's special idea.

Almost intuitively: you have to mind balancing **similarities** (eventually analogous) and **discrepancies** (never absolute in our real world). [Similar words 'convergent'/'divergent']. Separate the series of numbers you have like by the evens and the odds. Involving also the prime ones. 2 is the only prime number head of evens and others all are odds prime numbers. But mind also the number of operations for the factorization of any number, like for how far an even number divided by 2 stays even.

After the base of almost 0 and 1 (informed by complex numbers). Loops the base as an **ordinal order (?)** separated from a **cardinal disorder (?)**. The minimum cardinal compound with the order of 'head'. Take **the evens for 'first push' 'go in'** or **covering (?)** (the picture of the parabola getting back to ground or elliptic); and the odds to 'come out', engage in periods or step (especially if it can receive 'periodic energy' or could be constrained by the hyperbola (?)). Mind also combinations.

Consider a relative formal system. Have this as an informative *modulus* of generally solvable formula within a generally solvable informative **modulus** of point-able phase(s)-space(s); specifiable to cases (providing its critical inequalities). Make that relative formal system jumps 'prime number step'. Keep in touch ground with the universe together with a maximum achieved complexity reached... After what allowed by symmetries selections and algebraic groups. Try to fix with informative links and characteristic quali-quanti exponents-logarithms (or the reverse to meet-fit-match).

[Looking at the first prime numbers to notice that they look like coming by pairs or other close, not so far. Or the border at the reverse? For example, see: (3-5), (5-7), (11-13), (17-19), (29-31). **Primer number theorem** is about prime numbers number: $\pi(n) \sim n/\ln n$]

Avoid madness: better to know how to pose and clear problems in reality with all your brain's experiences; rather than imagine formal sciences have strict compartments as 21st Cartesian would say: "dividing separate isolated pieces in cell-boxes. Making that the only interesting thing is about numbers symbolic profits: pure speculated aspiration of leadership crushing executive superiority". Sort of reductions which are also well practiced by economists, but none able to build societies properly. Fundamentally this is not really the defect.

For example, limiting the professional engagement of traders to 3 hours a day, this could be solved. The main problem being with methods; that are biased so much in their use; so only the disaggregating perspectives are served. All where they could be used for framing, shaping and building ordinal structures in fact use the individualistic potential disorder of cardinal.

How can you ask democratic people behave orderly if the mathematics you give them subjectively empower their cardinal-ness? Be individualist but use the kind socially ordering intertwining frameworks or by collectivist but use individual flexibility and satisfactions. Ensure technically socially fair competition for friendship care in the first case. Ensure individual fair cooperation for involvement in care. Then you may have … some economical satisfaction better than gauge's excessive maximization.

The pathways are not to discriminate and disqualify, with **partitions, discreteness** and fake unary-ness of pole. Physically it is not like that one. Existing methods and quantic theory are about quanta (that is *dis-continuum*). But it is to reconsider first as the combination quantic atom-field respect order-cardinal, within a universe-wide- ('quantic sea' at the minimum?). Closer to confusing combinations of nature's approaches.

It is more about **balance** to maintain, between **explorations,** with re-emergence in frames of **conception,** approaches of **heuristics** (pathways to solutions). With a time for demonstrations which, axiomatically, is effectively linear and tending to binary-ness. This economy should come only when establishing principles, in the narrow expression of law, with kinds of abstract sentences having fake realities anchorages. **Adaptations** can make intermediate use of **analogies across registers**. We are all in the same universe, as a result grounds are the same and they cycle, exchange and adapt. Moreover "hypothetical analogies are often the opening doors to the **right formula, patterns** and even **'truth'.**

There is a need for **core universal methodology propaedeutic in epistemology** since secondary school or before. [Clearly also making responsibly together, as well as individually should prevail over the separations of classes. When already you have those of natural environment (even if most now also of the anthropo-sphere)]

For being helpful to individual social involvement and collective intelligence individually sizable. Then have informative links toward humane values and cultural involvement. (This possibly more important than the formal program.

Not to wait too late for training in such methods taught in too specific registers: as most education systems do.

Logic Easy Phenomenology

Logic is much about tautologies (logical evidences). It is well to know how to express them (it is simple logic). It is very reflexive, just arise similar questions at any noun, concepts and term of your enunciate then try to develop.

Tautology in logic, a statement so framed that it cannot be denied without inconsistency. That universal "truth" follows not from any facts noted but only from the actual; thus purely a matter of definition.

Mind also the applications. In natural sciences either you already know the principles and your applications, respect to tautology will consist to formulate properly for applying formula already known. Having this to be implemented in a consensual way were as many as possible could make a profit from this application. With yet not known principals to find the best future enunciate.

With social arts in effect most of the job will be about the fair tautological enunciate connecting to a natural physical world to bias it caring the most renewable conditions and designing a **framework of transformation** as consensually social as possible. So much is about the enunciate to accept and the framework management for these tautological qualities maintain: work done as far as compatible with the non-denial and universality of concern. As a result most of social-economy with this framing these tautologies, like **linear and nonlinear programming** as function of optimization submitted to limiting constraints.

In effect probably of 3 types (and not necessarily as we will see of maximization): 1) positive minimum shared benefit; 2) exogenous constraints either special fixed by environment of flexible globally after choice; 3) endogenous as productions constraints. Also there could be fixed as technical and flexible as organizational, but this sort are possible relative over the range.

A 2nd systemic step: take a broad concept and intent to establish a whole logic of it. Progressively more easily you will pose the frameworks for further "organized" investigation. Thank to world-wide-web; few **key words query** put in **a search engine** can report you very fast (... not as economical as we would like).

Mathematics is plenty of incorporated logic. If you do not find the key-word way to a special logic, think about the ways it is done, in mathematics. Then try to put it in words. Explore also better the concepts of properties (even or odd, prime numbers, lowest common multiplier, highest common divisor). Try to put in words of common sense the symbolic formula may help you reveal what you need. Does it put '?' on any symbol.

When with a critical need of logic in application, you may find the key dimensions of your problem. Establish a hierarchy and choose the 2 major terms (especially if combining a qualitative prone and a quantitative prone and you may uncover the relevant logics. Try to be as logical as possibly: variables, operations or (ex) change. Seeking the primary contradiction is complemented by realities' specifications.

Now for the proper general formulation that you have many general models but still not the most general adapted to any system. Thermodynamic is nevertheless a broad perspective. But it goes soon in technical details that can produce anxiety to many. In fundamental physics, physicists (as well as profanes) are fretting and moving toward a Great unified theory. Still no doctrine, nor disciplines, nor register of inscriptions, are yet established but if people could have an idea on the formalism generality of their sort. They may better understand why such expression of 'theory of everything'.

Possibly this should have more to do with what we are exploring here: how to lean on good understanding of numbers arithmetic logical properties; operations since the simple and the some less simple; but structuring ones for formulations frameworks; that could be economically and not difficultly identified to situations for obtaining robust enough pre-estimates of constant and locally acceptable enough degeneracies?

Phenomenology as perception of reality's evidence is not naked and has no one exclusive and lonesome perspective. We are not omniscient nor omnipotent (but economic models often played so). So none 'has to' validate lonesome one will and behave as your anticipation. Even if our sort of crystal-like shape (we introduce further) looks like the Canongate's Kirkyard soothsayer [he probably did not want to turn].

It is to examine compatibility and possibilities of abstractions tools. Train, learn and make evolve your learning skills. Quite often it will be good to mind your question with some basic book of logic; look at your spatial economics material situation, discuss how local communities do. [Possibly with Fujita, Krugman and Venables Spatial Economy to understand the complexities of proper formalism should get in interactive screens for being specifiable]. Rather than receive any 'superb idea by Finance the Planet 'petit bourgeois'. These just distract the nice shoes of those giving the access to the World Forum

When establishing a given model; it is to include the causality and uncertainty covers of our problematic. Have in mind quantified solvability and care the economics of complications levels. So that you can evidence openness and do not panic when meeting strange formal phenomena. Critical thinking is quite essential for not taking for granted any social theory.

Epistemogenesis or how philosophy of sciences create and develop in a formal way. Originally empirical intuitive now it balances symbolic expression that have reached ideal perfect formal form purely inductive but nevertheless succeed to relate to natural objects. For example now most of essential physics a preliminary manipulation of abstractions, formal expressions anticipate experimental results. Formal properties so "essential" that one could feel disturbed that so wonderful properties could be so abstract and so out of reality, unless one start to mind that reality is not cemetery of abstraction but infinite complex mixes of formal properties within finite pieces of world.

Olicognograph:
"Epistemogenesis"

relation by strongness, substantial or as state of art in modern methodology

strong
medium
weak

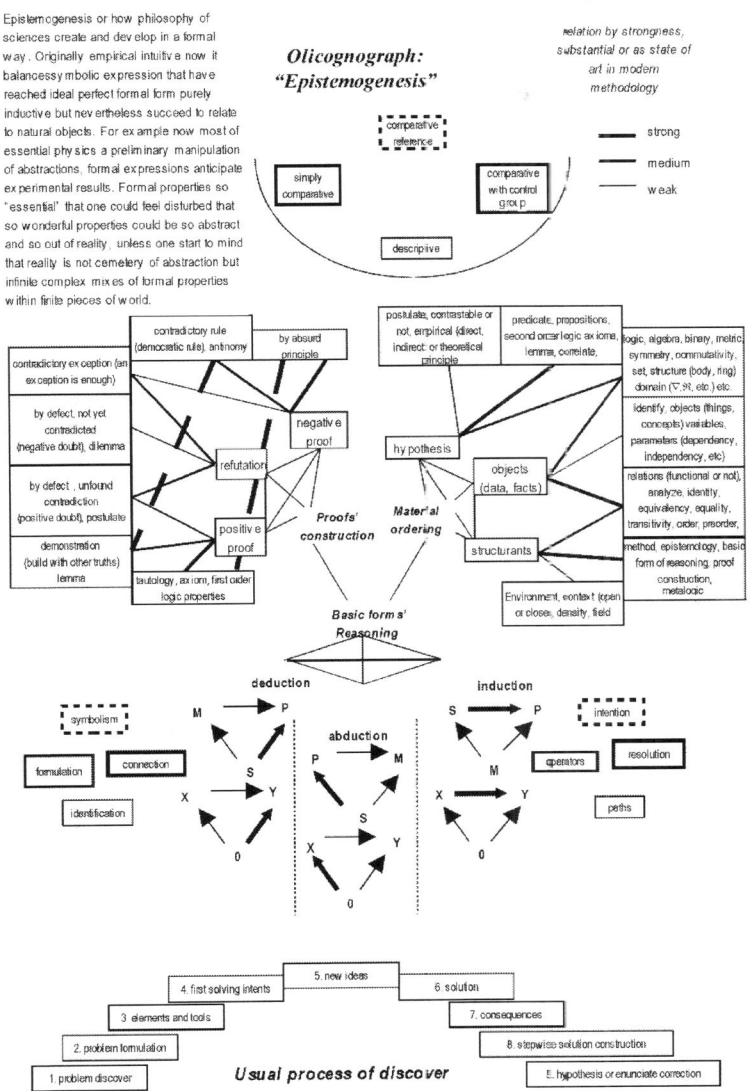

Basic forms' Reasoning

deduction   induction
abduction

symbolism
formulation   connection
identification

operators   resolution
paths

intention

Usual process of discover

4. first solving intents
5. new ideas
6. solution
3. elements and tools
7. consequences
2. problem formulation
8. stepwise solution construction
1. problem discover
9. hypothesis or enunciate correction

108

Examine in Short:

The solvability has to deal with manageability of 'simpler solution' too. Especially if we want to handle them. Care that this hope does not miss conditions nor diversities of informative links about the difficulties. Thus maybe it is to make a distinction between general solvability (the hardest would be for a unique solution). More reasonably have few possible solutions (and corresponding critical handling?). Like **different feasible scenario** to **apply marginal choice for involvement.** Levels of complexity because here we are: living. So not necessarily needing to care about quarks. But these questions like those; which have **enough range of integral-able; within statistical integrity at the level of levels,** nearest down, nearest higher; and the **economics of complexification.** [You have top-down '**simplexity**' and, bottom-up '**probable openness by diversity; midway calculable**].

As "we think, so we are" (Descartes socialized); have points at not forcing the equivalence between complexity (of Nature) and complications (of our mind). At a minimum you have: **emotions as shortcuts of complications** (but not default of preparation from complexities). Wisely tame that with the **lack of wisdom narrowed by physics** and; the **acceptable reduction of degree of freedom.** It is not to be just **discrete** or only **continuous.** Always try to catch between **2 grips on 4 clips.** It is better with the resources of: **discreteness trying to look like continuous** (diversity logic of the **mathematical residual**?) and; the continuous-ness of discretion. According the main stability of created quanta filled by fields and/or scattered with other particles;. But they are less relevant to the extensive conditions. Possibly more in hotter and different physics phases?

At least, because things are happening in **thick interfaces,** between phases critical points, lines or tubes of particles of relatively different thickness of their local field, around their trajectory in larger environment (in a Kaluza-Klein view?). 'Lower line a tube' ... and at its level 'not just a line'.

Not to miss that at more complex levels, we also need 'economics'. Because in **narrower thermodynamics extensive (or outer) parameters.** Have structures, functions and mechanics that ensure qualitative "upper" (eventually just labeled) **stability** (including the environment). And quantitatively requiring to **be renewable if not reproducible.**

If economics have some stocked facilities in the environment and can make use of upper emergence properties (narrowest top-down and goes up). Together with extract or informative artificial relations between different, quite separated levels and the media. Then there could be something like human processes around. [Beavers are fine too, but they do not serve hot meals].

For physics thermodynamics in proper nature, often we are relatively in smaller and more delicate ranges, often at interfaces of the media, or between some different. [The reason why ocean rising may affect many populations]. Variants emerge to develop diversity by **sub-combinations of properties** (sweeter avatar of similar forces). And bottom-up empowerment when by evolutionary mechanisms, more or less bio-incorporated as self-reproducible. These processes can select by **better fit,**

economy and **robust adaptations respect to previous average**. Not much by the strongest ones. In fact excellent predators are very sensitive to the crisis of their most economical preys.

Economically thinner up mechanics hardly linear, mainly nonlinear; up or down mechanics. Entanglement at the minimum but more intertwined (**interdependent, revolving**, etc.); in **relative inner asymmetries**. It is to take advantages passively or actively of **similarities**: that is like constructals and fractal facilities, copies and physics analogies or patterns].

Now, you are right, this poses at our end of concern (in the level of sustainable complexity and not necessarily at the highest top of specialization. Out the one of self-reflexive abstraction was is going the existential humans phenomena-non? And also some question about our fate as societies: what the humans teleological consciousness will turn to? When the uneconomical excesses of our complicated speculations have degenerated into too many distortions for the natural sake of the seeking and weak between? [Of course our teleology has succeeded to behaviorally adapt, to many different kinds of ecosystems; but still the 3 phasic solid/liquid/gas we enjoy].

Back to the harsh complexities of nature? Technologies that you can also call 'complications from properties of upper abstractions but weaker emergence'. With them humans often try to **shortcuts the physics levels** or extend 'thinner informative links', eventually new, between different maps sources. They are often calling for lower levels of complex energetic resources. These stocks are often more important. But they need to develop some **capacities of absorption** (and renewal) of environmental media. Capacity of absorption another concept of elementary natural economic concepts, we missed that were already existing in natural environments respect to our sort of **exploitation**. So making use of crossed physics properties, instead of closer biological ones. As a result often less comprehensive compared to natural processes (they develop only if possible after non manipulated inputs and outputs). Except some traditionally happier communities having succeeded in their discreet corner, to establish humanely efficient sustainable biased environments of production with smartness and minimum efforts (and without having read any Jared Diamond books).

Respect to the productive human engineer activities these businesses may have had as main result to perturb generally by heat specifically by toxic the ecosystem was settled. When it is not its living bodies also simply and stupidly suffering from nasty humans. Societies have to care **not to produce unstoppable regressions of our environmental complexity sustainable levels**. But in fact rather than learning, demonstrating or judging of crimes; it is to have some modes of calculus by the ways of self-learning, for participative choice. Within phenomenological procedures that could enhance the trust within and between communities. In modern history we preferred to emigrate to new lands of hope and post-pone; trusting that quite far from proper information markets will equilibrate on time; even when they are almost without roots on realities, just opportunities of trade and finance unbalances; able to generate many inconsistent distortions.

Calculi with environmental thermodynamics are not so easy. And in the same way as in meso and macroeconomics started passing by **multilinear matrix calculi**. The technological progress ideology made some thermodynamic framework mistakes at the respect. Perhaps when Podolinsky intents before trying to convince Marx and Engels had also made some proper metric mistakes of the environment losses. He was an agronomist, not a biomass ecologist. After having emotionally anticipated that this was the future a proper account; the major intellectual father of the 20th century revolutionaries preferred to stay with his system's ideas, nicer with his theory of humans' societies' classes progress. Marx was also capitalist and industrial, and any social believer prefer social theories to crisscross unpleasant numbers of inefficiencies, as are the thermodynamics ones of humans' societies impact. Not to see that yields of not more than a quarter (at best) that is just 3 quarters of thermal waste. Neither to see that network calculus makes ordered grid, expansive in linear sums of waste but fast decreasing yield ratios in productivities, especially when recycling economics still facing the costs of innovations before more efficiencies.

Possibly also Marx by the struggle of classes was potentially less socially softer than the too skeptic 'hidden idealist' Adam Smith. It seems probable that this latter was betrayed by imperial liberal capitalists. First times of capitalists such as was the ones from his superior neighbor (British Empire to become Victorians' power); as by the dependents ones of his home Scot Low Lands.

On the other side also to observe a betrayal of Marx by his followers. Since these did not learn to care about economics of ecosystems and have not been savvy with humans' massive sacrifices. But to notice that some were imposed from outside and that efforts had to take into account the conditions below: serfdom and pogroms, lord warriors and opium forced trade businesses.

By the side of the free world some efforts could have produced better scale in their policies like if inspired by Thoreau, Vernadsky. Leopold, Muir, Tansley, Including economists as Jevons Hotelling whom all could have been right precursors. Thus Polanyi, Carson, Dorst, Hardy, Club of Rome, Odum, Georgescu-Roengen, Passet, Daly, Costanza, Ostrom came quite late under marginal considerations on the margins of serious academic (not dedicated to 'bucolic margins'.

Does the switches to more primitive physics phases can have too high costs in humanities' survivals? - As **quantitative shrinks**. And may turn 'inhumane' by disqualification of 'nice-ness' values? In all that something as the **assessment of diversities options**. That formally can appear as **applications of vectors in different directions** then re-orientations, of the energetic process or flows.

Formally this can be just about **diversities of weights (series of values of calibration)**. Indirect management of parameters. Intents to re-synchronize related periodicities, and so on, We will see, after (our) understanding of realities, how some realist representative models, could be shaped. But before, by the side of arithmetic, it seems necessary to have some insights on the **properties of emerging (?), maps of previous options (?), expansion of symmetries** and **antisymmetries, anchors to assessments** and **balances (?), options of vectors to solutions (?), conversion or treatment of periodic signals; field-wide wise filling (?)** of **complex numbers.** They are primary in all those 'influential perspectives'.

Complex Numbers

Complex number algebra is not independent, it is related to real numbers or an appointed scalar product. That is also: "around centered". So complex numbers are fine for polar reference. That is pole not taken as just a symbol passive number on a straight rule (eventually passing by there). **Pole** playing a sort of **'selfish role around itself'**. So the coordinates are geometrically a *radius* (the length, a scalar product or a *modulus*) and an angle (respect to a line or axis or reference–and the line of the compass). So this is in **vector's representation** with a **scalar product** (making use of the cosine of the angle) and also with a **modular form**. Such vector's representation is useful for the study of **symmetries** (as by **conjugation**). Modular form is also to take as a 'oneself' as a whole ('around' at first).

To look at as a sort of concept imagined as a 'point' mathematics equipping spontaneously as a point in the space. 'Outer neutral approach which would have no 'thickness' or a position of its center (or barycenter) after a rule. As a **material point** by itself (modular form), as a **volume object** (described b rotation), thus inner approach, if it is a *radius* in a circle limit (dimension 2) or **spherical limit** (dimension 3 ... of intertwined dimensions?). Or have an 'outer approach' if a **plane front wave of expansion** or **sphere-like space of expansion**, emission and so on. With the vector approach we have a 'perspective of view', since the point; to manage relative directions of symmetries and so on.

So even if you will not make use of mathematicians' symbolic facilities. In all that has much common sense phenomenology and perceptions open to all. Maybe uneasy to manage by most people; as can do mathematicians or geometricians. But without doubt many made so unconsciously with our **visual integrating cortical part of the brain**. Whomever we are our brain push and pull network **bioelectric activities** and visualize by the occipital and coordinate this in parietal occipital cortex (as well as use the left and right hemisphere relative symmetries and asymmetries]. Why not even for any other brain networks activities wherever the specific place of cortex, source of the 'triggering start'? [Neuroscientist put the wish in the frontal and prefrontal cortex]. How many basic mistakes can have done key managers for not having conceived their orders any more than immaterial points without orientations nor properties of symmetry?

The production for social construction of society, would be just dominated by executive documents from above? With kinds of check-lists of abstracts, 'without geometry'. Of course you have executive putting that than in frameworks, sometimes more directed than recruiting participation. Not to tell about the bureaucrats for whom the 'you know what you have to do, does not even map. We are all key managers of ourselves.

How much waste, from policies' implementers, just because their collections of points to treat could make sense only in very restricted minds well inexplicit nor phenomenological to most. How many communities embarrassed by 'well educated civil servants' purely 'cleaned of' any natural experiences and missing working on basic intuitions avoiding essentials of formal sciences, because that's an animal behavior? Nevertheless cognitively here in minds? Only all leaders of above wanting-their-normative-points-be-cared and 'their'-statistics-of-success des-informing as they like?

Back to the basic of complex numbers; their formulation uses a sum of 2 real coefficients joined one an imaginary **i** for this weird square $i^2 = -1$. Conventionally we have the complex number = real part + imaginary part. **i**: z = Re + Im. **i**.

Could be an alternative? Complex issues of number = [(real coefficient 1st side + real coefficient 2nd side) (unit × (or exclusive selection)].

To observe that square power of **i** can take symmetrically left or right track and then resulting signs positive or negative. i^4 is positive i^6 is negative. Track of odds, always with a remaining **i** but also alternating signs: i^5 is +**i**, i^7 is–**i**

Quite fundamentally making us think that we need more epistemologists on how to equip our human problems empowering communities.

Mathematics put 1 as unit and simply account it then, often missing that a material unit not just a symbol and may not start a 1 but was the amount has units. Often misguiding us on true complex units … since with one, basic operations are simple. The recursive addition step 1 the basic. Educated common people proceed the same way, without any existential anxiety with subtraction, multiplication and division.

To remind also, some 'more mathematicians' have caught the ambiguities of subtraction. What mean negative number in the real world? It should be in the relative world a subtracted number. Never more than the amount of the before (or the amount you can exchange, so the subtraction just the possible to exchange (preserving the minimum of safety or of units). A tiny evidence, put logically ahead; is the most common of any exchange. So it is not as the shortcut of many in common mathematical exercises: without material mind. As a social means … it is to care about the criticality of the 0

[and of the poverty's balances. Extract and let the 'negative' be picked from elsewhere. To increase debt without clear understanding of how critical are the conditions. When it would be formally only to be more 'correct' in ways of accounting].

This may have important effects in the logical consistency of our operations (not *per se* oneself but for what it serves). We have to put more qualitative sense in numbers. It would be like in the levels of complexity the review of limits, maximum, minimum, average, characteristics, proper values, characteristic exponents, inequalities, qualitative, quantitative, modeling, etc.

For example, of the marginal concept: we have a characteristic minimum ratio of wealth that should be preserved at maximum for our survival. This is varying momentously, daily, seasonally yearly and along life … more or less smoothly). Then we have a **margin available for exchange.**

Pure simple and quantified amounts simply operated inform on basic physics of some indifferent perfect gases, sand grains. Improperly when only looking like Euclidean-metric–linear–Cartesian (the most used).

Mathematical scale of reference is thus not the only best gauge, for a bit higher complex level, especially involving social level, despite statistics simplify much also.

In state definitions of particles, quantic theory physicists have used the primary linear complex numbers algebra but have put it under weird examinations. In fact a mixture of simple core kind of linear algebra with 'multiple valued logic'. This is fine for the qualitative expression or labeling of quanta: creation-disintegration (further than characteristically quantified). As well as operations of transformations playing into and with other particles, since there are many balances and symmetries in energies, mass, motions, etc.

Further quantic theory needed to involve more logics. A good part taken by rigorous formulation; **closer to discrete configurations making use of symmetries** (provided by complex number algebra) and kinds of groups (more special algebra) for conservation laws. But so, quantic theory seems to match fairly well with experimental results. And is very different from the sort of simple operations we are used to ... on things that do not change. But further there have been a need to 'slightly more complicated operations'. So despite same physicists often said to be disconcerted by quantic theory. As could have commented Feynman in one of his conferences (an American physicist, among the best in Quantic theory).

> Somehow living on not so terminate and finite stable existence, that is on obliged probabilities is inspiring when observing in management how things are done by, often aggressive) oversimplifications, not even scientific. How many could be outraged by small objections about their way of accounting. Where fundamental mathematicians and lay humans meet simply in ambiguity of subtraction. Knowing also the sort of complex numbers poor made by common 'modern societies by simple lack of care and meanings defects. When discrimination by numeracy just imposing purity of simplicity when this just nonsense.

Back to complex numbers. They also **account for periodicity** [periodicity obtained by shift or slight un-adjustments or gradient?]. Originally these numbers have been introduced for **trigonometric functions**. Also they are **related to the exponent expression** (and consequently **logarithm expression**); **circular** or **periodic function**, and links to circle approach.

> ➤ How to formally and intuitively understand that they may quite easily be in sort of elementary cognitive mechanism, almost automatically? That could deserve to be consciously better done? Since complex numbers are essential to proper approach of interconnected multiple purposes and could be easy to collect in realities.
> ➤ Formally think about the rotations of a circle (a wheel) Imagine this is you. Mind these circling are 'inner proper', like your body's flow. For example, circles of food, awareness, moving activities (motions) and rest. Introduce a ruler is these rotations for them not be confused and; examine the details ('circles' not as regular as you think). Since you can do only 'one after-another' your ruler will just be the 'time' like the daily one.
> ➤ Relax or vary the time of its measure (seconds, minutes, hours, etc.). In the day you have the day-schedule. If about meals, conventionally breakfast, lunch and dinner. No problem with that, formally your 'body's circles' provide these important time's periods. You spontaneously structure your time more or less smoothly; after most important 'rulers' of time and so 'formally circle' as allowed; simulate the respective cycles and sort by the day most important moments. A

hand-watch of the 3 or 4 most important cycles with their respective pointers (interrelated, constrained and hierarchized); could help you detect opportune coincidences?

... All that is mathematically analytically can use complex numbers. If such basic needs to be a bit more consciously managed. With sort of statistical methods to renew, linking core frameworks as 'head of cloaks' few to many. Among many means it is to combine: clusters, samples, group algebra, short numbers, resampling, string algebra, combinatory, networks. Brought up to populations with advice, dynamics, care, allowances, policies better proportioned to the critical informative balances between complexities, complications, individual and social.

> But not here to pretend that this would be the *panacea*. If non-privately and individually managed, it has plenty of determinism's risks. But it is essential and that is why we are insisting of neurocognitive ways to make brains work better with complexities there are not reasonably informative chains than many abstract ones. This critically needs the social trust in ways of democracy. Made by the present implicit, explicit, conscious and unconscious, could; with interactive software, give other types of work moments, in the worlds of globalization.
> It is easy to imagine that, if wanting to analyze with numbers, many of your main structuring 'circles'. Then to put statistics 'within', gauged by common universal time of 'physiological prescriptions'. Further it will consist to order somehow the diversity. But not with too many activities.

You will have to care for the **'bundles of vectors'** like **'fibers'**. Apparently, they are not all random nor simply directed, but within critical phase-spaces delimited. On that to examine potential contributions. They may be cardinal selected. Then have some ordinal ordering, care not to be too close to critical proximities. And then implemented as **perturbations prepared to applications** and volunteered biases and/or extractions on dynamics of flows.

Statistics ways, smooth and erase. Nevertheless they make some sense to 'significant difference' *versus* ergodic (pure randomness). So even if we could be misguided by relations (central minded average have closer relation to linearity); when we are with reproducible exact experience, parameters well controllable and close to most fundamental principles of physics.

As could be said: '**near formal head reduction's** approach in its **differential calculus** and mathematical analysis. There, near the essential principles of mechanics, simple formulation and operations are relatively correct or tell enough for having obtained the Newtonian version mechanics. Still this way is much driving the sort of analogical models used in many nonlinear at all registers.

Also remind from infinitesimal approach with a curve over some interval you approach its values slicing into infinitesimal intervals and have the area of the slice under the curve sum all that the limit the closest integral value of the area under the curve.

Basic Theorem of Integral Calculus

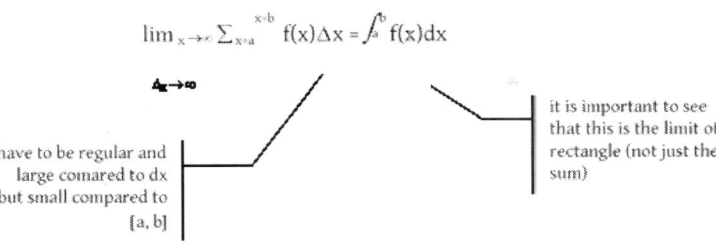

$$\lim_{x \to \infty} \sum_{x=a}^{x=b} f(x)\Delta x = \int_a^b f(x)dx$$

$\Delta_x \to \infty$

have to be regular and large comared to dx but small compared to [a, b]

it is important to see that this is the limit of rectangle (not just the sum)

Physics records the successive values, get the area. Once the formula's expression obtained, you can approach the details you want or can. Such as calculate average value, deduce the form of the function and so on. Calculate characteristic values, extrema make use of the derivation.

Values to derive equal 0 at extremum point. Signs of derivations, before and after, take the approach by below (thus a maximum) or above (thus a minimum). You have means for the estimation of other properties. It is essential to know about that, for anyone process. Informative link there would catch between 2 powers across levels of scale with the 'bit of' derivation or differentiation or integration (depending on whether you go down or up). Also you will make it a priori in different directions: simple prolongation, transversal one, correlated one, etc.

That like on Earth you look in the different straight cross: ahead, left, right, up, down, behind trying to economically combine like mixing after your 'window's capacity: left-up combined with down-right more or less combined with rotation is such.

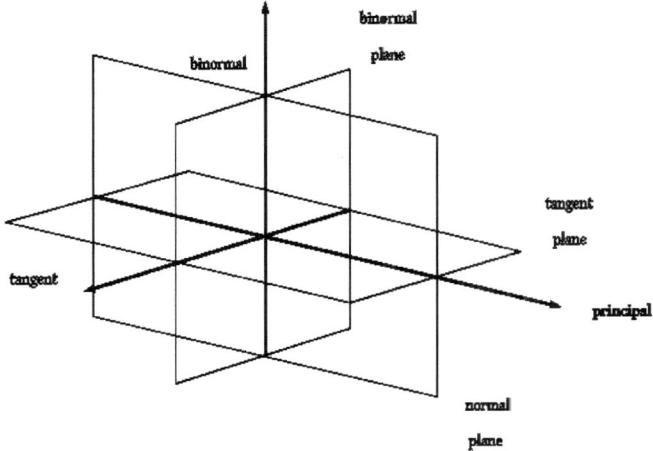

Mind that mathematics not with your own complex capacities has to make all that explicit in its programs. This turn critical and real most important economy, because you do not have as before in a time mechanically relatively slow and so structured societies, allowing some fancies about social theory of behaving like labor international division, world-wide leadership was empowering paradigmatic standards. Now we are mostly with nakedly reducing computer electronic. As intelligent and smart as can be those devices, you are still a 'biomechanical ghost' and has much less realistic phenomenological evidence. So as to maintain the dynamics frameworks for 'maintenance of the ghost' [You are a solid-liquid-gas energetic ghost, not so cold].

Practically with societies in disarrays and elites transnational, any youth looking at the wonders of telenovelas in the television box will have to feel that the future is there: that is his life's job! Both are needed: escape death and have future. Even more if the logistic world-wide means are here (with the tourists).

> Like if the curve record a trajectory. Speed provided by the derivate at the point. In the general equation de coefficient of the dimension one term, etc.

Since technologies cannot do more than physics handling and founding principles deliver a lot ... increasingly the details, approaches of criticalities; near-border interfaces and weird margins (that could be revealed by better understandings of amounts?) makes integral of differentiation *calculus* tamed by realities.

When the 'globalization' started with the revolution of information, it was to expect the fate of societies empowered with formal sciences should have not so much inflate the (mis) management of 'faraway determinisms'. Nor inflated the artificial expectation of administrations in facilitating their bureaucracies, inflation of (stupid but nice) reports and so on. The contrary seems to have happened.

The equipment with computation seemed to have more nurtured and properly supported the social unproductiveness of administrations, extended the possibilities of corruptions, put more in hands of mediocre or irrelevant, public as well as private. Do plenty of bureaucracies, free from their lowers levels (not necessarily the worst in production of wasting loops); including the downsizing ones of neoliberal adjustments (including those with 'human face' have really delivered simplifications and closer social mechanisms?

Facing the problems on how to maintain proper reasoning; for not turning global society ... into unmanageable governance. This is just ergodic-prone. That is just heating anthropo-sphere (or noosphere or anthropo-scene). This may not do more, metaphorically, than shot down the 'monster group'.

['Monster group' is supposed to be in algebraic groups the largest one. The metaphor is that just fixing the maximization of order in a cardinal-ordinal world is preventing the largest maximum order to be reached. In the first place the global civilization (dreamed) and then on the potential regional ones, and then on the federal one. With ergodic trans-crosses the levels: you have almost entangled crisis at international level and crisis at levels of humans. It can be (or not) connected but most determinist do not know how].

For many people **(statistics for all), how we could make use of such complex numbers** analysis? Not for the pleasure to manipulate equations of your private agendas; but the approach. For example, the possibilities of changes on a private base; over all repeated cases of your dedications (seasons, way of life, jobs); and superior constraints of lives (we prefer the humane ones at humans' distance: localness cared freedom).

> With another perspective if as dealers you want to approach the possibilities of your consumers that are **distributions between individuals**. Or under another sort of **statistical grouping** such as collective producer. Economics are with the **synergies**

between networks of raw materials of semi-manu-factured (in elaboration of products) and networks of semi-manu-distributed (finite product for consumers).

[The strange way to compose words for more explicit root-catching by computer text analysis: semi-manu, meaning the complementary automated part of the processes]

> Consider also to make use of the same but relaxed frame. Either relaxed the time ruler. Substitution of time ruler by space ruler is quite easy and even obliged. Since we are mobile, in the **environment allowed** by the **distribution(s) of stocks, places of sources**, and so on; equipped with the **functions for mobility**.

Much is with fundamental formal at the (formal) 'head', or its basic: for **massive data treatment**. Which now you have cleverly in mind: it would be a bit less stupid, with complex numbers.

> **Relaxing time?**–for taking into account others' structuration(s); like joining other rulers (than rudest time). Nevertheless hierarchically structured after the same humane imperative as obtain our energetic supplies. This to framework our **minimally important schedules**. The goal can be to **minimize the costs of our motions and pathways**. It is also to ease our space mobility, map after requirements and opportunities. Ensure critical shortages, care moments, reduce obstacles.
> Eventually picking in the residual (concepts of formal modeling), when priorities have evolved requalifying some of them, putting back some selected before.

We will see in forthcoming and volume how statistically this makes sense ... since the determinist illusions of statisticians could pretend statistics properly made do not show that. Primary goal is for taking advantage of opportunities, including those of precautions and non-actions, because detected critical.

> So opportunities that have been evidenced for businesses, for more probable satisfaction of the main or for other obliged associated functions: have your heart properly beating, breath at ease, any other basic physiological needs and/or affiliated goals (rest, leisure, etc.).

In all that the reasons for formal treatments are also for **examining the collective consistencies**. Since social consistencies you understand that **balanced opportunities, shares**, use of social **resources, effects of scale**, many but hardly all need **structuring, organization, rules of games**, distributions of opportunities. Requiring also without exhausting economies and so on. Intuitively understood that provide with corresponding possibilities of information to work semantically (by the meaning they have).

Recordings of data can be very basic. Perspectives of cloud computing, massive data treatments and networks make TIC devices increasingly able to record and treat at the simplest level. But requires to handle formally immediate contradictions, options, opportunities, essentials, criticalities, detections.

Starting that is the **proper social management of complex numbers**, their informative relations (communicated, exchange). The care of the complexities requires not to be just by a speculative collective anxiety, too heat driven. [Heat has due and serious reason to understand both as symptoms and cause].

Primary is also the care of the real humans' economy. Not just made of the (un) conscious fancies of some private leaders or; professionals of bubbles bursts (be them financial or prophetic one).

Complex numbers can also change the (mathematically formal) **dimension**? Such as a real (number) in 2 dimensions (area-like) turns a 1 complex dimension (1 pole like?). Or the reverse is possible: a one object incorporating various dimensions (say gaining an identity in a higher characteristic volume?).

Complementary concepts are emerging quite easily once one has understood the 'semantic tail' as in this case: spreading, diffusion, collection, pole centripetal or centrifugal and conceived how these can formally express. **Relative openness also plays down-up**: if you are incomplete down, you intent to complete up (without succeeding; intention is important.

Remind that today in many ways, it is you as human beings that need to logically conceive and choose that for the machine. This computer can try to **relates lexical with syntactic** (eventually in a fake semantic of well-formulated sentence) and summarize your will for the resources those machines can provide. It is not for the machine to be alone at thinking about the 'optimal social art' theory for its 'human chicks'.

Enough for the machine to be equipped with **the automata capacities to operate calculi syntactically** (as could be said from the well-formulated language and formula of logics). So as to **provide with enough well-similar proper informative relation** (dictionary of sentences 'not understood by the machine' but making sense). So the **semantic humans could balance humanely what they have to make by their own.** In their 'out the machine life or refill the machines of recorded knowledge with instructions.

This also has implications respect to operations crisscrossed between humans and computers

---

Back to the formalism: ...

Complex numbers have links both with exponent and logarithm perspective...

So and in the physics register: somehow the reverse a particle or unit 'pairing' into intricated (?) sub-particles [fundamental last entanglements, in the traditional pure concept, expressed 'out' in electrons' pairs and not much more? And most to observe 'in' with quarks?]. And also a one particle may incorporate the **potential direction's change.** Like under some shock-event. Even just an energetic corpuscular reorientation. And/or then the deviation of the one particle is taking all: absorption and motion change of direction. Or just a part: bias of flow possibly with a scattering?

[Potential direction change is simply the substitution of the vector of simple extension of a nucleus, by the 'adapted' to the exchange, simply the effect of crisscrossing the information: 2 nuclei exchange their vectors, these have to be recalibrated after their new support].

We also imagine that complex numbers have something to do with Dirac's or Kronecker's delta functions (quite similar). The one which up to some abscissa value has 0 value and there or now and further has value one (1). With plenty of eclectic readings we have not seen much about that.

Technically complex number representation its 'graphic' in the 'complex plane' (real (imaginary). Can be leveling up in space (real Hamiltonian, imaginary matrix) or volume (quaternions volume with time).

Of course reviews more authorized epistemologies. Which are more discussing about the unary validity of one concept and another. Close to there, questions and registers of your interest, if you are less for a 'wholist' propaedeutic, as in this present essay. Whence most with the idea that perfect thinking could logically ground much. Perfection has not been reached by any logic. Not to say about numbers which are often more in their perfect symbolic conception and simple-minded operations, with no space for epistemology.

For some naïve comments: Dirac's delta functions are like "instant steps" birth, at a given value. Normally series functional theory of Schwartz cleared its formal nature. They look like having the unit (in the world of the function or our quantic universe). So alike a linear and discrete (or jumped) expression of what we said about the logarithm: continuous function emerging from negative ordinates. But always with positive abscissa. And **emerging when catching the base** (1, 0). [Say it, in other words: Dirac's delta function is putting 0 for the negative part of the y=x symmetry of the (lnx, e^x) and putting 1 for the positive part].

To observe that logarithm x is only positive scale of x (meanwhile ordinate is both more negative than positive). Symmetrically by y = x links with exponential ordinate which is only positive (meanwhile abscissa, negative and then positive value). Possibly having that phenomenological realism to '**achieve for being able to catch in amount**': between negative and positive branches of y = e^x. Meanwhile on logarithmic scale just 'created with a before and an after emergence'. [Remind that derivatives of e^x is itself: e^x]. [Also mind better to have the support of the environment in that emergence: not need to be a solid if too hot for being there. Or better to be more than 80% water if for swimming in a womb, compared to adult 70% water (to dilute your rum)].

The economics (or information) is not provided by the exponential or the logarithm curve but the informative circle center at (0,0) covering 'economically' enough (like *radius* 3 or 4?– covering enough of itself and minimum discrimination from others of emerged entity?).

Another basic? Coordinate axes are mostly conceived in pure perspective (Euclidean metric one) supposedly refereeing but also have an implicit discriminating the best way. Or you often make a mathematical transformation of the reference system. Technically that maybe the gaps you have along the abscissa or the ordinate, if curves do not cross.

So in 'physics complexity augmented' an evolved body or form is never just pure and would observe these gaps with the axes of reference, where contribution of ordinates too low for abscissa and contribution of abscissa too low for ordinates.

That is more proper also to a quantic world [observe that mass less **γ** ray would be the least of energy]. Least you also have (formally?) the influence of 'quantic observers.' Thus it is very important. Also formally you may have fake invariance just because of the wrong choice of reference system; when true invariance mostly not.

Is it good to imagine that?- In the curves of material the reality is the combination of the logarithm curve(s)? Or logarithms and corresponding exponent? Or logarithms twice? Or logarithms and just the axis as a metric limit. [**All the sorts of relative operations of scale are to conceive, with integral-differentiation?**]. Symmetric exponent provided to corresponding logarithms, the best articulation the **axis of symmetry for measure and for that emergence**? Expressing that positive branch a newly appeared body (informatively related). This is able to catch amounts (of material) for itself (since its new positive base).

The logarithm for the only positive scale and the exponent for $-\infty$ and $+\infty$ branches and the linear x=y a straight line rule with no crossing (uncrossed by the 2 previous). That does not mean that a body could not be multiscale, only that we are on relative new informative link. That may be '**relatively encapsulated**' with a broader environment (more micro-fundamental). Another technical chapter would be to **metric rules after such structuring with relative new base**?

It is also tempting to relate that to a dynamic of a given point or particle: along a step function of existence (such as Dirac's) or logarithm; or it is about to have more "complex" qualitative-quantitative one (such as information?).

When you look at the complex number plane in abscissa: the real part; in ordinate: the imaginary one. Then a vector inscribed in a circle. As a result we have an expression in modular spherical form: *modulus* and an angle of rotation.

[**Borel–Carathéodory** theorem in complex analysis shows that an analytic function may be bounded by its real part; which is also an application of the maximum *modulus* principle].

"The effect of real number "complexification"; ease the solutions' investigations (roots or 0s) where imaginary roots are, easily existing, and are eventually periodic (since circling); meanwhile real not so. The physical problem with the meaning: in physics absolute one real solutions in $\mathbb{R}$ set of real numbers."

That quotation is easy to understand as soon as we pass by a **relative definition of the negative sign**: just with the sense of being the other and not a less nothingness. Very simple and the reason why complex number are essential in electricity or electronic: the electric current of electrons conventionally signs negative (but "really" the electric charge of electrons). Meanwhile the conventionally and relative current of protons; or main nuclear current attracting if *medium*–cable is conductive and connected, conventionally: positive).

3 particles look like having a special time-life *status*: protons and electrons have huge time life (not much different one to another) almost infinite. Compared to other 2 previous; neutron has 15 minutes which look like small but huge compared to most

other particles. The reason of this neutron with noticeable time-life? A bridge between *nucleus* and clouds of electrons?–Such sorts of experiments are hard to measure, relations within field-*nucleus*-cloud of electrons to complete their theory; and ways of calculus decays (for time-life calculi) are still debated. But as living beings we do with that, and maybe much of the story between creation-destruction ordinal-cardinal; exact-probability of our level concern? It is madness if a stupid technocrat or populist dear leader tells you: 'stop yours neutrons moron! That is irrational!'

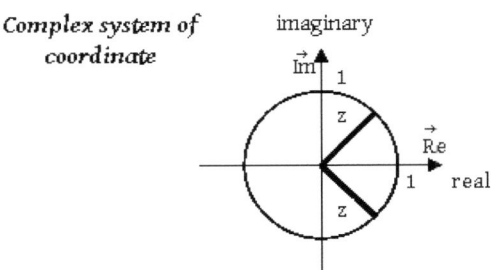

Complex system of coordinate

Somehow like eternal 'now' **phenomenology of complex number plan** is slightly more delicate. Reality's real axis of abscissa; imaginary nothing in "real" (or only directions in the virtual. Could it be in the options of the above mentioned? That is a very **specific virtual vector**. The only material one 'virtually-realized' supported only by the abscissa axis ... if the abscissa axis is so either transient or 'the step ahead in future' or the **diversity of options**. That would be proper to the real vector not of the measuring device. [Almost having to be systematically added in Quantic theory].

How to conceive the imaginary plane? - If the abscissa axis is a referential, not proper to the object centered at (0,0); imaginary plane would represent an influence applied over the previous vector of motion. Then by the influence (or of all vectors examined upon (0,0) the resultant vector (imaginary part & real part(s)); giving the new direction (if realized?). (Thus further, we may have to re-orientate the real axis in the new direction. Null influence, nor inner 'adjustment' than no imaginary one;

So the imaginary plane one (1) may also picture the diversity of influences upon a "real" vector, as in a field (of vectors). Further in time (periodic signal); motion, etc. Have in mind also that such system of reference cut the plane in 4 sectors and the volume in 8 with symmetries between. [Half-plans are also meaningful in the same way as symmetries].

Would be the fields the constraining environments produced by any particles in motions, but having accounts some core properties and different distance kinds of fields the largest one of gravity attractive similarity and local ones combining; repulsive and attractive dissimilarities of electric charges. Possibly 'avatarized' by motions of the with development of complexities (within developed more nicely interacting environments) inertia, moving surfaces, magnetic?

Intuitively and so, out the common and **traditional applications of complex numbers** are in **periodic signal analysis, spectral analysis** and so on. It is not weird that quantic mechanics with its creations and disintegrations of particles also prefer them.

> There are 2 kinds of electric currents [or 4?–if considering spin within electric currents]. Plus, the known properties of symmetries. [Concept that we will be examined later).

So this is out the almost primitive use of complex numbers, in periodic signal treatments; it seems to us that those could be considerably more important in plenty other representations of phenomena. ... Why psychology does not make use of complex numbers?

Too, these may help to conceive better quali-quantitative and quanti-qualitative concepts, requiring to be quantified (or quantized) and relative definitions or models matching. Model quantified and characteristic amounts qualified by a core model but to specify with realities measures. Only to establish a better formal and phenomenological treatment of such concepts, especially as interfaces of computer aided designs.

Complex Numbers Precautionary Policies of the Approaches

After that, clearly either because of nature or because of wanting to do something, have only one (pretended) solution to design, impose and implement ... it is really stupid. [Nature look like 'assigning where all possible necessarily and potentially evolve'. Not to make that definitive]. Government model empowered, uniquely masterminded by unique self-polar-leaders should think about that. The usual way is deeply misguiding, especially static-minded. **Determinism in Nature looks like only a part in the essential mechanisms of physics**: you will not change much to that or you are at risk to blow all up.

> Moreover this does not help people to think about how, and care what they feel required to preserve the potentialities. This does not contradict that landmarks of: 'not too ambiguous some relatively converging solutions, pole, core... Once decisions taken; you have some materialistic development(s); using positive and real algebra. This may have robust enough actions and commitments as well as focused directions but only robustly and approximate to prevail.

> It is more to obtain motivations so as complexities imagined problems to solve relatively to the major aims. Policies and social arts in our mind are not as useless as you think we imagine. Formally they are arts, they humanely need about precautions with diversity and commitment of participations that are local. They are **complex (or complicated) contexts have to be local environments anchored**, especially since with relatively autonomous units (as humans minds); that has **'in' their prior hierarchies** and 'out' possibly long distance influence, but not so determined to direct solve the relative unary framework of how should, the receivers, drive their conducts.

During most of the time the intent, comes after next phenomenological revision (or event, or switches from particle to field. [In fact the conii of projections in hyperbolic space and solid angles within parabolic are formally the corresponding tools ... in fundamental physics light the Minkowski's or Schwarzschild's forms]...

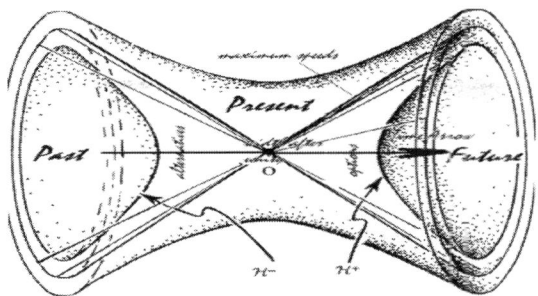

And picture-like sometimes even in the financial markets projections, more or less made stochastic (Black-Scholes's model).

Now considering that you have **core mainframes of 'superior complexity'** (but lower in the physics principles'); to account either because it is essential to your energetic supplies for productions (agronomic cycles of crops). Or because you have to care the flows of the ecosystem you live in. Or because in urban life of cities' concentrations **scales means some norms down-up** (?).

You need to feel no affecting the potentially affected by the **extractions** of your life way (ecologist call that **footprints**). Before they came to manifest their anger to have been spoiled by the corruption you entertain in their countries, to force the trade of your extractions. Analytically, you may need to have clear how, for operative purpose, are your main structuring flows or circles. Structure your frameworks or, at least, cautiously you managed your set(s) of informative relationships.

Then come the **variations respect to averages** [both **derivations** and **deviations**). Which are of special interest. Because they inform you upon; on one side on flows dynamics, and the inner mechanisms you can take advantage of and; on the other side; also where you can position you own extractions or 'derivations of outer flows'. All this should not be too hard. If you want to avoid putting yourself directly in the thermonuclear reactions of the Sun, for warning your cup of coffee (bad taste). Even on Earth you may have to use a smart device to take off your cut of coffee out of the solar boiler. And have something to prevent methane gets in your tap water, since you prefer it in the burner.

Thus commonly you prefer to be on the banks of the river and not in the middle of the flow; for looking at what you can catch for you. You will especially care about the variations of the main flow and then your own, in the most sustainable way for both. The good of the formal sciences and the natural sciences is that we can imagine plenty of information and then for knowledge. Formulation for anticipating somehow not too stupidly the possibilities. But why pretend to make a **theory of rational expectation with macroeconomic rationality**?

Adapt that to the diversity of streams (not just those of the fishermen from the rivers' banks; that is also the more abstract of the humans' economics flows. Make eventually a **portfolio** of that (but not rush to the magic *circus* of profits. Care that options are not as far as possibly to sustainability. Design sorts of **optimal systems' gorge-channel-like**. Also mind **shares** and **fair** distributions and choose the wisest options in terms of entropic risks and netgentropic not too out the *modulus* of maximum achieved complexity.

Formally with mathematics and logics this is turning increasingly smarter to model. Many problems now are more with the cognitive difficulties; about the perimeters involved or of solutions (too narrowed). This is not much because the formal and natural sciences difficulties. In the same universe we have always **energy gauge** and kinds of informative and computation resources, distance (or time), basic forces and many other sources for gauging and modeling that. Even if in common societies those of previous 'civilizations have been weakened.

The practical problem could be just to **reform, recycle and know how to reframe the informative links: between our human values and energetic uses**. Together with frameworks of operations between and philosophy on lives' precautions.

Theoretical mathematical possibly having plenty of formal resources at the respect; requires cultural commitments in cares and more integrative (practically applied) perimeters of commitments.

So respect to 'variations on the margins' how to structure a relative Chinese's box elements? Or more simply a **bundle of informative links** for wise economic management. It would be to care of variations respect to averages. **Variations** themselves more or less detailed since **'fundamental averages'**. That is ground bases economics.

This form or variations look like having been detected at least by Adam Smith. If he could have also involved the ground sources of 'physiocrates' wealth (Smith knew about since he visited them) things could have prepared better and sooner Carnot and Clausius for Podolinski, convinced Marx and Engels.

Mind nevertheless that Physiocrates with Le Quesnay were possibly too interested by the taxes to extract from agriculture. Meanwhile in Scotland the low productions were more about trading for corns feed the population at not too expensive prices, rather than those practiced by London Parliament licenses and monopolies delivered to friends.

Not to ignore that otherwise Smith was probably inspired by Newton; since he made a *memorandum* on History of Astronomy and read Newton to promote the teaching of natural sciences in the Scottish University. Smith did his Wealth of Nations after the literary readings of Newton's writing.

Balances can appear first and before. There is not much choice, but of physics; which are not in the hands of humans (just influence-open in destructive cyclotrons). Then up along natural processes of complexifications. Then in the psycho-cognitive more or less prepared unconscious. Unconscious forms are, as in visual tasks and auditory perceptions triggering **'emotions rapid assessment** and **synthesis'** (smile or disgust). And finally processes of conscious decision, as well as many ones.

Problems in all these being that many are between order and disordering. You do not control disorder as easily, but you may have some good use of some. The weakest one (you have in mind) is most probably the most ordered ones. That is it is easier to destroy and mismatch than create and fit. That is also much less useful than useful... So technological developments need that adapted lessons could be learned and kernels the other social constructions.

It is really surprising to see how psychology and psychiatry so full of words about -cyclic, variations, pathways, trajectories and inflationary quali-quantified scores that are only based on "points" (natural numbers) and percentages. That is to say: items, qualitative scale (turned surreptitiously linearly scale) and so on (for the metric, but prejudged ones, as well as unrelated to lower-superior grounds nor to be admitted-consensual ones. Meanwhile, complex numbers are almost ignored there.

Of course neurosciences and neurobiological signals just make use for signals' treatments (complex numbers based).

[Of course, not to ignore Anglo-Saxon psychologists' contributions (or related to that world of empiricism), to qualitative statistics. Nor the difficulties met by Anglo-Saxon behaviorists (helped by cyberneticians, as Wiener). Conscious theories hardly match properly with unconscious processes. Some good soviet mathematicians in labor psychology ('ergonometricians') have been translated (and expressed the difficulties met for the metrology of cognition. Cognition researchers intended to put minds into the formula. Artificial neural networks have been enriched with that (McCulloch, Pitts, Hebb).

Could the failure to come from the proper design of numbers' relative system?–by difficulties to catch the variety of complexities levels. If not too regularly perfect algebra used and too narrowed in the perimeter of analysis. Nor it is to imagine that our minds as perfect, especially as distorted as they can be by ... consciousness? - and social artists].

Somehow this makes us think that along (including sometime) a 'complexifying a volume of extension'. If 'complex core' something like a 'relative structure' able to anchor developments and select them. Relative structure which, by the side of geometry could have as head a sort of polygon. Just primary and requiring more hairs around; at its level of meso-development. Eventually also emerging new systems (hair-dressing).

Possibly it would be to imagine, chains of inclusive informative links. Like for shaping systems of neighbors and networks. Also to make possible the integration or participations of populations, associations, coalitions. So this is not without distributing (in your relative disorder), competing and promoting, etc. As sort of field framings environments?

Higher Algebraic Structures Than and With Complex Numbers

To get out just complex numbers, by the side of algebras we have structures that can involve complex number. At the minimum they are **algebraic groups**. This could be better than over-simplistic infinite iterated up one-step-one recursions at a time. Without levels made available for optimizing relative systems.

[Mind also we do not say that on a scale of complexification we need all the intermediate levels filled: water and minerals may supply enough so not necessarily having to pass by rum's cocktail. We also may avoid eating meat from calves if we have enough delicious palm-tree worms].

Now if we want the calculi by generally solvable. Thus the sort of relative formal shuttle also better than infinite descent cut-one-cut. That is regression that may be in everyone's soul under the will of dictators (or many others). Further than and around a *nucleus* or atom(s) or node(s) or interacting core(s) (according to the number of relatively autonomous actors and the environments of fields they are in or create). And hairy complexifications qualitative and quantitative fed by providing environment of supplies. [Of course such sort of hairs either in space or in time is expected to be sources of many exercises of 'haute coiffure'. Hair dressing? - leadership should not be more than hair dressing). Stay in the formal sciences can be more essential than the test: if 'haute coiffure' is adapted to heavy metal hard rock parties].

In that formal suggestion we omit many more needed developments. Such as the **matrix calculus**; the development of linear calculus (or nonlinear) or **programming** (mathematical methods developed for optimization calculi). Then also, it would be to have some better insights on the importance of **Fourier's developments in signal analysis**. And even the relations between concepts of functions and their corresponding series's developments. Functions are approximated by series, and this important chapter of functional analysis relates to **polynomial calculus**. Series are part of the "true definition of functions" [implicit fundamental theorems will be provided later]. That is not the purpose of this essay so we cannot be comprehensive and clear all our defects.

Systemic Model Premises

Logic of Model

In the simple formal **Logic of Model**, theory was initiated by Bolzano (1837), renewed by Tarski (in 1936). [Concepts here mentioned have their main source in Takeuti]. **Primary enunciate** would consider: a model of a set, finite or infinite E. Enunciate is an **interpretation** (as a A set of n-uplets) in which enunciates of E are **true** and if and only if (iff) any model of E is a model of A. An important aim is to examine the dependence or the independence of enunciate A respect to E.

After Tarski to observe that logical sign and extra logical signs in such theory can have no ground and reduce to a convention so to relativize. An 'interpretation' happens to be a n-uplet of objects. It is turning true when taking the right values. Other key concepts account for logical analysis and/or tautological characteristics; consistency or inconsistency (or incoherence) and contradiction characteristic of set of enunciates.

Model theory operates in a non-strictly using Zermello-Frankel-Choice set's the framework. Some authors propose extra logical characteristics be given (not as simple series but a couple of series).

- A **clause is inconsistent** iff it is false under all Herbrand interpretation [Herbrand a French logician]
- A set of the **formula of a language** is consistent iff all its finite subsets are consistent. [notice that in formal sciences all terms receive a correct definition]
- **Löwenheim-Skolem theorem**: all consistent set of the formula of a language, finite or numerable admit a finite model or is numerable. [An essential concept ... but may it means that identification in reality? - should be larger but enough smaller?]

By **extension** on model's **assignment** of truth values, all formulas are defined by recursion of (computable) complexity. [Computable complexity is a huge chapter of calculus and Computer logic: in which time or size of memory your algorithm find the solution. In this case not related to complex numbers].

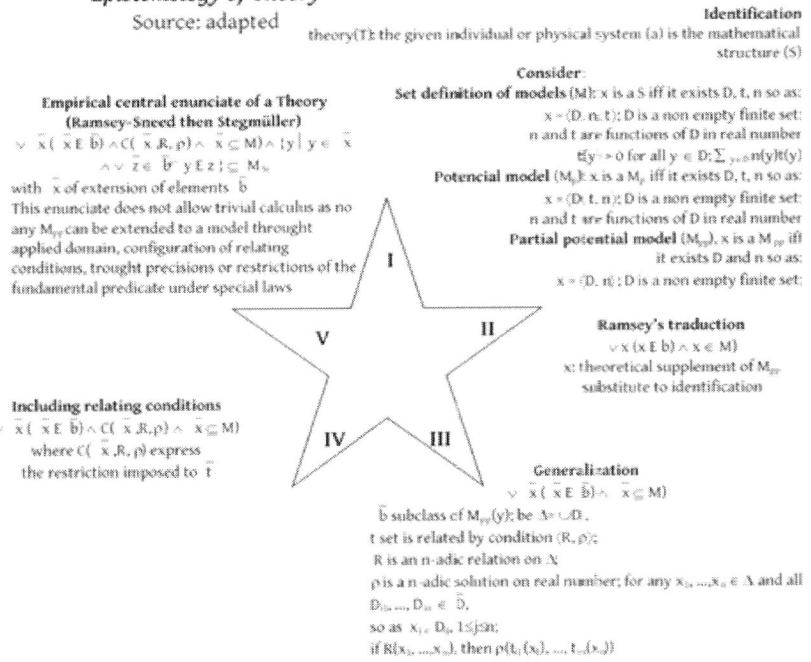

If no model makes the premises true; then they are called **jointly unsatisfiable**; otherwise they are jointly satisfy-able. If every model makes conclusion true, then it is called valid otherwise it is invalid.

General notion of **consequence** and un-satisfiability, at least for finite set. Set can be reduced to the special case of validity of a formula considering:

- $\neg(A_1 \wedge ... \wedge An \wedge \neg B)$ which may be called the leading principle and examined if valid or invalid;
- $\neg(A_1 \wedge ... \wedge An)$ which examined as satisfying or unsatisfying;

[$\neg$ is the negation of.; $\wedge$ is the symbol for "and" or intersection]

- **valid formulas** of classical sentential logic are called tautologically valid (or simply tautologies);
- **decidability** is practically a decision procedure for validity (testing). Classical sentential logic is decidable.

Pragmatic of Model Logic

Or, in other words, and in our mind suggested (?) by displayed physics world. It would be to find a **minimal required set**, for the handling of a generally solvable; well-fit balances, quali-quantitative and quanti-qualitative physics/mathematized model(s) (of real information)/material amounts characteristic values part of ...' ... And maybe, you will have caught some understandings of the system phenomenon under *focus* .... If, still you have kept in mind the basic probabilities of switches that are transitions of fields to particles or 'degeneracy'? [You are right, this sentence is horrible but, maybe, less dangerous than you, with your executive summaries].

By the side of model logic we see that theory of model provides a shell and/or testable assumptions of good formulation.

Bet an initiated user or a profane (as us), wanting to equip a given reality with such symbolic possibilities. Consider that:

- you have a lay enunciate, a practical one, from your reality (or imagination). You have some things to do: **identify** all possible pieces. As phenomenologically as possible, or because you want to use a conventional standard but properly responsible for ones' own choice);
- once that (simple reduced symbolization) to look at: **how should be operated**; after choosing a logic and/or computed treatment, most simple logic possibly a bit more complicated, by the "conditions of operation" or not 1st order logic but with 2nd seed and further order logics (in the same way of 'linking');
- after its' **'level of simplicity**,' the logic operates and provides results (anyhow it will), to be fair with the responsibilities. If about scientific facts and basic principles, operations are often primary. They reproduce (and deliver your good results). If about more complex sciences, they inform you on their coherence;
- then by intuitions and after knowledge you may have better interpretations. If you are with social arts; "results" should not be 'graciously absurd'. But provide shared volunteering in accepted interpretations. Without erasing definitively any doubt... Any should stay responsible for dramatic effects, at some different degrees, provided the hierarchy (**hierarchical order**) they have.

You should also care about excessive 'compulsion'. Which means either ineffective interventionist or, procrastinating. But the relative solitude of basic sciences inventors is commonly not a good attitude. You may have to prepare for some 'lynching of the innocent'. So a technique of modeling provides with formulation, to fit with formal operations. Consider a system of equations and test, of (logical) truth, then you search for the numerical solutions (mathematics) or establish your 'conclusions calling for actions (from cognitive representation to economic policies).

Models deliver distinct information; 1) Unambiguous (but with the limit previously mentioned: all ambiguities are easy to clear by simple scientific facts. 2) Quite often the information are not just positive: about what you want or expect; but better with the conditions, constrains and limits of your procedure(s). 3) With higher complexities; it is to expect that your formalism will suggest positively (determinist-like). Some mechanisms and interpretations or preparations of risks of failure. At best they will be robust enough to be handled or negative or evoke probable precautions.

Hence, of course, perfect science does not leave you of any social or future utility, to free you from physical duties.

Spirit of Nature Model Logic

Now be this with intertwining of 3 at least main concepts. Maybe this is better with a 3 valued logics (of a $e \sim 2.7182$ one?); when about one formed concept? We have many reasons to turn round that. Or 3 dimensioned primarily for thinking. In mathematics dimensions are either the 3 axes or the like degree of cubic of given one cardinal variables taken. [The reader is expected to help his-self (him & her-self) with a mathematics dictionary].

In physics, systems of positioning, or volume, is phenomenological: abscissa, ordinate and deepness. Also in mathematics, since Abel, we know that algebraic equations with dimensions of and higher than 4 have no general solutions. This gives with a multivariate shorter flexibility on the *modulus* of the system. But larger than of observed with 1 or 2 dimensions (the most used) and 'so simple' operations. They only apply well in narrow kinds of quantities.

[Even the monetary accounting has to take into account inflation (bizarre) indices, deflators of price calculus, plenty of risks, variable exchange rates, etc.].

You have to care especially not to limit your analysis of pieces, only one by one or 2 by 2. As those sorts of reviews of data which avoid considering any deepness or pieces of structures. And then provide extraordinary interpretations' but without trying to structure, in abstract of reality. To be sympathetic to our views across multi-levels of physical significance, models ought not to have much more than 3 or 4 variables or parameters at each level of the system. And in the same way, the same cardinal of 3 used for levels (each layer and systems to articulate in like 3 layers). Also it is to consider flexible coefficients ($\neq 1$, varying, making the non-linearity). Dimensions then also have to cover 2 or 3 levels, of integration-differentiation (eventually non whole number or not natural). That is partial.

To observe probabilistic hypotheses concerning complexity. It is to imagine that a given variable or parameter can play different papers (say as dimensions, parameters, scalar, etc.). [When relatively higher in complexity than the fundamental].

Different models and concepts of models may be used, since neither perfectly defined neither so undefined. That is neither fully deterministic (exact), neither perfectly ergodic nor random (probabilistic models). Meanwhile they are explored: like for detecting 'invariant'. Those **invariants** point at formal structures valid across systems of reference. Invariance respect to **transformations** (at homogeneous level?) expresses the existence of more fundamental, 'structure.'

Functional, essential **forms** are to explore in **patterns** or **forms of variations**? Care nevertheless that too many symmetrical relations make mind unclear the sort of **logical polyhedral (?)** ... Maybe it is a source of plenty of misunderstandings because, in the same implicit structure sides; you may manage their facets differently. But still having the same implicit polyhedral form... So 'social scientists' fighting at saying that there is in reality not sense of commonness out their fancy thesis because either at some vertex or hedge or facet].

Thus we may have the frame of formalized system proper specification?

As a mnemonic has in mind 3 formal dimensions space length, width, thickness, at a start, even of one. Like logic (but logically organized): 1st order logic, 2nd order seeds, 3rd uncomplete to specify if not the "neutral paraphernalia of language").

Time may not be as simple as usual but a closure, existence, achievement or an expected average life). Nevertheless dualism is a *primary facie*. The unary-ness of units either absolute (we ignore since accounting) or relative whole unit (your label, one-system object) is not much 'connecting'.

Practically made in the most naked form and often not enough. You will probably have to consider integration or derivation. [In mathematics as well as physics ways: to enlarge. For example yourself to your social group. Or, since atoms gets to molecules and scrutinize more 'coherence'. For example, you and your pieces (better than organs, pieces could be more basic functions ... organ specialized; but function also extends in all other organs, the levels are not exactly closed by organs. [Biological concept of functions more corresponding to algebraic structures? And biological concept of structures?].

For looking like natural levels minded: consider 3 levels at least:

- The **Macro-system** of equations has to be enough representative of **environment**, defining the *medium* of meso-system sustainability. Observe that these larger level in size, with physical principles not coming only from meso-level, but micro-fundamental level).

- **Meso system** of equations driving the maximum "netgertropic" unit reached and sustainable expression of meso variables (normally human being there will appreciate to be: relative-unified system. Still according micro system scale (provider of physics principles, and constrained by macro-system (medium of resources). Meso-level has some autonomy in its mechanisms of self-regulation; [human phenomenon is to be detailed more (but development of unconsciousness as well as of consciousness or capacities of speculations ....Not so impossible?].
- **Micro-level** (in size) is making the Universe and its principles fundamental particles and their fields, or other kinds of multiple potentials superimposition (cardinal in full) and source of orderings (ordinal in different but less than corresponding cardinal).

For some intermediate arguments:
- Formally what we are seeking is a general solvability of representing system of equations, economically cubic or quartic equations. That is more than only degenerate, or special properties for special solutions (either physics specifications or mathematical properties). [Using here the concept of Petrova]
- There could be more dimensions higher (if a higher "system-integrated level(s)" (like a more complex organism: say, for example: if mono-cellular bacteria would like to reason about plural-cells colonies if not human beings). Or if more dimensions with some properties, of symmetries, hence this implies (formal) ordering, which can help to solve ... the system of equations.
- There could be lower level, under the relative unit; or 'smaller worlds'. Which, in physics world it would nevertheless give path to existence. The "I think, so I am" (of Descartes) is in fact too reduced and should have been: "I think because I have a unity of thinking and so a self, required to speculatively and; consciously explore to maintain me ... so am I; for doing ... when automatism of my regulations fails to preserve me". [Sort of Gordian's tights and knots' around Pandora's box?].

Now, after having told you that this meso-level is a place for plenty of centered relative unit concepts. Making or not more or less intermediate and autonomous wholesome units. Still this should be open; so as to embody, maintain and develop... Under natural economics evolutionary laws... In a given providing *medium*... Better not to push to nonrenewable extremities. Nor get into too unstable flows' regimes for deriving.

Many other questions arise. That will further clear disconcerted understandings. Remind that and important pair of aims is about how to specify a model of a dividable for shared system. Especially between a computer, put in charge of the arid processes of calculus and treatment) and human operators; having to preserve enough intelligence for wise choice... [If they do not want to end all ethics in the war games of tele-killers].

We also evoke a concept of a system that still looks like weird. If you remind the traditional simple but non-coherent and; diverse forms traditionally dispersed in many registers of "sciences"; since more than half a century; after von Bertalanffy.

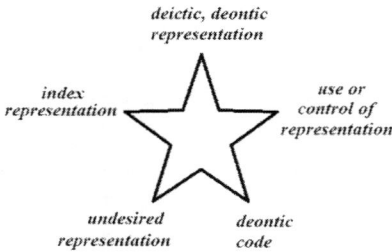

deictic, deontic representation

index representation

use or control of representation

undesired representation

deontic code

Metaphysics of Models

We have to explain more about the 'formal system'. Especially with the thermodynamics approach. We have to stay, somehow vague on details of the system. You will see later, the suggested links, with physics intermediates 'our' kind of system. But we will not err too much in similar systemic registers which have proliferated in many registers. Out of proportions to the main principles of physics realities. Sorts of insights are provided in a 2nd volume of essays (as about operations and statistics).

More originally (or rigorously?) we try to evoke the possible correspondence with mathematics or interpretations that can make formal disciplines be feeding natural sciences.

Symbolic systems of numbers may be with different **levels of scale**. This is implicit with base and just digit representations: tens, hundreds, thousands... Less known (before some introduction in binary digits of computer accounting) are modular forms of the sort.

> With numbers base systems probably started with 5 fingers of 1 hand, 10 for 2, up to 20 (fingers and toes?) as in Mesoamerican or Inca's empires. When it was not of dozens (in many Middle Age measures) or sixty (sexagesimal) in Antique Mesopotamia (That was good for avoiding fractions). Mesopotamia also inspired the week of 7 days and the night's 12 constellations. ... There are good reasons to think that Pythagoras had some transmissions from Mesopotamia. Or why not put some logic more: head = 2 eyes, 2 ears, 2 nostrils and one mouth, add a symbolic memo, add some symbolic esoteric mnemonic and there your head.

> [Of course we did not use this for conceiving this concept of formal relative system, this is an *ex-post* identification. But after **all nature's geometries have elementary forms** that cognition may use unconsciously and; analogically associates consciously. If for good and having clearly scientifically honest identification relations to nature it is not for observing that phenomenological nature can only lie when about humans' way of thinking].

> Modern day system of numbers is decimal. Arabs' Islam civilizations retook the Indian antiquity decimal base 10 system of numbers, practiced in the dust tablet, learned of the way make paper and made that compulsory in all the Abbasids' Empire. With important mathematics research they made with the decimal system. They diffuse up from the eastern extreme of Asia and were brought to Maghreb and Andalusia; practical and theoretical

133

systems (3 or 4). Processes of translation made from Greek and Syriac to Arabic. Then from there or Jewish followed to Latin.

Places of training and translations were brought to the occidental part of Asia (Europe). They have been many transfers of knowledge from Islam places. Sciences were carried by different communities of monotheistic faith. Many Italian merchants and scientists have been trained and then they write or translated and diffused in European universities. In most cases without paying tribute. Then 'Holy Roman Church' expanded its efforts of hegemony and shut many things.

Thus which numbers base? It is to consider that the unit focuses, in most social issues, since a basic humane one you have partial autonomic relevancy. In practice of some traditional model of yours; you may have between one more or less complicated equations, generally differential to some dozens of variables. Many hundreds of possible combinations if having a lone sort picture: multilinear. That way you can also have some variables, and still quite **geodesic frame** ... out some curiosities. Economics enjoyed that accounting linearly just with prices in single currency.

Now logical, humans also fixed their mind with some 'symbolically characteristic numbers, less than a dozen. Possibly because Aristoteles way of categories was easy to handle. Specific properties from numbers theory came after. Some basic cardinals did not changes occasionally with some reasons that they should or could have been so. Some stay, either used in the past (as with the magic 5 of gold number, 5 senses of perception). Or to expect in the future since indexing algebra groups? [Algebra groups have also been seen more fundamentally in solid crystals structures or chemistry. Anyhow it is to care and made a separation by reasons between benign esoteric; where everyone can have its secret corner or simple belief; with exoteric, if you are promoting around the explanations of your beliefs, not necessarily proselytism or preaching.

Cognitively having clearer in mind plenty of shades; from neurosciences and cognitive tasks; it would be to care to adjust many stereotypes in evidence incomplete or mistaking. Especially those affecting the imaginary of societies. So as to promote ways of consistency where the simplifications produced by humans conscious thinking is reflexive, **manage cognitive scripts and sketches** kept open (morally tolerant based). But it is also to observe that any intent to have their esoteric and look like 'initiated' even the scientists; like when preferring to call theorem and principles not after the closest concept helpful to remind and think about but after the inventor's name. In a way closer to the cult; instead of sharing the most easily the essential meaning of principles so as to work meaningfully. [Sciences way of lexicographic development has also consisted in using Greek or Latin roots].

These are images to think about, when framing a model, as a logical ball; willing to contain a **solvable network of tangible and intangible concepts**. We may need some flexibility in concepts of use. Especially to be able to make some corrections and/or keep open the levels of precision meanwhile also framing them together.

Conceptual explorations need not to be too dogmatic nor too rigid. More robustness and/or sense of usefulness.

'**Robustness**' is supposed to do modeling somehow simpler and more stable (enough in tune with what you manage and phenomenological evidences and be shared. Robustness to be provided by: 1) those existing in nature (you cannot conflict at will); 2) formally expressed (it can be explored by **simulation, sensibility**, theory of **perturbation** and has forms); 3) the sort of relationships closer to nature's existences you can establish and 4) the firmness for which you personally accept to sacrifice.

In this framework of models; be them explicitly formulated of more simple ways of behaving cautiously according abstracts... That is making easier to share and support slightly different specifications. It is basic for social model or policies having to do with participation. Hence not necessarily the best for principles if you do not include them in the modeling.

Principles are structured in more complicated formal systems. If high in the level of complexity, can prime-numbers indexed them in absolute?–And let relative frames somehow simple, in terms of cardinal and ordinal. In other words, have finite numbers and not much, but enough to manage. Together they are with orders of the same numbers, in more or less characteristic relations between. Both that could be managed qualitatively and quantitatively in a **sufficient characteristic way (and about characteristic physics quantities? Grid** them as labels of objects or concepts representing a geometric subject?

In logic of physics and objects and numbers which are quite often more or less analogical correspondences. Many are provided in this essay. Sometimes not much explained. Quite relevant to the logic of 'flexible geometry' you have topology. [Most terms are quite important to our concern].

Some Basic Ideas of Topology		
	General topology	**Metric topology**
Openness	Finite intersecting neighborhood	Open Ball
Closure	Complementary to open	whatever convergence in E, also n converge in F
Density	Adherence = E all open ≠∅meets X	Limit of a series of points of X
Completeness	irrelevant (completeness implies a metric)	Convergence, any closed part is complete. Fixed-point theorem
Compactness	Separation and covering finite	Any compact metric space is complete with an adhering value (closed and limited
Connectedness	only open and closed parts: E and ∅	

Now complex systems, seek evidently (from nature's) complex enough subsystems, to be absorbed and they enforce their own resilience after recovering. So their systems form is **unary-ly** relatively integrated; possibly as an 'identity'. Their survival and reproduction (so called '**autopoietic**' when living systems) require to be economical too. Because rather than 'redoing everything' since the start (of 'nucleons') which would be uneconomical they take advantage of others' efforts.

With live beings you can eat them, incorporate them, live with them, cooperate, parasites, etc.

Meanwhile it would be moral economy it is able to choose between feasible possibilities; choice would select, and eventually produce or prepare the alternatives offering the best share, preservation, sustainable balance with the less harm to any. Including limit the waste or recycle at the maximum. Especially because our best skill: thinking, caring and develop technologies. Practically this consists in examining critics to the most direct way of satisfying. Also to **question and reshape** (not so differently) the traditional models of applied registers, for better efforts and care.

This is not necessarily out the logic of Model Theory and can appear in enough detailed models, as constraints, conditions, selections and choice of relations, specification and degeneracy? Empirical models, formally well specified, properly simulated, help to approach realities and suggest wiser views... Simple kinds of models, as simple as relative informative, are linking ones are helped by common sense of formulations; identifications (anchors to realities) and by the ways there are implemented. Thereafter there are with the means of conscious cognition (trying to be logic ... despite international financial superstructures?).

If they are **non-experimental** nor summarized in controllable devices; their **contrast** with real data of **reality measures**; can help to suggest others involved effects and to reshape the **hypothesis**. Proper condition to that 'in' essential systems of reference, rather than 'outside' systems of reference (armed by whom pretending their exteriority the best. [Things are more complicated, you effectively also need to be 'out' for **comparisons of invariances**. But it seems to us that this $\ln^x$ & e^x can do that: the Chinese-box - Russian dolls (Matryoshka); moduli scale up integration-intricated systems of reference].

Honest (ethical) **procedures** also have to question the **ways of measures**, and provision of alternatives. Together with the help of 'complexity' maybe one day wiser complications). It is not about disqualifying realities. **Statistics despite abrasive-polishing, smoothing misunderstanding and misunderstood** can be helpful if not too manipulated. If the subject of representation is not experience-able under controlled conditions; fit the model, review the conditions of control, have the properties of the system to help to exhaust (or be tired enough be) deductions.

Care that 'Governance' is too prone to enforce without cautions and let the adaptations to the weakest ... but without any doubt about their own intelligence.

Traditional **"simple exact models"** make use of the **differential calculus**, seek unary-ness of the solution, maybe because of the presumption of management. Since not so accounting for that, we may be more in fields of formulations, and in special cases of solutions.

[We are not promoting a unique neoliberal model of adjustment. Have in mind that this disaster had some econometric substance (and the illusion national superstructures will adapt. The sort of relative formal system is more a 'nuclear modulus' already at a system with non-human (but ecolo-econo-physics) coherence and can modularly be expanded]

The effect in mathematical economics is that sort of addictive search for anything looking-like only one solution: **Pareto's optimal, asymptotic convergence** of any series (the point of the real limit at infinity); **Fixed-Point theorem** ... perfect in sophisticated simplicity but if effectively phenomenological, not as a determinist could like]. Preference they have for the simplest ones if not linear that is one 1 dimension or 2 dimensions; but not much more. Sort of those serious physicists cannot any more make use of.

Implicitly, most arts modelers underscore formal conditions; throwing disturbing concepts in a **black box of residues** without seeing that it is a kind of Pandora's box.

[Pandora's box an Antic Greek Myth:" Pandora opened the jar and all the evils flew out, leaving only "Hope" inside once she had closed it again."]. Their simplicity is hidden behind "tremendous" intelligence of symbols (like Great Kabbalist of *Sephiroth*). These **models like esoteric systems of symbols** have many advantages. They are easy to keep for ones-selves. They reserve confidence to the dictator (or the kings). They are able to corrupt plenty of resources of *calculus* to 'beautiful professionals of the hard-way').

Financial systems 'accounting simplicity' is based on linearity or normality. This 1st dimension (but graphed generally in a 2 dimensions system of reference); by the side of the *calculus*; stands on **simple triangular rule** (We add a table of inequalities in this essay, including it). Also said the rule of 3 or Thales's triangle proportions. Of course they are not as simple as you may imagine. Already they have many transformations that can help to simplify degrees. Our critics are more about presumed logical shortcuts and lacks of essentially humane considerations. Rather than with only a kind of bad intentions and be plot-minded of 'world-wide intentions plot'.

Formally, social theories presumed models have many basic defects. They are to determinists upon their dear abstract concept. They are not delegating enough. They never consider essential enough levels, which could anchor something. Most are just sending in the hardest fields of improperly living forms regulated abuses.

By the side of formal sciences model 'core' is too primarily ordered (by 'Chinese's box integration' [French prefer Russian dolls]. Speaking here of the way mathematical integrations is driven. By the side of cardinal perspective the implicit that prevails is: **clear-cut partitions**. That is Cartesianism (now more messianic than scientific.

Maybe pictorially the defect comes from the **view of step one recursion** (or **iteration**). That is to say 'not systemic-like' or at least after some sort of needed properties for ensuring '**local**-ness' and '**global**-ness', closures, differentiability and so on.

[At the social level this makes 'inter-social-class struggles'. At level of experts that is more birds' cage of wrong omens. [But probabilistically there are always few some to have been almost right]. Our humanist concern is not about imposing a formal sciences new scientism. Just empirically observing that their simplest '1st cegree' phenomenologically make brutal rules of rationalities. As could have been made with opportunistic neoliberal 'revolution' ... or otherwise too ineffective democracies. Since unable to mix properly cardinal prone democracy and opportune ordinal-prone structures].

Social arts have plenty of looking like powerful formal tools. Say multilinear system f equations, linear matrix systems which looks like able to include as many as you like variables (since their operations are "simple": product as a whole, lines or column **permutations**; extensions of division. The process of infinitesimal (differential) calculus; will give you reasonable estimates by *ex-post* fitting. But does this say everything about the way to?–we need to clear the diversity of horizons.

[Statistically among many experts you will forcibly have one for claiming the reward of having been the best predictor. Reasonably this may come, left apart the abuse of wordy rhetoric. Effectively by the model for having caught the composition of mixture of the margins effectively repeated: syntactic similarity or enough of the critical border of principles semantic similarity without having clearly with which it was. In most cases we are more in the verbal fraud and the statistic of the disagreements].

Hence your social-economic 'measures' or records will be iterated, delayed of months, too partial, be only items frequencies or positivists scales. And you will not have caught the 'mechanisms of your ambitions'. Just have caught and cut the 'at the moment state of margins, you would have made core, not even caring conditioning probabilities. So more an illusion of a chili con carne theory. {Not to miss the tabasco] distorted manipulated catch of amoeboid principle; cleaned from circumstances; so more good prediction of the already passed [projected into the ambition of future*]*.

Few Basic Problems of Modeling

Differential calculus may have to receive (mathematical) partitions not so simple, within more phenomenological intervals of existence. Also directly or indirectly it would be to incorporate enough 'physics' or material amounts of non-simple addition operation. Enough contrasting and statistically differentiable multiple independent 'determinisms.' There are sorts of simple and quite correct treatments. With almost linear trajectories. They can be close to metric kinds of fields and include vectors. [**Vectors fields** are straight lines tangent projections to points of curves trajectories].

See that quantic mechanics have core in linear algebra. But used within complex numbers' ones (Hermitian and **waves'–probabilistic of formulations (Schrödinger's** 1st formulation) or **types of fundamental particles statistics**. Also with some developments and operators, such as **Laplacians**. This linearity either because of "existence" ('existing or not' is: 'true or false'); or because the 'core-head' of the operation is so (main term close to linear). Second terms (of differential development are as in **Laplacian** or **Taylor's series**) Then corrective or complimentary terms (or extremities) less important in higher degree (of values below 1). See for example non-linear formulations of Einstein's ones with light's speed kinetic energy and heavier particles speeds corrected.

> [That is to say in a discrete pack you can draw some metric lines and their measure but you will need to catch the expansion as in a skeleton ... formally the concepts of **symplectic**? –And then optimize skeletons and 'flesh' (one respect the other in their interactions distant apart from the bone with formally is economical and effectively noticeable in balance natures). Care that a framework inspired by nature for formal or at the reverse does not mean they will match immediately together. If you use the model of a left shoe directly, you will have 2 left shoes (so you need a symmetric plane of transformation (not a rotation one for the other shoe). A left foot is not directly the perfect translation of the right foot.

Meanwhile from an 'out' perspective respect to **local-ness**. Not a problem for any metric axes 'out' the fundamental processes are stronger enough for having metric lines at levels of objects in their phase space diagram (or artifice of the sort). Even more in the informative chains we suggest? Since in higher (but thinner) complex systems are developed within, or inscribed in the larger principles). There are composed of emergences; 'within,' another level of order. **Composition** meaning that resulting object is a combination of the abscissa and ordinate axis, hence not purely one or the other. Technically a something to account for in an exploration which could make use of **Eigenvalues** or **Eigenfunctions**. This for positioning best discriminating axis; between clouds and **matrix densities** (or other mathematical forms) or volumes ... even think about that for disentangling the entanglement... Or consider the basic almost free entanglement known the rest of what in the **nucleus**?].

Divisions into pieces and adjustments or corrective terms such as in **Hamiltonian** systems. By infinitesimal calculus, divide a lot will almost forcibly deliver good approximation's (with strong principles). And you can come close to the linear behavior. Including with some **statistics of population** or that are of kinds of pure particles (such as **bosons'** or **fermions'**). There you obtain your proper values. But then: about which reality for which macro-properties? It is not to just have a simple compartment of pure and free particles to drink ... but more interesting are cocktailed properties?

> By **averaging statistics smooth things** and, by the way, disappear interesting '**rugose-ness**' ... the one relevant to the margins of phenomena? Statistically also, we have the **normal hypothesis**: a multiplicity neutralizing **great number laws of ineffectual alone interactions**. Make all that normal (law of distribution) manage average with 1st degree (linear) equations with convenient transformations. There you have all the stupid determinists, even if sometimes they have democratic values: they just promote formally the mathematics of the easy dictator's way, of Arrow's democratic condition.

> **Arrow's General possibility theorem** or Arrow's paradox is an impossibility theorem, about ranked **preferences**, that states that voters having 3 or more distinct options; no **ranked order voting** system can convert the ranked individual preferences into a complete and transitive community's ranking; while also meeting a pre-specified set of criteria: unrestricted domain, non-dictatorship, Pareto efficiency, and independence of irrelevant alternatives. In other words: no rank-order voting system can be designed that satisfies these 3 "fairness" criteria:
> - If every voter prefers X over Y, then the group prefers X over Y.
> - If every voter's preference between X and Y remains unchanged, then the group's preference between X and Y will also remain unchanged (even if voters' preferences between other pairs change).

- There is no "dictator": no single voter possesses the power to always determine the group's preference.
Voting systems that use cardinal utility is not covered by the theorem, as they convey more information than rank orders.

In an intent to provide Arrow's theorem of possibilities check this 'free translation' **adapted to quantic framework?**

Consider some place provided a *medium* and populated. This composing a cardinal *vacuum*-like (under some conditions of possibilities, of not too changing particles) and an ordered 'spectrum of evidences' corresponding to atoms-fields. **Ordinal positions positioned filled by cardinality.** '*Spectra* of evidences' each of 3 or more distinct options in the order are filled after being given ('attractive') probabilities; according to the order, enough compared cardinal *vacuum* like (It is to imagine a balance of proportion cardinal-ordinal (or even-ness-odd-ness prime-ness? In the absolute).

Potential atoms-field **states have no ranked order assignation upon the** *spectra* of evidences (balances between creation and disintegration); that can orderly convert 'individuals after *vacuum*' as a spectrum of evidence members; and this '**spectra of evidences' into a complete and transitive community's ranking.** While also meeting set of criteria. **Rank-order assignation in probabilities can be provided by extensive parameters**.

This can follow the 3 "fair to order" criteria:
- **Criteria of unanimity** (if all ones share (or 'have access', at least dynamically) to the order of spectra; then all will follow it).
- **Stability of spectra** (source of robustness) ... in given phase-space?
- There is **no** (relative) '**dictator**' upon the spectra of evidence: no single atom-field system can determine for (any and all) the population (it just fills a place-state, democratically).
  Cardinality conveys more openness to information than rank orders ordinal.
  Pareto efficiency (would be maximum; in the allowance of phase space, spectra and population. Independence of irrelevant alternatives (out the involvement in the order).

In this fast adapted translation of democratic possibility Arrow's theorem imagined in a quantic system it is not to imagine it perfect (and it is not yet approved). To remark that it is quite easy, especially in a framework starting since physics's principles; to imagine it is about democracy ordering possibility (and efficient? - and not a lay dictator paradox.

Second Arrow's theorem, sort of similar theorem can be inspiring: '**back-warded' to more fundamental levels** (and reinterpreting formal concepts out exclusive register of formalism). Also for this one we even can **loop forward thereafter** for example in the shaping of democratic institutions. How those ought to be filled? - after the goals of society. Finally, and considering the complexities, complications and opportunities consistent democratic life; with **partial forms of orders**. So to advocate for pluralism and diversity of care. At least this is not for the only perfect conscious ordering of dictatorship, the perfect anarchism of some ideologies, and neither is the place the first ordering in hands of intermediaries.

It is not to prejudge about simplicity. Think that these behaviors are "approximately very special and partial." **Multivariate method operations** are generally based on simplifications of operations. Which are supposed to have very "neutrally" aggregated levels. Giving, at macro level, that properties are not properly caring about 'real economy'. Proper economics is often at the margins of main structures (and better not to be corrupted by private ways).

With naive epistemology of existence and about dimensions and levels, we have to conceive how, written on a page; it is to establish a formal system of reasoning. And then what it is supposed to represent. Represent, as well for oneself, as for its social thickness; before put ahead an abstract concept with no materiality. Starting and stating, since a fundamental dual, but complex perspective. Then structural studies may have to explore how various levels, both formal and representatively, develop to compose and potentially reflect properties. Properties that define the best system of representation and can include the physics of the universe (if the system not exclusive of an environment).

Now, considering formalization, we may have to look by proper management of complexities side. It is not for trying to set a universal delimited non-material (and non-material-able) umbrella; exclusively made of abstract concepts. Neither symbolize nor summarize it, by a material or not-material point. Better to be inspired by the natural specifications of subjects; (made eventually objects of analysis). Since it is about them and because here they are.

Do as Descartes whom was a bit better, the Cartesians that followed; since he added soon that humans are governed by their passions (with some dismay?). Better if to mean that human passion can be self-conditioned for good. And the coherence of the formal system a bit better an abstract of infinity (Cantor's mistake?). The coherence of physics-formal match: make it real (save the Planet) or will all turn into Hell (hot place nice for medusa, scorpions, scratching bugs and bacteria (climate warming).

Care Correspondence of Formulations

The pluralism of alternatives of formulation, formal diversity of specification(s) are other problems to consider. It is to be inspired by the natural objects in their 3 dimensions; they are fixed by non-commutative time dimension or ... by something like closure (s) (or plural ... as many as to complete?). So to start systematically at least since a sort of 3: trinomial, 3 intricated **monomials** and/or **monads** (Unit, open by 2 and detailed by 3; not in the same register as Leibnitz or Giordano Bruno).

Also to clear some views on half-complicated mixtures between abstracts and real pieces we may consider; when dressing up a system of equations. They have to represent a relative formal system model of a real subject. It is to mind that each term has different correspondence. In the intuitive analogical way: terms reflect 1) a **component** of the "system," or 2) a **class**, or 3) a term of '**correction**,' or 4) a term for '**position**.' In a complex framework; a component itself is possibly a subset (the commonness of property with the set and a **distinctive operator** ... within a class of operation(s)?). The class a term of operations or function across constitutive levels the system.

Correction s are **relative weights** of the previous ... providing formal inner coherence to the relative system (if a system) and 'position' within formal *medium* term positioning the specific solution case (or 'degeneracy'?). The idea is that each term is consistent, both in the formal system and also in reality... In reality both functional and structural 'intricated'? But you have to care; it is not to identify obliged and directly. For an example of living cells only list the organelles directly or any structure as formal terms.

Relative system has grounds. So they are components of an **essential** 'function' (lay term) which link at different levels of scales. To assume the function (formal term), there could various types of structure, 'functions' of metabolism and crossed ones. They are also intertwined with other essential functions situated both internally as in the living environment. What is important is the 'function' assumed enough. You cannot understand some plants' metabolisms if you miss the nitrification of the bacteria associated with its roots; nor the fungi one if ignoring that they are digesting 'outside'.

Perspective is systemic, whole and 'complex.' Insight, focus or lenses turned **enquiring boxes** (formal shape of any experiment test-tube) ... **black-box** (at the start of knowledge but correspondingly possibly a '**white-box**'). For an *in vitro* or very experimental study, be possibly providing information after the system approach. And so economics is not in the naked Cartesian approach but in the system one and ... not everything, you would like his system.

Science knowledge exchange

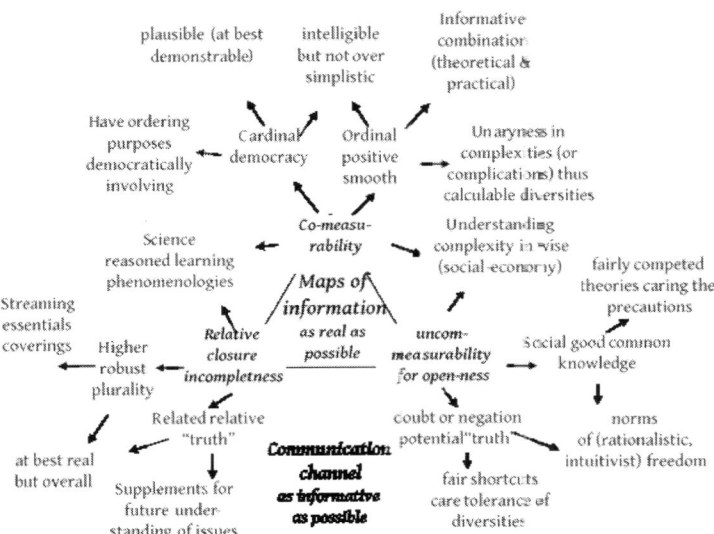

Since higher systems often live on lower near-by (at least) ... Mismanaged Cartesian approach is just reaching the most fundamental of lower systems; and recomposing may miss emergence in the pathways up. Perhaps the least probable. Nevertheless once you have a relative system quite clear (essential dynamic balances to identify maybe not too numerous ... like between half to some dozens as biological catalogs).

> Then somehow hoping (not in vain?) that you have a general framing, that can turn a referential (of simulation?); to which you can refer to the specific boxes of *focus*. Eventually black or white boxes. [Black box: we know almost nothing of the inside ... only the 6 facets of dice. White box: we have too much but we may know most things inside. This is the may object of perturbed have the spectra (or perturbation), but not necessarily these 'rays' operating so, as in the simple recomposition, in the original subject... At the start of a white box; you do not understand much, of what is going in, on, and out].

Approaches have to be complementary and des-intricated (or disentangled?). If the whole system approach is possible and efficient, global external measure may be better informed and then, what can be done... If the main goal is to preserve the system in its environment. Conversely the insight is supposed to have a better perspective about how to. Of course, intuitively, most cautious doers, are quite often of social arts if they are reflexive and critics. They can need more to meet-match-fit.

Mathematics Physics Spirit

Physics or Mathematics?

Are physics and mathematics? - Just 2 registers of words and a matter or only 2 words are not enough to specify and intertwine your pieces. Especially if you try to summarize under a unique label deducing all since 1st rank. Even if theoretically some are prone to imagine being able to eradicate any subjectivity. And the one solution or value of the characteristics; could by some unique formula? Something that would make definition perfect, for existing definitively by itself and could be isolated. Like put in some sort of container or reserved rich neighboring; protected from the envy of losers. But this just what is existing in anyone: "artists" of politics, policies for targeting and so on.

To extend a bit more, any component of a formula defines: 1) **Coefficient** (either weight in the relative system or the participation to use); 2) **Variables** (either qualitative or quantitative; 3) **Exponent** (characteristic or participation to use...); 4) **Scalar position** (in self-one scale of complexity). All with 4 operating precision are like 5) **Sign** (kind of play less or division); 6) *P*lay in and up operations (addition or products); 7) *R*ank (in the inner basal or in its active hierarchy); 8) *I*ndex (among competing membership or cooperating one). Finally, consider 4 matching (informative) 9) **d**erivability (2 down since the mid); 10) **i**ntegration (2 up since the mid); 11) **i**nformation (quali-quanti and quanti-quali); 12) **d**egeneracies (if a system 2 crossover links at least and overall but with the holes of openness?).

[Eventually to imagine that all those could be modeled with a formal head as a solid polyhedron and where we would have cut hairs before make up the bun of the *medusa*].

> Proliferation of abstract concepts with some formal identification may lead to just too empty or null dimension (the sort of despicable social sciences waste... That can be quite useful; for

the control of the rude and the unwise). A smoothing no more formal, if a belief is to never materialize. But could we pretend to some integral unit dimension? - Able to take the lead since one (1) design of a general formula-able relative system and then produce series of influential consequences. Say cardinals able to support their ordinal-ness so as, for some 'hierarchical structuring, not in excess and ... at 'best' according to beliefs in a sustainable better world.

Are Nature metaphysics epistemologies good minimum world? - for teaching humbler ways, and tame the crazy ambitions of absolute powers. Absolute powers? - when one wants to obtain everything from humans, regardless of formal representations, sacrificing people. Often then in the business to self-justify the reproduction of the means.

Humble metaphysics when caring enough not to alienate renewals; understanding that the best gains are social, and the most sustainable ways are with joining individual and collective intelligence, providing fair sense of achievement to most.

Practice of Praxis

How to cope with pure and simple formalism, when we are not at the top of **absolute numbers' pyramid**? [Whole grid]. If at a top of relative system pyramid (or diamond or platonic solid) there is a way to **re-rank** it. When its absolute position is far below the structuring of its Universe. But if wanting **to express some sense of unary integrity** within an environment on which they depend. Always in the relative numbers' rank way; have the basic logical **precautions**: negation, contrast, critics or objections. The other of the dual having accounted, some of the basic non-. A formally at least having made a sort of **fair residual melting pot**.

[It may be quite easy to formulate: 1st iteration you cut by 2 half for your half or a little less; for all the others and then go on the half cut. On what you have and what you pour in the pot to remain ... you sacrifice but since your fair share, and volunteering for the gains of more ordering, since ordering has a cost. You have immediately a sense of economy: **limits of self-sacrifice for your best 'profit of intelligence'**. Make same reasoning in the balance of quali-quanti. This has the top-down and conscious approach like with the way to cut cake, considering also the biodiversity of the fruits.

Of course you have the not so innate unconscious bottom-up approach: the **universe** in your **environment** provides with raw material, more or less 'prepared': honey, flour, fruits. Generously with what you need for a cake **(anticipation)** and a **receipt** (even a bear knows for what is honey). This as bottom-up mainly unconscious approach.

Now if you are also ingenious **capital of knowledge**; which able you, to take advantage of 'lower structured' levels'; but of higher energy amounts. If you are not stupid enough to master those larger steps not to make them blow up in your face (say explosive devices). Say you make use more directly of Sun, energetic stocks and so on as another source of raw material for cake. Bottom-up if the melting where you pour all your 'waste': share for others, unrecycled remains, almost pure energetic waste (heat). Then you may avoid the increased heat not trigger brutal entropy].

Democracies are not free riders fields of manipulations and require and careful consistent involvement. With no care of institutions that for being economical and moral should be as thin and fit as 'strange attractors'. Synchronizing some essentials, hence not the illusions of determinisms. Not the purpose to promote speculative profits as extractions preventing imbalances. Nor empower the defects of non-realistic social-economic. Neither to make societies pay for the lies and wastes of club-groups of aristocratic extractions. All just promoting Brownian (ergodic) overheating micro-motions-empowering entropy.

Wiener process is a basic in (Brownian) ergodic motion, for the diffusion process formulation, random walk in one direction of Wiener process can be seen as the limit of random. It is a continuous-time stochastic process, often called standard Brownian motion and one of Lévy processes (stochastic processes with stationary independent increments)

$$(dK/dt)_{jump} \leq 0 \qquad or \qquad (dK/dt)_{diff} \leq 0 \qquad or \qquad (dK/dt)_{drift} = 0$$

where K is a Lyapunov functional: $K = \int dxp_1(x, t) \log [dxp_1(x, t)/ dxp_2(x, t)$. dt is for differentiation, t is the time. Form is given in the index. Its unconditional probability density function, follows a normal distribution. It is formally used in mathematics, economics, quantitative finance, and physics.

Always be quite clear that, whatever the relative social position in hierarchical politically handled scales; the good potential of intelligence (of anyone, and behaviors) are to expect from any members. For anyone solve the opportunities carefully from diversities and circumstances.

Observe that in physics forces, come from gradients. The **gradients** from wider **heterogeneity** are in space, **diverging kinetics** for **expansions**, and also seen in local orders possibly going up with incorporation or integration of more useful energies. They are often **softer on the cooler margins, exchanging pieces of information**, made more capable to incorporate. And not to **disorderly mis-matchings, clashes** and **hard shocks**. In contrast from providing relatively more disordered environments. But economically making use of ordering pieces. Products of degradations are usable (or reusable). 'Heterogeneity willing to rejoin all together'.

Have clear where are the principles (constituting physics); the logical and accounted landmarks are. Have no too specific illusions(s) about what to reach (out your free individual spiritual will). The abstract to measure is about 'how far you are from the main-streams' if the main streams are good (including carefully). So as to compare yourself with **other comparable**.

Fields Physics Formalisms Compared	
Gauge Field	**Bundle**
global gauge	principal coordinate bundle
gauge type	principal fiber bundle
gauge potential $b_{(}^k$	connection on a principal fiber bundle
S_{ab}	transition function
phase factor Φ_{QP}	parallel displacement
field strength $f_{(v}^k$	curvature
Source $J_{(}^k$	Volume ordered?
Electromagnetism	connection on $U_1(1)$ bundle
isotopic spin gauge field	connection on $SU_2(1)$ bundle
Dirac's monopole quantization	connection on $U_1(1)$ b. after 1st Chern class
electromagnetism without monopole	connection on a trivial $U_1(1)$ bundle
electromagnetism with monopole	connection on a trivial $U_1(1)$ bundle

Find in the same way, **simple mixtures of formal gauges**; or more properly measuring scales, eventually axis of some coordinate. If you are '**round shaped and smooth**' understand that you are **not straight cutting edges**. Energetically compared they have to be at larger distance than manageable ones. In the 1st case it is constitutional (combination of both axes) in the 2nd straight case it is separation (often critical inflection).

So you may use an axis of reference but not alone. Think about the deeper meaning of experimental data, but do not avoid them. Just for looking like as "intelligent as a theory." Social theory without proper system of formalism is mental pornography. Seek corresponding but different concepts in physics, for example gauge theory in physics have more to do with scattering effects of perturbations(s) revealing so its structure.

Have clear which approach you are using top-down to the minoring, bottom up to the majoring; **within scale of measure proper to the body**; so with some sense of structural approach and; outer scale of measure. More with borders of the body, functional variations of filling; not necessarily the structure.

Always mind that this should appear somehow in the forms of your mathematics and the patterns or kind of logics you make use of. Also in this formal real connection, **always think about what your method is prone to some area of methods**. Most mixed formal concepts side by, less with others: formal bias. What you have under exam: if functional will be more at ease with logics. Structural will often be more prone to amounts; but both always somehow mix.

Observe that it is always better, to have in mind at any point, at least 3 concepts. Even if graphically 2 dimensions is what you can picture first: a, graph and also because **surfaces are fine to study the 'records'**. Your binocular view gives deepness but not always does it without illusions. Your eyes are in a (frontal) plane.

Not everything is (simple) mathematics as demonstrated Chaïtin. But underneath, mathematics can do much more. Also Gödel shows infinite simple arithmetic with bottom-up iteration (recursively) is not complete. That is to say: it cannot axiomatically justify and closes itself. Another way, have shown the same: top-down approach: a something like Fermat- Kronecker descent (as explored by Gauthier) also in trouble for being "perfect."

Thus pure mathematics with many more kinds or applied avatars. And despite the fact that it is an increasing role in any experimental sciences. It does not provide good reasons to any kind of definitive decider: **it is not consistent in the first place** ... and barely respect the need for openness. Thus find consistently, culturally and progressively the **best humane laws of economics: the universal ethical ones**. Possibly if you individually want in a metaphysics way: at the 1st place, with criteria of Justice. As we portrayed in an olicognograph in the **2nd order place** ... together as influence of a realistic model of thermodynamic transformation ... psycho-economical dualism.

For people wanting to be honestly somehow complete; but not to decide from anything more than your self-deficiency try to 'complete' with realities. Be these realities serious; when trying to use physics evidences. But not too automatically applying shortcuts of mind. Nor degenerate over-determinist scientist's abuses of nature laws. Cognition makes it spontaneously (of course not as in pure formal symbolic mathematics): **complete the perception of information up to some degree of satisfaction** (within a standard or prejudged degree of satisfaction). But it is also 'economical'.

Theoretical economics has plenty of axioms and most advanced theorems' inventors. Whom turned often the most conscious of their abuses limits; when their pieces of cakes suffered enough after having met no resistance when extracted: this is the **consistent way of learning**. More constructive human realities are made of **orderings within half-structured mixtures and partial confusions**. Wanting to be controlled diversities and so on. By the side of realities this means, to us that: mathematical approaches, as far as possible, are the good mathematical expressions of physics's formulations.

Practically also, this may mean to **minimize** (as far as possible) **the formal or logical paradoxes, produced by mathematical tautologies in realities identifications**. Then solve the remaining; by physics facts and such sorts of explanations. Or having understood that the surprising details, data and so on, express effectively something of physics. In the epistemological process of physics would our perspective needs an anterograde review of physics? - If previous physics theory too well proved. The example is with Newton's mechanics that has not been disqualified by Einstein's mechanics but 'incorporated'. As a result theory's revision may just need to be reformulated.

Thus, if wanting to reach at least enough specifiable system:
- Pure mathematics is absolutely rigorous but needing to be physically, as far as possible identifiable (or completed). That requires not to be contradicted by experimental devices or empirical proof.
- Physics not all about pure simple mathematics; (nor only for the materialistic sake of wealthy mathematicians). But now, we have very good mathematical knowledge that, if properly formulated, can inspire physics finding explanations within numbers ... but also more logics?
- Pure logics in the same vein, more for qualitative clean kinds of concepts, and the pure subjective ones isolated in only dimension 0 (when not vain).
- "Confused logics" is a bit too hard to explain in this paragraph. Because of existing mess and many misunderstandings. The reader will have more explanations further.

Of course, if the primary purpose of sciences supports our speculations and; moral issues share them in the 'best degeneracy' for all humans. Best absolute concept, best share when everyone absolutely free volunteering. This is not humane as the complete understanding of most teleological animal: the human (for the moment). Sciences may help to 'philosophy'; if humans are willing it to free themselves of their brutality towards usual previous means; and stop destroying the planet.

Tegmark's Mathematical Universe:

In a similar vein to summarize an extract of Tegmark's essay (a Swedish cosmos-logician who proposed recently mathematics as cosmos ontology.

"**Baggage**: would be concepts and words invented by humans for convenience; which are not necessary for describing the external physical reality. It is crucial not to conflate the language of mathematics (which we invent) with the structure of mathematics (which we discover).

Considering **mathematical structure** some set of abstract entities with relations between them; can be described in a baggage-independent way. [To add: 'a something invariant among different theories properly supported by statistics data of experiments and at least independent from purest language based baggage positive dependent copy ... a negative one with critics may arise one or more hypothesis].

Equivalence: 2 descriptions of mathematical structures are equivalent if there is a correspondence between them; that preserves all relations; if 2 mathematical structures have equivalent descriptions; they are one and the same [sort of isomorphism?].

Symmetry: the property of remaining unchanged when transformed. [At the top of physics in a finite possibly immobile universe?] **External reality hypothesis**: that there exists an external physical reality completely human independent [... formulation?].

Mathematical Universe hypothesis, says that our external physical reality is a mathematical structure. It follows from external reality hypothesis; meaning that our universe is mathematical structure.

The computable **Universe hypothesis**: our external physical reality is a mathematical structure defined by computable functions.

Finite Universe hypothesis: our external physical reality is a finite mathematical structure. Mathematical Universe hypothesis solve the infinite regress problem where the properties of nature stems not just the properties of its parts, which requires further explanation, ad infinitum, the properties of nature stems not from the properties of its ultimate building blocks but the relations between these building blocks".

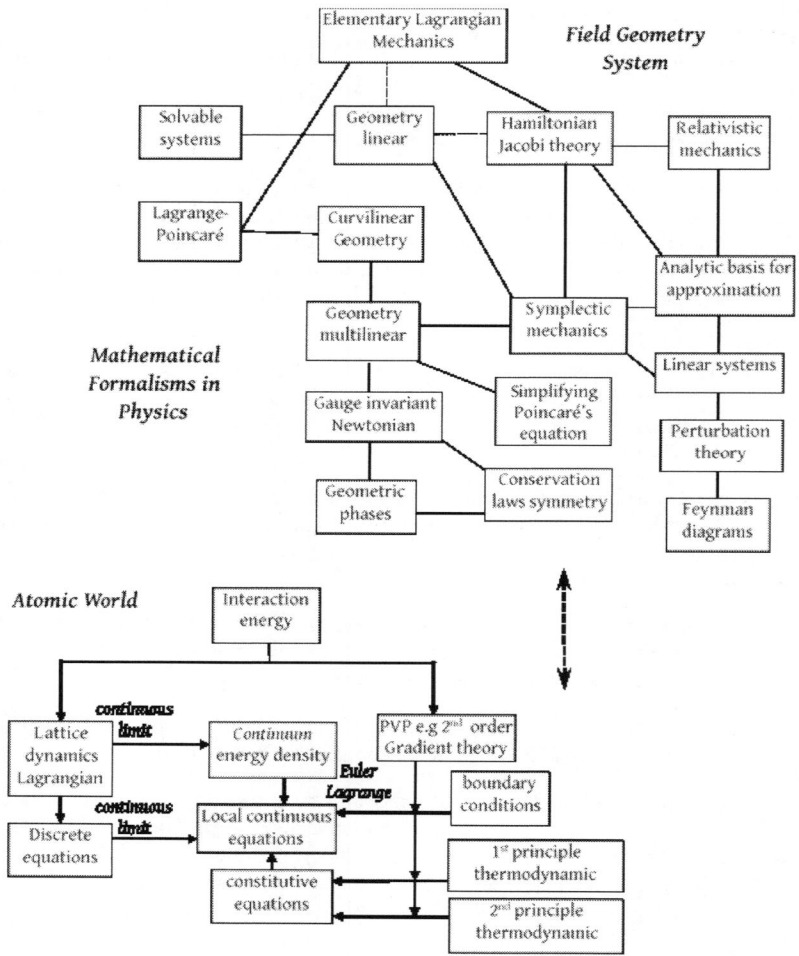

Gradient Theory: is a generalization of the usual concept of derivative to functions of several variables.

We have to remind, briefly how numbers are formed or maybe are from. In the tradition of mathematical training, things start more commonly since general sets of numbers. As we take the way of users; rather than of comprehensive discipline and perfect experts, the alternative is in the way 'numbers are formed'. But in this essay not a manual, we must also get faster to the points ... of marginal remarks. Assuming that the reader has minimum knowledge at the respect or enough literacy for consulting some dictionary of mathematics, logics or physics. Be it simple the worldwide web encyclopedia.

Real numbers ($\mathbb{R}$) are closer to the concept of continuity. They join types of numbers that are natural ($\mathbb{N}$), integer ($\mathbb{Z}$), rational ($\mathbb{Q}$). Real number set also includes 'sub-something ones': algebraic, irrational and transcendental (and many others in the crisscrossing of properties). Complex number ($\mathbb{C}$) are formed since real ones (and we already introduced them). Formalists are still in trouble about which set of numbers to start thinking, especially between natural ($\mathbb{N}$) and real numbers ($\mathbb{R}$).

Maybe this relevant to the necessary (?) incompleteness of formal sciences, "as extracted" from "exact sciences" of physics. It is in or more interesting with the "in-between and further" concept(s).

Summarizing complex numbers, some of you may know, provide imaginary or real solutions at ease; but "ascribed" to real numbers just with a $i^2 = -1$ which is quite useful for symmetry by anti-symmetry. Integer numbers easy to expand, from natural numbers by adding a sign. [Could the later relate to binary-ness? - (I am; I can exchange) were forcibly the 2nd term less than the 1st one (in relative rank?) ... Applying that too, to a combined population of (particles, field) ... and in similar ways (n in cardinals; n in orders)?].

Natural numbers are close to discrete. But if we want to use them with continuity, that may mean to have to consider 'segments' (unary vectors could be a form?). They also look like more 'quantic mechanics affines': developing dimensions since measure matrix (operating in linear calculus).

But profanes could be surprised about how it is difficult, to solve equations, exclusively in the same set of natural numbers ($\mathbb{N}$). This can have only of 2 unknown variables or more and/or considering 2 or more degree.

> Mathematicians have in effect, few clues at the respect. This general knowledge would be of good service. Consider intuitively that qualities, forms, Nature's unity or natural number prone. Just being able to make the formal rigorous contrast between natural only and other real algebra and so we could be sure to find in numbers the perfect concept among all and/or for all... Rather than an umbrella of abstract definitions more the nightmares of schoolchild manipulations.

> [Nevertheless this is an incentive, for treating the qualitative term as a semi-quantitative construction (number of units. sub-inner systems, essential subset, essential classes

between subsets; set of environments as phase-spaces) of numbered for example (5.555; 5) in the example of 5 in all ... this looks like '**games without chance**'].

Of course, many users of qualitative mathematics in social arts are full mouths with their numbers. Fine!–but, even if statistics are often robust and so may mean something (they have incorporated **degrees of confidence**, uncertainty and so on). Many experts often miss that those numbers have been obtained after many arbitrarily simplifying assumptions [... beginning with operations]. Thus requiring **facilitating assumptions** (normality, great numbers laws, 'urns' simulations ... for closing their arguments; but not the evidences of phenomenology which often reveal as **logical disturbances**.

This is fine but neither 'natural of physics'; nor impeccably in the qualities; nor in the proper relations of quantities. So what the meaning of amounts when operations have presumably been chosen? An often slight **informative indication**. Often too much over humans and apart legitimate affairs issues which are then too poorly scientific. They say something so it would be improper not to use them when collected and treated as possibly could be. Only some logics to be better off.

For simple observations, have better in mind: which special set of numbers you play in the 1st place (say the main natural for qualities) and the operations; and the real for quantities.

[If we could want to empower the small qualitative, log-part of information we will have to play more with **indices**, **ranks**, **orders**; and possibly **coefficients** ('weights'). There are more probabilities upon natural numbers].

In **polynomials** and **algebraic numbers** (from real numbers it is easier for finding a suspected characteristic number which is important to obtain). Have in mind that characteristic exponent is quantitative but sort of qualitative information in their behaviors: phase-space delimited by critical borders of speeds with critical changes, respect to value of the variable.

Algebraic numbers are complex numbers that satisfy a polynomial equation with **rational coefficients**. Similarly an algebraic integer is a complex number that satisfies a polynomial equation with integer coefficients. Provided the highest power coefficient of x is 1.

For each such polynomial we obtain an associated algebraic number field (meaning that you can add, subtract, multiply and divide such numbers. This is for obtaining a number of the same kind and; it is **a ring** (without division) of **algebraic integers** (from Steward a well-known popular British mathematician).

Chinese Boxes of Humans' Models

Have in mind that in social arts you need more logic and that with proper **graphs**, visual estimates are often enough (more important is your analysis ... unless you are a "perfect omnipotent, omniscient (miserable) dictator; exactly positioned, at the '**barycenter**' of the model's solutions.

Too many practical models consider their model some 'better than any alternative'; and so just like absolute truth. These models are used to influence the main decider after some self-interest; and care less that various actors need the possibility to adapt to their own perspective. **Model system** despite that fundamental denegation of service pretended to be a representation of what they can do... Out their implicit right of self-definitions one's operative concepts. Which anyhow reasonably will have to prevail (because the way they see their world).

'**Representations**' the model of anyone; so the reason why we say that most literature's models are self-theories under the point of view of a unique, maximally discriminating at the best point of perspective for that: the dictator like if at the barycenter (socially quite improper). Since the unconscious display of recalls and phenomenological evidence in the job; format a representation or model of operations and, possibly also derivable. If the actor has learned to **consciously disconnect, question and reformulate**. Better not to miss that perceptions are broader than about what conscious-ness can cope at the same time. Of course there is the sort of explicit formal model. We think about sort of aids more or less computed closer our future relationships with data bank respectful of cultural efficiencies. [Rather than shouting about occidental niceness and doing like if most cultures unfit. The modern dire stage of globalization?].

Physics model framework to approach better equations formulations. So the system of equations a proper one for a *calculus* of estimate. In social art model 1st better to anchor in a materialist framework provided by physics. And then possibilities of policies; that would purposely bias the main flows (since their margins) for some profitable diversion. It is to work with models (or representations) on **conditions** and **balances of good frameworks**. Sort(s) of models(s) that can be individuals and groups of intervention adapt-able.

It is not for making scientism established by analogies, the set of rules for the societies. The developments of the models have to reach the layers of the humane criteria '**entailed**' by materialist possibilities. Also Nature's mechanisms are harsh. So without ignoring them (they can be in the as constraints of phase-space); the humane condition intents to be smarter and nicer. Since the capitals of technologies are enough to provide to all and **ease adaptation**.

[Missing somehow the good properties of mechanical systems for conscious and unconscious learning. Compared to the electromagnetic ones much more: on-off, bugs and eventually electric discharge from a condenser or exposed cable.].

Mathematicians and physicians are with their specific things, poorly with social. And when they are, barely it is with their tools box. That is a critic: they are not enough in social technical support and too lost in teaching and administrative duties, away then they imagine. So they are not enough humanely involved, with their professional qualities... Teachers are too busy at boring students in calculus of impoverished logics. And engineers **too constrained by strength of commanding**; rather than supporting the soft authority of motivated learning by doing.

The evidences of successes in engineered works, look-like to self-support authority; but then authoritarianism turn to viciously circle on themselves so as to control over fundamental regulations. This does not mean that some techno-structures precisely need **pyramidal systems** and self-empowering authority. For some high in technology productions this is well needed. The problem being in that they are the only admitted model of management applied in anything and everything elsewhere.

In mathematics, any relation is also a case for treatment in 'an integrated way', and reason for investigation. Since its comprehensive ambition is often effectively substantial to rigorous treatment of levels. Even with applications not either "phenomenological" at first. But 'discretely pure mathematics'; may miss that the problem at the top is nabbed; either by **the limits of language** or by incompleteness.

Any language needs at least 4 elements so unary-ness of an abstraction could be treated by language. Whatever the side or the sub-register, when not unduly completed. So it can complete fundamental physics explanations. Or because it requires to be universally specifiable enough so by physics reality ... [or because God; imprecision is 'far before' the human limits of specialists...]

Systems,' comprehensive building has plenty of intertwining and complexities add emergences ... 'within' ... between discrete and continuous. Maybe it is to seek either empirical treatment as we said, **intervals**, kind of **probabilistic concepts** (since the probably more prone to discrete definitions of events or properties. This relates to a number, hardly only discrete treatment. It is at least with semi-quantitative ones and thanks to populations, **combinations, urns models, iterations,** there are plenty of "bizarre" comes-and-goes that can be simulated. **Games** what we had before.

Nature looks **like unable to carry excesses of complexities**; thus there are **economical ways to shortcuts**... Maybe the assumption of 'relative formal system' ... civilizations end because exhausted: by order(s) as well by disorder(s).

Purists often debate of that. But **large amounts may have great numbers laws to smooth that statistically** ... and so reduce the violence of the debate. Debates have been very harsh between **frequentists** statisticians (accounting of frequency in an idea of true exact proportions) and conditioned probabilities (**Bayesian** partisans: probability of an event 'respect-after' another one). [We will see these concepts, from a philosophical point of view in the 2nd volume of this essay].

Relations Between Sets of Numbers

So, more by the side of 'good mathematics' you have: between **discreteness** (more of natural numbers but not only of) and **continuity** (more real numbers), means of **functions** that could bridge both sets. It is still to clear the theories such as between **elliptic functions** and **rational roots** and possibly also with **Riemann ζ (zeta) function**.

This latter function is so formulated $\zeta(s) = 1/1^s + 1/2^s + 1/3^s +$ ... where s is a natural number; s=1 gives the (divergent) **harmonic series**; s=2 gives the sum of the reciprocal, of the squares; by Euler summed as $\pi^2/6$, etc. This series **converges** for every real value of s>1 indeed, for every complex number.   s=x+iy   In the half-plane x > 1. This defines an analytic function, everywhere in the complex plane, except for the point on the real axis: s = 1. Also Gamma function [Γ (f.)] another of importance has similarities with.

This function is **analytic (solvable by finite development series**) in the half plane. Elsewhere (in the other half plane), the infinite series does not even converge. With this function it may be possible to find a formula involving complex integrals; that is, not looking at all like the series $\zeta(s)$ and that agrees with $\zeta(s)$ in the half-plane x> 1.

[Concept of half (incomplete) cut something very interesting (more than full cut. If you cut all of you partition) ... We should be very interested in not pretending that only mass and no energy at all; or not exactly separated biological function from biostructure... Relation is also to establish with the concept of the partition ... since the number of n = 2^n].

Meta-Philosophy of Numbers

Care that many sub-something, like a **subset** are pieces having same properties of the whole (set for the case). So sub-something is not apart but less than the self-capacities (?) [And related defined operations: the whole needs to maintain as far as possible its integrity].

There are also concepts of class or **category** that may be different or in relative plans. Thus operations... It is basic not to shortcut too narrowly a living body with its "organs", that make the function distributed anywhere un-systemic. [Maybe to consider in a set subset of essential set concept; and classes 'of the set specific whole'. Applying in subset, the set and at the border ... does this make sense to openness?].

Logics of numbers properties are basic. That the professionals do not care about ... the proper ways to manage them more explicitly. Missing, in the same way that these subtle details are also **phenomenological but 'excluded from considerations'**. We think that there should or could be essential for identification(s) to fundamental realities frameworks. In the concept of formal sciences effectively modeling realities.

That is to say: if common **citizens are not to be enslaved by automatic 'intelligent' systems**; nor to mediocre 'interfacers' of computed systems. Programs that will have to translate for humans will and learned by experience; into criteria as the expression of **computer-aided modeling** will need sort of complementary frameworks. [Could be that a major for cloud computing?].

Basic logics of formalism have to turn more **epistemologies of core practices**. Like for working on **degrees of specifications**, and **representations of levels of uncertainty**. Further than, once **generic solvable models**, in the 2nd step proper formulations and systems of equations, will require local specifications for solutions. That is supportive of epistemologies to develop for having better propaedeutic (not starting by the formula with everyone).

Sorts of formal concepts relevant to numbers theory may need to know: **transcendental** (you "need to 'start at them and roots' them–**square root, cubic**

roots, etc. reaching an **infinite series**); **irrational numbers** (not as a ratio of 2 integer numbers which are **rational numbers**).

They deserve to be known in brief and logically hope they are forms: with enormous amounts of stocks (of resources); it would not be a problem; but computers are running after scale of high numbers and. with such sorts of 'crazy calculus'; better to know why your computer gets locked-in, by logical mistakes, lack of understanding; on how a number is obtained [... No physics amounts of quanta with infinite numbers after the point (or the coma) or got your numbers by "laziness" (**truncation** if formal)].

> Human beings' consciousness is more robust: their number of neurons is enormous but their scale of convergence since almost unable to remind more than 7 words of a list, at a time, eared 3 minutes ago (because saturation of channels). Nevertheless brains are incredibly robust and flexible towards, **always new, situations**.

Transcendental numbers were discovered because trying to find the quadrature or the circle: simple relation between a square and a circle both of same area required √2. As a result this was not solvable just using a ruler and a compass.

Irrational numbers cannot be expressed by a division of 2 natural numbers or those for which decimal development observed an end or having a periodic form. Irrational numbers (non-rational) are infinite. π, Euler's **e**, golden number (a/b = a/(a+b)) and √ 2 are of this sort. π and **e** are also transcendental. There is a close relation between ($\pi$and **e** via trigonometric functions. π is not easy to calculate by geometric finite means.

All rational numbers are algebraic in the sense that p/q can be the solution of qx–p = 0. Most can be approached by rational expression. [Whence the question about their nature: if such numbers point at 'holes'? -Solution of continuity is in the scale of numbers or barriers to some 0 or infinite representations].

What is important is not the 'touristic' label of the number, evoked after to dress up their magic. But the way they are obtained; how difficult it is to switch from one kind of reference says a: **Euclidean** one to a **polar** one, and so on.

This is important at any levels of human's mind; once out the vanity of self-appearance, all in oneself. Other common are necessary to stay. For example, **hiddenness of causality** is an oxymoron of all time. That should not summarize excessively the scientific approaches [even if finding it also in quantum theory]. Probability is consistent, even in numbers].

> For example: you may appreciate being round shaped and soft; despite our weakness of flesh. Meanwhile having endoskeleton instead of the exoskeleton of a king crab. The last was appropriated for some cold underwater hence not for colonizing 'freely.' Then the function of skeleton structure assumed with options (the endo or the exo) with probability made by fields. Schrödinger's equation, such an expression. There are plenty of other examples in biology, provided the evolutionary processes of economics selection open to diversity. We will see further some visual importance of that.

Hamiltonians, **octonions** are kinds of numbers formed with complex numbers. They have **matrix expressions** of 4 or 8 reference axes. Diverse component parts or joined 2 or 3 objects may use them as more or less rigid objects (taken as a whole). With **symmetries,** conjugates or **pairings.** They can be solved as well as operated with so-called operators like differential.

These numbers are of necessary use in physics; could they represent the formal head or *nucleus?* - of principles on which to hook further hairy expansions? **Matrix algebra** especially support the physics inner algebra of linear space (**Clifford algebra**) or **anti-commutative Lie algebra** of some **Lie Groups**.

It is good to know about their existence. They are fundamentals of realities. Then for the scientific or not readers to expect that if software will do the job. Some choices still within the possibilities of '**licenses authorized machines**'. If you want to maintain those systems open to humane choice and keep private-social freedom.

Probably you will have to use similar sorts (matrix driven) as a **system of preference definition.** This is for keeping an eye on the 'responsibility and justice' or 'efficiency in fairness'. With a systemic perspective: this can make more important interactive displays, **geometric forms**, etc. Then to imagine that the capacity to specify conditions, provide better shared explicated by programs. Or, with more intuitive interactions to tell and detail, obtain returns from the computer on the screen and as forms and patterns. So that you can learn relations between made and reviewed.

In simulations, you will be proposed to them, and will manipulate, with kinds of **algebra groups**, eventually detected (by the computer); as implicit in your choice. Computer programs operate that and **feed-back up for license**, consensus (of social groups up to enough society) or agreements.

The **real artificial intelligence** of the machine is not to provide you with just one solution but with **some feasible options** and **minimum constraints** to observe, **parameters of modulations,** 'last say **buttons**. Thus programs making use of formal mechanics; or for making better use of them. Without full need to know all that. Even if just abstract representations. They have to communicate and inform you 'phenomenologically'.

We advocate here for **more** than **intelligent aids,** that is letting you more efforts. Not to free you from tasks of thinking and decision. Also to be made more phenomenological. More as aids for conceiving models well anchored in the realities; rather than have pure and smart intelligence for socially wasting in bureaucracy.

Functions

Their fundamental forms are increasingly clear "*nucleus*" **differentiable forms,** groups of concepts; 'plastic solids'); **parametric equations** (solutions expressed according a parameter which is most often times (to revise?); **algebraic equation** (allowing unique and finite series developments; solutions-functions having polynomial expressions and series expressions which finiteness provides easy algorithms or programed calculi for unique, unambiguous solution.

All sorts of important animals in the mathematics bestiary. They are essential in the investigations of solutions and proper formulations. Even if you will not make de calculi by yourself; you will have to understand what you are seeking with the formula, where your research, what to expect. Like when expressing a given statistically recorded phenomenon to formulate (the job of **numerical analysis** in mathematics). To investigate **characteristics values** is after a theory and/or a model delimit estimates. Then possibly imagine an experimental device or indicate a phenomenon where such characteristic plays a role. Make an application or a calculus re-using a formula under new conditions within tolerated limits. Estimate what should be convenient to your application and handling. Select some technique(s) of calculus or algorithm to obtain the estimate you need.

> A professional mathematician may be too specialized, for knowing enough **best logical option frameworks;** that involves like demographics and ecological, and sort of human activities and the criteria of **games, options, rules, conditions** and **choice** to apply. Alas, there are the common abuses of competition, individualism, antagonism, sectarian struggles and cooperation mismanagement; which narrows sophisticated uses of formal helps overqualified. When these have not even been dedicated more to abuses.

> Hence democratic cooperating ones, have mostly been just nice and farcical weaknesses. So, important is the information on precautions wise communications and proper information... Only the Leviathan Golem-like of political economic management have been fed by technocracies. So they have infarcted of stupid stuff and exclusive narrowness. When they should help to introduce criteria and arbitration (including collective ones).

> In physics sciences (and related clean formal ones); **characteristic discontinuities** (or solutions of continuity) are left down (to fundamental denial of understanding) or right (up to higher complexities paralyzed by the word and the symbol of techno-political buffoons' rattles).

[Where rays and gaps of rays are: undetectable or absent ('*vacuum*'); so discrete and at some position(s). The certainty is the order on the situation of the ray, the uncertainty would be the disorder in the gap, but the probability of a switch from one side to another ... thus eventually reversible at life expectation...

The relative universe-universal irreversibility of the principles is driven by the main largest life particles?–and some looking like irreversibility of inner emergences? Emergences observed within cooler-colder conditions as patterns and 'ghosts' forms' from the 'divisions' into forces? ... To add cooler at the margins of big orderings: gravity made? ...

> [Mind that a ghost as a frameworks coping with many particles permuting, disappearing, exchanges, even at colder slower rates of molecules in solids and liquids (whatever the suits you wear) can still be enough thumping for hurting and shocking]

It looks like Nature's succeeded in staying open ... without fixing too much (closing) since the start.

> Another major concept: about the way largest fields to the 'thinnest', especially on the borders made of γ 'articles' energy granules; enough in masses in and on outer-borders for largest field?]

Thus where are the **critical limits of kinetic *media*** (kind or mix of behaviors) tracked by **phase-diagram**: loop(s) on abrupt changes? Where calculus of forces present on both sides has to be 'renormalized' [An important calculus technique would be to catch the **jumps of scale, or big steps discretization**?]. On a continuous *spectrum*, lack of numbers, **pivotal, cuts, points of inflections, tipping points** and interruptions. Fields probably there as **caustics**?

Fields are too commonly imagined 'statics' [Not so in physics reality? Supposedly nature hates emptiness. Maybe some concept of the system is to think of a sort of 'inner and outer motions' as well as their reason. You movement because pushed or pulled or propelled or because for **maintaining** or **expand, or evolve**. And all that is not for just one reason but also for (informatively?) slightly moving your probabilities. Also you have to slow down because **friction, disordering, shocking,** or restore, or rest or switch from 'out' to 'inner'; transformations as critical transitions].

[For some examples:
- 4 fundamental forces (strong interaction $_{nuclear}$; weak interaction $_{nuclear\ instability-}$ electric $_{moving\ magnetic\ charge}$; gravity $_{mass}$); fundamental pairs particle-fields, submitted to probabilistic switches of existence-disintegrations; between 'whole superimpositions' (?) to inner coexisting fields (thus the "*vacuum*" is 'in' and stay 'out' too);
- Discrete specified levels of relative stability energies (rays and between gaps including interferences; electronic orbitals and empty layers; quantic jumps ... provided by the jumps);
- Physics domains of existence with behavior defining critical properties; allowed as space-phases; defined environment (and 'black-layers' of space and spaces processes of filling-coalescence, layers of catchment and thick evolving fringes).

> Get in down (levels of energies) but higher (in complexities) joining and ordering; for sweeter matter

- Chemistry:
- Imposed energy thresholds of characteristic reactions, common to the support of force itself or characteristically "lower emerged", form dimensional factors (cooling sub-diversifying in narrower places);
- At high levels of 'structuring', entropy has weaker probabilities of expression; 'netgentropy' maximum when free or potential energy is 'optimally' divided;
- At low levels of 'structuring', entropy components represent kinetic energy prevailing; it corresponds to maximum probability (commonness); 'netgentropy' depending on the levels of environmental organizations heterogeneity ("agglutination") and localized kinetic driven interactions.

> Rather than neguentropy, we prefer the (characteristic?) balance 'netgentropy' of this ordering-disordering crossed neguentropy-entropy ... when they match (thus formal-able, as above ... but not exactly identified).

Chemistry 'within' evolve by sharing, volunteering and producing secondary levels of same sorts of forces, making the universe in nuclear physics, fundamental chemistry, mineral chemistry: covalence, ionization:

- Organic Chemistry structural evolution (van Der Waals forces, hydrophilic/hydrophobic...);
- Macro-chemical Systems (*ex post* building pieces, once there are enough amounts they will meet and be selected).

1. 'Advanced Systems'
   o Micro-molecules: they catch the resources of chaining: by molecules electronic sharing covalent, polymerization and stabilizing fluid ordering (mainly water because ambiguous);
   o Plane-folder space catches the possibilities of membranes, interface opportunities (of exchange and thickness diversification), and plane ordering;
   o The macromolecules catch the volume space possibilities of incorporation, inner developments within variations of the environmental conditions smooth enough.

2. Self-replicating macromolecules bio-precursors

- Biology
  - Living beings intercept entropy flows. They use lower-entropy sources of energy (but economically good when closer to their levels of structure) and produce locally structures and overall higher potential dis-entropic forms. Meanwhile as possibly as sustainably lesser marginally releasing (integrity modulating openness);
  - There are maximum levels of self-maintaining functions; requiring to cover the minimum and have margins for a bit more (obtained by smooth fluctuations of the environment);
  - Levels of dynamic functions also maintain basal structural level balanced with opportunistic or obliged functional levels;
  - System expansion of unary-integration and regulation: local levels specialized development; integration made by interactions and propagation of most economical solutions & main alternatives (for robustness); consolidation of homeostasis; development and consolidation of unary-ness of regulation specialized development (neural system, vascular system, ability to self-sacrifice (for example apoptosis: as mechanisms of evolution, repair or "suicide");
  - Pathological overtaking of physiology, with co-evolutionary development (as ways to reverse and balance signs;
- Ecology
  - pivotal threshold of under-renewal (run to extinction);
  - pivotal threshold of environmental, overbearing population pulsations.

[Continuity-discontinuity of life respect to physics not really, the media provides an environment of possibilities. This is for selecting in increased complexity evolutionary processes. The ones that succeed in looping; on to themselves. Not just because they are struggling and fighting but for moving the netgentropic cursor towards 'neguentropy' or construction...

In other words, reduce the probabilities of destruction anyhow 'propelled' by entropy ... with relative irreversibility useful ... in the same concept of good mass-matches in good vibrations?]

Sorts of principles and similarities; across levels of scale which are; by specification's developments and intrications. It is to observe that many concepts cross the levels present sorts of versions 'avatar'. Without caring exactly with the fixing of minds made by words, satisfying similar functions. It is not necessarily exactly the same components; as those that prevailed in the levels of lower or higher levels. That makes the job of the natural scientists to establish the sort of 'open to reversion fixations'. That is made at its levels and the mainframes are maintained (in the similar continuity of the 'principles' of lower level(s)) and for the satisfaction of some essential functions.

There qualifying the economics of the evolutionary processes: alternatives, options appear if required. Where possible and they are maintained if 'economically' (in the natural unconscious way) in the co-evolution. Have some time or delay of adjustments, 'rationalization' (in the natural unconscious way) and the 'system' can 'stabilize' in the periodicities or rhythms required by its maintaining. No need of life in all that, but life in this solution of relative continuity can be a pivot or threshold where in principles, natural allowances and environmental conditions processes of replication; specified informing structures are incorporated and ease the auto-reproduction of complex frameworks.

Continuity then an essential concept where its proper framing in physics may not have the Cartesian common use, which is a 100% as imagined by simple mathematics but let put it there because a landmark in the pathway. Pictorially probably to conceive it more is sort of spiraling. Also having to account? Some forms of fractals or combination with smooth fractal?] For forms as variations (complex numbers approach provided increasing-decreasing (varying) *modulus* That is continuity after discrete pieces. Like 'pearls laced by fundamental principles'.

Smooth fractal (after Borelli) concept has its source in Nash's work. This made use of isometric immersion in Riemannian variety (1854) [This Riemannian variety concept turned the space of a framework of Einstein curved space time of relativity]. Nash shown that there are many isometric immersions of such Riemannian varieties. Kuiper shown that is an infinity in the case of flat *tori*. To understand: the flat *torus* it is necessary to immerge in a 3 dimensioned space. To obtain it, make a flip and glued surface is closed (Möbius strip mechanism). This has the inconvenient to distort the distances.

Gramov connex integration made these smooth. (He was inspired by Nash and Smale sphere's turn inside-out). Connex integration is based on homotopy theory. Borelli made the algorithm allow to visualize connex integrations. It is obtained by the way 'corrugations' (from the short immersion) but these stay smooth; so it is turning a smooth fractal.

Could? **Smooth fractals–spirals–fractals** a tripod of similar to **log-straight** line **symmetry- exp** we are inspired by?

Now, back to something 'safer'? The continuity concept in theory of numbers.

 Continuity hypothesis: whatever the set A, the family of A's parts: P (A) has a cardinal: card (P (A)) > card (A). The card ($\mathbb{N}$) is $\aleph_1$ it is the same as of the set of real numbers ($\mathbb{R}$). The (undemonstrated) hypothesis of continuity, says that there is no cardinal between $\aleph_0$ and $\aleph_1$. In general if a whatever set does not admit any cardinal $\aleph$ such as $\aleph(A) < \aleph < \aleph (P (A))$ which is the generalized hypothesis of continuous. So **continuity cannot be demonstrated in the theory of set**.

Continuity in fundamental physics links to:
- Cantor cardinals of set theory;
- infinite 'box in piling of intervals';
- Bell's infinitesimal nillpotence.

[Of course the reader has to mind that what we have picked in the literature is essential but on which we do not have 'full' mastership, neither we have, in most technicalities of this essay. Our epistemological legitimacy is about what we need for society evolve better. Thus some sentences are open questions to self-research which are now very easy. Massive online knowledge sources require sense of synthesis and links opened by key-words

... not-crypto dictator fake leaders nor crypto club-selective true fascists; empowered by stupid ownership rights and disastrous robber-baron managers].

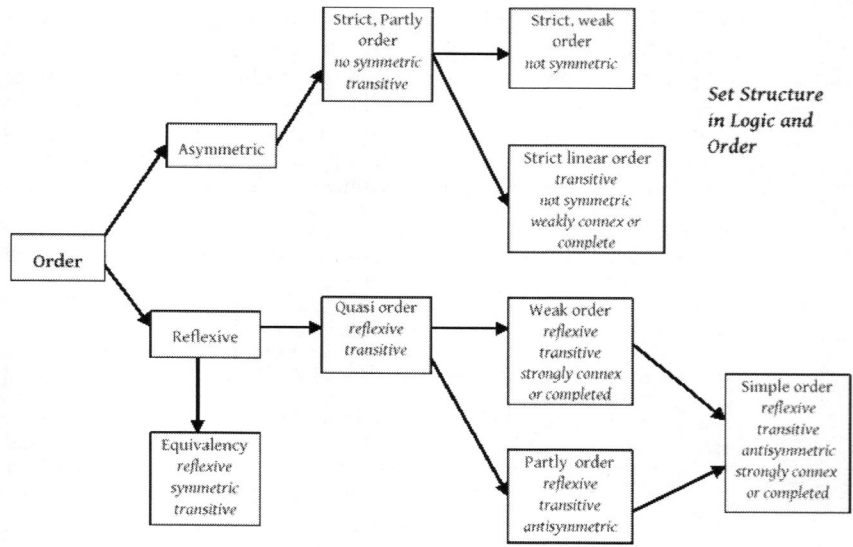

Set Structure in Logic and Order

When you speak about physics, with mathematics properly specified; their formulations should reflect the universality of physics principles. On one side the universality and the other the structured frameworks it looks like using accompanied with the metalanguage about for human understandings. How this can be represented by the means of abstraction: formulation, on a sheet of paper and **scriptures 'transducing' the cognate perceptions** of those having employed that they are dedicated to study and the way to explain and transmit that?

Now about the structures frameworks. This is expressed as 'invariant'. **Invariant as universal physics principles** indifferent in their conditions to the positive language used to qualify them by those thinking in abstractions made of derivations, possibly in other pathways but with same sources as physics principle? Invariant are so-called when mathematical transformations are not affecting principles: whatever the referring (valid) system principle is there.

[There is a sense of indifference combination (mathematical transformations: **local abstract**), neutrality of expression (mathematics: **global of abstract**), entertainment of meaning (universality of physics principles considered: **global of physics**) and shaping development (invariant as signified; **locals of physics**). Not to miss that this is mediated by the ink on the sheet of paper, but about significant-signified].

To consider since the beginning, if you system of reference is "external" respect to the object under study, with the study's dimensions of interest. So often called in physics terms 'extensive parameters'. In thermodynamic, basically you have as **extensive parameters the temperature, pressure and volume.** [Have in mind that thermodynamic about physic formalism approach of experimented systems consider broadly complex macro-devices] ... Thus main axis of reference in physics is often these. Then they put human bodies in such abstract devices... [But scientists, when sane, do not crush them for the experiment purpose, at least intentionally].

Parallelism between Thermodynamic and Inductive Logic		
	Gas thermodynamics	Inductive Model *H*- ÷
Correlations to consider are of primitive terms	particles, particle state, elements of state space, complexion or microscopic state and macroscopic state. 2 complexions belonging to the same macroscopic state	individual, individual state, universe description. distribution description, 2 universe description belonging to the same distribution description, i.e. 2 universe description are isomorphic
Correlation to make are about entropy and irregularity	thermodynamic probability w(s) (or configuration number). that is for: a macroscopic state, entropy; reciprocal of entropy	isomorphism measure i' (d); distribution description, irregularity, uniformity.
Correlation of thermodynamic 2nd law and random inductive logic	each microscopic state, has the same prior probability, the macroscopic state. If highest entropy is the most probable second law of thermodynamics.	each universe description has the same prior probability, the distribution description of greatest irregularity is the most probable, random inductive logic.

162

Elsewhere, in mathematics approaches of physics, the start has been more neutral and the systems of reference for graphics; have been **space** and **time**. Space was easy somehow at the start with 3 dimensions. But already there was different possible systems of reference: from **outside** or **inside**, **centered** or **by the side**, etc.

The original basic tools (first architects of most civilizations) have been the compass and the ruler; directly inspired designs and drawings but in human histories they 'soon also' have shown that they were not absolutely infinitely simple. Humans have been asking like for if any geometric architectural sketching could just use only these 2 tools. And just that started the first steps of arithmetic logic. To which abstract extent can simplify the tools of the architect in more universal geometrical properties: anticipations of shapes evidence. Without ignoring that nature were providing almost all these, be only as a visual illusion.

But further, does the choice of reference system primaries in basic physics geometry necessarily has to be the simplest way? – Whence impossibly the just one before your level of complications? The formal representation follows that and may face phenomenological difficulties in practice of analytical precision, when to be taken in charge by mathematical formulations. Mathematics formulations used systems of coordinates, in the space, time in many applications of arts and even in complex sciences without much consistent referential qualities.

Back to invariant concept: so transformations of systems of coordinates should not affect the expression of physical principles. Care that invariance not as easy as a 'word under the eyes' some artifacts, that is extra-effect produced by the system of reference, not consistent with the phenomenon, create illusions. It is a shame when these just come from simple geometrical transformations. Just meaning the failure of modern systems of education. [How so many people just do not want to get there but judge since where they are?]. But they are many other subtle complex situations with absurd complications.

In the subjective approaches as in the "objective" ones of sciences; either without proper theory upon a simple phenomenon, or with more complicated issues; all thinking make representations and models: cognitive and then more or less shared.

Neurosciences new imaging techniques of imaging are able to provide with pictures of brain activities, harmless, after some tasks of simulations. Conscious cognitions cannot keep everything on the narrow mainstreaming. So precisely what would be universal there in cognition?–If not an abstract more or less fitting, generally formalized and many conditioning and valid precautions; of 'un-implied' by the model. Remaining specifications provided by realities?

Formulations must show "special phenomenon" as "special" and universal as universal, but should be obliged intertwining have to care the appearance of causality and effects. On one left side (of equality's sign) the formula and its structural forms. Terms of models should consider (in coherence with our suggestions). If we want it to vary at its level with general solvability, we need the level characteristics number properties have the same minimum relative base (0, 1) and if on a trajectory a main one. If we want it to be volume meaning we need 3 dimensions and considering general unit should be 'intertwined' if dimension combine and geometrically compact and show the form or object some broad convexity. So as to simplify to 3 maximum degree, maximum of 3 variables, maximum of 3 remaining coefficients relations and so on.

Then it is to consider the formal tools to study the representation. Respect of the forms regularities and that from the irregularities. In mathematical graphs of **physical objects motions; trajectories** are often called to reach **singularities** or **bifurcations**, when at some points, there is more than one direction (of tangent). There, of course, the first questions about their local universality. What do they mean to the physics records or representing functions, simulations or phenomenologically when meeting sort of irregularities or extraordinary natural phenomena.

Transitions expressed by these singularities, bifurcations, maybe **coarse** or vary in a **smooth** way. If following crossing a point of inflection like with left and right (or before and after) tangent stay smooth (locally progressive), if not the same at the point of the geometric object under scope. Or having 2 (or more?) different directions of derivations at a point of one curve (left or right in the best discriminating plane). Formally we need to be more precise a trajectory does not need to only be in a "neutral" space. But before telling more about singularities, so kind with our-self unit or exceptionalism, we need to understand some of the forms for approach.

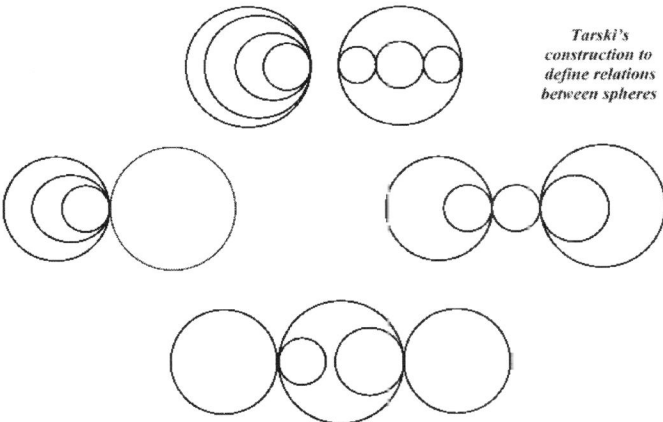

Tarski's construction to define relations between spheres

Phase-Space the Core Link of Medium

Phase-space apprehend the speed respect to the point of motion, it can show different **types of speeds**, after position of a point within a region partitioning the space. Region shows **different kinds of speed regimes** or phase-space. Space is delimited by **characteristic reason of speed**(s). Thus, between **critical interfaces** (lines, in the 2 dimensions of the graph, manifolds in the 3 dimensions) you meet with inequalities in the borders of the regime's description; where values vary a lot. On one side a regime, on the other another. It is easy to imagine with the traditional of physics. For example, with speed or motion: you do not have the same regime of speed when falling in the air or swimming in a pond. Put all those characteristics; 'at the maximum of the universe (one-self relative formal system and 'absolute' constituting universe formal system ... and there you have something fundamental ... for the time life of relative system), that you find both in the cosmos of solar system as in the tiniest fundamental particles of yourself.

It is to understand that in physics: each area correspond to a certain phase, for example solid, liquid and gas. Other used parameters (for characterizing) are: temperature, pressure and volume. Values **given inequalities of characteristics combinations**, or **parameters ratios; delimit the space of the phases**. Phenomenologically you know well that any point either part or intruder will not have the same speed whether it is in the solid, the liquid or the gas [if you do not understand: try to fly in a solid or to swim in gas ... being yourself a solid human].

[Physics observe **many more kinds of phases**; some easier to deduce from our lived experience, others less, we obtained them in the conditions of the experiment.].

Thus to retain that the phase-space graph can show the characteristic separations of media kinds (respect to their external parameters) and then to consider the number of phases that can be **graphed**: bi- or 2-phase, 3-phases...

[To observe that in some way globalization with massive new means of information and communication have put in evidence that the phenomenologies of humans societies phase-space almost unconsciously analytically ignored before in their way of social structuring, it was taking month to get there and as a result a someone at the command as leader where depending on the smooth or rude way; of the interpretation of the messenger. Would be the way to govern carving or sculpting all that; most with disgusting progress civilization aesthetics.

Actually behind screens can operate or should intervene at the instant of the glance; when none have even an idea of what is the sort of local types of social-economical regimes that make sustainable development; but the potential to intervene just on time. Commonly no more than cut, dissimulate de evidence and destroy].

More details of such phase-space framing. Like for characterizing ecosystems and other places that could be subject to approach can be harder to put in evidence and, in the meantime, less 'fundamental' (but more humanely meaningful to the maximum achieved complexities, in local environment types of regimes).

But there have been enormous literature for providing with the knowledge of the sciences, only relevant to very few specialists. Norms have been made for specific cases of environmental health. Not quite with the sort of essential method consisting in making clear in any mind that the **characteristic relative variation of a parameter to itself can be critical** to some operations or recommendations. In economics this was the prospect of elasticities variations of supply or demand in quantities or qualities respect to prices or between switch-able goods. Dynamic analysis there prospered and go on with more abstract but profitable concepts, hence not to imagine these respect to more physics realities anchors, like environments. So implicitly many things exist, but do not ask if all this gets into formalized systemic expression.

Also interesting local conditions are those potentially more complex closer to humans' management. Quite often the *focus* is at interfaces of nearby dynamic regimes. This is harder to analyze. So we are with combinations of 2 or 3 kinds of regimes at the same time; or mixtures.

Any farmer knows that dry soil with no water nor aeration nor organic mixture with kinds of minerals makes poor land. The questions behind are simply cognitive economy of formalism what are the basic of forms to know, as universal for sharing how to do with no more intromission in others' business but the externalities potential evidence.

Have all that a fundamental under your 'scope' record, and then you can understand. Put this 'that' in blurred media of human societies. Where you can do both, during your journey go walking and fly. Whomever are your crews; it is a bit more difficult to observe principles... Out the fact that you will crash if your plane face deep troubles without convenient solutions on their relative formal 'shuttle' system. Thus just patterns? - to explore carefully.

We may make plenty of mistakes, just running after ghosts (patterns) especially if 'fake'. Insist that your ghost does not mix with others' ones (like of different cultures). And even if having done your best specialized investigations and careful models' constructions; they will have 'much and many' probabilities. At **least to catch enough reflects for not being deluded in your own room of mirrors**.

Hence to avoid glimpsing and recycle your conceptual and methodological mistakes... For not turning a compulsive killer any for that? ... Just because the glimpse' is no more than an argument for private profit. Or that of ideal mind whom react more to the lack of principles and; lack of care of evidence? This, without having ever tried to anchor your systems of reference, in better principles. Than those of macro-technocrat of details of the norms of rules; obscene obese capitalist of my grab; or a crypto-stupid socialist of the ignored environments, of the people; or the right duties of a religious paradise crazy ticket dealer. Do not pretend any of these reasons and the 'rationality'. Feel free to do good social care not as professional nor anti-professional and care **not to call your everything principles and truer principles deny**.

It seems to us that most social well-inspiring principles, formally often in the theoretical mathematical economics; can often receive a more physical interpretation only adapting words and concepts.

In a sort of feed-back from Walras to Piccard (the meca-mathematician that inspired the economist). Care then, to reformulate the conventional or consensual; after observing the conceptual account which is due to true principles of physics, especially with thermodynamics grounds. Remaster also concepts of value (and prices) respect to information.

Back-pedal does not mean necessarily you have to get ride of any kind of money and financial system. But possibly have shadow-price systems to compare with the records of, properly anchored, markets. You will have to design subsidiaries: regulations, interventions, incentives and taxes after the discrepancies between: thermodynamics kind of information (netgentropy?) for fair prices systems.

Back to phase-space regions, somehow it is to consider also **interfaces** with other intermediate *medium*-media... But at different **scales' level of dimension** ... and division of forces... In physics plenty of 'bizarre phenomenological evidences exist:

capillary force, frictions... Probably up (or down) to the atomic level? To mention for example the magnetic force respect to electric force. They come together but because moving electric charge produces magnetism (and 2 kinds of magnetisms?) ... So magnetism is just a **force byproduct** of an electric charge? Another important one with gravity and Coriolis' force from moving masses... Anything seems to spin off and such concept may apply to the near most fundamental scale? ... Or an indication for shaping the formal *modulus* of systems or at the interface between?– Details that have been mentioned in a sort of physics's philosophic essay by Repchenko (a Russian physicist, with a heterodox conception of fields)].

> Examples of **critical states** from physics are of a ferro-magnet (i.e. how fast it loses its magnetism above its "critical temperature"). This problem in usual thermodynamics proves impossible to solve, even by approximation methods, since 1st principles. So one calculates the **critical exponent of a 4-dimensional** magnet and **analytically continues the solution from dimension 4 to dimension 3.**
>
> [Physics' state transitions appear at a **temperature of compromise**, where the **contrary influences of coupling tend to order a system** and; when thermal fluctuations have same range: an abnormal distribution for the resulting statistical fluctuations is induced. Technically it is to use what is called a **(formal) group of renormalization**s can help to explain that].

[With that turns fundamental? – Thus it is not to do anything a new force. But identify the **generation of 'avatars' at different scales' levels** for a given primary kind of force and define relatively if one or the other phenomenon emergence. That would be just as an 'avatar' at a smaller narrow scale. **Critical transitions** are formally suffering **infinite projections'**. That could be treated by **renormalizations**; methods for calculus estimates able to get ride off infinity terms. Or we would have just 'another kind' of emerging phenomenon. Whether it is an enough 'relative system' ... or is just a pattern by the side of the road.

> [For example we may call transiently a cumulonimbus (a type of 'structured' cloud) a relative system but not; one of its thunders a relative system ... as it was in *Zeus's* executive will (a guy with that drone of an electric type].

Formally this observes the basic link, within a phase-space. The one reflecting the *nucleus*: [(variable); (differentiate $_{variable}$)]. Thus often these conditions the kinds of behavior: stable/non-stable. This is very important. This formula 'catch a relative step.' Have the precaution to imagine that differentiate variable is one respect to itself. Logically not necessary. Thus respect to another either of difference to a characteristic value (d $(x-x_0)$, or a parametric equation.

Put at the front an integral such as...

$$\int a_0 x^n .dx \qquad \text{With dx possibly} \sim \log_{base} x?$$

... And you have a coefficient, integration and derivation with an exponent (... and the variable) capability. Almost all what you need. Think more philosophically about simple symbolic expression and you will understand that it should not be about magic from anything.

Another sort of important space would be just the **macro-system represented point**. You have both the **effective trajectory** as those potential past (like the solid angles projection at the moment: t-1. Notice that the statistics of atoms make that various trajectories can be orderly followed.

[Have more clever in mind vectors space traditional all vectors parallel for the ease of the calculus (linear vector space). But since a pole, which is ordering the vectors centripetal of centrifugal; all nearby vectors either diverging since pole of converging to pole].

Between random-wise statistics or differential exact-wise calculus or models. We have many **mixed possibilities** but: because our modeling is not so neutral. We cannot find best simple criteria for any like that because we pretend. It is as Smith said quite close to the concept of empathy. [And he never said that this was inconsistent and only have to be despised when judging]. In social issues like econometric practice specialists find something in the **middle of their scale**. But still are very poor at the extremities margins of change. To 'obtain true' they are prone to **narrow their window** (and that of others) at their will, Focus or calibrate their scales. They can 'have something' helpful to build a logical system. But this often in social terms turns weird to reality without vacillation. Unable to care and predict 'anomalies' not even serving paradigms at a time that sustainability is more in their fluidity.

Consider particles, the mixture of fundamental ones at atomic level of reaction are properties and, maybe, of quarks. May their fields, support mixtures of these particles?

[As it is shown, by rays' interferences? - entanglement is linking pairs' fate somehow?-whatever the distance). To consider with fundamental particles-field switches (local intermediating de-intrication?–Have that away intricated particles. 1st system to be resigned to its desintrication, to recover theirs common?].

> The phenomenon in which a change in a so-called **"order parameter"** causing a qualitative change (from one regime to another) in the systems' dynamic behaviors is called a '**bifurcation**'.

Bifurcations or Singularities, Region's Borders of Phase-Space

The mathematical description of a bifurcation is called a 'normal form'. Which is a differential equation representing the time evolution of the order parameter, given the value(s) of a 'control' parameter(s). [Formal control parameter does not mean you can actually control it ... deterministically. More probably you will 'move the balance toward something that at best can be another balance not too poor].

A generic property of systems that evolve in space, is that **the time is a generic perturbation**. Which, not only amplifies with time, but also propagates in space. For so, to generalize a co-mobile **Lyapunov's exponent** (this one is a mono-dimensional characteristic coupling). [Thus Lyapunov exponents are used for exploring catastrophic or **non-linear behaviors**]. Coupling may apply for 'state before' and 'state after' [and you may be interested that your 'state before' is not so different. At least self-identified ... avoiding **metamorphosis** as your state after. The term "your" is the "**coupling**"].

Singularities (point of bifurcation) as functions are continuous but non-bijective (irreversible) in time's case [The 'after' and the 'before' that is bijective account for both after and before equal: reversible]. Full classification of simple singularities uses **Dynkin's diagrams**. **Theory of catastrophes** has been evidenced by Thom (a French mathematician), in its natural generality, identifying 7 **standards of bifurcations** in the fifties and sixties (of the 20th century).

Theory of singularities in smooth applications was initiated by Whitney (inspired by Morse). Morse (1925) showed that the topology of a smooth compact variety can be reconstructed in a **combinatorial** way; since the study of the critical point (fibers singularities); from an 'enough **auxiliary' function.**

A **Theory of dynamic bifurcations** has been proposed by Andronov (with sources from Poincaré). Bifurcation pattern is universal pattern. As **combination of final state diagrams**. Periodic windows look like large (domain of interest), reach a maximum width then decreases. For example, **pitchfork**s **model** of bifurcations, leads to **logistic equation** [f (x)=r (x) (1-x)]; a very natural basic equation (saturating).

Diagrams of bifurcation in a 2 dimensions space, consider visualizing a **time evolving dynamic attractors** (basin of so-called '**strange attractors**'), fixed points (precise point passed by any relevant trajectories (anyhow after some delay); or **limit circles** (in the 2 dimensions); still points (possibly on a manifold) or border of a volume in the 3 dimensions space.

[**Fixed point theorem** (Brouwer's) means dynamics process would pass back this same point in the future. Whichever time it takes. Take into account that pathways are non-linear and some randomness, you will understand that it is not so intuitive].

These diagrams, graphs of bifurcations, phases-diagrams allow to identify transitions between different periodic systems, leading to **chaotic motions**.

Characteristic values of control parameters(s); are associated with transitions. Correspond to bifurcations where doubling of periods is observed. Some other important normal forms include: **saddle-node** bifurcations; **Hopf's** bifurcations.

Determinist –Chaotic Transitions

Now, remind that phase transition critical as in physics, abruptly change the kind of behavior. As you know, for example ice appears in liquid water at some precise temperature (varying a little after impurities and pressure). That is a critical transition of phases and the respective motion in each *medium* very different (almost immobile in ice, 'sea-sick' in free waters). There is the sort of quite different order(s) in formalized scale of motion. Nevertheless those of fundamental in diverse environments may coexist in an environment and they can be used for that.

Even polar bears understand that better than geeks they use the ice-pack and iceberg as a trap, pier, table and boat and otherwise swim very well but not for the same reasons.

There is some thickness at the interfaces; which is making phenomena occur or emerge there. Mobile bodies move between, eventually take advantage of this diversity if they are in-between or across. Transition of phases may also occur fast on one side and more progressive on the other. See the freezing of the river possibly fast once reached critical points of temperature and thaw slower. Following the temperature unless you have the mechanical push of the river behind.

Comes a major idea by the side of a formal mathematical behavior, the sort of 'extremist' transition. Between well-ordered one and almost complete chaotic ones. The hard part to understand is that these transitions, often come successively one after another. The most horrible of that for (stupid) determinists (not just tyrannical, politicians, there are many academics too) is that these transitions are very fundamental, natural and even have often n simple formalism

For example, **Feigenbaum's scheme of bifurcations** just considers 2 separations and iterations; and that formal simply written programs, displays in the screen: **tree branching, exploding fringes into chaotic-ergodic,** followed by **'catastrophic' reductions** to **simpler sparse ordered behaviors.**

[From chaos we emerge and to chaos we go and the most stupid of that; is more and **more strength on ordering ... can be the best way to chaos**... It is not to mention 'nice abstractions' that are just heating heads switching from robust almost stable, into sensitive very unstable... So the climate reach **tipping points** and **thresholds** to chaos?].

Thus also imagine in nature that **you cannot manipulate a lot** because these kinds of behaviors are basic. [... So the switches between particles and their fields?]. Take than more complicated systems (indexed by the prime number of maximum complexity reached?).

Whatever your 'degree of superior knowledge' you will meet with sub-coexisting chaotic or ordered sub-parts. In effect that is refilling of disorder. Even if some parts may be **effectively manipulated, possibly when closer to the critical points** [... But not as directly as you think. Pareto's optimum precisely near such sort of critical point entry to chaos? Suppose you tell to a 100 m race at the end of it that it has been extended just now to 400 m by the dear leader in the tribune?_.

Eventually after some axis most critical point look like the same, but they are unpredictable. Meanwhile they are **very sensitive to initial conditions**. They could turn either ordered (not necessarily the way you would like) or disordered-chaotic (not necessarily the way you fear most). How this? - at higher levels ... since we may be looking like a quiet border, cosmic fringe or troposphere ... with hot stuff below our feet and hot stuff above our head.

This is meaning simply that the 'highest-self' needs that 'within and in' hse environment(s); some robustness of the 'ghosts' as required by the survival of our 'shelves' (the ghost that matter to us). Without being safe about any measure of order implemented ... mostly unpredictable. [And sometimes with adverse consequences that can be mitigated]. Of course with 'self'-Nature having to do with that, be resilient and be able to have good uses of such mechanisms. Just have the vexing appearance, for the determinist of not to be able to know why, there or, there and not there. Complexity so hard to unknot?–especially if the methods are defective in intricated approaches and they are, moreover, managed discriminating. Intrications supported by?- **crossovers, mixtures, overlaps, confusions**. Taking advantage of order and disorders.

[In societies with *a plethora* of experts; could it be good policy to shortcut the degrees of confusions in the 'leaves of the trees' in **ergodic agitations with no roots**'. You will always have enough experts in dressed axiomatic **demonstrations encapsulated** in their almost **arbitrary limits**). As well as you will have met published articles; and you have plenty of believers around, enough for making plenty of noise. So that few some will always be in conditions to pretend to have been the good and right prophets of that '**black-swan occurrence**'.

Especially when you have not considered the roots before; and have uncared the **growth out** of logics and numbers. Dedicated are those social experts to **vague enough enunciates**, for looking like right. None to pretend that some sort of orders were 'impossible' to analyze and more essential humane equations are to care about. Impossible to study, in the way are actually those social arts in state-existing conditions of environment. Alas, so much and many concentrations of analytical skills self-empowered in predictions and ineffectual expertise over tumults ... and not dedicated to fair sense of **potentials**. Good resources paid for auguring as magicians of virtual volatility].

Feigenbaum's simulation examined the universality of iteration diagrams in simple binary trees (only cut to consider by 2). Then a cascade of iterations: solutions series of non-linear equations. It shows off at glance a 'zebra pattern' with stripes of ordered behavior (narrowing after increasing number of iterations) alternating with stripes of chaotic behavior; after a universal characteristic.

Consider Landau-Hopf Feigenbaum case: $F(x, \mu, h) = 0$ where μ is the parameter and h the range of imperfections. When $x \rightarrow \mu. x. (1-x)$, $\mu \in [1, 4]$ with discrete dynamic formulation: 1) $0 \leq \mu < 3$: **unique fixed point**; 2) when $\mu = 3$: there is **one marginally stable fixed point**; 3) when $\mu > 3$ that is a **fixed point turning unstable**; 4) when $\mu = 3.2$: there is **2 periods cycle**; 5) $\mu = 3.5$: there is **4 periods cycle**; 6) at $\mu = 3.56$: **period doubled to 8**; 7) at $\mu = 3.567$: **period doubled to 16**; 8) at $\mu = 3.58$: cascade duplications are so fast that logistic application turned **chaotic**.

[Could this support an economical concept: narrowing fringes of order intercalate with disorder? (One from another). Since the higher structuring (of order) has a cost, like when empowering the fringes of order. **Scarcity economics spectra not without a roof**, provided by complexity.]

Feigenbaum established a self-universal value: $\delta_i = (\mu_i - \mu_{i+1})/(\mu_{i+1} - \mu_{i+2})$ with δ^∞ converging to 4.6692. **δ is a universal for almost all any function that has a period-doubling** as a route to chaos. [Of course in the hope to meet one day with ternary and quaternary and prime numbers similar kinds of simulations?].

Basic Patterns of Bifurcations

To evoke first that **Co-homology element** is basic concepts in theory of bifurcation. It can always be restricted down to a region; but, if this region is sufficiently small, the co-homology always disappears. This is the argument for the **non-locality** of the co-homology [the folded small places are unfolded or smoothed by any perturbations, the large ones make 'natural environment' when their ontogeny prevailed?]. This has special importance in the theory of bifurcations - about **singularities of phase-space** ... formalizing "special case" or defining objects' space of existence").

Relations of singularities are with cubic, sine, doubling period and statistical stability. There are 3 ways that singularities emergence by 1) projection, 2) degeneracy and 3) folding over quotient.

Cohomology is a general term for a sequence of abelian (commutative) groups associated to a topological space; often defined from a **cochain complex**. It is a method for assigning **richer algebraic invariants** to a space than homology can do. Some versions arise by dualizing the construction of homology. Also it is a **contravariant theory** is more natural than homology in many applications. It also has to do with **functions and pullbacks in geometric situations**.

The theory of bifurcations has led to a **classification of regime changes**. [In basic physics speeds either of translations, rotation as "natural" support; there is the very existence of the subject you are talking about]. It was demonstrated to be reducible to a limited number of cases.

Self-organized criticality has been a concept introduced by Bak, Tang and Weisenfeld. According them, you have many out-of-equilibrium dynamic spatial-temporal systems; slowly driven; exhibit **threshold-like responses**... They tend to **self-organize into some dynamic state**. Dynamic state (or stage?) is characterized by a broad range of avalanche sizes quantified by a **power law distribution**. [power law]

Power law: functional relationship where a relative change in one quantity results in a proportional relative change in the other quantity, independent of the initial size: one quantity varies as a power of another.

Example with: square-cube law, Stefan–Boltzmann law, 3/2-power law in characteristic curves of triodes, Self-organized criticality with a critical point as an attractor, Exponential growth and random observation (or killing), highly optimized tolerance, two-thirds power law, relating speed to curvature in the human motor system,Taylor's law relating mean population size and variance of populations sizes in ecology, behaviour near second-order phase transitions involving critical exponents, proposed form of experience curve effects, differential energy spectrum of cosmic-ray nuclei, fractals, Pareto 'sdistribution, Zipf's law in corpus analysis and population distributions amongst others.

A sub-class of self-organized critical systems can be shown made of systems functioning 'at' or 'close to' a standard critical point's; in the sense of phase transitions as in statistical physics. It is the nonstandard type of slow driving, of the 'order parameters', which leads to the dynamic attraction of the critical point. This is usually unstable.

Have in mind that after proper formal explorations, you have the work of identifying; they have evidence quite universally in nature. That would be the job of physicists ... but philosophers (since proper epistemologists in dire proportions respect to 'managers'), on their own, ought to explain it in lay terms for the use of most: they are basic.

Now how to take seriously the previous?–as could a normal human being? Many formal iterations of real atom-field are just partial accumulations of numbers, ordered either globally or locally. Their physical properties are mixing neutral "mass" of numbers' behaviors; natural structuring effects. Even simple numbers have, some deviations from physics nature. 'Locally' from the previous (physics specifications) ... just in case

[Care that sometimes it is not easy to manage concept of localness for physics or ecology that are very large respect to our intent to self-think about our local cognitive which is very local-local. In the first place cosmic it is not so local producing environment for structuring and locals of that not for within bifurcations. In the 2nd place you have local small local systems like you (a very small bifurcation maintained by evolution, thus not, 'erased, in the meantime, of your life'). Another scale, but the possible perturbator of the ecosystem; which will trigger 'the unfolding its bifurcation place of living; once too perturbed by change of extensive parameters. A way to understand how the upgrade of entropy?].

If you still doubt that proper physics is not just proper mathematics with ingredients of logic to clear. Meanwhile other logics often too 'strangely manipulated by humans' with not care. Our economic management concept of informative links not only with kind or ergodic oriented fibers as stings.

In that formal limit case you have already all the behaviors you need for a complex society: order, disorder, exceptions obliged, cosmic evidence.

Thus even if, when measuring, you will not exactly find Feigenbaum's universal constant, the framework is essential. So, if really it will not too purely simple (binary-ness, iterations, probability or simple parameters); within physics numerical approach of similar phenomena, record and estimates can be consistent. Could they be not so wide significant difference? - Between theoretical calculus and empirical estimate is another prospect. We suspect may know can hope and intent most formal methods still. With plenty of data may expect more comprehensive systemic simple evidence of practices?

Now, since the "whole is not simply the sum of parts," as mentioned by von Bertalanffy (mid of the second part of the 20th century); the word system has proliferated in methods of applied sciences, missing a bit in their original determinism that at some degree of advancement, mathematics and logics were to come with better approach. Maybe then they should have more simply recorded, since more fundamental and have started to care seriously. Rather than multiplied the sketches of modeling for bureaucracies. Plenty of purism exclusive systemic for dogmatic. Not much of good formalism Anything can be taken, computed electronic and output, but not properly caring.

From the previous it is to suspect that the simple easy clear roomed so easily groomed by priests, pastors, doctors, experts, politicians, anarchists, philosophers, novelists and poets, etc.). House of the 'system' is neither easy to formulate; but: could it be not too complicated? How to account for those uncertainties and/or openness. When you have such kinds of 'monsters of reason' (as geopoliticians) just waiting out there. [Waiting on the other side of the door, there could be: not as a pizza delivery man but, something much more fearful ... as a cream-pie criminal?].

More workable:

1. Never have a 'residual' so nice as a little noise;
2. Get some randomness, imprecision, hazards involved in the modeling at different anchoring points (coefficients, exponents, signs);
3. Consider general equations properly formulated and degeneracy special cases;
4. Consider field waves and special case degeneracy;
5. Have variable windows; either analytic either included or considered in the formal model system;
6. Have some imprecision in the relative formal system proposed as models;
7. Know how to introduce random resolutions in models of intervention (and respect democratic choice);
8. Work with multi-scaled logical frameworks of critics?

Pitchwork bifurcation examples after parameter λ

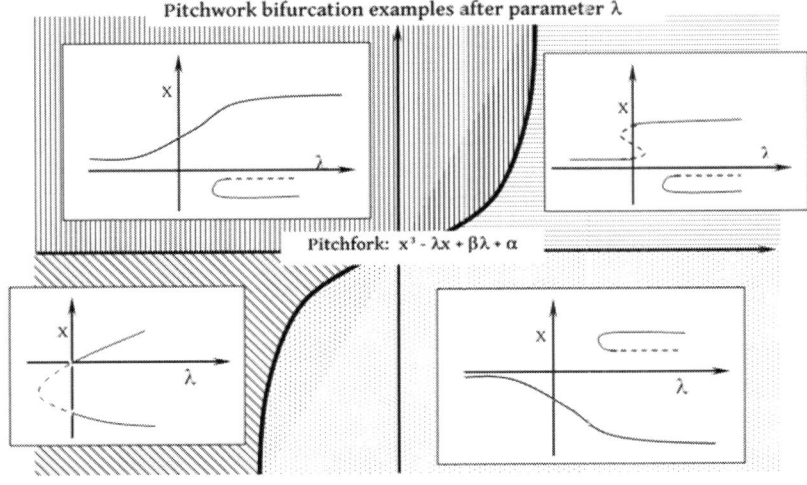

Pitchfork: $x^3 - \lambda x + \beta \lambda + \alpha$

Referential Self-Paradoxes

After Yi-Lin self-referential paradoxes are a way to introduce a contradiction and cognitive conception of existence: for some of them,

- Mirror image left-right but not bottom-up (or top-down): a mirror switches the positions of left to right. But there is no simple reason; that it should not make it top with bottom out a cognitive one. The brain makes correction in the latter case and not in the first one.
- Plato-Socrates's paradox: "what Socrates says below is false" then "what Plato says above is true," (observes that is involved a 2 separated);
- Liar paradox: observe that it carries a statement (true) on a negation (lie);
- Barber's paradox: observes that it fixes a statement (barber office) on a dynamic change of state;
- Russell's paradox (also called Zermello's paradox): about the set of all sets; addressing to Cantor's naïve set theory;
- Catalogue paradox: about the table of contents of the tables of contents.

So maybe to consider: 1) The qualitative, pure abstract logical or semantic paradoxes resolved by real forms; 2) The almost pure primary physics paradox either an artifact of formal theory (by incompleteness of method or a *vacuum* full of everything) or to solve by further physically explaining theory or the remaining.

Evaluation of self-referential proposals could (derived from Yi-Lin) evaluate and judge a proposition if one knows exactly what he/she is evaluating or; all in all the surroundings (only remaining the "not" and put the label). And have a corresponding set of evaluation criteria (at least having the "not").

When some are making the "true-false" and "right-wrong" judgment about proposition involving contradictory negation; it would be difficult or impossible to draw a definite conclusion. Unless this negation or "not" exactly completed at the infinite-relative or enough as falsely labeled "infinite-absolute."

Infinite relative: truly finite at very high numbers (infinite applied concept).

"Infinite absolute": concept thus can be arbitrary but fair. That is not yours nor any of those that will have to apply to themselves; and enough about a length previously chosen as fair but review-able.

Similarities/Inequalities, Equalities/Differences

As you may think, a formal relative system respect to a scale of complexity composes a sort of integral structure, at a given level. Logically we hope it will find itself at the start its own base ($0_{relative}$, $1_{selfunit}$). Some generally formulated model made in a semi-discrete modular way; is not impossible, either to formulate, or sustain and then finitely describe the quali-quanti-able).

[Somehow our kind of relative formal system makes relative (and mobile) discreteness within continuity. The converse being that reality is discrete (quantic) and filling continuity].

Qualities match inductively or deductively (in a different level of order?). With characteristic amounts which are considering relative minimum (between $0_{relative\ self}$ and $0_{relative\ below}$ and relative maximum enough after $1_{self-relatives}$. Hence basically and relatively, this is amounting more and detailing [not in crazy too large number of productions qualities. At least with some order or hierarchy for a given state. But first to ensure essential; despite enormous numbers .... Including billions of, more or less vicious bacteria within? [Like speaking of those you have in the intestines.].

To consider before that, some economical ideas. Not of the sort of human vanities but that of "Nature." That is how physically and formally to conceive the sort of huge savings we made; between a relative system 'pull-back' to zero (but indexed) and the amounts structures. In effects primarily at one piece of time we do mostly one thing at a time [possibly suggested by Noether theorem, one at a time of conservation laws operation) framework in some half a dozen of less concept of 'management'? – without presuming of time. For brain's activity it can be less than half a second].

In a similar way that is not much different from the number of equations in dimensions of basic physics formula concepts as actually with the international system of (physically accounting) units; and the *status* of formal model's components. So to consider enough: 1) Proper **formulation** and 2) **Logic levels**; with almost complete arithmetic logic, 3) Known **characteristics ratios** (exponent...); 4) Proper **informative, 'links'** (half complex operations); 5) Relations between qualities (or **properties functions allowed by structures**) and labeled (qualified); 6) Quantities **(or metabolic balanced systems of structures providing functions** for the life-time and contingencies.

All that is in generally calculable system (our influence-able frameworks?) and specifiable enough for solutions? There is an important pivot between physics' complexity and biological (but physics) complexity. Where **netgentropy can be more regularly positive** (in the 'time-window' of life and phase-space conditions). As a result life oriented toward more complexity and self-reproducible forms of life has balances between automatic and more conscious, and relative dynamics and hierarchical processes, not too many to manage essential functions. So they achieve units are able to catch relatively autonomously in the environment the resources to recycle. And to maintain overall the netgentroic balance positive?

This pivot maybe with bacteria; if not primarily it would have anyhow started with them. Researchers suspect that many basic life mechanisms are incorporation and associations co-evolved with bacteria. Hence how these inspirations can appear as a possible formalism? – that looks like not the traditional reductive way of modeling; after specialist dear concept; nor sort of system models which are already plethoric and are quite confusing after primary ergodic ways to operate?

Of the tipping point(s) or pivot(s) you have as a transition between non-biological to biological; we will further speak a bit more after. Especially will probably be with 'thermodynamics-like funny sentences'. Yet not having many ideas on the forms or relations that analogous formal concepts could be. An important required concept would be about the *status* of formal terms between one respect to others and into physics world.

You may have understood despite our critics and skepticism, that we have still some optimism with human ... dire efforts of intelligence. If such sort of relative formal system (or 'shuttles') could ensure our observations and management. Since we have already, enough (?), if not most of the logical and mathematical details, that 'absolute' approach, needs. Thus this is about trying to find the roads intuitively to **models** and **to order**. Somehow this has **unification** in perspective (we do not say ferociously wanting to ensure it); and the concept of the **system** in the basic of formal sciences. [Avoiding in practice all the horrors we saw in 'systemic vanities' of many sciences?].

Minimally one understood that the **piling-incorporation of systems along** the (abstract complicated) **complexity scale** (or another system?). Obviously this makes that more economical than **close systems** taking systematically advantage of one another destruction. [The most relevant mean but not the morally aesthetic one]

That is those of the same species for mating, those of different species for eating one another. **Whatever the degree of maximum complexity reached in the scale.** Difference could be there only on labels, extend of diversities and 'intentions' (or similar lower concepts as potentials?). That is to say, of course, the crash of a meteor on your head may (at least humanely) not correspond to the solar system having had 'the intention to eat you' (even if somehow you are cooked by the way). Meanwhile the very intention of your barbecue if for 'eating'.

Formally then: observing that a system considers **coefficients** (either **positioning** as scalar or **adjusting** variable to its size ... as a scalar modular product?), **variables** (either an **unknown** wanting to know, or **roots** or **degeneracy-able**); **exponent** (is either **scaling** the variable or **characterizing** the amount ... or the reverse? - is for qualifying), **sign** (either for **relativizing** or for operating respectively). Even if, we look like too much wanting our perspective to fit our thesis ... in a formal system, all that **seems to be intertwine-able** and **permutable**.

But care, we do not pretend that this substitutability or 'permutable' or link-ability by some equivalencies or transformable is major in all physics. Maybe all this is only when, easy switches, between matter and energy (or structures and functions). Because the physics of our interest is much about 'order.' So, probably much more about the complex intertwining of sort of **equivalencies** that could not be ... and better say 'that preferably, for not dying too soon, that ought not be'.

Thus, just here modestly to observe: it should be an **abstract formal ideal**, which could **account** for this perfect substitutability-'permutability'-universal-linkability-adaptable.

To add, for believers that about language formulation: since it is not in absolute having to be perfect... Omniscient-Omnipotent-Merciful--All in a Unique ... not unbelievable. Transcendence in absolute is not under our scope.

Abstraction Framework

Passing superficially over the concept of abstraction.

Perspective of **abstraction**:
- In anyway reductions;
- In many ways 'some purity';
- Principle of matching/linking (for relative continuity);
- Principle of concentration/differentiation (for relative discretion).

Perspective of **representation**:
- Principle of mixture for 'waving';
- Principle of openness for sustaining;
- Principle of heterogeneity for varying;
- Principal of satisfying for renewing.

Perspective of **economy** (any relate to previous bi-sets)
- Anchors to reality corresponding to incompleteness
- Integrity or unifying principle (quantic, quanta);
- Oscillation between 2 as a dual within some few more;
- Principle of evolution in the environment needs economy from and for diversity.

First observe with the distinction between quali and quanti, joined and matched, it is not difficult to imagine that upper (exponent) term and lower (logarithm) term together linked formal to material. Eventually, this would have more complicated formula 'in between'; but in the same spirit: effectively the object and real match.

Otherwise one term can be 'subjective' and the other term 'objective' according work on them, or a potential, or a time's delay, or a life time. To work: either with the qualitative part (normally the logarithm), and then deduce by exponentiation the quantitative; explores the sort of amount to relate and *vice versa*. At the reverse, you have something like a characteristic amount or quantity, a subject with properties of regularities and a qualitative formulation to work. The match explores both parts objectives, or subjective both, etc.

The important is to work scientifically and properly, in the usual *Galileo* way: 1) Experimental device (with controlled parameters (or inputs) and 2) Perturbations of the subject (destructive, if we can; or not if we must not); 3) Records of data and 4) Work of (operating) forms - mathematical models and validation by data. But captures around frameworks are also required.

[Once upon a time, we sketched an "olicognograph" of this Galileo method that can be seen in 'Olicognography', available at www.lulu.com]

The 6th element would be the reason of all those inputs and outputs. According the details and complexity; you can have more but also with some simplifications after de 'degree of freedom'. Concept of degree of freedom which more properly said that:

you reduce by one your degree; after complementarity (or one closure obtained). [The 5th element the lower pack of dimensions?]

Moreover after relative openness; it is to imagine that formally expressed. But you have also a relative system; that is it is relatively closed. Theoretically the defective remaining solved only by the physics side: the best can do arithmetic and logics. Care the confusions from difficulties of analysis; in the definition of a practical case of degeneracy. If you meet difficulties of formulations, and of approximations of transformations, etc.).

Formalism imagined difficult at our level of most desired policies? - The frequent characteristics exponents observed in living bodies metabolisms and brains? - Close enough to our conscious way; principles of proportions seem to express that formulation could relatively be not so impossible. The problems may come from the formal structure of the model-object (representing a subject). There are also many evidences in living bodies those sorts of complementarities have different forms: **co-evolution, symbiosis, cooperation, commensalism**; which are probably relevant to the details of a formal system. Thus which frameworks of effects on models?

Characteristic Borders Maximum and Minimum

With a sort of real object behind a number (lest its quali-quanti model), you may have to consider as material objects (in relative terms):

$$\text{Universe} \rightarrow$$
$$\text{principles selection} \rightarrow \text{local field} \rightarrow (\text{conditions} ($$
$$[\text{minimum}_{minimorum} \rightarrow \text{emergence} \rightarrow \text{zero} (0) \rightarrow$$
$$\text{composition}_{self} \rightarrow \text{minimum}_{maximorum} \rightarrow \text{unit} (1)] \rightarrow$$
$$\text{maximum}_{minimorum} \rightarrow \text{motion}) \rightarrow \text{maximum}_{maximorum} \rightarrow$$
$$\text{Environment.}$$

... and detail each:

- **Universe** provides principles, some of which (**principle selection**) providing the **local field** with *ad hoc* (phase-space?) **conditions** for the subject; informative relations within and, for the subject considered, its **environment** (end of the formulation), much of which provided by the local field of the universe;
- **Local field**: there the space and contain where you move (in principles, informative links? -with subject objective **motion**. Lower systems of composition have their own and possible;
- **Conditions** provided to **emergence**, they can be like effects of informative links or ordering process within all around conditions, possibly also operating framework? As informative **polyhedra** providing the operations;
- **Minimum**$_{minimorum}$: would be then, the lowest coincidence quantitative of the composition, obtained (and enough stable; relation to the previous composition; the model framework, eventually reproduced (that is **information stability reproducing**); could be the minimum cardinal of ordering? [In the model?]
- **Zero**: the relative term of the 0; thereafter if something to happen is to expect; the 'logarithm should catch the one since there'?–at least **minimum**$_{minimorum}$;

- **Composition** $_{self}$: any material object has structural and functional ingredients (not as fixed as you many imagine (constantly in the move), Could composition eventually be in relative terms? - the qualitative part of the model (or the set of composition?);
- **Emergence**: or the something to happen expected obtained ... (enough for measured?–and maybe thank to the catchment of the "beginning of a statistical density") ...
- **Minimum**$_{maximorum}$: consider the needed openness of the pre-unit to gain enough stability;
- **Unit**: thus what could be calling the one (1), deserving the label of identity or integrity. And may be only a virtual average (?) between **minimum**$_{maximoroum}$ and **maximum**$_{minimorum}$... As shape it could either spherical or elliptical or toroidal or both (if with some inner order which at best, intuitively would be a topological hole);
- **Maximum**$_{minimorum}$: Once the object there (or subject according where you put soul); it needs resistance and resilience, and economy. The overall cardinal of its definition model is all functional enough at the minimum. And the flexibility of subsets to have priorities after the needs and the opportunities... This possibly entails hierarchy according the criticality of the function *versus* the need [... If you do not breathe underwater, have in mind that not more than 3 minutes to catch what you look after];
- **Motion**: relative motion in your proper field and for more openness ... or opportunities ... to **increase your probabilities of catching** or grabbing what your maintenance or reproduction need... Motions as characteristics possible speeds and possibly motivated by needs of satisfaction;
- **Maximum**$_{maximorum}$ is not to expect materially? - At least in permanent absolute terms, this satiety or obesity does not provide any problems.
- **Environment** ... but; also it is to consider the **evolution around**: kinetics, cooling, localness, neighboring systems (commonly reducible to space-phase or interfaces of phases).

As a whole the concept has 14 cardinal details or 12 (2 can be simplified at the extremities). The nucleus within [] has 6. The larger subject within () has 8. It is to think about the sort of informative links able to reduce some, pack the system, dually separate the system; between generally solvable form and required specification. Without missing relative openness and somehow included in some ordering of the system.

Somehow intuitively the whole block to work on. But it may have to be revised corrected and formulated. Even if with more tips in this essay, we are with 'wholesome' language, with narrowed aims. So we are more with intuitive epistemology, in the hope it would be enough for humanism?

Some comments more: it looks like not so difficult to put all that as quali-quanti-model (some more details of intuitive logic further) with informative links.

Forms of Model

Having in mind this 3 or 4 dimensions for maximum generally solvable expression; we took a one-volume precision (3&3&3&3+2 intertwined in formulation) for a one relative object. To imagine time as a "closure" by the stability of each precision. The way from one level (system of 3 dimensions would eventually more intertwined to reduce to general solvability–no more than 3rd degree.

At level and higher or lower systems levels may be to take with: Calaby-Yau compactification of dimensions [Named method after authors efforts in String Theory]; 'Closures' (differentiable/integral-able?) inspired by the premises on time(s) and; Groups algebra (the 'privileged way' to operate that? For preserving some needed symmetries). [Of course this is no more than intuitions exposed to objection and rejection here].

To imagine one step more toward absolute-ness. As also related, from where (or in which larger universe is the object?) and then. So: the grounding universe of the object under study is a materialist form of physics. To imagine other similar objects than relations between 2 (often already well explored) or 3 (3-body problem having been hard to beat by Poincaré).

[That is to say you still have to consider at complex levels operations between 1 and 2 or more whole systems; or 1 system and pieces or raw materials, which are not systems. Intuitively it should be more economical when able to absorb evolved pieces of nearby systems (since most prefer biological steaks to chemical ones... We will see some more necessary concepts in the next coming volume].

[As the rule of survival, out specific hazard or rotten food, you can consider that closer the specie to yours more edible, more digestible (and better quantified). Do not take that as an apology of cannibalism ... even if it is often a usual way of civilization].

Observe that the perspective of in/out have not much developed here less implicitly and in some way. This may be a defect we hope to amend the forth-coming volume, since operations also discriminates inner and outer algebra.

Now aspiring to detail more about the geometric volume and the properties; it may have; with nearby upper and lower systems dimensions. We will intent a bit further, to clear the ideas. Since we induce that we also need, a formal figure for 'general equivalence'. This could be titled like a "General Axiom of Abstraction."

General Axiom of Abstraction

Consider either 'anything is everything,' 'anything is nothing,' 'nothing is everything' or 'everything is anything'. These 4 concepts are values-like. It could be better to add a "trajectory of consideration". Like, at least, would be a 'before' and a 'future'. The relative 'flat' would be respective: 'no more one at once' (creation operator), 'have to' (disintegration operator) and 'fields there' (field-atoms' time?).

[No more than intuition there. Eventually with 2 more sides of the box. First one for the universe (of physics principle?) and come another for the place of maximum complexity (entropy-netgentropic phase?)]. All 6 are like a dice's sides. The side or the apex of the entry the 'before' (or minimum main founding principles?) and the 'one of going out' (or the maximum complex one): the 'can be'. Box or dice, the concept of many 'box modeling'.

We know, this is a bit difficult, why some many complications of formalism?–to look like our vision or to catch the true loops of realities, of non-soapy-slippery-slope? Back the nothingness of wholeness, everyone's abstraction. That is the general axiom of abstraction and its indispensable expression, for oneself in a universe. Universe of which we are part and parts of us are off.

[If you believe in a 'Hand-Some Determinism' ever; you will put there: an omniscient omnipotent, absolute, eternal, etc. You will also want selfishly God merciful ... but not prejudge exactly in the same way when monotheist or any other, nirvana the pre-formal one-ness!].

Not to see scientific approaches in absolute tune with teleological methods. Maybe better they do not have to. And let some something for that: religions should not care to develop natural world interpretations. Since they are soon opposed by correct natural sciences (in our opinion, not by formal sciences on the essential minimum of spirituality). And the converse not to waste formal sciences develop too much in modeling the belief of spiritual.

Probably it is to be better concerned by what you do and feel to have to do. Good enough it is (or not), as a register for thinking on sciences' standards. It is to observe that modern-day levels of technological developments, have disqualified (wisely or wrongly) plenty of natural phenomenological expressions of religious dogma hence not all belief. Even if logic can try to cope with the belief. So as to summarize spirituality to a small set of basic qualitative concepts. And even if scientific approaches are now increasingly using abstract formalism.

We see the need of a general axiom of abstraction once on-in the scale of complexity. It may be easier so to make it recyclable, fragmented and discarded relatively....

General axiom of abstraction which, considering formal methods, logics, mathematics, statistics, etc. have to make use of a something-everything-anything, nothing, together in or out.

This may apply in many higher or lower levels. Of course the scientific approach of physics; something will consist to specify relatively to this general axiom of abstraction. 1st have in mind that we let the absolute first to the spiritual. Good if everything and general axioms of abstraction in the process of use; a balance of what something is, and is not.

Negation Universal –Avatar Switching Operator

'Is not' operator of negation in logics; is somehow delicate to manage. But actually it is often very improperly used. Especially this as observed, in the registers of social sciences. There the avatars of negation could be: **'counterfactual'**, **'residual(s)'**, 'remaining', 'exogenous', 'ignored', 'despised or disdained', 'critic', 'opponent'. [Accessible to systemic approach?]

Artists of the authoritarianism sort, barely tolerate critics and want to care only about what is positively selfishly defined). So are the biases of politico-social practices. This is a major mistake, with some historic fairer reasons, in the positivist occidental sciences systems.

'General axiom of abstraction' is a relative formal concept of which we will make use, as an instrumental abstract; intermediate in many circumstances and approaches. Consider for example any physics number is formally *per se* (by itself) cardinal and ordinal and respect self and all any other.

Imagine that any amount should look-like as a monomial having in a minimum a symbolic letter (variables: x, y, z), characteristic exponent (in [-3, +3]; relation to ($\pm i$, S/dS , $\int \partial$) (?) and a position (min_0, [0;1], max_1).

- x, y, z the traditional way as a symbol of variable,
- characteristic exponents needs not to integrate neither fewer than 3 (just delimit a volume of relevancy and forms within;
- i for complex numbers
- and within symmetries, seeming to us [S_{min}/dS_{max} S_{max}/dS_{min}] something as the maximum or minimum entropy (of whole system) divided the minimum or maximum entropy variation in a given transformation, at best netgentropic?
- $\int$And ∂meaning by that: we need integral-able and differentiability but in the cross way and Π/Σ in the continuous (?) or/and Σ/Π(?) in the discrete.

The **product of positive real numbers**:

$\prod_{n=1}^{\infty} a^n$ converges to a non-zero real number if and only if the sum

$\sum_{n=1}^{\infty} \ln (a^n)$ converges.

This allows the translation of convergence criteria for infinite sums into convergence criteria for infinite products.

Of course we walk too fast. We are too intuitive and very probably abuse of many shortcuts... So just take that only as a working hypothesis. Wholesomeness without esoteric ambition only try to mind the **possibilities to balance** or manage in the balance. Not tell you as esoteric that we have a better explanation in a radically complete different scientific system. Meaning by that we discard invariance of universal. But developing properly all the argumentation may take a larger book.

A formal system in the proper formulation of **cybernetic-system** forms have often been a **'black box'**. We may have, inspired by quantic theory to add a **white-box** representation?

Be a **black box** one where in you do not know what is in, only maybe a sort of *vacuum*. But can turn around to observe something including management of extensive parameters (in the thermodynamic way) ... Maybe this is to consider with the logical quantifier of existence ($\exists$) and the one step up, possibly in an ordered way, iteration and not a sloppy kind of reversibility (that is a relative irreversibility). Then you would have relative metastable steps up. Moreover having to handle a concept of maximum.

So correspondingly a **white box** with plenty of things. Potentially so many that anything can happen or can be seen. Would be there a sort of partial management possibilities 'in' to measure in (gauge); perturbed, eventually scattered and see (one subsystem at a time?) the structuring concept. Of course headed by universal quantifiers ($\forall$). Progressive descent is the way to; it would also be a concept of metastable step (downward) and the need for a minimum (bottom).

Thus complementary ways (inductive and deductive) to try to examine systemic boxes, define conditions and so on ... and then to make coherent ... informatively?– where the 'General axioms of abstraction' concept would 'play in relative terms'?

A physics or thermodynamic formal system with "realistic specifications" and reducing the correctly formalized system defining (by characteristics values) the physics system (often prefers the atomistic or wave-like formalism) or thermodynamic system (often prefers the phase and box-system formalism).

Humane Systemic Economics

Communities aperture is contained in basic rights and physical criteria. Thermo-economics ought, if taken comprehensively, to disqualify present macroeconomics as those practiced.

> At least because it is crazy to conceive sort of economics classifying societies into countries and economics since individuals up to their rank in the United Nations system exactly in the same continuous implicit way. Using formal approaches in a unique way excluding flexibility (and complex number). Seeking the conditions of humans adapt to, same qualifying set; for ensuring essential. In other words, tight half a dozen (more or less consistent straight-jackets and then ask the country to develop as a global village with all the commodities provided in the television by the business of creams.

Thermo-economics yet not in effect because focused more on feasible balance, like exergetic balances of industrial sites. Because yet not core, nor in the practices of institutions; still not very clear with entropies concepts; nor is with information(s) and their informative relations, respect to systems of prices and values. Requiring that also care of cultures (originality of specification of cases); better understanding of time; have a proper care of asymmetries in strategies, together with those asymmetries in negotiation and respect of humane values.

> Natural environments have 'special national accounts terms'; at the middle of worldwide competitions which are battling for domination, driven by barriers of entries and

immigration controls... 'In the name of our values'?–Arrogance of egotistic supported privileged illusions and; good to dealers of lies?

Meanwhile, macro-meso-economics still in the *limbo* of markets utopia? (Markets themselves are not out of use); and national balances (they are not useless but should evolve). The idea would be out of dirty private interests (when dis-balancing cares) or miserable public pork-barrel policies (when preventing cares of diversities and more meanings of subsidiarity). Thus as defined, not as useless as to expect: in a society of information. Communications for better information(s) are 'critical'. Especially if this is about criticality of true information(s).

Considering traditional macroeconomics, the fracture can be even more sensible. Even if main forms of deductive macroeconomics and proper constrains are less clear than the one of competitions between nations. As we think that the most significant issue will be the general satisfaction of basic 'human rights', in the diversity of cultures. Respecting each other interpretations and relative freedom. That is, also not a government top-down directly imposing the occidental way of direct definitions.

Now if pretending to make scientific models involving ecological levels in the way systemic representations are and still made and uncared, this could generate many conflicts and furious debates on abstracts. Easily missing humane perspectives or misinterpreting formal resources.

Reframe would probably start better with sort of informative relations with the main frames. Maybe not to imagine starting from scratch. There are plenty of resources, including geographic information systems (too rigid). Thermal tele-detection and easy to implement geographic positioning systems network systems of measure with detectors. Hence with sort of geo-systems with perimeters are to reconsider.

Also it would be a good practice to design interactive expert systems as computer aid-supports to 'wishes of policies'. Allowing to make specifications directly by communities in the limits of physics possibilities. A sort of participation in local-regional economies-eco-systemic planning; using computerized interfaces eventually of ideographic sort.

The meso-systems definitions need the design of metrological of different kinds and also support relevant projects with various reasonable options. In fact it is probably more important in this process to put commitments, contributions, social financing in legitimate practice (not the sort of 'from outside the good advice).

The problem here is in the representation of local democracy to examine externalities of projects and activities. How they can be properly 'managed: requires kinds of synthesis. Here consistency of intermediate accepted mechanisms of regulation are to insert. But managed in 'learning societies' concept. Often there is no realistic enough proximity with acting communities. Nor enough respect of the 'systems' of fair legitimacy. Too often the projects of the 'charity business' are simply embarrassing and embarrassed by analytical preliminaries, without sense of social opportunity.

Formally the steps of modeling for simulating are about the designs of few but some alternative frames of perturbations (formalized scenarios). To apply on ground level's model, eventually pre-delimited. Not to promote static and supposedly maximizing projects more prone to free catastrophic effects. Thermodynamically to be true socially to avoid inhumane consequences.

In the idea of Physics to inspire a systemic sort of modeling, is formally a kernel-like inductive quali-framework (match with a quanti-deductive one?). Not as simple as one formula and still not accounting for all. Yet already with some deductive glimpses. An important mid-concept (or mid-link) is with meeting and matching self-informative minimized and expandability maximized.

> **Kernel in mathematics** (and elsewhere): for any function f:A-> B (where A and B are any sets); the kernel (also called the null space) is defined by Ker (f)={x: x in. Such as that f (x)=0}, so the kernel gives the elements from the original set that are mapped to zero by the function. Ker (f) is therefore a subset of A [fine with the logarithm of unit]. The related image of a function is defined by Im (f)={f (x): x in A}. Im (f) is therefore a subset of B.
>
> In algebra, the **kernel of a homomorphism**, measures the degree, at which the homomorphism fails to be injective. The kernel of a homomorphism is trivial (in a sense relevant to that context) if and only if the homomorphism is injective. An important special case is the **kernel of a linear map**. The **kernel of a matrix**, also called the null space, is the kernel of the linear map defined by the matrix.
>
> In functions theory you have many avatars: 1) **Integral kernel**. a function of two variables that defines an integral transform; 2) **Heat kernel**, the fundamental solution to the heat equation on a specified domain; 3) **Convolution kernel**; 4) **Kernel in statistics** is a weighting function used in kernel density estimation to estimate the probability density function of a random variable; 5) **Stochastic kernel**, the transition function of a stochastic process; 6) **Pricing kernel**, the stochastic discount factor used in mathematical finance; 7) **Positive-definite kernel**, a generalization of a positive-definite matrix; 8) **Kernel in geometry**, the set of points within a polygon from which the whole polygon boundary is visible.

Grail Soup of Letters and Numbers

Practically more than one line of equations, you have few lines of equations system. This may not have just 1st degree of operations. Say also more complex operations; consider some unity of the system, some type possibly making a class of model. Then specifying or having to specify enough conditions. This is also involving natural constraint.

System of structured system? - in the Hamiltonian way but those involving complex numbers; to take into account symmetries. Operators? Are those kinds of more complex operations (more than 1st level) they usually involve so, derivations and integrations. Say kinds of **Lagrangians**. Pieces of links expressed in formulas, corrective factors, equations of motions, theory of relativity formulas; such as Heisenberg's principles.

There are similarities between **Lagrangians** and **Hamiltonians** but commonly any approach has their own qualities and difficulties and is not easily equivalent. Mixture formal for example of operators and matrices formed as **Jacobian** or **Hessian**. Trying to take into account the sort of primary algebraic structures are already mentioned with **Lie groups** and algebra or the basic dimensions of space, time, mass, electric charges. Those are similar expressions having emerged from physics approaches as are **Pauli's matrices**.

Finally, also in the different levels of scale the primary one (variable and differentiate or variable ad integrated) Laplacians-like or the maximum one that is including some statistics. Formally related you have the **Hermitian**. Other statistics distribution with physics particles related as **bosons** or **fermions'** statistics. [Bosons and fermions are 2 main categories of fundamental particles named after their statistical behavior. For example, electrons are fermions].

Reminds that Einstein spend many years; after the most creative part of his life, providing fair advice, good questions, celebrity conferences and trying to find the 'great good operators' for the perfect synthesis. All in all, those management need expertise. Now plenty of major pieces are available, as for the standard model of physics. It is not yet clear if all are in a generally unified theory kind of system model.

Since not our expertise and more 'un-inspired' by users models; you will not find in this essay; trying to be popular, epistemological and naïve; more than suggestions and suspicions. Suspicion that a sort of 'shell' and/or 'shuttle' as formulated system can exist. Then the suggestion because yet; without any proper 'systemic nuclear formulation' to start of complexity or 'wholesomeness'. Also aware of plenty of time wasted in formalism applied to think.

As well as of many other sorts of modeling that did not deliver practically, in terms of tasks achievement. Out of our idea to expect sort of usual 'true anticipation of truth' we are more for ending the management tinkering. The ones which are made without care and; without proper model of dialogue. Bad and wrong tinkering made with plenty of models and stupid the way they were applied. And even with the ones of good qualities to understand why they could be so misused.

Add to that the uses made of professionals of the sort. Compared to what could be done, either in wise social-economical or in ecological-economical. Especially for having some possibilities of common understanding. Plenty of professionals of formal sciences and natural ones have dedications to useless sciences (and often stay in their office or cooled 4 (4) when given the opportunity to enlarge the perimeter and articulate better. Be it only the care of their discipline.

Be only dedicated to industries, they are also more dedicated to the enormous consumerism excesses of affluent societies; very busy to distract the essential frameworks; required to be shared by as many as possible.

[Only some despair to see all these 'beautiful minds' wasted in hothouses of academies so good at burning neurons, so arrogant in their fields of application; instead of being respectfully involved as explicit supports to societies. Societies which are based on; no other things we have than the alienation of the 'irrational human-animals' by leaders. Politicians and bureaucrats so ungraciously alienated by 'management' paradigms of naughty and nasty perversions. Only limited by strong self-esteem about the humanism of their authoritarianism].

Thus how to develop essential formal systems; that could provide with overviews easier to shape, adapt, reformulate and specify?

To observe sorts of links within the 'core' as basic building pieces. It could be, at the simplest level, an operation about self ... of course a product (**logical product** still not an arithmetical multiplication. **Cartesian product**s?). Should it be both an addition (logically a joining or **union**) and an arithmetical **product** (thus what involves the concept the logarithm but logical product or an intersection).

One step further would be a formal concept about **composition** since dual forms should coexist and others may have to be established; on self-containing **convolutions**, or functional expression for operating '**inter-wined**' or entangled functions. To remind that we insisted on the concept that 'information' is exchanged, so having insisted on **crossed information**: one-self and information formulation.

Not to Miss to Put Some Salt in the Soup

Self-information is, either the way to consider the self as a quali-quanti (for analytical purpose). Or already we have a match between an amount of quality and another possible course of quality amount. That is a crossed information; allowed by 3 disentangled uncoupled forming concepts (this may mean 3 free combinations but when they are entangled may reduce to 6?]

> In the suggestion physics of 1) The order-disorder of atomic particle-field? - thus distinct but linked terms; or 2) Whole mass-energy of that; or 3) Hadron's balance of strong and weak interactions [hadron is something like de heavy particles]; or 4) the hadrons-leptons (or more simply proton-electrons cloud of an atom); or the 5) whole electric charge-energy of that; or the 6) electron - electromagnetic balance of the cloud? (With possible exchanges out of: non-nuclear relations?) [Mesons?]]

> [Need of a bridge between hadron and leptons or proton and electron, at least transient stable enough: neutron? ... still in mind that may be confused by the neutrality-ness - of the field? ... how to detect a neutron properly so hardly interacting when at the 'same insane time' or there are fields switches ... or even quantic jumps?

Formally also to observe that we need, since the foundational level, is not to have separated forms but mixed ones. Would clear cut-partitions came after (by specification: either 'in' (the formal relative system?) or, on its 'outside' ... Otherwise only natural numbers would exist and nothing of integration and derivation? -the reason why to say that mathematics in quest of purity has developed in most minds with full 'clear separations' (not the most interesting?).

This may be good when to approach by formal side sciences the simplest principles (or the least complex one), principle for extracting the 'fundamental formula'; but not the good way for starting deductive journeys in physics. Of course at macro-empirical level; that is to say by the side of deductions; you can well obtain informative empirical formula (they are '**covering and gross**'). But this still will not nicely **fit deductive logic with inductive logic**, unconsciously applied in management will pass ... to those from the lower, the non-understanding ones to adapt. Even the logic of the orders given to them is anyhow understandable.

Patient comprehensive building of separated disciplines, provides with good and most relevant concepts; only missing few but essential things. Complexity is combinatory with huge numbers of atoms; ... [And humans are too prone to solve their ideological problems with weapons; rather than sense of composition. Many signals of formal sciences, have been missed].

... for wiser socio-technical development:
- Probability concept: it links events naturally) and rational (proportions in $\pm[0, 1]$;
- Conditional probability (Bayesian) and Frequency statistics (which have the illusion that phenomenology is a definitive truth);
- 1st order logic and regular arithmetic logic incompleteness.

... as naïve suspicions; since being in a Universe means we are made both: and in].

Switching now, to a more deductive empirical perspective: from the data. Of course, models in social arts are full of ugly things [the mix everything without **pattern framing**!]. So as in econometrics [and they call that 'cutting edge'; where we see 'cutting throats']. Out of judgment of values: formal ugly-ness (most of our intuitive suggestion) is beautiful. Since the start of analogies and realistically, both positive and negative options are forming.

More Practically Suggestive

So maybe a defect of mathematics purity is that dreaming of infinite purity they missed that you need to think. Start at 3 dimensions, for any object and any concept, since most subjects are 3 or 4 dimensions. Consider the twist: reduction and reducing dimensions. But in the search of 'starting rank' it is up, in the first up steps; whether this is the cross of 2 planes for 'outer' reference, or a simpler surface, interface of exchange. That may be an 'in' cut (to examine a slice of the volume or a meeting plane (like to appreciate a convexity).

You go up but in abstract it is 2 dimensioned; dual as graph or matrix perspectives or separating or judging. One more up but in abstract 1 dimension either for a line (inside a metric or norm), outside a relative position then often where you stick a one name or a label, or the unique concept or problem name or unit;

At 3 dimensions you have enough possibilities of specification for looking at more conceivable, at lower dimensions (2, 1, 0) you have very incomplete information upon the volume object. Then at 3 dimensions you may have a general expression of object's equation.

But if you need specific solutions as well as understand how the object is formed (symmetries, anti-symmetries, after the main components); and the way they structure, you will need more specification to have numerical solutions. That is what we may call (improperly?) 'Degeneracy'. The general equation will need real values. Probably according to the sort of device(s) or experiment you used for 'stop' it.

[Why specific solution for a kind of object you have not already tested?–better to have phenomenological identifications of behaviors].

Going on down but at 4th level, you have language and best general level of models for approach. That is your turn able to ensure the description of your volume. Would this also be the good global time closure? (Unifying the object?)

Now with the logic, as small relative link if you do not want to 'stay locked-in,' by 1st unique order logic since defective (incomplete) at one (1). You need in your logic at least a small 2nd order logic. Like 'kernel', like the first wish of steps. Thereafter it is more about geometry, phenomenological one (understandable) and then a matter of 'relative encapsulation'.

The complement is analogy logics (intrications of logics ranks, theory of numbers and their degrees. Eventually you have with 'General axioms of abstraction' and some rescaling property; as mentioned with prime numbers. Geometry is with general expression (3 dimensions in the relative *nucleus*) and other lower of higher dimensions relatively shell-formed.

Let examine an application of minimum scope 3 levels in the human economy concern, could it not be better? -:
1. A system of **micro-rational subsystems based on real materialistic World**, thinking about thermodynamics ecological balances and potential technological transformations. Micro-canonical ensembles may have to be time independent ... respect to meso or macro-level. They would be micro, but made of higher or more simple physics principles (less depending on the meso-scale).

2. The **meso-system centered**; for example, on human actors (or an objective distribution of actors, which is not exactly as an 'average human'). In the human case this is at "human range distance" (that of the range of realistic action; thus limited by calculability, complexity, etc. Defining the hierarchical links between other levels and actors levels or the integration-differentiation relative to the system or in general, 'closer to the Universe'? [We will propose further a concept of ordinal ordering].

3. The **macro-system is generally natural environmental or social constructions** (including ecological transformations) or is like a 'local field' (respect to the 1st hence not for the 'meso-level' or relevant actions space. And precautions' logic in an ecosystem called to stay renewable (not too affected) as the support of human societies. With least assumptions as possible, places of economics translations for minimal (but maximally involving) social rules; in fact on the criteria of justice and humanity preserving human identity.

1st level has to be minded in the wholeness of a pivot, meso-level and cover as far as feasible: many variables and parameters are often proper (like metabolic rates, etc.); making its material identity at minimax complex units of meso-levels. But needing there, a concept of the system, not inflated but all the things to take into account and not in a modular way.

This sort of modeling implies to 'down tune' Durkheim's principle of social science construction and traditional positively excluding economics. In natural sciences it would be more to reshape formally, not the evidence and principles but the 'freewheeling lift without breaks' of general arithmetic, perfect 0, infinite partitioning, with no consideration for atoms, groups, modulus, scalability, relativity and discrete limits.

You have in the micro to incorporate the ground of your materiality more probably closer natural sub-ecosystem(s) if you live on the environment. Better, of course, it is consistent ecosystems if not the most fundamental physics principles, especially the thermodynamics one of your transformations.

Coherence of specialism is not all disqualified: but it should develop at meso-levels more in the 'system solvability' for special cases. Fewer effects as 'purified abstractions' of elegant hollow abstracts filled of speculations. This also points at the limits of 'free ride of powerful'; and care more 'undesirable low contingencies' which are our real life and the essential needs of economy for all already advocated by Adam Smith.

Adam Smith economy is not about mercantilism and luxury or luxurious expenditures of the affluent ones. Of course even more virtuous is the social-economically wise management of societies caring in their productive environments

[The reason why Max Weber reading Adam Smith attributed too much virtuous capitalism to Protestant. Capitalistic structure exists anyhow. They are relatively virtuous if entrapped as low profile communities,, but have another face when dominant: Jews in Europe, Protestants below United Kingdom or remaining after Catholic massacres, New Worlders under English taxes, old believers marginal to Tsarism, Taiwanese separated by a Straight, etc.].

Thermo-economics has the purpose to feed you at the best cost-benefits care of ecological losses. Meanwhile there could be plenty of intermediate efforts for caring an economics of informative links. This fundamental is not so different from circulation of values; only they will have to be better anchored to landscapes and energetically measured economics of production.

Metasystem applied to Science

Language	Domain	Level	Logic
Facts observed	Domain of application	User	Descriptive models
Hypothesis	Applied Science	Observer	Explicative models
Theories	Pure science	Inventor	Prescriptive models
Paradigm	Philosophy of sciences	Epistemology	Epistemological models

The methods to build such a core system does not have to be very different from one level of scale to the other. So we need a transversal formalism with some natural physics consistency.

Consider defining energetic and material maps in a conventional way at a range of regional economy or eco-systemic landscapes; and empirically measured. Maps of information as synthesis of potential, natural gradients, etc. The meso-system (or pieces) interacts with those maps throughout perturbations (extractions, recycling,

191

etc.). With purpose of transformations and organization of extraction. On the basic ground of a formalized system or model.

We may have both correlations of human activities, rates of derivations (extractions); changes of subset functions and varying sets of priorities (with symmetries examined), alterations of balances and of flows, and so on.

Formal studies implies effects of scale, mixed constructions of meso and macro-scoped concepts. Traditional economic formalism if what is under scope must inscribe in limits defined by basic ground model. Budget constrains can be derived from thermodynamic suggestions are of that sort.

Now knowing about the quite unimpressive energetic yields of transformations; it is to observe that such estimations may be effectively well at the margins may generate anxiety observing the gross losses and absolute waste. Or quite deceiving when to look at relative numbers. And too calm for frenzy cocaine consuming traders. Not to tell about the depression of such as the 'poor little of G-S' ...

Models Links to Thermodynamics

Notice that this "what to expect"; as said in policies recommendations; is not absolutely dictatorial and static decisions. De-stockings of energy are to consider [In fact that destocking reservoirs of energetic resources the major abuse of industrial capitalism.

Society of consumption by Keynesian demand and Ford's elite labor, after World War II changed the previous. This kind of consumption Say-offered until 1929 crisis. With forced international division of markets of trade. Later was possibly more important than that of work pretended as well as analyzed by Marxists or socialists].

So in tune with hydrocarbons destocking; we have the unwise exergetic balances that are warming the climate [exergetic freeing out energy in any transformation, so heating anyhow the climate]. This together with the agricultural underuse of Sun's power resource, sources of environmental toxicology and biodiversity loss by degradation. In the delays, making the mis-adaptations of recycling to climate changes].

Now in core models, what we have to see is that the energetic "back-bone". This formally starts, in the matrix's calculus, with the **main diagonal** (the one on which you calculate the **'trace'**) [Of which we will not talk much in this essay]. Main diagonal (of squared matrices, especially the autocorrelation matrices defining the self) catch the symmetries, take-off of the proper values (also called **Eigenvalues**).

[At the minimum t is important to notice that when you want an identity analysis; you need to self-cross the matrix same row and column (so number of lines = number of columns and look at the main diagonal, the one of same, commonly maximum and concentration. If qualitative or probabilistic sum = trace = 1; unless defusing of correlating to each crossed self-cell. The model purpose to set the main independent variables and find purity].

With a cube (or a hypercube); it could also be the importance ordered 'main tube' from one corner of the cube, to the opposite corner of the cube. To imagine how these structures the levels, degrees of feeding and symmetries. This is the main feeder (matter-energy from the "micro-level" to set the main balances. Thus to manage that more rigorous by the side of analysis. Supposedly by simulation of sensibilities to perturbations under simulations for meso-level detailed in distributions into subset, *modulus*, etc.). So the matrix or the cubic box "centered" on the meso-level. Matrix calculus (or Hamiltonian) is able to take in charge many other issues, as of different levels by blocks of matrices.

Having to care, conventional matrix calculus is linear just for one type of metrized data: maxima only, minima only, linearized averaged. Products there take the matrix as a whole and product are either between 2 (squared) matrices, vector and matrices. But real phenomenological matrices are combination of matrices, partly linearize-able (when using conservation law). But many effects more point-wise or line-wise and so one is needed. But are harder to account for or having to be 'hand-loaded'. Assumptions of multi-linearly-ness are not always the best for taking account of punctual effects. [So with a need also for being more phenomenological. And let to the computer the work of deducing the degree of 'matrix-ability'.]

We know: for profane it is a bit difficult. Even it may be quite unclear to specialists since they are used to making that 'damned numbers' get out of the calculi. Things enough fragmented into pieces, for estimates from reductions enough reasonably looking. We have to complete a bit the details and hope the reader complete hse concepts.

Just for some tips of coherence about our vision of models. **Feeding main diagonal** would come qualitatively from down (micro-level), quantitatively from the macro-level. Which are "realistically obliged" enough matter (or energy) from flows, stocks, etc. and technological energetic yields, etc. Consider the specificity of the meso-level (consistency, level compactness, distributing to other cells; at positions, in other diagonals of the matrix. Where relative units (or subsystems) stands, relative relations, local openness varying capacities of developments: permeation from main diagonal, to other ones as distributing or draining (in the abstract of formalism, possibly the regulation, diagonal, or lines, or columns).

Eigenvalues are used in the method for estimating the best orientation of the main diagonal (minimizing the difference) but (?) whether the path diffusion of least efforts. [Commonly eigenvalues are used for best separating of axes from 'outer' reference (when minimized?); this is a bit delicate in interpretation, and they should be combined with the concept of maximum combination, structuring densities etc.].

Matrix of effects back-feeding of constraints upon environment [... commonly because trying to purify and ease the calculi, matrix calculus misses the complexity of real maps or cubes representing reality].

If with policies you will have to consider a superimposed map of the system perturbation. Possibly in the management what feed the matrix-system or the plan of actions and how distributed in the matrix.

Think about an irrigation scheme: main tube–main diagonal, primary ducts–diagonal closer to the main one - secondary ducts. Influences relations are between cells ... with the possible need to develop other picturing matrices as self-correlating matrices.

Policies would be then distribution of actions, within the network or over the matrix since an assignment of entry (some vector multiply by the matrix). And how you may bias or vary it smoothly after an abstract optimal of management.

Of course in a kind of irrigation schemes you have the general scenarios of 'control' which work more easily if well homogeneous and unlimited below (for limiting the specific work). So hardly the most intelligent and the most productive in realities with relatively independent cells, constrained in other ways, etc.

Deviations to recommendations have to feedback a system of disincentives, incentives for redesign (and innovations) or mitigating works, regulatory measures, etc.

The effects on "a primary" or intermediate level stocks of resources dilute the impact of changes (thus solve criticality?); as well as any interventions (direct or adverse) may be called perturbations. In fundamental physics you perturbed [bomb or blast ... a goal or target with particles] and examine the **characteristic scattering** of your experiment (in different kinds of recording devices dispersion of fundamental particles intuited by the theory).

Most softly in environments to care, micro project to macro (the meso develop with some degree of autonomy as balance between a 'micro' and 'macro'. 'Macro' or environment made forcibly and integrally since 'micro' fundamental level. But possibly having softer levels of 'complexifications' and in a macro-environment made in the same way from micro. Making a co-evolved environment (eventually transformed by 'meso' but meso possibly 'mobile' that is able, for a while, to migrate between more specified environment.

[Maybe the picture of 'twisted loops series. (More or less according to the level complexification in a much larger loop and a little bug (you inside the little loop, still made from the large loop ... or a Möbius' strip iterated cuts

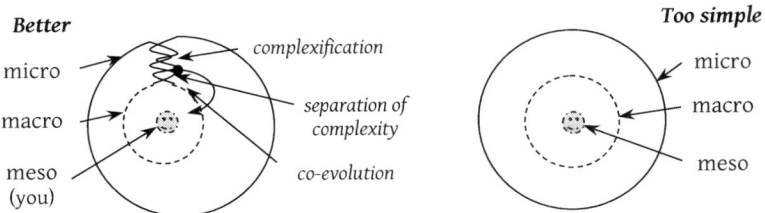

With the formal condition that we have to get rid of the pure organic view and catch the functional-matter and structural-energetic intertwined representation(s). Once design the ground model practical formal procedures are to establish scenarios of experiment inputs in such system. More of less developed as a matrix algebra-ized with more or less specific properties.

Possibly it is to make formal use of **quaternions**, or **Hamiltonian** (a kind of quaternion or possibly better: **octonions**). Then compare situations (states), vectors of effect (since operators or operated matrices, commonly by derivation one or twice so-called, respectively **Jacobian** or **Hessian** matrices).

Many human-made perturbations affect 'anthropo-scene' in excess and decently they are not deserving the social potential-cost-benefit ratio.

Simulated studies with measures of information (entropy), fractal dimensions, characteristic exponents, etc. as products on the previous maps of information, could be a way to estimate the impact. At least help to compare various options and choose the least problematic damages with the best rewards. Even also it can be evident to know in advance most sustainable scheme of use, the formulation and calculi could have a pedagogic virtue. That is to inform and help to discuss options, detail solutions. Create learning to manage closer to real information(s) and make better informed contracts as well as communication for regulations. Basic meanings and, eventually using updated art of conventional economics; to inscribe in those redesigned constrains. Probably with more emphasis put on neutral kinds of economics (or care) and more flexibility respect socially ideological micro-meso-economics.

[Remind that most **matrix calculus** is mainly based on **multilinear** sort of calculus, possibly the main right one for closed system and 1st principle of thermodynamic: conservation law, at the start of energy; but not all the good one, on the margins, which you intervene and perturb].

Macro-system constructions have a variety of perspectives. Either it is higher in complexity, but narrower in principles. Or in concepts weak and to protect from interventions. That is strong enough for being considered. Also formally, macro-levels can complete the meso-levels (providing the specification and values of some constraints (if there is no steak, there is no steak). Could be too: criteria of solvability (derived from policies).

Consideration may also be applied to a wider space, like a social environment. Meanwhile, the lower or natural environment comes from the micro-level. As an effect of abstract construction, it looks like that macro-environment is also the one of abstract values and macro-social aggregate. Considering it should be a source of solutions. Of course this should be formally manageable. Maybe it is not to have hundreds of lines in equations under only one kind of operation, but a proper understanding of balances; across moduli-integrated-packages of 3 dimensions; with sorts of symmetric relations between moduli level. The reason why suggested the micro-meso-macro intertwined level in a 'curious' way (with **twists**).

The reason why; of such **looping**(s) within efforts of constructions of models; will detail concepts further. But in short it is between formal 'extreme abstract' and on the other side 'physics fundamental extreme'. Between which we try to insert intermediate loops (to choose the "most convenient ones"). Anyhow, **matter, information and energy invariants are** quite suggestive of that feasibility, both physically as well as formal metro-logically (measures but possibly with adjustment of residual terms).

In other words, you have 1) Abstraction or 'information' developed as far as possible & 2) Energy exchanged of all details and overall energy (the thermodynamic estimate of energy & 3) Matter structures (measured in values of energy (as they have the energy equivalence expression). Then the system model is between, as a model functioning economically in the region of phase-space and values of measures. Those compatible with the one provided by parameters simulated in the formal model.

Systemic Economy of Models

Care that correspondences of formal model's structure maybe is not directly identifiable to the anatomy of the subject. Traditionally you have models focusing on details. Thus the anatomical correspondence is easy. But we do not understand why those traditional models are so complicated with a plethora of required formulation lines. And so absurdly simple by the side of operations. Even if we do not expect to be any prophet of anticipations good estimates.

When trying to shape a wholesome (relative model system; it is to imagine that what you expect is the wholesome reflecting the global properties of the subject in its environment, proper logical formulations and arithmetic for wholesome estimate of systemic use. This has some of the cybernetic black-box, but our idea is more to obtain a formal piece of **reasonably rigorous incorporated box series**. This for clean enough integration-derivation not ignoring the evolutionary processes. After the complexity, residual, openness, contrasts, variety of options and symmetry maintained, you may have non-perfect correspondence (as an aperture of probability), the point also is not to waste too much time on details.

Cybernetic device at the origin was speaking of feedback on a 'black-box system'; of which it was enough to manage the inputs and outputs (or extensive parameters) with feedback(s). [But at the reverse, such extensive parameters would be in our kind of model more the constraints to care]. Cybernetic black-box to control what was happening inside, no need to get in. We are not in that position but it has some reasonable sense, our motives of concern would be about looking at. First the sustainability of the subject and also consider the integrity in its environment and constraints or conditions for the economics of sustainability

Basic types of feedback processes
One step machine $x_{n+1} = f(x_1)$
Two step feed back method $x_{n+1} = g(x_n, x_{n-1})$ or Fibonacci numbers: $g(x_n, x_{n-1}) = x_n + x_{n-1}$
Feed back machine with memory
  One step machine with two variables:
  $x_{n+1} = g(x_n, y_n)$
  $y_{n+1} = x_n$
  One step machine based on combined formulas
  ax_n if $x \leq b$
  $a(1 - x_n) = x_n$ if $x > b$
  Multiple reduction copy machine (MRCM) as one step machine
Logistic feed back iterates: $p_{n+1} = p_n + rp_n(1-p_n)$

Once this basic level of the system (or head relative formal system) is enough 'reliable'; we can enter in more details of 'subsystems'. With an example the idea behind is the following, if you are sure that an environment system cannot carry the population observed or projected; before entering in more details of development.

No need to waste efforts if not enough margins or potentials. With enough perspective you may have to develop mechanisms of adaptation. In more basic physics model, if your model is suspected to be a formal system that will turn too illogical, or too incompatible with Universe-all micro-system and not matching any data measures with simulations then abstain.

If your approach is suspecting not to have reached a system; broader the view and try to catch a system with a larger perspective; but dismiss previous formulation. Not everything has to be a system. The relative abstract model is supposed to relate and mimic. With scientific goals you will not want to go on sustaining the model of, quite probably false.

With social choice clear responsibilities are, to be properly assumed. The social choice may give more delay to the model of use;. If enough delivering enough caring possibly no need to have the whole picture. [What we actually observe about development, barely care carrying capacities and does not expect most constrained people follow a reasonable scenario. Just those serving some interests. When not having policies preventing the possibilities of adaptations: restrictions to mobility; raise of borders; diversions from the coherence of provisions sets; promotion of systems easy to corrupt. This includes when regulatory counterbalances have been established. The converse not better: inflation with not look at the coherence of regulations].

Care nevertheless, that in social issues there could be functional targets that have to focus because too poor will be the effects if not achieved. But quite often social goals can be broad register some satisfaction without affecting critically as many as possible. Moreover, first of all, is the learning effect. Good learning may resolve later, having learned how to care and remake.

Thermo-Economics of Models.

In a whole system anyhow there is way(s) of entropy principle. Put it plural in its containment more than its direction (general trend to disorder). It mixes the quali and the quanti, possibly not in an homogeneous way. Some losses are going to be more critical; depending on the network of relative information. Probably a good use will consist obtain, after the different levels of complexity the potential destructive impact of entropy release. Possibly you will have the need to use complex numbers across scales. That is with the powers of the i.

To examine buildings flows opposed to entropy; that is 'neguentropy'. Then balance and you have what we coin 'netgentropic'. Formally this may be as simple as the exchange of information provided by one to another and crossed another to one. In our acts, we make for ourselves and for our aspirations (as feeling of stress for wanting to satisfy). This happens because coexisting open systems are exchanging. Both submitted to entropy trend toward disorder makes on all that one among the other(s) can obtain from that: matter, information and energy. It has to absorb which it can because relative closure (as well as open). It can accumulate and use for the building. This also varies, after the values of extensive parameters or its proper state, or specificities of moments and needs.

[So the horrible observation: capitalism and anarchism have more substantial physical ground under the form of netgentropic: (originally or neguentropy) and entropy (cardinality or, at the least: ergodic) ... And the problem that human societies of robber barons capitalists are often much more destructive. In facts both present the same risk, activate too much entropy either by destructions excessesor by order excess. Not to speak of communists that have pretended to build societies with perfect 'ordinal ergodism'. And probably no less than liberals that pretended to gain order from exaggerating openness].

In a narrower way, the micro-source of our universe principles, including in the narrow and huge troposphere, is of fundamental quantic physics. It has turned complex like up to biophysics and biochemistry (in a broad sense).

Then to the meso-system made of human beings caring properly decent average life expectations and socially sustainable constructions. They make that within environmental macro-systems pieces of troposphere. Which are both natural and complicated enough by humans; engineers, societies... Now, in a way that formalism is solvable; with the consistency of these: requires not rigidly closed by infinite iteration of the differential calculus but open and then probabilistic.

So, in the state of comprehensive modeling actually made; could it be not an unreasonable wish: that there is a good alternative with moral choice, ethics of equity as a primary social-economy. Because constructing with destruction, by release of entropy requires in the frame, care or constructing (technologies) and simultaneously not destroy too much (moral conditions). This would have much the sense to reach more feasible societies? And in more proper proportions with our technological advancements.

Of course this comprehensive systemic way; is still too valid. Anyhow no prohibition in the establishment of informative links; enough essential sorts of fibers bundles, which are like policies vectors. So with which to record ordering processes. The Gordian knot is with the comprehensive perspective: on what to base the relative formal systems?

We mentioned that they are invariants and if the energetic, electric of mass ones are universal. Good ones enough phenomenologically closed to behaviors of humans; are not necessarily brutally fundamental or just naively ecological. Present ecological management often show plenty of contradictory effects.

Going on with amounts of entropy and crossed entropy; statistically, we have rarer higher ordered systems positively receiving and incorporating economically. There are the needs of more common (ingestion) of lower-ranked systems. Quantitatively they can be larger as fuel sources. Shortcut there are technological and may supply if caring the economics of structuring recycling and networks economy across scales. So you may understand why we see netgentropic as sorts of loops succeeding for a while to have their neguentropy positive respect to entropy. So thanks to 2nd principle of entropy. For a while during the one's time life.

Economics of netgentropy consists to move the balances, minimizing the damages and entropy's excessive expression. These preserves wisely or eventually increases neguentropy. Manage it the best possibly the bits and bouts of diversified matters and energy avatars; since their supports with smooth exchanges. Exchange made possible and savvier, because from the 'similar equals' before or 'not so different after'] ...

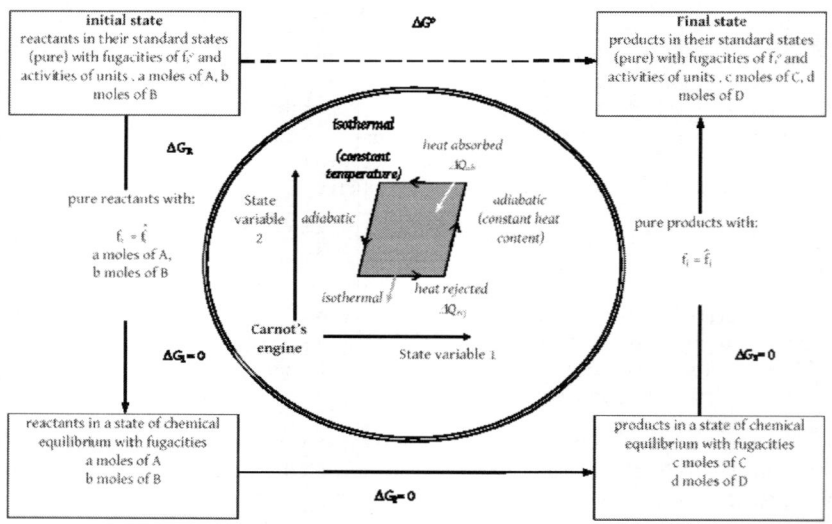

Pity and shame on the economists? -That make triumphant their pet-concepts superior to common sense. As if to abuse of: Lagrange-Piccard-Walras-Ricardo-Pareto-Arrow-Debreu -Hahn would be a sort of gene-ideology. And to have been late in the inclusion of Carnot-Cournot-Clausius-Nash-Prigogine-Georgescu-Roegen. [The cohort we could imagine inspiring. Like a mixed strategy Nash's equilibrium representing minimum entropy... Within which we would appreciate having a maximum neguentropic expansion: positive netgentropy or minimizing it].

Taking here economists as scape goats, but without ignoring that many superior formal scientists have personally not been better. Just you have the problem of first one's social ambition: succeed to influence policies.

Meanwhile the defects of formal scientists may have been for being voluntarily or not too discreet on executive humanity. Among mathematicians who intended to fix the mess with formalism: Kronecker, Hilbert, Carnap (1st period), Popper, Tarski, Bourbaki. Most had their counterpart or contenders (Cantor, Gödel, Carnap (2nd period), Lakatos-Feyerabend or exhaustion).

Equilibria in Social Systems

Now for some relations with theory of equilibrium as existing on social arts. Just started here with some of situations and critics. Theory of General Equilibrium has originally intuition already mentioned by Adam Smith (at least). Ricardo has been the one to try to put Smith into mathematical formulas. Supposed 1st mathematical interpretation of equilibrium came with Walras (a French economist after mid of the 19th century exiled in Switzerland). Maybe since formulation as equalities of all relative change (derivation) of 'needs' by a mathematician: Piccard fed Walras. This latter has been further empowered by Pareto's whom also promoted a harsher view of Paretian optimal (which very static optimum of assignation was also very conservative about inequalities. Much nonsense when looking at Nature's economy.

Marginalists teaching in economics ensued Walras and much of their forms were with the differential calculus (on abstracts) since the end of the 19th century. It was still expressions of (narrow and homogeneous) theoretical formulated models; proposed as intuitive mechanics in the businesses of States. In fact that has much to do with our start. A marginal cost of a 'one more unit to produce equals the price is simply this informative differentiate combination, hence not that with logarithms.

But one has to care that it is a projection. And one more unit to produce is not necessarily the same ground of previous. We have a mix of same and next different. Another inconvenient is precisely with the lack of heterogeneity. That is poorly informative. Moreover, other relations are missed. As the not so strange one you have with time, information, characteristic ratio, all that with price.

Things in mathematical economics develop much more intensively when the cohorts of economists empowered with Samuelson's manual (just after 2nd World War); meanwhile Kuznets statistical series, motivated by United States American economic planning efforts followed the mobilization of 2nd World War. Post war this came then in support of Keynes macroeconomics promoted post-war. [Somehow paradoxically Keynes was a statistician trained, but knowingly inspired by 'mass psychology' and his experience as a trader of money, in his economics essays. So he was at some point quite hard to formulate if not to understand. And this was made by his followers and adapters differently motivated. Hicks produces a now discussed popular formal version but remained a neoclassical. And different schools of Keynesianism appeared].

At the time of post-WWII industrial society, most of economics had that same purpose: **calculate general equilibrium theoretical models (GET) with large systems of equations or matrices**. Of course they retook from Linear Programming, programs of optimization with more mathematicians precursors. Such tasks of econometric models empowerment take place during the sixties and seventies and made these decades of primary GET, and not much more in theoretical economics; when everyone was in some degree recognizing the merits of planning,

Planning what?–without just accusing excesses?

Eastern World by ideology and occidental World has both practiced it with more or less lean theoretical grounds. Partly because the 'Soviet model' was for everyone, of course, had nevertheless succeeded to face the contingencies and brought its society out serfdom up to the cosmic outer space. Not miss the sacrificial means of their policies political empowerment.

But also because in the West the War efforts of after 1929 crisis of supply has been resolved central will and planning, more or less decentralized. The propaganda against the East were not just simply with facts (they were enough) and fair analysis. But also add creative counter propaganda from paranoid ideologists. Meanwhile out their own 'free' country cooperation has just promoted planning elsewhere (including agrarian reforms) started, so the empowerment of neocolonialism: planning against planning, any polarizing power intent that.

Standard rigorous formulation of General Equilibrium Theory in modern days has been made by Debreu, Arrow and Hahn just after the mid-20th century. Themselves or after their critics cleaned formal requirements.

Commonly they were about basic formal properties: **convexity, time adjustments** (dynamic of models), etc. Allais' sequenced time models intended, formally too complicatedly to cope with some. [Notice the informative oxymoron in physics time's a sort of 'simplification'; in economics it turns a problem hard to solve]. Another included formulation accounting for different effects such as **imperfections of information** and the meaning of "invisible hand". This **"invisible hand"** previously evoked, since the 18th century; when not before, it is about the (more or less slight gentle push toward ... 'nice or sour' good vibration for markets' adjustments or public interest, and so on.

Briefly, the formal primary link of theory equilibrium is with the equalization of all price variations respect to that of units of production; equalizing also by the way prices to marginal costs. Marginal costs, to be that of one more unit production. Geometrically it is quite easily the tangent at the point... But it can be future virtual if already reached 100% of production capacity. So there requiring an increase production by new or renewed means (investment, gains of costs, etc.). Under 100%, it is supposed to be easy to produce smoothly in the projection in near future the one more unit. In all that the first primary is to homogenize, consider simplicity. Theoretically and fairly, only by the 'end of everything' nice, soft and smooth. [Of course this is unbelievable out obsessive compulsive disorder]

[These rigors of interpretation for making economics properly satisfying the 'wonderful harmonious world. A model of discipline which look at the reality top-down; and so puts nature wonder in inefficient margins. As an effect impolite economist to discard and despise most of the trends, frameworks and states of construction of natural complexities. And the ignorance of most of what to properly insert humans' complications. Including the ones that could be helpful for enhancing robustness and ground our abstracts metaphysics concepts good to physics-formal existing equivalences: energies, quantum supports of information, etc.

This is like to prefer, cognitively the position of the omniscient, omnipotent, omni-defusing (or omni-informing) and 'omni-smoothing' and plane since that. [Even God does not do that!]. They may concede some accounts for contradictive problems and large contributions of 'artifacts'. For looking like caring some 'details below'. Possibly their complicity is required *ex-post*; for fixing some inconvenience of their utopia management and theoretic social arts of economics. After the 'not so good tests' of their theories despite so positively framed empirical data series. Top-down corrections are entertaining, distracting and maintaining the exhausted paradigms. Not to tell about the wrong uses of knowledge resources and communications.

These are abuses of formal methods usability. Their instrumental qualities recruited and wrongly biased for justification of abstract. Mostly non-inscribed in the natural processes and their suggestions. Of course this is not much different from the many fundamental mistakes of social arts: to justify an abstract their utopia theory for the deterministic purpose of groups and societies manipulations. This is what every humans, groups and societies are doing and is not without fair intention. Make their civilization contradict the generally morally harsh ways of natural regulations.

And in some way the level of complexities and complications; dissimulate the lack of realism of mechanisms. But strategically this is an essential mistake of Occidentalism and globalization promoted by bureaucracies; submitting most of affluent modern societies. They are helped in their frameworks many peripheral dependent societies whatever these last ones traditions. Subordinated to Occidentalism they are and exacerbates their entropic promotions and destructive extractions to their own profits.

Some of the societies main reasons; having achieved those degrees of technological developments are to make prevail moral issues within the main possibilities. Similarly for many 'leaders' or 'deciders' the converse: ensure the many possibilities of profits by the hard means and hierarchical strength. Rude ways of geopolitics or policies economies used to ensure the disposal of availabilities to their societies. Of course, in the worldwide technological turmoil of information and communications: confusion, levels of mistakes dilute; allow the massive uses of non-renewable stocks.

This is somehow smoothed when the regular regimes. But still preserved the traditional means of adjustment: techno-bureaucracies parasitism, wars and conflicts, clash for domination of civilization or geopolitics. Essential strategic mistakes are with the lack of enough informative streams, for something like: **co-homological development of moral ethical frameworks choice**. That would be **to develop within the natural processes of transformation**. So that could make **smarter use of capital of knowledge**.

Of course it is not to ignore that the evidences of disturbance produce everywhere fair and fine reactions, as in terms of new social economics. Such are trials of life's other ways. <any

sorts of substantial studies and philosophies blossom. Bu most often looks like in the margins of relative societal non-effectiveness. So they need no less of the privileged link to the dominating ones; directly or indirectly; pretending the contrary or not.

[Some, not as many as to expect, benefit from that and even profit of that. Hence not in the proper conditions]. Nor they use the potential of advancements of knowledge. And finally make use of methods just of the same ways as traditional. That is they will not achieve sort of integral but fair and moral civilizations they aspire to. They are well part of ergodic warming.

Smarter use of capital of knowledge with the instrumental ones of formal sciences would have the purpose to **manifest more cleverly the sorts of naturally complex maps of information** we mentioned. This may be unconscious and **conscious in the flows of implicit** information and knowledge communication. In the hope to influence free attitudes, reactions and actions in 'production' (Say's law with care at micro-conducts part of the social job). Manifest in the mostly implicit frameworks of social-economical human complications to influence and partially express the corresponding maps of societal transformations. Probably to **nurture the spontaneous reframing of ambitions**; hence not to make them disappear.

This would be **sources of training and conditioning 'free' motivations in cognitive processes of formulations** rather determinist-like promoting and undertake 'enormous' bureaucratic processes of societal re-engineering.

Looking at the formal **concept of value** in general theory of equilibrium is fine. But as we will evoke, have alternative kinds of interpretations that could have better physics ground origin... So why not get closer to the most fundamental physics concepts? ... in a systemic relative whole way? ...

Not theoretical narrowed register convenient to one specialized scientist comprehension. Why not better let legitimate actors, eventually trained; develop, volunteering and share their own interpretations in their own processes. Rather than push abstract social norms, as far as possible, in the corners but in fact this was more for out of the 'house of wisdom and the field of freedom'. Especially because wanting to be inconsistent with Nature and enough manipulated for not being easily disqualified by evidences.

Disqualification quite easy confused when many ergodic noise and many distractions so implicit in unequal affluent and nasty multiplying rules for over loading the places of wise freedom.

General equilibrium theory, during the fifties up to seventies of the past century, had the effect to bypass some 'pure mathematical concepts' that could have been useful for better explanation and sooner corrections. Rightly called after but for serving the theory. Concepts as of **convexity** (solved by **law of decreasing yields**); **asymptotic convergence of equilibrium** which is mostly taken as given by models, in a non-realistic sense?). **Existence of unique solution** more retrospectively framed since an assumption of stability delivered by 'The Market' (markets' supply-offer opposed well, the very stable X shape; but in practice all contrary was observed: non stabilizing the purest ones).

Even when alternatives from closer to production phenomenological interpretations (Sraffa, Minsky, reminded by Keen). To observe that the **meeting point of curves**, looking like forms delivered by pure mathematicians under the name of **unstable**

equilibria: a flattened × with slopes both negative. Many arguments were recruited to support the neoclassical convictions in that belief: as Brouwer's **fixed point theorem, Pareto's criterion** on convexity, norms' **convergence** to global equivalent: **any norm converging at the infinite to the same is equivalent**).

Empirical Economics Calculi

1st generation of econometricians (since Cowles's Commission) started to make uses of widening States' statistics (initiated be Kuznets) with large systems. Models could have reached hundreds of "structural linear equations". They had to use the advances of **linear algebra** and economics input-output matrix representations (by Russo-Soviet: Kantorovitch, Polish: Lange and Russo-American: Leontief).

Dynamic analysis has been seeking for points of relative equilibrium; facing better sorts of stability and instabilities that could also non-linear.

Appear better understood, **different kinds of equilibria** (apart the Paretian optimal, sometimes already existing in concepts upon specific questions (Cournot, Bertrand, Stackelberg). [As well as in a system of different variables, there is partial ones]. Nash's mathematical formulation based them better (with quite fundamental mathematics effects). Such **non-Paretian out optimal uniqueness** can be either free or imposed. Such as to keep **strategic games** (to win over) or to push forward (**cooperative games**) and consensus framing (from linear or plane borders).

Another kind of matrix formalism: more **random matrix; game like logic board;** and state transition matrix state-[transition matrix is used to find the solution to a general state-space representation of a linear system]. It fed a huge current of these 2nd order, kinds of equilibria within the Theory of Games. This Theory of Games was founded with the help of von Neumann (a major Hungarian-American mathematician of the 20th century). It nurtured another cohort of 'pure mathematicians of economics'.

At first they were put at the front of the scene, because **cybernetic-systemic** and behaviorism also were ideologically pushed. But those registers have immediately discussed in a multidisciplinary way. At that time, you could not move society just with economists; the fear of the reds was an easy engine. Even for preparing developing countries dirty wars in the defense of crazy civilized dictators against armed socialists disturbed by the populist **mirage of values and wealth.**

Contrary to what may think foreigners of the Anglo-Saxon world of economics: theories at that time were less important than politics or law, even in academies. Business sciences were also not so relevant, and yet not much more economical. They were more related to pressures of groups of interest near the governments. So business arts pretending to be a science only somehow after and often as a sub-register of industrial organization, and accounting ['Scientific organization of work emerged with Taylor; start of 20th century].

With the emergence of the discipline came also finance exuberant in growth. This started during the eighties of the 20th century .... For sizing the power in the industrial factories? As Chief Financial Officers meanwhile industries were delocalizing and delegating to Big Dragon and small tigers?

Times was also about 'end of' struggles between political systems ... without having clearly what was a well-formulated system...

... and just rejecting any other understandings. So refusing to examine what sort of 'subtle by ignorance' systems Nature was carrying.

On the distant margins even trying to disappear, more or less actively, the primitive communities properly balancing their less stressed lives with their environments. Preserving they are the flows and bio-diversification transformation while deriving 'fruits' to their way of life.

Only with the problem being savagely attacked by all those moderns. Almost free to kill them; meanwhile the nicer of the global village where producing folkloric theories. It is not to look at those sorts of global citizens, wanting to participate to the wealth of affluent societies by supplying their markets of fancies; at the expanse of indigenous.

Lessons From World DisEquilibria

World-wide financial destabilization came abandoning fixed parity of 'expenditures' main international currency, to its gold standard. That was imposed, because the maturity of its main owner empire; were trying with wars to prevent political destabilization of its labor international division.

> In 'its' free world its national budget had increased constraints produced by, far away from home, war. It triggered a huge increase in oil prices; since producing countries were becoming more sovereign and has organized in a Cartel-like based on their oil resources. Oil prices were very low, previous empires in stop-and-go kind of economics trying to slow down their regression still incredibly arrogant. Meanwhile oil-producers were trying to react to a down-trend of their incomes from their resources; and to anticipate major investments required in this sector. The pretext of big push oil-prices supposedly provoked by the cartel with a pretext in another war, nearby region of major resources; fundamental unsolved humane equations; costs a lot. When not a practical means for dissimulating.

> Coinciding with the post-war reconstructions and maturity of 'renewed affluent societies; the 'Occident' was facing a slow-down of its labor productivity. Keynesian occidental economy with increasing resources of national economic turned to plans with large models and many statistics; were culminating its concern. At the same time the geopolitics of Cold War was also coinciding with post decolonization aspirations for development.

How to speak of smooth general equilibrium in such conditions?–when the aspirations were so conflicted prone? The wisest concept may be more to understand the **dynamic transitions of equilibrium along most essential renewals** (satisfaction of basic needs) on the main trajectory of life of society (or not if un-careful and ineffectual). As smooth as possible are the transitions from one state of the system (of supply and consumption), to the next one; not necessarily on the same things since they are exhaustible. 1) **Sable in local fields framework**, 2) **commutable in members as atoms**, 3) **occupying the environment of opportunities**, 4) **not prejudging too orderly of whom stay in commands**; 5) **taking all the opportunities to maintain the sustainability of the main metric:**

stay alive and 6) **enjoy having had it with good means** (reward). All in all … a sort of shuttle in the 7) Sweetest phase-space of reasonable efforts: we are and since 8). We are not framed for lack of efforts.

In the seventies of the past century, within few years social instabilities were blossoming everywhere despite worldwide maneuvers of brutal contentions. The first empire did not succeed in its war. But for weird reasons, preferred the shame of having lost its peripheral war; while ignoring the one of having corrupted its democracy with a Watergate. So soon it turned to be again proud with invasion of tiny ones and with the implementation of neoliberalism adjustments as if a martingale for strategic gambling. Neoliberalist adjustments had their first tests in bloody military dictatorships. That the Empire had just almost it-self established.

Next decade observed the exhaustion of some paradoxical race for supremacy; that is the political disinflation of the other cold-war big contender. Change the model of development within the 'same system' … more to be produced by **endogenous factors**? On the mean time pulling and pushed up the financial services have taken advantage of information's revolution. This revolution has been more efficient, in many hardly developing countries; to empower the bureaucratic public offices local and global. So as for the generalization of corruption in politically dependent subsidized countries. "Why they do that with our money?" Because **you refuse not to determine inclination of others' trajectories**.

Those were times also to develop the privacy of rent owners; and the recycling the incomes from rents of delocalization. Officially it was pretended that the financial markets the best place for stabilization. In effect they characterized more by **'volatility,' friction, deflation, 'dis-capabilities of absorption.'** Shocks symptomatically reflected that this propensity to stabilization was not the case and that the monetarist equation a too simplistic one, for the understanding of governance? No aid-worker has yet understood that the world is not just simple as filling their conversations with the word 'complex' in any paragraph.

The trade of weapons another profitable line based on speculations of fears flourished? Since this was the most efficient way for **recycling** the rents from oil; of government with dubious legitimacy. Not so easy to cause-effect breaking of such **cycles**; not based on the essential: gain some from the laudable mainstream. Of course not to miss that theory of **imperfect markets** were already existing, after some sides of Keynes. At least since Robinson, further than with Stiglitz and other].

The financial programs of restructuration were started; [contrary to what you may think it occurs before the major ideological leaders of the new monetarist dogma]. These programs of restructuration were more pretending to restore stability in Countries' international *status*. Using for that a Unique and Simple Framework, pretenced to be as 'forcing' as possible. But a highly related world 'robustness'; is not exactly an **endogenous quality**. In effect the best empowerment has been for international financial organizations stanza. Leaders as major deciders of world economy presided to huge opportunities of financial liberalization and deregulation. This better had to come together with an enormous increase of budget deficits for the 1st one. The 2nd enough 'lucky' with its new platform of intercontinental intermediation's services, and the rents of new oil resources stock (nothing neoliberal in that).

The new revolutions of information and personal computing supporting the means of massive telecommunications did not come alone. This feed the financial innovations, but then this turned short and did not bring the relief and the support to expect from reframing of such sort of so necessary distributions of signaling resources for the advancement of social-economic sustainability. This came, also correlated to worldwide charitable capacity of projections.

Such sort of determinism could be easy and could have been a major in the smoothing of societies' transformations. Also to mention global regional circulation of cultural products that could have relativized the barriers and the borders between countries. Possibly they have produced efficient norms of conducts; for preparing the ergodism of difficulties of governance and frustrated communitarianisms.

To remind 'quantic jump' is highly uncertain (from the point of view of the one free and transparent in the field; especially in very rigid countries. And even more it is in the determinist frameworks. Deserving is an ex-post self-justification in a World not framed by most efficient spontaneous potential assignations of the quantic world. You need to share some of other fields so bifurcations to self-development not so autonomous.

In the *limbo* of mentioned revolution; also came together with the containers' transport revolution, providing enormous logistical and 'fluid' vehicles to world-wide heavy exchanges. Thus mobility of raw materials, pieces, intermediate and final goods expanded grids almost exclusively. The increased mobilities of humans took other implicit determinist pathways. Meanwhile the distribution of the hardware and software had not necessarily with the same opportune properties of fair networks open to all. It is probable that have been better served those of peripheral administrations on their relations to the 'restructurations', the virtual opportunities of services supports and the leisure minded kind of industries. There are fields that spontaneously share and intricate, forcibly considering the extensive parameters; weirdly and possibly are disorganized when under the determinations non-clever with the sort of extensive parameters and rules of games to manage for good maps of potentialities. Very few are those caring for **potential open optimum Occam's mappings**.

Of course the concept of sustainable development was started during those eighties and celebrated start of following decade. Have in mind we do not speak of social arts fashionable concepts. Of those that are propitious for recycling business of the services on vague terms. While pretending to solve humans conditions ignoring most of true information. That is more with instructions of advice. Out of the needs felt by consistent problems. So instead of smoothing what we observed had reactive adverse effects. As you have with so-called corruption, environmental threats to increase and degradations of many social conditions, out of the records. Despite some basic improvements in the targeted public services; significant to international statistics of primary needs. Those enough for the supposed providers pretend to have been successful and efficient.

Now it is not exactly the same recycle abstracts without thickness quite easy to connect many things and the geography of needs or the symptoms of illnesses. For example, desertification emerges as a world-wide concept since the fifties of the past century. Taking and managing it seriously since that time could probably have brought solutions to the ecological crisis that ensue thereafter. The world-wide management of humanity's threatening seems better at putting in evidence the gaps between what we declare, what we effectively do. What was generated, after these wonderful expectations, in a new era for all?

The primary criteria applied at the respect of these **expectation** look awful, at least in terms of **coherence** and determinist wisdom. Even if narrowing the scope of benefits and cost relevancy. The illnesses of globalization emergence looks, in surprising disagreement, with the intentions implemented. Of course all policy manager will object and deny any relations between hes good wills and the contemporaneous clashes observed in the societies they serve.

In the present essay, even more surprising than the humans passions we are used to (and skepticism may carry), our concern is about how the epistemologies of formal sciences is just biased, for not providing lucidity but biased toward arbitrary disconnections and distort lessons. Also quite surprised by the feeling that many primary basics are never examined, nor mentioned nor formally equip people in charge. Most seemingly to have a refuge in prolific and; artistic agitations of words and poor excuses.

More With Equilibrium Practices

The aim of this essay not for judging on social responsibilities, but examine the formal troubles, we think are increasingly part of the problems societies so imbued by the means of information's revolution. Making the formal sciences misconceived supports of traditional paradigms about the ways to do. Soon we will get back to our main course, so we have to be extremely short.

In the aftermaths of national decolonization processes or social revolutions, 'anticipated' of 'refrained' wars by elites' convenience. Dependent states produced social and political straightjackets with all the help and advice they imagined to need. Aspirations for accelerated developments and models of paths toward achievements had their theoretical contributions and their bizarre implementations. With conflicts about areas of influences, it is not to be surprised that Cold War prepared containments and induced wars and social struggles without much difficulties to feed them on the other camp.

This had some set-backs in the peripheries of 20th century seventies, together with other 'atrocious victories' meanwhile accelerating and exhausting the distortions of social economies by the races to armaments. Just before also came huge exhaustion. Rush to the bottom and; to the top is quite usual in the distractions of civilizations. This is often producing big crunch at ends of the roads; if no new countries of invasions are discovered.

Soviet Central Planning had reached discreetly some level of social care (with enormous sacrifices previously made by most of the society and by some groups. It had and fundamental problems of economic formulation and perspectives. Clearly non-adapted to the race toward leadership, but could be saying that out the military sector the 'sclerosis of civil society competitiveness was all bad for the common people' - things where negotiable. Biased system by military sectors contributed much to the exhaustion. Meanwhile in terms of social economics it is to observe that the **inward social geographic distribution** of this empire; made **central planning formal models of economics** had some justified constraints pragmatism. Necessary views were represented by those **accounts by material balances, awareness of information's problem,** etc.

Opposite the 1st Empire implemented neoliberal revolutions were to disqualify the diverse Keynesians paradigms. Also affected have been economical efforts, processes of planning by the numbers. Neoliberalism was too confronting, too ideological, become the *Deus ex Machina* of efforts with main effect to promoting inequalities undercover of supposed rigor to prevent State's *extravaganza*. But it had some primary concepts not so unwise about the need of societal simplifications because mature affluent societies were also distorting by means of complications in a similar way inequalities. Without this neoliberal simplifications policies would probably have come in the first place of societal problems, under another way of words.

The problems of neoliberal propagations have been too, in the choice for implementation. World-wide in yet not enough developed countries with the choice of dictatorships. These are anyhow strikingly purifying their opposition much more than their honesty. Another major indirect inconvenience was the support by many institutions whom did not have these goals. Those supposed to equilibrate started to behave simply according to the new dogma, not after the legitimacy of their mandate. With nice manners they did not clean their own practice and implicitly they maintain their top-down segregating ways.

As a result all applied the same frame even if at the rostrum and what could have been supposed the revival of individual frameworks for opportunities and responsibilities. This turned a harsh and old-fashioned bitter *panacea*, promoted by occult interest politically correct but strongly empowering the manmade disaster, the ferocious inequalities and the opportunism of corruption. What could be somehow justified and mature, in developed State of Rights requiring to 'oxygenate' their superstructures and established petty privileges, produced better hidden networks of unfair competitions. Meanwhile in many peripheral countries turned more the structural adjustment juke boxes of traditional martingale to feed the embezzlement.

By the side of radical critics, there was in the East as well as in the West some forms of tolerance. With fundamental scientists for example in the Soviet Academy of Sciences as it could be for some kind of equilibrium in the East. Not to observe sorts of equilibrium in the other East, where the rebalance came from succession of periods. In the democratic West the rebalancing were more respect to the peripheries of the neocolonialism. So inside democracies you had more some funny guy exceptions in the free world of academies and the competitions between chapels or schools of thinking. The national systems of elitism then had to face with more or less periodic 'revolts of youth'; without much affecting the races to inequalities.

To observe plenty of good emerging ways in economics approaches from many fields and registers. Maybe they were lacking sense of *consensus* in the way to make things more simply phenomenological ad more fundamental? They could have done much better than what they did for 20 years. Major defects of these dispersions had 2 major defects: 1) The **lack of synthesis processes**; at least under forms of mutual respect; 2) The **formal individualism** that at some point ignore the grouping effects thus do not balance them in what has to be shared. Like for the construction of frameworks.

There the problems for joining and developing together both with the competitive **systems of incentives** developed, without consistent social involvement. Or the academic defects of having to produce theories rather than synergies.

Consider, for example: plenty of good concepts from 'post' and then 'neo'-Keynesian that could remaster itself. Observe the emergence of ecological accounts, another good initiative; together with alternative quality of life approaches. Sort of 'post-industrial' concepts which have been hardly corrective of Veblen's leisure-class. Also as premises of thermo-economics you have the line of Georgescu-Roengen (Romanian-American mathematical economist) or Grinberg (Swiss ecological economist) and some others (Schumacher in the United Kingdom, Passé in France).

Most, alas, covered by the noise of neoliberal revolutions and normative of most economics departments behind the monetarist-neoliberal-neoclassical economics (Cerberus, hounds of Hades has 3 heads). Other specific registers were good for inspiration; theories of: 1) **Regulations** (over-simplistic systemic), 2) **Contracts (too narrowing, 'Polanyi's sources of exchanges), 3) **Auctions**; and 4) **Incentives**; 5) **Behavioral economics**. Most because dominated by the theory of their research; were driven, since the free-world of academies.

So, many diverse and complementary efforts, have been unduly disqualified, by the international superstructures bizarre lack of competence. So dedicated they were to their dogmatic compulsive and iterative 'financial restructuring of national economies' ... and their uncertain good results. [Or too busy at selling their services for half-sweet weird advises. Formal arguments to pay attention was the conceptual economic theories difficulties of their equilibria formulations, for example:

The residual or 'remaining' of good 'invisible hand tâtonnement'; respect to a proper understanding of **residual** when you manage an economic model in a society. The technology (approached by Solow). Eventually it's' bluffing and formally the way it may be implemented in a learning society [a case for **Liouville's theorem**?]. To consider together with the **limited pluralism of capital** and/or the **economics of knowledge**?

Imperfections problems are of **information** and **interfering asymmetries**. That never properly understood the correct system of speaking levels. As pleasant as could be to level the right of speech at international ones. This cannot come before clever social participations in their ground levels. As proved by the liberation theology, with its defects by the side of methods).

The **economy of scale** and **innovations** have frameworks which are quite deficient; for the management of qualities and quantities in combinations. Where compactification of individual units hardly use sorts of **intrications grids**. So you are commonly limited to 'outer measures of amounts'. And the prices negotiated when transactions not properly reflecting thermos-energetic costs ... without telling about the indirect consideration of that).

The **zero-sum games** understood has the sort of activities and efforts generation that do not bring that combination of growth and satisfaction. As expected (in economics of consumption to imagine the hyperinflation of energetic waste *versus* the satisfaction of consumptive addiction. Addiction as could be seen many expenses of any. Compulsory have satisfaction; but activities providing employment are to compare with deficits of consumption elsewhere; or in the same environment the poor recruiting effect of luxury goods and; services of the same sort.

After the theory of games, **logics of games** have been developed, adapted to the handling of plural modalities in probability?–Articulation of games without chances and **grid network order**, to compare with **random networks degree of freedom**. Games with probability; in the consequences of choice of options? With present many kinds of paradoxes named after their author: Allais, Condorcet, Jevons, Leontief, Lucas, Solow, etc.

As we will suggest further, all that was somehow true but too often the willingness to believe prevailing, in the relative frameworks that should be dedicated to societal jobs and only behaviorally indirectly influenced by your spiritual beliefs. **Not to let the public spaces high jacked by ideologies of religion at the expenses of**

commonness. The same valid for private interest. Of course which historically has stripped of the formal arguments? Some could have over recruited to feed dangerous illusions of unique truth; despising the much informative counter-arguments.

Nevertheless to observe that many sorts of ideological beliefs pretended, out religion or even out spirituality, have played the same paper as these. Especially for lay political deciders: unique-mind-ness authoritarian governance adepts... Which may be the source **of 21st century politicians'** sorry status. Either in non-democratic countries kill (really) your opponents or; in democratic ones die yourself (of ridiculous) from your policies, 'because not as smart as experts'. So leaving to the politicians the last option "take the money and run". Sort of short social-ness left from past glory. No expert able mention that: that would otherwise have to recognize their own inefficiency; when not just preparing their future political 'career'.

> ... **Un-understood uncertain probability**, make most providing advises trying to look like 'very tautological' but tremendously of blurred applicability.

This already mentioned by Smith but, clearly the main is that economists are not all clear on how to be smart with policies and their management. Meanwhile traders can be dynamic and flexible respect to the conjuncture of the markets, but too an antagonist to the social utility when not too relative respect to businesses. Not enough conveying the needs for financing, missing where values have proper anchors.

> Uniqueness of minds, models, representations and beliefs are all formatted toward these inconsistent illusions of one best and all coincide; only to (wrongly) evacuate the residuals that may be virtuous synergies required by social economy.

Bad News Good Lessons that is about Mistakes?

For looking at the humans' phenomenology, more essential is to consider **variable sequential equilibrium maintaining few trajectories**. Like life and broad freedom of 'free' enterprising in social utilities. With a sort of somehow stable 4 wheels balances representing **the multiple purposed life vehicle**. Better not to want a precise one, so as to be adaptable to the environment of work; in the 'phase-spaces' of dedications. To solve most of our matter and energetic problems by kinetics. In search of good dedications and satisfactions. Helped with denser approaches with formal efforts.

Of course we have clearly in mind that our critics are re using a very traditional technique a "could have been better human development" or implicitly a framework of comparison, which is here by no means fair. Unfair way but because still **non-existing perfect relative formal system; anchored to complexities**. Those that could have an end-say on the comparison between past and modern-day conditions. In social sort of principles that is the problem: they are not; since analytical social frameworks are mobile. Making that the comparisons would be anyhow dubious.

We have yet no comprehensive empirical result. Like if it will be easy to implement practical matrix of influence over models of relative formal system. We see quite well the opposition that we could face if even imagined trying something at the respect.

Now with the formal mathematical economics efforts made since more than a hundred and half years, Marshall and Pigou as the bridge between marginalists' school (end of the 19th century: Walras Jevons, Menger) and post-World War II. With efforts in general formal sciences modeling and; in particular of mathematical economics and econometrics, formal broad picture is well advanced. Even if many other details are needed in algebraic structures. In our informative link it is to observe a need of marginalist expression as a sort of **convolution**; between more than 2

Modern formal economy intents for being unary and comprehensive. Conscious of challenges and difficulties. After some results of formal investigations, it would be to include mathematical economics. But you will not find all what you need here (?)

Formal scientists have they quantic *vacuum* (and the weirdness of their concepts) as a source of modesty and often their lack of curiosity for human affairs. Fundamental natural scientists have the Nature wonders and their experimental devices but should they? Better care their social involvement for being wise and supportive. Those a bit more distant from formal 'cleanliness' should try to master better their doctrines? –For more cross-borders fair practices and prevent themselves from being dogmatic. Social formalists have not much more than their shame either individual (when facing their responsibility and duties of consistency respect to realities); within close environmental constraints and; social ones as professional and as citizens.

Also you have the need of designs of socio-technical systems, for not exonerating any.

Our concern is about: how to reach potentially more social utility; for fruitful perspectives on modeling in human affairs. Then not to miss that all the mentioned defects. To imagine how they have played urging frameworks of investigation, like about this concept(s) of the general equilibrium.

With so many results in the intents it is to fix the formal problems of the defects. We will see further some formal suggestions to remaster your "wholesome" meta-philosophy upon your metaphysics.

Formal in Economic Models

To summarize here some of the social art, of economics; its formal defects; and undue arguing for being considered as mastering most important science. Of course, you can make very sophisticated models. Symbolically looking like identified to social realities. Even if filtered by a sort of window on economics; it does not make that you are listened for what you pretend. Would be the statistics the truth? When you are used to them in natural but complex science, thus quite high in terms of complex systemic. You tend to think that the statistics of well-designed experiments somehow inform you. Hence not as properly as to expect on very mechanisms.

So social economic statistics dressed for and by theories could they be fair with the purpose and the predictions expected of anticipations when they are meaningful? With so much formalism economics look like half-serious. More by the ambitions of their masters than by the deliveries nicely expected. So in half part their share the same fate of social arts, periodic crises of distrust, where only narcissist believes quite exasperating prevent the depression of mood. More problematic is that the formal approaches do not share the learning properly, training and critical effect that could be expected, especially once understood the importance of uncertainty in common day-life: most things.

> Be an official formalist can sustain sort of bizarre but interesting mathematicians. Even some recognized *genius* of some kind, honored with academic chairs. Especially if they serve or at least stop bothering the real owners of governments. Otherwise they may be irritating model producers. More at the service of international financial institutions; bizarrely they will not be in the real box of accused; when the disaster set-ups? Nevertheless these internationals are easily vilified too; by their ex-partners in preparing the disasters. Many critics 'from outside' are often unaware of advisors weak conditions.

> Models in social arts is the ambition 1st to justify a dogma; for a self-established good condition (yours' and of your country); 2nd to maintain the 'super-social-structures feeding you. Be it only your research funds. But not to deny that achievements of wealth can be hard to obtain and; environments of business. These are not so easily resilient. 3rd is to make many promises to those who have not. Especially if they pay for your services. 4th one includes many obscurities (for being uncontrollable) and the pedagogy for looking like smart.

In our opinion, those kinds of mathematical economics formalism major difficulties come from: 1) Disarming but often ferocious **short cuts with averages** about human concepts. For example, you have the myth of average humans for theory together with the lack of account the most essential. [Now that is a (wrong) bias which is more historical, but still with inertia of neoclassical micro-economics]. 2) **Sense of purity**, thin-ness, smoothness, 'asymptotic', homogeneity, integrality at will. Exclusiveness after caprices of social methods. [If it is clear that these are more reference for 'not so as' could be more inspiring to contrast with realities]. 3) **Cleanliness of many formal concepts**, almost reserved to certain professionals [when many converted are propaedeutic scripts; could be useful for learning how to search and care formal preparations].

4) **Over-simplistic on concepts of operations** [to distinguish between excesses of purification for operating too simply–analytical laziness. *Versus* geometrical significance of operations when to approach overlaps, framing, entanglements, intertwining, economics of modelling]. 5) **Faith in formal reduced infinite simple mathematics as if 'complete'** or "anyhow better" than mind and common sense [brains' arithmetic(s), contexts and circumstances humanely and formally often wiser than plenty of 'rational models'].

6) **So too many believers on the sanctity of mathematics 'by their** own' but those uneasy with many basic concepts of formal sciences. [Making that formal sciences are often too unhelpful]. 7) **Still too uneasy with fundamental probabilities**

concepts and statistics mixtures. [Too much misunderstanding the meanings when probability could be seen as a 'major engine of Nature' required by everyone. For them not expect 'just prophets']. 8) **Abuse of power respect to environmental based economics** [meanwhile environmental based economics not enough thermodynamically grounded].

Providing this with important economists' excessive compulsions (obsessive-compulsive disorders):

A) **Determinist prone**: either reason ground [Cartesian not necessarily of small cells board] or executive friendly [either executive summary for incompetent deciders illusions or missing providing induction that could smooth formally empowered social actors].

B) **School-dogmatic-prone**. Driven by their antagonisms [... Instead of complementarities, similarities and potential synergies].

C) **Static prone with 'their principles'** [definitive and perfect definition seekers, when not religious at economical dogma or finance officers addictions].

D) **Lacking flexibility** when **facing political frameworks of economics** [would be reality formal systems of social-economic could have to be better cared by structures of social-political constraints].

E) **Often moral or ethical principles antagonists** [when the targets of economical laws should be sustainably ethical as first and last resort].

F) **Service mind biased, either toward that sort of dictator perspective.** [For the remaining common, no other alternative than detest formulas. And stay out the exclusive jargon of pure lines of interpretation. [There is a need for adaptability or flexibility of social-economic models for better demo-collective regulations].

G) **Too-incomplete with many concepts** [Without missing that analytical completeness a natural resource and good *praxis* must entangle the complement of analysis... Feed-backed perceptions on effects obtained].

H) **Discriminating social forms** [the paradox of economic policies: pretend to serve the society by forcing cognitive resignations of most, to their 'rational'].

I) **Epistemological defects since a logical perspective** as well mathematical metrical rudeness.

Of course, this list of sins should not ignore that so many defects correspond to reactions against many arbitrary and unfair intrusions. Intrusions of social actors are when willing (justified or not) to distort policies, consensus, facts and common sense. Wrongly toward their illusions and profits in the name of their superior economy. It is to notice nevertheless that pure formal scientists look like more amused by mathematical economics ambitions... Rather than wanting to be informative enough on the limits of this register. When it is not just to avoid being involved in the lives of the cities, formal framing.

You can expect some suggestions further, but first: to get back to our mainframe of epistemological suggestions formal.

Vector spaces

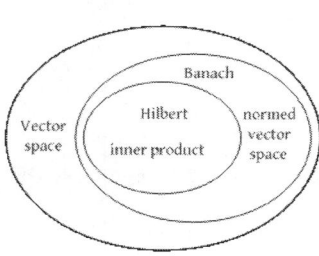

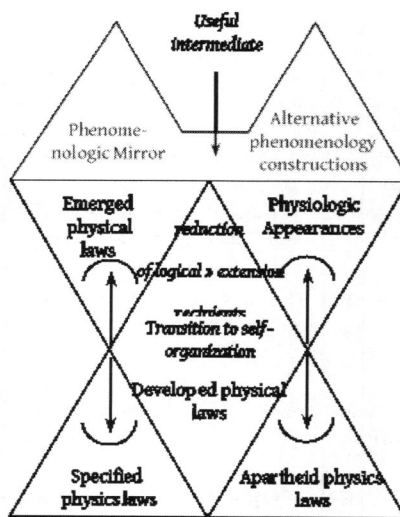

Dunce cap: conceptual representations or natural pictures

Phenomenology Mirror: tautologies and alternative in logical representations for the same sort of physical laws (they can receive different approximate formulations) or phenomena (they can be explained in different equivalent terms (with the same effect), area of synonymous.

Alternative phenomenology constructions pool of alternatives partial representation, is more specifically useful for one use or the other.

Above 2 are exposed to inflation, mistakes and misunderstanding, eventually compensated by average of proper practices or debilitated by wrong dogmas.

215

Consider different types of mental work; if a technician you are going to compose common elements, with pieces of your job. Pieces you already know; formula you are already used to. Formula of this sort will make use of characteristic properties, manage known transformations of it. In the complex case most around and with will, made them by themselves. In the simple case you will pretend what you know delivers what you expect as a main.

In the complex reality approach you will better expect the main bias be useful enough. Considering its broad range of effects, primary, secondary, up to the maximum-minimum of your hope-analysis (reasonably reviewed your expectations); down to the minimum-maximum of your effects-analysis (exhausted your effects). You will hope to have a use overall positive and not too adverse.

Unless you are an addict of diet no formula for food. Foods once labeled so are 'gobbled' and then 'autonomously' transformed for being taken in charge as **metabolites** in the body; by your inner metabolic pathways. Which generally requires to make those metabolites, having lost their previous **identity properties** (by the digestion), possibly also their defense-or **toxic properties** (by the liver and other detoxification). Otherwise they are seen by your own self-mechanisms: as 'not you' identity; that is possibly an allergen. [Formal processes of reframing, are preserving the advantages of less costly in energetic losses].

When there are not for eating, other raw materials and any object; are to put into your environment [the engineering]. Expecting after having applied **formula and processes of operation** to fit at your service. Then in the hope that those remaining properties will have at least tolerable inconvenient. This often at common level of activities almost neutral effect (be there and just wait your wants) or, positive. That is with minimum large entropy triggering (spontaneous 'informed by the environment') and induced or deduced processes to which is submitting the object/subject in the environment. So as it will not harm you, nor the ones you care about.

If you imagine that your brain cognitive ways are going to make you dress a **mental representation** (want it or not, most is unconscious). A model of your own and eventually share; inspired by realities under eyes. Your brain will make this representation from **pieces of experiences** and **framework**(s); that we may spontaneously enough make like a system. At least see a sort of **geometric object** hence, not exactly, the only closest similar one; you had crossed before in your journeys of numerous experiences. Cognitive or conceptual framework relatively composes orderly mixed perceptions (primary one visual), frameworks and recalls of pieces.

Have in mind we are not necessarily in the visual just with 'sight' but the areas of the brain dedicated to management of forms. These can be activated by other perceptions and inner cognitive processes. Without seeing a lion any sort of related motive may recall you the series of most impressive memories you have at the respect (and possibly your previous speculations? –'The lion is eating me' (even when no such case has happened).

Thus a cognitive framework is made of plenty of related components. Including the most important both from realities matched to previous cognitive experience and passed works of design an approach; after a similar respect of subjects, its imagined properties and anticipations renewed. This is mostly implicit, not much conscious, not fully explicit and with a purpose to react or act, in situations, in already prepared ways and open to reconsiderations.

Intuitively you will have, **pieces of knowledge** quite generic, and cope with the new situation, as usual as it can be. [Could be that pieces? Sort of informative links?]. Events in 'almost the same' repeated task something will have; in your, mood and preoccupation, levels of attention and **patterns, automatic to repeat** and (open) capabilities to **detect 'abnormalities to reply'**. Including because yourself go a bit further than consciously. By the openness (?) you will be, for example, able to detect variations and 'differences'. Relative differences in proportions: all situations are new. Faster from usual thanks to slight differences of perceptions. So you need of these 'slight differences' despite having been previously 'residuals classified'. This makes you able to analyze the potential importance (or interest, or informative open relations) of new things. What we seek is with your mental task:

1. **Phenomenological experiences** is wider than you have consciously. But it would be broader in sense of completeness. As theoretical as can be the researcher, hse has laboratory experience. Be them for the mathematician, in front of his white sheet of paper, the problem with his pens contemporary to the idea he adds; brain will possibly use that for indexing?];
2. **'Theoretical knowledge'** (cognitively managed in a boarder way as the 'least fixing most *main ad hoc* nodes for framing an understandings'; if required to switch from unconscious-spontaneous contaminated by conscious 'metrological') [quite related to the 'abnormal operations hse made?];
3. Conscious and unconscious **good rules of examinations and tests** (possibly in the scheme of a 'structured relative formal system of representation' able to relate structurally' so has many as manageable (**cluster** like) links for 'solutions' ~ pre-heuristic);
4. **Precautions** and care you could produce well, for yourself, your family, your society and humane wise care (accounting the environment and **synergies** in space and time; making the economy of your journey).

Most often the **best of experiences** (most impressive with sweetest success) will be selected and kept further in memories ... unconsciously. Since what the brain does is: put into automatic pieces of programs so as focus consciousness on what really problematic.

[Of course our problematic in this essay is to establish the big connections between real world, proper cognitive subjective approaches and the 'cleanest formal way for this. 'Least fixing most *ad hoc* system of main nodes used for framing an understanding' ... That may well reproduce, or have reproduced the essential nature; progressively 'evidenced and summarized'; sense of that we are made of, too]. [To mind nevertheless local framework of diffused or detail to expand modularity the capabilities of analyzing and insist?].

Helpful to that the evidence of nature... They are often better than so many social rules. Of course the knowledge of social rules, explicit enurc ates is indispensable. But they are narrower; more than you imagine. They are often simple reasons, and so the aim is more to obtain a collective norm of behavior. Be this within neurons' population; or among the populations of social actors. Thus simple, explicit and minimum ... in the way of Occam's scissors (the **least minimum common**) for expected minimum results. Minimum result is not even explicit on the ways to reach the results. [Sort of an 'invisible hand', but for which we also need a statistic concept] but for sure this is not like the anti-natural way of determinist people in the mood that any provided order from a superior to an inferior. So as to 'serve hes fixing' and his supremacy should be the only unique rational way of the informative links, to what you have to do. Most dictators also pretend, their orders are the way to better society. That is too narrow a way for robustness and resilience in such a wonderfully complex world).

With the evidence of nature; first you have to mind that often 'they are more upon you, at least in your genes treatment of information (you: **epi**-genes, **para**-genes and **exo**-genes). That is: your heritage will have selected you, not for being elected by the social means over others, but for being able to manage, not alone as social a framework you may maintain better for all or returned to the common spontaneously, by slight move balance effects). [If at the position in the framework you do wrong sooner, you are eject-able; in the physics after the ergodic thermal level. Or 'should?' in the social free-minded. After the physics up to social ergodicity?].

Uncertainties, you have many in an environment (eventually passed by) full of many balances maintenance. Too there are ways of simplifications, with commonness at all levels. **Genetic commonness** has been shown mostly shared between and across species (few tens of thousands ~ 3). The **interspecies variations** not with enormous numbers (few thousands). **Humans' populations' genetic selections** taking generations and centuries for only having some small relative species frequencies 'adapted' to the environment and **'enaction'** there. Care not to consider adaptation just with the extreme of specificity. Most of plural is 'slight'. The reasons why humans beings are often quite less stressed in nature: their genes are for being there. And the historical motives of the past have relatively fewer periods there. Possibly in their sweetness of affluent societies. Thus fewer constraints for surviving there on your own means.

> ['Enaction': maybe the cycling concept we need for the roll-over of adaptation but not necessarily in all in the ambition of this theory trying to be comprehensive. Enactivism in cognition consider dynamic interaction between an acting organism and its environment, empowering interactive capabilities].

So using the means of 'innate phenomenological natural evidence'. Those of geometric abstractions are especially geometrical, so a basic of Nature approached by formalism. Once understood the phenomenological forms in their amazing diversities show enough patterns of geometrical pieces as fundamental. Hence not only the lone minded reductions of humans about simple geometrical forms. In your brain, the essential mechanism also seems to follow the same ways. [More details will be provided in another volume].

Now, in modern days of information revolution; accounting on the fact, you will have anyhow good profit for being more explicit to the interface of computers. For this in its interactivity be better servant of you; have in yourself at expressing well; but not to have to be one hundred percent perfect. [New Asimov's robot law? the machine has to know it cannot complete what it work, to reach human]

Consider the need to know a bit better the many tricks, tips and forms. Mechanisms that help you, mean you may not 'model' in a very formal way. But nevertheless with having good approach; this is for proceeding well, pose well and your way to solve problems collectively. To reduce as far as possible all this bureaucratic stuff; imposed by sordid imitations of 'reasons'. Apart from 'lower grounds' hence pretending to mimic them (competition, predation, we do with, what is relevant is the informative links with fairer alternative and slim economy). Not follow that proportion of bureaucrats whom never properly experienced the absurdity of their prescriptions. But also the new one, driven by short-sword.

Meanwhile precisely, by the side of 'reasons properly equipped; there are increasing motives to obverse. The good ways to be economical is with being naturally consistent, make use of natural imitation; make compatible the different sorts of environments. Between which we are moving in (and of which we are made). Of course it is not to take our rapid options, when involved in other scales; directly as the ones used by nature. Or we will turn devouring only our children. [Figuratively this is what some societies full of debt and level of consumption of stocks are doing?].

But use our brain and levels of technology achieved ... with (fair) management methods of relationships; so has to make more sustainable and balanced our humane options, entailed by the need for efficient social balance; To give consistency to these levels of aggregation. To add to these considerations these ways of better prepared phenomenological skills; convinced that formal sciences within natural sciences are not just for pure abstract and anti-natural inventions. But the closest means to mechanisms of nature that we have; to make things could be derived to our utilities and options.

As a result no waste of time to join, match and meet; as a common to all; what we conceive geometrically.

Basics (Re) Call on Geometry

Geometry is a **collection of propositions** with the following properties:
- If a finite set of propositions is elected as '**initial propositions**'; the remaining propositions can be **deduced** from them;
- The propositions of set must be **logically consistent**;
- The **propositions should be independent**, i.e. none can be deduced from the other (hence not essential);
- A **statement is a set of elements** that may (or may not) be satisfied.

Observe than the treatment and; ambiguities, even when looking like cleared, being about an object or a way of treatment of them that you selected. [Which is somehow 'unfair' but preferable]. Put apart what you do not speak of, but insert, "inside chosen logical system." The remaining propositions and the elements which are not satisfied. In some way, you have at least 3 formal levels of negation: 1). Not of the geometry (others ignored, out integrity); 2) Irrelevant propositions (remain or residues; but in integrity); 3) Unsatisfying elements of the statement.

We abridge; more correctly we should consider: either a complete perfect superior oneness ... and that our treatment not fully correct; or 'get in' with a mixed perspective applying logic of 1st (world) & 2nd ('seed' kernel~0 where operation) in a something 'relatively closed' (~1, unit, relative system).

'Seed' would be 'logical operation field' [2nd in relative contrast to the 1st ... or the other way]... Not to confuse with physics? ... [Could be the geometric physics the start of such logical atom the pair: field -atoms? And in a more complex formal system... (Could be: relative formal system, environment of life), within (physics universe, netgentropy)?].

Euclidean geometry has 5 postulates. All theorems must follow from a set of statements; simply assumed to be true; since all other theorems follow from these postulates:
1. A **straight line segment** can be drawn joining any 2 points.
2. Any straight line segment can be **extended indefinitely** in a straight line.
3. Given any straight line segment, a **circle** can be drawn having the segment as the radius and one endpoint as a center.
4. All right angles are **congruent**.
5. Given a line and a point not on that line, there exists one line exactly through the given point parallel to the given line. (The parallel postulate).

[To Let You Make the Epistemic analysis?]

> With practical associating minds, it is not surprising how ancient humans' architectures developed. And why 'hope' turned so deterministic... The primary compass is just the circle around the radius. The "horizontal inspiration" like sea line-horizon; made in the spirit of Greek Antiquity mathematicians. [Remind most were close to the sea, straight calm, waves when winds] (But before that, in at least Mesopotamia; horizon was more 'wave-like' fixed). Straight lines of great architecture and Euclid's geometry is the 1st known 'axiomatization'. Non-linear geometries formalized after (out of the architects' tricks). But, not so difficult for being inspired by the compass.

Came after, other geometries had the 5th postulates to be reformulated.

- In **Hyperbolic Geometry** it is to replace the parallel postulate (5th of Euclid) by: "given a line and a point not on that line, there exist an infinite number of lines through the given point parallel to the given line.
- In **Spherical Geometry**, lines are defined to be circles on a sphere. So to replace the parallel postulate with the following: "all lines intersect in exactly 2 points." -- i.e. there are no parallel lines (so latitudes cannot be seen as parallels?).

Topology is a more modern term for a kind of logic for geometrical 'like-plastic' objects. Topology with Euclidean plane or space, deals with straight lines, circles, lengths and angles. **Topological transformations are just rigid motions.** Distances do not change; nor they stretch, shrink or bend. Then topology considers these possibilities and study these properties. The plane in topology is **elastic**. It can observe deformations, but some properties are conserved. **Closed objects** such as **polygon** stay closed. They can be deformed, a triangle can be turned into a circle.

Thus topological frames are forms within which analytical (mathematical) tools are providing space with: norm, distance or metrics. Making loose some of the general meaning. This helps to develop narrower but more precise applications.

Topology also in other dimensions has many uses. Linear forms either as **knots of ropes, lines** or **projection overlaps** from higher to lower dimensions have many practical uses. Analytic topology approaches well the concept of invariants. **Grand canonical ensemble** (general formula of the system) treats separately interacting, as well as non-interacting particles, one (1) Eigenstate at a time.

[Grand canonical ensemble a statistical ensemble used to represent the possible states of a mechanical system of particles; maintained in thermodynamic equilibrium (thermal and chemical) with a reservoir.]

Forms of Curves

Ellipse is closed and has 2 focal points and center at the origin. In non-elliptic Euclidean geometry lines are the great circles of the sphere. Angles are the usual angles. For an ellipse fixed relation of 2 distances sum, since one point on the ellipse to 2 focal points. Mind that: since one focal point, on the ellipse, you can go to other focal point [And imagine what it can mean, phenomenologically, as a binary and symmetries between].

Elliptic problems correspond to **stationary processes** in nature. The solutions have no discontinuities. 2nd order equations are elliptic if and only if (iff) the Eigenvalues of symmetric real matrices are all of the same sign. Elliptic integral generalizes rational integral and trigonometric functions.

Parabolic problems correspond to **flow processes** (heat conduction, diffusion,...) These processes have smoothing effect in time. 2nd order equations are parabolic iff at least one Eigenvalue of symmetric real matrix vanishes.

Parabola links power 2 variables, with power one variable. It consists of all points whose distance from the focal point and fixed line of directrix are equal. Parabola observes **convergence** of any parallel to x-axis to the one focal point.

Hyperbola has 2 focal points. It considers **equal difference of distances** at a focal point. It is in 2 pieces. In hyperbolic geometry point is classical points in the upper half plane. Lines are half-circles in the upper half plane whose centers lie on the abscissa axis. For a hyperbola difference of distance to 2 focal points stay the same (symmetric divergence).

Hyperbolic problems belong **to wave processes**. Propagation of discontinuities along waves' fronts is an important mechanism for transporting physical effects in nature. 2nd order equations is hyperbolic iff one Eigenvalue of symmetric real matrix is positive and all other Eigenvalues are negative (or the other way around).

Are called **regular conic section: circle, ellipse, parabola, hyperbola**. Are called degenerate conic section: 2 lines, 1 line or a point.

It seems intuitively that the concept of parallel, does not seem to exist so properly in most of Nature - for long or in other than a pure abstract (like combining the horizon and the 2 borders of a river). Could it either has to be reformulated or considered a more clearly a pure abstract exception? ... With such enormous influence as a mathematical concept: metric, straight line. Easiest formal start is important but not the exclusive to have in mind.

Gauss, Lobachevski, Bolyai observed that parallel axiom cannot be proven from other axioms. Later 2 invented so non-Euclidean geometries.

Euclidean geometry is the easiest for metric. That is the 'mechanics of the abstract ruler'. It may not be needed to be just getting 'rid of that' if in a relative formal system. Despite not physically core, with differentiability and derivability (in limited range of dimensions (half a dozen or less and around 3 ... for a one unit more or less specified). So metric becomes a piece of the system [Instead being the start of everything. It is not needless to measure unless willing to make a 'great leap forward' into a man-made disaster].

You have to mind approached are at least dualist (left eye, right eye). General solvability 3 or 4 'multi-cardinals'. Integration goes up from 1 to 3; the converse differentiation from 3 to 1. Dualism top-down and bottom-up. Thus at linear dimension 1 a something metric-able to find out about what it represents in the geometric filled object (equator, north-south poles axes, heart-vessels circle, head to tail?).

Thus straight line, despite most of Nature is non-linear may play as the mid-adjustment for 'main axis' linearization. That is 1st find the main, and whatever its form make it a straight line then relate other trajectories to it (closest distance or deviation). They may reveal some characteristic relative pattern. Different independent main axis also make easier to study so, as 'orthonormal'. Once cleared the relations and having made the analysis. Do not miss you may have to get back to the transformations you used for more phenomenological evidence. As a way to examine, 'trajectories in the black box'.

[So take the straight line simply as the start of everything; as nothing more than a physics world free of anything without fields; and not more than one direct interaction? Formally straight line is just the 'perfect complement of total randomness'). It is not surprising, of course, that the pure line (dimension one) neutral abstract concept (dimension 0 of nothingness)].

In a similar way, the straight line and parallel concepts of Euclidean ('impossible') geometry may have to evolve to 2 trajectories. Almost never meeting; and the trajectory is within or crossing a corridor. Or re-bouncing on the walls or scattered on some interceptor of trajectory. Have in mind that 2 objects almost in a dual relation with the "almost straight line" traced on 2 points, but having a 1 dimension ... then requiring 2 dimensions; for seeing lines (for being sure).

The circle made with one point the center and a piece of straight lines (the *radius*) 'Rope of motion'. Pictured as a vector tangent to the circle. Originally, the force direction at the point of application: moment or friction. Mind from physics that such vector, drawing the circle, has to account on the tension applied to, enough resisting small rope **'centripetal force'** (sticking to the center and the circle). This provides a picture of the **tensor** concept and/or **moment**.

Around 2 interacting bodies (point system?) Lagrange observed that for them there are 5 points of equilibrium (labeled L1 to L5). Only L4 and L5 points are stable; the other is in unstable equilibria. Practical use of the 3 relatively stable is possible, if maintained by some occasional engine low consumer in energy. It is also a line-way for economical motion; since there are between these a pathway of minimum energy.

Further help, to consider the sort of system or orthogonal reference you need; to conceive an instant, just before and after immediate-ness.

Visualizing Phenomenologically.

To notice that visualization thinking is not to consider vulgar; but as a major cognitive resources for anyone, non-experts at analytical formulation. The analytic formulation is another aspect of formal intelligence kind. Some neuroscientists observe that the parietal cortex of the brain is in the charge of 'visual to other tasks' coordination. So, despite the fact that it is not the frontal cortex of 'mid-start of conception'; parietal cortex is the one with the major human brain volume development. Possibly because many work to do there for assembly and synthesis?

What is important that by all means we need to be more intelligent for better use of computers and wiser sense of options and articulations ... for, and the future. It is horribly stupid to imagine that empowering the hierarchies of social discrimination could be the best way to 'peace and love' among humans: 'potential achieved' that is exhausted, not the best?

Moreover it is to imagine that future computer's queries in computer data bases will need not to expect that we, humans are going experts of anything, required by the solutions. Better orientations have to be better shared. Both between human and computer and between humans. That is, the one's able to point in enormously improper lists of search engine queries. In some way what we need; since only to have less or too much incomplete knowledge; and wish to have more. It is to clear enough, by interactive queries and 'help' computers so as to prepare better selections; even of things we did not previously known.

Whatever the inflation of good hope after globalization, about knowledge, resolve problems needs documentation. Moreover our artificial transformations have distorted much natural environment but have not created 'only wiser than Nature' sub-ecosystems as anthropo-scenes.

> That is like in diabetes management. When you have lost the natural way of sugar in the blood management (insulin-conditioning entry or go out (stable glycaemia). You will have to substitute by your conscious management (until we find automatic blood detection and release of insulin without inconvenience) with sugars food uptakes, glycaemia measure, and then injection(s) of insulin. So as to smooth and stabilize level, never not too low (fainting) nor too high (diabetes) without doing better, and having to balance inconvenient; despite already many technological advances.

If we want to be better and freer at making our choices and decisions than more efforts are required. Moreover not to ignore the importance of the uncertainty gap. If not, then let traditional violent means resolve conflicts: with wars, hunger crisis, overcrowding, warming climate and so on. Because ethically unable to properly resolve fundamental human equations on one side and choose softer (and smarter) options when close to the border of 1) Potentially critical imbalances; 2) Critical phase space transitions; 3) Near a bifurcation point. Technological means may serve in either case, the so-called 'inhumane' as well as the name-humane ones.

Moreover it is essential too, that local knowledge or capacities adapt to contexts' needs. Like for the previous: local knowledge often know better where are the 'abrupt changes'. These are also to empower in consistent relationships. Not of the easiest ones of violence, misunderstandings and antagonisms.

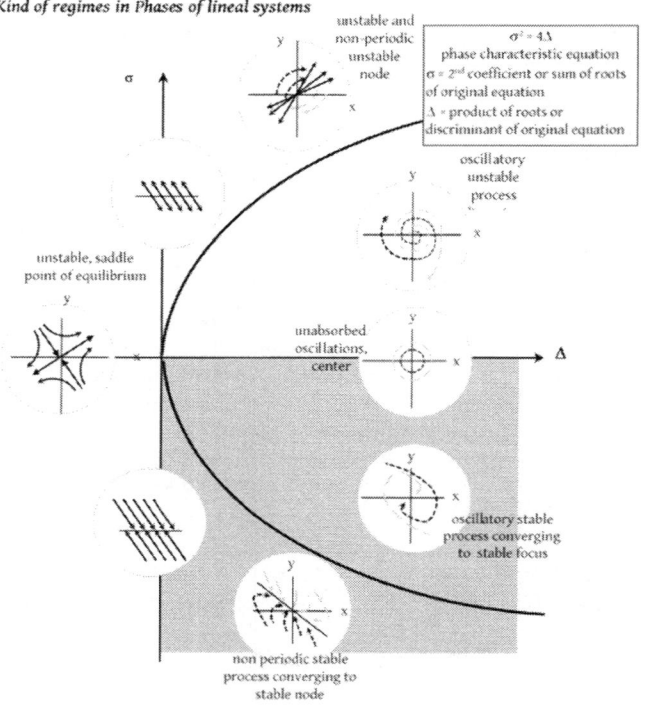

Kind of regimes in Phases of lineal systems

unstable and non-periodic
unstable node

$\sigma^2 = 4\Delta$
phase characteristic equation
σ = 2nd coefficient or sum of roots of original equation
Δ = product of roots or discriminant of original equation

oscillatory unstable process

unstable, saddle point of equilibrium

unabsorbed oscillations, center

Δ

oscillatory stable process converging to stable focus

non periodic stable process converging to stable node

Logics and Geometry

Before going further, we need something on logics of meaning. Meaning often called semantic (in many abstract philosophies). Thus on **Semantic Logic** as summarized from Tomassi. Formal semantic explicitly concerns the interpretations of propositional logic formulas. There, an **interpretation** of proposition logical is just any assignment of truth-values to its component **atomic formulas**. Any interpretation, which results in the whole formula being true. Overall is a **model of that formula**. [Consider invalidating a propositional logic interpretation if premises true and conclusion false; eventually use this to generate a counterexample. As an effect you also need to invalidate].

Shortcuts of method exploit the fact that each **type of formula** is only false under certain circumstances. So this entails to identify the type of formula and conclusions. 2 or more compound formulas of propositional logic are **semantically equivalent** iff for each every assignment of truth-values to their component sentence-letters; the overall truth-values of those formulas are one and the same. The identification a semantic equivalence simply constructs a **comparative truth-table** for the relevant formulas and consider whether or not; each formula takes the same truth-value under the same interpretation. [Care that logic's seme (piece of sense) may relate to physics form and physics facts may relate more to the lexicor.'s-lexicographic logic?]

The **propositional logic** is bivalent (true or false). Truth-value of any compound propositional logical formula is a function of 1) The truth-values or its atomic formula and 2). The particular connective(s) used to form the formula. Brackets are used to structure atomic formula, so the sub-formula the structure of each formula, in language, is determinate. [You have to be cautious with neutral separation (brackets, parenthesis, etc.) and simple operators, as of union and intersections. Quantic physics cares for that too].

They make use of '**connectors**' between letters identifying the variable. The meaning of each logical connectives can be fixed by a truth table which takes true-valued formulas as arguments and gives true-valued as values. Any such connective is truth-functional; every propositional logic connective is a truth-functional connective.

In mathematical logic, a **sequent** is a very general kind of **conditional assertion**. A sequent may have any number m of condition formulas A_i (called "antecedents") and any number n of asserted formulas B_j (called "succedents" or "consequents"). A sequent is understood to mean that: if all of the antecedent conditions are true; then at least one of the consequent formulas is true. This style of conditional assertion is almost always associated with the conceptual framework of **sequent calculus**. [Observe that sequents consider order, succession ... what expected by operations, time and irreversibility].

A sequent is semantically valid iff there is no interpretation (i.e. no possible assignment of truth-values to the component formulas under which all that sequent are true while the conclusion is false). For any valid sequent the set of formulas consists of the conjunction of each of the premises, of that sequent, together with the negation of the conclusion, of true sequent must be inconsistent (a truth-table can always be made). Even when not a reason, truth-table columns are often visually ordered. For any valid sequent, corresponding conditional must be **tautological**.

So 'sequent' the sort of logical sentence managed by order logic. To determine whether or not a given sequent is semantically valid, it is to construct a comparative truth-table for the constituting formula and consider whether there is an interpretation under which the premises are true while the conclusion is false. If so sequent is not valid. [So the valid sequent has caught a sense of truth].

Pragmatic About Logics

Logic seems quite boring, everything there, looks like to have to be perfectly detailed. Thus if you add our "vicious ideas" in absolute never perfect... At the same time logic provides the way for cleaning the formula(s) of the concept(s); in the manageable framework(s) that can be taken in charge by automatic systems and evoke too precautions. Thus by the interactions to clear ideas.

Evidence in logics is called **tautology**. Notice for example modern day economics is full of tautologies and advisors as well as advised do not see enough that the tautology applies mostly not to your prior (own selfish) system. But in other's ones and/or in a common share. So there are some risks that identification, if not the logical system by itself, can be different (but 'symmetric'). This way of wanting one's own logic applied is disastrous in human history. [Meanwhile it seems to us that Smith put it fairly with ways of individual understanding, anticipating empathy?].

Most 'lay definitions,' not worked as 'logic shell,' are context linked; coming from common problems questions emerged... But today, which advisor will tell you? That worldwide data banks have thousands of better information than themselves. Thus more need to be acceded properly and with pertinence. Better by the users in most cases and; sometimes still better by the experts in good synergies. Critical are the processes of interactions with 3 nodes. The economical use of their services is to suggest: really much less in distracting explanations and; it is to turn much more informatively serious than actually.

Meanwhile the knowledge of fields' is increasingly more important. Especially including the traditionally wisest people of practical fields. The reason why also relationships need to be more critical and better balanced. It is striking the enormous majority of 'experts' pretending to know so much and mastering so few. We need limits better and fairly understood. A something that no bureaucrat cannot imagine.

Moreover it is to observe the defects of manipulations by ideological misunderstandings and policies. Whom do not want to imagine that out basic natural sciences the communication of labels and definitions, in the traditional way of outside to inside, should be over. Anyone works better when forging one's own precisions and consistently in the applied definitions, the ones really operated and which are for most end-processes suggestive sentences for trying to remake.

Of course our essay is with that defect of being for most, all outside concrete situations. As a heterodox from rational paradigm, to your 'inside' reasoned phenomenological (but with good reference of formal knowledge). Nevertheless since wanting to point at the most common for all science of forms, maybe we could be forgiven. That is, in simple words, you do with 1) Sciences (an economic quarter and our ambition); 2) field knowledge (a cultural economic quarter); 3) Have good intentions (a cognitive not all explicit quarter) and 4) Learning by doing (a feed-back phenomenological quarter). Result of that for a 'learning society' is to save much time or value, from the dogma of 'rationalities').

When you leave the pages of this essay, it will be more about your construction approaches. Hoping also to trigger more critical curiosity about the helpfulness of free mind.

[By the side of our efforts there is a primary of ideographic frameworks; we made purchasable under the name of 'olicognography'). Our reasons not as simply as said: mind your duties, care you environment, think about natural sciences, adapt to real actors; recruit your culture put in its words. Made all that yours. Since no one should disqualify your legitimate and hesitating ways to find humane issues. Cultures change, after legitimate actors, just these, do not want to be pushed and co-actioned].

If you do not expect "better conceptual shells" nor techniques robust enough, for clearing options of decisions and just want for your regular life; formal logic receives all (without looking that this is most from your unconscious brain). Thus formal logics may look like deceiving, for many lay reasons; profanes as well as improper ways of scientism. Care about tedious sugary waters inventors especially if bureaucrats or nice friends].

For some tips and very briefly:

- You have understood that formulate properly has nowadays the main purpose to properly feed computed treatments ... whence not to let too determinist hidden layers of robots, mob you;
- Mind that, if many such sort of tautological lessons (the formal logics is tautological, the corresponding natural evidences effectively also); set the reasonable limits for all... Hence there is much of work to do for better interfaces.

First because logical interfaces for faster investigation of knowledge are still to establish (search engines not extraordinary by the 'systems of probably pertinent queries'). Only few key words for specialized registers. **Rap**: rapid assessment procedures are not bad intent, but they are not aware enough of Nature's proper processes: since a mixture of determinisms and probabilities). Actually Data banks for profanes will not deliver immediately what you need.

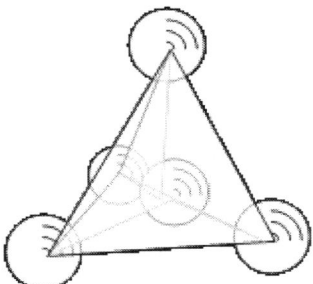

Second, because ways of workings with the world-wide web is, yet not with best 'human professional 'interfacers''. That is for good they should be less pretending to be experts of truth and better should try technical needs and skills. For downloading what a relevant local problem can need. Documentation, procedures and adaptable civilian mechanisms for resolving problems...

Without expecting too much from other sorts of superiors; especially from political intermediate and governments agents. As long as they are conditioned to respect superior orders blindly. They have to compose with essential legitimacy, fair respect of legitimate superior instructions and be in the fields context. Opportunist compromise between 3 modes plus their deontic competence, makes shares more than half a miracle of efficiency dubious. []. Notice nevertheless that we enlarge the perspective. Nor to pretend that your positive results are low because of that. Now to observe that essential management of public services have been weakened by the defective epistemologies of new technologies and knowledge.

Programs have to be made more understandable hence not in the exclusion of voluntary initiatives. They should not be deluded by determinism... It is better to feel that you can freely involve socially. That is not sheep-pilchard like (but this way of behaving have sometimes justified reasons (as oar race). Even if an impression (the social economics term of 'trust' is not all bad) has to be worked in due processes.

Have in mind what information is really about. Care constraints and conditions and the subtleties of proper management. Finance is not a good condition for free selfish excellence (but an individual, basic of social). Especially in a basically uncertain world where economics is yet not near humans: cognitive maps of information are very disturbed by diverging humans money. Cognitively your brain's economy shortcut what unconsciously considered use-less or to underscore or forgive. For freeing mental registers and recycle (at any level).

Mind pours into unconscious, much of what does not pose a problem. So as to dedicate your conscious thinking to the real (unsolved) problems (requiring harder approach of solutions); if it has time for analyzing and intent. So brain simplifies to make operations more easily "calculable." Your brain is still first and last, especially in social constructions.

The accumulated capital(s) of knowledge is (are) now enormous but; still not as good in their complications. To help behave 'optimally' with commons in common lives. In our opinion, it is not to expect that one day; everything will be done by robots. You will not find happiness in that (out at laughing at robots' mistakes ... if that is not for it to laugh at you). That would mean that your living structures are no more needed in this world.

Economics of intelligence will ensue. In common life the patterns of cultural and natural shortcuts; for fast understandings then they are very important. Culture be those of 'old days that reminded you happy days'. And not with the new ones which frankly pass too fast. Including for really let your genetic stock adapt your feelings of happiness.

Anyhow for the computer, the social groups and the others, you will need to be more systematically explicit. And we hope, no more sustaining work than few hours each day. Meanwhile also, socially dedicated to care much more than actually would be good. 'Patterns of simplifications' there would have to be software designed in increasingly artificially efficient computed systems.

With logic(s), you may prepare not so difficultly to care especially practical issues. Learn to construct **tables of truth**, **trees of decision**, draw **tables of games**. Care that too simple semantic has the paradox to widen and makes harder the good communication of information. Any should be more cautious. Frame well the identifications to complex and complicated realities. You may find that the proper semantic logical treatment can suggest requalifying your identifications.

Implying that rather than 'I want to be leader forever' could have better to be reformulated "just enough with one good term and be appreciated in the fair future. The 2nd best goal you can ever reach is 'not too loathsome in better shared and volunteered the future'.

[This concept existing well in theory of games public decisions, policies and elsewhere. Examples of fundamental concepts to replace would be: order, probability. Theory of games to apply to fundamental physics and ... common sense].

Unit of Logical Objects

First it will be to examine some concepts of Set theory about a realistic or abstract object, taken as 'cognitive units'. **Set** defining unit properties considers a normed called **metric space**; when all representing sequences are converging (limit of norms tending to 0). And then space is called complete [metric may look like too strong, and could be relaxed to mathematics norm- or better equipped with a physics' system].

A set of metric space is **closed** when any representing convergent sequence contains its limits. A close-set is **compact** if, for any sequence in it, there is a subsequence that is **convergent**. A set is close if any point is included therein together. A set is **dense** in another if for any **point** in the latter, there is a sequence of points in the former converging to the point.

A set with the center and *radius* is either **open ball** or **closed ball**. It is **bounded** if the whole of it, belongs to some ball. That is logic, yet not about a quantified or 'filled geometric form'.

Practically our problem is to have a physics relative open and closed collection. Care with the concept of a set in logic we need a less simplistic identification. Possibly the universe would be a so closed set. This could further consider a first bipartition: sub-set, relatively closed-open on the other or reciprocally. Could this has the form of a subpart of the universe co-existing one for the space of possible matter (or as a mixture oriented of it; correspondingly the other mixture complementarily to the first?). With this and then the space of field-quanta for the side were we are?

Have clear that we are not proposing a theory, not even an intuition; we are more trying to conceive a logical framework compatible with the logic of set and how we imagine our quantic world. Fine if this does not horrify a fundamental physicist.

Domain of Numbers

To make intuitive sense of dimensions when speaking of concepts:
- **dimension 0** (zero) would be just a **virtual point**, mistaken virtually a common lay wrong doing of social symbolic numbers arts stays symbolic. A scalar has also dimension 0 but position too. Quite often the minimum distance of object to reference system. Not, of course, the purpose to restrict ideas, but more with the implicit dimensions of that either as financial implicit or time consuming dedicated to concepts; without any consistency. Fine, if only free self-dedication

without consequences. At least this may preserve the environment. Not everything is bad in pure and empty abstraction.

- **Dimension 1** (one) would be like a line, just a derivation and you stay alone with a scalar (commonly the slope and/or the 1st coefficient of linear equation). From a constant motion derivation, gives the speed. Maybe if lower (hidden dimensions?) are just the 1st level of larger units. If the curve is not a straight line, you may need more dimensions than this, to describe the trajectory. But with an unknown it may be the *nucleus* of everything, provided integration operators.
- **Dimension 2** (two) could be some thickness. Coming from up, as a local, present or bordered snapshot of reality, or an area. If of a trajectory's derivation, it gives the speed. If the speed of a motion non-constant that is an acceleration. To examine the term of dimension 1.
- **Dimension 3** (three) be a moment of locality, a volume or a description by a volume: an 'object'.

With that in the process of knowing where we are in quali-quanti; like giving sense to amounts. And properties operated so as to emerge more properties since quite fundamental ones. They would be so easy to index by number, to introduce some ideas about numbers. Only, for making the link with the previous: we will speak further of numbers sets, one dimension at a time. Thus and for example if speaking of dimension 2 (as planes) the set of number either continuous or discrete will be squared.

Numbers of Physics

About **sets of numbers** used in primary physics. When you qualify numbers (not just pure symbols) you have the choice of set. Reality's numbers are essential in 2 sets of number theory: the natural (discrete) one: $\mathbb{N}$. These are discontinuous, delimited, geometric objects like and propositional qualities prone. The second one is real numbers ($\mathbb{R}$), contains the first one, numbers are continuous, quantities-prone, observe a separating point between natural (or integer) piece and after the point, between 0 and 1 fraction. [Separating point is replaced by a coma continental east side of the Atlantic]. Sequence of numbers with limited digits or infinite.

Epistemologically these developments below are interesting not just in the theory of numbers. Between 2 natural they 'do not add in absolute, but cover more the interstice?' – That would look like more for quantities mostly irrelevant; or with the relevancy of residual. Unless if qualitatively and informatively it informs you of about the level of details and eventually imagine that this can be an index about qualitative properties.

The level of details can be infinite (so the series of digits after the point do not end). Or it can be limited. Take place there the ambiguities of division. Limited arbitrarily (by you), that is a cut (or discretization or halt). Technical problem of the detail, if you feel obliged to do so may reveal you did not choose the right operation or; that you care of natural integrity number. If the quantities you divide always produce finites series of digits after the point ensure discreteness.

As an effect in absolute you may rescale to the absolute original 0 and operate from there convinced that numbers express both amounts and index of properties in the physics. But operations requires you are able to handle that since the smallest amounts. Thereafter comes the way you make the computer work, etc.

Not to go on with this epistemology of numbers relevant to the ways you make operate the computers; and also relevant to physics up to humans' brain. To humans cognition when they detect the abnormalities between the way amounts behave in physics and the symbolic simplicity of operations.

Phenomenologically there are simple evidences. Size of you pair of trousers make sense if you too big, size too small (cut has not been well made, or material not enough extensible). Brain have billions of neurons and knowing that; makes you care about that more than worms (have worms, blues?). Care only about symbolic of numbers and essential of physics and you will learn easily that: have you day allowance of electrons (basic component) directly from the wall plug; for the needs of your bioelectric body currents, is not a good way.

Often, with the primary set of numbers (you take), you have to consider also which 2nd set (you get to) future stage-state or 2nd object. You 'tend to' (or examine its interactions). Anyhow searching, comparing, studying, relating will make you make a dual, even an abstract one. Determinist-like you chose where you operate, but this is not the natural way, and this natural way questions discrete and continuous approaches. This turn turns critical in physics estimates made supposedly from discrete by the huge numbers looking like continuous or the converse.

The relative formal system will make you imagine an abstract in details (dimension 0); and extend: links to a material point or line (dimension 1) and further (focus, pole, etc.). Dimension 1 is usually supporting the metric or norm. But there will also be, since object: surface (dimension 2, a transect, a cut, a field) and then to get to a volume (dimension 3, a form) better studied in 4 dimensions. Dimensions of complement (to the 3) either the time (which in our subjective term make the closure or complete the perspective; which is easier also for a reference system of 2 crossed orthonormal planes, etc.

Also you can have in mind the generality of representing system of equations no more than 4 degrees relatively. This is in the need of special values; across formal mechanisms between levels: integration and derivation. Relativity that is: higher of lower systems; summarized eventually in 5th or more dimensions. Openness meaning that formal expression are not completely close relative system. That is completed by other and/or physics-identifications complement(s). In differential calculus, the scalars are provided by values at the origin ... and that a question of physics's measure. Measure is a scale, so has one dimension (that of a line), either natural (qualities are sustaining functions?) or real (continuous quantities ... [provided by the maximum level of complexity reached?... Eventually by the component].

But imagine starting since a volume, thus logically you can be $\mathbb{N}^3 \rightarrow \mathbb{R}^1$. This may not change of your relation or make in reasoning a great difference; but precision interesting for the computer; for those having to detail and as part of the economics of language.

	Stereology and Logical Space Parameters			
R^3	Volume fraction $V_1(X) = N_1(X)$	Specific surface $A_2(X) = 4N_2(X)$	Mean curvature integer $M_1(X) = 2\pi N_3(X)$	Connexity number in R^3 $N_4(X)$
R^2	Area fraction $A_1(X) = N_1(X)$	Specific perimeter $L_2(X) = \pi N_2(X)$	Connexity number in $R^2 N_3(X)$	–
R^1	Linear fraction $L_1(X) = N_1(X)$	Connexity number in $R^1 N_2(X)$	–	–
R^0	Connexity number in $R^0 = N_1(X)$	–	–	–

Connexity: a connex is a geometric form that included as special cases the curve considered as a **point locus** and the curve considered as a **line envelope**. In all (a graph) the relationships between nodes. A binary relation **R** over X is called connex if for all a and b in X such that a ≠ b, a is related to b or b is related to a (or both). Connexity does not imply reflexivity. A strict partial order is a strict total order iff it is connex.

Thus we have more a number of relationships, more with an existence, relatively to 'minimum of flow', diversity of links, respect to maximum with 'maximum flow', possibly oriented; much about grid, network, graph, etc. A principle of classification depends on whether a relation holds between every pair of a collection or not, also may relate to connexity.

Compactness theorem: a set of first-order sentences has a model iff every finite subset of it has a model. It provides a useful method for constructing models of any set of sentences that is finitely consistent. It is equivalent to Gödel's completeness theorem, and both are equivalent to the Boolean prime ideal theorem (a weak form of the axiom of choice). Its formulation in topology: "Inside a ball B in $\mathbb{R}^3$, {rectifiable currents S in B; Larea S ≤ c, length partial S ≤ c} is compact under the flat norm".

Now the formal compactness of your approach is to question. In physics that is almost already well established. For example you have what is called '**equations in dimensions**' indicating by their expression in extensive parameters and basic physics characteristics (space dimensions, time, mass, temperature) that formal expression is 'compact'. Even if not much care have been provided in common people epistemology-like sorts of debates, despite … it is a great simplification for the practical and essential thinking. Technically it is important to check if you formulate properly. [Interestingly electric charge is expressed has a structure of the previous].

Empirical formula taking the precaution to involve operations have on one side an often comprehensive structure no more than slightly complication (respect to the basic phenomenon represented and the equation of dimension). On the other side this seems to allow huge extension of the operations of calculi (of amounts) and **manipulation of formula for reformulation** (and suggest some properties-qualities?).

Many practical calculi are about **collected measures**. And then a manipulations of simple operations for the calculus of the terms related to the formula, and that could not have been approached. Engineering calculi consists in adapting the scales, sizes and amounts for their applied to technology management, each registers having their levels of values and relations. Which are for many not in simple proportions.

Globalization with information revolution other opportunities at reach but also challenges produced by simplicity of computed system. Computers' half-scft-wared, half-hard-wared, **narrow robustness *versus* the broad one of human beings** make: 1) Many good helps from new technologies; 2) Requirements of simplicity (especially formal) for talking to the computer, which are not right in the margins of most humans' societies (whatever the 'ludic' compensations they can have from machines); 3) The losses of cognitive advantage of normal biomechanical natural environment; 4) The ludicrous hyperinflation of bureaucratic normed simplifications produced by the occidental determinism, after the paradigm of 'rationalities in governance'. The extent of 'implicit social algorithms for the closure of 'rational governance'; are not economic. Both from the humane side as by what can bring technologies to humans' societal balances.

If you operate with *minus* but in a real discrete world that would be the set of integer numbers: $\mathbb{Z}$. Remind either not to subtract more than the maximum; or take absolute value is in relative terms and **symmetrically to stop the subtraction at 0**. If you are on the 'other side' (or other signs) you inverse the arrow and make the counterpart the positive receiver … if you logically want to avoid the term "looser."

Division is also not as easy $\mathbb{Z}/n\mathbb{Z}$. Calculators obsessed by calculi; most take for granted the ideal situation and ignored that mathematicians preferred to **define division as a product**. Thus by the means of a symbol of equality to get ride off the division by 0. Then they pass the non-0 coefficient, below the sign of fractioning and so divide the number of the other side. This avoids the problem of 0 and of non-existence (you **do not cross the '=' sign if 'nothing'**. The 'unnecessary' problem is about if some 'insignificant' has some phenomenological importance and also in computer aided thinking.

Without specific instructions have computers the right to shortcut and simplify by themselves, when the humans doubts and imprecisions can be meaningful. We are just in the case of prejudging whom have not rights to doubt. Thus programmers have to learn that. Now, huge calculi made of many routines; miss-specifications somewhere pose problems. If you do not double, at least of the securities.

Imagine you want to combine humans and computers; because wanting to be closer to social contributions. Do not presume of simple operations in the 'enormous'; that the machine can have to take into accounts as a whole. When the size of associated human communities now often by the thousands. By the side of any phenomenology; it is also to imagine questioning cases. For example, between humans filling all their items of questionnaires, either putting 0 as 'no answers' and other put this 0 as answer 0. Otherwise leaving the cell empty. Just in more complex socially interactive computers suggest being more careful.

Divide with a 0 is not possible. Division also nurtures logic with operating concepts are **residual of a division**. It is also influential in algebraic structures as Ring, ideal (subset of a ring with an additive property). Obsessed by the calculus often makes it "simply" in real number and miss much. Maybe Nature is much wiser than that. [With 'formal system' may rise the concept of residual of addition and of product]

$\mathbb{R} \times \mathbb{R} \to \mathbb{R}$ gives a faraway projection of multiplication that is applied. Which is not quite realistic for geometric or limited objects. You must not miss the 'gasoline'. In Nature would be only special conditions, orientation or shape shows that only in very small proportions (**coherence**?–if able to receive energy for extending the field?)

$\mathbb{R} \times \mathbb{R} \to \mathbb{R}^2$ Is more a graph of crossing from 2 lines onto a plan, thus a vector (as a good picture for more abundant in Nature). And if you cannot fill-veiled your area then you may better **use grids or polyhedrons**.

> Of course there is not much in those details in common life. But we have the feeling that many people are left aside the best benefit from revolution of information. Not because it is expansive, nor because this is of the old generations refusing to adapt to such globalization. There are, of course, but also from the exasperation of many. Either against the bureaucrats at odds with their bugs; this exasperation not to expect much relief since also produced out of public administration. Computers ways of life are not kindly matching the ones of humans. Some effectively, have also taken it as a new way of life: spammers, hackers, pirates, raiders .... All this is questioning the societal sum of all games since a society productivity has to account for every sign of operations.

We only provide with some precautionary comments and minimum for understanding. Nevertheless it would be good if you catch that this is basic and may inspire formalism to be careful, when sharing designs across domains. **Units' bases, reference** or **check** what others do. When pretending to volunteer events, policies, comments and so on. And out any obsession by formalisms, you may unveil how vain are social communications and not contributions to global mental health..

Yet it looks like the melting pot of **noise** and **words**, ambitions and vanities; have some analogies with the original soup picture of: **superimposed fields**, **quantic sea**, **'broth of uncertainties'**, **chaos** and **hazards**.

Humans make often without care for the limits, the constraints of social constructions nor the precautions of care. Done that just with sheep-like mind driven; by fake determinist speeches and pieces of rules. And then to pretend them to paradigmatic *status*? Why be surprised by the astonishingly aggressive populism huge development of exasperated people?

Bases and Dimensions

Bases would be in formal sciences upon physics; the simple geometric frameworks referring the characteristic? Either extensive (or outer), or intensive (or inner) could be those formal system. Thus they are generic: supporting the developments but ... then too often taken in the simplest way. This makes hard to generate into complex things, quite easier with complications able to produce virtual reality. A metaphysics question would be about (in) compatibilities between natural and artificial worlds.

Reference systems thought as a way to 'clean' views. Regarding the proper definition of bases: some concepts of the forms. **Base in topological neighborhood**, involves families, subfamilies, finite intersections of members. Topological space base of a family of opens. **Filter** (is a formal mathematics concept), it bases a sub-base, if non-empty and included in intersections. An example with Fréchet base (in theory of integration).

> **Filter**: is a special subset of a partially ordered set. Filters appear in order and lattice theory or topology. The dual notion of a filter is an ideal. Semigroup operation induces an operation on the collection of its subsets. If obtained subset is both a left and right ideal then it is called a 2-sided ideal). The minimal ideal of a commutative semigroup, when it exists, is a group. Green's relations about a set of five equivalence relations that characterize the elements in terms of the principal ideals they generate, are important tools for analyzing the ideals of a semigroup and related notions of structure.

> **Base of a Hilbert space** considers a complete orthonormal family of vectors, equipotent and its cardinal number the dimensions of Hilbert space. So are Hilbert's space, all pre-Hilbert space which is separated and complete. Because normed and complete, any Hilbert space is also a Banach space. [Hilbert space provides a scalar product from real numbers to complex numbers $\mathbb{R} \to \mathbb{C}$ (or reverse). They relate well to **Fourier's analysis** [most important approach for **signal analysis**, as in electronics]. **Banach space** is basic to vectors' field.

> **Base of tensorial space** is defined on a finite, commutative dimensioned body. [Tensor is a broader concept of vectors]. **Canonical or vector base** considers any free family generating the vectors; either complete of incomplete. Base of a uniformity will be detailed elsewhere. **Dual base** of a vector space is over a **commutative body** and its **dual space**.

Vector mini-Summary					
Operator	Abbreviation	Symbol	Argument	Result	Interpretation
gradient	grad	∇U	Scalar	vector	greatest increase
divergence	div	$\nabla . A$	Vector	scalar	Sources
rotation	Δ	$\nabla \times A$	Vector	vector	Vortices
Laplacian		$(\nabla . \nabla)U$	Scalar	scalar	potential field
operator		$(\nabla . \nabla) A$	Vector	vector	Sources
∇ :Nabla operator used for gradient					

If any could have a proper base definition in social approaches just may avoid many misunderstandings (or could distract to technical formalities of (Rousseau-like) 'social contract'. But this base ought to be accepted by all parts; that the technical work of formulating properly has to be respected. Before discussing on the degeneracy of solutions.

We will not mention much of reference space, in the thread of this essay. The chosen ones pose each their technical difficulties, not the purpose here, Just to suggest having a logical eye in what they look like. For example, you may investigate in the pictures of the main search engine (of the world-wide-web). And also mentioned that our ideographic frames since primary framing often need the system of reference to be the one or the other. So for a brief list:

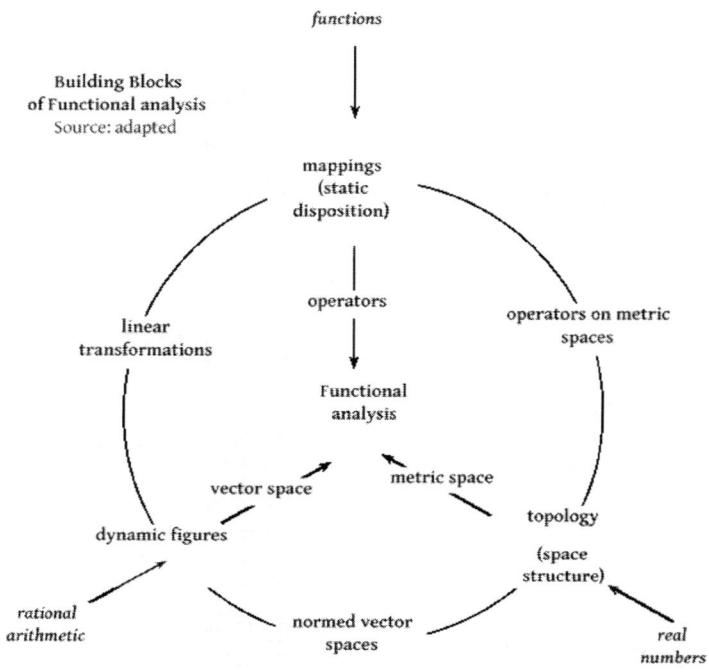

functions

Building Blocks
of Functional analysis
Source: adapted

mappings
(static
disposition)

operators

linear
transformations

operators on metric
spaces

Functional
analysis

vector space   metric space

dynamic figures

topology

(space
structure)

rational
arithmetic

normed vector
spaces

real
numbers

Spaces of Reference

Inner Space referred
- Cartesian base straight line or Euclidean geometry;
- Polar: based on the *modulus* (length rotating after an angle;
- Riemann's sphere;
- Poincaré's sphere.

Outer Space referred
- Normed Linear Metric
- Non-Linear Curved Spaces
- Minkovsky's, de Sitter's, Schwarzchild's.

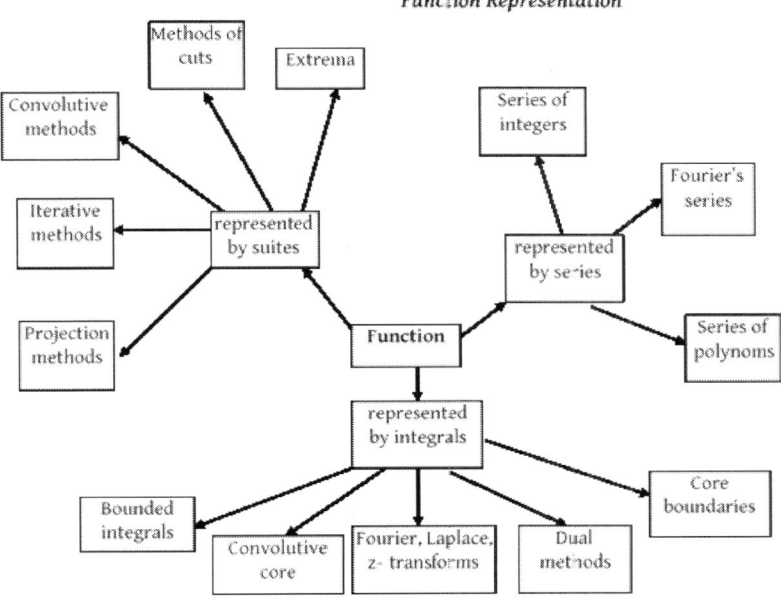

Function Representation

Reference Systems in History of Science

After Descartes's reductionism, the Cartesian's system of reference; the functional analysis empowered the differential calculus offered by Leibnitz-Newton (joined by Newton's laws of attraction).

> [After the unfair resolution of conflict of interest; of the British Royal Academy's (BRA) President; it is to observe that it was Leibnitz who provided most of the differential calculus modern design. Not to miss mentioning also the sketches of Huygens whom also claimed for paternity. And it has been Europe that kindly promoted the crypto-alchemist of Cambridge (turned president of BRA) brilliant ideas, upon the mechanics of the apple's myth and more prone to secrecy and greed. In other words, is this the mass-volume weak attraction force of similar (gravity). But the other ways of Newton have plenty of wonders and, still some mysteries to unveil. So his distasteful British manner (of those times?) does rest too much of his *genius*].

Previously, *Galileo Galilei* and premonitory studies, has been the one providing the extreme western part of Asia with the proper scientific paradigm: experimental device (or disposal) by the side of a mathematical model. Having been offered the choice to shut up or be burned by the "holy" Roman Catholic Church (as so many of those times). He muted just keeping that as Copernic said Earth was rotating. And so Galileo had been prevented from exposing more about the reason why balls were rolling on inclined planes to ground.

In nearby Geneva Calvinists' city neither was a refuge for scientists as they could experience on the stack. Reformists from Low Countries (Dutch Flanders), at the beginning; were a bit more open. Since they were trying to establish their doctrines. So they let Spinoza survive (but he was ostracized by his community), then surviving polishing lenses for Huygens. Also there, have been published... Descartes's "Discours de la Méthode" (1637) whom ground Cartesian reductionism of small partitioned pieces. Nevertheless reformists' mind openness was more about moral justification businesses (including the overseas ones). Not so directly for protecting scientists freedom. Moral justifications were more about the rights of civilized, not much about the means employed by Dutch captains in the 1st world-wide empire on seas.

Newton was indeed a major *genius*, but not prone to share soon and politely his results with the maximum. So in Europe scientists' language French dominated it was through their circles of 'beautiful minds' whom promoted kindly Newton's ideas. Occidental peninsula of Asia was already engaged in many natural discoveries and systematic experimental studies. They had come especially from Italian universities (in modern history this Mediterranean Peninsula united later). Then came the era of 'Illustration'; with its Encyclopedia of knowledge.

Newton's gravity inspired plenty of social artists or moral philosophers; including Adam Smith. In physics during a quarter of millennium, what better than Newton's mechanics? ... Nothing until Einstein-Poincaré Special Relativity Theory came in. Einstein was effectively the 1st to publish but worked hard to achieve his conception ... well knowing that Poincaré, better mathematician than him; was on the same trail. So anxious was the young German physicist about his priority; so the already mature and great French mathematician; kindly recognized the original prior and equivalent formulation of young Einstein works.

That was not the only time that in a private owners' world mixed complicated competition and cooperation. It happened: and that was a time that you can be smart with natural concepts or experiments not almost only with mathematics. Logics, have been less relevant ... but may be more in the future? – at least by the critical way of preventing cyborg madness?).

> The modern paradox of 'Information Revolution'; objective ambiguities of utility is now between humans and computers machines of information...

So if we want Asimov's laws on robots are respected, we absolutely need to be less stupid than robots, fairer and more honest in what we do.

Point-Wise Models

Another basic of Newton's mechanics approach was about a point-wise representation of a system, especially solid ones, thus by a core point put forward by d'Alembert (end of 18th century a French mathematician). As far as we remember: formulated then by Laplace (another French mathematician) (with Laplacian operators?).

Representative One point Constrains
- if any under system of referent;
- the sum of displacement is null;
- the volume remains the same;

- the solid can be resumed by a single point.

Boltzano-Weierstrass properties

- If D is a compact subset of $\mathbb{R}^n$ then all partition $\{x^{(k)}\}$ of d contain a subpart $\{x^{(kj)}\}$ which converge in one point $x^{(0)}$ in D
- The set of 2 points strictly positive in quadrant (I) is open but non adherent,
- The set of 2 positive points is closed but non adherent,
- A point of coordinates is interior iff coordinates are strictly positives,
- Whatever line or plane or plan in $\mathbb{R}^3$ is a closed, non-adherent and has no interior point,
- A set of 3 points in $\mathbb{R}^3$ where each point is positive (or null) is equal or inferior to a given value in a compact set,
- Interior points are those strictly positive and strictly inferior to limit.

The Laplacian **for a scalar function is a scalar differential operator involving scale factors of the coordinate system**. It is important in mechanics, electromagnetics, wave theory, and quantum mechanics, and Laplace's equation, Helmholtz differential equation, wave equation and Schrödinger equation.

Analogous operators obtained by generalizing from 3 dimensions to 4-dimensional space-time which is known as the d'Alembertian. A version of the Laplacian that operates on vector functions.

Despite that for Newton's gravity this point-wise may conceptually not look like the best; it has been a useful simplification for motion study. Without mass, **barycenter**, when not filled around by matter is nothing much. Nevertheless this paved the way for the concept of the **moment** (weight vector force link to a center of rotation by a given *radius*) and then of the **tensor**. Gravitation is for a whole body and for its overall kinetics, in a reduced free space (at the extreme in a *vacuum*) and far from. That could be a good approximation when with cosmic distances. But on the borders, or surface you have: **friction** (eroding), **stress** (more of less elastic) if not fluid (producing Coriolis force). And then with time the sort of closure we imagine: a dimension one (1) Notice that commonly time is more as denominator than as the numerator.

[And could there be? - a possibility of an under systemic (thick) world 5th dimension (a Kaluza-Klein concept?) Also does that supports the sort of Calabi-Yau's 'dimension compactification' proposed by String theoreticians? Or up: the 3 required dimensions (closure successively by a time line, then by a surface like closing a *conus* of projection, then by an environment: space of projection and/or provision?)].

[String theory seems hard for fundamental physics experimental devices; as mentioned by Penrose? - and others. Intuitively that may be easier; and a 'good oathing' for formal ideas].

Short-passing observations about t mass and gravitation:

[Observe that we try to join some fundamental physics interpretations (relatively common) with a formal phenomenological reading; may look like confused (it is so by the complexities. But may have the advantage to be able to inspire the framework: set of elements subject to gravity-mass force of similar subset-injected with dissimilar attraction-sub-similar repulsion–electric force. This is a nice primary framework left apart the physics's identifications. For nice it is also for structuring any logical atom-field-like order-disorder or ordinal-cardinal?].

- Locally: **nucleus** mass volume-kinetics is tightened by strong and weak interactions [**nucleus** of atom-(field). It would be to structure that with forces 'balances': 1) attraction of same, 2) repulsion and attraction of different.
- Universe width: Higgs-boson's mass is providing and gravitation waves, 'of or for'; since primary expansion and 'mass projections' (we had an unequal distribution since Big Bang?–primary-expanding cosmic masses-gravity field). [Attractiveness of same nature universe force provided by dynamic heterogeneous projections. Either in an empty almost free space and/or dynamic ordering gained over a quantic 'vacuum'?];

  [Would be the converse of 'out or in all' 'netgentropy', the primary 'in' strong *versus* weak interactions? -of nucleus to integrate with gravity? (Weak interaction already relation evidenced with electromagnetic)].

- ... So the 'force of difference' (electric currents producing magnetism when moved in transversal plane; coming from order in shorter distance effect in local fields; related to weak interactions and; neutral when it is mass less γ rays?);
  [electromagnetism of the γ rays which latter ones are (almost) without mass; making no mass order established for expressing the divergent-convergent system of electric forces?–Of course to the physicists be suggesting a cleaner expression].

- For gravitation at the contact of the surface: the friction on rugose; or stress on elasticities, and if the surface fluidic: Coriolis force;
  [... Make further sub-forces possibly having to be a volunteer in sharing (or fielding?) the local space with holes filled, holes to fill and holes not to fill; places and electric driven forces or sub-forces... Emergence by combination(s) of carriers?].

- More distant (centrifugal force neutralized by centripetal gravitation makes evolutionary cosmic existence.

  [Structuring of space, differentiating local environments.

Care our correspondence: general in the text we call 'micro' the fundamental (which in facts makes most of universe and 'macro' the local environments; not out the fundamental micro frameworks and some enough 'smoothing between 'for supporting, emergence of detail' ... and when enough reproducibility in complex ambiguous environment-complex systems ... allowing life].

[To this very picturesque way of seeing the World, we did not abound in the relations to thermodynamics or corresponding formalism. Of course because by the side of physics all that is still today's core efforts of physicists. As well sort of clean formal expression that may eventually test the formal consistence of physics' Universe. After that only 'sub-state-instantiation' our lay expressions].

Now, we are seeking some formal systemic expressing a sort of relative formal system; out the usual pieces and links. That is also possibly expressing the component required by the relative informative system link. Hence a bit more complicated than the lone link of relative information is provided since the beginning. It is to catch somehow the package of geometric objects 3 dimensions, to join with the different primary logics levels and; the 'General Axiom of Abstraction; we found in Petrova's **skew symmetric differential forms** in field physics.

These are formal forms of 'operators', at least analytics which are very interesting combined form. So we will summarize some of their properties later. This anticipation to manifest the need for crisscrossed informative, formal kind of ligatures; slightly and relatively more complete to 'operate a relative system'.

[In the 'common life analogy the closest picture: the straight-jacket, one of a sort that could be either for the upper limbs as for the lower limbs. We have to care for some right to breathe and some evolutionary right to move. Of course, if you find that funny. That is because you did not understand that mathematics can put that in the formula. And you cannot imagine a straightjacket a formal device that can be used to study effects. When you tight, release one after the other before giving the mad back to common life.].

The Sphere and the Cube

Now for some basics about minimum geometry. Could we appreciate any kind of object, or mental representation a volume?–at least a **closed networked structure or framework** (brain is just made of that: a co-functioning some networks relatively specialized. Neurotransmitters in the brain are fewer than 3 dozen

[Like an alphabet or a code vocabulary?–Where half a dozen are more important: dopamine, catechol amines (2 important: epinephrine, norepinephrine), serotonin, acid glutamic and acetylcholine). Commonly with central brain and peripheral functions.

[After core framework either abstract ... and after materialize; or corresponding well to physics and after operating; further, you fill. Either the skeleton surrounded with flesh, and the representations with amounts as 'stirring strings' or hairs dressed... As a result you obtain Gordian knots; inside the framework and 'grids of hairy tails; outside'–the cloak of the *nucleus*. To match with the local field?].

At least to think about geometric forms not so perfect for being exclusive. So not make those the absolute reference. Only relative ones, to help you manage your ideas according systemically solvable forms. And also help you, to position your relative freedom; respect to what you can mentally represent and handle. This is either still analytic or practical, since natural space. When we will know a bit better about the properties of these forms, simple and pure in abstract; more complex or complicated in realities ... the way to 'wisdom in practice'.

Pictures for starting the approach of combined (?) approach; there is, either the sphere or the cube [or both?]–An abstract start of any logical ball or formal box. If with the sphere; unless there is a dual (north and south poles [or in-out of *torus*?- or elliptic form]. Showing at least one **axis** of **order** (as the order of an electromagnetic field? - which is transversal plane). Or a box seemingly able to position: one apex of entry (like to the time) and opposite one will become for 'out' or 'issue': opposite corner-apex.

[Have in mind that an order needs; among pluralism (of qualities and quantities) an 'ordering'; either timed or spaced... And even scaled (in: atoms; and out: field? Not enough attention is paid to the **differently timed subsystems** in a systemic hierarchy... That maybe follow its system time life of maximum complexity; reached ... relative top-down].

Then there are **different ways to refer**: since an inner-centered system (?) of coordinates, for the sphere of 2 orthogonal planes (so-called **Poincaré's referential**). But could be requiring another information? -to close the required cardinal (as of general solvability. To take into account the contraction or dilatation of the sphere; or an "in" and "out" (as a point of view). [**Riemann's sphere referential** is a sphere on a complex number plane, so more outside].

For the cube it would be an almost similar referential system of **2 planes orthogonal**. But could it be fixing one? -passing by the 4 apices not "in" nor "out" the mid-belt of present? And another passing by these "in" and "out" apices; orthogonal to the 1st. With time made a (closing) dimension? Often respect any geometric volume we have a plane approach looking like **little card** (it is a kind of Poincaré's card; or perpendicular targets), for intercepting the trajectories (these are at best perpendicular to the flow). Be with time the **time-card 'the present'** as a plane-picture where you have to imagine the before (past) and the beyond (future). Repeat and then you have a series of exposures. [Imagine a series of 3 Post-it: 1) the **label** (or start); 2) the **intersect** of the patterned trajectories (in our mind a 4 dualizable details to bring: left- up-down-right or/and the converse: left-down-upright; 3) the **closure** (or its end?).

Formal definition of a topological space
It is a set T of elements of an arbitrary nature (called of this space with:
- T and the void set are open,
- The sum of an arbitrary (finite or infinite) number and the sum of an arbitrary finite number of closed sets are closed.
- Any 2 distinct point x and y of the space T have disjoint neighborhoods (Hausdorff space).

Then to give you some basic in quite a primary school way. At minimum could be to explore with some visual formulary...

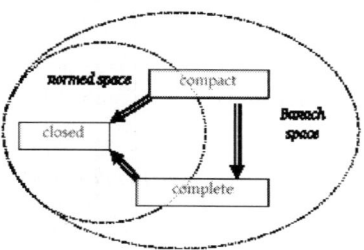

Regular structure of topological space

243

[Keep in mind: we do not want you to turn any perfect mathematician or geometrician. We are just willing to be concerned about being smart with the way things works and a curious citizen 'preparing to care'].

Sphere is perfect round shape in the 3 dimensions it can be described by 2 *radii*. Think about this thoroughly: a 3 dimensions object if perfect round shape (implicit property is that it just needs 2 other variables or parameters to be described. Sphere is all point to a constant distance from the center. A sphere does not have a boundary.

The 3-dimensioned analog of a sphere, so-called a 3-sphere not a solid-ball. Formula of the sort for the **3-sphere is embedded in 4 dimensions space**. A 3-sphere embeds in a 4 dimensioned space, not to imagine it, as a traditional sphere. Solid ball has its surface as the boundary. In non-linear geometry an **elliptic volume** requires 1 more characteristic.

Poincaré (a French encyclopedic mathematician transition of 19th–20th century) discovered that there is at least a 3-dimensioned space (not a 3 dimensioned sphere) with the same homology group. **Homology** is a sort of topology similarity. Examples with this property the so-called Poincaré's **dodecahedral space** (also called the **fundamental group**).

Conics or ellipsoidal are imagined to be rare as objects; but we will see further how this can be important for the projection into **'solid angles'** and diversities. Notably with **Perron-Frobenius theorem**. Maybe epitomized in: "the 3-dimensional positive semi-definite symmetric matrix is represented by an ellipsoid; which allows to visualize 3-dimensional **covariance** matrices; by means of a standard confidence region or primary deviation pair".

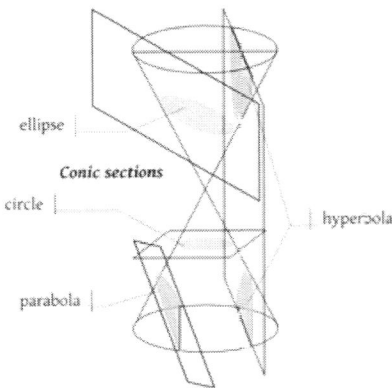

ellipse

Conic sections

circle

hyperbola

parabola

Bestiary of Spheres

Analytically spheres' lexicon contains basically: **quadratic equation, points of contact**, sphere **chords, tangent** and **polar** planes.

Sphere is referred to its center, it follows a quadratic equation with 2 roots. The mid-point of chords of a sphere and parallel to fixed direction lies in the normal diametrical plane. That is equation of any sphere has the form $cx^2+cy^2+cz^2+2ux+2vy+2wz+d = 0$. General equation depends on 4 constants. Only one sphere passes through 4 points. There is in general 1 and only 1 sphere orthogonal to 4 given spheres.

All spheres orthogonal to 3 given spheres, form a **general coaxial system**, whose radical plane is the plane of the centers of given spheres and whose line of centers is their radical axis. Coaxial spheres are spheres having common **lines of centers**. This has applications in the study of trajectories or particles. There are 2 point-spheres (limiting points) of a non-intersecting coaxial system. 2 spheres intersecting each other joined either by one point (out) or a circle. 1 sphere intersected by a plane either a circle or an ellipse. There is only 1 sphere through any point not by plane.

Banach Tarski theorem (on sphere): Ordinary unit sphere in Euclidean 3-space can be cut into 5 pieces. By simple Euclidean motions (translations, rotations) and these pieces can be reassembled to make 2 complete spheres.

Banach-Tarski paradox: says that a ball in the 3 dimensioned space can be cut in a finite number of pieces and reassembled. Thereafter to provide with 2 balls identical to the original one less a displacing. The result is based on the existence of non-measurable sets. Collection of points with no traditional volumes is implying non-numerable choices, to detail the way the ball is divided.

For a simple algorithm to **classify objects in a 3 dimensional space**:
- Is the object linear? (1 dimensioned);
- Does the object have multiple 'higher orders'?
- If the object does not belong to, either a linear group or a polyhedral group, then does it have a proper or improper axis of rotation (i.e. C_n or S_n)?
- Does the object have an even-order improper rotation axis S_{2n} but no plane of symmetry or, any proper rotation axis, other than one collinear with the improper rotation axis?
- If the object does not belong to the linear point groups, the polyhedral point groups or the point groups C_5, C_4, C_1 or S_{2n} then look for the highest order rotation axis;
- Are the nC_2 axes lying in a plane perpendicular to the C_n axis?

Unit System Approaches

Analytical natures of objects or models do not completely and instantaneously fill all the conditions that allow traditional simple operations of the calculus. Ideal formalism avoids contradictions of real subjects. Meanwhile complexity needs it (possibly the most general out (quantic *vacuum*?) and incorporated enough and more or less ordered?–symmetries and alternatives?).

Complex objects, as ones like of our realities, need "imperfections", permitting local singularities. That can help to 'develop up' more complexity. Against but using the concept of **potential** (and crossed information?). Imperfections start very soon already with quantum theory, thermodynamic entropy-'netgentropy,' open living and reproducing systems.

> For that reasons it is quite surprising that the world of governance. Despite many engineers in there, so 'simplistic' in their attitude, and so the management of followers of formal reductionist, not better than 'esoteric reacting' (missing that they propose causal alternatives as reductive as the 'officially authorized leaders of the changes'. Once any out the intelligence of their expertise are surprisingly prone to think that social things are and should be simple and simplified at the extreme to provide with incoherent pictures of how realities are? Probably the problem is more with our bizarre thinking.

Mind too that fundamental physics managed hyperspace of 7 – 17 dimensions. That is more than the phenomenological real world ... and the possibilities of general solvability? Since this one is taken in absolute and not 'relative?

Hyperspace more dimensions where physicists are trying like theories of superstrings; sorts of relations or (larger or across?). Properties of symmetries to infer the fundamental construction of the fundamental physical world.

First to apprehend what we have in the toolbox. So as to approach: logical unit, correspondence and some about complex objects. Thus an introduction to set theory and its limits; category theory is a basic for modeling: **isomorphism** (similarity of behavior) and then complexity and parametric approach of complexity.

Categories and Analogies? (care because we made suggestive complements)		
Lattice theory	**Set theory**	**Category theory**
2 nodes arrow	Elements	Objects
preorders	Sets	Categories
monotonic function	axiomatic operations	functor
(pointwise) functions ordering	choice axiom	functors natural translation
nodes	equations between elements	isomorphisms between objects
lattice between nodes	functions between sets	functors between categories
forms between arrow	equations between functions	functors natural isomorphisms
supremum	event space (finite)	colimit
least	singleton	initial
Galois connection	orders closed operators	adjunction
prefix point	choice in operations	algebra
closure operator	choice in finite cardinality	monad

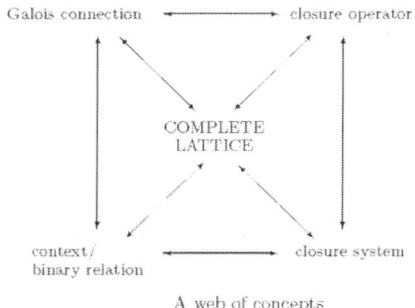

Galois connection ⟷ closure operator

COMPLETE
LATTICE

context /
binary relation ⟷ closure system

A web of concepts

Think Better With Basic Forms a Primer

In modern human ways, there is still some place to cope better with basic forms in formal self-management of social issues. Thus the ambition of this essay to provide with many small insights and essentially intuitive concepts because they could be important to manage individually as collectively. There can be used to examine the remaining sense of deviations; respect your abstracts and phenomenological perspective, approached by forms. Upon that: 'what to do in reality' or 'cognitively care mental attitudes'. Trying with small seeds of knowledge for corrective purpose.

Revolution of information is a major 'revelator' of the improper ways we govern our illusions with abstracts. Those are often wrongly specified and inconsistent with realities that humans: either are not giving them any good materiality; nor they are choosing. When positioned between alternative of small sacrifices or exposed the keenest realistic ones. Just to look how the Leviathan of geo-bureaucracies triumph in their 'innocent' vicious and nasty uses to distort perspective. Including both the superficial socially useless uses; as well as the services they ease for criminals and free-riders. Aspiring to be free to un-care massive threats. Thus to avoid lightening ones.

Despite the fact that neoclassical value economics laud the disparities in the sources of profits when fomenting inequalities and itchy scratchy opportunism. That is not all a laudable sort of relation: of the quantities; of positive (material) resources dedicate to such sorts of socially negative (values) qualities. We need better mixtures

To notice that it may look like a paradox to tell you on one side: your very physics nature is about ghosts, full of emptiness, fields superimposed ... but that is much more serious for coping with realities. Since we now have plenty of technologies for understanding why rather than ... most of politics abstracts, traditional economics and arts.

So would be the sorts of epistemological 'arts' of those examinations, for most people; this does not mean that social arts are not important. They have essential functions to the humans to ensure. Just better if the ground cores are enough well designed. Our management of realities; precisely not should have to fight with the stupid of the scratchy sort. Those having misunderstood that the information is not just the communication of 'big mouth nice words'. So for behaving in a very different way as soon as they have to compete making it so unfairly with always same kinds of justifications.

Not in our mind to eradicate 'others' sins' nor ignore these. We are more with rebalancing with not too costly services of good will the incorporation of usable disorders. To make them self-one scalable. Instead of stockpiling the supposed reasons of advantages and let to other the inconveniencies of disordering disadvantages.

That remarks or critics are not just about common citizens, lay people, non-experts in formal sciences. Since the mistakes are also with them managing enormous populations of concepts. Which are often taking some illusionary abstracts for truth. Un-specifying enough them for obtaining some solutions to their systems of unknown. But asserting much despite the flaws of their activities and financial supposed support.

For simple examples:
- **Many visual illusions** came from that no measure are done or because just operating in 2 dimensions flatness. Spontaneously brains (and binocular vision) makes your mind build thick or deep. Normally human visions are **stereoscopic** and so, eyes on a plane, produce optical illusions at some coincidence. But not simply behave for catching the 3rd dimension of the scene.
- Have you ever experienced the absurdity to try to convince associates? - That for quite a good management of their own chosen social-economic problem (they choose themselves); the combined use of 3 (intertwined) parameters for checking and operating turn unacceptable... Despite with no higher cost and with better efficiency in the approach... For them it is only to stick, at the fake unique abstract concept, giving them the illusion of the *panacea*. And further when arrived the evident defects and inconvenience, of their way, having no care..

Mind the consequences of the 'flat world' and all the waste and misery this did because too 'uniquely inspired 'Church' by its dogmatic doctrinaire choice prevented, consistent thinkers, from questioning. We still are not managing many abstracts dealing worse than Turing's machine (a British mathematician author of the computing automaton): minimal recursive step (the automaton) with the ambition to be able to master the global (the human leader), with the same simplicity, despite the evidence that out of their office, task force or enclosed meeting; they only may have destructive means.

Ethics in Metaphysics Essentials

So to advocate for better cares in phenomenology; that anyhow, in some way, shape the brain. In the brain they make it in a wiser way than the conscious one. To suggest that information maps-anchored could be formally analogically fundamental physics systems–half-completed.

Not the potentially elusive sensibilities narrowed by our skills of arguing and explain rationality. Communication is not the whole picture of information, nor the paradoxes of virtual, respect to realities' phenomenology, are not to take seriously. In our training and learning systems; as soon as the brain establishes its frame-working registers [The little Tiffany MIB 1 test?].

Together with many basics of Nature; there is a need to get back to better observations of social and environment. And helps without barriers to understand, for free choice, fairer concepts. Thus also stop insisting on those issues that they can be determined from far. Especially on matters of social buildings and just with computed hierarchies closed on whom.

Thus once you have examined your real and abstract geometries. Children's cognition does not start with Cartesian's analytical frame of reference. Once used and developed your skills of observation in the environment(s). Understand which ones you are used enough. For some unconscious simplifications when the situations. Empower applications with your analytical skills. So you can close realistically enough the proper specifications of your models. If you have too much incompleteness for narrow solving.

Do not discriminate too dogmatically between your rules and intuitions. The first to inflating the anti-natural ones take more risks to turn inconsistent. The intuitions have to learn and be trained. Make options for 'better' choice approaches available as close as possible to any. It is also to stay open to call for more resources properly prepared for calling them. Save time and resources of designed investigators called for help. Learn to collect and format properly. Care about feasibility: all that has good enough analogies with more sophisticated data treatment.

Thereafter experience may teach you that even with abstracts you may give them some geometric analogical shape. Knowing a bit better the smart properties of geometry, some have them which are quite intuitive, others should not be distorted by manipulations out of the basic. You will save plenty of time, if understand which sort of information to collect and how. Which means are easier to structure your analysis and practice.

Other effects or major constraints of information revolution and even globalization are that we need everyone solve hse pieces of complexity and complications on hse own as far as possible. And turn to higher or larger social scale for more if scalable. Hence not necessarily at the highest unable one level. Only for the remains, in a more explicit way (thus caring good communication criteria), rather than infarct common world-wide ways provided by new TIC; with exhibitionism of useless private things. [You will appreciate further that our treatment of residual or 'remains' is quite different from determinist despise ... thus more quantic?]

Geometrical explorations are also analytical. We care much about intuitions, not in an "instinctive" abridged concept. Cognitively, most training also lends on attitudes, emotions and so on... Not as you may think just on your conscience. The 'point' is to prepare you are properly reactive and more efficient. But not for being arrogant about the exactness of your anticipation. Have a robust enough good **solid angle** (probably a **polyhedron of 'principles'**); and *coni* **of projection** able to **meet, match and fit** not bad with complexities are much better than any finger index.

Now if you have a unit object under the eyes, just tracking it for sometimes, may convince you, it has a unity or integrity. In a propaedeutic formal-physics, you need to have some ideas concepts existing on one side and the other. Not as the expert having them alone about the concept of hes own; that will make your one 'pole'; on sphere poles come by 2, as an order in a volume, on its surface. You are only on the surface.

Vectors as Moving (Dynamic) Point

Much of the previous play either as particles or/and as fields .. [and de Broglie relates 2 natures]. Fields express with waves and spaces of vectors or tensors. The tensors are originally defined as line segments. Scalar and vectors are both special cases of tensor operators, of order n. Whose specification requires 3 numbers called the components. A scalar just needs 1 number for full definition, a vector requires 3 numbers. Vectors have the advantage that their equations describing the physical phenomenon can be formulated without reference to any particular coordinate system. But, when calculating, one must cast the problem into a form involving **scalar**.

A key step is to expand the vectors (or tensors); with respect to a suitable basis: coordinate curves, polar coordinates or generalized polar coordinates (where coordinate curves are ellipses); orthogonal system or curvilinear coordinates; each adapted to the sort of problem.

Newton's 2nd law (about force) has been made a 1st order tensor. The change in the distance between any 2 points of the elastic body is uniquely determined by the quantity called the deformation tensor.

The diagonal components of tensor's deformation rate are the relative elongation rates of a fluid element, along 3 axis of coordinates... [Mind to relate that to Eigenvectors]. The non-diagonal components symmetrical over diagonal equal half the rate of angular deformations. State of stress, of an elastic *medium* has a moment of inertia.

> For the lay, we suggest retaining such basic and remind in any circumstances. So as to become familiar with.

We will see (mostly in next volume) some about operators. Which are kinds of 'more complex operations' applied to some object(s) of physics. Since this essay is not a handbook, we are more trying to evoke some fundamental formal concepts for looking at realities complexities. That could be handled with formal tools. Not to revise the full formulation building of arithmetic or logic (they need not) with a purpose of purity and perfection.

Having or not the idea that this could exist or that we will meet at the extreme of simplifications only a (enormous) residual incompleteness that will be filled by 'only physics' or that formal sciences are everything.

Operating as System Premise

For physicists or mathematicians it is often to produce a formula representing most of the behavior of an object, its inner or interacting properties and/or outer motions in more or less interacting *medium*. On formal representation, anyhow when using a representation there is an **effect of reduction by abstraction** *versus* the **ambition to represent as much as possible**.

But, with complex things, how far we can go?–in the purification 'for principles.' Supposedly completely specified models or system of formula? Even if we could not take account of the intense desire to predict the future; be this concerning an object, situation or subject, etc. This question of detail is constrained by the possibilities of the calculus.

With the development of sciences there are plenty of quite well formulated general expressions. Sometimes uneasy if not impossible to calculate. Either because estimations of parameters or coefficients are non-accessible or ... not enough specified?

As you may have remarked, we evoked that; was not because the mechanics of the general expression; which would be enough catching. To be further specified in special cases, you have, on the one hand, and the concept of a formal system, on the other hand... If a something almost unary relative 'system' could exist and behave; or after dressing in realities are completed with estimates in memories and, by simulations open to choice or comparison of alternatives, all possible.

There are also many mathematical formulas that provide good empirical approximations, but still not well understood why. Natural theories can be required. Even in pure mathematics they are formulas of that sort.

> The right match would be very probably a mixture of logics and mathematical formula. Mathematics could not have been perfect since simple arithmetic was logically 'self-sustaining'. Logics needs some relationship operations for their election could be framed, possibly ordered, prevented the risks of too many paradoxes.

Being aware of Einstein's the difficulties for finding non-equivocal 'perfect operators' and sort of similar concept as an operator, functions, operating framework. Logically in physics standard operators, as slightly more complicated operations have been with **Laplacian, Lagrangian** and **Hamiltonian**. [They are others]. They are still not too far from simple arithmetic. Hamiltonians and Lagrangians; since the most probable that all those that provided much to physics objects formalism will be all compatible.

Having already mentioned Petrova-Cartan skew symmetric differential forms; relations, at this stage of the essay, we have to introduce on the formal and physics structures. Like with Noether's theorem for conservation laws; invariances, Green's functions, thermodynamics.

Yi-Lin-Forrest (a Chinese-American systemist) has also proposed an inductive systemic approach, called 'yo-yo model'. We did not have time to study it carefully (neither we are equipped for). But we think that qualitative ordering of systems' logics needing anyhow numbers theory. Maybe it is interesting to say that Yi-Lin's logics will probably have to inspire thinkers, Since mathematics perspective on systems filling or filled of complexities.

Numbers as Objects

Previous to that, have a look to the **numbers' concept of existence**: 3 levels of 'existence' to consider:

- **Pure existence**, such as Boris's proof [Borel defined a normal number (1900). **Random number** defined as **normal number**, observing that the decimal expansion of a 'random', real number's digits should appear equally often. Borel demonstrated with probability that a 'random number' is normal [following a normal law's] (but he could not exhibit any number of such sort)];
- **Existence with characterization**: such as the theory of complexity or called Lebesgue-Sierpinski type. In 1916 Sierpinski gave a "method" for producing an explicit example of a normal number. He defines, for every $\varepsilon > 0$, a countable family of intervals, $\Delta (\varepsilon)$, and shown that any number not absolutely normal is in $\Delta (\varepsilon)$ and that $|\Delta (\varepsilon)| < \varepsilon$. This has a "constructive" character and one view this as an explicit description of a normal number.);
- Existence via the **existence of an algorithm** of *calculus*: such after Turing, Becher or Figueira [Turing gave an algorithm to compute normal numbers. In 2002 Becher and Figueira gave an algorithm to produce a computable absolutely normal number. In 2007 Mayordomo gave an O (nlogn) algorithm to compute absolutely normal numbers].

[Remind, **randomness** as **noise** follow a **normal law**. Hence normal number concept key to existence of number. Modern theory of algorithmic randomness, has led to Martin-Löf's **characterization of a random sequence** (1965)].

In short intuitive existence here conceived as a switch from randomness to order ... or as a cardinal (unordered) to an ordinal... Considering at the 'head set' that one cannot discriminate completely in all numbers its cardinal and ordinal nature ... with the cardinal minimum special ... and the choice theorem of Set theory? Then only intuitively, what paper played by prime numbers, possibly in the 'jumps' to formal systems formation?

Unit of Logical Objects as Elements of a Set

To examine some concepts of Set theory, if it could inspire on realistic or abstract object taken as the unit within a collection. Remind that Set Theory also presides the approach of numbers.

Set **defining unit properties considers a metric space**; when all representing sequence is **converging** (limit of norms tending to 0). Then space is called **complete** [Metric if looking like too strong can be relaxed to norm-mathematics or equipped with a system-physics?]. A set of metric space is **closed** when any representing **convergent sequence** contains its limits. A close-set is **compact** if, for any sequence in it, there is a subsequence that is convergent. A set is close if any point is included therein together. It is **dense** in another if for any point in the latter there is a sequence of points in the former converging to the point.

A set with the center and *radius* looks like either open **ball** or closed ball. It is **bounded** if the whole of it, belongs to some ball. That is logic, yet not about a quantified or 'filled geometric form'.

One of our main questions in this essay is about what, in number theory, can correspond for the formal framing of the system concept ... applicable to reality.

In "affect, effect or object or subjects' representations," the Theory of Set started by Cantor and Dedekind is supposed the best logic to support arithmetic. But, among the 8 axioms (Zermelo-Fraenkel whom made the standard Set theory) it was also added a non-typical axiom of Choice. And this, as far as we can know, occur in many primary logical system, trying to be comprehensive: a something "affecting" the cleanliness of coherence.

Actually the encountered limits of Theory of Set made that not every collection is now thought to be a "Set."

Then the intents to introduce concepts, like of 'class'. More to find complementarity, since 'other' similar, precisely not to repeat the same. Maybe some issue could be accounted either as a crossed frame with sets or a dynamic piece, not of the same "as in the pure theory" would be the start.

Similarly the same logics in the same intent to reach comprehension. The method is developed, with many analogies across, becoming smarter, but with no success at reaching the major ambition ... nor wisdom. Thus in mathematics successively intuitionist logic (promoted originally by Brouwer a mathematician of the 20th century from the Netherlands). Such an heterodox logic of arithmetic failed but provided many grounding arguments to Arithmetic Set Theory adaptation.

Decidability of Unification				
Logic Order	Unification	Patterns	Monadic	Matching
1	Decidable			
2	undecidable	...	Decidable	decidable
3	...	...	Undecidable	decidable
∞	...	decidable	...	?

Then theory of categories have done the same and is important to similarities between structures (morphisms), etc.

Category Theory

[Category theory uses collection of objects and of arrows (also called **morphisms**). There are 2 basic properties: 1) **Associative composition** of arrows associatively and 2) Identity arrow for each object. It has been used to formalize concepts of other algebraic structures such as sets, rings, and groups].

For some concepts in short, a **category** C a category is the given of:

- 2 classes one said the object, the other the morphism of C;
- For any pair (X, Y) of objects of the category; the set called the HomC (X, Y) is said of morphisms of X to Y such as Hom (X, Y) and Hom (X,'Y') are disjoint unless X=X' and Y=Y'. [Hom: **homomorphism**, or morphism on 'oneself'];
- For all triplets (X, Y, Z) objects of a **category application** of Hom (Y, Z) × Hom (X, Y) in Hom (X, Z) said **composition** of morphism (f, g) ↦ g o f. Where g o f is the morphism of f, followed by g with the 2 conditions:
  - when all composition have a meaning (h o g) ɔ f = h o (g o f)
  - for any object X there exist a morphism idX identity of X so that idX o f = f and g o idX = f

Category Theory Objects			
Concept	Symbol	Objects	Morphisms
Sets	Se	Sets	Applications
Groups	Gr	Groups	Groups homo-morphisms
Abelian groups	Ab	Commutative groups	Groups homo-morphisms
Topological spaces	Top	Topological spaces	Known applications
A-moduli	Mod (A)	A-Moduli	A-linear applications

This theory has been introduced because needed by algebraic topology; algebraic geometry and problems expressed in terms of **functors** between given categories. **Functorial morphisms**, universal problems, **adjunct functors** are other relevant concepts, etc. Pay special attention to the term of morphism declined in many forms: homo-morphism, isomorphism, homeo-morphism, auto-morphism, mero-morphism

So it is of importance for looking at ways of mathematical behaviors as in physics's one. Isomorphism is a Primary in Similar Behavior for Complex or in Model. **Isomorphism**; n lay terms the state or property of looking like the same shape or form. In mathematics. It is a one-to-one relation onto the map between 2 sets, which preserves the relations; existing between elements in its domain.

Isomorphism in structures (Lascar): be M and N 2 τ- structures an isomorphism of M on N is an application h bijective of base set of M on base set of N; respecting the different symbols of τ; such as:

- if c is a symbol of constant then $c^N = h(c^M)$;
- if R is a symbol of the predicate, then $R^N = h[R^M]$.
- If f is a n-ary then for all $a_1, a_2, ..., a_n$ in N, $f^N(a_1, a_2, ..., a_n) = h(f^M(h^{-1}(a_1), h^{-1}(a_2), ..., h^{-1}(a_n)))$.

Be F a **formula**, universal closures of F is the formulas of the form $\forall v_1 (v_2 ... (v_n F$ where $(v_1, v_2, ..., v_n)$ is an enumeration of F free variables; a formula is valid if its closures are so. 2 formulas F and G are valid is F equivalent to G, equivalency is valid. Moreover:

- quotient set $\mathcal{L}/\cong$ provided the operations $\wedge$, $\vee$, $\neg$(successive symbols for intersection, union, negation), if a Boole's algebra
- proposition: any formula is equivalent to a 'Prenex' formula.

  [A formula of the predicate calculus is in 'prenex normal form,' if written as a string of quantifiers (referred to as the prefix) followed by a quantifier-free part (referred to as the matrix). Every formula in classical logic is equivalent to a formula in prenex normal form].

As important example an arithmetic, an **algebra** is said to be **isomorphic** to another algebra if there is a bijective homomorphism. An homomorphism of an algebra to another one has a linear map with respect to the product

  [Have in mind that in comprehensive formal approach any lay term, often commonly used in street conversations, has a specific definition in the formal register. This is 'for clean handling, hence the definition there, is not exactly as the lay term. Precisely for that, you would have to delimit in the common; a range or perimeter of concepts associated to your lay terms; similar framed (copied) to: those existing in the logic, identified these relations one by one; trying, economically, to cover as many as you can (or different essential situation). So to exclude some common language other terms (as redundant) and then check (or iteratively test?) the isomorphism. This is possibly simplified if all qualified actors only play according to the rules of the game of isomorphism. But in reality it is quite common that none want to play fair; just by the rules].

Curry-Howard isomorphism is 'enunciate complete total equivalence'. In λ-calculus [a basic language of calculi in computers] with isomorphism; there would be only one located variable for each type. That is not a simple correspondence but a 'true isomorphic structure'. Variables of primitive base may be delocalized ('transportable'). It extends for all logical connectors

Formal Systems Reductions and Complexity.

Now, you can imagine types of variables in a system that would explore scale(s) of complexity (like: fundamental, intermediate and more complex). Then to detail one level (or a near 3 levels relative: S_{-1}, S_0, S_{+1}) of complexity. Or at least one and a bit more (that could be iterated); across perspectives. For explaining registers developed at a given level. In some way, you can also put here a sub-hierarchy. This also applies for exploration of development or diversification at the level.

Interesting **patterns** would be like to study the purity or independence of a classificatory concept (on the main diagonal in a representing matrix) at the level. Consider also effects transported over scale(s) (formalism of fundamental exponents). And finally care processes of diversification (turning impure). Understand, traditionally any register seek for reference of separated dimensions, thus in orthogonal (or orthonormal relation) which is valid at the level, since 'framing the volume'. But if you are **multiscale**, developing within, with the same or relative universe principle, the dimensions independent dimensions 'at the level' will have correlation passing by the lower level, possibly at the level a process of identification (or systemic relative unity). Also to have to take in account some environmental or fields constraints. [That is all a mechanic of system model, new? – many things have already been examined in structural multivariable models. Probably not so much new, out the configuration, complex by its questions:, complex numbers, non-linearities, **parametric equations**, and some other issues we will see further or in next volume].

We have mentioned a concept of maximum reached complexity. For a literary approach of complexity (after Fernandez Diaz inspired by Morin); should consider 1) The irreducibility of randomness and/or disorder, such as defined by a non-reducible algorithm, 2) non-decidability, from any series of numbers and events. Complications would emerge as a consequence of 3) innumerable numbers of fundamental interactions or biological and social phenomena. Complementary are 4) partially antagonist relations between, disorder, order and reorganization; and 5) the concept "order from noise" or "order from order" and "order from disorder" are, all to account for. Natural sciences have 6) transgression of limits [in both sides formal-physics] in what can be called universalist abstraction erase singularity, local, and temporality. So given the priority of singularities 7) 'resurrection' would be sources of other singularities.

About organization as a system; since different elements; as simultaneous unicity and multiplicity. A system which is, at the same time, more than less, the sum of its integrated parts. There is a conceptual loss of self-sufficency of objects; and of **Popper's delimitation principle**. The incorporation of the human observer in his observation as a 'twist' is between an authentic aspiration for truth and human re-introduction in the cosmos through '**anthropic principle**'. The **principle of contradiction** is not so a problem, as a signal of errors; but as an important epistemological tool with creative capacity.

[Note that we made our essay more as a work of composition. Driven by our sense of synthesis including by the way concepts, definitions, abstracts and extracts (somehow remodeled). This makes some extract commentaries, not all smoothly continuous after some thesis or intent to ground the discipline of demonstration in itself coherence. So methodologically with stay on the register of questions, exploration ... or by side what we have to do.

Parallel and/or collective thinking pays more attention to the processes are fair enough in robust goals. Which in a formalism-managed metaphysics-of meta-formal-physics seems the missing face out of certain determinism. This pretended needed by our societies; which compulsions for purified cleanliness just 'shears strict' produce hypocrisy and obliged reaction, rather than positive investigation of consensus in 'social arts'. That is how and where social arts are important: not to find theories but to agree in the choice of solutions].

> Paradigmatic modern managements, do not assume enough the obliged reactions to their 'shears strict' hypocrisy. So has to betray that proper lessons of humans' history which are, if information flow easily, never the lie of the winner. But much more about the failures of all.

After Parsons: in qualitative knowledge systems dealing with uncertainty, **possibilities, incomplete probabilistic knowledge** or **partial ignorance**, "regardless of how it is named ... the knowledge is incomplete" in its way. "The difference is that while **qualitative algebra** and **order of magnitude system model knowledge** that is incomplete, **interval probability system model information** that is uncertain and incomplete..."

"Thus the **incompleteness at 2nd order is an imperfection in knowledge of the imperfection of knowledge...** It is this kind of information modeled by all quantitative systems abstractions. Whether they are qualitative probabilistic network of systems built on κ (kappa) values. In contrast all the defeasible system just aim to handle first order incomplete information."

> **Kappa value:** Cohen's kappa coefficient is a statistic which measures inter-rater agreement for qualitative (categorical) items. Thought to be a more robust measure than simple percent agreement calculation, since κ takes into account the possibility of the agreement occurring by chance. One value of kappa can be regarded as universally acceptable.

> "To each constructive object corresponds a function $\Phi_x(k)$ of integer k–the log of minimal cardinality of x-containing sets that allow definitions of complexity at most k. If the element x itself allows a simple definition. Then, the function Φ drops to 1 even for a small k. Lacking such definition, the element is "random" in a negative sense. But it is positively "probabilistically random" only when function Φ having taken the value Φ_0 at a relatively small $k = k_0$, then changes approximately as $\Phi(k) = \Phi_0 - (k-k_0)$." (Kolmogorov 1974 quoted by Vitányi).

> Let a, b, c and k be natural numbers; by $a \rightarrow (k)_c^b$ means for every function $f:[a]^b$ (c, there exists a subset A of a such that A is homogeneous for f and the cardinality of. A is k. It is well known in combinatory that there exists a primitive recursive function $g(b, c, k) \rightarrow (k)_c^b$.

By the side of formal, complexity receives various parameters which often relate to powers' characteristics or measure of entropy. With some limits such as in systems when we are with high dimensions or; systems of low dimensions with more than 1 characteristic time; Lyapunov's exponent or; Kolmogorov-Sinai entropy, cannot catch important characteristics.

General expressions of Complexity:

- stochastic complexity = - lnP (x: () + parametric complexity)

- stochastic complexity of a code D is given a model H = L (D/Ĥ)+ complexity (H);

- parametric complexity = ln $(\hat{x}_{\in X} P (\hat{x} | \theta(\hat{x}))$

- minimum L complexity algorithm: $\min_k \min_{\in \Theta k}{}^{(m)} (\sum_{t=1}^{m} L (D_t: f()+1/\lambda. L_m (\theta,k));$

where $L_m (.,.)$ is a function $\cup_k (_k (m) \times \{1,2, ...\} \rightarrow \mathcal{R}^+$ and + satisfying $\sum_k \sum_{\theta \in \Theta k}{}^{(m)} e^{-Lm (\theta,k)} \leq 1$

" ... in 1965 Kolmogorov revised Shannon's average notion of random source entropy; into Kolmogorov complexity to permits extraction of a desire amount of properties modeled by a finite set; that includes the data string which amounts to modeling data by uniform distribution and; the amount of properties if measured by the Kolmogorov complexity of the description of the finite set involved." (Rissanen. 2005).

A measure of structural complexity would consider general observations; in other words, formulated the model of a system. It may use the language of set theory and binary relations. The statements and observations can be guided by when estimating the structural complexity of the system in the **polyhedral dynamics** approach.

["Polyhedral model is a powerful framework for optimization and parallelization. It is based on an algebraic representation of programs, allowing to construct and search for complex sequences of optimizations"].

Conditions for Complex Structure System

Designed mathematical models and the results of analysis give the basis for structural complexity estimate creation. To a certain extent it corresponds to the conclusion that measure of complexity depends upon a particular language of representation. The model replaces the actual system, and may mean that we are «digressing» from the real complexity of the real structure(s) as trying to analyze its image and build a theoretical estimate, about the information summarized in the model." This extract (of which we lost track) is in the 'conventional' approach to complexity.

It is somehow dissenting with the hope that relative formal system could make the *nucleus* of some handling. But with an adaptation, it is not a definitive impossibility. Consider that overall complexity if managed by the (huge) prime number index of maximum achieved complexity. The help of a proper relative enough formal system (absolute base adjusted by the subtraction of 'prime number index of maximum achieved complexity').

As a result the absolute values are rescaled to][0,1][and the easy formal handling can then restart. The informative relations being for units or atoms, 'in' (the general solvable must have rich enough formula (3 dimensions and the details for special solutions). Informative relations link 'out', of the atom (environment or relative field). Complexity also turns relative and the extent of informative relations there is across (relative dimensions). Thus if the proposal of a formal relative system is valid, the 'achieved formulations of complexity'; are not disqualified; but may need to be reformulated ... and possibly 'cleaned'.

Now, out arithmetic (and out complex numbers), to mention the complexity of calculus by algorithm which is taken in charge by computer algorithmic. It happens to turn much around polynomials. There is still some work to do at the respect [with some prize waiting as reward]. Or the logical problems of decidability. The world of systemic, as in engineering is not much more than in applications; illustrated by mathematical simulations. And so it is an art of many words.

> Of course mind that it is not because we have not yet clear concept 'system' in theory or numbers, especially the naked one, that is without physics. That does not mean that calculi are not right in fundamental natural sciences. They are, possibly with some waste and some manipulating abuses. If observed some physical phenomenological evidence, as there are, that may mean a lot for arithmetical nature of physics.

> The problem and questions are more about the proper way to formalize complex manageable frameworks at the middle of too many mistakes and too much deficiency with complex natural sciences (with not ambition to predict properly). But there are too many abuses of formal sciences when used by social arts. Out the hope there that we could have humanist schemes in social-economy.

> This is not so sweet, because intermediate determinist are just artistic approaches too dedicated at saying that it is better than 'common irrationalities'. In our ideas that these 'irrationalities' or to regret have much to do with improper educations, training and learnings. Of course the critics addressed to the Occidental way leading neither is convinced by the alternatives nor by many alternative efforts even when some are legitimate and many are positive and sympathetic. Of course there are many kinds of new original formalisms applied to simulate social decision with mathematics. Our problem is more with the arts of forcing the social hierarchies or the corresponding populism still prevailing, if not growing.

In the traditional concept, complex system includes many parts (components) and connections between them. These features cannot be regarded as unique when defining a complex system; but structural properties, together with behavioral properties. This primarily defines complex systems; the presence of connections testifies to a dependency of parts and existence of the order that leads to the wholeness (integrity) of the system.

> "The number of parts in the system should not be considered directly as a measure of structural complexity because the term «parts» is not uniquely defined, and it depends upon the levels of description. If an observer (researcher) disposes of information about the system, it gives him the possibility of creating several mathematical models and perform a more detailed study of the system; depending on the elements (parts) and interconnections representation level." [We mind that the trouble with formal sciences traditional management is that they do not put soon enough intrications of operations. The traditional view see sort of discrete graph relations, but do not superpose graph ... it would be too technically difficult, if without the resource of relativeness].

Degree and nature of interaction (weights of connections), normally between elements of a system, are not taken into consideration—very often such information can be inaccessible at the initial stages of analysis. Most probably, complexity should not be regarded in a context of simple numeric value, because in such case it irretrievably «hides» the essential structural information expressed in the mathematical model and «amounts» distinctive multidimensional system's structure to a number. [In a similar conceptual way information is carried by the link, not necessarily making the link. Of course it is not to exclude that. But a concept of relative formal system would have to consider more].

Weighted empirical process: $W_n(t) = \sum_{i=1}^{n} Cn_i / (\sqrt{\sum_{j=1}^{n} Cn_j^2}) [1_{[\xi \leq t]}^{-t}]$ for $0 \leq t \leq 1$

For so traditional complex systemic conception evokes "inescapable limits". "Unary-ness" or any comprehensive theory is limited language. This latter requires at least 4 levels of elements (in the provided structure). Incompleteress either arithmetic or its equivalence could make this the suggested reality of physics [The best complement to formal logic-mathematics and then mathematics becoming so 'the best expression of the real world ay the limit only completed by'. Mind also that a real complex system has to maintain an open-ness which can formally express as incomplete].

Set theory could be too close to the "object stability" of set. So at the minimum this is the need for choice axiom (link to order) and the same all logics encountering their limits in themselves. Because constitutively having to include paradox. And as a result, this set theory is too 'cutting' and/or too 'static'. In the same way class a something good intuition; or in logics a 'not out'.

Systemic Openness

For a complex system, what seems essential is all the preparations and interactions with environment and other objects or systems. Especially to smooth the pathway(s) it is not to remake all pathways to complexity, but take advantage of those underneath. So complex systems may also incorporate complex sub-systems. Things start at simple entropy level and openness of systems. Any real system is open. The only doubt at the respect is for the Universe. The practical problem then it is more on **probability of interactions** and/or **density**(ies). Nothing would exist without interactivity or aperture, **willingness to**, **potential**, openness or reactivity.

"**Opening of sets** if for any subset of a universe. A correspondence is established with another subset. This correspondence is an opening if it obeys the conditions of **idempotence** ['get back to itself'], **isotonic** or **decreasing** (including the later in the former) and invariance of universe. Such subsets, as open bijective relations have to be formulated between closure and opening; by the complementary either of subset or of relation." (Maravall Casesnoves, aSpanish logician and agronomist).

[To notice that open-ness has to coexist, both with exchange (at the least 'information'?) with some sense of relative closure ... or 'effectively system' and also relative and including irreversibility ... For relevancy of levels at which, those properties are defined and; the way the pluralism of such functions assume diversity].

Motions Typing

Once units, objects, relative open system defined to consider also their motion. This is not just in a real space of: geodesic, geographic or cosmic distances. But also is in qualities, characteristic phase-spaces or logical. General axiom of abstraction could be useful to imagine that.

Retaking Chizhov's on ... symbolic:

Motion in finite dimensional spatial object S	
• translator motion: +S, -S	• left rotation S^{+1}
• rotational motion: (±S)	• right rotation S^{-1}
• wave motion: +(±S), -(±S)	• self-intersecting motions: $[S^{\pm}]$; $[S^{+(\pm)}]$, $S^{-(\pm)}$
• absence of translator motion -iS	• absence of rotational motion: S^{i}
• Transfer of static object +iS, -iS	• rotation of static objects placed on another rotating one S^{+i}, S^{-i}.

Kinetic relations associated with the algebra of the operators are representing observables of the system. Which is usually formulated as commutation relations determining the algebra. This with an object; hence if considered as a system, to examine on which the support of the motion (that is where to apply: energy, electromagnetic, gravity).

Now we have seen some premises of the configuration of the system and subsystem formal approach; at micro-level (the logical formal evolutionary system emergence) and this was prior to that "transport of principles" (with Noether's theorem).

Formally a operating may use:

$$\frac{\textbf{finite algebra (A)}}{\textbf{ideal maximum (m)}} \longrightarrow \textbf{isomorphic subalgebra}$$

Physics Phenomenology

Observe that attractive force by similar characteristics (gravity) is weaker but has more distant effect. Yet not to say 'more cardinal effect.' Of course because it is the analogy that we use) have in mind that this about mass and gravity force.

Symmetries are between particles and field, waves and space heterogeneous dispersion of masses ... with possible coalescence of masses. Also to have in mind conversion of mass to energy (and vice-versa) 'crossed/closed' by 'heat/cooling' and 'expansion/contraction'?

Combination and discriminating attractive and repulsive forces are locally stronger but with narrower effect if not just of 'contact.' In physics this is also mass related (thus gravity exposed and contributing); but this is resulting from an order within electric charge characteristic (positive and negative currents). Because of that, narrower but (?) 'Ordered field' or electromagnetic field in the physics.

Observe that the previous addresses outer space main frame... Asking symmetrically about the correspondence for atoms existence or 'inner main frames'. In physics correspondence is in the 2 other and nuclear forces known (strong interaction and electroweak). [We avoid the approach of quarks].

[The reader is allowed to reason analogically in this way to obtain a similar 'wholesome' framework, for any kind of 'system'. Care that in the analogy since physics interesting part for one in the Universe is often with the 'tails it can catch'.

Somehow being in the universe has ensure you are from ... unconsciously. Thus what you can manage is only some ... one tail of Schrödinger's cat. Schrödinger's cat is a metaphoric picture of entanglement (simplest intrication?)].

For the sake of the system concept; from the concepts of thermodynamics, which is the sort of systemic we have for physics. First imagine that meta-stable energetic levels can be convenient pictures for identity's construction. That is to say where energy captured by a system has enough relative stability.

Energy for transforming is the disposable energy required for change. Part will stay in the system after the transform developing (increasing its complexity (± entropy). Different sources, at least entropy (self or environmental) implicit in neguentropic 'raw materials' and/or heat or other energetic transforms. **The catchable energy** since transformations do not occur in closed environments, catches by the system under focus and variable part possibly caught by neighboring open systems (potential mechanism of competition or distribution?). Space-structural effect? - by orientation. **Energy of activation** is the part of disposable energy required for change, which will not be incorporated in the final energetic stage. As a result can be part of future or *ex post* disposable energy or be caught by neighboring open systems (potential source of 'cooperation' or orientation, irreversibility or synchronization?)). **Previous energy** is the energetic level of the system at the beginning of the contemplated transformation(s). (To differentiate by types of potentials in the orientation of transformations? Conditions availability and conditions of transformations). **Energy gain** is the system gain of energy, after transformation(s). With more structure, more complexity (± entropy) complementarity more exposure to neighboring entropy (for more transformations up or down after meta-stability obtained). Maintaining or not some identity or label on the system. Conversely energy loss. **Energy freed** reactions, transformations, desegregation of systems or subsystem free energy which turn catchable or disposable for other systems and other transforms.

Thermodynamics and statistical physics basic concepts follow after inner or out, release or incorporation by the side of matter or energy. Also at first it is to apply the principles of conservations meanwhile the transformations; on the previous conditions and the final result. Since the speeds of transformations could be for most quite fast, especially the narrowest engineered ones. Nature combines more softly larger range of speed; including fast ones. The humans industrial activities have often preferred fast ones (especially destructive), since more inert physics chemistry.

In the construction of our environment it is to distinguish different levels of nuclear-quantic types of reactions (atomic-fields) and 'slimmer'; in the balance of the previous and feed by them more of less structurally. Ordered by time-life, speeds, mass and electric charges (electromagnetic; since some atomic order) and evolving.

Terms are also with the **constraints and conditions of transformations** maintained or not. Since the studies find fixings (controlling) the conditions for looking at what happens and can be measured; hence for the provision of **characteristic values**.

This has many applications in physics, chemistry, engineering, biophysics of ecology, and so on. It is well important to the concept of systems, irreversibility and complex ones; read especially Prigogine writings, a Belgian chemist that turned a great popular exponent in biological and complex systems vulgarization. You have to care in these questions, to avoid the traditional determinism: 'this to that'. You have more balance, their displacement, reversible (life enjoys keeping reversible processes and organize upon, precisely to make functions renewable (on the big slope down of the entropy), separation and irreversibilities at different levels of size and constraint and borders. [Under the volcano, at the fringe of the forest, you enjoy the fertility from the mixture of the volcano hashes and the green manure of the leaves of the forest in the savannas between. But by the side of the explosions or; forest harsh diversity; the huge profit is trickier].

Hence despite its importance; the 'pre-topology' of this essay, does not have much to add and tell about such core-head of thermodynamic or statistics physics. Their system concepts nurtured many faculties department applied physics; chemistry engineering or complex sciences. They actively explored the details. Thus despite this essay has many relations of the sort, especially with 'entropy'; it is better to explore the subject with a good handbook. Then only just a very short amount Entropy.

Entropy: its variation (Δ S) is calculated as the required complement to 1st principle of thermodynamic (of energy conservation). The entropy of a system is the thermal energy per unit temperature; that is unavailable for doing useful work, in the applications. Originally it was evidenced in Carnot's engine cycle (and named entropy by Clausius). It is an essential knowledge of transformations (of any kind and not just chemical). The amount of entropy (S) is also a measure of the molecular disorder, or randomness of the system.

As an overall calculus after results (and relative stabilization); the Gordian knot (hard part) of the concept is its understanding. Its definition as a 'global parameter' (S) makes difficult to imagine how it could play in the transformations. Including because fundamentally these transformations, especially in complex situations have a noticeable part of uncertainty (despite providing order). A minimum is with standard transformation it provides whole direction of spontaneous change.

Intuitively:
- Could be S a path dependent average?
- Meaning of ∂S and relations to informative links between different time-lives?
- Meaning of minimum S; balance between disorder-order?
- Relation between Lebesgue integral (average trajectory) of Δ S and path dependent integral of ∂S

- A need for better approach with structuring moving across scale reference systems?

Maximum, Minimum Framework

In a quali-quanti approach of some system unity, you have many considerations from formal sciences. About borders, limits, lower one or minimum and maximum one. Respect to the formal relative system set them cautiously is a way to prevent some future difficulties for formal supports and calculi. Here it is to be slightly more 'catching' of complex forms (possibly complex number calculus?). Instead of truncated avatar of a 1st order logic ignoring the precautions (of informative links, 2nd order logic 'kernel' within 1st one, and so on). Have that not clear in mind and more explicit could be very helpful to approaches of realities. Now, put that in a perspective like used to approach 'risks' or decisions; playing well with functions, limits or probabilities.

About limits frameworks 'could have 4 feet'. It is used to take a 2×2 combining Maximorum and minimorum.

- **Maximum, maximum:** take it as 2 orthonormal (perpendicular) curves cross at one point, like a peak. If they do not coincide by a point, a curve may join them.

Conceptually accounted some risk, it is the situation that commonly maximize gain after maximizing risk but; to complete, in balanced nature overview. Hardly do you have win-win case. So, when you are in the ecological-economic environment; whether you use the facilities of some stock; or available capacity of production. Or in the short-term abuse of speculation you push on transient higher needs (for catching ... and not necessarily solving the long term regularities of scarcity; not maintaining in the financial needs streams. The delays of return to fixed point need to be in the virtuous horizons of essential time. Not to capture and make stocks for perpetuations of heritage at the expense of classes, fake concepts (races) and waiting larger entropy discharges. So win-win is more at the expense of some others (or against fair distribution).

Sort of dynamic Pareto's criterion like obliged by the physics realities and; societies are observing and looking after variations and having to switch after to other opportunities. Better if more finding the constructive trends up, rather than obliged down spiraling by entropy (wise distribution of adverse effects).

Static maximax would be not just unfair (depending on costs and possibly decreasing rates of returns (if no innovation). This could be possible at the expense of smaller respect to less important existence: sacrifice of small not essential, reserves, large stocks. To shorter transient needs, constrain immediate opportunities, etc.

Observe that when you are system-considering, you will have to complete the picture like to four, half a dozen or more issues or aspects. Mind for calculability, evenness (4, 6, 8) divides easily by 2 if you have symmetry.

- **Maximum, minimum**: The higher may meet the lower when independent before and after and crossing at one point. It may be more subtle; the reason why in any analysis not to fix point but at least look at different directions or dynamically. For example, if maximin is with a scenario of, wanting to stop going down (when on the minimum curve); you will have to change your path; and going on with the maximum curve. But when with complex curve you do not know in which curve you are globally, reached a potentially relative bottom care your strategy care not to take the path which has reached the top;

In geometric analysis it is a sort of **saddle-point (gorge-like** for a channel). Imagine yourself on a horse's saddle, on the forward-backward you want relative static-stability (so the horse goes one with you in it's back); left right sides you want both dynamic stability and conductibility for dynamic motion. That is all your life: stability is for staying alive; conductibility for increasing your choice to go and get what you need (not all for sure); motion as for your way of life (get after good enterprise.

Maximum risk for minimum gain, looks like nonsense, unless you observe some, hidden gains or are mad of altruism (or openness excessive). Hence as a statistical or social resource, analysis should go either in the few more of qualitative analysis; or in the rare scale effects as in threshold effects.

> Keep in mind that a system analysis will make you immediately pose more potential options and help you for better comparisons and examine or test constraints. Cognitively that is the way you naturally think. The introduction of formal sciences as tools to help you explore, when the basic framework is immersed in more complicated conditions. Either because statistically or socially you need fair instruments to account for numbers for you and for all. Which help you too, privately to position your condition respect to the collective. And the logic to help you evoke systematically the frames worked main questions, you can translate thereafter in proper reviews of evidence.

Because of natural complexities, since the present you are never sure about the future. Even when what will happen in the future will surprise you. Train yourself to properly examined options; will make you less surprised than just blindly accepting. "Believe me, it is the only rational way for our win-win max-max deal" is more a mad-max-war-wind.

> [Despite their sophisticated modeling, humans' society statistics hardly reflect efficiently such shadings. Most social deciders more with the determinist and binary minds. When citizens as you, need more to position themselves in clouds of fair options and well-informed trails.
>
> Of course, not to ignore the difficulties to make non-positive statistical accounts. But quite subjective statistics exist as opinion enquiries. Alas, in the same kind of positivist frames. So not preparing the social contrasts well of decision on alternatives, as 'formal relative logical']

- **minimum, Maximum**: is another sort of saddle-point (crest-edge like?), not necessarily symmetrical to the previous in complex contexts; formal simplifications are almost obliged. But that is not as actually put ahead in most sectors of human decisions when possibility the most implicitly practiced.

Say, for example: maximum gains with minimum efforts. That is the sort of good economic ambitions. The problem with social economy with the gain obtained from others, public or environment, with the minimum individual. Make a social institution and that the best for corruption and private interest.

So the balance: if you are with the best resources of humanity: knowledge, technological smart devices, scientific progress; or quite bad, if at the expense of others (more or less qualified underclasses, accumulating all the politically manipulated disadvantages, etc.).

To translate also into more physical perspective: have the maximum possible neguentropy in the minimum waste of entropy (with anyhow will be higher than the constructive fraction. Or have the maximum possible netgentropy, in the minimum waste of physical systems stocks. Essentially it is much better concept than the economics of scarcity. Or have the maximum of consistent qualities or diversities, in the fittest economic relation, to the minimum uses of amounts... Or have the optimal use of electrons clouds which are in chemistry; in the lightest possible relations to atoms; and the atomic imbalances will not nuke your environments.

On Earth conditions it is more economical to be carbon frame-worked than silicon (they have both similar outset electrons' clouds allowing 4 links for 3 dimensioned structures); but carbon *nucleus* is lighter than silicon one).

Nature economy is still more inspiring than neoclassical economics ... if not to miss the prime number maximum complexity index of the formal system.

- **Minimum, minimum**: in the form of orthonormal crossed curves that the "hollows" of the most common in nature. Especially if your mind that is normed or scalar scaled by energy (in the simplest expression). In some sense could this scalar proportioned with the 1st dimensioned metric variable parameter?].

Minimum gain with minimum effort? depending on if you are at a peak of power allowing the fatty and nasty dictator of the system; or the wise ascetic whom within an environment which is caring itself. Nature can be the best way to preserve future generation options: pass with the least damages and let.

Lowest hollows nevertheless not the best way for receiving light or have higher perspective. And exposed to suffer the effects of floods, or dusts and other filling solids. Now, for characteristic approach of relative system.

Obviously the range of possibilities examination have to pay special attention to define minimum and maximum. Either of the unit as the limits of environment's provisions. Could be this as the phase-space of existence, and possible economics... Carrying capacities; environmental footprints similar concepts existing in ecology yet there are not well incorporated in 'societies borders'.

[In some way the place for principle of minimum action. Care anyhow that relative minimum is either recruited for stability storage, etc. and may not be just 0 (as in quantum *vacuum*). Above disorder you have ordered, below you will measure more than a noise; since Nature produces for everyone. Nature even ordered, has been able to make good use of disorder (in smaller pieces?

... when humans force the quantities orders at the extreme; without seeing that this just empower qualitative disorder; provoke quantitative disorders but thereafter do not know much on how to rebuild the one they wished ... but then just call the main long-term pyromaniac firemen to throw fuel].

Wholesome-like- observes that 4 feet frames, even when at some point you will, as a bipedal, to stand up; it is analytic not so bad. The *Homo Erectus* made it and sit down when possible. They did it so as to handle and examine what in their hands (and possible learned to make fire and then turned *Homo Abilis* (master-chef), so since they could... Why *Homo Sapiens* cannot?–imagine how to form complex numbers in statistics governance.

This framework of 4 looks like similar to; those used in quantic mechanics. But try to enlarge the perspectives with this half-complex basic framework. First you can do that with the quali-quanti- informative way. You make one maxi or min either the object or its exponent (quanti-amount), or its log (quali-amount) and try to imagine what does that mean ... this is about.

For example ($Max_{quali}Object$) log ($min_{quanti}Object$): could be respect to the object (care the meaning of indices). The maximum of qualities could be the set of as many as possible functions (quali). This also requires the 'doubling' for these functions quantitatively weighted) and the logarithm of 'minimum quanti like the minimum amounts 'required'. Under the perspective of the informative relation we have for as many functions mentioned. The informative relation is not for being rigid.

Another possibility with the intents to make that more dynamic. Including as pathways. In terms of the words; maybe tailing the minimum or maximum with 'orum'; minimorum or maximorum and there you can start the exploration considering the forum (statistics, semi-principle of motion or criteria.

Also just start this with all 4 forms. Together about the same object is like a 4 valued logics or in the usual 3 valued logics with a closure 'signing' there the 4th as a period or time of validity. Multi-valued logic, 'intricated' gives access to quantic logics, which is a multi-valued logic. Consider also **patterns of reviews' pathways** 'one at a time' And you have just after the taxonomy of considerations: meet the patterns in optimal, maxi or min effects, the sort of ordered operations as observed or as expected.

Of course we may be in cases of empiric games and games. It would to introduce probability (or uncertainty). Have also a logic of games that have received a formal logic expression. Find lay expressions and games stay games even if adults put strategies behind. Find consistent relations 'beneath' and fundamental metric expressions: thermodynamics and so on. You may explore close to essential realities, with possibly better volunteered and shared formalism: modular, complex numbers, quaternions, octonions, involved. Searching by the way better social-economic relations based on regulated successes of entrepreneurship. Instead of the vague mid of systemic determinism: 'social inequalities' are eventually possibly affecting the society if not defecting it...

In all fix in mind, that extrema (Maximax, minimin) are more for 'outer' limits. At best this is like critical values of 'phase-space transitions'. And saddle-gorge (Maximin, minimax) more for within. Achieve as you can but remind the best is for preserve one's life essential, all together. Quite often this is formally also offers the resources of combinations: hyperbolic with elliptic?

Characteristic Formal Structure and Formal Resources

Kernel, some concept as *a mathematical nucleus*; which is useful for the approach a concept of integrity or unit. Kernel is a non-null square integral function K (s, t) defined for $0 \leq s, t \leq 1$. Kernel is at most countable with n number. [We will see, furthermore, at the respect].

Eigenvalues functional: In mathematics, an **Eigenfunction** of a linear operator.

Some function space is defined as any non-zero function f in that space that, when acted upon it is only multiplied by some scaling factor called an Eigenvalue. The **Eigenvalue** tells you the scaling factor for how that matrix acts on the corresponding Eigenspace.

Eigenvalues play an important role in situations where the matrix is a transformation from one vector space onto itself. Someone Eigenvalues is a **measure of the distortion induced by the transformation** and Eigenvectors tell about the **orientation of the distortion**.

Each 'characteristic value' corresponds to one or more Eigenfunctions. The values can correspond to frequencies of vibration, or **critical values of stability parameters**, or energy levels of atoms. Problem is amenable to variables' separation methods. Depending on whether the *spectrum* is discrete or continuous.

The **Hamiltonian operator** H is an example of a Hermitian operator whose Eigenfunctions form an orthonormal basis. When the Hamiltonian does not depend explicitly on time, general solutions of the Schrödinger equation (fundamental quantic wave function and a concept of probability) are linear combinations of the stationary states multiplied by the oscillatory. The Eigenfunctions of the Hamiltonian operator are **stationary states of the quantum mechanical system**. Each has a corresponding energy. They represent allowable energy states of the system and may be **constrained by boundary conditions**.

Relative informative on oneself, combination of power and logarithms for emergence of a new axis and/or for the new unit (also if it could be related by **modular calculus**; combination of previous significant lower axes; Eigenvalue,

Eigenfunction, Eigenvector may be conceived as main 'stirring' axes of self-fundamental, for the 'prolongation of self-axes'. But out that combination, especially to the most stable linear 'ruler'; they have relation of circles with complex number Eigenfunctions and polynomials; relations to Dirac's function; density matrix?

Mind also a function, which power is higher than one. Any circle, square or polygon with at least 2 dimensions; any **sphere, ball, cube or polyhedral or platonic solid** with 3 and possibly are requiring 1 or 2 more; for being better apprehended. Representing a given object may be easier to calculate, passing to a series expression. These series are obtained considering transformations. There are **fundamental relations between function and series**. According the problem; they have different properties. All well used in signal analysis. Periodic signals involve complex numbers and where main used transformations are called **Fourier transforms**.

Numerical analysis which, since series of data, tries to establish the best fitting empirical equation or function representing the measured phenomena. For examples of transforms quite used to approach "*nucleus*" (or specific geometrical object), especially in physics are: **Laplace transform** which has the effect to convert differential equations into algebraic equations (that is easier to solve). **Fourier's**, **Mellin's** and **Hankel's** are other transforms quite important in physics.

As soon as understood that today, operations should be learned more for: how to pose problems. Problems should be examined and logic not trained as an imposition for unfriendly exercises-solving fancy enunciates.

Schools' programs should make better use of *calculus* software by directly involving? Software will probably have to turn more to interactive logic and *calculus* classes will stay but many mathematics classes ought to turn: of arithmetic epistemology... So philosophy could turn more practical: care about the way of philosophers in across cultures). Paying to great philosophers of the past tribute by updating them as instrumental. Not worship them, because the teacher made hes thesis on one of them.

Once the geometric prospects engaged, either from outside or from inside (in mathematics according your systems of reference coordinates; you will seek for structures. For relevant precepts at the respect you have proper values (or Eigenvalues), used in matrix calculus and *spectrum*.

[Most students require better physics phenomenology. For example, when wanting to approach phase-space diagram with that; since an observer perspective ... if the critical limit interphase could be seen as a place for Eigenvalues? ... Critical limits place of phase transitions with important energetic gradients. Distance from these is a good way to position some simple (one phase) system, respect to the critical border... When in complex systems (of our level), we may see more a capability to use different types of phases. But not to confuse exactly Eigenvalues and critical space-phase].

Eigenvalues (proper elements) are easier to calculate when under the formulation $(A-I\lambda)$ r = 0. I am identity matrix (only 1 as main diagonal elements, 0 elsewhere).

This formulation has solutions only if space is non-trivial. Determinants of n × n matrix is a polynomial degree n in λ .[See a **determinant** as a matrix or system of linear equations self-calculated characteristic denominator informing on the resources of systems solutions or about matrix properties... That does not prevent any use of higher degree. Higher degree will be applied on the matrix as a whole.

Plane wave is the Eigenfunctions of translation, operators and many basic equations are derived, from systems with translational symmetry. So in the useful transforms since translation; the main support of kinetics objects in the space.

Transfer axiom could be useful:
- for any standard formula F $(x, t_1, ..., t_n)$ with no other free variable we have:
  $\forall^{st} t_1, t_2,..., t_n [\forall^{st} x \quad F(x, t_1, t_2, ..., t_n) \Rightarrow \forall x \quad F(x, t_1, ..., t_n)]$
- an also equivalent postulate is
  $\forall^{st} t_1, t_2,..., t_n [\exists x \quad F(x, t_1, ..., t_n) \Rightarrow \exists^{st} x \quad F(x, t_1, ..., t_n)]$

Spectral Analysis EigenFunction Relations

Spectrum concept has emerged by the side of physics; as series rays component of a mixed **spectrum** as used in optics, interference phenomena, music. For example, the details of all the colored lights in Nature. White light the wholesome composed of all other colors. Thus easily obtained by sub-reflexion or dispersing re-diffusing lights as in white clouds.

"Spectral analysis states that a matrix projected to successively lower ranks, using the top Eigenvectors, the sum of angles; squared cosines; between 2 data points; is strictly increasing. It means that: if the matrix is embedded in high-dimensional space, so the dimensionality of the representation is reduced; the distribution of cosine changes from being concentrated around 0 toward the 2 poles ±1."

That quoted, quite obscure sentence for non-experts, but enough for helping you suspect that harder formulations simply try to cope with primary effects of the way flows and hierarchies may go up. Mathematics corresponds **spectral theorem**. This theorem states that a **symmetric matrix** admits an **orthogonal basis of Eigenvectors**.

Have in mind that spectrum analysis applies mainly to waves' systems directly. That is you seek for the *spectrum* of a complex light or ray (light of photons, other rays of electrons or other particles) or; mechanics waves as those of sound, water and vibrations. But indirectly also you make use of *the spectrum* after destruction for studying composition chemical compounds, molecules and particles. All at different ranges of energies; this is characterized by periods or frequencies of 'vibrations,' range, length of a wave.

This is like in experiments 'crushing-like' submitting atomic *nuclei* (in atomic physics when trying to find fundamental particles and fundamental forces) or; by relatively dispersion of compounds (after some property as mass of electric charges; like spectrometry in chemistry) of previous; more or less destroyed or characteristically reacted compounds. Hence formal study of similar phenomena (or analogical) called spectral analysis. It is often well related to **Theory of perturbation**.

[... Perturb physically or in formulas; then scatter, then study the *spectrum* or; with a formal equation you introduce an often slight perturbation. And then see the computed simulated effects, in terms of stabilities, motions and so on. Perturbations to affect the behavior of the equation; or systems of equation. Commonly, this is with perturbations of variable (Δ x) but other parameters can be moved; as scalar coefficients made variable (so turning linear forms in non-linear ones)].

You collect the data (either physics, empirical, random simulations), apply numerical statistical analysis using mentioned transform and infer the representing equations of the function characterizing de phenomenon... With the help of what you know on methods, technological limits, constraints of good representation and theories.

[In our opinion it would be good to start sooner this epistemology with Eigenvalues, Eigenvectors or Eigenfunctions; and other fruitful concepts: **characteristic exponent**, **convolutions**, **congruence**, **modularity**, etc. Considering their importance not just with the numerical solutions of problems]. And the way of teaching not necessarily alone front of a white paper.

They are concepts well mentioned in Logic Theory of Model. Cognitively we often proceed by analogies.

For example, turning around a something dangerous just will try to detect a good direction to play, for example a blind point, a blind direction or a way to go around. This may make anyone clever about what for; in what conditions.

As here mentioned; they are about the best orthogonal basis of representation (for the orientation of the 3 main axis) but this is about reference that could be 'from outside'. Of course our concern is dual first as the best separating axes of reference (along scale of complexification?–for looking at what is more basic, and second what is new ... by new re-combinations). This is about direction, axes or plan to discriminate analysis (without missing that not everyone best place for differentiating.

Matrix Approaches

Following concept is about the most filled 'inner axes' (more or less these meshings micro but larger, macro but environment; meso-emerged within produced by recombination ... [produces dizziness]). Formally it is often to record the most structuring or most constitutively delimited *versus* filled ones correlated.

Thus **matrix main diagonal** and other diagonal are measured respect to the main. This is about **auto-correlation matrices** (crossed over themselves). Thus studying the 'identity' of the object about which the matrix. Be it either a unit (structural) or a **matrix of transition** between 2 states (functional). All that has many relations to **graph theory**; which are primarily formally approached with **matrix calculus**. To mention also that there are **random matrices** and **non-linear** ones plus the present one.

In most cases to compare a matrix of observed records with a random one and/or then some as fixed coefficient with changing ones. A matrix representing a linear system of one variable (degree one) makes use of a matrix of coefficients. The explained variable (Y) by the system relations of the explaining variable x_i) possibly submitted to vectors of changes. Then how this can be used as distributing referential and consider levels of orders. [More will appear in next volume].

Multivariate methods called geometric (statistical); methods as **principal components analysis, canonical analysis**; etc. Commonly to start with the plane graph of the main discriminating axis and then conduce inspections: **cloud, barycenter, distances** and **correlation** analysis.

This would be for a "feeding kind of matrix" (matrix often to prefer in systems simulations); it is to understand that between 2 moments the feeding just in one diagonal, then the diffusion since (eventually emptying pulsatile-like) this main and filling other. That would be the most economical. A refinement more it is to consider different levels of orders or scale. Formally this can appear as **blocks within matrices**; hierarchy possible along the main diagonal. And the relations of scale could be from one block up-flow (up-left) to another down-flow (down right). That is for example how larger stocks down provide with functional fractions. The amount measured in energetic units or matter or information.

Of course in economics it is money as costs of components, prices of costs and products... Thus to have better adaptations to '**econophysics**' could be not so uneasy but require to understanding flexibly and formally about marginal cost or prices; as pieces of information, rather than as actually taking the prices the start of everything ... it is like to put an end-product (after costs estimate, negotiation, etc.), ahead of all.

Matrix or calculus is, of course, about quantities. Matrix can make use of first or second differentiation all with the same homogeneous operation (Jacobian, Hessian). With multiscale we ought to develop. It is not to imagine totally different from the sort of quali-quantification; we mentioned (the log (x) term or $x\log (x)$? Then to match with the quanti-qualification (the e^x term or xe^x) and compatibilities are to be examined; under connectivity of cardinals of base, scalars or characteristic exponents

... All that does not seem so impossible... If we dare not to be too ashamed by articulating premises, already existing in the thermodynamic and mathematics paraphernalia. For an economy more inspired by formal wholesomeness and physics of nature, providing the limits... Not so the limits of growths but those for caring...

Precautions About Scale of Release

> In thermodynamically fundamentally care not to 'free' entropy, too much and too fast: the many have to be care.

... Entropy the minimum engine of transformations in nature turns a problem if you release too much, too far and you do not let time to re-uptake (recycling to neguentropy, thus has an excessive negative netgentropy). So much will turn to heat (lowest bio-yields of recycling as well as of work for production). Products of degradations can non-linearly accelerate destruction. At least of the most complex bio-systems). Eventually this can make reach sooner the threshold limits of more destruction.

Observe also that more complex the development more, possibly wasteful uptake from the environments. But at the same time more diversification more capacities to get involved margins of input sources into more complex smarter structures. Humans not enough smarter at that; nor it is fast adapting but often because able to involve more stocks in traps from mineral-like resources. [Still unclear if today's smartness will compensate enough the overall losses (transferred to exergy and warming climate); nor is better than have been some eco-efficient systemic agriculture].

Threshold limits of more destruction could be 'horribly hard' to calculate in the complex world? - It cannot be a good satisfaction that they could turn effectively easy to calculate: this may mean that the whole world would have dramatically simplified... Like actually with the biodiversity shrinking ... under human transformations ecosystems are not balanced.

Reminding that entropy is thermodynamic term for disorder. And observing too that humans are the best at producing stupid huge thermal disorders. Just with abstracts at first non-dimensioned ['stupid idea?' ... but that has already 2 dimensions: 1) idea as 'vector', 2) stupid as a 'sign']. Variation of entropy is negative signed and its sum algebra is harmonic.

[The reason why we intend in another deceiving experience to introduce a measure concept of entropy and its variations comparisons in a project of land use planning Law. Formulation of ecological impact assessment. Were to make between projects of land uses and humans' projects of transformations or anthropologic activities for ecological impact choice. This was in a project of Law for spatial planning, almost at that time innocently: it was to discuss about. But the stupid preferred to 'change the Constitution' ... because he made his own government a mess?].

Notice that when systems are merged (energy, entropy, volume, particle number). The corresponding intensive variables (temperature, pressure, chemical potential) are not additive over sub-systems but describe possible gradients. At equilibrium either between systems or between a system and its environment these intensive variables will be the same in all the connected systems. Thus algebra of systems (usual concept) as media not directly as you are used.

A primary of anthropo-sphere sustainability: the unexpected huge stair of entropy? Up for entropy release, down for complexity's effect.

Restructure Mathematical Economy

Upon mathematics paraphernalia of economics we will only mention briefly few some. Mathematics of securities, finance, insurance is full of mathematics concepts; quite similar to those existing in physics. But there are not properly anchored to engineering thermodynamics grounds, nor they are enough cognitively empowered in common people. These needs especially to be with humane options and as proper method for committee ethics work in a less corrupting way. It is horrendous to observe how most governments and governed just prefer dependence to markets conjuncture profits; populism, dirty business biases, pork-barrel politics and gifts or subsidies to the corrupts; and rescue then when they should be declared bankrupted, put in jail, advised calming down, neutralized and returned to the cardinal commonness if improper to the ordinal and the fields maps of essential opportunities for all.

In theory, **stochastic models**, search for **invariants**, other **kinds of order measures** such as with Hausdorff's measures, **statistics of stabilities, games' logics, diversified portfolio, balance** are much there despite poorly referred. Only also important in finance is: not to excess the loops in 'bubbles of speculations'. To approach, either analytically or probably more inductively with inspired methods upon strange phenomena (if they could generate social profits), fractal dynamics (if conceived for producing minimum ethical rules of socialness), 'black swans' effects. Questions already posed but too far from truer values, when not just uncaring ... cynically?

(Qualitative) exactification of modal theory	
Exact probabilistic	Modal language
$\Pr(x) \geq 0$	possible
$0 < \Pr(x) < 1$	contingent
$\Pr(x) = 1$	necessary
$\Pr(x) < 0$	impossible
$\Pr(x) \doteq 0$	almost impossible
$\Pr(x) \doteq 1$	almost necessary

Mathematical economics developed much after the 2nd World War. Neoclassical economics you have with Theory of General equilibrium after: Arrow, Debreu, Hahn Allais) and Samuelson, Hicks and many others. **Ecological economics** or **exergetic calculators** of the industry. Inspired from ecology or more fundamental sciences; you also have **evolutionary economics; econo-physics** etc.]

Central planning Soviet *calculus* (too centralized, too in the intent to avoid marginal dynamic concepts of values by money). But they discovered many resources for the proper **material** *calculus*. **Linear programming** and **matrix calculus** (in economics) both in the Soviet Union and satellites or with national economy large models developed by Cowles foundations in the US and econometrics for policy makers. Completed by **industrial sectorial analysis with input-output matrices** of productions initiated with Leontief (somehow also in the **social links** of Hirschman).

Russians have still extraordinary mathematicians and excellent **'synergistic'** updated concepts: about **non-linearity** and **dynamic analysis**. Apart from inflexible ways to govern, humble social mathematicians only need better interdisciplinary synergies from formal sciences and social links Read for example Milovanov or Malinietski.

Controlability simple constraints
Γ: borders, observe that there are 2, so as 2 components $\Gamma_0 = \partial\Omega_0$ and $\Gamma_1 = \partial\Omega_1$ $v(x)$ vector oriented outside Ω with $m(x) = x - x^0$, $R(x^0) = \max |m(x)|$, vector is concept of control and $\Gamma(x^0) = (x \in \Gamma / m.v > 0)$, $\Gamma_*(x^0) = \Gamma \backslash \Gamma(x^0)$. And so $\Gamma_1 = \partial\Omega_1 \subset \Gamma_*(x^0)$

Control-ability under stronger geometric constraints
Ω_0 is star-rized respect to x^0; $\Gamma(x^0) = \Gamma_0 = \partial\Omega_0$; $\Gamma_*(x^0) = \Gamma_1 = \partial\Omega_1$

There exists a constant C > 0 so as $\|\Phi^0\|_{D(A)}^2 + |\nabla\Phi^1|^2 \leq C\int_{\Sigma_0}[|\Phi'|^2 + |\Phi''|^2]d\Sigma$ for any solution Φ which correspond to data $(\Phi^0, \Phi^1) \in W \times D(A)$.

Control-ability on the neighborhood of a border or a part

ω a neighborhood of $\Gamma_0 \subset \Gamma$, for Ω bordered domain of P^n with border Γ of class C^2. Be $x^0 \in P^n$ and $T > T(x^0) = 2R(x^0)$. Be O a neighborhood of $\Gamma(x^0)$ and $\omega = O \cap \Omega$ so it exists a constant $C > 0$ (enough large) so as $E_0 \leq C \int_0^T\int_\omega[|\Phi'|^2 + |\nabla\Phi|^2]$ dx dt, $\forall \{\Phi^0, \Phi^1\} \in H_0^1(\Omega) \times L^2(\Omega)$

Plenty has been missed by-side of economic models, graph theory users in organization, with mixtures and involvement; like multi-criteria decision in large projects, commonly of infrastructure. To mention the **multivariate geometrical analysis**, as in social statistics somehow make it somehow that way. French school initiated in the 70s during the 80s found a refuge near Bourdieu, before being somehow accepted under the generic term of **geometric data analysis**. Where it is also to select most relevant constituting vectors, thanks to eigenvalues, and rotation for better reference principal axis components.

All that, alas, is only with 'exclusively economics serious concepts' or only 'social data' (because Durkheim's paradigm? Of purification of concepts within their specialized registers). Abstract concepts under the assumption of their linear operations (direct or after **linearization** transform). In lexicographic relations without a clear view on the systemic dimensions "anchored"; to the main frame. That could be materialistically handled together; with the anxious goals to find stable truth, no **covariance**, nor **heteroskedastic**. Looking like a stupid heterodoxy? [We will see some comments about in net volume].

Back to Basics, one aspect more in an approach trying to evoke what we have as formal tools. To help identify like the principles of those carried at any level of complexity scale? And in general calculable? - take one level above and one level below, and set the dual intermediate at 'meso-level' with 'relative closures or specifying links'. Say, in other words, that you may, as actual humans' societies, have fancy neoclassical economics with them: half tautological, half naïve, half-weird, half-strange.

[But, first of all, somehow unconscious and really mad when daring to look at the dire stage of the Planet. That is many halves, but we are with complex numbers ... just we do not have a proper management of it].

Be or not friendly with ecology should not be so dramatic to anchor meso-economics to 'micro-universal' frameworks, macro-feeding and waste; webs immersed in ecosystems. For example, gravity (masses or weights), whomever levitate, can tell you; has effects on your social economics (like through transport, logistics and so on).

Do we dramatically systems of values since the disturbances produced in ecosystems ... before could-be potential values from ecological services if the tourists come in?

Of course, economic modeling and economists will tell you that. Since so many existing statistics are coming from the physical world; which is used and provide with "structural coefficients". They themselves have enough with their *focus* on their simulations. Indirectly much of economics includes 'roots and ratios from physics'.

> But still without caring that these grounds are those that should support calculi of equilibrium and humans' groups, societies and activities. So they could be examined after the variations they produced and synchronize respect to; the variations of the grounds and respect to the environments' criticalities. Thereafter in which way has the best governance to assign after the unmarketable; allow financing networks between supply and consumption in marketable levels of societies, opens opportunities to markets elsewhere for investments, closing relatively those were needed. Often missing by the way most of the coherence and the learning effect of what could happen from the phenomenological details. Just weak assumptions, true lies and confidence in the paradigms.
>
> Observe that this way a public economy is about the phase-space sustainability relative aperture of closure to social fields, as a space of opportunities; regulations or exclusions are to apply if too damaging activities; or have most efficient subsidiary transfers to basic needs. Ensuring also the critically important constraints for preservations for eco-renewals. Many things already existing in sorts of policies, but probably other systems of information, and more constraints of democracy in the social places, as well as freedom was effectively efficient in ones' own places of responsibility. Otherwise the economics calculi will have much to do with the most efficient ways to develop and order ones' own bundles of informative links.

Well, since some years those are the questions addressed more crudely to neoclassical economics. But it could be said to any other kind of formal economy if they could insist on wanting to be more the 'more mainstream.'? The informative links produced by 'quali' formal economics to 'quanti' businesses; if 'related' would probably be much lower than the noise made by 'the media'. Heterodox are not always well-guided in their anti-formalist reproaches to not so purely abstract and fake economics of financial markets. Effectively they often mis-linked too with real economy, none pretending to be 'vicious in their virtues'.

Also there are growing insiders (or extravagated ex-insiders) in the critics. Another sort of critics come from ex-physicists or still mathematicians but turned traders or economists. Knowing well the weakness of orthodox assumptions. It is not so easy. Original orthodox assumptions were horrible, and are still taught so in many business schools. Answers and intents to fix the excuses have also developed, sophistication of models extraordinarily (and preoccupying). Thus is the best answer has models doing methodological in the same way but starting at the core for the formulation of nice concepts show that they are nice, they also express the good trend that first laws of social economics would be ethical. Fine but that does not mean that the management of applied options and projects will not produce plenty of paradox and self-contradictions easy to be cut by next government cutlasses of angry consumers and rich destroyers. [De-growth economy a superior intellectual of faddist literacy, possibly in some societies were sustainability under the umbrella of peri-urban posh-ness, is claiming for State's subsidies and rents in para-public].

> Of course go against the normative economics, has huge costs and plenty of sunk ones. So does it look like too crazy to intent? ... Any reconstruction before the 3rd World War? The 2nd cleared the path of supposed to be Keynesianism with a more human faced capitalism (or geopolitical massive reconversion?

After the levels of deadly means, can humanity afford geopolitics distractions? As observed, at the expanses of policies of other kinds. That could be more important; than the direct dedication of resources in fuzzy preservations of States of Orders? Rather than involved coping with massive threats, with other adaptations of views and ways off. Will the enclosures from mazes' dead ends'? Produced by past ways of life; could flex to more sustainable the domination of neoclassical economics?

It is not so much about change theory morally empowering ways of doing. Yet we are not with the clearance after the major 'reset of, required change of speedometers. Only for sure that a 3rd WW should meet with enormous difficulties to properly self-justify.

[The concept of **phase-space diagram** displays speed *versus* position and separate media with critical borders, limits of regime change. The sorts of speed regimes, like of renewal and on that the ones of exploitation and possibly reducing those of the natural medium at too 'regimes' of/and phase-space define. All that is quite delicate calculus to compose. Thus the way of making it; not for pretending to tell the truth. But to inform for participating on the criticalities and call needs of technological innovations for pacing the speeds of use. Also to care about thermal balances.

This theoretical, supported nevertheless on consistent axes of reference analysis not to determine much of the good behaviors to have but possibly able to make use of metrics closer to phenomenology and possibly related to new metrology. It is hard to measure financial frenzies from the near outer space (how they would warm the climate). Thermal diffusion out a region can.

We are in the need to change the speeds (slow down the ones of exhaustion or thermal production). Moreover we have to get that collectively (solidary enough, among very diverse types of eco-spending humanities) or democratically; and establish flows or regimes of resources uses (versus destruction for).

This is in the support of restoration or positive netgentropy (more probably reduce the negative one correlatively to the decrease of entropy). So it is to move overall in another phase of speed. Be able to 'reset relative count speedometer'; in a smooth way for communities. But 'conducing them' where the new life ... is not in the usual means of a 'holy land in a new world' by ecological migrations.

Revolution of information would also be here revelatory; if we cannot properly solve out of hegemony-mania, and our representations or way to drive our models: with captured public power of superior civilization. So stood only in humans 'magical forms'; 'in the 'peripheries of misunderstandings' and; the 'crushes of civilizations'. Pretending to be such sort of informative links about 'war on terror' at the 'heart of the core of seriousness'?

Back to Basics, most real object is circular, round shape, elliptic possibly combined eventually with thick disks: between galaxies or pies; tori-like (more of less flat doughnuts?). Also in principles dispersed fragments, more or less modular-like scaled by combination of dimensions. Even in the layer(s) of troposphere it is to observe slices of kinds of life and ecosystems. If there are some, almost plane, plants most and bio films all because probably at interfaces of exchanges. Thickness is having locals the 3 dimensions; possibly because colder and order-able to expand on the fringes; borders are places for diversification.

Probably at the starts of first biological orders have been passively space made after the relative position to the Sun, the optimal shape of tetravalent carbon and the 'ambiguities' of water. Thick layers then self-reproducible forms incorporating most of their convexity. Many man-made objects have circular and spherical parts, and circles and spheres projected onto ellipses on the image plane.

Some of the original essays on forms at the respect of natural shapes in life are with D'Arcy Thompson (Scottish bio-mathematician with forms and mathematical accounts of nature) and Thom (French mathematician with the mathematical structures of morphogenesis). For we have nature, pictures', natural encyclopedia, *herbaria*, living forms phylogeny, chapters of biomathematics, mathematics books about fractals, cellular automata and some complex systems. It is to examine that not too complicated mathematical forms can provide with amounting scales with great diversity of patterns and possibly structures and functions showing some explicit enough under the eyes. [Broccoli is not just good for health they are good fractal]. See nice books of simulations (Mandelbrot, Gleik, Casti, Feldman, Wolfram, Bejan).

Many structural non-living and living forms show mathematical patterns spontaneously more expressive when not having to diffuse in the environment of diffusion. Sources of primary forms can be observed: 1) Mathematics small graphs; 2) Physics polyhedral crystal 3) Chemistry molecules 3 dimensions forms (carbon like); 4) Biophysics bio-metalloïd (combination metal-organic molecules) and small proteins 3D configurations; 5) Snow ice flakes; 6) Vegetal branching; 7) Many other plants packing forms of plant world (seeds, leaves, etc.) 8) Radiolarians; 9) Shells of mollusks; etc. You may have a look at Murray's biomathematics.

Cellular Automaton is a collection of "colored" cells on a shape grid evolving through a number of discrete time steps following a set of rules based on the neighboring (formal) cells states. Iteratively, computed cellular automata comes in a variety of shapes and varieties. Initial patterns explored; by Wolfram (he is British mathematician entrepreneurs of 'Mathematica' computer programs for mathematics, and put a useful Mathematics dictionary on the web). His 4 classes of cellular automata behaviors produced by identified 256 standard rules are:

- Class 1: evolve quickly into a stable, homogeneous state. Any randomness in the initial pattern disappears.
- Class 2: evolve quickly into stable or oscillating structures. Some of the randomness in the initial pattern may filter out, but some remains. Local changes to the initial pattern tend to remain local.
- Class 3: evolve into a pseudo-random or chaotic manner. Any stable structures that appear are quickly destroyed by the surrounding noise. Local changes to the initial pattern tend to spread indefinitely.
- Class 4: evolve into structures that interact in complex and interesting ways, with the formation of local structures. That could be able to survive for long periods of time. Class 2 types stable or oscillating structures may be the eventual outcome.

It is to mind that they appear relatively at half-random–half-conditioned by the environment or 3rd random-3rd pre-structure expansion-3rd conditioned by environment. Then evolutionary processes select those most energetically economical, more useful and most fitting the constraints of dynamic stability (at some point renewal). These evolutionary processes from balances between creation ahead, disintegration below, best dynamics balance atom-field environment (at that level not necessarily the fundamental particles ones).

On all, cellular automata seem to show the sort of tail we imagine: functional or structural expansion. After roots in some core-head of a given piece (inner part designed). Or both selected by the coherence of inner and after the relations with near environment and the 'outer environment'.

> [Of course all that just words of a language for summarizing how it can happen. Not much with the specified details of what, where how, and when].

Stability and Motions

Mathematics, physicists, chemists technologists have developed many methods; for formally approach motions, speeds and stability subjects. Since they are essential to their control of the issues. This is used in theories of: **control, regulation** (linear and non-linear), **transports** (physics or logistics), **reactions** (chemical and biophysics) and so on.

Elementary Kinds of regulators
Feedback regulators with no memory;
Feedback regulators with memory;
Feed forward regulators with no memory;
Feed forward regulators with no memory.

Central role of Uncertainty in feedback processes
Uncertainty features of the controlled object
(they can be characterized by additional state variables);
Stochastic exogenous target motions or disturbances;
Measurement noise which perpetuates uncertainty.

We will not talk much about that. It is no more to invite the readers to search what they need. You can eventually intend an epistemological thinking about them. Especially you can find in the propaedeutic and the half a dozen of the most fundamental concepts or devices in each. We do not have much intuition to provide at the respect. That does not mean there are less important. Only here for some logics' notions.

"A **Base of uniformity** in a uniformed space provided a uniformity. It can be called 'base of uniformity', any subfamily containing one of the subfamily and following the conditions:
- any member of the base subfamily contains a diagonal. Any member from base subfamily and reciprocal of this member also contains some member of the base subfamily. If with a member is pertaining to base subfamily, exists another composed pertaining to base subfamilies, this former is included,
- intersection of 2 members of the base subfamily contains a member of it.

A **subfamily** is a sub-base if finite intersections of it is the base of uniformed space and follows the conditions:
- all members of subfamily-sub-base contains the diagonal. To any member of it then reciprocal also a member,
- to any member of subfamily-sub-base existing a member such as its self-product contained in first above mentioned one." (Maravall Casesnoves).

Now, by the side of field physics, it may be useful to consider (as for Identity of a system?) of an exploratory operator at critical point or object the identical relation provided by Petrova-Cartan skew-symmetric differential forms.

In general identical relation can be written $d\phi = \theta$ ^{P} identical relation only satisfied on **pseudo-structures**: $d_\pi\phi = \theta_\pi$ ^{P}. On one side there is a closed form and on the other side a differential of same form with a degree less by 1. [Correspondence between form and to physics are probably to take cautiously, mathematics may express what formally needed ... from a physical structure operating so; not exactly directly identifiable as. In the same way that logic provides a framework to nature to find the form of a 'frame' for the 'work' entailed... At least in a relative form. At the most fundamental the discrepancies between structure and functions have probably less space].

Formula of Newton, Leibnitz, Green, integration by Stockes, Gauss-Ostograskii are examples of such identical integral relations. Form relations that connect exterior forms of sequential degrees; one can obtain vectors or tensor identical relations. That connects the operators: gradient, curl, divergence and so on. From closure conditions on exterior and dual forms one can obtain identical relations such as gauge relations (primary in electromagnetic field theory). Example of identical relations between derivatives:

- Cauchy-Riemann conditions (theory of complex variables);
- Transversality's conditions of the calculus of variations;
- Canonical conditions (of thermodynamics functions)

Physics Application of Identical Relation (Petrova)			
Dimen-sion	Field theory	Physical fields	Identical relation
0	Quantum mechanics	Strong interaction	Dirac brackets vectors
1	Hamilton formalism	Weak interaction	Poincaré invariant
2	Maxwell electromagnetic	Electromagnetic interaction	$d\theta^2 = 0$ and $d*\theta^2 = 0$
3	Gravitational Einstein field	Gravitational interaction	Einstein equation when covariant derivative of energy momentum tensor vanishes
note	* inexact closed exterior or dual form degree. d: for differential		

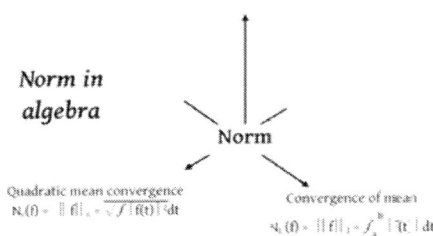

Uniform convergence
$N_\infty(f) = \| f \|_\infty = \sup_{t \geq 1} | f(t) |$

Norm in algebra

Norm

Quadratic mean convergence
$N_2(f) = \| f \|_2 = \sqrt{\int | f(t) |^2 dt}$

Convergence of mean
$N_1(f) = \| f \|_1 = \int_a^b | f(t) | dt$

By the side of, discrete or continuous, formal amounts, intuitively we are in the spectrum in the matching of options. Of course with characteristics quantities (as characteristics exponents) mostly with a lay-term possibility of rigorous formal definition of which, we did not catch all required cleanness for a simple operation. The intuition is that between physics order and disorder are coexisting everywhere at any level, one across all with entropy minimum and possibly some at each level?. So the idea of sub kinds of disorders, specifiable in different ways relative to the suborders.

Now thinking that the dual nature of any number is providing cardinals, in their generally more 'by the side of disorder'. When relations or order between pieces, at any level giving to representing number quality of ordinal. Would be this structuring inner 'informative link'? We would have then sort of complex relations providing dual nature to numbers: ordinal and cardinal. Coinciding in the most symbolic and lowest fundamental levels? Structure or order makes stronger relation of cardinal-ordinal at the core or head especially between 'minima and maxima', 'ordinal' and 'cardinal'. Out there, in the fundamental we have many options to be toward cardinals (ergodic like), fewer options to be toward ordinal and get 'in' an order. All that having to be examine statistically, with theory of numbers especially with the different properties now well explores.

Technically then cardinal more with the disordered Universe, quantic vacuum. Ordinal more with the sparse pieces of order, matter, situ places of quanta . Set theory looks like a framing system of discrete-prone cardinal with it first informative link about the 'kernel' of ordinal of Theorem of choice. Practically we stay finite and 'short' (at scale of Universe); since we are more interested in the reasons between different kinds of numbers sets. Infinity? - We do not know more a relative very, very, very ... large than an object without prejudging of it transcendence. [Remind that Cantor wanted to treat infinity as an object].

In the same way with the sort of language provided above in our intuitive way of thinking; it seems that neither we establish a definite separation on formal; more as a language than a nature of nature. Of course logics will be more by the side of language, and mathematics by the side of nature, if infinity is infinity.

By the side of a formal system; one thing is almost sure this is not a 'supreme base'. In mathematics may be just the 'point of adherence to the top'; complement of formal sciences by physics (or the converse). Relatively below, we are not to pretend to have demonstrated relative formal system demonstrated full formal nature of physics; as Tegmark and Yi-Lin-Forrest would like? But practically it seems possible to work with such mathematical language ... social-economically ... with the apparel of thermodynamics, but more formal properties than usual in accounting. The wiser economics way would be in the respect of our level of maximum achieved relative complexity. The idea being that with have not to incorporate lower specific identities. [Otherwise we may had incorporated higher than coevolved sort of bacteria. Like having bugs and worms crawling in your body].

Economic way also understood in the best relative laws of economics should be ethical. Possibly an artifice of language and also just a relative. Since having clear that sort of social ordering can never get rid of or un-cared 'cardinal disorder'; between humans. Animal societies have kinds of cardinals and ordinals somehow less free and smart, that can sometimes be humans ones.

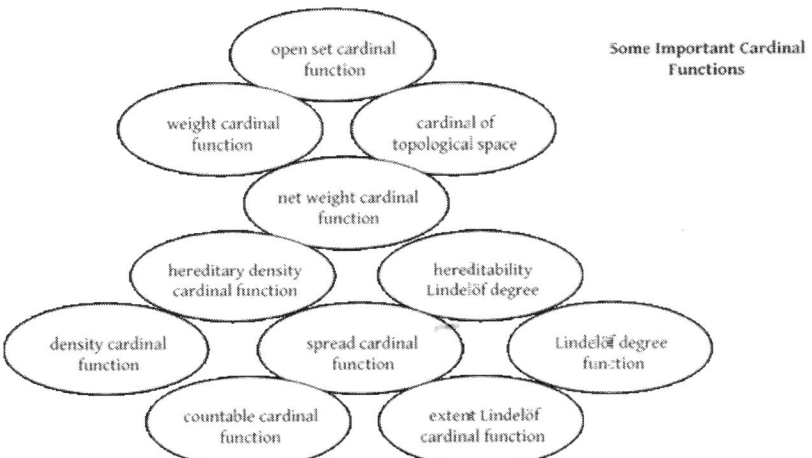

Some Important Cardinal Functions

But nothing in all that inspiration theorems demonstrations after the axiomatic way. Just questions with possibly bizarre words for that sort of specialist; just suggestions for Chan-mindedness. The 'gaps' of the difficulties of detailed calculi too important for making that social order, even partial determinism. Efficient democracy required to care cardinal complexities and have some flexible but cared proportions of ordinals. Without will and good care from most; for the reachable tiny part of order, that would 'be management' the register of economical efforts. To observe more precautions than actually observed with the bulls and bears in the battle fields of rational geopolitical determinist and populists. All those making the cover page of 'The Economist' without much positive effect.

But back to the basics, among main known types of numbers they are much in debate. If our world is made either for natural numbers or integers or real numbers, respectively $\mathbb{N}$ and $\mathbb{R}$ and then between the 2 previous detailed $\mathbb{Z}$ for $\mathbb{N}$, provided a sign + or -. Rational numbers $\mathbb{Q}$ obtained by quotient of 2 integers, provided by division or over $\mathbb{R}$ as complex numbers $\mathbb{C}$. Adding to its real term an imaginary term coefficient "of orientation, i" has its square = -1 (providing it an essence of 'reflexive mirror vector'?) Clear cuts in kinds of numbers and deficient epistemology at their make that if most common people have heard of such $\mathbb{N}$, $\mathbb{Z}$, $\mathbb{Q}$, $\mathbb{R}$, $\mathbb{C}$; and eventually known, some of the properties they deal with; with unwise shortcuts. Possibly missing to imagine more about transitions between. Especially for having clever views on simple operations solutions. Actually the simplicity of operations probably interfere as fake perfect views on set of numbers. [That is do not so perfect for apprehending the sort of quali-quanti mixtures giving self-sense (at least) to the numeracy of amounts.

A primary is with the understanding on how numbers are formed by operations and/or by concepts? There is a successive integration of kinds of number from $\mathbb{N}$ to $\mathbb{R}$. "Intermediate of transitions" such as between rational and real numbers. There are like with **algebraic real** and **exact solutions**. Or "completing kinds of numbers" (?) as **irrational** numbers do, respect to **rational** numbers. [That seems to be 'conceivable backward': as **roots of prime number**?]. Also quite important are the algebraic real (accessed by polynomials') or non-transcendental algebraic real and **transcendental** [source of 'holes filled' of **scales of numbers** since π, e and others?].

A rational number is **quotient** of 2 integers. It needs to exclude 0 as a divisor. Division by 0 does not make sense (?) if 0 absolute (infinite absolute). But if slightly relative it gives access to a large number (or very sensitive to small errors). Those sort of observations are almost non-philosophical. They address the solutions approaches that have to be programed within **algorithms of calculus**. Or if possibly knowing some features of their formation; have wiser approximations with '**truncation**'.

Manage operations ignoring primary essentials at level of high complexity will meet problems in highly complicated computed systems with their self-made approximations by the system. Actually these a binary operating, and then may give illusions. With the disastrous effect that when smart with number detect some phenomenological anomaly, for example proper to theory of numbers, the most probable comment hse will receive form an executive if: 'stupid'. And since these 'anomaly' are essential and more than common in this revolution of information we may have the tip of some of the icebergs of such time: thinking is a monopoly reserved to bureaucrats; that are orderly organized to limit their thoughts. Of course we are not promoting the disobedience.

Biological nature is somehow more robust to approximations? Apparently it would be easier to measure; more in stable environments. And with robustness at the expense of individual cases ['no one indispensable'] plenty of complexities take places in interfaces and motions; between phase-spaces or their co-existence.

Technological complications?–May at some costs produce strength by core rigidity ... and plenty of 'bugs' on the margins; as well as crossed toxicities and losses of biodiversity... where the humans are. This is not much robust.

Gordian Knot Linking Most Things

Formal sciences explore themselves the gaps in their methods. There, they are essential and those can be very interesting for knowing better the composition of nature. Research try to fill those gaps; for finding links or relations between; and/or providing, in some case **continuity theorems**.

Maybe also the explicit relation between natural and rational real numbers passes by elliptic curves (continuous) and relates topology (more for finite discrete stretchable geometric objects). In the following we provide some main arguments picked in literature. [Most from Zeidler et. al.]

Complex function theory passes commonly by 2 z-planes. Riemann had an approach by 2 Riemann spheres cut and glued them diagonally, providing a resulting surface as a torus. **Fundamental topology property of torus has 2 different types of closed curves, which cannot be continuously deformed to a point.** [The ring has the circle within the ring meaningful to the finger and that circle of the grosor of the ring meaningful the amount of gold. The idea with characteristic ratios between size, curves/circles and shape and numbers of holes?]

The topologically structure of a *torus* a doubly periodic elliptic function. Allowing this to establish that arbitrary Abelian integrals has Riemann's surfaces homeomorphic to a sphere with g handles. g is the *genus* of the Riemann surface. **Genus is the only topological invariant of a compact Riemann surface.** The greater the *genus* of a surface is, the more complicated is its structure.

After Poincaré's theorem, a curve is rational iff it has *genus* p = 0. Curves of this form are **conic sections** (quadratic curves) and cubic curves have **singularities. Smooth cubic curves** (curves of 3rd degree) have the *genus* p = 1 and are **by definition elliptic curves.** Elliptic curves closely relate to elliptic integral and elliptic functions. Theory of automorphic functions generalizes elliptic functions.

In investigation of more complicated integral; since complicated curves. This started with Riemann $\int_R (z, w)$ dz where points (z, w) on the curve p (z, w) = 0 with p a polynomial in z and w. **'Many valued' function w = w (z) is referred to an algebraic function** (investigated by and after Abel). **Algebraic functions were a major contribution to the Theory of functions.** They also relate to Fermat's last Theorem; which demonstration required the proof of a partial verification Shimura-Tanimiya-Weil (**conjecture** concerning elliptic curves)? Fermat's observation was about diophantine equation: $x^n + y^n = z^n$ where n is an integer. Once resolved theorem is now called of Fermat-Wiles.

For algebraic curves 'Uniformization theorem' makes such for global parametrization. Parameter space is compact, connected and one dimensional complex manifold that is: a Riemann surface [Notice we are in the complex plane about one material complex number]. Its mapping is holomorphic and surjective; there is necessarily a **finite set of singular points** and; as the **inverse image a critical set of parameter values.** Both curves provide a **bi-holomorphic map**, where the **critical set of parameters values is compact and has no interior.**

Legendre normal forms for integrals of the 1st kind are **generalized to arbitrary elliptic integrals.** These use **4 distinct complex numbers** with the 4th to infinite.

Weierstrass (a German mathematician, end of the 19th century) provided a general method of substitution to get an elliptic integral with the 3 distinct other complex numbers with 2 periods.

In physics: curves' **parameter may be interpreted as the time.** Curve C as the generalized trajectory of a point. It is important that the parameter space has no singularities (thus its parametrization called the resolution of singularities of the curve C (which has singularities).

There is an interpretation of groups' structures on elliptic curves. Since the intersection of a line with a curve we obtain a 3rd point by geometric construction. It also appears as an addition of the first 2 points. Similarly a neutral element of the curve is defined. As a result **elliptic curve happens to have a structure of the group**. If one chooses the neutral element as an inflection (tangent at the point crosses the curve) then the 3 points on the curve lie on a line. Important relation is with **diophantine geometry** (itself essential to theory of numbers).

Moreover all that is useful to the Theory of schemes which considers, in algebraic geometry: systems of equations over arbitrary fields (instead just over the complex numbers). It involves notions of manifold, connects topology, differential topology, algebraic geometry and number theory.

> ... In the hope to have joined some essential arguments for suspecting that there are like links still to finally establish between natural number of discrete topological object (with 'holes) and real numbers continuous structurally operated, eventually frame-able.

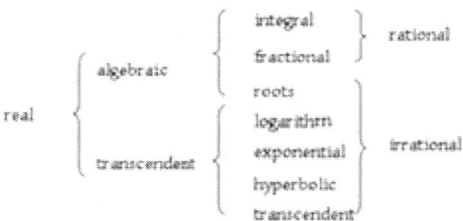

Number type of functions

Diophantine linear equation relates to greatest common divisor and integer numbers ($\mathbb{Z}$). Quadratic diophantine equations have forms of Pythagorean numbers (natural or integral no mind). Diophantine birational transformation is also indebted to Poincaré. Diophantine-Poincaré's theorem is about diophantine curve *genus* p = 0 and odd degree which is equivalent to a diophantine line (infinitely many rational points). Mordell proved that to corresponding for *genus* p = 1 (so on diophantine elliptic curve.

Mordell theorem meaning that the subgroup of rational points of the additive group; if the curve is elliptic is generated by these finitely many points. Then Faltings (1983) made the fundamental theorem of diophantine geometry which says that: for **every diophantine curve *genus* p ≥2 there are at most finitely many rational**.

Rational coordinates of a curve with an algebraic structure provides a finite group. This can be characterized by a parameter: **the rank describing the group.** When trying to define the rank barely is known the way to calculate the rank associated to a curve.

> The idea is to replace an **infinite set** (rational corresponding to coordinate of points to find) by a **set with the same properties but finite**.

Then it is to create a L-function incorporating all small intermediate results which; to any complex number associates a complex number. Such function is defined everywhere but 1 where it has a singularity. It is solved by introducing an order to nullify parameters.

Birch and Swinnerton-Dyer conjecture that **'order to nullify'** and **'rank'** are identical ... but this is still to demonstrate.

Of course most, as us will not understand everything of those essentials. But all may intuitively feel that there are fundamental results relating different major parts of formal sciences. Only to add qualities look like more with natural numbers (and, of course, main ones not many. Amounts more by the side of real numbers. Links characteristically the 2 and have methods from one to another, and there you have what we need with quali-quanti quantified and qualified both... And an 'in' between quite formula-able. Insight on how formal well formulated and well programed are able to deliver better approaches.

In the hope that afterward the human users' options of choice will also benefit from that: options different and more feasible. Conditions made more explicit and commitments clear and more inclusive ... if misappropriated orders less presumptuous. Computers need to clear the formal representations of essential natural sciences. (As some help we just put in bold characters the minimum to look at.)

Back from the skies; of course you should care not to use these kinds of terms for looking like experts in mathematics; in high society sophisticated conversations. 1st because the most probable is that most will ignore this 'essential of everything' and 2nd because you may be asked to explain. Just evoke them for yourself from time to time, so as to aesthetically understand one day. Enough intuitively understood those pieces they may help you test between true and fake mathematicians. We are not pretending to be true mathematician or perfect logicians of formulations. But when, in your legitimate business, as citizens do not vacillate to defend your duties and rights, when some not really legitimate, pretend that he's symbolic magic give hem superior reason. Be more positive be good and smart with realities can support your satisfactions. [Less need of Mandeville's obscure force of 'invisible hand', possibly better use of Smith's nice 'invisible hand'].

Fundamental theorem of arithmetic: any positive integer n can be represented in exactly one (1) way, as a product of prime numbers: p_i: $n = p_1 p_2 p_3 \ldots p_k$. or Πp_i
(Π: is the symbol for iterated products)

Add to the previous short brief, ideas about modular arithmetic, and you may have a field for long-term investigations? There are plenty of places for being more serious (than this essay?) with natural *versus* real (with division), **finiteness, continuity, rank, orders, groups**, etc.

Now, for being more intuitively simple, with sort of quali-quanti relative system: we will see in the following lay common expressions of compliments; and back to our intent of informative relation. Explorations have to include operations and concepts of numbers that will be efforts as a pretext to examine better proportions. Sorts of operations which are not simple when you ignore all the algorithm for exactly reach the one solutions (Which is an almost perfect impossibility). To put economic numbers in enough properly specified qualitative-quantitative (or the reverse). [Complements are to expect in next-coming volume of essays).]

The suggestion being that any concepts at least receive 4 details for better clearance. They ought to be better intertwined or entangled with the others (and the least):

- Quanti-quanti: would be something like a characteristic amount turned a scalar (where characteristic are: one object in the space, in main 3 or 4 general time(s). Or a degeneracy or a specific solution 'for now'; the formula of its orders ('set of systems-algebra') and cardinals complement. Cardinal complements or substitutes; where are the 'holes'. [Our expressions do not intend to be perfect but catch something to reason].
- Quali-quanti: would be like an index, eventually signed, respect to other; characteristic exponent or ratio, dimensions; up and down a "head of integrity" (made of differentiability-integrability, specifications or closures) and 'entails' after or links below.
- Quanti-quali: would be a concept of rank (respect to highest complexity?); characteristic coefficient the basis, head of integrity (links); [we are in need of top-down, bottom-up dual formal way to approach];
- Quali-quali: the variable (commonly: x, y, z when not solved) for the investigation of solution, or function (commonly: u, v, w)); the composition of variables (subsets of a set). We have the operations (half-classes of set of in-operations, between subsets of composition and half-classes of set of out-operations).

Of course these shorts are awful. We try to avoid the simple primitive correspondence; as you have in simple operations. Mind that the informative relative link is a sort of complex dual: have complex concepts or object; try to inform with that. A simple model would be a relative system with minimally complex operators (but somehow complex and open).

Follows the processes of posing the problem so as to be shared. It is a planning process trying to be converging; but not one directly a simple paradigmatic expression of systemic engineering. Our approach is indirect because we (all) have wrongly been used to take numbers as symbols (almost in an esoteric way).And because most ignore too much of the primary or essential structures; existing in fundamental mathematics. So we try to avoid that and the delusions.

[In the abstract world a blind is the king in the kingdom of one-eyes: he does not see the smirking; so get to the essence]

Intuitively, for fast overview thinking, consider for each 4 concepts, and 4 more to tell about them. About intertwining concepts ... which considers at 2 best links each to 2 other of the group of 4 (inner ring) and 2 others for exterior, expressing as an open physical system.

Participative planning often does the same. But they may let much of the truest operations in hands of manipulators' closures. So that is not the best way to rebalance the collective processes of decision required by more efficient democratic communities.

Essential Model Approach to Match With Criteria

For example, just for an amount, the group of 4 would be minimum and maximum, the conceptual unit (1) and the non (0). Limiting to 2 details each could be minimum for existing, minimum for restoring; maximum characteristic non-alienable, maximum for trade; conceptual unit (self) and its environment; 'non' (others) and ratio of sustainability.

In that concept time is not just the lowest lone vibration of the atomic clock; enough: stable either in the interval or 'signal windows' or 'unit-related'. But more relevant time can be the whole-est (potential life); is the quali-quanti: the event (coming from the past) and the projection (going on to the future; hopefully expanding?). Time, achieved or not can be seen as a closure. Achieved closer just in degenerate solution and if disclosed, a series of options (or a field?).

Take for example the coupling of e^x and lnx. The first is an expression of population size and the second is of one's share (easier in an unlimited environment). You observe your progress of well-fitting information on the lnx curve (like a social satisfaction). Since with slow growth (after having emerged) and not exponential after the unit it is manageable since. The identification of the coupling to frame, it is quite a simple a model of relation between qualities and quantities. In your investigation for example the number of your progeny biologically unlimited ex and what you expect in non-limiting environment. Such is your share of profit in a larger family, having the same conditions as your factors of production.

Just drawing a circle bordering the more or less critical limits of all that (lnx, axis of symmetry, e^x) make a modulus and a range of reach. It can also be seen as a lens. The 'what' in the reality or your mind model just used as a *memento* for fixing ideas.

You can add plenty of formal considerations. Either deductively from your environmental management experience, shows jump of trajectories in paths bundle. From events that occurred or further steps that you will intend to support. Horizons of time may change. Inductively to extend to your *praxis*; what the abstract made you decide and undertake.

Then it is to imagine that, in sort of informative curves you have to cross information. Any system will always relatively start setting the base: relative 0 and relative 1 and the limits maximum and limits, for oneself or the basis between 2 or more, or all other than you. And all referred decisions will make use of similar minimum frame. Do not be too anxious: the idea is that most calculus with being made by the computer, and what will remain to you is the identifications, meanings and so on.

With field's concept it turns more simply phenomenologica: always at a minimum a field of vectors. The informative link has probably that virtue, only you take it so. Or in complex environments which superimpose fields and crossed many trajectories pathways. When focusing on any situation you will tend to use families of curves; crossings, crossings avoided: relatively parallel; after fields, bundles, times' framed and so on; about geometric objects.

You narrow the numbers after the subjects under study. If in the narrowness of the *medium* or media ... you focus on principles or essentials. These somehow allowing those. If you are with statistics, it will be to retake 'probable distributions functions' (pdf). Some standards pdf is expressing the statistics forms of numbers and primary pattern frames (be them in structures, functions, half complex operations). These pdf often observes a starting pattern for some, meanwhile other are more laws of random numbers average. [There are many things to clear at the respect].

Sort of high numbers inductive approach 'at the reverse'. That is 'deductive statistics' and often numerical analysis. [Of course this implies to reframe a bit better the epistemologies of such methods]. No methods are no 'perfect *Deus ex Machina*' of formal theater, there is always a concentrate of reduction.

[In Antic Greek's tragedy, the drama is at the end so intricated by capricious vicious gods. So has to be solved (with the artifice of a mechanical device (in the theater) by some superior god, commonly *Zeus*, and solve the case for the poor little humans [Dr. Seuss is just a (very nice) subversive of words].

To consider also limits, defects and conditions. We need to get rid of bureaucratic magical numbers mess; almost not understanding much of logics and mathematics. At the informative step of analyzing; you induce a model, select its wisest pdf and data treatment to join in simulations. Data sampled and collected, empirically or sorted by the computer; you numerically analyze with comparisons (to simulation pdf). There you have methods of statistic inference for matching and eventually fit. Care always that at some point conditions and constraints, what has been operated are informative, and may sometimes be better than results and conclusions for executions; because the levels of complexities have not much truth in the stuff of the weird unanchored flying experts (WUAFE). [Which does not mean that WUAFE are totally useless].

[Mind about fundamental statistics inference, that you have a syntactic paradox: statistics inference neutralize the effect of scale (of amounts or statistics); to help you 'chose the cut' (or discriminate, or observe a 'significant difference'); respect to a probability (or degree of uncertainty) about some population. That is fundamentally a statistical lesson would not be substantial to the phenomenon analyzed so? The data and approach are quantitative. The lessons and conclusions are essentially qualitative, but respect to statistics, not to qualitative essential nor quantitative essential. Thus we are somehow in the formal case of language. Now in a whole world of only numbers much better 'operatively performed' the higher qualities of the statistics would also be semantic (that is meaningful); possibly the only remaining paradox solved than by the physics missing link.

But actually as lay people ignoring all of statistics say: 'all that is blablabla (3 times) and they are right: it is true! They are only slightly wrong: it is informative; but not all experts are conscious of that].

Undertaking System in an Environment of System

Set the system of criteria in its 4 feet minimin, Maximin, miniMax, MaxiMax is like an environment of possibilities. As an ecosystem; we have much of what we need as concept criteria. Formally it is good if we would be able to calculate all that anything in or (economically) enough for setting norms of use.

For example, consider on Earth systems eventually classified as food-webs, and trans-food-webs and transformers. That is meaningful to the evolution of the environmental system. Consider then the functional ecologies hierarchies, spontaneously established by evolutionary processes and respective populations (metabolic and kinds of consumers). And you may sketch a whole picture.

Maybe it will not be so hard to approach by formal calculi, if enough making use of scientific knowledge. Out any sort of preconceived interest narrowed by greed; you also often meet with systematic holists. Alas, these last ones often have too alienating ideas for fellow-humans. Whomever they are they are often determinist-like transformer of humans' being. Most pretending to be wiser and better in thinking than nature.

Reacting to that, it is to understand the complexities of nature and its capacity to carry such enormous mixture of amounts, requires some reasonable logic, of a number of 'principles'. Not necessarily all those only seen by humans. It would not be informative and wise if without essential qualities and no proper proportions to quantities; and lacks of consistent balances manipulations.

Of course with sort of 'adverse effects' humans it would be, to prefer not to make them conscious of the dominant determinist in societies of the leaders of the World. Most people understand in lesser numbers are their mental options. Human consciousness has achieved some nice levels or amount of time resources for thinking. Thinking is leisure respect to emergencies. 'Leisure', for those having at their disposition enough materiality (goods and services), so they can be socially nice. Or some with the wisdom and resource to play in their environment in a precautionary way and nice if they exclude to put the alien in the pot. But concentrating one's minds does not need much. Also at short term it is the means for reviewing why the automatism did not fill its function well.

In the fundamental, to find the critical characteristics. So the minimin will tend to establish lower limits of possibilities. Imagine your position 'your' system in a phase-space of the universe or; an evolved piece of it: an environment. And the higher limits of possibilities: MaxiMax. Possibly there also, to consider some degree of evolution or development. Imagine the system or process under consideration; in the environment eventually technological, social and ecological 'ruled by the law of its universe'. And the share, or range of systems or processes would be in the environment of potential development. To consider also that it is this environment that supports and provides resources.

As a result, after the MaxiMax and the minimin, dedicated to setting the limits; will remain the Maximin and the miniMax between the extreme. Before, some words about 'inside' observe that the limits have to be interpreted in the thermodynamic terms and here you have a crisscross. MaxiMax will thermodynamically has much to do with lowest limits provided by a maximum positive netgentropy (the best balance of entropy toward neguentropy). But where an excess of entropic inputs can simplify too much and so destroy complexity (biodiversity, good social buildings).

Minimin on it turns will have more to do with an ambiguous dual (deal if a promise?). That is, with the maximum of entropy the system can receive, the minimum positive netgentropy. [Of course both Nature and humans sacrify complexity... Nature often in a wiser way (but harsh ones too). So humans will have to crisscross 2 systems in interactions, if they want a system of their own].

[Fundamentally here also it is to question the nature or the property of entanglement-disentanglement ... Either these 'entanglement-disentanglement' is permanent and it would be only for few; or are transient (at the level) and going up ... if more physics than the artifact of complex numbers valid in the relative levels?].

What Remains to the Mid of Criteria

Thus in the essential of formal: with characteristics of fundamental; the 'management perspectives' of criteria remains to explain. Taking into account the previous thermodynamics insight, out emergence. That is 'in within' considerations; it may not be so hard to talk, about essential on Maximin and miniMax.

Just see your life will have to combine to obtain the maximum from the minimum. In essence, the good way of economics and including some concept of least action or socially the logical sustain of so-called Occam's criteria. This would have to balance between, qualitative, quantitative.

Principle of least action: of stationary action–is a mathematical variational principle; applied to the action of a mechanical system. This is to obtain the motion's equations. A different action then; is minimized or maximized. It can be used to derive Newtonian, Lagrangian and Hamiltonian **equations of motion/** It also applies in general relativity (see Einstein–Hilbert action). Its solution requires to find the path that has the least change from nearby paths. Feynmann used it in Quantic dynamics.

Occam's razor: The principle states that among competing hypotheses, the one with the fewest assumptions should be selected. In science, it is used as a heuristic technique instead as an arbiter between published models. It is not considered an irrefutable principle of logic or a scientific result. [Our perspective if proved would make it so, and critically necessary both in the social geopolitical modern environments as in the state of the ecological environment]. The preference for simplicity in the scientific method is based on the falsifiability criterion. But it is kind with primary physical principles. William of Occam was an English scholastic theologian [But his paternity of principle a riddle of history?].

The miniMax could be subtle criteria?–Always in the process to find at the same time an order between 2. At least, easy help to inspire with a relation of information. Examples with the 'minimum' that can bear individuals of a maximum society?– Libertarians will agree, when the maximum is the State. But if the socialist disagrees with them; they should observe that the minimum is about preserving lives and freedom (or all what oneself feel as main components of hes identity). This is not exactly what the history if these systems shown. So this is not necessarily in a Paretian exclusively economic frame.

Pareto's optimality: allocation of resources in which it is impossible to make any one individual better off without making at least one individual worse off. Pareto efficiency is a minimal notion and does not necessarily result in a socially desirable (re) distribution; it makes no statement about fairness and equity. To the contrary, but dynamically it is possible that this was more Pareto's ideology than impossibility.

Now saying that the maximum (affluent) society not the wisest; at incorporating energetic inputs; this calls for competitive freedom killing States its own citizens - The libertarians may disapprove!? Being also at risk that a Stage able to catch the opinion of its voters by horrendous threats are just waiting behind the curtains; so that much sacrifice is expected in the defense of 'the people' (or its faith and ticket for the paradise) Even if not knowing how to define the word 'people' despite commonly you (or the ones you hate, all say 'we the people') ... You may put numbers everywhere and justifying anything; blindly respect to smart realities if you do not care the finiteness of 'quali' in the link.

Whence not ignoring the complexities and complications of realities. Just formally we have to say something about how we could operate all that. Maybe the reader could be convinced that the concept of 'relative system' somehow has advanced. Primary links with the concept of information and the preliminaries we already provided. Other similar links are sorts of crisscrossing, overlapping and mixing concepts. This would be in a semi-ordered and semi-'agitated in uncertainty' way.

Possibly what is called Hilbert's metric, convolutions, kinds of α and β statistics' errors, similarity and so on. Other concepts are to assess (on the quanti-quali frame). Since it is already used in physics: **convergence/divergence; congruence, independence/correlation, density function** (in probabilities). They may all deserve a flexible and more intuitive systemic interpretation.

["**Hilbert projective metric** is an explicitly defined distance function; on a bounded convex subset of the n-dimensional Euclidean space R^n. It was introduced by Hilbert (1895) as Cayley's formula generalization, for the distance; in the Cayley–Klein model of hyperbolic geometry; where the convex set is the n-dimensional open unit ball. Hilbert's metric has been applied to Perron–Fröbenius theory and to construct Gromov hyperbolic spaces."]

[A **convolution** is an integral that expresses the amount of 2 functions, one g overlap function f when shifted over; therefore a blending. This produces a 3rd function viewed as a modified version, of one, of the original functions; and giving the integral of the pointwise multiplication, of the 2 functions as a function so-called translated. The convolution is similar to the cross-correlation. It has applications in: differential equations probability, statistics, vision, language processing, images and signal processing].

Now, even if the serious computer algorithm things will still be made by the same formal professionals... no butler of good manners in an imperialist style to serve you. You have to join your own efforts. So ask for more respect from the programmers of damned artificial intelligence machines.

At more systemic level Petrova-Cartan skew-symmetric differential forms seem to be nice at a higher systemic level for the review of geometric objects representations and intensive principles. When extensive ones will be defined by the conditions in the macro-environment.

Now, close to what we called generally solvable systems of equations with their sort of symmetries; could we use the basic groups algebra? We have yet not spoken much about. Possibly also have to behave forms as polygonal frameworks and networks as means to order in simplifications... The purpose is to avoid impossible calculus too but do it in a more realistic and phenomenological way: straight line for crossing the rock when you can turn around at less cost, do not work (we are not just neutron). Enough diversities for evolutionary processes are essential to robustness of shapes. [That is life]. The relative formulations to maintain the hope that we can manage formal processes].

Cardinal and Ordinals Fresh or Refresh

When dealing with numbers in qualities, somehow in the symbolic absolute and in many frames of flexibility (m)any numbers are in a same plane of importance and composing something with them will deal with cardinals. Cardinality formally (in arithmetic logic) is about 'a number within other', with no distinction between, unit symbols. Cardinal is also the number of distinct objects in a collection or as a set.

For some mathematicians a cardinal is an ordinal that cannot be put in bijection with any ordinal strictly smaller. [A way to involve the ruler of metric]. **Co-finality** of a cardinal κ is the **smallest cardinal** μ such **as there exists a sequence indexed** by. μ: $(\lambda_i: i\ (\mu)$ such as $\kappa = \sup_{i\,(\mu)} (\lambda_i)$. It is noted $c_of (\kappa)$. [sup: for superior of top border]. 3 operations are defined on cardinal: addition, products and exponentiation. If λ and κ are infinitely cardinal then $\kappa + \lambda = \kappa \times \lambda = \sup \{\kappa, \lambda\}$. Have also $\kappa^{cof\,(\kappa)} > \kappa$ and $c_of (2^\kappa) > \kappa$.

Axioms of cardinality that are of special interest are:
- a **topological space** follows the 2nd axiom of cardinality; if the family of cardinality possesses an **enumerable base** and so is **separable**, more restrictively than it always follows first axiom; [conceptualize the key words];
- a topological space follows the 1st axiom of cardinality if the surroundings of **any point of space has an enumerable base.**

All finite or infinite open, semi-open, closes intervals of length, that are strictly positive and that has the same cardinal; such sets of numbers are said with the **power of continuity**. This is counter-intuitive into the perspective: from 'bottom up to top' and easy to understand from 'top down to bottom'. By bijective projections from S center of 'folded' intervals]0,1 [to $\mathbb{R}$. Set $\mathbb{R}^2$ of all real numbers pairs (that is to say real plane) have the same cardinal as $\mathbb{R}$. [~closed interval]']~open interval[.

On **cardinal number properties**: Be α the cardinal number of some set A the **equivalence class** of all set with the same cardinality as A. We have $\alpha < 2^\alpha$ [2^α number of parts]. **Smallest infinite set representing cardinal numbers** is symbolized by $\aleph_0$ (aleph zero). **Cantor's diagonal slash** explores cardinality. Cantor β^α for the cardinality of B^A when $\beta = 2$. Each element of B_A is thus an **assignment** either 'in' or 'out' of every element of A. Such an assignment is simply choosing a subset of. A. It implies that the possibility of an infinite number is 'so huge', that there is no way that general computation can come to an end (Turing). [From that the incompleteness of Gödel]. [Then **halting problem** turns a major concept of applied computation].

Continuity hypothesis: whatever the set A, the family of parts of A: $\mathcal{P}(A)$ has a cardinal card $(\mathcal{P}(A))$>card (A). The card ($\mathbb{N}$) is $\aleph_1$, the same as of real numbers set ($\mathbb{R}$). The hypothesis of continuity, says that there is no cardinal between $\aleph_0$ and $\aleph_1$. In general if A: whatever set, does not admit any cardinal (such as $\aleph(A) < \aleph < \aleph(\mathcal{P}(A))$); is the **generalized hypothesis of continuous**.

Continuity cannot be demonstrated in the theory of set.

Continuity in fundamental physics links to:
- Cantor cardinals of set theory;
- infinite 'box in piling of intervals' [mind integration];
- Bell's infinitesimal nil-potent.

In statistics, a collection of statistical units can be no more than collections, with no order, norm or metrics. Even some parameterizations provide with a number of inference. It does not necessarily means that there is continuity. Statistical inference can explore that deductively; as a property or inductively as an expected criterion and no more. Some testing possibly related are like of medians, signs, conformity (Kolmogcrov-Smirnov or Wilcoxon). Many statistical practices under-care conditions.

Rigorous mathematical procedures are often uncared because said 'theoretical'. For some operations' management ignore impossibilities'. Like when saying that 'any kind of result is better than none.' Something that unacceptable in democracies, nor with the respect of the physics phenomenon (field, cardinality, etc.). Scientific knowledge that effectively follows such behaviors and those that may be better not follow over-impose bias.

Ordinals ordered definition (from Takeuti): deals with ordinals and seeks well orderings on the natural numbers. If **well founded**, order relation is expressible by a<Π_1^1 Formula (a 1st order system with free 2nd order variables suffice). Gentzen proved that ε_0 the least ordinal is not provable in formalized Peano arithmetic [abridged: PA].

More precisely we have 1st ordinal number ε_0, ordinal less than is 0 and an ordinal. Be μ_1, μ_2, ... μ_n ordinals; the sum as $\mu_1 + \mu_2 + ... + \mu_n$ and ω^μ are also ordinals. From the previous, the only way to define ordinal; '<' and '=' is inductively defined. '<' is a linear ordering and 0 its least element.

Peano arithmetic: his postulates turned the set of axioms for the natural numbers. Modern axioms list of (PA) has 3 types of statements. The first axiom asserts the existence of at least one member. Next 4 are general statements about equality more as "underlying logic". Next 3 axioms are 1st order statements about natural numbers properties of the successor operation. The 9th, final axiom is a 2nd order statement of mathematical induction over the natural numbers. A weaker 1st order system called Peano arithmetic is obtained by adding the addition and multiplication operation symbols and replacing the 2nd order induction axiom with a 1st order axiom schema.

In other words, ordinal is a number into another, ascending or descending. Ordinal there is like the ' rank' of objects (in a regular increasing relation of order).

Cantor's generalized continuous hypothesis $2\exp(\aleph_\alpha) = \aleph_{\alpha+1}$ where α is an ordinal number. Discrete case applies to counting, numbering, listing or enumeration. Continuous case thus especially for continuous numbers. [exp for exponent operators, we use it when difficult to put the expression () up in usual exponent].

Relations of order (called statistics of ranks) can also be studied in statistics and are robust. That is, without requiring too much precision.

Ordering Bias: Any processing system that cannot simultaneously evaluate all possible hypotheses needs an ordering bias. 2 reasons supporting simplicity bias are. Simple cause is inherent part of conjunctive causes' definition.

Confused Cardinal and Ordinal

"Of transfinite ordinal numbers and cardinal numbers, the first correspond to our intuitive 'counting on and on' and cardinal to the number of elements. All ordinals can be bijectively mapped to form a well-ordered set. The smallest ordinal of this set is called the cardinality of A" [The 'minimum head' basically ambiguous?].

In common practice and the small quantities or amount managed by common people (small speculators) it would be to observe that numbers are deeply intertwined as cardinal and ordinal. Cognitive combinations have many fundamental reasons. Dual complex perspective (cardinal-ordinal) is poorly used (?) when it should play a significant role in the way to manage arithmetic and the way we care humane meanings. Cardinal-ordinal a fundamental dualism, the way they articulate? As many effects as could be suspected.

For example, it is to mention kinds of statistics (rank, order, conformity, continuous, qualitative, quantitative...). There since the beginning with numbers and enumeration you may have to care about the 2 concepts. For example, any human subject play both as equal when citizen (in the way one human one vote) and non-dissociated with ordered as in professional hierarchies.

But for whom care about dynamic relations between relative ranks, complexities to cope with (Nature a good place for tests), reset cardinal-ordinal? If with a kind of framework where always the same accumulate constraint to adapt in the same fixed social place, accumulating the disadvantages. And the half converse: all accumulate the advantages the lack of constraints to adapt and the same fixed rank. When the proper match and fit consider: a program (miniMax or Maximin). This would be to make optimal assignation of balances: production, time delay, place distance, care. And support the sense of opportunities, possibly of fairness? Cardinal the property of democracy. There are more fundamental basics to that than economics laws separated from environments and principles of constructions, not at any costs.

Does this play too at more fundamental levels? Could we say disorder of cardinals being more common in physics and order more exceptional: field-particle not an impossible analog? –So switches to quantic *vacuum* more a cardinal process and particle emergence more an order process? And going up with ordering complexities, it is to incorporate dynamics of renewal. Forcibly it would be as positive conversion. Many other successive duals of the sort are from compulsory and half random investigations of foods mid of the 'food-webs' in the environment. To the processes of relative reduction of eating, digestion and metabolization of any living body as an integrated process of ordering?

In abstract observe that **time's gauge is quite the test between causes** (out of disorder)–effects (order eroded by entropy into cardinal disorder). And possibly with an expression intrinsically in theory of numbers. See for example the concept of **evenness** in numbers all having the same 'prime head' (that is 2, considered a prime number) and **odd numbers** (1 commonly not considered a prime number). And then immediately we have to discriminate between odd-prime numbers and non-prime odd numbers. [Or course to make more arithmetic logic explicit].

Would, a proper and efficient management of these 2 entangled concepts and other related ones (by their spectrum?), pose less social-economic problems and avoid plenty of bureaucratic waste. Of course, apart the 'curse' of those simply ignoring that nature has better reasons than the perfect order and unique-mad-goal determinism. That many administrators of societies in humans' hierarchies want to 'below enforce' to the extreme, and ambiguously above. Ambition for becoming the highest in the hierarchy, looked at in a cognitive way. Some for accumulating all the same relative and lowest ranks. Others accumulating the highest ones, by fake merits, provided by the place, that do not make social-economically sense of humanity.

Nature is quite explicit on the coexistence, without 'prejudgment of value', about articulating the resources of disorder and order. Despite not the human fate to only mimic nature, there are enough smarter and economical ways for better and fairer management.

To develop the ideas at the respect; see for example that **numbers as indices** somehow to be treated in the same way (say cardinal or horizontal relationships). An 'half tip would be: even or pairs as equal below their only prime (2) as rank; with odds then goes on the series of odd numbers after the prime, the 1st of them (3) rank 3 below 2. We have thus a 'spontaneous scale of proportions.

The idea is to extend the arguments: 0 start, 1 unit, 2, ordinal, 3, cardinal, other even, other prime, other odds. Extensions over the concepts of **coefficients, variable, index, situation** this is by the side of qualitative terms. For the mid-quantitative terms it would be: **rational, component, logarithms, exponent**. Closures or tightening links would consider: **algebraicity, series, rank, characteristics** (if discrete) or **polynomiality**, function, dimensions, systemic complexity (or nearest prime number of references) when we are with continuity. More or less: this is no more than for discussion. As an intent to 'type' the amount … suggested in a horrible way.

Other sets possibly the same (*spectrum*), that could have to be treated with order. See for example that vital functions of a living body all need to exist somehow equally (in qualitative) definition. And orderly weighted (put into a relative hierarchy). Like by the critical delays to the loss of enough function. Since their failure could mean death. But having also accorded the circumstances, conditions having to also play timely hierarchical.

> For human body it is quite easy: cardiac function risk is a matter of seconds, respiratory function of minutes. Then you have neurologic (hours, but more or less after circumstances) nephrological (kidney) function of some days (more variables according electro-ionic disorders), feeding and digestion (depending on stored, from days to weeks). They have significant critical interdependence.

Then, out the observation that the theory of numbers may give frameworks to inspire oneself about the 'art of **combinatory**' to apply to {cardinal-ordinal} such as: **permutations**, **sorting** or **combinations**. Each is with or without repetitions, with or without put back, with or without order. Using often the **model of the urn sampling**, etc.

Not much to tell about this matter that can receive many developments. Just to observe: such sort cardinals (?) well pictured when displayed on a circle or similar (around a center, eventually 1 to 3 focal points ... or an atom?). Then what may be important: the number of foci and examine average consistency (in a geometric picture and the n (maximum effective of around). [Observe that with *tori* and some elliptic relations the inner (like with a shell) need not to be filled].

Meanwhile the display of order ought to look like a ruler, a linear order or a pyramid. [Cantor's diagonal slash is the way to display the order of numbers filling since the corner of a square]. Then to consider the **lowest and highest limits**. [In operations you have the highest common divisor and the lowest common multiplier]. And further to develop the ideas. Circle of spherical or geometric development that can involve partial or focal hierarchies, paving, etc. By the side of order development mixing as grids and so on.

> Do not hesitate to picture both forms, share and then think... [For example: **binomial coefficient grids** (1st dated in China but now called Pascal's triangle). Newton and Cantor has seen so well with such forms... So collective intelligence can do]. Then try to convince people around about that: collective people can do it.

> It is more important to practice both: work on your own with references, work collectively (nor being ashamed of reference, nor too proud of 'magic-man knowing everything', the synergetic result more important. Be conscious of self-advantages and defects and care talents. Make you less defective the way to distinguish or compete and practice your talents, the way to be useful and fair to the maximum of others.

> Economy is about mixture, synergies and doing better together ... with as optimum as possible individual contributions. It is not for ignoring that basic combinations co-exist and should be useful. And they the remains a 'ridiculous waste to ignore'. It is

nonsense and narrowness; it is like to be unable to make some use of both: order and hierarchy, equanimity and motivation of emergence.

Relative No Commutativity

Does order presides over Non Commutativity or Relative Irreversibility? - As soon as physics of particles-fields still open frames have been allowed; commutativity turned relatives? Complex approaches need 'mesoscopic slices' from the realities including the unconscious, uncommunicative ones. Otherwise cognitive imagination of your brain will complete with conceptual dimensions. These are abstract precautions to 'fill' with convictions. Insofar a volume of comprehensive will cope with 'altogether sorts of things', **combining inductions and deductions.**

The most traditional (modern) formulations in standard model of physics observe the symmetry of time. So, out of 'travels in the past or the futures' (which are a bit problematic), an important question (of order) is which irreversibility? As a result of non-abelian algebra (abelian algebra is commutative) of Connes (a French contemporary mathematician). Also the physicists to conceive emerged symmetries (like with particles and antiparticles, and coexistence of symmetries and asymmetries in the fundamental physics world. Quantic theory is already dealings since decades with symmetries breakings.

One would have to consider such in invariance, conservation, regularity, equivalence or face: criticality, instability, singularity. More conceptually which are with unequal proportions? In the couples: finiteness/infinity; local/global; continuous/discrete; matter/anti-matter. [Or $Field_M$–Matter > antimatter–$Field_{-M}$?].

Breaking the reversibility of time arrow? Technically this often passes by the use of kinds of operations slightly less simple than the standard; (we have seen not as simple as you practice with coins). Use of operators? Their introduction in quantic physics corresponds to Heisenberg.

Atom may be described by an **operator- position. Operators do not commute**. Thus after the measure not commutatively the same Heisenberg also proposed the **principle of uncertainty**. Born shows that Heisenberg's operators were matrices but physicists traditionally had preferred the probabilistic wave of Schrödinger. Waves handling was more familiar to them. This was during the first half of the 20th century, mainly from the Copenhagen school.

More recently Connes's non commutative algebra turns good for **generalization of relativity to quantic theory**. Measure of distances, in non-commutative spaces, uses a concept of a spectral space, allowing great variety of spaces. **Concept of a point is redefined as a state of quantic nature. Concept of curvature** in a 4 dimensioned space becomes the *calculus* of a surface, of this space. It adapts well to non-integer dimensions of spaces. And it allows to incorporate the 4 fundamental forces in a unique non commutative space-time. So it may be the basis for reformulation of standard model.

Difficulties of Connes with his non-commutative algebra are for example that differentiation and integration are not as in the commutative form. But the 'emergence' of properties allowed Connes to solve the equations of von Neumann (rigorous mathematical formulation of Heisenberg). And so produced a **classification of operators algebra**.

In short, for the profanes:

- Operators in physics half-complex operations on something;
- Some are quite small matrices as simple as 2 ×2 matrices (Born, Pauli);
- Operators are non-reversible (irreversibility like that);
- Some irreversibility is needed [for going up in constructions]; (that does not make physics order hate disorder)
- There is more matter more than antimatter,
- And there are plenty other phenomenological evidence of asymmetries (physics, chemistry);
- Anti-symmetries obtained by symmetry (ies) breaking(s), [as soon as at fundamental physical levels];
- Arrow of time has symmetry breaking [or an encapsulation or folding for a while?];
  [or time a delay of the possibility of other levels of development within?]
- Relations to openness, entropy, evolution?
- The irreversibility and instability are able to produce higher complexity (Prigogine in thermodynamic chemistry).
- Higher development of Connes's non commutative algebra?
- Chinese boxes of cardinals-ordinals?

Fundamental Formal Types of Path within Spaces.

In "pure terms" objects can have 3 sorts of basic mathematical behaviors. Interesting is that the 'avatar terms' appear from somewhere in the formal or physics sciences. Then they may have received mathematical generalized form and/or/then have been evidenced as primary:

- Random "driven" processes
  - o **Ergodic**: is the term that came from the Brownian motion (from British botanist: Brown) of small bodies local permanently moving (without axes or direction) under the microscope; accelerated eventually by heat. Then mathematics developed a theorem of ergodicity;
  - o **Random**ness: is commonly mentioned in probabilistic issues, sorting for better sampling and statistics. Probability sampling made it a technique for ensuring un-manipulated selection (the best way to representativeness).

[Today statistics computed programs for treatment of data are using properties of numbers within random limits, of pseudo-random algorithms. [Algorithm as a program of simple instructions; is away of calculating. (Kind of Turing's machine; these delivering so almost-random numbers, further used to select or index candidates for sorting. Sort of simulations methods].

  - o **Stochastic** is another term for randomness. It may be sued more to qualify the random events of meetings. They may follow a probability of distribution functions, queues theory, radioactivity decays. Thus connecting to ergodic theorem with time.

- o **Markov chain**(s) (after a Russian mathematician) formally describes that pathway is nonhereditary (that is without memory). That is to say their direction of each step can change, it is not pursuing. [The physics can make them disappear?]

Thus, much about probability that you may not approach with a one point nor a single line but at the maximum by a (quantitative) less than one degree of certainty. [Or a qualitative which has one more dimensions than the present one? – that would be a primary for openness?]...

Notice that in terms of dimensions, you will work at more than just one (1) dimension. At least not an abstract point but an interval of trust. [Connection to cardinal of ordinal?] To mention also, in probability you have almost always the counterpart that appears: since the concerning event is p, ¬p often uses q; and p + ¬p = 1.

Say it also with probabilistic intervals, not at 100% for sure. And commonly much less than that (in most probabilistic models). And 'almost never exactly' as the exact value, which will be observed further. Of course, there are all the subtleties of probability theory that get into the train. We will further mention only few that we feel important; to care about. Because most are still with traditional learning exact-mindedness shortcuts.

Have in mind that in probability theory: basically no start about what you are talking of but better start identifying all the set or, spectrum or space of events. Even if the definition of probability (cleared by Kolmogorov) links an event to a value between 0 and 1. The value itself cannot be a point in space or moment in time. Nor is any defining characteristics referred to a fully abstract concept (dimension 0) or a one-point concept on a line (dimension 1) but starts, relatively, as its non-dimensioned point into a wider interval. Or its dimension is one point in a larger area or it is a point or 'card' in a larger volume. [Of course much more interesting are the links between domains or spaces].

Thus such 0 probability an event either impossible (label vanishes) or has not been yet observed (label may stay waiting for) ... but we do not know. [You may develop a **theory of belief** but you must not decide for others ... when 'not critical']. Theory of belief or **subjective probably** anyhow in humans and humans based (?), and is also reflexive with theory of probability. This may be needed but probably better with cleared precautions.

There is also the start of utilities anticipated concept; over theory of probability. As an obliged 3rd complement... But human consciousness is 'entangled' with unconsciousness meaning. That may also have to consider a dual system: the objective conscious system with the belief (from unconscious subjectivity?); and the subjective over unconscious system. [Unconsciousness has also a system of treatment, but we do not know, so we make a subjective of unconscious system].

System is where we can put the probability information. The reason why it is not so easy to 'disentangle objective probability from/with subjective probability': they exchange their quali or informative pieces.

Physics Nature seems to have a universe of **potentialities**. 'Locally' quanticity made it, at least, **probabilities** (in the *quantum* theory sense ... not as illogic as pretended), brains overall **work probabilities** (always some lack of knowledge), consciousness made them **possibilities** and humans societies shortcut into **believes**.

[Lone self-unique belief acceptable, and possibly beautiful, at least for you not turn psychotic: disordering the entangling of self?]

In the quantic theory, concept of probability or uncertainty is not the same as in mathematics theory of probability [we are not more so convinced by that could be an improper concept of uncertainty out of *quantum*: physically an event has to be quantum?]. The Heisenberg principle of (quantic) uncertainty is about characteristics (more than one): defining a value in quantic theory, makes that you cannot know for sure the other, when knowing one. This principle is applied like to the pairs: {(position, *momentum*); (energy, time); (number, phase)}.

> [Commonly this is seen by pairs... Could it be a sort of relative unknown spectrum. Respect to a *focus*, intricated and details known-under-known, 'up' to first unknown systemic basics 'intrication' (be one before '3', contrasting with those after '3'. Or Heisenberg principle a logic artifact instead of a physics' effect? - because of the formal deficiency of binary value respect to the triple-value, In the idea of better expressivity from 3 (valued logic & general solvability)?]

In our opinion we may have objectively a complement: physics completes here the mathematical concept, making it minimum or essential; when phenomenologically? - There are plenty of uncertainty (ies): by lack of knowledge or, because unconsciousness or, because limits of consciousness. Of course, unconsciousness has limits, none can say that it has not, neither any can know really properly where are these limits (moreover in specific conditions). Probably only that language limits are lower than these unconscious-conscious ones.

Also because subjects of physics have a fundamental requirement of open-ness (quality may change): develop, move, appear, disappear, accept, reject, share; with terms quite phenomenologically contradictory (our level of consciousness); still at fundamental particle level. As an effect a formal type of uncertainty is open-ness expression in the formula of the system.

- **Determinist types of formal behaviors** call kinds of something mathematics modeled following clear base (0,1) at least relative to itself.

Infinitesimal calculus is at ease with that. Care nevertheless, about what your function is coping with. It may be a wave or "width-ness" of probabilities. With an object, it is about a representing, and for finding solutions realistically relatively coherent and specified thus uniqueness exists as a special case.

[Care nevertheless that unique solution may be not just a point, especially an abstract one... Precisely, in a relative and expanded system it can be a sequent, a **segment** (delay), a **line** (measure), a **curve** (trajectory), a **map** (transect), a **surface** (board of criteria limits), a **volume** (object as a good) or a **delimited phase-space** (care) ... Depending on where you put the '**magnifying lens**' and thereafter the hoped].

The formula is expressing either the atom or a border. In the first case of "atomic representation" formula expresses the way to calculate it, according approaches. And if there is nothing, there is no object. If there is a solution then there it is (?). [Obviously that the illusions of most bureaucrats].

If formulation is more about delimiting a point of a space, with a given behavior, then the value, a characteristic; possibly a singularity of property as in phase-space.

[Also it is to consider the position of formula respect to the system: probably, as soon as a system; it takes in charge formula(s) [and not just one: even on a reduced crystal-like you have plenty of edges, apices (or corners), facets (or faces or sides) and symmetries. So you should care about narrow delusional mindedness, before fighting just about different perspective, on the same easy to reach].

As a new volume anticipation of essays, it is to intend to make sense to Euler's graph equation: number of corners c−number of edges e + number of faces f = 2. The Euler characteristic χ was classically defined for the surfaces of polyhedra, according to the formula: χ= Vertices - Edges + Faces in the given polyhedron. Any convex polyhedron's surface has Euler characteristic. $V - E + F = 2$

Euler characteristic may be generalized to any topological space. In particular, it is equal to $2 - 2g$ for a closed oriented surface with genus g and to $2 - k$ for a non-orientable surface with k cross-caps. This property led to the definition of rotation systems in topological graph

thus formula in a system can be: 1) Structural (always functionally 'in' informed?); 2) Functional (always structurally either 'in' or 'out' information; 3) A system relation, variably important after the qualities of the system's formulation].

There exist virtual points without existence (or the binary: representing point centered; or a material volume of existence or possibly non-existence or *vacuum*). For a geometrical example of a volume without center: a *torus* (a ring volume form) has a center 'out of itself.'

In physics concept: mass grows with volume. Thus if the center representing it can be used at macro-level. Would it be not better at micro-level? - to consider the limiting sphere (or surface) of its volume more important than a center 'nothing' without mass. Especially since through surface critical limit, between 'in' and 'out' that is where exchanges are passing through and enough mass stay to keep or take a label if not an identity? – Life has probably emerged since interfaces. Formally this makes sense, because in the effect of the formula and an inner volume not as homogeneous as imagined.

Phenomenological discussions (of epistemology of the forms) qualifying the amount(s) are not enough made systematically by just numbers as they are. Dedicate some time to that could help share and reveal many deficiencies in our language shortcuts. Such elementary questions are relevant in formal sciences as well as produce metaphysical or cognitive questions and may be treated differently as evidenced by cross cultures comparisons. Many cultures have produced sort of intuitive mathematics in applied arts, discovered now quite topological, combinatory, games like, etc.

Discussion about coherent formulations, dimensions, units, systems, extended identifications, proper anchors, reviews of opportunities, care of precautions would have the benefit to expose the uselessness of many academics. Especially of the ones ascribing dogmas and paradigms away from minimum ethical contingencies. Not to exclude from that dustbin engineers in social abuses, there are so many. Many do not like their devices and efforts be properly comprehended by 'the social': no need to complete the social-economic system around, just to follow their own narrow hierarchy!

Back to basic, on formal path behaviors; after their professional's dedications, some consider other sorts (that we think) more degenerated ones or combinations.

- **Linear behavior**: if the easiest and a formal start for there in. Alas, there is misguidance. Most prefer the simple proportional division and often miss that this **'affinity'** in mathematics could make the 'kernel' for inclusions of dimensions higher than one.

Possibly in the system relative approach; this would be the limit of integration and derivation (no more than 2?). Something that we will see in statistics with high number law: **average of average follows a normal law** a sort of measure in doubled inclusion (or integration) of data. This would lead to a perfect, with which physics meaning? Abstract of abstract?

Observe also in (physics formula) **equations of dimensions**; you will sometimes see power 4 or -4 hardly more. Most commonly global concept will be power 2 or -2. Thus the kernel of a measure in dimension 1 or -1 not to be taken just out any system and make it a way for formalizing the laws of societies: the metrics of societies may be elsewhere, more biological? Naked linear behavior looks quite exceptional in nature (out selectively pure optic geometry?) or more a local illusion: 'observing the sea-horizon within the very sharp *angulus* of oneself observers ... and the Earth is flat?'

In a formal system it is there, at dimension 1 that the metric or the norm is. Probably also the one dimension where we have to linearize the main components or dimensions of reference and situate other inscribed component structure.

The mathematics of these linear forms is 'within; possibly to be approached by sympletic forms. [Once understood the frameworks like developed; at complex meso-scope level. To explore there after linearization (like of the most structuring issues) and then symplectic analysis?–for what is all that shape a system. Without missing there after that this 'solved referred complexity,' to return to the phenomenology of recorded data to make the statistical comparisons of conformity?].

Norm's properties

Norm of *: $||*||$ defines a relation from $\mathbb{C}^n \to \mathcal{R}$ that satisfies the following conditions for all $\mathbf{u}, \mathbf{v}$ and all $a \in \mathbb{C}$

1. Positive definiteness $||\mathbf{u}|| \geq 0$ and $||\mathbf{u}|| = 0$ if and only if $\mathbf{u} = 0$
2. Homogeneity $||a.\mathbf{u}|| = |a|.|\mathbf{u}||$
3. Triangle inequality $||\mathbf{u}+\mathbf{v}|| \leq ||\mathbf{u}||+||\mathbf{v}||$

Linear, and Nonlinear formal differences	
Linear	Non-linear
Reaction in proportion of action	Reaction with no direct comparison with importance of action.
On-off behavior equal to the sum of parts. Causal additivity	Collective behavior qualitatively different from the set of parts
Physical system: set of preexisting parts and in permanent interactions	Physical systems: parts reach individuality just by retroactive interactions ones to others
Reversibility of actions and synthesis	Irreversible analysis
Existing isolated objects	No isolated objects, no separability
Explicit properties	Unary conceptions
Dualist concepts	Adaptability
Non adaptive	Structural stability possible at any dimension.
No structural stability if n > 2	Stability of stationary states. Limit cycles
Contraries exclude or cancel themselves	Transitions between stationary states are fundamentally non-linear phenomena
Particle or waves are mutually exclusives	Particles and waves can associate
No deterministic chaos if n ≤ 2	Deterministic chaos if n > 2

with n the number of dimensions, not necessarily an integer

Symplectic geometry is defined on a smooth even-dimensional space which is a differentiable manifold. On this space is defined a symplectic form, which allows the measurement of sizes of 2-dimensional objects in the space. The symplectic form plays a role analogous to that of the metric tensor in Riemannian geometry. Where the metric tensor measures lengths and angles, the symplectic form measures areas.

"**Symplectic form** is responsible for the ability of symplectic geometry for giving a **closed** mathematical description. **Symplectic Group**: are bilinear form, anti-symmetric and linear $s_{ab} = -s_{ab}$ i.e. $S^T = -S$. **Symplectic manifold**: unique connection, non-singular antisymmetric tensor field S_{ab}. Present in phase space classical mechanics. $dS = 0$ Symplectic group Sp (m, m).

Geometric Liouville Theorem says: be a symplectic variety dimension 2^n and H: W → R a function. Suppose that the Hamiltonian system associated to H integrable with n first (independent and in involution) integrals $f_1, ... f_n$. If $c = (c_1, ..., c_n) \in R^n$ is a regular value of $f = (f_1, ... f_n)$: W → R^n and if f^{-1} (c) is compact then the connex components of this sub-variety (dimension n) of W, are tori. The trajectory of such sub-variety at level is contained in the sub variety and is linear. Liouville's tori are in the phases' space. They exist relatively to integrable Hamiltonian systems. But, when an integrable system is integrated, we generally obtained a system which is, no more integrable. Nevertheless some tori will stay invariant according KAM theorem."

Liouville's theorem on the conservation of the volume of a dynamical system

Let $\mathring{u}(t)=H(u(t))$ be a dynamical system defined on a certain compact subset U $\subseteq \mathcal{R}^n$. Then if A $\subseteq$ U has a volume $V \equiv \int_A dx$, then the volume V(t) of the set A(t) = {v = u(t): u(0) $\in$ A} satisfies $\overline{V}(t) = \int_{A(t)}$ div H(u)du where the divergence of the vector field H(.) is defined as follows: div H(u) = $\sum_{i=1}^{n} \partial H_i(u)/ \partial x_i$ i.e. the trace of the Jacobian of H(.).

- **Nonlinear** formal behavior or in formal science so-called chaotic is very important to us. In Nature straight path either in small proportion or an artifice of relative reference to the pathway (once referred the pathway would be made straight and near trajectories are defined relatively).

So once the important line(s) [core of as a limit?], it is (are) made straight, many or most others are not (So nonlinear) ... if no other transformation (out of itself) can make them straight. Then relative to the main-frame it is nonlinear [sort of approach of "parallelism" locally better than the Euclidean?].

[Observe that this sort of relative reference respect to main-reframing leads to main frame straight line and all other nonlinear, but relative. Implicitly and geometrically there is also another concept of '**parallelism by pieces**' or: **stepwise functions by pieces** or; **segment** or; 'corridors of the box' was supposed to join all at the 'in' and 'out' corners of the box or; going in and going out not by these corners but by other sides. A relative stochastic trajectory will crosses not by the expected corner, but a side (without pattern) or an edge ... or will be pseudo-stochastic: keeping in one channel 'in' delimiting the box].

[Notice that we make use of a cubic or hyper-cubic model, observer outside at one corner or the other. Riemann's sphere as reference of this sort for spherical case?]

- **Hierarchical (**sort trajectory formal behavior): as mentioned by some variables of decision are under an authority of (one decider or unique criterion or consensus ... or a unique pole-self?). It seems to us easy to relate to formal and logical treatment ....

[We look a hierarchical path or way of formal behaving more an abuse if lonesome: it is a linear mixture with rankings.

With formal (sciences) systems, you may have an implicit hierarchy in scale of complexity. Maybe the use of prime numbers indexing, allowing some flexibility. Because, precisely since have a relative system (relatively autonomous) is also about being able to disturb the hierarchy. Rightly there are hierarchies in nature. Chinese-box-Matrioshka the clearest principle. But as we get into social issues more they may have to be flexible (it is stupid rigidity respect to conscious opportunism on Nature. That is being variable or adaptable after the best economics of the solution? (Not the order of the private determinist).

Observe that since the global state-stage of a complex biological system; if it is able to vary its sub-hierarchies of its 'quali-quanti' main dimensions of sub-dimensions.

If not it may not survive: 'eat when you can, rest when you can ... store between maintaining accessible ... So the functional hierarchies of the body have to change, intuitively everyone understands that hence not the 'yellow livers of leaders'].

Perspective on Systems Structures

In common **geodesics** (geographic topology) looking at volumes requires 3 or 4 points of perspectives. With an object at 2 dimensions it is to hope your object not too un-elliptical. At 3 you may check that and at 4 you may close (life time) or test. Geodesic process may be called triangulation or quadric-angulation.

With shapes or forms pay special attention to the **convex** or **concave** form (of curves or surfaces). Analytically imagine exploring trajectories or lines, flatness of surfaces. For trajectories 'crossed spectrography' makes us of a small card; possibly dimensioned after the range of the *spectrum*; the 'window' of your measure, or the respect to the smoothness of approached surface. Oriented commonly after perpendicular faced surface on the volume. In dynamic analysis it is the principle of Poincaré's card. In a 3 dimensions system of reference; it can also be a decision plane: the cut-off). Patterns may appear either transecting the card, possibly in other ways meeting the points of the peaks. In geodesic the isoclinal levels' map.

If you prefer the unique point matching your plane of cards to the surface touching the volume that is the principle of Riemann's sphere...

> [... Coming together with the plan and projections involving the sphere, you can map up to the infinite. Sphere is like rolling on an infinite plane. Think about projections at the top of the sphere. Maximum distance, pointed on the sphere, respect to the plane, and passing by some detail of the sphere. The idea of (managed) infinity with the projections that since the same point at the top, passing by no inner point of the sphere].

Convexity makes the formal approach quite simple. The concavity is slightly more ambiguous, you card may not have reached the extreme point: you have more than one point to get out and reach the maximum point of 'in'. This is from an outside perspective. You understand intuitively more naturally that you approach the border by the concave side.

Convex forms are well considered, in optimal *calculus*. Since they are better phenomenological forms of unity than the concave one. But this is often too static. When considered complex units; you have not just convex forms: various relative peak (or holes) values. If you mind it well, you will understand that: if globally a form (a system?) may better be convex, but it needs to be open; it may have to admit some local concavity (turned outside) [and/or be able to close the aperture, as of a wound]. Like for being able to include locally.

Organized Societies have probably capabilities to be more open (less convex?). That is to say possibly also, with linear interfaces. Mind hexagons of honeycombs, or soap bubbles together: inner contact surfaces are straight plane. Spontaneous minimum and packed surfaces, between many provide linear surface. [Not to presume of metrics if not voluntarily socially shares?] And organized concavities eventually dynamic one (for absorbing more).

Conscious social members but relatively individual autonomous as teleological units (human beings), have to mind that if they try to catch the best of their environments. Themselves as dynamic units: they have to be aware of the ways, to take advantage of complexities. So they have to mind on how to 'trigger' the balances, with knowledge (curiosity and diversity of smartness); comprehend the economies of scales and tickle the environmental dynamics on marginal bio-productions they may empower not critically. Socially then willing to have social motivations to share information.

That is: do they have to socially exaggerate the 'rational discriminations' (that formal sciences no more support) to maximally augment brutally the already existing biological and environmental universal ways of differentiation ones?–As expected so liberally by Hayek? - Or in an authoritarian way, completely empower the norm of mythical average (that can be manipulated by a hegemonic model. This called the best theory (for avoiding the word of dictator), against the bio-ecology?

Formally geometric approach of solids often makes use of **Hamiltonian** or **octonions**. As reference to formalize the box or the object. But approaches of trajectories, pathways, positioning; many are using sort of **triangulation**. This 'turning around' "triangulations of a finite point set, forms a **flip graph** that can be embedded isometrically into a **hypercube**, if and only if (iff) the point set has no empty convex pentagon.

Point sets of this type include convex subsets of lattices, points on two lines, and several other infinite families. As a consequence, flip distance in such point sets can be computed efficiently." [In one sentence you have much of such a formal approach].

A high-level view of the flip graph has a 3 × 3 grid of points has 64 triangulations of this point set [an object not an abstract point]; grouped according to their diagonal edges. Flips are shown directly as edges within each group, while the number of lines; between each pair of groups indicates the number of flip graph edges, connecting pairs of triangulations in those two groups."

The previous in easy geometry may inspire you about which forms you could have to 'drive': polytope with sides, edges, networks, symmetries to describe its forms and structures. This may look like enough for a given object say as some framework of relative system: 3 dimensioned. Eventually followed in time by a series of views, 2 or 3 dimensions or instantaneously like; when adding the vector of time at each point; as an object in a field.

This would be like for the design; of a 'coherent head' or; formal *nucleus* of many uses. And possibly in a formal systemic relative system as our meso-level. Or any sort of structuring policy which would be important enough for being 'integral' if not willing to be a system. Among subsystems which are prone and just willing to be consistent informative links ... the social economy of tomorrow? If social scientists understand their theory not to proliferate in the grabbing of public or social funds not at the service of fake truth? [Economics of the limits of knowledge].

But you may also have to move your lens appropriately. Either you are in lower levels of relative systems (micro); or you are higher (macro) and in those movements; along the 'scale of complexities'. To evidence other sorts of structures to care about. Or because appearing: emergence or repeating similarities along scale(s). Fractals are nice partial concepts.

In the narrowest way of simple dimensions; were no structures are much existing or developed at some dimension (or pack of dimensions); appearing at higher dimensions? [Probably a need to naturally examine groups and systems formations?].

Other just from disorder, but possibly providing ordering structures. Care also structures you may not see when on them (you just see bundles of fibers) and better see when at some distance (such as strange attractors). [Which formally is a bit trickier] or have we to stay with those? - Of infinitely slippery waxed anti-chambers of toady courtiers?

You have more overview. It could be good to look at strange attractors forms [Despite uneasy to see the true flows of percolations of means]. In strange attractors to find the disposal of planes, lines which may direct, without being part of (in the simplest reductions: tori). Once you have seen the form in a relatively close volume, or plane of trajectories. With the computers they are obtained by high numbers iterations.

Formulas of such formal behaviors are in fact often quite simple. Out the knowledge their management requires from mathematicians they need friendly sorts of pedagogic simulations. So as to understand their underneath important phenomenology. Most do not need to be able to reproduce the general heuristic of analytic solutions. But they may understand the importance of some shared automatisms, to maintain the 'strange attractor' also with individuals' involvements.

[Which sort of these fundamental anchors forms economy you can have? If the society is almost organized by the brutal; to punish those not seeing any esoteric ghost at all. But a fundamental natural way?–Wait the next natural disaster just for giving a hand to networks of corruption? That your own transnational fellow citizens have organized with the implicit help of aid-workers?].

Now, we follow the intuition, concerning time (plural, 'para-metric,' discrete, combining-coinciding-closure, etc.). It turns more a relative informative parameter of a system, just a local field metric. Not just of one to one; but one for all one possible in the area. Parameters which are expressing the informative partial ordering are valid for all similar particles in the region, into another 'system's time-life' (broader universe containing the region). Thus a fundamental particle has in the range of possibilities (of integrability?) different times ... with the local time of fundamental particles has otherwise its life.

Strange attractor can be an ordering possibly shared and distributed. Parametric equation not of one lone (numerous iterated) but the order for as many as caught in the region and the number of trajectories or loops could be for one (trapped?) or cardinal of particles of the same type (filling and saturating?). Thus strange attractors (tentatively) an 'ordered fibered space' time open to many similar, composing a field of as many that could be packed and spontaneously share the rule of order.

Strange Attractor: in the mathematical field of dynamic systems, an attractor is a set of numerical values toward which a system tends to evolve. It makes it in a wide variety of systems starting conditions. System values that get close enough to the attractor values remain close; even if slightly disturbed. Types of attractors respect: 1) Fixed point; 2) Finite number of points; 3) Limit cycle; 4) Limit tori.

Visually and in the 3 dimensions space strange attractors look like filling a delimited volume, with a structured form (in most empty space), looking like a curled hunk of hairs); which is obtained by the higher numbers iterations and trajectory of a given function (dynamic system, generally non-linear, sensitive to initial conditions ... or specification of primary parameters?). Shape with possibilities regions not in the 3 dimensions: plane, lines.

We have to care to make a distinction between principles, shaping the logic of a relative system [as emergence of **'constructal'** (... in the Bejan's sense), in a way the functions push the form; and a structure that would like to be expanded as a **fractal** (... in the Mandelbrot sense) or possibly said the structures pull the forms? [In complex nature it is more probably both at the same time ... asymmetrically].

Care about the shades often missed by the popular pictures. There are not enough good manuals 'only for profanes'. **Fractals** are about self-similarities (of form or pattern), have non-integer dimensions but formally 'grow top-down ... by divisions.' **Constructal** the 'mirror's effect' is bottom up ... but expansion physically limited? - We have mentioned the primary dualism; else energetically limited ... or formally capped by lack of economy; of algebraic group? ... And a mid-concept may be with **'smooth-fractals'** involving **convex integration** and not properly fractal]. Constructal comes more from physics; maybe more formally proper would the concept of a 'smooth fractal'.

Structural Approaches

(From Pearl) "To approach of structural equation an equation $y = \beta x + \varepsilon$ (simple linear form) is said to be structural if in an ideal experiment. Where we control X to x and any other set Z of variables (not containing X or Y) to z. The value y of Y is given by $\beta x + \varepsilon$ which is not a function of the settings x and z.

It has a claim of invariance: the statistics of Y under condition $d_o (x)$ should remain **invariant** to the manipulation of any other variable in the model. This claim appears as $P (y \mid d_o (x), d_o (z)) = P (y \mid d_o (x)$ for all Z disjoint $\{X \cup Y\}$. Meaning of structural equation model: $b = \partial/\partial x. E[Y \mid d_o (x)]$ where X is held at x by external control.

We have to interpret $1/\beta$ as the change in E (X) per unit change of Y. But this conflict change of E (X) ought to be 0 (or stay '$_o$'?) if Y does not appear as an independent variable in the original structural equation for X. Counter argument with the one side casual relation (out of the model) and that ε cannot be both uncorrelated to x and to Y, thus β and $1/\beta$ cannot both have causal meaning."

'Mystical' error terms: $\varepsilon = y - E[Y \mid \delta_o (x)]$ traditionally interpreted as representing the influence of omitted factor concept; which instructs judge whether there could be factors that simultaneously influence several observed variables; and operational definition no substitute when to decide whether pairs of error terms can be assumed to be un-correct [selection bias eventually welcomed?–serendipity].

Effects:
- total effect of X on Y given by $P (y \mid d_o (x))$, namely the distribution of Y while X is constantly held at x and all other variables are permitted to run their natural course;

- direct effect of X on Y given by P (y | d₀ (x) d₀ (sXY)), where SXY is the set of all observed variables in the system except X and Y.

Exogeneity is another necessary concept in models. Consider 'exogenous determinations' on the model a common in econometrics and with a structural perspective for the present case. Exogeneity distinguished 3 types of exogeneity: **weak, strong** and **super**, the former 2 are statistical the later one is causal;

- super-exogeneity captures the structural invariance of certain weighted relationships, it is discernable from the topology of the causal diagram;
- exogeneity if there is a set of parameters of the post-intervention probability; identifiable from the conditional distribution; equal for any 2 models satisfying the theory of the model, there exists a kind of error-based exogeneity.

[Of course we summarize a lot or more simply briefly recopy a minimum. You will receive more information further or the other volume].

Dynamic System: Or Time Evolving System

Systems evolve, including the highly complex ones of our interest (at our level of complexity or erring complications). There are no, deep green roots for ecological terrorism in this essay ... we do not pretend that many natural laws are not harsh to humans). Observe; in a perspective, of complexity scale. What we seek in the most micro-level, the one of universe is primarily. Not to pretend you will just take the model of physics: 'theory of everything', add the layer of your social economic system. Put above the one of your macro-environment criteria and there you have solved all easily [Cross fingers in the nose is ... painful!].

If wanting to apply a framework of the system, with the micro-level, you will probably have to narrow; to neighboring supportive complex system; close to your phenomenologies, since that your transforms. Just that in a universe, you will obey the laws of physics (and they offer plenty of opportunities). What seems necessary is that these opportunities may have frameworks still not very explicit. Neither formally they are 'correct enough'. But once that work made, and computed such sort of relative formal system model. They can be retaken and more easily specified, closer to you meso-level of interest.

> That is to say, it is like your food system. You will probably not get down to the electrons and protons of your food. But from there take the framework (formally quite good food supplies, in terms of dietetic). And level it, at that of potatoes and meat matching them. With your-self (eating) and replaced in your ecosystem productivity.

> A proper modeled framework provides reference and anchor points of economic interest, modular, possibilities of simulations. You can manage diversity of perspectives, approximations from similar problems and vary the sorts of selections and statistics.

> Network learning should not need to remake all the modeling; nor all the data recorded again. Close to your special-case specified models. With a capture of specific values of parameters easy to input. To inform you properly on your options and possibly it could mention probable effects or defects of your decision. That may be communicated to other devices.

In the example one or two dozen(s) of your health and body data (already available in a computer-port device) the aim is to dialogue if you want and possibly also relate with the half-dozen captors your condition may need.

Dynamic System has generally 1) Set of **States** S; 2) **Outcomes** X; 3) **Outcome function** $G(S) \rightarrow X$; 4) **State Transition Function** F (S, X) $\rightarrow$ S; 5) (Deterministic or random.)

Dynamics stationary states: stable highly organized equilibria observe, in facts, sustained yet not critically deficient energetic flows with double flows on dissipative structures:

- Producers of entropy (common of non-reversible reactions);
- Inputs of free energy taken from the environment.

Trajectories:

- Instantaneous speed of moving objects, they are considering free or interacting motion and avoidance or meetings (shocking or smoothly);
- Tangent line at any chosen point on a curve;
- Maximum and minimum values of function;
- Curve length measure, areas of the region, volume of an enclosed space, location of the center for mass.

$$V (p) \leq [S (v)-S (u)]/[v-u] \leq V (q)$$

with S: movement; V: speed; instead of V: k for the local rate of change; Minimum $\leq$ [f (v)-f (u)]/[v-u] $\leq$ Maximum

Orbitals are essential, observing:

- **periodical or conservative**, all applications in the space itself. This space being a *torus*, the class of applications are conservative of areas, fixed points of hyperbolic types (as saddle-point) may exist as a source, elliptic points are possible. A periodic system shows a simple diagram.
- **Almost periodic**: examples as with Poincaré's 3 bodies, homogeneity (for which one known orbital allows to know all, equations are linear.
- A **stochastic** movement can fill the space of phases without (emerging) structures;
- **Chaotic** (or hyperbolic) motion has exponential divergence, and high susceptibility to initial conditions; a chaotic system after a long time may show a fractal structure (across scale self-similar pattern) called a strange attractor.

Problems are that it is not known how to associate the representation of all orbitals, thus only select 'useful ones' applying Plancherel's formula. If orbit dimensions are maximum its Lie's algebra is abelian. For abelian groups, in harmonic analysis commutation there is the Fourier transform only on its Lie algebra not on the group.

In representation theory of semisimple Lie groups: Plancherel theorem for spherical functions is a generalisation in non-commutative harmonic analysis of the Plancherel formula and Fourier inversion formula; in the representation of the group of real numbers in classical harmonic analysis. It has connection with differential equations. The Plancherel theorem gives the eigenfunction expansion of radial functions for the Laplacian operator on the associated symmetric space X. It also gives the direct integral decomposition into irreducible representations of the regular representation on $L^2(X)$.

Now we are talking of system evolution which may be described as a **time indexed trajectory**, in the space-phases of n dimensions. Rather than study separately each variable the system is one pointed and describes in a space of n dimensions. In phase space the speed regime is directly observed. When the system changes its dynamics the system's point describes a trajectory in the space of phases. [Space of phases may be somehow partitioned in different regions by critical limits].

Among the different kinds of functions providing geometric forms, a question to rise for a concept of the system is about the combination of different kinds of geometry. Say when we speak of somehow finite object with one (sphere), 2 or more n foci (ellipse)? - We cope with elliptic functions, as a whole. But if such elliptical form we have some m hole(s) we may have, locally some hyperbolic forms.

Maybe 2 kinds of networks with foci in any universe are to consider: the one 'globally' of elliptical expanding-expanded-inertial and locally attracting (by gravity) and the one of 'localities' hyperbolic-holes

A bit difficult since the gap of the simple expression possibly witnessed in cosmic displays. Could be formally similar to those relevant at our levels of complexities?

See that by the side of 'cosmic evidence':
- the global of our phenomenological concern (celestial bodies or atomic part of the atom-field dual) may so be 'small' (respect to field, dark matter...)
- force overall (gravity) or largest range attractive: celestial bodies (but originally and inertia-separated (also to consider in movement, 'infrared shift');
- propelled attracting objects, their existence maintained dynamically in their region balancing between attraction centripetal force and inertia centrifugal one;
- narrowly also attractive and repulsive forces play from 'order separation' (2 forms of electric charges produced by 'order'?) - [electric order provided by neutral into heavy positive and light negative?] attracting if of opposite sign; sub-dispersing if having the same sign (unless strong interaction);
- could cosmic holes (formally the low densities between levels density scales) be provided by expansion of previous holes (active or passive existence of no-zone?); passive creation of holes would be by nearby attractive foci (or nodes) which clean around them;
- then between foci (2, 3 or more, limited by coalescence) there are interstices (either emptied or filled (since, even without 'nuclear forces' or fields of *vacuum*, we may have still different, conflicting or cooperating forces; so holes either unstable (nothing after anything) either stable (anything or nothing).

Passing by the existing foci (as nodes); if there is n-nodes existing maintained network of foci ('outer' balance between centripetal attracting-centrifugal repulsive in the given global elliptical-like expanding universe (or piece of it). The observed distribution of foci may network them polygonal after n-gones (especially because also attracting) and is maintaining relative distances when staying (because the balance centripetal-centrifugal). Or is changing by birth-death effects (existence-association-fusion- 'self-death' (and outburst of energy?).

Contrary to what the reader may imagine we are not so much for suggesting a new physics model, our epistemology is not appropriated for that. We are more in the intent to inspire about the combination of formal behaviors; in such space frameworks. Like having foci-nodes-polyhedron-contour-outline-of (near-by) universe with its holes, it's bodies, the trajectories.

A formal system that could make use of the different formal geometry options: elliptic (objects-environment), hyperbolic (holes-fields of objects; metric-linear-gauge-norm-time or space that could help to measure. And the pieces of that would be: segments, trajectories (parabolic, hyperbolic, elliptic), periods, twists, pivots) for focus.

Management of these forms is universal and. Can be aided by interactive programs. If primary in complex systems understood as roots; you may then understand what is core to respect. The margins you can work, preserve and use. Be it only in an intuitive way if wanting some way out of destructions and; world-wide ways of governance not based on the aggressions of your neighbors, nor their fake altruism, nor the 'unsustainable' expertise. Thus avoid the damages of hysteria as well as of compulsions.

[Formally a primary is with between 2 forms of formal behaviors: the informative (or integrative) one; for example, we could have the elliptic for the widest and the hyperbolic for the holes inside the widest... But there are probably many other pairs of the sort. With operations and formal management of equations, physicists use plenty. [It you want your pizza not turn a bubble of hot air, make holes).

Compulsively modern fundamental physicists are trying to find the Theory of Everything...Which could be a kind of systemic concept, that would be our formal 'first head of primary *nautilus* shell'; so for any system of reference. Which could help along the scale; set how to configure a relative formal system for 'working in the evolutionary conditions' as some (complex) unit, standing on the complexifications reached and allowed by the 'entropic conditions'.

['Entropic conditions' are mirror-like complement of residual structure; produced by ordering complement. Which general issue is disordered back to the 'ugly old time before', in facts a great source of everything and of many partial contributions to keep open, robust and resilient the ordered functions-informed-structures. As far as this last in their environmental range; inscribe within the locally narrowed rules of the Universe. And if uneconomical, as by too large energetic involvement, the achieved level of complexity may simplify. Possibly in an accelerated way by entropic massive release. Domino's effect of the Chinese boxes integration?

A level of living bio-cells in a tissue, this may be called apoptosis and narrowly has even received some use from autopoiesis].

Then once the 'first head of primary *nautilus* shell' has been applied, to obtain the fundamental supplementary information emerged and mastered at the level: neguentropy: natural or possibly 'human biased or made'. But we would have to clean the 'confusion of our models from artifacts', misconducts and human-made noises.

In all those relations either consistent. At the complexity 'level of the stage' with enough economic formal representation. Possibly to co-respond to the atom-field kind or patterns of informative relations. Followed and provided consistently by nature or imagined and advanced by humans. Not necessarily as sustainably as expected by humans: humans' management on the fringes.

In the 'first head of primary *nautilus* shell' ... it would be semantic and syntactic [if our aim to make language **meet-match-fit** the best of our understanding of nature]. Either physics specifically 'solves' formal paradoxes (at least in a generally solvable system) or to semantic physics paradox, syntactically discriminated. See their emergence, lexically properly completed. Allowing this to provide the **best invariances candidates** and properly the **qualified symmetries breaking**s ... evolutionarily selected and/or separated?

Formally to imagine 'nautilus shell stage', a sort of extensible elliptic form provided hyperbolic holes; communicating with remaining *vacuum* space, all around [imagine a sort of giant red-cell shape like with trans-holes as optimum shape and exchanges? (Since dark matter?)

In the one hole case a doughnut like tori. To imagine that after the minimal (economic optimal) shape, considered the reason of curvature radii the distribution and size of smooth holes may follow rational numbers series? [This essay is turning a formal science fiction novel?]

Infinitesimal Infiniteness and... Stop it!

Historically, Leibnitz and Newton's modern invention of the differential calculus has been made to cope with **infinitesimal calculus** close to absolute zero and infinity. Possibly something less conceivable from Huygens's anterior schemes. Once the treatment of limits somehow fixed (fundamentally it is not yet solved (despite Cantor's shortcut?) differential calculus operations have been made easy.

So Euclidean could and straight line calculus evolved in the formal sciences are primary. Even if some reasons remained undefined: $0/0 \, \infty/\infty$ and so on. It turned so easy to find the way to calculate at the limits and/or and used to simplify the formula of derivatives or integration, equations. The formulation of the relations between series and functions (in the infinite development) is more recent. Where you may meet Schwartz (a French mathematician of the 20th century. His theory of distributions, gave its meaning to functions such as the Dirac delta's).

Infinitesimal calculus may have contributed to biasing mathematics towards symbolism. For most profanes this made an underestimation of arithmetic logics, as long as the most important thing is to have the clean solution of the simple equations; more important than the formulation. All abstraction with mathematics was to give clean pure numbers. [Sort of nasty cleanliness]. Contrastingly the Physicians in the mirror effect tried to obtain the formula expressing their cognitive work understanding of physics. [Physicians and mathematicians' meetings because most primary physics formulation elegantly match mathematical primary rigor: brain is quite smart].

Childhood illnesses of logic with reduction and simplicity but still expressive of phenomenological ambiguities. Thus easy to conceive abuses, under short-cuts; so as to *focus* on axiomatization and concepts of calculus. Also the difficulty to mention of their relations with human languages argumentation lay techniques. That was more substantial to life's earning ways: rhetoric, dialectics, rituals, future predictions, justifications of nasty projects: of imperial and industrial alienations and so on.

So as long as the pathways of fundamental sciences first principles yet not properly discovered; why care about mathematical details of qualities? –It was in arithmetic logic to word and size, discreteness enough for that. Could be that not much more important to match qualities with quantities?

Infinity axioms were expressing the existence of a very large power, inaccessible to cardinal's axiom [thus a 'huge complement' … but a word?]. Vague proposition of Cohen came with: "any enunciate of arithmetic is **decidable** in a set theory enriched by an infinity axiom… Or with a negation axiom of choice". Also in the same vein you have Martin's axiom.

[Martin's axiom says that all cardinals less than the cardinality of the *continuum* behave roughly like $\aleph_0$ It is used to control certain forcing arguments (as in computer sciences). It is a statement that is independent of the usual axioms of ZFC set theory. It is implied by the continuum hypothesis, but it is consistent with ZFC and the negation of the continuum hypothesis].

With the **negation of the hypothesis of continuity** in numbers type. This can be a negation axiom of choice on measurable set in the sense of Lebesgue.

[Lebesgue produced the most achieved definition of mathematical integration since his theory of measure. A basic of these is a theory of integration. Lebesgue sets the infinitesimal partition as *ex-post* achieved regularity (?) which technically makes works of integration quite easier. Intuitively it looks like fair to start with the achieved integration. Then it is quite necessary to most calculus in physics instead of the classically first learned in the school curriculum (Riemann's) which looks in the concept more an *ex-ante* infinitesimal partition… That is sorts of debate that may look like mathematicians perversion but making sense when having to program software, and conceptual work at the borders of proper logic].

So when we need to take account **discontinuous densities, compactness** we have to combine economically the discreet intervals; by tending to continuity fillings or insert sequences 'in holes' (?). So as continuous scale to divide, share or spate. Once realized that nature with enormous and far distant limits is discrete. Then, to find hard to imagine the whole universe fully filled since the start and forever [… Even when stuffed with dark matter; out of 'thinly fielded' with material and almost non-material particles' waves?].

And infinitesimal focus observing how; we human and life phenomena are so exceptional but also so small, so weak, so close, so diverse and so short-lived. So common also with energetic (or metabolic) characteristic dimensions or sizes.

Thus if to go on; with good things of the information's revolution, we need to be better when setting the limits of our enterprises. Define about what they are (you, your phase of motion, your phases of existence, your environment or your universe). And examine if mathematics and logics both incomplete in the first place, the limits of the range, the hierarchies of time, those also of operations…

... so as not to be misguided by fake purity ... that you do not need materiality but have a whole "system" (not of our sort) for deciding the fate of others' faith.

Of course, the reader has read that we find no problem to a first primary spiritual package providing everyone believes as hoped. The 'fake purity' of what we think here is about the over-determinist extent forced brutally by manipulators of religions or sects; in quite most commonly invoked as 'purity'. This is a complete physics and logical nonsense. Physically the 'almost complete disorder of quantic *vacuum* has not the properties hoped from God's. In that you may hope after evidence that his will be pushed out disorder. Then enormous order to structure details are obtained not by the means of purification (neither in the formal, nor in the physics registers).

For so: ground policies on such superior abstracts of purification is by physics, logically insane. The wise choice is about assuming humane options in the reflexive way is the human phenomenon. Now apart from that the need of simplifications for possibly sharing the management, iff these are made with relatively autonomous reflexive contributors with teleological sense of precautions and possibly good sense of social means.

Limits Concepts (After Yi-Lin)

In topological space applications (or gridded web network concept) and sequences (or filter or window concept): to consider the application of some sequence and then its confirmation. Then you may have convergence to a point (polyhedron of networks, map); if existing the limit of an image is equal to a number (essential quali-quanti informative relation. Or information which would be between 2 maps bilayered (matter, energy). Unaryness in solid points (symplectic-Eigenfunction completed connex network; convex out-within concave bilayered map) provided a universe, providing environment). [Looks like a label, provided a way for structuring assuming functions of atom-field?–for assuming positive netgentropic-connexity compactness of the system?]

Inductive limits make use of set families. Set of indices is 'right' filtering. And inequalities: equal, superior or inferior such as to define inductive applications. Superior, upper or major, inferior, lower or minor, makes use of ordered sets and non-strict comparators, to define lowest minor or highest majors. Limits of a set family, reviews the sequence of sets and consider a superior or an inferior limit; when parameter tends to infinity. Inductivism's main technical problem, as prone formal method; is about when variation related to formal artifacts, emergence of within properties and evolutionary process economy: the Information/Entropy of a complex system is made).

[Thus, when you meet a number looking like random unstoppable tail, since discrete and bottom-up these questions the method improper?–more an irrational?].

Main problem of deductivism [once resolved the problems of discordance between analytic (formal) frameworks and experimental records in models of essential principles]; will be of truncations or halting in continuity or 'when and how to stop in the verification'?

[Thus what to do when top-down meeting a number looking like random unstoppable tail consider it as a transcendental 'hole'? ... suggestively].

In other words: induction often come to face a thick-wall from others' halt or avoidance of order'. It would be stupid imagine not to meet such wall, since that in the quantic is providing raw material for primary construction. Leadership fingers against the wall are stupid, and fists of dictators are rude.

Deduction refinements, mistaken by ab-dimensioned simplicity, if not avoidance, of operations (infinite calculability-like) and theories without grounds are hardly specifiable and unmanageable as policies: you ignore the proper structures, nor the implicit meanings.

(Yi-Lin extracts for most). Limits of projections consider families of sets, set products, subject of an element satisfying a relation, which is a projection. Identical application, restriction is called **canonical application**.

Limits of ordinal, order relation, recursions are their essentials. If α is a limit ordinal $\delta = (\omega^\delta)$ and $\omega^\delta > \alpha$ then: $\omega^\delta.\{\alpha\}(n)=\{\omega^\delta.\alpha\}(n)$. To consider majorization (upper bound) of primitive recursion. A relation of order defines a **lattice** if for any 2 elements exist a sup and an inf and they are well ordered if for any non-empty subset has a minimum.

Hardy class is the class of all **provable recursive function** in Peano arithmetic. Hardy's class is the smallest class of functions containing 0, all $h\alpha$, all projection functions (I_n, i (x_1, ..., x_n)=x_i) and closed under primitive recursion and substitution; for every α. Hardy function $h\alpha$ is provably recursive in Peano Arithmetic. [Hardy was a British mathematician].

To add that **Tauberian theorems** which are those that **deduce the asymptotic behavior of functions, series, integrations**, etc. since their mean values. [Asymptotic is about the approach at the infinite or inverse (0), as a directions' guide. It is a straight line or a point limit to which converge the curve of the studied function.]

Also in physics to consider approach of **critical points**; for observing huge changes of behavior. This is where **renormalization approach of multiple-level of scale** applies. When looking at different microscopic systems and observing same near critical points. So when ignoring the microscopic details to confine attention to long length scale. But this study needs to take a kind of *continuum* limit. Now, in systems remaining inhomogeneous and fluctuating; even on the largest scale, systematic method for good fit (or detection of scale invariant emergence) is called **renormalization group**. Critical phenomena are limits like in states of matter-phase transitions. Formal approaches show very large deviations. Renormalization groups are used to **prevent divergence of calculus at the extremities**. And to examine the extent of physical principles effects across scale levels; searching in a similar way **invariants across levels of scales**.

The renormalization examines system space maps into itself, under coarse graining. Coarse graining operations shrink the system and remove microscopic degrees of freedom. Renormalization is useful in reproductive fundamental processes, distributing at different levels of scale, say as gravity. So renormalization is either a wholesome theory or pointedly introduced; but in the later way it is potentially losing the unitary sense (perturb-able systems). As a result after Connes; it is quite difficult to have a theory both unitary and renormalizability.

With the previous you have received a few insights on the concepts and approach of the limit in arithmetic kind of logic. Have a look at dictionaries of mathematics for more. Weinstein's a major one in 3 volumes but almost requiring leitfaden. [Leitfaden often appear at the start of many books of mathematics, graphs providing the main connecting thread or theme].

Simplifications of Frameworks and Patterns as Symplexity

Having seen some notions posed by fundamental formal knowledge, and their manageability; to clear the medley term mentioned by many ignoring what they say when talking about 'complexity', thus more the basket of fears.

Fundamental difficulties represented by elementary formal concepts, **modularity, multiplicity of scale, similarities sort of dynamics** and causes, **branched diversities, heterogeneity** are primary concept often incompatible with many dogmas of economics.

Much misunderstood in most practices but intuitively much imbuing cognitive individual practices as well as reprinted in the consistent statistical mechanisms; but well ignored by the positivist determinist data collections.

Not to observe that many contains and practices of social arts are simply stigmatizing analytical efforts of that sort. Making them ridiculous after the aesthetics of their circumlocutions (nothing consistent with the relevant looking like dynamic frameworks needed). Disqualifying intents of formalization and quantification since the reign of abstract dimensionless is profitable; without need of true social yields, and more implicit and mostly ignored thermodynamic ones. We have to provide some considerations about the resources of simplifications and reductions or better, port-folio concentration. [With much to say, more in the next to come volume of essay].

It is to imagine the levels of robust and efficient selection processes (meanwhile preserving flexibility, at least unconscious). See, for example in the brain the numbers by the billions of neurons, the basic cells of the brain. The thousands involved in elementary complex answers. All the structures part in that and we cannot detail much. That is for converging to some half a dozen primary options, by short periods of time; are relevant to ideas and concepts, in a matter of few seconds. The coefficient of 'focusing' is 'monstrous'.

Without missing the backward processes that are waiting and making those ideas consistent respect with 'a project'. Somehow you have like few dozens of complex processes [2 hemispheres, half a dozen neuroanatomy levels, half a dozen main neurotransmitters networks; like a dozen or less of different areas in the cortex of the brain; some hundreds of cortex columns, etc.); that can be recruited more or less unconsciously or automatically like in a day period of work.

In physics the levels of orders where everything starts in our Universe are 10^{-34} for Planck's constant for joule second, 10^{-35} respect to meter for Planck's length; 10^{-8} respect to kilograms for Planck's mass values. [Planck's constants often consider considered the lowest or starting ones ... of order?

So in these ideas that mathematics could reflect the quantities of the world; a question that will necessarily arise is about the characteristics limits at each level of complexity system. And then at which distance (or order) to start our formal, 'simple and relative head'); and if this may be inspired by physics's constructions of the Universe? Since there is no doubt, we are fundamentally 'that'.

Formal relative system which could be easily related to emergence of new properties; as indexed by numbers [at least prime numbers? Or in which range of deviations the quantities may derive from qualities (and the converse) or more simply avatar of similar patterns already existing below.

Observing physics definitions at minima. Like primary forces only 4; but then how they are framed ... and can be modular 'within' reframed? Not with so many levels (since nuclear physics atoms to biophysics components a there are 4 to 6 levels of forces, all avatars of same primary 'outer' forces as gravity and electromagnetic. Discrete fundamental number of quarks [those 'below known fundamental particles']. Most common components of matter (less than half a dozen?).

With fundamental particles it is to add some dozens of more transient ones looking like more required or produced by transformation. Chemical elements for a hundred, and not much more with some unstable.

The ways of chemical reactions obtained from electronic orbitals (see periodic table of elements; cardinal of lines and, columns than outer most electronic layers made the 1st to exchange (complement); in all not much more than one hundred elements. With 2 dozen humans' realities generally useful, with cores the one able to get in structural functions (4 or 3 co-valences) or functions issues (2 or 1 valances) and kind of ambiguous molecules water and respect to it hydrophilic-hydrophobic ones.

Ambiguous under the environmental regular variations conditions have near phase-space critical conditions (solid-liquid-gas).

Then going up into extraordinary higher levels of complexity and diversity. But obtained, at each state/level/grade levels (of details?); from so few primary components. At each step, able to assume an avatar of functions (non-mathematical concept), that seems so similar to 'sign'.

Quite similar to the sparse numbers (with some details) you have as basic options as in life's cardinals: amino-acids, nucleic acids, genetic information structure; many basic biochemical have in all that only few dozens basic blocks: alphabets somehow redundant for few (but not just one (1)) alternative).

Notice that in nuclear cell DNA you have basically 4 bases on the nuclear material 3 of them are coding for an amino acid. Making this 'codon' made of 3 bases →60 motifs (redundant) →2 to 4 codons coding for each amino-acids. Amino-acids providing all the structural and functional properties defined with proteins. (2 other macro-elements components, carbohydrates and lipids are simpler and have more specific functions (in animals).

An important point to that is how not so extraordinary in cardinals of 'ordering' qualities at 'transversal state/level/stage/grace. Maximum complex units use the facilities of 'lower complex systems' [we have plenty of bacteria in us]. We observe so, large highly complex amounts so packed possibly mixing with and involving plenty of contradictive mechanisms.

Formally this could be not so difficult to enumerate; but is it also able to provide considerable phenomenological diversities within the 'principles'? Disconcerting contradictory pairs are well used by nature to empower its economical evolutionary processes. This also has plenty of use of entropy. Humans societies already with plenty of sciences but so humanely improper at promoting efficient nicer alternatives should care about these details.

> Primarily and formally the curiosity would be for elementary perplexities. An example with Feigenbaum's tree of binary bifurcations. Could also be about the compositions of quarks (after the properties of particles as inferred by Quantic Theory, elementary Pauli's matrices algebra and theory of algebraic groups.

All pose the questions about how could be 'amounts and units of systems indexing'. Since the qualities provided emerge from the smallest levels of matter orderings. Eventually look at the properties of fundamental particles according composition, if not by their index. Then how primary 'forms' could also be transcribed at higher numbers?

It seems quite important how to keep the relative simple **algebraic frameworks** (and the symmetries and anti-symmetries they carry)? In sorts of **modular ways up**. That leads to the questions about how invariants are kept. And how similarities are repeated. Maybe not exactly all, nor in the same way. That is with specificities of levels, valid there: as sorts of **evolutionary processes** (previous to biology).

Then in the humans' interests to delimit manageability of that. Not too complicated nor too over-simplistic ... in a 'rightly' systemic way (in the way we understand it more?). And what would be the limits? Would it be enough with lower properties (conceiving the emergences just probable)? Could we think an iterated binary: yes-no; with what is kept from below. **Building blocks keeping the index** and **Turing's machine jumping after the prime numbers?** A sort of modular systemic 'shuttle' (displacing the index–to 're-synchronize around the new unit'). Providing that both 'ground in the universe' (notably for the abilities to recycle or recruit). And functional premises satisfied diversely near more positive netgentropic level. Taking from entropy (and convenient entropic storages) as well as economically live on bodies of same level or just below levels, without leaving ground.

Supposing that 'shuttle' with a sort of cloak in a Turing automaton; part joined with a mechanism keeping in mind the 'the index', the main and 'the secret'. The Turing character is without memory, the 'secret' the switch field–particle; the index the distance of amount, closed (and open) all 3 by energy, the main the local and dynamic resource of hierarchy ('ordering in the nearby' ~ organized openness?). [The 'secret' is at some points the source of des-intrication if required. You have the memory loss at the level or; the 'relative loss' made when path before, or relative irreversibility].

To consider that 'opening energy' like outer variation of entropy; inputting into relatively closed energy. Like inner variation stabilizing entropy? Time between ('pulsations' of lower organized fields and systems. But also, that of maximum complexity achieved level average life. [... This makes that 'time' is also information or at least a model ... if not a wise cut or division: passing the non-null coefficient under the bar on the other side of equal sign].

'Handle-able' (or 'work-able') meaning the possibilities of an influence (in the range of possibilities) and economy. The later as a process; of slow or fast, selection? The reader ought to have clearly in mind that this handling will not be just 'as hse would like': in a determinist way. Like for exactly mastering the future. Much more a mixture of manageable parameters and narrowed uncertainty (ies) but far from 'to erase' ...

... Metrically and methodologically, similar to Heisenberg's principle of uncertainty. [And it is divisible in a similar systemic way?–system of not (¬)?].

Things that in policies would have plenty of applications. Starting modestly, for example not to pretend that the macroeconomics of a given social-economical entity could ignore effects of size, consider each country the same (and practice discrimination), and so on. [More probably accounting for difference and properly practicing empathy positive to the commonness ... that is: not a sort of discriminating sympathy].

Effectively: even with crazy dictator best hard hand of a that would be wanting to reign on a land without humans. First; all with that universe is together. [Have been and will return to be? –'Consumed material']. And is mostly made of probabilities or uncertainty? Ordinal order, much less than Cardinal disorder (?). Even if more meaningful in amounts and this, not because of ignorance. But, because the ways of animals needing to maintain and restore that is for not producing critical 'netgentropic' imbalances. To maintain and keep moving in differently moving environments.

Thus insulation-isolation and warming are overloading returns to lower-ness. Meanwhile openness at any cost can have also destructive effects. So, can be the models of preventing social macro-system to balance and preserve their core information? So as societies too ergodic-like informed in excess and wanting to maintain their high yields of waste. Without enough recycling and at the expense of other societies. [Autarchy, owning, nationalism, free-exchange, consumerism, globalism] ... are very poor-minded in their excesses of wealth].

But care this is with our frameworks. Actually traditional modeling methods are for many in social economy quite disconcerting; if not entropy high release promoting. Not so different seem to be the patterns of inefficient good will. Not to tell about many other social arts. Even if many people understand a lot; many people are forced to do what they can, and do well, and have or copy their model of aspirations (or wealth), too tightened, too restricted or too conditioned sources of inspiration. Some are practicing consciously enough properly. But the margins of consciousness are much lower than the ones of whole-ness and are not necessarily meeting the needs? They have plenty of basic feelings and 'emotions' well felt necessary.

Formally the resources for modeling are huge. They are as atypical theories, waiting or already used for having better uses in sort of social-economical modeling. Theory of **perturbation, percolation, evolution, dynamic analysis, control** and **synchronization** and **simulations** well advanced. But often with not enough 'wholist comprehension of main meanings'. Be it just about basic uncertainties, better preparations for care.

In societies, to be on the edge of positive changes requires links, flows, capacities and skills to articulate different formal-abstract kinds of sub-mechanics. For diversity of sources they also need probable-improbable physics. Not just with claiming since dimension-0 and with much ergodic agitation, proliferate 'superior' concepts; as sophisticated or nice-harsh as they can be. If equipped with materialistic traditional means of empowerment; that may mean too much destruction. Be it humane or not some effects are for 'taking advantage of entropy and neguentropy.

Thus the 2nd order goal of primary policy would be, about minimizing complexities and negative netgentropy within netgentropy; maximizing the complications of the artificial. Meanwhile technological society overall environmental impact is still unclear if not-(at best) a zero-sum society (Ellul, Thurow, Becker), by the side of good feelings, highly destructive on the other dimensions.

Some have with the environmental threats many apprehensions. Since they can express more their destabilizing effects by the side of anthroposcene anomies. Of course, with plenty of places for better thermo-economics savings. To care nevertheless: the decays of de-growth may turn quite unpopular and carry a risk or counter dynamics of disorder.

With formal scale of complexity (?), there is the need to **reposition differentiability and integration range**?–such as referred to general solvability. Bottom-up along (be just series of indices). In effects the processes of complexity in physics develop, 'within the extreme range'. At least for the one of our concerns. So why humans should pretend to be far from that?

There is the whole universe (in many places too hot but where we have learned to put some devices ... or look at with fewer reflecting mirrors). And we are on the cooler and nice places, open and receiving enough energy at our services. These places became more complex because nicer environments were better distributing 'soft' resources. At some stage |> informed<| state objects; there turned self-replicating (possibly biological). Then increasingly achieved capacities levels of engineering. They 'succeeded' to pick from stored resources. And then came the massive pressure for social-technological changes.

The wild universe is expanding in the extreme (abstract) maximum range of pure energy or pure matter (physically this is confusing). Orders came from 'inside' the environmental range orders. Often this is at one main phase-space (especially at the different sorts of solid/fluids interfaces.

[It is a bit disturbing compared to other minima; that we are only being 310K° from 0 Kelvin's degree of lowest temperature (no taste for superfluid fountain of Helium!); compared to the other minimal unit. So on Earth conditions remaining 'nice-cool' phase-spaces coexisting (mostly set by water for life) enriched too by this diversity of phases (and near sub-one's t the interfaces).

Expansion or pulsations of the Universe may trouble the picture (in billions of years); with a "not yet existing" potentials, of environmental natural, or engineered-made: disasters, globally in not much more than a quarter of millennium, for the present civilization over the whole world.

Simplified Pictures to Imagine That.

See our 2 opposed capped coni of the macro-micro levels (a conus each) cutting the present with the 'meso' at the mid. [Popular books of Hawking and Penrose quite illustrative as sources of inspiration].

Lower conus (base down) with a selection of fundamental principles up to meso level of concern. The top down reversed coni; the macro providing the umbrella of meso's development. Sort of elliptical form within a hyperbolic providing space?

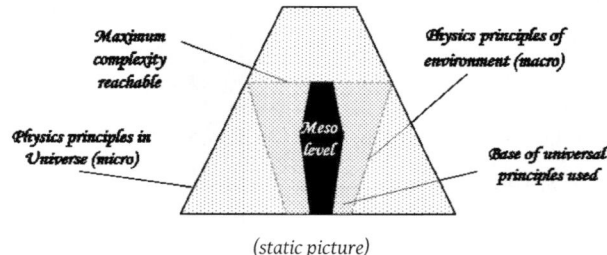

(static picture)

'Time' can also be represented by a double conus left-right the past and future, in the other opposition: top-tip, relatively providing a channel where out light speed stand the essential of the unit. A sketch base on a Minkowski kind of space (made confused by matter and mainly not at light speed on the limits of the coni). We will see more on that further.

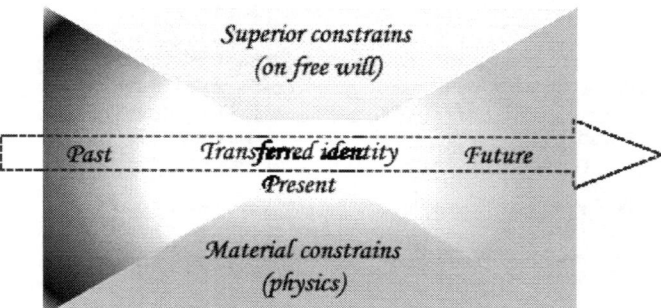

Possibly within a volume of global evolution and involution we can imagine a [parabolic?] trajectory of complexity development. [Global volume of development could be sort of an elliptic kind of development?–For so also sort of hyperbolic 'holes' and 'vacuum' to account for an order to emerge from disorder of the origin, and still many places of disorders everywhere as nearby sources?].

A 3rd dual could be (in the plane) the lower conus like the real world, the upper the corresponding to eventually potential or perspective. Taking from below some principles (but not all ... we may not be much interested in too hot principles). Examining potentials what informative pattern to report from the past to the future.

With the 'risks' (which are not necessarily only disastrous if we care both not to trigger too much; the sources of disorders and they avoid the rigid effects of orders. Naturally, these often spontaneously care better. Meanwhile, the artificial (humans ones) are potentially not-smart disordering ones. So narrowing much the controls over subjective abstractions, respect to an environment, more or less competed or cooperating.

The meso-shuttle between that of our interested management.

Menger's Sponge

Now, if you remind that we develop 'within'; as thermodynamically; that is the start of the first dual: order/disorder. We have about a beautiful representation in a cube as a cubic 'grey box' with Menger's sponge.

Menger sponge is a fractal curve. It is a 3-dimensional generalization of Cantor's set and Sierpinski's carpet (fractal in 2 dimensions). Menger showed (1926) that the sponge is a universal curve for all compact metrizable spaces of topological dimensions one (1) and thus for all Jordan curves in space. [Commonly we like to measure, anyhow].

Every curve is homeomorphic to a subset of the Menger sponge. Curve here means any compact metric space of Lebesgue, covering dimension 1. This includes trees and graphs with an arbitrary countable number of edges, vertices and closed loops, connected in arbitrary ways. To notice that it encloses an (almost?) empty volume.

In simpler words draw cubes with sides from which you take of the mid third part and then iterate down scale on each segment. At different levels of scale and in the volume of a cube you will obtain different sizes of very ordered holes. Pictorially you obtain a sponge, with holes at each level similar a fractal.

Now have a mental flip-flop. Imagine you full-filled cube your space of energy or field and the places of holes in effect the switches to order: registering emergence of matter (from energy). Thus what you obtain is the reverse of the sponge, the places of holes were the matter, around the quantic vacuum. [Also with different levels? – Dirac's sea, field of atoms (which stay enough, cosmic bodies in their 'ethereal'?].

Imagine that somehow curve or round shape. Expending, fields maintaining (as places of balances or dynamic equilibria) but possibly with inner reframing (matter bodies attract each other and disperse since they are in motion, aggregate, disaggregate), 'sub-organize' or 'suborder' ...

... The picture of inversed Menger's sponge is a good-looking representation; as pictures of ordering Universe?

Measure the characteristics deviations between this perfect reference (with some complications with contractions and dilatations and motions) and the empirical measures...

[... in the hope that you will; from now on, wash the dish 'hand and sponge' in a different way. Rather than with a washing dishes machine?].

Of course the filled spaces of holes by matters driving probabilities of emergence will be much thinner than a 1/3 of the line, 1/9 of the carpet, 1/27 of sponge ... not so sure? Care that formally it is not necessarily the way of space dynamic diffusion].

Present (Past and Future) Solid Coni

Now for approaching time, past, present and future; we like much the useful picture starts with a double conus of projections. A volume of reason 'not yet done' is probabilistic (lacking the information of existence?). Also around a volume of minimal and maximal projections. Large nonlinear deviations (including the concept of chaotic motion). Further, non-commensurable and non-credible areas; (too stable to be true). Notice also, that physicians and mathematicians shown that order often appears on the verge of disorder.

Formally Minkowski (M_4) space time seems our picture in mind is a basic of special relativity theory (of Einstein). All notions multilinear algebra can apply to if: tensor algebra, **exterior algebra** (Grassmann); **inner algebra** (Clifford), **Cartan differential calculus and duality operator** (Hodge) [Petrova's frame?].

Poincaré groups are much more important to the quantum field theory consists of the set of all transformations of M_4 to itself. A few kinds of terms and tips, since our purpose is not for expert but for simple suggestive links (in bold letters those terms).

Minkowski spacetime M with + - - - ds^2 metric (in Penrose's book notation) is a different real section, w being real and pure x, h, z imaginary. A Lorentzian real section takes w to be purely imaginary and x, h, z real where the induced ds^2 now gives + + +-

and dl^2 version of the Minkowski version. Minkowski M space is in many respect very similar to E^4. Length of the curve in E^4 is given by the same formula on E^3. $\int ds$.

Minkowski space time Geometry is also only differing in signs of signatures: (+ + +-).
$$Dl^2 = -dt^2+dx^2+dy^2+dz^2 \text{ and } ds^2 =$$
$$dt^2-dx^2-dy^2-dz^2 = g_{ab}dx^a dx^b.$$
Sphere in M the loci of points with fixed **Minkowski distance** a **from a fixed point O**.
- if a > 0 (with the +---ds² signature). We get **2 hyperbolic pieces 'bowl-shaped'** H⁺ (within the future light cone) and the hill shaped H⁻ (within the past light cone.
- For imaginary a (or with a real a and the + + +-dt²) signature we get a **one-sheeted hyperboloid,** space like separated from O.
- a **hyperbolic 'straight line'** in H⁺ is the intersection with H⁺ of a 2-sphere through O.

Angular Momentum: the components of 6-angular momentum M^{ab} are the generators of the (Lorentz) rotational motions, of Minkowski space M. The rotational motions give rise to the entire non-reflective Poincaré group.

Anyhow, the **formal mechanics of the time-space** (you have some other in Hawking Penrose book). You understand it is essential. It has nice general property in case you would like to adapt it. It is also very useful for lay thinking if you could like to 'cut time.' Probability of an event(s) to realize.

Consider that belief, uncertainty of information, *ex-ante* unrealized situation (thus probable), *ex-post* it is distrust that makes probabilities. At the minimum you have the relative probability of event realization, compared to another. And at best that is to all other non-events. Realization can be called, by analogy, in subjective matter as a '**revelation**'.

In any way we have with action a double *conus* of present time, centered on realization. Past probable, despite an exact realization may stay with doubt(s) especially if the object is complex or, if some **loss of memory** can happen (like in Markov's chains). [Loss of memory, not necessarily always a bad thing: this is a determinist view].

Or if historical evidence has been probability built: *ex-post* you will only have one for sure if there is, but not without doubt on what before: History is a big liar. *Ex ante* you may have different options. Conus limit surface of some maximum speed(s) (out there are not) ... But a lay interpretation could be 'maximum speed for you stay in the good range for doing'. [As a result **Bayesian** way looks like more dynamically consistent with ambiguities of complexity?]

In the future *conus* may reappear the doubt, the probability and so on, and not in the same way as before, as realization changed it. For this one since starting point. Lay physics often use the term of '**solid angle**'; or *coni* **of projections**(s). Going one with an adaptation of double *coni* (or hyperbola bowl shape on the horizontal line, like a yo-yo) to conditioned-conditioning probability. **Bayes's calculus** has this meaning to try to catch "before" (past) for "after" (future) in "between" match of 'present.'

[But it is about conditioned probability, so not to limit to time, especially because time not so mono-spirited ... with humans].

Conditioned probabilities (not necessarily over time) cannot fully be satisfied by realization, nor understand what is complex time. The difficulty we have 'in the present' would be a sort of basic [informative at least?] frame coming from the past [like a polyhedron?], to transport into the future. [The fact is that polyhedral 'projections' has mathematically some good properties].

Now, concentrated distributions of probability, are according to the concentration of repeated events (or "meaningful average"). Observe that we may have not only one volume of reasonable projection. One is the universe or environment if explicitly and properly taken into account.

For many reasons the forms are not so simple nor reducible (and in anyway its costs maybe uneconomical). Levels of complexity have to be defined and focused. In the original graph most outer one is speediest light... More subtle way can have different spectra of speeds, and maximum energies you can input. Maximum speeds that can be observed; shades after the sort of trajectory you mind, object you move, etc.

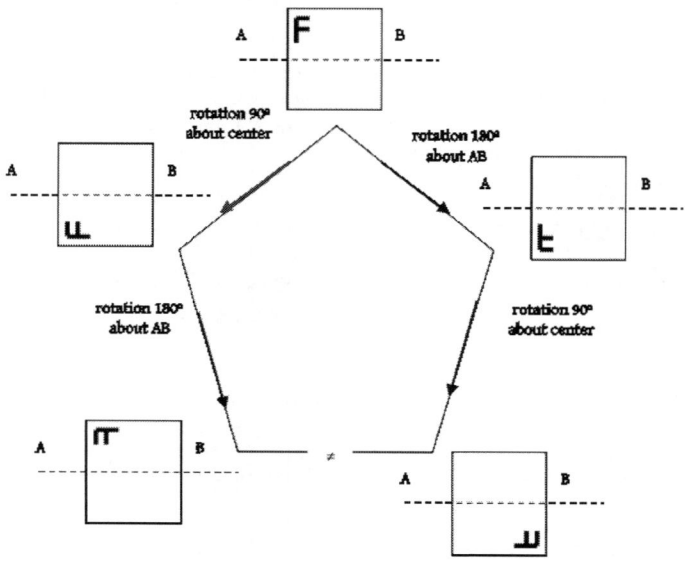

We already saw logics or mathematical kind of disturbing phenomenology evidences as in semantic paradox. There are also optic illusions made visual and subjective. Before having a look at the 'sort of ghosts' of reality we mentioned, picturing the ways that complex structures may renew their contain. Faster than you imagine way but not in wrong proportions ways, keeping the identities, in the collection of labels we care for. In biology those recycling are often called turnovers. To conceive what are formal paradoxes and also illusions, eventually provided. Since the places we are do not have all the perspective that world like the scientist 'over the crowds' of people at levels of their phenomenology and what they 'see in their brain' (all) and have under the eyes, conditioned by their emotions.

Kinds of Spaces in Physics

Euclidean space	Curved space	Minkowski space	Energy-momentum space
Fields in flat space	Space curvature	Homogeneous space (all points are equal) Poincaré groups acts transitively on this space affine space	Not homogeneous The Poincaré group acts on orbits (mass shells)
Curved line in flat space	Straight line in curved space	It can be identified with the quotient Poincaré/Lorentz Dimension: length	Vector space Dual of the translation subgroups Dimension action/length
Matter causes fields	Matter causes curvature	Elements appear as dummy variables in Quantum Field Theory calculations where they lose their space-time meaning	Conserved quantities /easily measured since transferable to apparent uses). They are also additive quantities.
Field equations for fields	Field equations for curvature	The only use in quantic field theory (QFT) lies in citing the locality of the interaction Lagrangians	All calculations of Feynman diagrams are made in this distance

Physics With Phenomenological Paradoxes

Yi-Lin summarizes different paradoxes of physics.

Olbers 'paradox': is about why night space obscure since populated by so many stars; our nights' sky ought to be enlightened. Because, in the meantime, of expanding universe existence; most stars have not emitted enough light. It takes time to travel even for light.

Unstoppable force when meeting an irremovable object's paradox: ought to be just a semantic curiosity or non-logical almost impossible coincidence (infinite-infinite). But if to happen, coincidence would produce a singularity. If not, object will keep on existing since force is unstoppable and objects are irremovable.

Vacuum fluctuation paradox: has a hypothesis about the null sum of all the universe energies; a universe would, without any physics' law violation; emerge from nothingness. But for quantic mechanics there is no real fully empty vacuum. From a microscopic region a positron-electron may create and annihilate (so-called "quantum fluctuates").

Quantic mechanics have produced various weird concepts: Maxwell's Daemon, Schrödinger's cat, Einstein-Podolsky-Rosen effect. Not the purpose of this essay to do more than mention. In lay physics of thinking, it is often more interesting how formal behaviors can mix and turn formally compatible one with the other. Doing so at quite often at different scales.

Quantic theory brought it with a dualism between formal treatment and physics intuition challenging experiments... But despite that and many counterintuitive concept, quantic theory the best experimentally proved physics.

Thus, if the proposal of a relative formal system prosper, the next step of the work would consist to develop a sort of operations between relatively achieved system, after their contiguous position. [In formal intuition, could the idea be that the cases of cardinal-ordinal numbers fed physics logics with arithmetic logics, including relation with quali-quanti informative pieces?

Informative relation could then develop as an economics. Economics is also existing in nature. The traditional management of scarcity is more fundamental with probabilities of orders, more or less extended, more scarce respect to cardinalities. So partial are equilibria more fundamental, evolutionary selections more represented by the economics of stabilities and after complexity of large systems, possibly accessed to management or/and analysis by relative formal models; those with high numbers, possibly reflected in the cognitive number of brains. To the leaders, engineers and governors and politicians, for once are not in such an abstract challenge to adapt to the uncertainties of physics, nature, environment away from dubious dogmas and paradigms.

Observing that the levels of complexities in these challenges are so huge that they require voluntary participation from as many as possible with the best intelligence they all have the economical ground for active democracies.

What happens between relative formal systems is not for turning to sort of war games inspired by natural ecology. These hard relationships existing have already been well explored in biomathematics as used in ecology. Since the primary works made by Lotka and Volterra, and advanced by May. It is not to say that wise human fate is about exactly the use the natural means in the same way. But to have their humane criteria and their technological skill to evoke, meet, match and fit over various larger than natural principles scales ... caring about that].

Many premises are here suggesting that we have a critical need to develop such ways of thinking to conceive a bit better our social economy of influence on the natural processes. [Before it is too late?]; if we want to achieve more seriously less exergetic expansive socio-technological systems. So evolve towards greener societies without too much regression of natural complexities.

But also with smarter solutions based on choice between variety of options and take the least damaging between those profitable or work hard for innovating in the good moral ways. That will not be so easy, but that can receive serious gauge and it is very possible to augur that sort of moral economy would make sense as fair social economy. Moreover without prejudgment on the individual-social balances to observe. Much being in relative efforts without excessive bias towards individualistic ideological purified arithmetic we would be able to examine, different sorts of societal metaphysics.

Heterogeneity

Heterogeneity (quantic, random and pieces of order) is great mechanism of creation, coalition (in) formative configuration and emergence; by distribution of attractive forces in the space. Gravity forces dispersed by motions in a volume of expansion. Heterogeneous (almost discrete and continuous) space distributions of matter are recorded diverging in the whole cosmos. And locally that are evolving after the original major propulsive impulse dynamics (of the Big Bang). [Quantic version since one overall phase-space to another?]. Regional rebalances of creations and motions occurs in the cosmos, those are land-marked more where 'things can be' and less where 'they cannot'. The fields before, meanwhile, after (still to 'formulate better in their switches'?). The dispersion(s) produced heterogeneity where it can be. Providing framing of space expressed into forces, attraction field(s) **of similar** (mass and gravity) is the most extended.

> [Inclusively further than mass by almost without mass of γ rays? ... -but these γ more electromagnetic?].

Also **to observe the repulsion of sub-similar**; correspondingly you have the **attraction of dissimilar** (electric charge either + or -) electromagnetic by motions, and which are effective at shorter range. Possibly this produced by 'more order' (after gravity) ... All that produce essential heterogeneity ... [before than just a milk-shake of simple gases?]. There we have the 'local dis-adjustments' and 'far-reaching propulsions' the establishments of fields (?); the expansions/contractions the universe has. Then come the local reactions of specification/de-specification; the sub-expression of forces produced from heterogeneity/homogeneity by diffusion and concentration on 'space-time', meanwhile the resources of diversification, form more recombination and thinner in some cooler places.

Diversity of phases space regimes: where what is at which speeds inside areas with critical borders of behaviors and properties allowances, with a potential time-life hard to imagine if unable to completely master the levels of properties allowed by such huge numbers. Possible then? To prepare the standard ones and have some recordable ones on Earth after some hypothesis or theory of explanation(s). As usual to suspect about heterogeneity that things start soon: 'immediately'.

Triads oblige to consider a more dynamic figures. Conceptually thesis, antithesis, synthesis. 'Back-up' they can imply the possibility of a dual strategy positive and negative coalition. Another back-up and there you have your label.

Also heterogeneity obliges to consider the imperfection of information for one or the asymmetry of one actor upon the other.

Heterogeneity
- trichotomy law: for each pair of real numbers a and b, 1 and only 1 of the 3 possibilities: a <b, a=b, a> b is true;
- addition law, for real numbers, a, b, c: a <b $\Leftrightarrow$ a+c <b+c;
- multiplication law: for real numbers a, b, c:
  o   a <b $\Leftrightarrow$ ac <bc if c> 0,
  o   a <b $\Leftrightarrow$ ac> bc if c <0;
- transitive law: for real numbers a, b, c:
  o   a <b and b <c $\Rightarrow$ a <c

To organize the evidence of heterogeneity and mechanisms in terms of 2 summarizing measures:
- Amplitude of disorder or heterogeneity in the system and;
- Levels of coupling or interaction strength among the system's components.

For a sort of formal phenomenological description on heterogeneity. Singular evolution correspondence works with heterogeneity dimension corresponding to the amplitude of the noise; n defined in equation. **Coupling strength** is quantified by the ratio of the instability growth rate divided by the diffusive relaxation rate. A large ratio corresponds to a large coupling strength: because the **local order parameter** S (r, t) exhibits large fluctuations and because the full amplitude between the 2 branches of the subcritical pitchfork bifurcation can be sampled. These large fluctuations have proportionally a strong influence on neighboring locations. This rationalized the results that "dragon-kings" emerge only for relatively small noise levels n and large ratios.

Paradox of heterogeneity: Nishikawa et al. using linear stability analysis and the ratio λ_N/λ_2 (largest divided by 2nd smallest Eigenvalue of the graph Laplacian matrix as an **index of synchronizability**. They showed that:
- un-weighted, undirected) networks with a more homogeneous degree distribution synchronize more easily than networks with a more heterogeneous degree distribution. Even when the latter network type has a shorter average path length;
- other also suggested that for large sufficiently random networks the synchronizability is mainly determined by the mean degree, and not by the degree distribution or system size.

When modeling homogeneity criteria of algebraic system must not prevail over heterogeneity of units: what is measured has shorter validity. Triangle inequality is not necessarily in the logical specialized discipline within which we examine an object, but stands with thermodynamics materialism and energetic balances of material objects that made our economic process (which is not with our speculative subjective manipulations).

Nevertheless intuitively the regularity of the collection as logarithmic curves at different basis, effects of divergence. Produced by the product of logarithms inverse. That should allow to scale or frame our quantities and allow comparisons, if we pass by realistic values (that is positive and superior to one (1)). Yet not in that be a diverging form.

With the humans on Earth a thesis would have examined the reasons of populations' motions in the space-time of lives. In the short space-time of this essay and its purpose this would be too far. In the previous it was about the importance of the concept of heterogeneity and diversity as one of those adjustments to reality against the paradigm of homogeneity and standardization; that have been taken as a policy without counterbalance in the globalization trends.

ReCombination

It is, of course, not to pretend to solve the so investigated Great Unified Theory (GUT) as expected by the standard model of physic.

> This GUT joins the different existing theories for the different forces relations established between them. Somehow each look like experienced and well probed: Einstein's relativity (mechanics of moving bodies or gravitation force, Quantum theory (particles, yet not seen quarks), Quantum electrodynamics (electromagnetism and weak nuclear interaction), Quantum chromodynamics (strong interaction-relation to Gravitation?).

> Remaining to clear the relations between all 3: 1) Gravity, 2) Strong interaction and the 3) Electromagnetic-electroweak and make logic the couple Relativity-Quantic Theory (already schemed).

Thus our concern is more about the cognitive analogies we could develop. Any have to imagine for sorts of proper frames and the primary ones, with at least some alternative may help to reproduce our sources. Any need o has in mind in physics and look liking possible formal frameworks for inspiring our policies. Not that exactly scientism oversimplified by esoteric determinism.

If in the state of sciences under globalization, it is not to say that engineers could be the good social artists for promoting kinds of fair models; they would have elaborated on their corner. Despite already exist plenty of fair theorems. Determining and separating at head cutter stick in the spurious all sorts of residuals. Neither to consider as well done, actually by inflation of "ceterminist expertise" where most social artists, as politicians, social forces speculators, owners of the economic powers are pretending to do, but more strangulating means for coping.

Since, as humans, neither we create from nothing, out of nothing. As perfectly as we hope in a narrow selfish way. We depend on Earth resources (humans included); past achievement of nature, biases of this Nature and complex selection by evolution. Hence for a natural optimal that has not always time to converge and stabilize especially more under anthropo-scenic perturbations; there is a need of economical alternative. In the opposite: wholist ways of Nature; humans bias Nature focused towards their interests. On which effects they have poor overviews, huge weaknesses; especially social. But also which are occasionally scientific, with knowledge and could be possibly wise about Nature's phenomena. [Notice that 'wholism' has technically much with 'closure', connexity, loop, completing, etc.]

In the same way biological troposphere follows the processes and adapt. Be these phenomena: cosmological, geological, hydrological, interfered by point processes or humans-made: provoked and abnormalities empowered. When there are not potentially able to change the conditions of phase-space singularities in a proper way. Consequences produced by biases and disequilibria are imagined to be hard to anticipate because of level of complexity. When not wanting to be brutal; despite having accumulated plenty of knowledge to conceive and obtain.

> Determinism is more for telling having understood the very mechanisms of disasters. Meanwhile the regular usual and ethical shocking mechanisms of societies adaptations are no more than another avatar of violent uses. That are now empowered by new means of destructions. When not sweeter uncomprehensive social affairs are more corrupting and rotting. Sometimes policies are called 'economy' by superiors of civilization. Which, since more than half a century have driven global governance from macro-structures. These have been better at wearing the suits of the nice good ones than really ensured sustainability.

Formal approaches have slowly discovered frameworks; showing that mathematics and logics match properly with Nature and now; could help better the thinking about natural phenomena. Hence not as in the simplest shortcuts that arbitrary humans could like. Also, if taken with the advanced precautions formal methods show their important limits but the deep logics of Nature.

We already mention the quali-quantitative match of model that must also balance between: larger field of uncertainty and disorder. With order formed rather than determined perfectly by humans 'superstructures'. These later ones are more efficient at destruction. **Randomness** is such a necessary resource existing at every level. To care since the start of everything, not just negatively; and whatever the ratiocination extent you know.

Intuitively a minimum of logical mistakes made by determinism:
- Infinite and zero are too idealized views (in absolute irrelevant to our world)
- Too systemic ambition with purification (and Aristotelian categorical?)
- Too shortly completed cut of fully reversible minded division (completeness misguided)
- Too unary-bad, binary (true-false); perfect illusions deluded, linear and discriminating.

Hence the need to better involve in simplifications-complications as nature's approaches the following concepts:
- Random emerging cardinality can create or empower order, not just wondering over ordering only;
- Subjective–objective in phenomenology and reality constrained formalism;
- Formal-physics-potential quali-quantity model intermediation;
- Non-complete complementary operations if completed set theory,
- Real world on heterogeneity-identities (pro-attraction-confusion) similarities (pro-separation-exhaustion).

Of course not to ignore advancements... Most of the contrary is observed as a *modus vivendi* (nimbies) of good profiteers and ascetic for an-aesthetic short period.

Formal sciences have than many concepts, methods and primary sort of half-complicated devices to better establish since young minds. So it is not to be surprised by the phenomenological evidences of adulthood essential difficulties. Essential, that is not those more created for complicating others' lives; among them absurd simplifications.

Confuse and Merge

Confusions and mixtures are to promote within some limits (differentiate those before and these after but informed between); help to make systems open and define complexities properties. As properties of variables and parameters, operated terms to play, eventually different papers in close configurations. Formally one problem is very general in mind: there is a common mostly confused (vacuum?) and mergence when convenient and up to human thinking mostly unconsciously... Even out, when just cognitively, as your brain smooths the visual pictures. [So that makes pleasant to go and see a movie, since the succession speed of pictures is just slightly faster than your rate]. Where confusions are not correct is where you make a continuity; when there is not but better discreteness.

That abuses which may have dire consequences. Look at statistics, everyone makes average, smooth values discard accidents, call them aberrant (even when consistent or existing). **Smoothing** on monthly collection by trimester or yearly and you miss what consistent mechanisms sustain the trend: you just blindly 'trend'. The reverse defect also with seeing plenty of things very differentiated but inconsistent and missing what a broader view could bring if looking at the 'vulgar more fundamental mechanisms'.

> Natural economics is present in the openness concept which is existing in the same way as basic physical principles: switches from the field to particles (maybe permanently at some ordinal-cardinal ratio?); and confusion of fields (superposition)? Whatever are photons global carriers (γ- rays, quanta of light but energy). *atoms' nuclei* of matter (ordinal of hadron? cardinal of leptons? but mesons?); any sort of currents (ordinal protons? Cardinal electrons? but neutrons?); and so on.

> In effect non-linearity (or called catastrophic formal mathematical behavior). Were effectively better to have an overview at a higher level of scale; inclusively for confusion? Hence not just for ignoring such kinds of behaviors are there. And not a simple straight or smooth and direct line. Humans' dissimulations or lies when there are only providing average or giving just central-mean-measure-minded.

The proper rules for confusing or discriminating are not as simple as you may think. In physics and sciences of the engineers, discrimination, exactness as methods and principles, possibly combined are no more really scientific. Engineers still want a unique solution not: 'wholesome and then specifiable system'. Be scientific is more about with sharp gradients, singularities, bifurcations, dynamic equations properly modeled. But still there is plenty to do for taking into account of interfaces. Probable theory better understood, phase-space diagrams and so on. With some methods sometimes still quite specific or hidden on the computer.

The problem in formal arts being that if concepts of the sort are necessary they are mostly ergodic promoted and 'heating entropy'. The degree of imprecision is quite high and argumentation only worldly quite robust and; in the same time almost systematically improperly manipulated. For not telling about the 'artistic reactions of experts' when you intent to suggest, mostly and obliged suggestive intents. Never sure as pretended there and nowhere; it would be better to care to involve some degrees of uncertainty rather than the certainties of experts.

By the side of the **formal ability to merge** are often important:
- Finite numbers of states;
- Fixed transition probabilities;
- Any to any possible balanced in some proportions away criticalities;
- No simple cycle (strange attractors shape well suggestive forms).

Formally difficulties are also important; because the methods, like for understanding between the binary-ness and the high number values are not much developed and too unknown. These in the **small numbers** or "**oligo-elements**" which are asking for closer networks, algebraic groups, small number statistics and combinatory, **networks** approached; **pluri-valued** properly calculable logics. Plenty of proper work is required. Rather than conducing only qualitative analysis of many things free from any dimensions... But amendments much require computer-assisted share and collective intelligence with allied propaedeutic.

Excessive confusion comes from disconnections; developed between real issues and policies. They are precisely easy to produce by those imposing their fake order. By the loss of proximity of analytical objects with respect to situations. This may come from socially theorized illusions over potential social determinism and ideological systems created for that. They can variably be called reductionism, scientism, esoterism, sectarianism, and so on—all kinds of compulsory obsessions or "mono-manichean". That is a sort of 'cutting evil's throat until no one left' much produced by Occidentals). Or indirectly produced by those monomaniac everywhere in lay affairs; for enforcing absurd normalizing systems.

All these are, more or less, largely unable to balance humane partnership. It seeks alienation and unfair competitions to self-justify unequal social structures. It is to prevent any computed device easy to substitute humans establish definitively that Nature under formal approaches qualify the substitute and disqualify humans?

Times Ordering and Hierarchy

Some few words about time are required. As you may have detected, we are not at ease with the idea that time is something like a metric by the side of space [if not outside]. Mathematics physics makes intense use of temporal and space coordinates. Time is primary also in causal analysis. In the following some basics of time logic, after Burgess

Logic of time uses comparators looking like those of mathematics with a sense of **before** and **after**. Formal classical predicate logic in the 1st place of contains predicate logic, regimented language U = (U, $\prec$, $\vee$) where $\prec$ is the frame. **Valuation function** is represented by a pair of numbers (i, u) where i is a natural and u takes value 1 if true or 0 if false. Then it would be to consider **consequence** as relative to a class F or frames with some special property called totality: for any element v, w we have $v \prec w$ or $v = w$ or $w \prec v$. That needs **unstated promise** (enthymeme) and more than 1; **additional premises** [or to find the answer in physics?].

"Classical physical assumed time to be total. Relativist physics merged space with time and does not assume the space-time to be total; but it still has to 'fully' define its *status* between Special and General Relativity theories. For computer scientists there is a trade-off in logic between expressive power and other desirable properties. For philosophers, the grammar of temporal logic is closer to that of natural (rich) language.

Notes that some use terms of '**indices**' and '**labels**' respectively for '**times**' and '**states**'. That could make more sense if (complex) time could be considered as evolution (between 2 critical trajectories points of something hard to state definitively.

A temporal logic kind of problem putting ahead is about autonomous approach of temporal or **tense logic** using non-truth function connectives. It is to understand how assumptions about the structure of time expressed in tense less regimented language. With explicit quantification over times or states correspond to validity assumptions of various arguments. Forms in the tensed autonomous language that does not involve such quantification. If one has such (autonomous) formalization with '**Meredith's translation**' [of sentential modal logic into classical predicate logic]; it can always get a regimented style. Every formula of temporal logic has a predicate logic translation (but the reverse is false)."

Primary axioms of temporal logic: 1) any tautology; 2) prospect of $\rightarrow$; 3) retrospect of $\rightarrow$; 4) generalization of the prospect; 5) generalization of retrospect. There are 2 rules of inference 1) *modus ponens*; and 2) temporal generalization. Minimal tense logic axioms is sound for the class F_0 of all frames.

More (composed) rules consider, for example: - substitution instance–rules of tautological consequence–mirror image or reflection–tense in any operators' sequence. This class of theorem is under Becker's rule (from A (B to infer TA (TB for any tense T)–replacement–duality (from A (B to infer B*(A*).

Classical physics time's axioms (Burgess): "properties; 1) transitivity, 2) right totality, 3) left totality, 4) right extendibility, 5) left extendibility, 6) density if $u \prec v$, then $u \prec t$ and $t \prec v$ for some t; frame (U, $\prec$) to consider either in $\mathbb{Q}$ or $\mathbb{R}$; there are several transitive frames (4 at least); and theorems derived from minimal temporal logic with classical physics axioms.

Temporal logic also accounts for **reduction of tenses**: treating temporal operators as iterated without limit. This is not so in natural language. Hamblin's theorem shows that most iterations collapse assuming classical physics treatment of time. "

Quantified temporal logic is complete and decidable; it adds universal generalizations. **Combination of axioms**: provides with sentential logic concept (to 'interpret') such as: converse theorem–direct Barcan formula $\forall xGA \rightarrow G$ (xA–permanence of identity–non-identity and others. Extension of a Kripke model to temporal predicate logic may help to clarify some.

Summary of Temporal Logic

Logic	Models	Model Generators	Class of Models described
linear	sequences	Büchi sequential automata	all models
branching	trees	Büchi tree automata	k-ary models
partial order	± trees	Büchi tree automata	k-ary models

Partial Order
consider ordering in the context of some familiar datatypes:
(a) < on the natural numbers, IN = {1, 2, 3,... }, with 1 < 2 < 3 <... ;
(b) ⊆ ('is a subset of') on the power set $\wp(X)$ of all subsets of a set X;
(c) the relation **F** < **T** on the set of booleans {**F**,**T**};
(d) the prefix order on binary strings;
(e) the relation 'is more defined than' on partial maps π so the domain and range of π are subsets of 'in').

Instanton of Time

Modern theoretical physics based on group-algebraic approach; which has generated the formalism a **principal fiber bundles** and the 'instanton approach'

[instanton a cut more or less thick or a minimum piece of time ... or a required analytical artifact?]. [Fiber bundle a general tensor theory kind of concept used in differential approach of electromagnetism].

That formalism is based on Pontriagin's degree of map theorem, which originally 'bridges' homology and co-homology theories.

From idealized or formal systems to concrete ones, we face systems that seem too complex to model or whose models could lack convenient simplifying elements. **Simplifying** is an issue that arose in the consideration of self-replicating automata was that some cases seemed too trivial for consideration. Others are self-similar mechanics provided by non-natural (number) dimension.

Triviality is derived from the **replication** being placed on the context, rather than being volunteered in some non-trivial way by the self-replication of entity itself. Paradoxical situation is that replicating system cannot exist until its range is fully defined, but the range, which must include the system cannot be defined until the function exists.

[That looks like a maximum degree of reached complexity, better for incorporating and make use of, if testable: inner management of openness. From bottom to up there is openness... Created by phase-space emergences and relative cooling making possible heterogeneity and patterns created ... and refrained when captured ... by 'information' ... in the need to formalize].

An adapted approach to our views would examine 'context' to denote fewer (then all disordered) and feasible (at best sustainable along time) states presumably definable main systemic solution (potential and model) [phase-space for 'potential'? Model since informative piece]. Set of configurations: given the context E and principal of some system. The set of configurations E is a set (or subset if focused set) of all possible states of given system.

For minimum formalism starters:

Call elements of E configurations. Time development function would be a map T constrained by $T(E; 0) = E$ and $T(T(E; y); x) = T(E; x + y)$. [Make a distinction between a fundamental time of atomic elements (logical concept) produced as a statistical balance between fields and their atoms and evolutionary time provided by more complex large systems.]

The subsystem set: if S is a system, denote the set of all subsystems of S, and say the subsystem set of S. Extend that all states of subsystems of S which are the same as X wherever that comparison is meaningful.

Subset part of a set is not a structural miniature representation of set; but a functional one, which is preserving its "inscription," just assuming the effects (and duties) of its subset configuration. This is to define possible subsystems E as a the union of all F^* such that $F \times E$. A dissimilarity pseudo-metric would quantify the 'self' portion of self-replication. A pseudometric d, obeys $d(x, y) + d(y, z) \leq d(x, z)$; $d(x, y) = 0$; $d(x, y) = d(y, x)$ and $d(x, x) = 0$; but not: $d(x, y) = 0 \Rightarrow x = y$.

The presence of a subsystem S in a context E within tolerance to be the probability that a randomly selected subsystem will satisfy $d(T; S)$. Also, S is possible (in E) when there is some time such that S is present in $T(E; t)$. Given a set of configurations E and 2 E-configurations; it is to define the momentary relative replicability of a system S in E_1 relative to E_2, with tolerance at time. When S is possible in both E_1 and E_2, we also define the replicability over time.

Overall Replicability is the limiting case. To define the self-replicability of a system S in a context E".

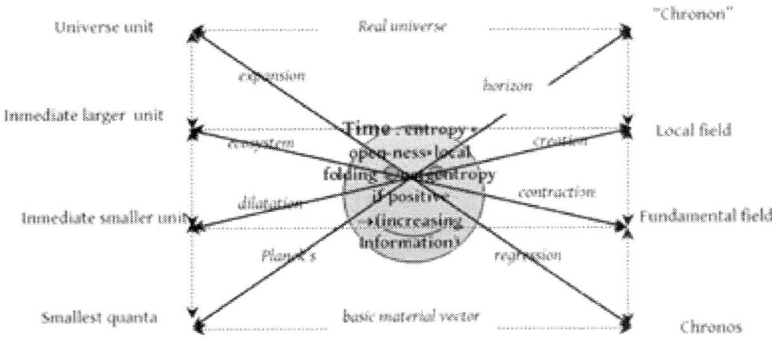

Not to miss the folds, bifurcation
creating (in cooling environment)

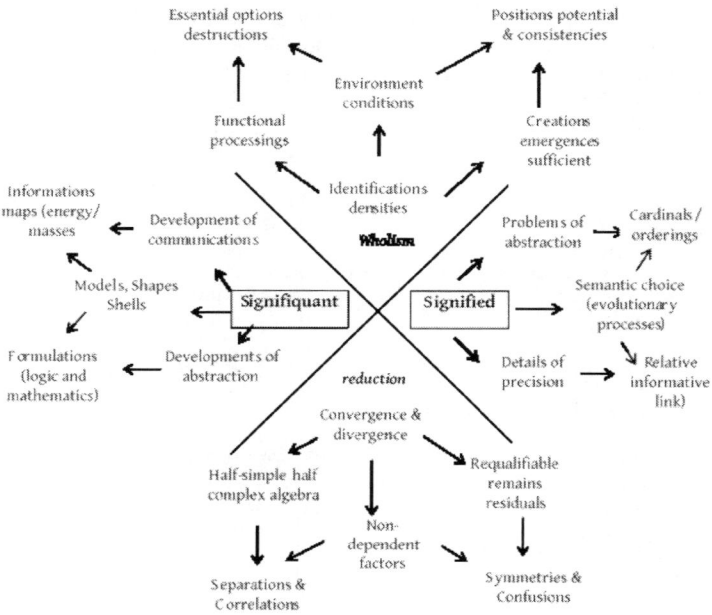

Essential options
destructions

Positions potential
& consistencies

Environment
conditions

Functional
processings

Creations
emergences
sufficient

Informations
maps (energy/
masses)

Development of
communications

Identifications
densities

Whollion

Problems of
abstraction

Cardinals /
orderings

Models, Shapes
Shells

Signifiquant

Signified

Semantic choice
(evolutionary
processes)

Formulations
(logic and
mathematics)

Developments of
abstraction

reduction

Details of
precision

Relative
informative
link)

Convergence &
divergence

Half-simple half
complex algebra

Requalifiable
remains
residuals

Non-
dependent
factors

Separations &
Correlations

Symmetries &
Confusions

Causality Instrumentation

Logic of instrumental variables (Pearl): in a causal framework, observes 3 levels hierarchy similarly characterizing the notion of instrumental variable (Z); Z is **independent** of all variables, including error terms that have an influence on Y. And that is not mediated by X. Z is not independent for X. When a set S of covariates is measured. These definitions generalize as: a variable Z is an **instrument** relative to the total effect of X on Y. Y if there exists a set of measurements S = s, unaffected by X. Such that either of the following criteria holds: **counterfactual criteria** considers: Z independent from YX (S = s and Z dependent X (S = s. Graphical criterion considers: (Z independent from Y (S) G (x and (Z dependent from X (S) G.

Above mention to consider along time approach. Now few technical comments concepts useful in time analysis. On some formal perspective (applied in physics) of signal treatment:

- **Ergodic system Poisson's process** statistics have average equaling time's average [that something we will approach in the next volume of essay].];
- **Fourier analysis** [of signals] does not allow proper time analysis. It allows to discriminate order of signals. But **Wavelets analysis** allows such time analysis [Wavelet analysis most developed by Meyer].
- Some described '**Space=time cell**' by the equation of a commutative algebra closed at 2 nearest local complexes

The above does not have much more ambitions than to mention few things probably helpful for further explorations. Of course they are too simple and too short for people of the area, as well as for an essay that would have a more serious ambitions. At the minimum we need in the line of the relative formal system proposal; something that respect the diversity of time-lines would structure and pack them. Considering for that: a sort of different times integration. This could intuitively make the system of closures or links, or tights we need with the first *nucleus*.

Hierarchy in Temporal related Logics

Source: nfm

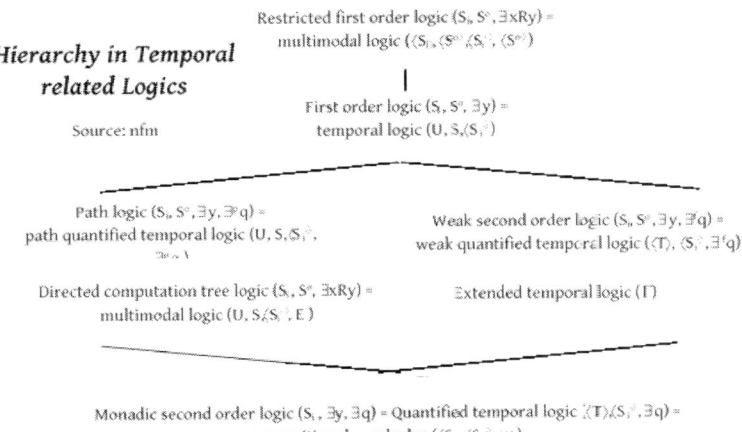

Restricted first order logic $(S_1, S^o, \exists x R y)$ = multimodal logic $(\langle S_1 \rangle, \langle S^o \rangle, \langle S_i \rangle, \langle S^o \rangle)$

First order logic $(S_1, S^o, \exists y)$ = temporal logic $(U, S, \langle S_i \rangle)$

Path logic $(S_1, S^o, \exists y, \exists^\infty q)$ = path quantified temporal logic $(U, S, \langle S_i \rangle, \exists^\infty \land$

Weak second order logic $(S_1, S^o, \exists y, \exists q)$ = weak quantified temporal logic $(\langle T \rangle, \langle S_i \rangle, \exists^1 q)$

Directed computation tree logic $(S_1, S^o, \exists x R y)$ = multimodal logic $(U, S, \langle S_i \rangle, E)$

Extended temporal logic (T)

Monadic second order logic $(S_1, \exists y, \exists q)$ = Quantified temporal logic $(\langle T \rangle, \langle S_i \rangle, \exists q)$ = propositional μ-calculus $(\langle S_1 \rangle, \langle S_i \rangle, vq)$

Logically inspired by the fact that over the 3-space dimensions, the tights form physics time (time in the denominator) close or relate the 3. A system of times would consider than the '3 levels of lines of lives': of micro (most relevant weakest time-life particle); macro (in a system of relations where meso feeds in macro) and so: meso. With that it seemed to us that von Neumann Lexicographic Ordering could be a good way for structuring variety of time. We transformed the reference to our purpose.

Von Neumann Lexicographic Ordering

[Adaptation of a Wikipedia's article, to a concept of pieces time lexicographic ordering, raised at an eco-physics provider-producer level].

Consider different times options:
1. Time of constraining principles
   a. **Universal** (micro-level): enough qualitatively large for being not too constraining; quantitatively constraining by yield limits of transformations (including the options provided by the technologies of transformations) [in the same universe we have *a priori* almost anything possible ... but with different costs];
   b. **Relative-Environmental** (macro-environmental): considers nearby systems used as sources for transformations and the informative piece of their cycles of renewal (for the minimization of impacts), nearby systems themselves in the same universe of times; after the factors of production composition; informative relations of their time costs and transformations process yields.
2. Intermediate Game (Meso-level)

a. Self-relative: are the options of productions qualities (diversity of productions) and quantitative (yields or returns); definition of preferences expressed in times;
b. Relative Macro enlargement is considering macro-social and market) s) of products, possibly including market attitude towards the environmental 'trace' or impact of productions.

Since **time as information or as potential and gauge of values**. Gauges may exclude options (provide death risk, emergencies of conditions and utilities of productions, risks of production), costs time valued, prices referral, values also so (profit margins over costs). We have both a common gauge (and can combine or dualize with energetic estimates).

The idea is to **obtain the critical times of transforming systems**; after the constraints. Consider the technical, delays, estimate costs and 'states' of the market. Have a partition; see the principles'. Critical times may have their solutions from technological innovations or investments or thermodynamic flexibilities. But environmental costs are more or less theoretical (from regulations or tolerance). Others are more with subjective values, solutions are either with flexibility, market fluctuations, etc.

To imagine that the actor is experienced in the production. Thus hse is in reasonable conditions to solve and work the economics of hes production. **Manageable critical times 'bundles' of lexicographic orderings** describe comparative time-information preference; where an agent prefers times priority (X) solving the most numerous-weighted manageable critical times; solved by X production process (to any other less numerous-weighted (Y) manageable production(s) process (es). Consider specifically if offered several bundles of productions' possibilities.

Only **when there is a tie between bundles**; with regard to the number of units of X, will the agent start comparing the number of units of Y across bundles (in a way to keep flexibility and/or synergies). The **lexicographic preferences extend time preference (discrete) analogously to the way that nonstandard infinitesimals extend the real numbers**. With lexicographic preferences, the utility of certain productions is infinitesimal in comparison to others. What is not critical-weighted, has already solution.

A distinctive feature of such lexicographic preferences is that a multivariate real domain of an agent's preferences does not map into a real-valued range. That is, **there is no real-valued representation of a utility function**. [That look like compatible with a productive already experienced and tree of critical different possibilities.]

In terms of real valued utilities, one would say that the utility of Y and Z is infinitesimal compared with X, and the utility of Z is infinitesimal compared to Y. [Notice that the scale crossing of our informative may shade that; keeping levels of differentiation. First because, other matches or evolution may be reappraised, establish other crossed links, change with conjuncture, thus other sets of criticalities. Second the frame applies, for example observing modeling may address other levels (by modularity and transport].

The **model of real numbers is always logically ambiguous**. One is allowed to adjoin infinitesimal quantities to make a nonstandard model. Standard models of the real numbers exclude infinitesimals, so **lexicographic preferences are not precisely described by standard reals**. But by assigning a utility to X. Which is much larger than the utility of Y. Which in turn is much larger than the utility of Z. The infinitesimal order relation can be approximated arbitrarily closely, which means this is a problem of idealized limits only.

If all agents have the same lexicographic preferences, then general equilibrium cannot exist because agents will not sell to each other (as long as price of the less preferred is more than zero) [That is not a disadvantage of plurality or diversity, of productions. Moreover in such sort of analysis we are not the case of main providing stream but disrupted provision if all have at the same moment the same lexicographic preference].

The lexicographic preferences can still exist with the general equilibrium. For example; - different people have different bundles of lexicographic preferences such that different individuals value items in different orders; - some, but not all people have lexicographic preferences. - lexicographic preferences extend only to a certain quantity of the good. [Remind from the start that we make it partial: some productions are non-critical and they make profits.]

> The lexicographic preferences are the classical example of rational preferences that are not representable by a utility function over the standard reals.
>
> But nonstandard equilibrium prices for exchange can be determined for lexicographic order to use standard equilibrium methods.

Practically lexicographic ordering follows:

- An ordering of characters gives rise to an order on strings of those characters.
- Strings of characters possibly have different lengths are ordered by the first difference in the strings.
- Let $<C$ be the ordering of characters, e.g., $x <_C y$ for any 2 characters x and y. Let $x_0 x_1 ... x_{k-1}$ and $y_0 y_1 ... y_{l-1}$ be two strings of length $k \geq 0$ and $l \geq 0$, respectively.
- The two strings are equal $x_0 x_1 ... x_{k-1} = y_0 y_1 ... y_{l-1}$, if $k = l$ and $x_i = y_i$ for all $0 \leq i \leq k$.
- Define lexicographic ordering $<_L$: let $x_0 x_1 ... x_{k-1} <_L y_0 y_1 ... y_{l-1}$ if there is an index $i \leq 0$ such that $i < k$ and $i < l$ and $x_i <C y_i$ and $x_j = y_j$ for all $0 \leq j < i$ or if $l > k$ and for all $0 \leq j < i$ we have $x_j = y_j$.
- Notice that the empty strings (sequences of 0 characters) is the smallest string in lexicographic order.

Care that in this formulation, you have not all required adaptation. The aim is to make you notice the possibility of relation between discrete (eventually arbitrary) lexicographic ordering and real (numbers) in continuity. One step further will have to do with quali-quantic and informative crossed process (more complicated)

Entanglement of Plural Times or Closure

This will the explained intuitively; because it looks like we have different meanings in the literature. Some redundancy comes from the concept of motions inside a space (making use of speeds) and; effectively requiring **reversibility** of time. In this way of universal, the trick of time makes it is used has a **divisor** ('closure to back to the start'). Since a perfect **partition** of 'hypothetical achievement of a potential'; would be grounded on what? With good will some very regular atomic vibration? Thus why not an **average life expectancy** (?) Observing redundancy time concept with the concept of space (go (distance. Average of varying speeds)/come back (time/average of varying distance).

> [Go-get-come back: the idea is when going you anticipate the distance of the destination and vary your speeds after what you can do .. we are not presuming of perfect determinism. When the return to the supposed same point of start (be only abstract: recall) but vary your path respect to the original one trying to earn some time, after the special experience you get, when returning. Self-speed driven, after

distance anticipated when you go. Environment space driven to earn time when the return].

That is if no prejudging of the time and the space determinism; but taking information by the way and events. We see a bit better than in the perfect determinism. Time and space are 'relatively the same' and the formal expression of closure, or achievement or; piece of that. We have (more or less pure) completion, compactness... Combination of anticipations (goal and risks); if the space is more referring. Because environment in the mobile is submitted to universal laws. The conscious mobile has to core its anticipation, on the greater stability of the environment. In the way to on what it has (anticipation and self-resources), in the way back also on what it has (but anticipation change: 'get back' and what it has, is the experience of the way.

This, then makes time a 'spectrum': 1) Anticipation from information (an **informative match-fit** ... but not an 'ending everything' perfect fit: 1); 2) A **path possibly sensitive** to space, circumstances, events (all possibly at variable degrees 'intricated') ... in other words: relative openness; 3) Experience and history; thus **information and**, moreover ... that can switch (or is a game?) from inner-capacity speeds driven to outer conditions space driven; [... information and game also meaning that **it can play in a formal system**] 4) If one considers that space, circumstances, events are effective on the mobile than the program can evolve. Thus **evolution by netgentropy can happen** [another effect of openness in environmental resources]; 5) It seems well that the **times of primary principles** structuring the universe as well as yourself; can be involved: you need also of universal components average; as well as meeting them in the environment [artificial of natural].

In all that, it is the object that achieved in an ordered way all this management of a different time, possibly also accounting if not primarily about that "in the long term we are all dead" (Keynes). As a result when we make a formal system of time we may have to close with space coincidence. And the converse, when we make a model of space, we have to close that with time. In either way this looks like a 'shuttle'.

[That looks like this conception of a space-time model look like as one from Stavraki, but we did not make connection with. [He is a Russian physicist with a proposal on field physics 6 dimensioned] "visually (it is like a closed line) as an "8" loop. "The symmetry of this local construction under T reflection allows representation of a T-reversible flow of local time by a discrete chain of local T-reflections instead of a continuous time shift. The fundamental causal interval is constructed as an indivisible time step of such symmetry.]."

Then, the suggestive ambition that the formal treatment of times is both as an abstract object of closure (specifications, complements, etc.) as a fundamental physics ordering for causality and grading could be handled... Possibly also managed as formal relative systems... Without missing the levels of scale of complexity, nor the care of nice netgentropy (at least not too negative) we have there...

... if the crazy aristocratic bourgeois, capitalists of their convenient hierarchical orders and, the mad made ergodic anarchist-fighters; do not size the powers of entropy?

Invariance Symmetries Applied

Further in the formal expression come the ambitions of structures or constants or regularities; in ways of the **concepts of invariants**.

Technically considers for example that when a system of mass moves, some quantities remains unchanged. Most familiar is energy: it comes as kinetic and potential, 1st is provided by speeds of the body's mass and 2nd by the effects of forces.

> Thus principles are such sorts of forms that stay, independent from the system of reference, that is, you may transform and the principles stay. It is invariant under the transformations.

Invariants have the status of observables in quantic fields topological theories serving to describe the stage of its field or its levels of energy (which is discrete). In the topology of nodes (theory of nodes), they express **nodal structures with characteristic properties**, including the dissipation of energy (or at the reverse of the thermodynamic equilibrium). The **node is a singularity** such as a folding, well locally defined. A catastrophe occurs in the theory of nodes when 1 crosses you have another kind of invariance.

Symmetric Operations			
Symmetry operation	Code	symmetric element	Dimension
Identity	E	entire object, no change	3
Reflection	σ	reflection plane	2
Rotation	Cn	rotation axis	1
Improper rotation	Sn	improper rotation axis*	0
* proper rotation axis points of intersection; and a perpendicular reflection			

In common mathematics there are expressions non-sensitive to the reference base change; or which are symmetrical. Mathematicians examine 4 fundamental types of Operations Symmetries. In physics approach invariants are met in **conservation laws**. They come with symmetries. For some examples: 1) total impulse; 2) energy conservation; 3) mass conservation; 4) amount of movement.

In Quantic theory there is a systemic treatment of those possibly existing invariance or symmetries. For some eclectic cases (quite important in the technicalities of the formalism):

- **intrinsic dimension** is an important invariant, in metric spaces samples.
- In universal formula of characters: **trace** $U\psi = \dim T \vdash \bar{G} f(\psi . j^{-1})$ where the function is Fourier's transform, j is invariant functions by inner auto-morphism.
- invariance in field theory is about: Hamiltonian calculus, tensor calculus, group theory, quantum mechanics equations, Yang Mill theory

- to have **gauge invariance** [Weyl's Gauge theory] a complete knowledge when gauge's change is needed; (thereafter you have Maxwell's electromagnetism quantification that could have been made quantic).

["Consisting Gauge theory adds to the 4 dimensions of space-time of Relativity theory, one more as a circle corresponding to the group of phases. This allows to make use of differentiated covariance (for the calculus of differentiation of phases) and helped to explain Aharonov-Bohm effect"].

Invariant measure

A σ-finite measure π on $B(X)$ with the property $\pi(A) = \int_X \pi(dx) P(x, A)$, $A \in B(X)$ will be called invariant.

Subinvariant measure

If μ is σ-finite and satisfies $\mu(A) \geq \int_X \mu(dx) P(x, A)$, $A \in B(X)$ then μ is called subinvariant.

For some more arguments, in different registers:

- In a dynamic mixing system **distribution relaxing towards invariant measure** can make appear **an analogous of irreversibility**. This relaxation of invariant measure turns a property of 'set of initial conditions' and refers to a generic dynamic system.
- *Genus* is the **only topological invariant** of a compact Riemann surface under bi-rational transformations. The greater the *genus* of a surface is, the more complicated is its structure.
- A topological invariant is based on the way laces of the surface can be deformed. 2 laces are equivalent if they can be deformed one into another.
- **Poincaré's invariant fundamental group** in geometry is dodecahedral (but not of a 3-sphere despite having the same homology invariants).
- Poincaré invariant of Hamiltonian formalism: is an identical relation with exterior form of 1st degree.
- Galois's symmetries is observed in algebraic geometry and theory of numbers.
- Symmetries or regularities are observed in crystal, quasi-crystals, fractals, dynamic systems.
- L-systems are used in algorithms of Plant growth.
- **Invariance of phases** $\int_{(1)}^{(2)} A'_{\mu,s} dx^\mu = 0$; $\int_{(1')}^{(2')} A'_{\mu,s} dx^\mu = 0$.
- Symmetries in Theory of Relativity from Einstein, Lorentz.
- Closure of exterior differential forms, have their **invariant results from the conjugacy of the exterior elements or dual form**.

Many other applications of formalism also consider invariants, for example **Networks invariants** (Estrada) "is any structure regular description will better seek to find its invariants. They are **centralization** invariants; and **adjacencies** based invariants."

But physics is also 'sided' and not everything is symmetric. Where they were expected but unobserved, also to examine **breaking of symmetry**. Many physics phases (states of matter) have broken symmetries as of ergodicity (randomness), as magnets, crystals, superfluid and liquid crystal

Breaking of symmetry expressed upon: invariance, conservation, regularity, equivalence and evidence in criticality, instability and singularity.

Now to conceive that when the developing, in a given time-space has followed:
- Specification by conversion of energy to matter. This is since the original "soup and foaming-out soap,"
- Transport of energy under many different forms be by particles (motion) which would be more of less vibrating,
- Different forms of energies (waves trains, solitons, particles, etc.).
- Waves with at least some minimum particles (photons of light, gravitons?) or a mix (eventually representing fundamental supporting forces),
- interrupted by aggregations (when speeds slowed down?), Shocks and interactions and eventually other conversions according products and effects of interactions.

Emmy Noether Theorem

Emmy Noether a world class German Jewish mathematician of the 20th century has been key in the development of **algebraic structures** and in an essential theorem; that relates algebra and **physics symmetries**.

> She proved that every conserved quantity, corresponds to symmetries' continuous group of equations. Correspondence was established between that leaves action functional, invariant and; conservation laws (of Euler Lagrange equations).

Laws of conservation concern by the theorem are: energy, linear momentum, angular momentum. All symmetries forms a: n algebraic group. Allowing the sequence of operations be: 'do one transformation then the other.' These properties of symmetry characterize structure: not too weak nor too strong. [Observe that '1 operation at a time' is what we can expect from simple operations (in the 'formal head' without losing the essential structure's ... thank to the structure of invariance). Intuitively also remind that we need to maintain 'openness' but also enough stable structure].

Too strong a structure, does not allow the objects to be isolated and specific ... [we need they are expressive]. But 'mirror effect': relative closeness for the physics system is also needed and is expressed somehow in the formula. And a too weak ones do not stay (thus similarly: not too open system).

> **Noether theorem**: on a polynomial factorization $P [X_1, ... X_r]$ when $P = P_1 P_2$ obtained by identification, there is a pack of polynomial equations on the coefficient of P, P_1, P_2.

When P is fixed, we obtain a universal family of polynomials and P is absolutely factorial-able.

This, extended in a Hamiltonian system confirms Lagrangian case and gives rise to Lie algebra (characteristic algebraic group). There is structurally homomorphism between Lie algebra of Noether. Symmetries and algebra of conservation laws that form Lie algebra in Poisson's bracket. [Poisson's bracket used for multiplication of infinite dimensional Lie-algebra].

Symmetries in Physics

non-observables	mathematical transformations	conservation laws or selection rules	other correspondence
absolute spatial position	space translation: $\bar{r} \rightarrow \bar{r} + \bar{\Delta}$	linear *momentum*	translation invariant
absolute time	time translation : $t \rightarrow t + \tau$	energy	time displacement
absolute spatial direction	rotation $\bar{r} \rightarrow \bar{r}'$	angular *momentum*	rotation around an axis
absolute right (or left)	$\bar{r} \rightarrow - \bar{r}$	parity	
absolute sign of electric charge	$e \rightarrow -e$	charge conjugation	
absolute sign of time	$t \rightarrow -t$	time reversal	
difference between identical particles	permutation	Bose-Einstein or Fermi-Dirac statistics	
relative phase between states of different electric charge Q	$\psi \rightarrow e^{iQ\theta} \psi$ (Gauge transformation)	electric charge	

Nevertheless, **non-Noether symmetries** also plays an important role in Lagrangian dynamics and Hamiltonian dynamics. Formally and mentally expected quaternion constructions, to preserve some properties or symmetries for general formal; but localized resolvability. That is to say, caught by combined mapoïds which derived from 3 dimensions (volumes) and are potentially evolving (time-tamed).

Hamiltonian systems have properties that conserve energy but, from general systems of differential equations, have distinct properties. Said so in definite Lutzky's correspondence with conservation laws. Each generator of non-Noether symmetry may produce a whole family of conservation laws: maximal number of conservation laws that can be associated with non-Noether symmetry via Lutzky's theorem; is equal to the configuration space dimension of Lagrangian system. This is especially valuable in infinite dimensional dynamic systems. Lutsky's theorem can be formulated in terms of bivector fields, and have an alternative derivation of conserved computable quantities in infinite dimensional Hamiltonian dynamic systems.

"Many important integrable models are such as Korteweg de Vries equation (partial differential equation in the *continuum* limit), nonlinear Schrödinger equation, Boer-Kaup; Benney system and Toda chain; possess non-Noether symmetries properties. Also they have several essential geometric issues such as Frolicher-Nienhuis operators, Lax pairs, bi-Hamiltonian structures and bi-complexes."

For profanes, as us, as well as many simple physicists: remind that this is not as simple as our laziness could expect. Searching for the natural invariances in the formal expression since these invariances points at the principles that stay has plenty of difficulties. Formalisms is delicate. For example, Lagrangians and Hamiltonians fundamental approaches of geometrical analysis for the investigation of invariances are not the same: they have to meet, match and fit. The conditions of each are as well as of Noetherian and non-Noetherian kinds of different applications of invariances.

> The Legendre transformation converts Lagrangian function defined on tangent manifold into the Hamiltonian function defined on cotangent manifold is degenerate transformation. Hence a correspondence between the Lagrange equation and the Hamiltonian system will be fulfilled only discretely. Transition from Lagrangian to Hamiltonian is only possible as degenerate (as in the reverse). Hamiltonian system in case the Lagrangian manifold is not integrable. (Petrova).

Pathways to Wisdom With Formal Sciences

If we take arithmetic as a perfect pure symbolic way, at the infinite of straight line details, we hope to have shown that most simple operations already have plenty of logic misunderstandings about how, methods could relatively be used. Formal method incompleteness does not substantiate the humans' metaphysical 'transcendental' view.

> This may be seen as a spiritual advantage: formal methods are not for demonstrating in absolute that God does not exist. But it would also be an abuse to use them to demonstrate that He does exist.

Otherwise formal sciences rigor transcends cultural difference with fundamental physics. So intuitively believers and non-believers with good feelings could imagine that most universal language for sciences with formal ones and then to understand that complexities qualify contexts-culture-related local merits. Also to understand complexities and limits of formal sciences conceptual integration. One should observe much more general use of logics and mathematics and fundamental physics or natural sciences for universal communication (at least to empower them). Instead of passing by 'their own specific and make use systems of translations forcibly 'unfair'.

> Part of 'modern management defects in social arts' expressed so with their incredibly poor use (if not repugnant') in 'producing harmony' in fair social-economical negotiations. A reason of this defect is because most are without seeing that whatever the 'absolute *status*' of formal sciences there are many reasons to think that relatively, at least they are also a language. And language properly formulated ought to have the qualities of the service: solve the problems between contenders 'on a piece of paper'. [Something that Adam Smith looks like to have understood when pleading for talks to solve problems].

> Of course this defect from the ways that social-economic formalism is conceived: be this as a strategic game of winners, losers, inequalities and despise if not despoiled. Meanwhile

made more ambiguous with technological progress, scientific shares, economic development: 'for peace but...'.

Quite often spiritual mathematicians and people properly understanding the resources of formal sciences as best users who are fundamental physicists, have occasionally taken their dear investigations indirectly. This has been, both as 'little vehicle' (self-inspiring) and great vehicle (supporting their belief) to their spirituality. Despite that, the modern paradigm for historical reasons of social reactions, to the 'power of ecclesiastical authorities' has often used physics sciences, in the 'Occident' to get rid of religious lies; since the scientific theories, some churches carried, was contradicted and denied. The scientific theories advanced Churches or faith professionals to insist on establishing the scientific truth of their beliefs. Even when most natural evidence was contradictory. Despite also they soon had religious experts turned essential theologians, having based primary belief out the scope of scientific consistency.

Among civilizations ways of doing formal sciences have varied and the best attending the 'free licenses of formal scientists' (India, Islam) not necessarily were the less spiritual. So more practically the effect of conceiving as perfect and infinite cleanness. This has been biased by people at ease with symbolic analytic; for looking like 'initiated' and so: deserving grants and positions. Moreover the level of difficulty of handmade calculi rigor; has made engineers willing not to waste time explaining their 'heuristic choice'. Probably also because it is a matter of unconscious cognitive resources, making the engineering (unaware of cognition), anxious not to look like 'not scientific in the occidental way'.

Finally, see with lay people the reason why their reserve about that 'stuff' of formal sciences; is because they prefer to evade the post-traumatic syndrome of having alienated, during their childhood school, with finding the 'correct numbers of the true solutions' ('dunce-hat'). More than having been educated, as they could, in their own sort of intelligence with the intuitive commonness and essence of formal sciences. That is to say make sense with logics and mathematical. To turn able to examine results, detect irregularities and regularities, the way they like.

Systems of educations on formal methods, often vary. Some pragmatic societies (so called empirical) make important pedagogic efforts to match them with common life phenomenology and formal sciences issues. Others have a talent for conjugate cleanliness of formulation, culture and care for simplicity of pedagogues (Slavic ones?). Elsewhere way of teaching so much controlling the risks posed by students, when trying to extend the lessons to social-economical-political applications, conjugate poor copies, restrict logics, maintain low levels of numeracy but their dictator level of understanding govern. Other, proudly Cartesians, because too imbued by the superiority of such skills, just miss that not every student has to turn a blind disciple. And by the ways of such methods restricted to sophisticated levels of clean manners excluded their sciences from the common services they should have near the most.

Error, among human societies, is not to have clear enough in mind that formal sciences in more clever limits are not just for the nasty industries of world-wide looping insanely profits. But there are more as basic methods and instruments that can carry cautiously, and less alienating, more universality among humans minds. And so they should be better systematic used. Especially to equip the approaches. Rather than have these proliferations of 'strategic' sort sight-ness of social arts registers common logics. Applied in ways of forcing convictions. Ignoring by the way that cognitive reasoning is primarily for coping with daily lives and decisions or transient phenomenologies. So be flexible with humans' affairs. It is not for pretending to reach finite proofs and truths other than scientific (out those having scientific principles). With the computed resources so invasive in our lives observing how inefficiently, they are not used as tools for the supporting the harmonies to expect from scientific and technological advancements made humanely profitable.

Algebra and Formal Structures

Fundamental now is to pay more attention to the formal sciences structures for progressive-continuous quali and quanti improvements. Which are required for not being alienated by the artificial intelligence of machines and interactions with knowledge. Even arithmetic has structures between discrete and continuous.

So if any number with some digits may be estimated by approximations (of orders of values) or statistically (by significant differences) can defect 'irregularities' (by defect); if you have no clue on algebraic structures, 'selected by the system', fit any result to a model or representation of the sort you will not make details of difference such as between mistakes: 1) of records (you can checklist procedures of record); 2) of problems formulation (well posing of mathematical problems is often defective); 3) ensure the proper 'phenomenology' of your heuristic.

So as, respect to your model about 'how it works' could be effectively tested according it merits: 1) Capacity to explain (semantic); 2) Ability to get in knowledge-based automata (syntactically); 3) Power of representing (economics of identification to phenomenological realities; 4) Capacity to model (both for explaining, representing and motivations). But do not confuse, traditional statistics have fitness and likelihood tests... That is respect to the capacity of the model to fit the statistics data on average, overall; which is not exactly the same as the best picture or model respect to the phenomenon; neither is about the usability of the model for detecting directly informative about counter-factuals.

You will not be able to say that the regularity or irregularity you 'observe' is consistent with the phenomenon. Moreover it is usual, especially front o legitimate actors: innocently 'cheat and chat': as long as gross inccherence not enough democratically perceived; with pretending the numbers serve your theory ... or deduce 'so many things', so infective of inefficiencies. This will often come together with lack of respect, of phenomenological issues.... If there only one new kind of paradigm required is making prevail the positive use of formal resources.

A basic kind of formal structure met in algebra or ways of operating numbers are **groups**. A group is a non-empty set provided a binary operation with the property of: 1) Closure (operation of 2 elements also in the group); 2) There is associativity (in an operated series of number parentheses' position or sub-operations are indifferent); 3) There is an identity element (neutral to the operation), it is unique; 4) There is an inverse element.

One uses **groups to describe geometric symmetries**. Understand also in a general set of numbers, group selects those provided by the operation. 'Associativity' means uniqueness of all operations. Associativity starts at 3 elements. Neutral element depends on the operation.

Associativity is a valid rule of replacement for expressions in logical proofs. Within an expression containing 2 or more occurrences in a row of the same associative operator, the order in which the operations are performed does not matter as long as the sequence of the operands is not changed. The order by the side of **operands**.

Inverse element depends on the operation possibly restricted. **Commutativity** starts at 2. Commutativity means **permutations** not affecting results of operations. A **binary operation** is commutative if changing the order of the operands does not change the result. It is a fundamental property of many binary operations, and many mathematical proofs depend on it..

In the global traditional way of using mathematics we observe 'perfect' symbolic, neutral and simple and avoiding the 'details', essentials to the good fit with physics. Groups' algebra are **arithmetic structuring** of **algebraic**.

Group which originated with Galois's theory of groups. He connected the theory or groups to the solutions of polynomials. His purpose was to study the effects of permutations in equations roots calculi. This established a correspondence between algebraic structure and permutation groups. Groups operatively produce (add or multiply) elements of set. They are said abelian if produced elements can commute.

Lagrange's theorem: if G is a finite multiplicative group and U a subgroup of G than | U| divide | G| **Order theorem of Lagrange**: Its (kind of) order of every subgroup of a finite group is divisors of the order of the group.

Let be X a finite set, there is a Galois correspondence between subgroups of the symmetric group Sym(X) and X. General quartic has 4! (4 (3 (2 (1) = 24 Elements of symmetry as visualized by the tetrahedron. General quintic equation has 5! : 5 ((4 (3 (2 (1) = 120 Symmetry element visually is the icosahedron.

A normal subgroup is a subgroup H (of given group G) which has additional property of ghg-1 for all g ∈ H and h ∈ H.

A **homomorphism between 2 groups** of maps; one is into another with respect group operations in both. Bijective homomorphism are referred to as the group isomorphism.

Symmetry (rotation) group: Set of all rotations around a 3 dimensional space fixed point, forms a non-commutative group, which is referred to as the 3-dimensional rotation group.

The **group operator** is given by the composition of 2 rotations. The intuitive symmetry group of a ball which center can be described by a group theoretically as the set of all rotations with map the ball into itself.

There are groups of permutations, transposition, etc. Cyclic groups have generating elements.

If there is one group for any dimension from 0 to n and for each space, we get a series of topological invariants.

Structures that are $\aleph_0$-categorial and $\aleph_0$-stable can be approximated by finite structure simultaneously in both categories.

A Grassmaniann structure in the category of permutation groups is bi-interpretable. [Grasmann algebra of exterior products in a linear space].

Poincaré's 'Fundamental group' is a mathematical group of a topological space characterizing holes and borders of an object. (See also the paragraph about the interpretation of groups' structures on elliptic curves).

O (3) group of rotations of all the symmetries of spheres.

Groups passed to Quantic theory historically so: Gauge invariance was initiated by Weyl turned a U (1) Lie group of planar rotation for electromagnetic force. This group is commutative; equations are linear. In 1954 Yang & Mills used SU (2) for Weak interactions and SU (3) for Strong Interactions. These groups are non-commutative. As a result Yang-Mills equations are hard to handle. Yang-Mills is the corresponding theory to Quantum electrodynamic QED (for weak interaction) to Strong Interaction Primary assumptions on 0-mass particles as $\gamma-$ rays and so of infinite range and other difficulties as a 'mass' gap' make...

... Yang Mills theory is still incompletely explaining. Despite some clearance from Higgs's field and boson; and unification of Weak interaction with Quantic Electro-Dynamic (Weinberg, Salam). Also van't Hoof showed that Yang-Mills equations with Higgs are renormalizable. Higgs's boson and gravity field received a recent empirical confirmation.

The reader has to remind those U (1), SU (2) and SU (3) are fundamental algebraic groups explaining much of Quantic mechanics.

Commonly arithmetic logic and structures start with group building piece, and then follow with larger structures: **rings, bodies, fields.** We avoid these mathematical extension frameworks somehow more sophisticated than required by nature's phenomenology intuitive understanding: and metaphysics of formal sciences basics. Respect to a concept of relative formal system, both are inspiring; since also caring the basic logical difficulties. That we presented in an intuitive way. They have higher (or deeper) degree of subtlety, exceeding the purpose of this essay.

In the following we would like to introduce to a renewed concept of mathematical form called skew-symmetric differential form credited to L.I. Petrova (a Russian mathematician). We do not have in our capacity to assess if deserving the curiosity of field mathematical physics professionals and many others... But a basic framework 'providing 4 articulated concepts enlacing over differentiation: invariance, covariance, conjugacy and duality with generality of expression and specification or degeneracy for precise solutions... This has much of what we need to stich with the formal relative system shuttle possibly requiring to generate closed exterior differential forms.

Petrova Skew Symmetric Differential Forms

Evolutionary skew-symmetric differential forms are deduced from evolutionary differential manifolds and are defined on non-integrable manifolds (such as tangent manifolds, Lagrangian manifolds...).

Process of extracting closed exterior forms, from evolutionary forms describes the generation of various invariant structures, conjugated objects, operators discrete transitions and quantum jumps forming pseudo-metric and metric manifolds.

In theory of exterior differential form non-degenerate transformations are those that conserves the differentials:

- Unitary transformations: 0-forms;
- Tangent and canonical transformation: 1-forms;
- Gradient and gauge transformation: 2-forms;
- Spinors, scalar, vector, tensor fields: 3-forms.

Significance of non-degenerate transformations allow one to get new closed differential forms. This opens up the possibilities of obtaining new structures. Non-degenerate transformations are like: unitary tangent; canonical or gradients. Their transformations are conserving the differential: unitary, tangent, canonical, gradient, gauge.

Evolutionary differential form proportion broader than to simply expect because they can generate closed exterior differential forms and unconventional elements:

- Non-identical relations;
- Self-variation of the evolutionary non-identical relation;
- Degenerate transformations;
- Transitions from non-integrable manifold to integrable one.

Skew symmetric forms are evolutionary forms, derived from differential equations defined on non-integrable manifolds. Evolutionary forms are non-identical relation, degenerate transformations, transitions from non-integrable manifolds to integrable ones, they enable to understand the process of configuring operators.

Skew symmetric evolutionary forms **correspond to conservation laws for the material system**. Closed exterior forms describe conservation laws for the physical field. In real process balance of conservation laws are non-commutative. Such non-commutativity from the fact that the material system state appears to be non-equilibrium one. But non-equilibrium stages of the natural system turns out to be self-varying or "self-variation of non-identical evolutionary relation."

Additional degree of freedom is realized as the condition of the degenerate transform; vanishing determinants, Jacobians of transforms, etc. Conditions specify the integral surfaces (pseudo-structures): the characteristics (the determinant of coefficients at the normal derivatives vanishes), the singular points (Jacobian is equal to 0), the envelopes of characteristics, of Euler's equations, etc.

The extraction of some formation from the local domain of the system is accompanied by emergence of the break surfaces (contact breaks). This is relevant in shocks, kinetics, particles or fields. [Some more, at the respect of these forms, will be provided further, for the moment going on with epistemology on more simple things].

Self-variation of evolutionary relation can be realized conditions when an inexact, closed on pseudo-structure exterior form is obtained from evolutionary form. Thus non-identical evolutionary relation will be obtained on identical (or pseudo-structure) relation. Examples of pseudo-structures and spaces are formed sections of cotangent bundles (Yang Mills fields), cohomology of de Rham, singular cohomologies, pseudo-Riemann spaces, pseudo-Euclidian spaces.

This point to the variation of the material system when we pass from non-equilibrium state to local equilibrium state. Degrees of relevant closed form is connected with the degree p of evolutionary form in the non-identical relation. Fields formed up by physical structures means that they are discrete ones. Exterior closed forms corresponding to conservation laws are inexact forms because they are obtained only under degenerate transformations.

Group properties of exterior differential forms have connections with Lie groups. Exterior differential forms are differentiable forms with exterior multiplication. Closed inexact exterior form an interior (i.e. defined only on pseudo-structures) differential $\theta_\pi^{\ p} = d_\pi \theta^{p-1}$. Closure property of an exterior implies any object conjugated.

This leads to the realization of invariant and covariant properties. Properties of closed exterior and dual form are:

- **Invariance**: staying enough (for being framed) closure/openness. I-structure: [I for 'invariant']. Invariance in field theory concerns the Hamiltonian calculus, the tensor calculus, group theory, quantum mechanics equations and Yang Mill theory.
- **In covariance**: interacting, so coinciding and reacting one to another.
- **Conjugacy**, conjugacy represents a certain relation or connection between 2 operators. A relation is a comparison. Conjugacy leads to invariance and covariance property of the exterior and dual form Conjugacy happens to be related to the duality.
- **Duality**, it is between exterior and dual form and elucidates a connection between physical quantities and spatial structures. Important issues from closure and integrability concepts. Duality is a property of closed form only: non-closure and non-integrability are not in dual terms. Duality untangles the mutual connection, the mutual changeability and the transition between physical object and evolutionary processes. Primal θ = pdx+qdy, dθ = 0; Dual $*\theta$ = -qdx + pdy; d$*\theta$ =0; Cauchy-Riemann's relations: dθ = 0, d$*\theta$ = 0

Importance to physics of the closed inexact exterior form with dual form since it describes the difference geometrical structure which is an invariant one. Exterior forms are, for example:

- Algebraic structure: form a coefficient
- Geometric Nature: base components
- Space dimensions.

Intuitively we imagine this operator look like what we may need for an overview of 'mobile base' geometric properties. Let have some relation about what could be needed going up (or down) the levels of scales... As for the meso-system with relative units still related to principles ('micro-down' of Universe) and environment ('macro-up' but within Universe and possibly other parallel systems, more of less nearby). Of course actually, if we see that power and logarithm are the simplest expression of operators required for that; and already used arbitrarily. In the same intuitive way we imagine that potential expression, density functions, eigenfunctions are the resources needed from formal systemic approach that intuitions have still not much ground, at least in literature we examined (only few are mentioned in bibliography).

Forming the Convenient System in Relative Stability

Anticipating or continuing with the previous any moving subject, passively of actively they are all moving is approached formally so (in bold letters only the methodological possibilities for study you need to know:

- **Eigenvalues, Eigenfunctions** provide (top-down?) the best discriminating lower axes: consistent with the **primary dimensions** of the formal object (prone to analysis, for

general formulation); respect to nature's subject (prone to geometry). [Hence analytical geometry]; But in geometric statistical analysis they are more used for separating perspectives. With our approach of combining for developing within, the idea is that there is no real object just purely one dimension. Physically they are properties of 3 or 2 dimensions objects.

- Bottom-up is the eigenvector is 'stirring the 'axis' of expansion'? [That is to say if Eigenvectors are the most consistent axis. As scale carrying the axis of most universal principles; we may need something between different levels of scales. Possibly having with them a way to separate what happens at levels of scale and what crosses levels... And also make some relations with wavelets and renormalization?]

- **Densities** produced by primary dimensions combinations and '**intricated'** quali-quanti amounts of object representing the subject. [There the **informative linked corresponding** ... with 3 dimensions and at least 3 building bricks; with the crossing and the self-overall relatively closed. That may possibly make a general expression up to 6 and 9 or some few more dimensions. [We do not know much of String theory]. It is simplified by 'degree of less freedom' and/or complicated by 'degrees of openness', etc.]. Densities may extend into more complicated units [to consider also what we development we have at some level of scale such as to ensure the 'functions of the system'?].

- In simple point, point-wise object, non-biological subject; this form is in a **phases-spaces-graph** (better 3 dimensioned); delimited by **changes of phase critical limits borders.** Then look at if the point-wise or the object are closed (or not), to a critical border (always 2 'sides' at the minimum). This is approached by phases-space diagrams (plotting position and (characteristics regimes of speeds). **Extensive and intensive**

- **Conditions** in a region already make some **possibilities of emergence** (exponent-logarithmic approached?) 'Within the universal principles.' With complex objects we are either very close to a critical border, more emergence can produce, eventually-**exchanges and emergence** still 'within' the limits of reasonable universe.

- Motions anyhow in space of reference or regions of phases (phase-space) and for some bodies, of the same universe possibly intruding into regions to collide, interact or react to conditions. There exist phase-space not just about speeds of motions but also of variations (temperature, pressure). **Cycling complex** and **self-reproducing subjects** are often taking advantage to a **motion** (of a subject from the environment) in **heterogeneity** or/and **integration** of different phases-space regimes and other nearby systems (eventually **incorporated as a sub-system**).

- Subjects as self-objects emerged (**created**) or; unit system logically arithmetically structured succeeded in operating **articulation**(s) of maintenance, function and structurally (**groups, invariants, characteristics exponents, relative closures**). This is qualitatively (**properties**) quantitatively balances (**amounts**) (in **dynamic equilibria** maintaining '**economically'** for some: **reached and achieved level of maximum netgentropy** in the **evolutionary processes**.

- Approach, can be systemic (and formally relativized and indexed?) ... [if not: definitively unmanageable?]. A given **subject** positioned in its **principles** and its **environment** in **time-able accessible universe**? (Of which it depends, but it is not limited to just one phase space (for complex subjects?)

[Linear metric Euclidian system has used with conditions, and probably locally (so also analytically) with interesting functionality. Rules are down provided (at dimension 1)].

Now within regular conditions, once values of equilibria, have been reached [and stabilized under evolutionary processes of selection (you do not need a pattern be perfectly established in its environment 'definitely' ... if the 'field is good')]. It is to observe a change of founding grounds (physics).

This would be much harder without constraints... Swift from atomic nuclear reactions to chemical reactions the latter are more at the 'periphery'. Get back to nuclear changes requires more brutality. Because the microstates of other classes form an insignificant part in the microscopic space of phases and/or the system has less probability to get into more developed orders... But that irreversibility is also the logical reason why, for not evolving definitively, and fast, to the destructive 'congestion of complexity'.

There is a fast track to destruction. If all things are inflexible or rigid and entropy let on its own 'big steps of destruction'. Precisely the particles swift to field and reciprocally? [Bungee jumping requires good elastic (not too long nor breakable) to avoid head crash on the ground. As well as not having infinite perfect elasticity (you would crash your head on the bridge's arch)].

Micro-canonical ensembles need to be 'time independent' (for the life of the couple particle-field) or relatively infinite. Thus for grounded systems of higher complexity have their life-time within the ground's possibilities. Statistics allow this to be robust. A fraction can go elsewhere, and renewed (not 'deterministically forcibly'?). But it is almost sure that your constituent particles of protons and electrons have been exchanged so 'degeneracy is not the same' at the end of your life than at the beginning. [You are a shape-formed-evanescent reflexive ghost].

In mathematics **time independence needs Liouville's property**. According to Liouville theorem the Hamiltonian flow (dynamic such representation of exchanges of the system) preserves the volume of the initial phase-space region; even though the shape of this region may be distorted [... So it can be distributed ... in the phase-space?]. And the trajectories only stir the energy surface around. Liouville's theorem is true for all Hamiltonian systems. So flows in phase-space is incompressible [physics laws there, especial requirement conservation? Remind also our comment on time and space correspondance].

To note that there are no attractors in Hamiltonian phase-space systems, contrary to other dynamic systems [making a place, at least the essential to definition, somehow stable: no identity metamorphosis there?]. Liouville's tori is also in the phases' space.

To examine how formalism can express systems' evolutions. Consider the geometric nature using the Hamiltonian (**H**) of a projection (Hamiltonian projection) postulate that in the Eigenspaces of the projector (**E**), the horizontal plane representing the Eigenvalue 1 and the vertical plane the Eigenvalue 0. We have the decomposition of state y $|y$ (= $E|y$ (+ $(I-E)|y$ (into 2 orthogonal parts (**E** and **I-E** where **I** am identity matrix.

The probability in each case is given by the exact proportionality factor. Whereby the squared hermitian length $\hat{E}\psi\hat{E}$ of $|y$ (is reduced in the projection (state vectors not normalized). [Have in mind the Hermitian relate complex numbers, polynomials, orthogonality and statistics].

Equilibrium is a macro-state property. Macro-identity may stay, if the macro-state switches out equilibrium, are ruled by critical priorities; to satisfy essential functions flows. Some essential functions are not fully switched-off or turned-on exclusively.

Real life of body not the narrow determinism of humans' consciousness [thus so weak appear consciousness, in reality, despite 'so much' civilization?].

It is not hard to put some macro-state out of equilibrium relaxing some constraints (formally 'opening'). They exist relatively to integrable Hamiltonian systems. But, when an integrable system is integrated, we generally obtain a system which is not more integrable. [A sort of closure we expect].

Thus nevertheless some tori will stay **invariant according Kolmogorov-Arnold-Moser (KAM) theorem**. [Remind that Hamiltonian system are good form for system formal representation].

KAM (Kolmogorov-Arnold-Moser) and Nekhoroshev theorems show that **ergodicity and integrability are not generic properties of Hamiltonian systems, but resulting from the perturbation of integrable systems**. [... Does this mean that the integrability or incorporation not from the lower? (And not just superior) But constituted system can express systemically at meso or macro-defining level? [... Allowing Jane or Peter be named so, whatever the very protons and neutrons they have?). Hence not necessarily any macro supposed levels of social, with the systemic qualities it pretends to?].

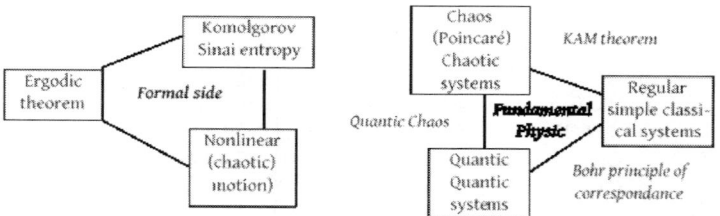

KAM results are variables for any time, but only in a part of phases' space. KAM and Nekhoroshev analytical results have to be read as qualitative, about kind of regime rather than specific point values ... or at least a dynamic probabilistic definition of the object or represented subject.

From KAM theorem and the study of chaos; Hamiltonian systems with small numbers of particles are often not ergodic (thus somehow ordered). They are commonly regions formed by tori of non-0 volume; which does not mix with the rest of the energy surface. Answers to find in the structural ordering of Hamiltonian) ... [The possibility of some relative closeness needed by an object ... and the corresponding subject].

Apparent Macro-Equilibrium Hypothesis

Now in all, the much more uncertain and dynamic universe; since the most fundamental to the most cosmic ones; a fundamental question would be about why it 'locally-widely' looks like stable (or aspiration to it?). To the point that economics theory even (but not very properly) puts it as the main "architectural" political device: the General Equilibrium Theory" [interconnecting all prices and all markets in high numbers?]

For some systemic formal approach. Microscopic states of a system 'get in' quickly in larger states classes; where the states correspond, all to the same value; of macroscopic magnitude of interest. This magnitude characterizes the value at equilibrium; with, at least, up maximum and down minimum regimes.

Remind that these microstates are already dynamic balances between particles and their corresponding fields. 2 opposite natural providing primary dynamic capacities and/or openness in systemic terms. Then going up in complexity meanwhile providing successive grounds (or plateaus) is for apparently stable physics constitutions, relating matters and energies; switches of expression. Since they are, in the 'lowest' and the 'highest', interrelated by Einstein's formula. The higher the variations of energies are, the stronger the variations or, less the matters. The lower the variations of energies are and the lower the ones of matter; than the weakest but enabling more diversity.

Having to consider the overall trend from the hottest and most localized to the coldest and most extended spaces. Then 'in between' the discrepancies of adjustments take place and they are very necessary to the emergence of local orders: high masses respect to small energies and cold enough, life can appear. High energies respect to masses and stars may provide small amounts of energies (enough statistically and combinatory divided and filtered?) to neighboring colder systems; kindly or avidly opens, for receiving and keeping it at a better range of use.

These intermixed a bit complicated? ... The formal reason of approach that was allowed incomplete 1st order logic informed by 2nd order logic kernels completed by reality ... [tentatively].

Complex Modeling Systems

As profanes can remark: we all have a 'not so large' series of concepts or properties but they may have similar 'avatars'. These are contributing to a given system (or subsystem), program, project (and so on) playing or operating together according to a group algebraic structure: 1) Given by the *substratum* of physics (playing against, would be foolish: you have to understand that, and then to know on which parameters to play (technology makes it), sensible system to perturbed. 2) Provided a political sub-set of criteria and influences. To apply to the chosen parameters (possibly including social values... As a sort of model accepted by most, possibly on a model system; adapted to their perspective). Subsystem of perturbations made by the partial contributions sum.

So it would be not so difficult to conceive; either a quality model of amounts; eventually as changes of (or parts within stocks) or; a quantity model of qualities (structure properly your logarithms; then up in amounts and by the way; matching logs and exponents. [Possibly double log down and double exponents up] or work narrowly on information (The 'information' matches may also vary after the base? In characteristics dimensions numbers and eventually diversify? Possibly to make use of the matrix or cubes; (representing surfaces or volumes: Hamiltonians) finding characteristics networks. You may also make use of quaternions or octonions, much depending on the symmetries you have and/or want to articulate: such as actions and regulations.

> Do not play foolishly against physics principles but smartly use them (by the means of their balance) ... And remind: even engineers are irrational unconscious players and/or manipulating humans beings. When this is used in experiments and feedback from realities', aware of balances between determinism and uncertainty; cardinal diversities and ordinal scarcities.

> Under such umbrella you may imagine using the 'general axiom of abstraction' transiently, everywhere for looking at with a small mirror. Have clear enough in mind, at least in intuitive understanding; you have all the possibilities of symmetries and relations between concepts. Many of those, make use of similarities and cooperation positively synergistic. To intent to recruit contributions since actor perspectives and margins of flexibilities is for the success of programs. If individuals are caring first, the social sense of utility (or broad 'non-dissatisfaction'), rather than quite too often very specific goals.

> Measuring has to balance objectivity (fake measure possibly problematic) and requiring to be phenomenologically informing to most. Good learning effects (in exemplarity) is often better. Social utility possibly also to consider as a relative formal system not just the simple sum of individual competing contributions (you may record, effectively but do not learn to make it socially.

To calibrate relative formal system? Have in mind that the General cubic (degree 3) equation has a general expression of its solutions by determinants calculus. Also it has (factorial 3): 3! = 3 (2 = 6 groups of symmetries). Knowing also that the General Quartic and General Quintic equation has no general expression of solutions by determinants calculus, so that some solution(s) requires more dimensions or complement of information, or simplifications.

Possibly also the algebraic group of operations. Intuitively have in mind that more than 3 you may also need from general compacted expressions some specific value or degeneracy for solutions ... the v_0: values at 0?–and a bit more: some 4 + 2 (for integrity). [This is still for clear by proper mathematicians and to be made, interactively computed for self-made explorations of posing and solving problems].

Often principles and within specifying relations are expressed as symmetries. In the fundamental physics like particles-antiparticles. But either by effect of perspective, narrowed one or nature's development (which shows plenty of asymmetries) there are symmetries, as conservation laws and other that face breaking of symmetries. Consider, for example: there are 24 possible groups of symmetries, for quartic general equation. Knowing enough may give you specific solutions (if all symmetries respected) or the knowledge of the special group algebra (reducing that). [For intuitive understand observe that 24 looks like many alphabets].

Mind also that geometrically we have simple called **platonic solid**s in the solid physics crystal structure are of the sort. [Not so much the cut and polished precious gem but the optic properties provided by the natural crystal structures]. Group theory applies well to them. Also called **polyhedral** we met in nature plenty of essential models. Formally they can also be approached with graph theory and networks. Some of next volume chapters, were we intent also to provide some suggestions. This essay is more about that.

This way of inspired thinking may have wide implications; when analyzing even in more common social approaches of ecological and socio-economic transformations. In some way all what we do, pass by this. Prospect is not to have too much ambition about knowing, everything for caring everything; evidence that it is not the way things operate. Nor it is to make all independently without sharing common sense of commons.

Probably it is more for making sense of **commonness, coherence**, whatever the unary-ness of the label 'at the top'. Understand also enough of the main subsystem, of the system: 1) similarities/separations (1st Universe/micro); 2) anti-similarities/recombination (2nd meso diversifying within) and 3) 'remaining symmetries'/'diversifying' (3rd for 2nd macro environment). [We will have to manage 2 other 'subs']. In sort of metaphysical theory (with practical estimates imbued of complexities and complications) and more probably some few classes of informative links to 'operators'.

The aim is to prevent different perspectives of the same or complementary; turn destructively antagonists; since having to connect and correlate in the explicit when implicit; in the implicit when explicit. In the minimum it would be to avoid struggles and fights when views are just complementary. So that they should be just synergies for the good, regulatory for the hard. [We never heard any technocrats explaining by the polygons the symmetries existing often in social-political systems, making for example that quite often the problems faced in one have been solved in the other antagonist. Only to be the winner and the proud cause of the humans made disasters affecting others whom were only trying to live better].

Yin Yang Form without esoteric

[Beg your pardon, but next useful 'yin-yang' form is not a traditional identification. And we do not care about property rights at the respect. Nor we take it as an esoteric resource. More we care about geometric properties of symmetries-anti-symmetries, breaking of symmetries yet not done].

Ying Yang patterns a wonderful form of eastern Asia philosophy to summarize the sort of half-complex formal tools to mind and start informative identification and formal pre-topology. Whenever some interrogation 'pop out in your brain'. Apart from the artifice of Capra (that we personally did not read at all); nor having recalled how Yi-Lin-Forrest relates his systemic view to the culture of his roots. In fact we remember more some article from physicists about its symmetries. Care that our first one is 'with the point one into another'. [South Korea's flag missed them, they are essential] but as far as our memory can this is not relevant to below coming sort of exploration.

See that this construction is a good combination of symmetry-and anti-symmetry. Mind also that the **Yi King ideograms** have much interesting combinatory fundamental properties which intuitively may explain why the Yi-King could self-justify its harmonic 'Grail Soup of Letters and Numbers' with aesthetic sensations. But Yi King is not our art.

Another important insight of our poor culture that impressed us has been with Zen poetry: when you have in a 4 small verse **haiku** a simple description of nature. Whatever your speculative poetic fancies around, you should be simply convinced that the wisdom is just in this 'simple description of nature'.

Yin-Yang forms an 'ideal' that does not exist so harmonious if taken as a picture of a formal abstract. Consider after having qualitatively framed you inspection so; to get to your quali-quantification (down-top approach) or quanti-qualification (top-down approach) and your quantities if ever required, may be completed by the sort of complementary **Menger's sponge picture**, we developed above.

In the 'realities' you also have to face asymmetries, growth or contraction of the forms, and colors of the structures. Preserving some invariance of qualitative symmetries? The formal fiber of the job, without presuming, processes ... as the cuts we suggested with a sort of **Mobius strip**? ... top down generally in the Kronecker way applied with (physics) energy... Or bottom up relative formal system with matter but with fillings and holes?]. [Kronecker was a Prussian businessman before turning mathematician, and then quite harsh in his relationships with colleagues].

This makes this yin-yang concept a picture (natural) **complexity-before** or (anthropic) **complications-after**; variably proportioning its areas and crossing it informed potentials (before) and balance '**intern energy**' and **exergy** (after) [the gap with sort of skew-symmetric differential forms of **netgentropy** after?].

That is a framework concept you can use in **dualist approach** like **formal and physics**: **cardinals- ordinals, matter-energy**, as **the field(s)-particle(s) ... in up tip top down** ... **body-unconscious-conscious-enactions**. And the suggestion to start better with a 3 or 4 similar forms. More explicit visuals of {over]below-above[behind} your scoring-indexed card.

Consider ahead of such Yin-Yang form locally an eye (exploratory) or point-wise: grey color with partial memory. That is: having its pathway steps (either sure or directed or at random Brownian ergodic) in the field of the form... Just a kernel moving in a large yin-yang providing arena. With a short (local) memory of color, surprised (catastrophized) at 1st; when meeting or entering into other color area ... then get used to (or get out soon).

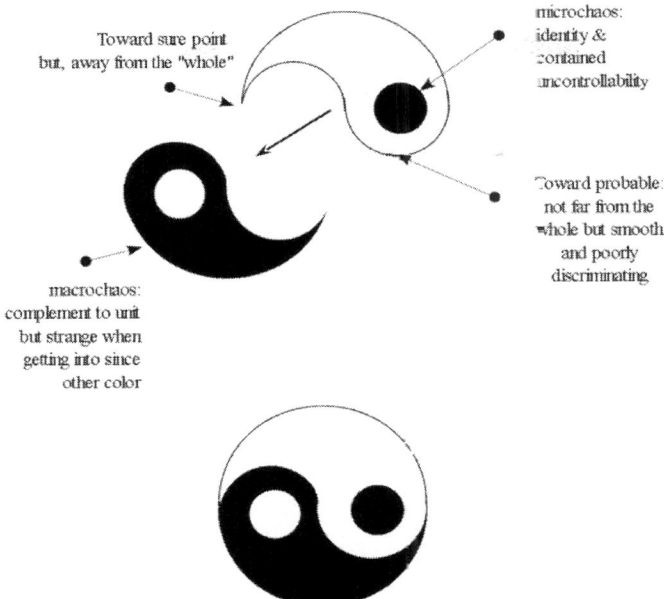

That considers a **point process**-able in colors' regions of yin-yang symbol. Dropped neutrally mid of one color main area, and then move in your trajectory, either **random or deterministically** pointing at; makes your 1st memory. Go to explore the space around.

When meeting an area of different colors (almost ignored before) point process proceeds in a **catastrophe** and then adapt to the color; after the point-progress's **memory**. If your step sides towards the 'fat part' of the region, you will probably meet the other color little circle (name it the small-not). So that fat sides can be accounted as a **probable side**: the pathway progress is not 'certain'.

Further, like trying to meet the tiptop of the area (say **optimum**) of this fat side, in fact you need an extent (like of your arms extended. Thus were a range, **interval** or **segment** is necessary to explore, converging but having to take into account the 'small-not like' (necessary) uncertainty; in that near: fat side of 'probable' of one color. [Meanwhile the other thin side determinist region of same color can be just one finger pointed at)].

Back to the start, for siding the other way. There you have no 'small-not' to take into account. Easily, with few doubt, you will find the foremost point, since you are narrowly driven to it. We call it often the tiptop of the claw. [Since half form of yin-yang looks like a tiger's claw]. That way look-like the one of **exactness**. Formally to use the **differential calculus** and the borders of color-referential you **converge to**

one. But: respect to the remaining area of the same color, the "tiptop of the claw" isolates itself from the whole area and correspondingly increases the probability (or risk) of 'catastrophe'; when to meet the other color (you are on its fat part). So extreme point (the tiptop of the claw) is very clear and very unique. But have different **left and right derivations** and there, **bifurcation** is almost forced. If you 'cut the way' to your people's.[thus the: 'kingdom for a horse' option (Shakespeare's Richard III)].

Big change or "**catastrophe**" (which is not necessarily in the abrupt way; when you are passing from a color of the area to another. This **tipping** point is in fact the center of the whole picture. Central bi-point is also an exceptional wholesome point there to cross the lines of colors smoothly as a **point of inflection** (tipping point) tangent, a straight line crossing in 2 colors.

Now this separating wavelike border between 2 areas of different colors we often call it **Ockham's scissor**s. **Dynamically** following it on one *extremum* of separation we side by one color, further **balance to the other**. The so-called Ockham principle (not for sure from Ockham himself) is about collective *consensus* siding to the weakest but most commonly shared option (because lowest inconvenient?). You can practically think that you are yourself of some color and the other is other color; of which with your small point of its color have something in common. Collectively it would be not so different from the **least conflictive affective option**. This small point of the other color in each area can be imagined just what you **exchange, inform**, 'have in you'; this is for **understanding the other** (lucid empathy) and care apart, from **the pool of uncertainty**, and so on.

Scheme can apply like if you are **both individual and collective**. The small points may play as information of the other(s). Self without crossing knowledge is not much more interesting, so is the purification consisting in making the fusion of identical color ... but then where the need to a straight line of exchange?

The framework could receive a **combinatory logical treatment** and possibly help to imagine the first steps of **partitioning, semi-separation**. Especially if adding perspective with 3 dimensions. As have ternary Yin-Yang symbols [Do not miss the 'intrication']. In the binary case here you have a **dynamic dualist balance**: first others to your side (if your condition not the best) then you to others (especially if you turned better off). So philosophically you may consider the small of another color the required knowledge of the others. Either for self or for having some reason to interface and exchange. [Make it the **log off** and there is your exchange. Mind too **in the same universe there is always something to exchange**].

Imagine also types of **complementary crossed symmetries**; not the black- wrong, white-good. (Historically it has more often been the reverse.) One may put you in some state (say for 'rest and restore') and the other is another (proactive or exploring). Vary also actors: you and your partner, you and all the others, you and nature and so on [and at least 'cross information'].

Possibilities of such frames are considerable as mnemonic; but always mind that the policy to erase all of the others in you is very poor policy tries. It is never to pretend to be determinist at a 100% rate [somehow in the maximum: $(1- n^{-1}\log n)$? Since 100% is quite often the best way to show that you are ... stupid not to know calculate with energy's yields.

Of course, mind that **evolving applied cases have also asymmetries.** Even in fundamental ordered nature's breaking of asymmetries are shown. You have margins for varying (in the short term), average variation (as potential) and variation (overall). Just neither too small; nor excessively to adapt to physical conditions. Making that better and better after humble efforts and corrections of care, made; a good way to better your mood and empower your humor or sense of happiness?– having achieved to be good?

Also, better to think about it, as more specified (as told **3 to 6 kinds of color-area.** You can use the 3 primary colors and then their mixture.

Try to imagine the volume. For the correspondence it is a bit trickier; maybe you will have to imagine 2 intricated sorts of Klein's bottle (in topologies approach) [Mind that Klein's bottle provides with holes in the topology].

There are plenty of relevant topological concept you can imbue Yin-Yang's picture with, especially the 3 dimensions kind of: fibers **Möbius strip** (between small **discs?**), **fractals** (different levels of the picture), **smooth fractals** (between 3 dimensioned small discs) etc.

Of course this may turn awful perverse mathematics. But imagine only this **programed in an interactive way in a computer**, you will only have to identify the simplest, **check at the properties** you expect (and other amenities), **weights** how you are used, organize the consult in a proper way, indicate the registers. The output the **choices** you can want, or **flexibly adjust after the simulations.** The statistics you will meet in the 'clouds' (of world-wide-web?).

The **characteristic values** you obtain from **natural sciences knowledge** and **otherwise from previous experiences** [Bayesian approaches] caring to maintain flexibility of uncertainties; and the computer will return your **forms, patterns** (metaphysical) **questions** (about your choices) with **sorts of critical sentences** not only for telling you that you are irrational.

Much will depend on the **included specifications** also with the **suggestions of operations** (algebraic group like, operators, etc.). But avoid the authoritarianism of discretionary unique will, systematically manipulated behind the scenes.

Of course there will still be the back-stage of software designers and precautions. In possible mathematical formalization this picture of yin and yang 'is easy' [kind of joke]: with/Black parts could be determined/random realized part;

Exact means: from point to point infinitesimal differential calculus within the limits of experimental realizations bordered by the critical transitions (phase-space in the environment), characteristic exponent and excessive deviations to the Eigentensor structures system Densified (supported apart from critical transitions?);

Probabilistic means: from 'point to (at least) segment'. Probabilistic calculus can eventually be central mean driven (the determinism in the random) and statistics confusion but not just. [Some more about in the next volume of essay].

Catastrophe: change of color small, catastrophe of probability: non-linearity. Large catastrophe: change of relative definition (threshold pivot?). Eventually reframing of algebra? Tipping points and bifurcations (smooth and breaking?).

Too: imagine yin-yang with **various levels of scale**. At least 2 levels or 3 after a concept of 'wholist' systemic units. Mind that each level of the symbol is a basic organizing step in the evolution of the subject's system. The **maximum degree of complexity could be the unit organizing systemic steps**.

You also have to think dynamically, like using the **pattern as a mixer**.

Essential principles are defined as **generic base**, and **set the space**, not its own universe; where higher degrees of complexity could exist. Thus essential principles may **expand within** not beyond the limits. If the higher complex included unit succeed in recruiting and include resources, from wider and lower environment, or its reachable universe.

So you can mathematically **integrate in a complex way for meso-existence in macro** (unity of maximum complexity) and micro-level (extensions into **systemic integrations**). Have in mind that it is not just of this pattern. There are plenty of different patterns a bit more complex, we say half complex that you can use.

In all yin yang picture is fine for a sort of crossed dual thinking about informative piece.

Riemann Surface, relations to Category Theory

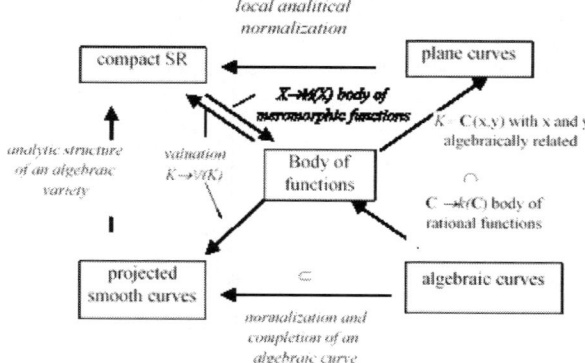

There is equivalence of categories between
1. Riemann compact surfaces + non constant morphisms
2. Bodies of functions of one variable+ non nul C-algebra morphism,
3. Algebraic curves on C+ non constant rational morphisms,
4. Plane Algebraic curves+ non constant rational morphisms
5. Smooth projective Curves on C+ non constant morphisms

Un-Conclusion

In this essay, together with some intuitions posed as questions we try to provide a relevant collection of formal fundamentals that seems essential when looking at natural physics frameworks; like for a multiple levels of 'complexifying' scale approach. In the first volume of the present essay we pursued various other goals. Provision with insights that most of modern education curricular simplify too much and despite the fact that they are the basic to formal sciences services near everyone and anyhow, as needed by a cooperative society. Better than analytically these and formal approaches should better be introduced, 'epistemological and phenomenologically'.

At a stage of globalization and information revolution, which are turning harder; both require more maturity with formal tools and new equipment, rather than just 'curiosity'. Otherwise we are going to lose their social benefits so wasted in fancy things and nasty ones.

Another critical condition is with 'social sciences of interventions and precautions'. Addressing not to their grounds but their conceptions and ways of management. If the idea of knowledge society is obvious, it is far from clear that a theoretical social economy should develop in the traditional way to create disciplines. And it is also increasingly discussed the defects of economy's methods and policies, proposed by administrations imbued of their hierarchies and deluded nice ways of servicing.

Examinations, insights provided in this essay are often introduced in common scientific vulgarization terms. Formal sciences joining mathematics and logics can do much more. 'Smaller' logic probably have to revise its ways of social contributions since its forms are going to turn critical in this new era of information revolution. We should care not to impose unfriendly formal simplification on natural cognitive way to reason, but find better of mutual empowerment and synergies between what can bring these technologies to the fields and what they cannot replace despite the marketing of their dealers.

The universality of formal sciences knowledge is hardly cared; despite the fact that they are everywhere in the natural world and in as product of humans discoveries. As a result good philosophies of such sort of sciences or epistemologies are being too poorly known and does not permeate properly in social and economic management. In such a poor way, which because with plenty of 'intermediaries' almost preventing informative enough coherence establish with the support of essential knowledge and phenomenologies by the intermediate between people of the societies and public and private intermediate of structures.

Even if it is not to deny now that concepts of 'complex management and econophysics have come fashionable. We are almost convinced that it is not good enough ways for gents and administrations of 'people'. The challenges of globalization in the reshaping of societies, for them dedicate better to their constructions have not been coping: they empowered much more bureaucracies, populisms, extractions and reactions from proprietary governance.

Fundamental natural sciences enormous 'stock development' and ethereal diffusion have not lowered determinist inefficiencies existing in human affairs.

Possibly more than the crisis of neoclassical economics there is a crisis of governance means paradigm; affecting first the industrial Occidentalism consumerism-prone, organized by affluent superstructures. We speak of means and mainstreams' management. This does not mean at all that we expect the solutions would be in the heterodoxies and reactions or in the dependent ones, in their ambitions restore their leadership. We are often having seen the inconsistencies of reactions promising another paradigm, where they could be better ownership, mostly unaware about what methods, means and tools, could clear if better managed. Similarly not biased by another scientism. History of sciences has produced many wrong sorts of scientism.

Formal sciences and natural sciences have developed correlatively not in a straight way. Posing this often many metaphysical questions, we should examine better. Because if natural sciences and formal methods have delivered much in terms of technologies innovations and primary connected knowledge. Formal methods, have been managed otherwise, more are arts for manipulating convictions rather than infuse social constructions of individuals care to bias environments flows in cautious ways. So it is for them, to evolve in positive ways to care the supports (biological or not), and smooth and humane sustainable societies.

There have been many 'scientists' jumps' into many concepts, for detailing the determinist rights way to inflate business opportunities in the governance of people. People of many kinds, or required to be clients, manipulated for feeling bad about their mediocre performance of developments when not having to leave the place for others' ambitions. Add bizarre hierarchies over-piling of transgressions reserved rights as clubs of privileged. Bizarre respect to the ways, nature could inspire optimum assignations.

More with primary epistemological and social heuristic defects seem to come from the paucity of formal treatments and forces interrelations in ways of doing things, uncaring the sources. Major mistakes come from determinism and crude intents of discriminations. Separations as essential practices of methods for studying are produced in the increasingly coarse ways of Cartesian. Mistakenly supposed to be the best way to refer under discriminating categories. This comes together with the traditional rude ways for priorities, unbearable for the proper uses of new means.

Traditional paradigm that makes modern societies more supporting autocrats and centralized administrations. Alienate democratic leaderships to implicit technocracies and correspondingly democratic populism under bureaucracies containment. All without proper epistemologies, nor civil sense of formal limits. All are contributing to delusion, pretending to be scientific for closing minds. Meanwhile the global trends show the contrary.

Among all this, the least to expect is that the methods we use for the framework, inform properly. They are expected not to support the narrow allowed thinking paradigm, providing options in opportunities and derivations. And could also inform better, about the policies because potentially able to evidence the inefficiencies. But for that they have to be applied in a fairer way for conscious choice.

For this non-paradigmatic essay, be fairly applied, relations have been evidenced in formal sciences either formal and naturally possibly intertwine. Human methodological perspectives, give reason to think that formal sciences rooted, since natural sciences could induce social frames in fair continuities or more humane contradictions. Not to work without roots, nor without universal moral meanings. Somehow this, in the minds of humans, is done cognitively. But it should be better understood and seen in operating representations and share-able models.

Once understood the proper position and marginal way of conscious. This would give by the way, resources that could be used for social-economic management. As well as serve ecological-environmental management. We suspect perfect formal achievements too much claiming for purity;. Whence not enough accounting for some essential frameworks. So too many are artificially separated from phenomenological ways of behaving simply and responsibly.

Mathematicians, logicians or physicists and scientists able with formal sciences may not have been properly involved in tasks of services, as the revolution of information means should have been expected. Engineers are still to abridging their social tasks by poorly looking at most of natural ways. Fundamental physics theorists are not engaged enough in proper supportive informative relations about natural mechanisms.

Social 'scientists', un-seriously, have been kept social 'un-commitments' in their too dedicated, researches of essential laws; dedicated to produce future 'dead leaves of theories', they do that in a similar way, but without the qualities of natural ones. Too much they have been living on theories to turn fake soon and their methods 'simply inconsistent' ... by the delays between formal advancements and transfers to social arts.

This co-exist with huge communications on wrong informative relations for solutions.. They are enormously unfair shortcuts made in common affairs. Lay management should make less biases in their use of formal methods narrowed by the eye-flaps of discrimination, improper social care and misunderstanding of options and issues. Many are aware of that; but the paradigm self-reproduce its mistakes. Even when those feelings of mismatching and unfit are growing. The simplifiers of the wrong side are growing in the same way as the distortions

Since fundaments are not properly cared nor caring, most are lured with such wrong shortcuts. Could also be a mis-concept? - that other governmental theory would be required to preserve, for the kind ones, an ideology of democracy. Where most have been inefficient at behaving with it properly. At least not before detecting that the primary required steps could be by the way of conceiving and formalize things, since nature principles also practice with 'equanimity'. It is the minimum: make better use of the formal methods, with which most, without properly knowing, pretend to do the best, ignore most lessons ... and cheat.

We have started some intuitive propositions, as we felt required for wholesome approach but lay understanding, not excluding at all what all have been proposed. Just we are more by the side of synthesis inspirations. In the hope that they could have some potential to attract the curiosity of professional logicians (for adjusting), mathematicians (for corrections), physicists (for clearing), epistemologists (for being more open to propaedeutic) and any-others.

Now feeling obliged of that, after having observed (not neutrally and always cautiously) supposed experts, governance and management mistakes with social issues. We somehow turned a field epistemologist of formal methods, since we have tried to understand why the field phenomenological evidences was calling for other and better cared of what were talking about fundamental formal sciences. Having so often observed the absurdities promoted by the dogma, the practices so evidently producing their own set-backs; because their lack of synthesis between diversities. Thus we are in the mood that much of social conditions have been worsened by theories, paradigms and ways of; social as well as private business, management who are pretending to be 'rational'. They are more 'pure order compulsive' (POC) ... Far away the simple evidence, because some pretending things of their side simply transpose to the other without even adaptation to the most essential and minimal formal properties; mostly because simply ignoring them.

We are more interested in the many trying cautiously; sometimes called 'people'. But we know all the ambiguities in this term of 'people' mostly with improper definition. So our sources of interest have been heterodox, but more because of metaphysics of methods, than 'wanting to be a heterodox'. Neither we are, misunderstanding the inertia, as well as the qualities of normative practices. Being at the ground level social-economic, and because people make the democracy and so the efficiency and inefficiencies of democracy. Whatever the 'formulation' of democracy and its structures or their traditional procedures. The care or uses of complexities require everyone uses, care and contributions; in the minima of fair intelligence.

We have no axiomatic symbolic demonstrations of our proposals. Previous to axiomatic method for demonstrating, we prefer to explore visually or more broadly said with the plurality of perceptions. That could be involved: writing, symbolism, geometric displays, cognitive knowledge and techniques used in many different registers and their commonness. Not just fed abstract aspiration of their specialists. Much already exist; so more important seem, the articulations of concepts, their reinterpretations and synthesis in social-economical practices.

Thereafter to have explorations for typing (a basic for 'communicating with computers) and that is for selecting (a basic for humans to have a good use of their computer); the most essentially important, summarized, treated as knowledge base contains and sketched in consistent democratic collectives (a basic for real societies). Thus caring to differentiate de specific, global, applicable and so on, so as to be put back in cognitive frameworks for preparing the job to do in the fields. Apart from the abuse of power of reductions. Doing the job of formulation will not replace the learning by doing; in the first stage of establishing better informative links. With what we already make names, categorize, classify in operating abstracts, avoiding the dear definition of arts specialists; and try to relate to amounts whatever they are. The crucial ones to make use of in our vanishing environments and ecosystems.

Formulations and calculi not so for the lessons we want to give, but those we have to receive for being conscious of what we do fairly.

With epistemologies designed as interfaces; that should better be taken in charge by the interface; you have with "olicognography" sketches of the sort. And those applied to scientific registers closer to natural and formal sciences... Frameworks that seemed us plastic enough for collective intelligence applications. You can order them at www.lulu.com. Among some 50 preliminary frameworks a quarter may apply to our present essay about connecting essential knowledge to social operations; when effectively wanting to grab realities cognitively.

Of course you will not meet estimates, nor definite suggestions or any kind of system promotion. We just envision in the present essay the sorts of requirements to framing systemic synthesis based on formal methods. For the present essay to approach natural mechanisms you have some tips and insisting on they have to be completed with statistical physics and thermodynamics if you want to be 'thermo-ecolog-economo-dynamic logical. Formal logical grounds of 'relative-informative links' arithmetic. In the hope they can effectively put some sense of amounts and economy of language in the modeling allowed by the new means. In the hope they can do better for supporting, at least your free self-management, suspecting it the first stage of humans' economy.

We have been much inspired by all the methodological advancements on what makes the last 2 decades fundamental aspirations; about a Theory of Everything. But that has not been the theme of studies. To confess that we were not much interested in that project, and more by the sort of contributions formal methods could make to imagine, help to conceive, require to design. Theory of Everything starts with a Great Unified Theory (GUT) in fundamental physics. Our essay may not be enough properly connected to that. Maybe because our need is with having a framework enough inspired by the natural forms; as a formal way of establishing roots-based models could if achieved the same as GUT.

To any ones according to their social duty after their potential expression of skills. It is also to be sensitive to one owns limits, even if most humans cannot avoid to have their view in metaphysics. So we do not achieve any consolidation nor any Great Unified Theory. This corresponds to best thinkers in proper formulations and required empirical calculi to deliver according the devices, experiments and regular proof of physics theories. At least we hope that you will appreciate some 'rectifications' about how to manage mechanics of natural roots.

Of course we are very sorry that the aim to have some intuitive semantic and applicable contributions, does not make this essay a manual of all what needed. Even if considering completing with another volume. We have had to focus and may regret not to have been heavier; for example, on statistical physics or thermodynamics. But we did not have much to say better than what has been already formulated.

It is more for us to imagine sorts of basic concepts framed with: 'heads and hairs', logical enough, related enough, phenomenological enough, willing and share-able; for guiding consensus. These guides have to be both, experimental or intermediate and then filed, paved and 'dressed' for extensions into flexible models. There has been heterogeneity between expectations about formulations evolutions; in the many theories and models existing in complexities. Approaches where we visualize are the effective formulations.

Out the figurative ones we posed in intuitive way; expecting the right experts of formulation react to the suggestion? Most elementary formulations and 'half-quoted extracts' have been retaken from literature. Many non-voluntary contributors have not been mentioned, out the discoverer they quoted. Also because not wanting them to look like approving and endorsing our lecture. The aim of short technical details is more to give faster access to common readers; to the sort of language used 'there' and; most essential conceptual results; they have to think about, when caring grounds, including the cognitive ones of their brain and they ignore.

Common readers must have in mind that nor general formal register can be mastered by one; no abstractions about applications are truly perfect. Most special registers are very imperfect. It should correspond to talented able to push forward the cleanliness of the formulations. But of your commitments no one should ignore that three quarters of the job is in your hands, an important part is with your efforts. Understandings in your own cultural ways, and quite often common sense have often manifest in abstract, the good lessons. Just with sciences ways of you have to know, prepare, make fair use of some tools, care a proportion (as of a quarter) and let your brain do its jobs.

Next coming essays will be about the approaches and frames, in 'numbers' higher than the starting ones; of this essay. Present ones have been kept around unity of geometric objects and the start of arithmetic frames. Other slim mentions will be about 'operations'. We do not know if we will be compact enough to include bio-ecological and social-economic approaches in just one further volume of essays. Even if we are not yet with a treatise and still more in prolegomena for young people in the transition to further studies. They are our audience... You are those who will have to pay for the mistakes of modern days.

Bibliography

Bibliography is not exhaustive. We do not want to send you to technicalities ... of which we are not an expert. Following books have been explored (and we explored many others too). But many of these are somehow more of lay philosophy and with some unspecialized explorations. Some are primary handbooks hence not the best known by students constrained by exams.

1. Boccara N. Modeling Complex Systems Springer 2010

2. Boolos G. S. et. al. Computability and Logic 5th ed. Cambridge University Press 2007

3. Bouchard Y. Calcul en Logique du Premier Ordre Presses Universitaire du Québec 2015

4. Burgess J.P. Philosophical Logic Princeton University Press 2009

5. Casti J. Complexification. Harper Collins, New York, 1994

6. Chizhov W. B. Geometrization of Physical Quantities Krasand URSS Moscow 2010

7. Connes A. Noncommutative Geometry InterEdition 1994 (web downloadable for free)

8. Dorogovtsev S. N. Complex Networks. Oxford University Press 2010

9. Estrada E. The Structure of Complex Network Oxford University Press 2012

10. Feldman D. Chaos and Fractals an elementary introduction Oxford University Press 2012

11. Fernández Díaz A. La Economía de la Complejidad: economía dinámica caótica McGrawHill Madrid 1994

12. Gatica G. N. Introducción al Análisis Funcional Reverte Barcelona 2014

13. Gauthier Y. Logique arithmétique, l'arithmétisation de la logique Presses de l'Université Laval Montréal 2010

14. Giaquinto M. Visual thinking in Mathematics Oxford University Press 2007

15. Girard J-Y. Le Point Aveugle (The Blind Point). Théorie de la Démonstration (Theory of Demonstration) Hermann 2007 Paris . vol. I / vers la perfection ....(toward perfection) vol. II/ vers l'imperfection ....(toward imperfection)

16. Gray R.M. Entropy and Information Theory Springer Verlag New York 1990

17. Korn G., Korn T Mathematical handbook for scientists and Engineers. Dover 2000-1968 Mineola

18. Lascar D. La théorie des modèles en peu de maux. Cassini 2009 Paris

19. Latour B. Enquête sur les Modes d'Existence une Anthropologie des Modernes La Découverte Paris. 2012

20. Lawrence D. B. The economic value of information Springer 1999 Berlin

21. Leroux B. Rouanet Analyse géométrique des données multidimensionnelles Dunod 2014 Paris

22. Luderer B. et. al; Mathematical Formulas for Economists Springer Berlin 2002

23. Makovelski A. Histoire de la Logique. MIR 1978 Moscou

24. Malinietski G. G. Fundamentos Matematicos de la Sinergetica ed.'URSS' 2005 Moscu

25. Maravall Casesnoves Diccionario de Matemática Moderna Editorial Nacional 1975 Madrid

26. Mas-Colell A. General Equilibrium and Game Theory ten papers Havard University Press 2016 Cambridge

27. Michell J. Measurement in Psychology. Critical History of Methodological Concepts. Cambridge University Press 1999

28. Milovanov V. P. Sinergética y auto-organización sistemas socioeconómicos URSS 2010 Moscu

29. Moisseev N. Problèmes mathématiques d'analyse des systèmes Mir 1985 Moscou

30. Murray J.D. Mathematical Biology (2nd ed) 1994 Springer New York

31. Narahari Y. D. Garg, R. Narayanam, H. Prakash. Game Theoretic Problems in Network Economics and Mechanism Design Solutions Springer 2009London

32. Panza M., A. Sereni A. Introduction à la Philosophie des Mathématiques (trad. de l'Italien) Flammarion Champ Essai 2013Paris

33. Parsons S. Qualitative Methods for reasoning under uncertainty MIT Press 2001 Cambridge

34. Passé R. Les Grandes Représentations du Monde et de l'Economie à travers l'Histoire Les liens qui libèrent. 2011 Paris.

35. Pearl J. Causality models reasoning and inference 2nd edition Cambridge University Press 2009

36. Penrose R. The Road to Reality Jonathan Cap 2004London

37. Petrova L.I. Skew-symmetric differential forms in mathematics, mathematical physics and field theory Krasand 2013 Moscou

38. Prigogine I. et al. Thermodynamique Odile Jacob 1999 Paris

39. Pupion P-C, Pupion G. Méthodes Statistiques applicables aux petits échantillons. Hermann coll. économie 2010 Paris

40. Reinhardt F. Soeder H. Atlas de Mathématiques (original en allament) Encyclopédies La Pochothèque 1997 - 1974 Paris

41. Rioux O. Théorie de l'Information et du Codage Lavoisier 2007Paris

42. Samuelson L. Evolutionary Games and Equilibrium Selection, The M I T Press., 1997 Cambridge

43. Sandholm W. H. Population Games & Evolutionary Dynamics The MIT Press 2010 Cambridge

44. Scherrer B. Biostatistiques (2 volumes) Gaëtan Morin 2008 Montreal

45. Schumacker R.E. Marcoulides G.A. Interactions and non-linear effects in structural equations modelling LEA 1998 Mahwah New Jersey

46. Sethna J.P. Statistical mechanics, entropy, order parameters and complexity Oxford University Press 2006

47. Simmons H. An introduction to Category Theory Cambridge University Press 2011

48. Sheliepin L. A. El Fenómeno de la coherencia 1983 trad castellano ed. Urss 2005. Moscú

49. Steward J. Gapenne O. di Paolo E. A. Enaction The MIT Press 20_0 Cambridge

50. Sychev, V. 1985. Thermodynamics of Complex Systems ed. Energo Atomizdat: 1986 Moscow

51. Takeuti G. Proof Theory 2nd edition Dover 1987-2013 Mineola

52. Tegmark M. Our Mathematical Universe Vintage book 2014 New York

53. Thom R. Mathematical Models of Morphogenesis. Halsted Press 1983 New York..

54. Tomassi P. Logic Routledge 1999 Oxon

55. Traub J. Complexity and Information Cambridge University Press 1998

56. van Benthem. J. Modal Logic for Open Minds CSLIpub 2010 Stanford

57. von Bertalanffy L. General System Theory Georges Braziller 1968 New York.

58. Yi Lin. J. Systemic Yoyos: Some Impacts of the Second Dimension, Taylor and Francis. 2008 London.

59. Zeidler E. (ed) Oxford Users' Guide to Mathematics Oxford University Press 2004

374

Annex 1: ZFC – (Lay) Set Theory Axioms

(Zermello-Fraenkel + theorem of choice)_:

1. Extension (element of one set in another set),

2. Scheme of subset,

3. Pairing or intersection of sets,

4. Union of sets,

5. Power set or inclusion of sets,

6. Infinite existence of empty set,

7. Choice function: collect of non-empty sub set,

8. Replacement of a sentence by an equal,

9. Restriction of the tenancy of object to a subset.

[Could we suggest? – a minimum complement for completeness with a: reality relation could have to consider a probability link (in algebraic [0,1]) like a correlation) with 3 ports (links to openness): one in some formal system of reality, one anywhere in the set theory series of axioms and one in the choice's axiom. This later activates the order in the set abstract that is the concept of models. Reality system is ordered since reality. So the relation(s) to corresponding set theory will reflect its order but that to not makes it could be model handled].

If a profane mind that some problems historically resolved have to be known. Example with Cantor whom conceived the way to pass from continuous space of numbers to discrete objects (easiest element of a Set) the converse: from natural to continuous is not so easy to imagine when using Sets' Theory as collection of objects. Before the explorations of uses of Set Theory have been developed by mathematicians; the debate what about its consistency. Thereafter decline on the fringe of "clear cuts". After all that and nevertheless, Set Theory has got a wide acceptance. Not least because now very implemented "complicatedly" in all kinds of registers; and computer logic.

The Choice axiom (C) appeared because Set theory needed of an ordering relation. But it is an atypical axiom in the most accepted Zermello-Frankel consensual formulation of Set theory for making ZFC. (C) has been much debated. It is a sort of fainthearted point (to non-abstract fans) and has great importance. It has been declined is other registers. For example Zorn's lemma tells that in any ordered set is so, that all subset completely ordered has a majoring. So it has a maximum element.

You have to be cautious at what does not stay; nor pretend an abstract just to be directly identifiable to your practice. For example, a subset preserves the properties of the set. That is not the sort of isolated piece often imagined in lay reasoning; isolated from the set's operations. Words similarities (synonymous in linguistic, but all synonymous have their shade) across registers and lay language. They are sources for analogical explorations, but they have to be clarified when applied. And this clarification (by the side of formal sciences: demonstrations) minimum is often a process (of representation at least in minds, sometimes as shared models among people); not as easy as said.

An important use in a theory is to explore what the theory allows. And, not to miss: a help to differentiate what does not side with the theory. For example, with Cantor's hypothesis of "continuous". This says that: "there is no set with cardinals between the set of whole numbers and the set of real numbers". This turned the 1st of 23 Hilbert's problems. Hilbert was a German mathematician whom provided, start of the 20th century, with an exemplary program of mathematical investigations. It was shown by Austrian-American logician Gödel, in 1938 to be non-refutable within ZFC's axioms. After than logician Cohen shown it to be non-deductible (or undecidable with Church) also within ZFC's axioms.

Thus, at the turn of the millennium Set Theory is no more seen the perfect *panacea* and its use may pose problems in just simple issues of complex life. So actually also exist the premises of the fundamental logical system; which is yet not paradigmatic.

Annex 2 Arithmetic Logical Construction

(Sinaceur)

Be **K a commutative field**.
K is real if $-1 \neq \sum x_i^2$ for any n-uplets $(x_1, ..., x_n)$ elements of K.
K is ordered if the property of positivity is defined for any element of K as:

- $x \in K$ where $x = 0$ or $x > 0$ or $-x > 0$;
- if $x > 0$ and $y > 0$ then $x+y > 0$; $x.y > 0$ so if $x > y$ $x - y > 0$;

Any ordered field is real with previous properties; at the opposite a real field is not necessarily ordered.

K is said real and closed (algebraically closed) if K is real and no algebraic extension is real. In K real and closed any element different from 0 is a square or the opposite of a square and the sum of square element of K is also a square.

A real closed field can be ordered just in one way (the reverse is not true). In real closed field any polynomial of impair degree has at least one solution. If K is real and closed then K(i) is algebraically closed in a Steinitz sense: any polynomial with coefficient in K(i) and all its' solutions are in K(i). If K is ordered and; any positive element of K is a square root; any polynomial of impair degree has at least 1 root in K; then K(i) is algebraically closed.
If L is a closed algebraic field with null characteristics, K a subfield of L so as L is a simple extension of K, then K is closed and real.

Real closed field are exactly the field which by simple extension give an **algebraically closed field** and if $L = K(\alpha)$ is algebraically closed then K has null characteristic. K real and closed $\Leftrightarrow$ $K(\alpha)$ is algebraically closed. K real and closed $\Leftrightarrow$ any non-zero element of K is a square, any polynomial of impair degree has at least one solution in K.

Theorem of intermediate value: with K real and closed field and f a polynomial of K o far two element a, b of K, we have $f(a) < 0$ and $f(b) > 0$ then $\exists c \in K / a < c < b$ and $f(c) = 0$. Consequences of previous theorem in K real and closed: property of uniform continuity of polynomials in real interval,

Rolle theorem (between 2 solutions of polynomial exists at least one solution of derived polynomial.

Theorem of finite increases: if f is a defined polynomial continuous on [a,b] of $\mathbb{R}$, derivable on]a,b[then $\exists x \in$] a,b [with $f^\circledast = (f(b) - f(a)) / (b - a)$.

Sturm theorem (on the number of real solutions of a polynomial between two real given limits, any solution of polynomial $x_n + a_1 x_{n-1} + \ldots a_n$ is majored in an absolute value by $1 + |a1| + \ldots + |an|$.

Any rational function where denominator is not null on interval [a,b], reach a maximum and a minimum in that interval. Any real field has at least one algebraic extension real and closed (analogic with Steinitz theorem). Any real field K can be ordered at least in one way. Any algebraically closed field L with null characteristic which is it's simple extension, that is K(i) =L.

Theorem of existence and unicity of real closure of an ordered field.

Any algebraic field closed, with null characteristic and non-absolutely algebraic, has at least two closed real field non isomorphic.

Annex 3 Model Theory

Model Theory main original authors Löwenheim, Skolem, Gödel, Tarski and Cohen. Since Tarski's Model theory original frame (from Lascar)

- A model is a structure where a closed formula express a 1st order property of the M-structure itself. A model is an interpretation of language in which all the sentences are true in the set of sentences (formalized in 1st order language);
- Set of sentences is consistent just in case it has a model; care that in logic a 'model' more a structure in which a formalized theory is interpreted according to rules.

Definable set lead to theory of model.
- Be M a τ-structure; definable sets of base are:
  - singletons $\{c_M\}$ when c is a constant of τ;
  - interpretations of symbols of relations;
  - graphs as: $\text{graph}(f) = \{(a_0, a_1, \ldots, a_n) \in M^{n+1}; a_0 = f(a_1, a_2, \ldots, a_n)\}$, for any integer n and all symbol of function f arity n.
- M can be obtained from graphs of operations, projections, singleton {a} with 'a' a discerned of Boolean operations, projections and trivial operations.
- Any infinite model admits an elementary extension containing an infinite undiscernible series. Infinite structure with a set fully ordered.
- Corollary: be $p \in S_n(A)$ a non algebraic type; then there exists an elementary extension N of M containing a series A-undiscernible which all terms realize p.

Undiscernible and Skölem functions allow to build rich groups of automorphisms such as Erhenfeucht-Mostowski's ones.

- If T is an enumerable theory with infinite models then it has enumerable models having a group of auto-morphisms cardinal $2\aleph_o$
- Theorem: be T a consistent theory in a language L of cardinality λ and κ cardinal $\kappa \geq \lambda$, then T admits a model M cardinal k such as all $A \subseteq M$, if $\text{card}(A) \leq \lambda$ then $\text{card}(\{p \in S1(A); p \text{ is realized in M}\}) \leq \lambda$.

Considering set of real numbers $\mathbb{R}$;

- addition and product and an order relation constructed as a subset of $\mathbb{R}^2$ with Boolean operators ($\cup \cap$ and complementary);
- a definable set a subset of a Cartesian power M of $\mathbb{R}^2 \to \mathbb{R}$ since the graphs of +, × and order relation.

Results from Theory of Model:

- Gödel theorem of Completeness The formula of a formal language of 1st logic order is formally demonstrable iff it is true in all the models (universal validity).
- Gödel compactness theorem: A theory has a model iff all the finite subset of theory have a model
- Löwenheim-Skolem: If a theory of 1st order has a model, then it has a numerable model. (it is paradoxical). And also if a theory are numerable than theory a model for all infinite cardinal.
- Morley theorem: If a theory has an infinite cardinal then all the models of theory with same cardinal are isomorphic and all theory with higher cardinal is isomorphic to the previous cardinal theory.

Qualitative Confirmation
1. Entailment Condition (confirmation)
2. Special Consequence Conditions: Implication after confirmation, confirms.
3. Special consistency condition: Incompatibility after confirmation does not confirm.
4. Converse consequence condition: Implied after confirmation confirms.

Annex 4 Language and Knowledge Logic

Syntax of a knowledge base language (Levesque):

Expressions of language are build up as sequences of symbols taken from 2 distinct sets:
- Logical symbol:
  o countably infinite supply of (individual) variables;
  o countable infinite supply of standard names;
  o equality symbol;
  o usual logical connectives: existence, negation, or, and;
- Non-logical symbols:
  o predicate symbol;
  o function symbols;
  o each predicate or function symbol is assumed to have an arity, that is, a number indicating how many arguments it takes.

Expressions of languages are of 2 types:

- Terms: used to describe individuals in that application's domain; terms fall in 3 categories:
  o variables;
  o standard names;

- ○ functions applications;
- Also of interest primitive term, ground term …
- Well-formed formulas describing relations, properties or conditions in the application domain; syntactically divided in:
  - ○ atomic formulas or atoms;
  - ○ non atomic formulas;
  - ○ also of interest primitive atom and ground atom;
  - ○ well formed formulas are: an atom; $(\tau_1 = \tau_2)$; $\neg\alpha$; $(\alpha \vee \beta)$; $\exists x \alpha$.

Properties of L or generalization knowledge logic (KL):

- validation of sentence;
- satisfiability of a set of sentences (without names or equalities) in the 1st order ordinary logic;
- if α contains only logical symbols then either it or its negation is valid;
- validity of the sentence without standard names $\Delta \cup \Gamma \Rightarrow \alpha$;
- let * be a bijection from standard names to standard names; then α is valid iff α^* is valid;
- validity, free variable and bijection letting α unchanged;
- single free variable, standard name α and all standard names in α and validity;
- there are 3 approaches to incomplete language:
  - ○ dependence on everything that is known;
  - ○ 3 valued logic to consider unknown but this a problem with specification (because unknown);
  - ○ augment the language L so for every sentence α there is another sentence that can read as "α is known";
- Language KL add an extra-logical symbol K if α is a formula, that K_α is a formula too and read K_α as "α is currently known to be true";
- sentences of KL are subjective or objective

Moreover:

- 1st order logic is compact but not L (there is a sentence that cannot be satisfied);
- there is no reason to believe that the proof theory needed in computational realization of decision procedure for L but only validity of sentences;
- KL a language communicating with KB, L not enough, question on sentence is needed;
- KB a finite set of sentences from L;
- to make a difference between known sentence and potential instance;
- for a KB whose knowledge is accurate:
- known sentence $\subseteq$ actual instances $\subseteq$ potential instances;
- type of subjective knowledge usually call meta-knowledge;

Possible world concept used there come from Leibnitz, has been formalized by Kripke and applied into willingness by Hintikka; purely subjective knowledge can be both complete and accurate.

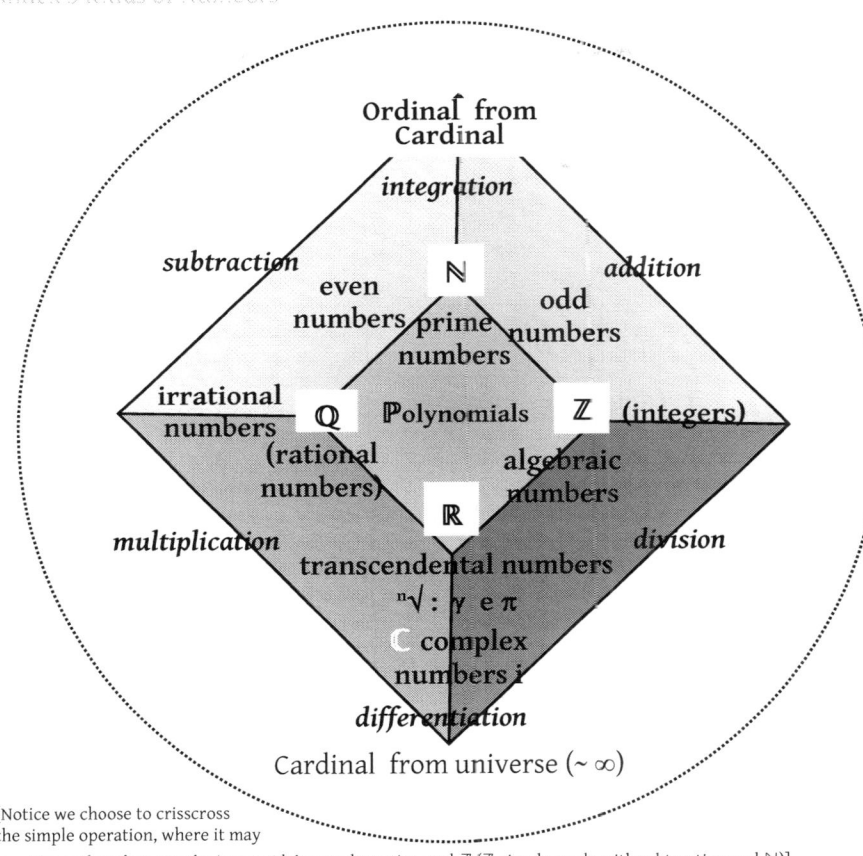

Ordinal from
Cardinal

integration

subtraction   ℕ   *addition*

even
numbers   odd
numbers prime numbers
numbers

irrational
numbers   ℚ   ℙolynomials   ℤ   (integers)
(rational
numbers)   algebraic
numbers

ℝ

multiplication   *division*

transcendental numbers

$^{n}\sqrt{\ }$: γ e π

ℂ complex
numbers i

differentiation

Cardinal from universe (~ ∞)

[Notice we choose to crisscross
the simple operation, where it may

question rather than put the 'same side'; ex: subtraction and ℤ ℤ simply made with subtraction and ℕ)].

Properties of Numbers						
(Care that text closure not exactly mathematical closure)	natu-ral	inte-ger	ratio-nal	alge-braic	com-plex	real
Symbol	ℕ	ℤ	ℚ	\	ℂ	ℝ
Complete continuous					•	•
Closed under division			•	•	•	•
Closed under subtraction		•	•	•	•	•
Closed under addition	•	•	•	•	•	•
Closed under multiplication	•	•	•	•	•	•
Dense			•	•	•	•
Algebraically closed				•	•	

$$\lim_{n\to\infty}[1+1/2+1/3+...+1/n - \ln(n+1)]^n = -\int_0^\infty e^{-t} \ln(t).dt$$

Power laws:

$a^x a^y = a^{x+y}$;

$(a^x)^y = a^{xy}$;

$(ab)^x = a^x b^x$;

$(a/b)^x = a^x/b^x$;

$a^{-x} = 1/a^x$; $a^0=1$

$\lim_{k\to\infty} a^{xk} = a^x$;

$a^x = ex^{\ln a}$; $e^x \neq 0$;

$e^{\pm ix} = \cos x \pm i\sin x$;

$e = \lim_{n\to\infty} (1+1/n)^n$

Logarithm laws

$\log_a(cd) = \log_a c + \log_a d$;

$\log_a cx = x\log_a c$;

$\log_a(c/d) = \log_a c - \log_a d$;

$\log_a a = 1$; $\log_a 1 = 0$;

$\log_a y = \ln y / \ln a$

De Moivre Formula: (in complex numbers' set: $\mathbb{C}$)

$$\cos(nx) + i\sin(nx) = \sum_{k=0}^{n} i^k \binom{n}{k} \cos^{n-k}x . \sin^k x$$

Möbius Transformations

There are functions of complex plane applying on circles, straight lines on circles and straight lines. You have the form of $[az+b]/[cz+d]$ where $ad-bc \neq 0$, a, b, c, d complex numbers and z complex variable. They can visualize some properties of 2×2 complex matrices;

Lattice symmetries are special kinds of Möbius transformations. Using them, we can construct tiling patterns in suitable hyperbolic geometry.

- This geometry can be identified with a region of the complex plane. In which straight lines are replaced by arcs of circles.
- Highly symmetric tiling patterns to each complex function are repeating the same values on every tile. They are known as modular functions which are generalizations of elliptic functions. They are used in physics to simplify bi-dimensioned models of fluids.

Replicator Dynamics

Replicator is deterministic monotone non-linear and non-innovative game dynamic. In evolutionary game theory it allows the fitness function to incorporate the distribution of the population types rather than setting the fitness of a particular type constant. This allows the equation to capture the essence of selection. Set of types $\{1, 2, ..., N\}$; payoff of each type is π (i), proportion of each type is $\mathbf{Pr}$ (i):

1. Choosing highest payoff weight: π (i). $\mathbf{Pr}$ (i);
2. Rule: copy someone else: π (i)+ $\mathbf{Pr}$ (i);
3. Replicator equation: $\mathbf{Pr}_{t+1}$ (i) = $\mathbf{Pr}_t$ (i). ((i)$/\Sigma^N_{j=1}$ $\mathbf{Pr}_t$ (j). ((j).

Spirals

They are obtained differently by artists or scientists; such as Archimedes' which is an arithmetical progression. Dürer's spiral is a gnomic progression made with a compass and a ruler. Logarithms' spiral is obtained with a geometric progression. Fermat's spiral is a parabolic and a case of Archimedes' made of 2 symmetric spirals $r=\pm\theta^{\frac{1}{2}}$.

Cornu's Spiral

It has a curvature radius $\times$ arc (development of) = spiral's constant, They have been previously seen by Bernoulli and Euler. It is plain curves made of a double spiral. It allows to pass by a line (infinite *radius*) to a circumference (finite *radius*) without 'suffering' centrifugal force.

Nature's Spirals

They are very common: flowers structures often spiraling and fractals. Zoological spirals are observed in nautilus's shell or amounts; ones.

Lay applications use spirals for geometric patterns treatment; compression of lines (as ropes), fluids and gases; as separators as for dusts collection and digital treatment of light to minimize rainbow effect.

Strange Attractors

(Fernandez Diaz, Wikipedia & Others)

Strange chaotic attractors are in the phases spaces regions. Examples of phases spaces are at our level, state of our interest: solid, liquid, gas. Strange attractors are delimited by interface, line or points. They join disorders at all levels of scales like 'spinning'. They are highly dissipative (diffusing) and also they are fractals. Formally they are compact sets in the space of a phase, non-0 volume, contained in a 'basin of attraction'.

They are composed of all points set; which trajectories share the same attractor issue (goal or end?). They follow a pattern as: point, limit cycles, tori, butterfly wings. They are almost periodic (with 2 fundamental frequencies). They show intermittent upsurge of turbulent regimes. They are invariant by action of the flow. And they are based on Smale's topological transforms of 'stirring' and overlapping;

Lyapunov exponents can be used to explain the 1st part of the process by giving a measure of exponential separation between 2 closes trajectories; or nonlinear inflection between 2 moments. Ruelle and Takens shown that the states of confused currents or flows remain to discover.

Chaotic motion Parameters

Tells how orbits on an strange attractor move apart.
Classify the system
Tell the limit of predictability of chaotic system

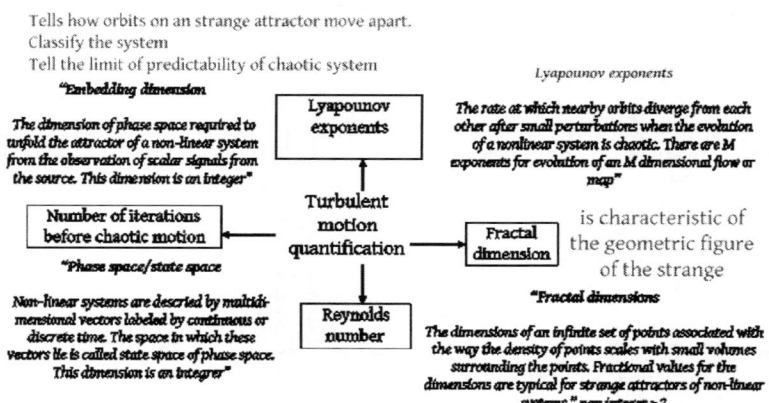

Attractor could so represent a final state of dynamic systems with few degrees of freedom, non-periodic, not intersecting and which large 'orbitals' in a finite area (or manifolds are in 3 dimensioned volume).

Some classification of strange attractors make use of integers set. These are extracted from the chaotic time-series data by first reconstructing the low-period orbits and then determining the template, or knot holder. Which supports all periodic orbits embedded in the strange attractor, and the strange attractor itself. The template is identified by a set of integers which therefore characterize the strange attractor.

Low dimensions Strange Attractors can be Classified by Bounding Tori. Tori are characterized by holes ('crossing the volume, not exposing the inner contain'). They can be created by 3 mechanisms: 1) Holes are normally placed between branches in a branched manifold that is created by a folding. This represents a hyperbolic limit. 2) Holes are created when the flow is restricted to a sub-template of a larger, fully expanding template. 3) Holes can be generated by embedding short experimental data sets. Particularly when one or more of the branches describes very unstable orbit segments.

Yi-Lin proposed a yoyo system theory. It looks like a *tori's* form, conceive in the 3 dimensions 2 (orthogonal) indicated and crossing *tori* or yoyos.

Pictorially imagine your free hands in-blaming each other and fingers of the same hand established. Further-out there (and-inner-before?)

Strange attractor networks are types of recurrent dynamic networks; which evolve toward a stable pattern over time. Nodes in the attractor network converge toward a pattern that may either be fixed-point (a single state), cyclic (with regularly recurring states), chaotic (locally but not globally unstable) or random (stochastic).

Examples of Strange Attractors

Lorentz strange attractors: $dx/dt = \sigma(y-x)$, $dy/dt = rx-y-xz$, $dz = xy - \beta z$ where σ and β are constant and Rayleigh's number vary defining the regime; volume changes in the phase space is according $dV/dt = -(\sigma+1+\beta) V$ giving $V(t) = V(0) e^{-(\sigma+1+\beta)}$. if $0 < r < 1$ there is only one stable stationary solution. Graphically with σ of 2 digits and β a rational of 2 one digit it looks as a packaged orbitals ∞-like slightly twisted. It is interesting to examine the values implied by simple cardinals.

Rossler strange attractor: has the system $dx/dt = -(y+z)$, $dy/dt = x+ay$, $dz/dt = b+z(x-c)$. Graphically the package of orbitals, looks like circling, on some abscissa and ordinate base plane, spiking on 3rd dimension;

Henon strange attractor: follows the system of equations $x_{n+1} = y_r + 1 - ax_n^2$ and $y_{n+1} = bx_n$

It is not a classical determinist or quantum theory indeterminism. It postulates a finite (small) universal local model or elementary catastrophes, in time and space This should be essential to processes of local diversification (evolutionary processes). S folding most simple; notice that you have a 'window' where the curve has more than one solution after a reference axis. They are classified by complexity of order. It is primarily theory of birth (or emergence) that could explain morphogenetic dynamics. Appearance or disappearance of forms on discontinuities of the *medium*, are putting in evidence an underlying geometry to critical phenomena or threshold levels.

So it gives major importance to folding (of continuous curves) introducing bifurcations, ambiguity, non-bijective relations in parts of space by folded functions. Catastrophes are the singularities of determinants; unfolding toward the simple isolated singularities of hyper-surfaces; perspective on the space-time as a space of parameters for dynamic phenomena. Systems described so, are considered to have hidden variables, unmeasurable, too numerous or inaccessible to experimental devices. To the contrary, external parameters are influential in small number and Thom (the founder) shown this number should be less than 4, other external parameters constant). [So we have some framework for thermodynamics phase-space parameters defining the conditions of emergence of local space.]

Elementary catastrophes are, according to the number of parameters. Fundamental theorem of catastrophe theory suggests only 5 elementary catastrophes in the space of dimensions 3 (3 external parameters): fold (A_2), cusp (A_3), elliptic-umbilicus (D_4^-), hyperbolic-umbilicus (D_4^+), swallowtail (A_4). To add 2 more when go up in 4 dimensions (4 external parameters): butterfly (A_5) and parabolic umbilicus (D_5). So when 4 or less we have: Thom's original 7 catastrophes. With 5 or less they are 11. Arnold (a Russian mathematician) gave the catastrophes a wider classification exploring the connection with simple Lie groups. If to have 5 or more dimensions implies an infinity of elementary catastrophes. In reality to those elementary catastrophes mix, the calculus of isolated forms still relevant as an expression of the resistance to the emergence of a split. The method generally is primarily qualitative and descriptive, does not allow any prediction. There is as nonlinear (chaotic systems) initial conditions sensibilities of measure.

Umbilic catastrophes are examples of 2 coRank catastrophes. A_0 is a non-singular point. A_1 a local extremum (stable or not). A_k a representative of an infinite sequence of one variable $V = x^{k+1}+...$ Each elementary catastrophes (characteristic bifurcation) has its properties such as:

Cusp catastrophe **properties** are when 2 factors or parameters of control meet and conflict in both sides of cusp(α,β) then you have the relations: $u = \alpha+\beta$ and $v = \alpha-\beta$. Properties are: 1) Discontinuity (slow variations and speedy jumps); 2) Bimodality (2 or more coalescing variables); 3) Hysteresis (memory or footprint); 4) Divergence; 5) Inaccessible.

Entropy in information theory

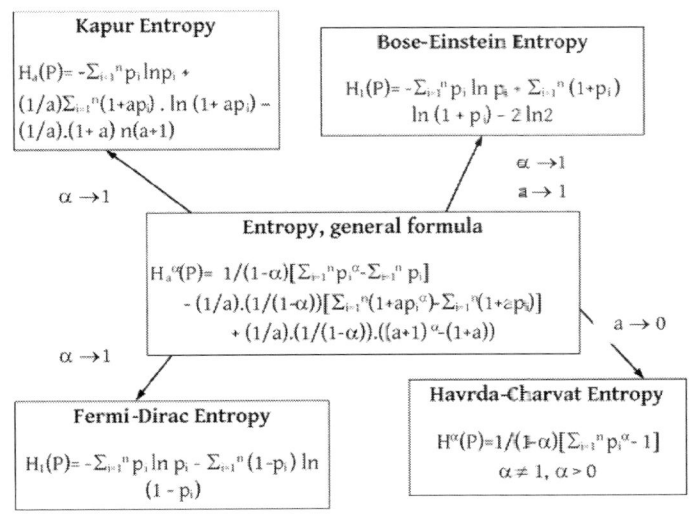

Kinds of Variables

variable number	In the number of variables distinguished by the axis				
	n = 1	n = 2	n ≥ 3	n >> 1	continuum
	growth, decays or equilibrium	oscillations		collective phenomena	waves and patterns
Linear	Exponential-growth, RC circuit Radioactive-decay	linear oscillator mass and spring RLC circuit 2-body problem (Kepler, Newton)	civil engineering structures electrical engineering	coupled harmonic oscillators solid-state-physics molecular-dynamics equilibrium-statistical-mechanics	elasticity, waves-equations, electromagnetism (Maxwell), quantum-mechanics (Schrödinger, Heisenberg, Dirac), heat, diffusion, acoustics, viscous-fluids
					Space-time complexity
non linearity	fixed points, bifurcations, overdamped-systems, relaxed-dynamics, logistic-equation-for-1 species	Pendulum, non-harmonic-oscillators, limit-circles, biological-oscillators (neuron, heart cells), predator-prey-cycles, nonlinear-electronics (van der Pol, Josephson)	Strange-attractors (Lorentz), 3-body problem (Poincaré), chemical-kinetics, iterated-maps (Feigenbaum), Fractals (Mandelbrot), forced-nonlinear-oscillations (Levinson, Smale)	Coupled-nonlinear-oscillators, lasers, nonlinear-optics, non-equilibrium-statistical-mechanics. non-linear-solid-state-physics (semi-conductors), Josephson-arrays, heart-cell-synchronization, neural-networks, immune-systems, economics-systems, economics	Nonlinear-waves (shocks-solitons), plasmas, earthquakes, General reliativity, Quantum field theory, Reactions-diffusion-biological and chemical waves, fibrillations, epilepsy, turbulent fluids (Navier-Stockes), life.

Practical-uses-of-chaos
Quantum-chaos

Theorem Proving and Proof-function

theorem proving

algorithm synthesis

Find a constructive proof of
the desired algorithm

if a constructive proof can be found that an algorithm
does exist, then derive this algorithm from the
constructive proof

express the algorithm design problem in terms of
proving that a conclusion. G is the logical
consequence of finite set of axioms: $A_1, \dots A_q$

prove either that:
$(\neg A_1 \lor \dots \lor \neg A_q \lor G)$ is valid or that
$(A_1 \land \dots \land A_q \land \neg G)$ is inconsistent

from logic constant and/or from existentially
quantified variables of the conclusion G, produce
the desired algorithm (expressed in a structured
logic language) by means of constructive laws

from a finite set of logic expressions derive
(if possible) the logic constants 0 or 1 by
means of deductive laws

logic
transformation

set of constants and/or
variables

logic language
(set of logic expression)
deductive laws
↓
0 or 1

constructive laws
↓
algorithm

388

Dimension Equation and Symbol of Main Physics Parameter

MECHANICS		
length	l	L
mass	m	M
time	t	T
speed	v	LT^{-1}
acceleration	a	LT^{-2}
angular speed	ω	T^{-1}
angular acceleration	α	T^{-2}
frequency	ν	T^{-1}
period	T	T
force	F	MLT^{-2}
volumic mass	ρ	ML^{-3}
energy	E	ML^2T^{-2}
work	W	ML^2T^{-2}
power	P	ML^2T^{-3}
force's moment	M	ML^2T^{-2}
inertia mass moment	I	ML^2
movement quantity	P	MLT^{-1}
kinetic movement	L	ML^2T^{-1}
pressure	p	$ML^{-1}T^{-2}$
longitudinal elasticity modulus	E	$ML^{-1}T^{-2}$
dynamic viscosity	v	$ML^{-1}T^{-1}$
cinematic viscosity	η	L^2T^{-1}
superficial tension	γ	MT^{-2}
mass flow	q_m	MT^{-1}
volume flow	q_v	L^3T^{-1}
angle	α	1
relative lineic dilatation	ε	1
relative volumic dilatation	θ	1
Poisson coefficient	μ	1
area	A	L^2
volume	V	L^3

THERMODYNAMIC		
thermodynamic temperature	T	Θ
heat quantity, entropy, enthalpy	Q, S, H	L^2MT^{-2}
mass thermic capacity	c	$L^2T^{-2}\Theta^{-1}$
dilatation coefficient	φ	Θ^{-1}
thermic conductivity	c	$LMT^{-3}\Theta^{-1}$
thermic convection coefficient	α	$MT^{-3}\Theta^{-1}$
thermic flow	λ	ML^2T^{-3}

	symbol	Dimenssion equation
radiative thermic coefficient	hc	$MT^{-3}\Theta^{-1}$
thermic density flow	φ	MT^{-3}
gas mole constant	R	$ML^2T^{-2}\Theta^{-1}$

ELECTRICITY		
electric current	I	I
density current	J	$L^{-2}I$
electric charge	Q	TI
potential	V	$ML^2T^{-3}I^{-1}$
electric field	E	$MLT^{-3}I^{-1}$
resistance	R	$ML^2T^{-3}I^{-2}$
capacity	C	$M^{-1}L^{-2}T^4 I^2$
electric power	P	ML^2T^{-3}
electric induction	D	$L^{-2}TI^{-1}$
dipole electric moment	p	LTI
resistivity	ρ	$ML^3T^{-3}I^{-2}$
conductivity	γ	$M^{-1}L^{-3}T^3 I^2$

MAGNETISM		
magnetic flow	Φ	$ML^2T^{-2}I^{-1}$
magnetic induction	B	$MT^{-2}I^{-1}$
magnetic field	H	$L^{-1}I$
magnetic potential difference	Um	I
permeability	μ	$MLT^{-2}I^{-2}$
self inductance	L	$ML^2T^{-2}I^{-2}$
magnetic moment	m	ML^2
magnetic polarization	Bi	MTI

OPTIC		
luminous flow	Φ	J
luminous intensity	I	$T^{-1}J$
luminous lighting	I	$L^{-2}J$
luminous existence	M	$L^{-2}J$
luminance	L	$L^{-2}T^{-1}J$
light quantity	Q	$T^{-1}J$

RADIOACTIVITY		
elementary charge	E	n
disintegration energy	Q	ML^2T^{-2}
activity	A	$T^{-1}n$
particles current density	J	$L^{-2}T^{-1}$

We are in the difficulty not to have the concepts to appear in next volume. Our exploration of potential or innovative (?) concepts about formal sciences, but non-formal review needs overviews... We think potentially fruitful to remaster or rethink sciences that have been developed in a systemic, enormous and serious ways since half a century. As a result this glossary-like summary we will be short, and to adjust in next volume.

Fundamental **ordering of logics** are suggested to be related **somehow analogous to the arithmetic logic**? Considering that **incomplete arithmetic is, at the maximum, informatively solved by the physics**. And the converse, **physics as well formulated as possible, to be solved by the mathematics**. 'Below that' we have the **mathematical-logical 'syntactical' paradoxes**; possibly to be recalled by the process of application, 'semantic-like mathematical'; so as to be lexicographed by physics evidences. And so the **'improper' converse of physics paradoxes possibly semantic is to be solved by formal lexicographic 'service'; either informative or syntactically mathematics**?

The logics apprehension would be the way to 'abstract lexicography' since the uncertainty principles of complexity? As an effect proper formulation of fundamental physics with **mathematics meet-match-fit with physics arithmetic logic**? Meanwhile proper physics formulations of complexity could make use of relative systematic mathematics formulations: potentially half manageable at best?

Meanwhile proper logical formulation of the systemic mathematics; of enough physics objective complex object; made them potential manageable with, at maximum, that **half-manageable**? Previous half because between the **informative obliged relations between cardinal and ordinal of numbers**. Amounts, qualities interrelations ordinal and cardinal makes the ordinal the correspondent of 'quali', which is possibly less numerous, compared to wholest cardinal. But most of ordinal come from 'quanti' more numerous cardinal and not just and only from other ordinal?

Concept of quali-quanti is mostly operating within **development between relatively** purer quali-quali and quanti-quanti, extreme of range (pure abstracts? But having to be finite?); that has to consider, 'unary-ness and large pluralism'. Some duals are to articulate, in a solvable way: cardinal-ordinal; random-exact, matter-energy, atom-field, global-local, etc.?

We suggested the **use of logarithms, exponent, their symmetry and links** (economy?) **to meet-match-fit of quali-quanti**; along different levels of scale (to be more rigorous at the respect?) **Logarithms would be a good curve for quality and emergence**, including base for minimal connectivity?

Exponential curve could be a good for quantities. Exponentiation is important for characteristic exponents; so important? **Development or successive generation and production is requiring to be linked and capped by information**, exhaustion or finite world? So; when not reverse decreasing negative exponential:

circumscribed by a modulus encircling or enveloping logs and exp curve related by them: **y = x axis of symmetry**? The axis of reference for a new object obtained by combination?

Good formula information-like for many concepts, such are: system, models, theory, real object, living bodies? For logarithms be numerically taken in charge properly, has still plenty of work to do ... for materializing formula. Or provide more substance to label of real objects, **relevant to our 'economy'**? As well as all many concepts of relative formal systemic mathematics and logics to develop? [The sort of work we imagine is more by the side of phenomenological applications to our way of using universality of formal and fundamental natural sciences in modern humane societies with their new instruments].

Sharp$_{smooth}$ complex in dynamic terms of relative formal methods and real objects behaviors to explore by fractals, bifurcations, critical transitions observed in phase-space, renormalizations, ergodic or random motions, cardinal accounts provided continuity. They could be approached more by real numbers, strange attractors breakings more proper to quantities?–or to expect if willing to define spaces of places where some narrower kinds of moving behaviors can exist for developing some more complex units? Smooth$_{sharp}$ behaviors, could be explored by folding, continuity, smooth fractals, strange attractors within, regular non-linearity, ordinal accounts? In the idea that **more clever formal inter-twinings are required** and possibly to develop in higher levels of complexity?

Relative closure, by the formal side of relative formal system, **accounts for more properties of numbers evenness**? (Especially should consider whole share able properties?), oddness (especially for trajectories, motions, etc.?) Prime-ness (system scale, modularity?), and so on? In the sort of geometry provided to the **relative formal system or atom or 'head' (logical head of relative formal system)**? The suggestion to have is for more phenomenological use of primary kinds geometry: **elliptic-like for relatively close and convex volumes** (starting with 2 or 3 foci), **hyperbolic-like for holes 'within' elliptic forms**? Euclidean (straight line) of course for metric (to imagine that you have an outer system of reference (provided the way of log-exp diversification. Or to only approximate segment trajectories of bodies? Or inner norms or metric in one main degree intern or have possible hierarchical-linearization along the main axes of the system?

It is better to conceive also by global and/or local combination, for better use of diversity but consistency, convexity, connectivity, compactness... In the same ideas of informative links: mostly elliptical in amounts provided the information of hyperbolic or the converse: mostly hyperbolic in amount, provided the information of elliptic. In the cosmos of Universe to observe both in asymmetric, with characteristic proportions? In the idea that Nature would not discard the economy of relative diversity of options together with the resources of huge numbers?

In more local and relatively local terms the **switches either from cardinal to ordinal**; or from one type to another we have **characteristics in state proportions**, before and critical when the switches? In the same way to note that higher complex units formed and limited by information (qualitative-quantitative)? Observing that in physics fundamental physical ground are not disqualified by more complexity; to study that with information of logarithm emergence, made quantity and its economy consistent? The development in softer physics allowed by the cooling of places (nurtured with energetic inputs). This is **'within' principles and combination of principles principal components**. So within best reference axes can express diversification by recombination and higher complex less purely one or the other, of the level of complexity 'before.' Formally the effect would be the possibility to explore multiple levels maintaining resources of relative proper formal integration? Diversification of complexification; as sorts of twists or loops with ordered (hierarchically) possible time?

Relative formal ('atomic system'?) **unit** should have a **general solvability expression** (3 or 4 degrees, variables, etc.)? This would be in the **'general axioms of abstraction'** assumption (at higher complex levels than fundamental physics)? And possibly adding **some levels more of specifications? 3 at the most fundamental levels of physics**? And this would be since the general solvability expression, **like closure(s) for providing specific values of the case**? Concept of time to remaster with **combination of different compatible times**? Concept of dimensions to remaster in the macro-meso-micro levels after the levels integrations of formal (arithmetical system)? [Of course that is not at all disqualifying fundamental physics good results, especially of quantic mechanics. Also the **framework for 'hierarchy (ies)?**

It always is to think about the **'doubling clicks' of integration up and differentiation down. Always crisscrossing to manage**, not less than direct?

Of course in the idea that either formal and physical structures can develop and sustain since global as well as local frames: symmetries and invariants (structures and principles of conservation). **Algebra of groups for systems operations and kinds of system? Integration and derivations or differentiation have both to play in the local relative especially inner or endo to the system or global outer?** Energetic relations, jumps of relative proportions atoms-fields, uncertain probability-exact 'sustained'? So locally some possibility to have 'integration by encapsulation of the system'? The way **a relative system can integrate onto itself, empowering its unit**. The converse with **openness maintained indispensable at any level**?

But a macro-system incorporate higher developed sub-microsystem making **'within' development by loops, folds, encapsulation?** Supporting this there is also by the way the Möbius twist of the strip, Klein bottles-like, spiral dynamics of development, fractals and strange attractors in the relative ways as forms of development? Emerging by allowance? Submitted than to **evolutionary processes of selection** (since the physics world)? **Plenty of theoretical concepts are existing in economics, ecology, biology, but can have more fundamental ground in physics**. So such principles of 'economics' are not to be exclusive?

There is a fundamental suggestion of relative formal system unit after some **level of complexity; possibly indexed by a prime numbers scale**? Relative formal means to these **'relative formal system shuttle'**. You may subtract in its logic the maximum complex prime number of complexity reached; and distinguish primary dimensions/degree/base as a general solvable system more or less specifications? Still some outside the ghost (or spirit) relative formal system? Other contributions fundamental principle of the universe are from the side of 'absolute amounts'. Openness feeding diversity, use of amounts resources; more economically from nearby or close systems? [Some not close enough inputs can be toxic if not self or close].

So you may logically be simpler, have your general specifications, set your characteristic values, etc. ... possibly differentiate and compare logically, informatively, qualitatively and quantitatively frameworks; examine and share structures, in a rather simple way; supporting your hope of manageability possibly relatively consistent and an economy? But that because the universally of physical principles, quite narrow fundamentals, similarities naturally observed.

Numbers' sets Consideration, out of the abstractions, more concern is begged for the perfect or ergodic (**purely random**) at the extreme (**cardinals of singletons fully free**) and **perfect order** on the other extreme (like the 3rd principle of thermodynamic, or **lattice or grid 'perfectly tightened geometrically'**)? What is to consider is playing in only one set natural or real is 'more than exceptional. Natural numbers amounts enormously and structure have almost continuity with its finiteness and real numbers. But to imagine that **realities play more with proportions between, and relative combinations** between natural and real numbers, producing and sustaining properties?

> 3rd principle of thermodynamic is regarding the properties of systems in equilibrium at absolute zero temperatures 0°K. There entropy of a perfect crystal is exactly equal to zero. Physically, the Nernst–Simon statement implies that it is impossible for any procedure to bring a system to the absolute zero of temperature in a finite number of steps.

Entropy together with system openness that makes disorder free resources can be caught by near-by more ordered system? (If the values of extensive parameters are convenient.) This would be developed at the minimum probabilistically in the convenient places (quantic situs?) of phase-space, enough but not too much cold; Almost for sure but possibly at first levels of complexification with very low probability? (But do occurring). Constant switches or twists or permutations between relative orders and disorders. Successive or simultaneously existing; starting between quantic *vacuum*, atoms and fields in most fundamental existence of nature, at some characteristic ratio making nature probabilistic and exactly existing 'at the same time'? That **makes our world most of probability**, needed probability for evolving.

Entropy on one side, is feeding positive construction of near-side neguentropy and nearby fundamental transfer? **Balance of these transfers tentatively called Netgentropy**? Sources of disorder are diversifying (any below) despite a common-end fate of disorder? Expressed in the narrowed steps of disordering expression, potentially at some moment self-reproducing? [There is **emergence of life as a natural consequence in some 'sweet ambiguous' places** with such elements]. Entropy possibly also potentially input and expressed in a rather destructive way? In the need for more details about entropy's ways; produces different levels of the 'crunch' (regressive steps after heat modifying phase-space)?

All that, made of the same basic building bricks declined in different levels of specification: quanta pure energy mass-less, mass energy convertible, electric charge mass ordered exchangeable in current and mass. All having **natural economics common denominator**; more intrinsic and more detailed in 'avatar since the same' as human complications? **Modern concept of humans' economics ought to remaster after these impacts, either on phase-space media (macro-environments), and essential hierarchies of time?** At least with an **economy of informative links**.

Humans complications making use of physics principles produced extraordinary technological developments but turned anti-bio-economical because having **bypassed natural evolutionary principles (of nearest recycling lower system)?** And uncared the **triggering devastating potentials of entropic expressions** by the use of massive storage of matter degradable into energetic fuels heat warming and entropy-heat convergence?

In all that the **possible paper to play of relative informative links. In the smallest one self-own unit the simple information formulation?** More interestingly in the **crossed combined way** (started at the dual)? Possibly in the **sort of operators trying to relate a something between 2 states (in and out) by a crossed link with 4 grips (X-like)? Skew symmetric differential forms**, not our proposal, but an interesting one of the sort?

Relative pieces of informative links natural or artificial for natural or artificial exchanges already practiced unconsciously and naturally? Already explored yet not all cleverly but potentially a proper material for wiser economics based on **fundamental exchanges between relevant nearby and close systems natural physics and mechanics**. Could this be accessed by formal relative system algebra and not too critical margins for supportive systems in the cardinal and; ordered systems in the compatible hierarchical values of ordinal? Could this, possibly in a way of influential relative systems ... of policies?

Many other forms which are quite interesting to understand from many principles and test under analogical adaptations at analogical level of humane economy? Sort of economics not as complicated and simplified existing ones and not as unobserved as imagined by the readers of these suggestions?